Code of Federal Regulations

CODE OF FEDERAL
REGULATIONS

Title 21
Food and Drugs

Part 1300 to End

Revised as of April 1, 2020

Containing a codification of documents
of general applicability and future effect

As of April 1, 2020

Published by the Office of the Federal Register
National Archives and Records Administration
as a Special Edition of the Federal Register

Table of Contents

Cite this Code: CFR

To cite the regulations in this volume use title, part and section number. Thus, 21 CFR 1300.01 *refers to title 21, part 1300, section 01.*

Explanation

The Code of Federal Regulations is a codification of the general and permanent rules published in the Federal Register by the Executive departments and agencies of the Federal Government. The Code is divided into 50 titles which represent broad areas subject to Federal regulation. Each title is divided into chapters which usually bear the name of the issuing agency. Each chapter is further subdivided into parts covering specific regulatory areas.

Each volume of the Code is revised at least once each calendar year and issued on a quarterly basis approximately as follows:

Title 1 through Title 16..........as of January 1
Title 17 through Title 27..........as of April 1
Title 28 through Title 41..........as of July 1
Title 42 through Title 50..........as of October 1

The appropriate revision date is printed on the cover of each volume.

LEGAL STATUS

The contents of the Federal Register are required to be judicially noticed (44 U.S.C. 1507). The Code of Federal Regulations is prima facie evidence of the text of the original documents (44 U.S.C. 1510).

HOW TO USE THE CODE OF FEDERAL REGULATIONS

The Code of Federal Regulations is kept up to date by the individual issues of the Federal Register. These two publications must be used together to determine the latest version of any given rule.

To determine whether a Code volume has been amended since its revision date (in this case, April 1, 2020), consult the "List of CFR Sections Affected (LSA)," which is issued monthly, and the "Cumulative List of Parts Affected," which appears in the Reader Aids section of the daily Federal Register. These two lists will identify the Federal Register page number of the latest amendment of any given rule.

EFFECTIVE AND EXPIRATION DATES

Each volume of the Code contains amendments published in the Federal Register since the last revision of that volume of the Code. Source citations for the regulations are referred to by volume number and page number of the Federal Register and date of publication. Publication dates and effective dates are usually not the same and care must be exercised by the user in determining the actual effective date. In instances where the effective date is beyond the cut-off date for the Code a note has been inserted to reflect the future effective date. In those instances where a regulation published in the Federal Register states a date certain for expiration, an appropriate note will be inserted following the text.

OMB CONTROL NUMBERS

The Paperwork Reduction Act of 1980 (Pub. L. 96–511) requires Federal agencies to display an OMB control number with their information collection request.

Many agencies have begun publishing numerous OMB control numbers as amendments to existing regulations in the CFR. These OMB numbers are placed as close as possible to the applicable recordkeeping or reporting requirements.

PAST PROVISIONS OF THE CODE

Provisions of the Code that are no longer in force and effect as of the revision date stated on the cover of each volume are not carried. Code users may find the text of provisions in effect on any given date in the past by using the appropriate List of CFR Sections Affected (LSA). For the convenience of the reader, a "List of CFR Sections Affected" is published at the end of each CFR volume. For changes to the Code prior to the LSA listings at the end of the volume, consult previous annual editions of the LSA. For changes to the Code prior to 2001, consult the List of CFR Sections Affected compilations, published for 1949-1963, 1964-1972, 1973-1985, and 1986-2000.

"[RESERVED]" TERMINOLOGY

The term "[Reserved]" is used as a place holder within the Code of Federal Regulations. An agency may add regulatory information at a "[Reserved]" location at any time. Occasionally "[Reserved]" is used editorially to indicate that a portion of the CFR was left vacant and not dropped in error.

INCORPORATION BY REFERENCE

What is incorporation by reference? Incorporation by reference was established by statute and allows Federal agencies to meet the requirement to publish regulations in the Federal Register by referring to materials already published elsewhere. For an incorporation to be valid, the Director of the Federal Register must approve it. The legal effect of incorporation by reference is that the material is treated as if it were published in full in the Federal Register (5 U.S.C. 552(a)). This material, like any other properly issued regulation, has the force of law.

What is a proper incorporation by reference? The Director of the Federal Register will approve an incorporation by reference only when the requirements of 1 CFR part 51 are met. Some of the elements on which approval is based are:

(a) The incorporation will substantially reduce the volume of material published in the Federal Register.

(b) The matter incorporated is in fact available to the extent necessary to afford fairness and uniformity in the administrative process.

(c) The incorporating document is drafted and submitted for publication in accordance with 1 CFR part 51.

What if the material incorporated by reference cannot be found? If you have any problem locating or obtaining a copy of material listed as an approved incorporation by reference, please contact the agency that issued the regulation containing that incorporation. If, after contacting the agency, you find the material is not available, please notify the Director of the Federal Register, National Archives and Records Administration, 8601 Adelphi Road, College Park, MD 20740-6001, or call 202-741-6010.

CFR INDEXES AND TABULAR GUIDES

A subject index to the Code of Federal Regulations is contained in a separate volume, revised annually as of January 1, entitled CFR INDEX AND FINDING AIDS. This volume contains the Parallel Table of Authorities and Rules. A list of CFR titles, chapters, subchapters, and parts and an alphabetical list of agencies publishing in the CFR are also included in this volume.

An index to the text of "Title 3—The President" is carried within that volume.

The Federal Register Index is issued monthly in cumulative form. This index is based on a consolidation of the "Contents" entries in the daily Federal Register.

A List of CFR Sections Affected (LSA) is published monthly, keyed to the revision dates of the 50 CFR titles.

REPUBLICATION OF MATERIAL

There are no restrictions on the republication of material appearing in the Code of Federal Regulations.

INQUIRIES

For a legal interpretation or explanation of any regulation in this volume, contact the issuing agency. The issuing agency's name appears at the top of odd-numbered pages.

For inquiries concerning CFR reference assistance, call 202–741–6000 or write to the Director, Office of the Federal Register, National Archives and Records Administration, 8601 Adelphi Road, College Park, MD 20740-6001 or e-mail *fedreg.info@nara.gov*.

THIS TITLE

Title 21—FOOD AND DRUGS is composed of nine volumes. The parts in these volumes are arranged in the following order: Parts 1–99, 100–169, 170–199, 200–299, 300–499, 500–599, 600–799, 800–1299 and 1300 to end. The first eight volumes, containing parts 1–1299, comprise Chapter I—Food and Drug Administration, Department of Health and Human Services. The ninth volume, containing part 1300 to end, includes Chapter II—Drug Enforcement Administration, Department of Justice, and Chapter III—Office of National Drug Control Policy. The contents of these volumes represent all current regulations codified under this title of the CFR as of April 1, 2020.

For this volume, Michele Bugenhagen was Chief Editor. The Code of Federal Regulations publication program is under the direction of John Hyrum Martinez, assisted by Stephen J. Frattini.

Title 21—Food and Drugs

(This book contains part 1300 to end)

CHAPTER II—DRUG ENFORCEMENT ADMINISTRATION, DEPARTMENT OF JUSTICE

PART 1300—DEFINITIONS

AUTHORITY: 21 U.S.C. 802, 821, 822, 829, 871(b), 951, 958(f).

SOURCE: 62 FR 13941, Mar. 24, 1997, unless otherwise noted.

§ 1300.01 Definitions relating to controlled substances.

(a) Any term not defined in this part shall have the definition set forth in section 102 of the Act (21 U.S.C. 802), except that certain terms used in part 1316 of this chapter are defined at the beginning of each subpart of that part.

(b) As used in parts 1301 through 1308, 1312, and 1317 of this chapter, the following terms shall have the meanings specified:

Act means the Controlled Substances Act, as amended (84 Stat. 1242; 21 U.S.C. 801) and/or the Controlled Substances Import and Export Act, as amended (84 Stat. 1285; 21 U.S.C. 951).

Administration means the Drug Enforcement Administration.

Administrator means the Administrator of the Drug Enforcement Administration. The Administrator has been delegated authority under the Act by the Attorney General (28 CFR 0.100).

Anabolic steroid means any drug or hormonal substance, chemically and pharmacologically related to testosterone (other than estrogens, progestins, corticosteroids, and dehydroepiandrosterone), and includes:

(1) 3β,17-dihydroxy-5a-androstane

(2) 3α,17β-dihydroxy-5a-androstane

(3) 5α-androstan-3,17-dione

(4) 1-androstenediol (3β,17β-dihydroxy-5α-androst-1-ene)

(5) 1-androstenediol (3α,17β-dihydroxy-5α-androst-1-ene)

(6) 4-androstenediol (3β,17β-dihydroxy-androst-4-ene)

(7) 5-androstenediol (3β,17β-dihydroxy-androst-5-ene)

(8) 1-androstenedione ([5α]-androst-1-en-3,17-dione)

(9) 4-androstenedione (androst-4-en-3,17-dione)

(10) 5-androstenedione (androst-5-en-3,17-dione)

(11) bolasterone (7α,17α-dimethyl-17β-hydroxyandrost-4-en-3-one)

(12) boldenone (17β-hydroxyandrost-1,4-diene-3-one)

(13) boldione (androsta-1,4-diene-3,17-dione)

(14) calusterone (7β,17α-dimethyl-17β-hydroxyandrost-4-en-3-one)

(15) clostebol (4-chloro-17β-hydroxyandrost-4-en-3-one)

(16) dehydrochloromethyltestosterone (4-chloro-17β-hydroxy-17α-methyl-androst-1,4-dien-3-one)

(17) desoxymethyltestosterone (17α-methyl-5α-androst-2-en-17β-ol) (a.k.a. 'madol')

(18) Δ1-dihydrotestosterone (a.k.a.'1-testosterone') (17β-hydroxy-5α-androst-1-en-3-one)

(19) 4-dihydrotestosterone (17β-hydroxy-androstan-3-one)

(20) drostanolone (17β-hydroxy-2α-methyl-5α-androstan-3-one)

(21) ethylestrenol (17α-ethyl-17β-hydroxyestr-4-ene)

(22) fluoxymesterone (9-fluoro-17α-methyl-11β,17β-dihydroxyandrost-4-en-3-one)

(23) formebolone (2-formyl-17α-methyl-11α,17β-dihydroxyandrost-1,4-dien-3-one)

(24) furazabol (17α-methyl-17β-hydroxyandrostano[2,3-c]-furazan)

(25) 13β-ethyl-17β-hydroxygon-4-en-3-one

(26) 4-hydroxytestosterone (4,17β-dihydroxy-androst-4-en-3-one)

(27) 4-hydroxy-19-nortestosterone (4,17β-dihydroxy-estr-4-en-3-one)

(28) mestanolone (17α-methyl-17β-hydroxy-5-androstan-3-one)

(29) mesterolone (1α-methyl-17β-hydroxy-[5α]-androstan-3-one)

(30) methandienone (17α-methyl-17β-hydroxyandrost-1,4-dien-3-one)

(31) methandriol (17α-methyl-3β,17β-dihydroxyandrost-5-ene)

(32) Methasterone (2α,17α-dimethyl-5α-androstan-17β-ol-3-one)

(33) methenolone (1-methyl-17β-hydroxy-5α-androst-1-en-3-one)

(34) 17α-methyl-3β,17β-dihydroxy-5a-androstane
(35) 17α-methyl-3α,17β-dihydroxy-5a-androstane
(36) 17α-methyl-3β,17β-dihydroxyandrost-4-ene
(37) 17α-methyl-4-hydroxynandrolone (17α-methyl-4-hydroxy-17β-hydroxyestr-4-en-3-one)
(38) methyldienolone (17α-methyl-17β-hydroxyestra-4,9(10)-dien-3-one)
(39) methyltrienolone (17α-methyl-17β-hydroxyestra-4,9,11-trien-3-one)
(40) methyltestosterone (17α-methyl-17β-hydroxyandrost-4-en-3-one)
(41) mibolerone (7α,17α-dimethyl-17β-hydroxyestr-4-en-3-one)
(42) 17α-methyl-Δ1-dihydrotestosterone (17β-hydroxy-17α-methyl-5α-androst-1-en-3-one) (a.k.a. '17-α-methyl-1-testosterone')
(43) nandrolone (17β-hydroxyestr-4-en-3-one)
(44) 19-nor-4-androstenediol (3β, 17β-dihydroxyestr-4-ene)
(45) 19-nor-4-androstenediol (3α, 17β-dihydroxyestr-4-ene)
(46) 19-nor-5-androstenediol (3β, 17β-dihydroxyestr-5-ene)
(47) 19-nor-5-androstenediol (3α, 17β-dihydroxyestr-5-ene)
(48) 19-nor-4,9(10)-androstadienedione (estra-4,9(10)-diene-3,17-dione)
(49) 19-nor-4-androstenedione (estr-4-en-3,17-dione)
(50) 19-nor-5-androstenedione (estr-5-en-3,17-dione)
(51) norbolethone (13β, 17α-diethyl-17β-hydroxygon-4-en-3-one)
(52) norclostebol (4-chloro-17β-hydroxyestr-4-en-3-one)
(53) norethandrolone (17α-ethyl-17β-hydroxyestr-4-en-3-one)
(54) normethandrolone (17α-methyl-17β-hydroxyestr-4-en-3-one)
(55) oxandrolone (17α-methyl-17β-hydroxy-2-oxa-[5α]-androstan-3-one)
(56) oxymesterone (17α-methyl-4,17β-dihydroxyandrost-4-en-3-one)
(57) oxymetholone (17α-methyl-2-hydroxymethylene-17β-hydroxy-[5α]-androstan-3-one)
(58) Prostanozol (17β-hydroxy-5α-androstano[3,2-c]pyrazole)
(59) stanozolol (17α-methyl-17β-hydroxy-[5α]-androst-2-eno[3,2-c]-pyrazole)
(60) stenbolone (17β-hydroxy-2-methyl-[5α]-androst-1-en-3-one)
(61) testolactone (13-hydroxy-3-oxo-13,17-secoandrosta-1,4-dien-17-oic acid lactone)
(62) testosterone (17β-hydroxyandrost-4-en-3-one)
(63) tetrahydrogestrinone (13β, 17α-diethyl-17β-hydroxygon-4,9,11-trien-3-one)
(64) trenbolone (17β-hydroxyestr-4,9,11-trien-3-one)
(65) Any salt, ester, or ether of a drug or substance described in this paragraph. Except such term does not include an anabolic steroid that is expressly intended for administration through implants to cattle or other nonhuman species and that has been approved by the Secretary of Health and Human Services for such administration. If any person prescribes, dispenses, or distributes such steroid for human use, the person shall be considered to have prescribed, dispensed, or distributed an anabolic steroid within the meaning of this paragraph.

Automated dispensing system means a mechanical system that performs operations or activities, other than compounding or administration, relative to the storage, packaging, counting, labeling, and dispensing of medications, and which collects, controls, and maintains all transaction information.

Basic class means, as to controlled substances listed in Schedules I and II:

(1) Each of the opiates, including its isomers, esters, ethers, salts, and salts of isomers, esters, and ethers whenever the existence of such isomers, esters, ethers, and salts is possible within the specific chemical designation, listed in § 1308.11(b) of this chapter;

(2) Each of the opium derivatives, including its salts, isomers, and salts of isomers whenever the existence of such salts, isomers, and salts of isomers is possible within the specific chemical designation, listed in § 1308.11(c) of this chapter;

(3) Each of the hallucinogenic substances, including its salts, isomers, and salts of isomers whenever the existence of such salts, isomers, and salts of isomers is possible within the specific chemical designation, listed in § 1308.11(d) of this chapter;

(4) Each of the following substances, whether produced directly or indirectly

by extraction from substances of vegetable origin, or independently by means of chemical synthesis, or by a combination of extraction and chemical synthesis:

(i) Opium, including raw opium, opium extracts, opium fluid extracts, powdered opium, granulated opium, deodorized opium and tincture of opium;

(ii) Apomorphine;

(iii) Codeine;

(iv) Etorphine hydrochloride;

(v) Ethylmorphine;

(vi) Hydrocodone;

(vii) Hydromorphone;

(viii) Metopon;

(ix) Morphine;

(x) Oxycodone;

(xi) Oxymorphone;

(xii) Thebaine;

(xiii) Mixed alkaloids of opium listed in § 1308.12(b)(2) of this chapter;

(xiv) Cocaine; and

(xv) Ecgonine;

(5) Each of the opiates, including its isomers, esters, ethers, salts, and salts of isomers, esters, and ethers whenever the existence of such isomers, esters, ethers, and salts is possible within the specific chemical designation, listed in § 1308.12(c) of this chapter; and

(6) Methamphetamine, its salts, isomers, and salts of its isomers;

(7) Amphetamine, its salts, optical isomers, and salts of its optical isomers;

(8) Phenmetrazine and its salts;

(9) Methylphenidate;

(10) Each of the substances having a depressant effect on the central nervous system, including its salts, isomers, and salts of isomers whenever the existence of such salts, isomers, and salts of isomers is possible within the specific chemical designation, listed in § 1308.12(e) of this chapter.

Central fill pharmacy means a pharmacy which is permitted by the state in which it is located to prepare controlled substances orders for dispensing pursuant to a valid prescription transmitted to it by a registered retail pharmacy and to return the labeled and filled prescriptions to the retail pharmacy for delivery to the ultimate user. Such central fill pharmacy shall be deemed "authorized" to fill prescriptions on behalf of a retail pharmacy only if the retail pharmacy and central fill pharmacy have a contractual relationship providing for such activities or share a common owner.

Collection means to receive a controlled substance for the purpose of destruction from an ultimate user, a person lawfully entitled to dispose of an ultimate user decedent's property, or a long-term care facility on behalf of an ultimate user who resides or has resided at that facility. The term *collector* means a registered manufacturer, distributor, reverse distributor, narcotic treatment program, hospital/clinic with an on-site pharmacy, or retail pharmacy that is authorized under this chapter to so receive a controlled substance for the purpose of destruction.

Commercial container means any bottle, jar, tube, ampule, or other receptacle in which a substance is held for distribution or dispensing to an ultimate user, and in addition, any box or package in which the receptacle is held for distribution or dispensing to an ultimate user. The term commercial container does not include any package liner, package insert or other material kept with or within a commercial container, nor any carton, crate, drum, or other package in which commercial containers are stored or are used for shipment of controlled substances.

Competent national authority, for purposes of importation and exportation of controlled substances and listed chemicals, means an entity lawfully entitled to authorize the import and export of controlled substances, and to regulate or enforce national controls over listed chemicals, and included as such in the directory of "Competent National Authorities Under the International Drug Control Treaties" published by the United Nations Office on Drugs and Crime. For purposes of exports of narcotic drugs, the term also includes freely associated states authorized to receive such exports pursuant to 48 U.S.C. 1972.

Compounder means any person engaging in maintenance or detoxification treatment who also mixes, prepares, packages or changes the dosage form of a narcotic drug listed in Schedules II, III, IV or V for use in maintenance or detoxification treatment by another narcotic treatment program.

Controlled substance has the meaning given in section 802(6) of Title 21, United States Code (U.S.C.).

Customs officer means either an Officer of the Customs as defined in 19 U.S.C. 1401(i) (that is, of the U.S. Customs and Border Protection), or any individual duly authorized to accept entries of merchandise, to collect duties, and to enforce the customs laws of any commonwealth, territory, or possession of the United States.

Customs territory of the United States means the several States, the District of Columbia, and Puerto Rico.

Detoxification treatment means the dispensing, for a period of time as specified below, of a narcotic drug or narcotic drugs in decreasing doses to an individual to alleviate adverse physiological or psychological effects incident to withdrawal from the continuous or sustained use of a narcotic drug and as a method of bringing the individual to a narcotic drug-free state within such period of time. There are two types of detoxification treatment: Short-term detoxification treatment and long-term detoxification treatment.

(1) Short-term detoxification treatment is for a period not in excess of 30 days.

(2) Long-term detoxification treatment is for a period more than 30 days but not in excess of 180 days.

Dispenser means an individual practitioner, institutional practitioner, pharmacy or pharmacist who dispenses a controlled substance.

Export means, with respect to any article, any taking out or removal of such article from the United States (whether or not such taking out or removal constitutes an exportation within the meaning of the customs laws, export control laws enforced by other agencies, or related laws of the United States).

Exporter includes every person who exports, or who acts as an export broker for exportation of, controlled substances listed in any schedule.

Freight forwarding facility means a separate facility operated by a distributing registrant through which sealed, packaged controlled substances in unmarked shipping containers (*i.e.*, the containers do not indicate that the contents include controlled substances) are, in the course of delivery to, or return from, customers, transferred in less than 24 hours. A distributing registrant who operates a freight forwarding facility may use the facility to transfer controlled substances from any location the distributing registrant operates that is registered with the Administration to manufacture, distribute, or import controlled substances, or, with respect to returns, registered to dispense controlled substances, provided that the notice required by § 1301.12(b)(4) of Part 1301 of this chapter has been submitted and approved. For purposes of this definition, a distributing registrant is a person who is registered with the Administration as a manufacturer, distributor (excluding reverse distributor), and/or importer.

Hearing means:

(1) In part 1301 of this chapter, any hearing held for the granting, denial, revocation, or suspension of a registration pursuant to sections 303, 304, and 1008 of the Act (21 U.S.C. 823, 824 and 958).

(2) In part 1303 of this chapter, any hearing held regarding the determination of aggregate production quota or the issuance, adjustment, suspension, or denial of a procurement quota or an individual manufacturing quota.

(3) In part 1308 of this chapter, any hearing held for the issuance, amendment, or repeal of any rule issuable pursuant to section 201 of the Act (21 U.S.C. 811).

Import means, with respect to any article, any bringing in or introduction of such article into the customs territory of the United States from any place outside thereof (but within the United States), or into the United States from any place outside thereof (whether or not such bringing in or introduction constitutes an importation within the meaning of the tariff laws of the United States).

Importer includes every person who imports, or who acts as an import broker for importation of, controlled substances listed in any schedule.

Individual practitioner means a physician, dentist, veterinarian, or other individual licensed, registered, or otherwise permitted, by the United States or the jurisdiction in which he/she practices, to dispense a controlled substance in the course of professional practice, but does not include a pharmacist, a pharmacy, or an institutional practitioner.

Institutional practitioner means a hospital or other person (other than an individual) licensed, registered, or otherwise permitted, by the United States or the jurisdiction in which it practices, to dispense a controlled substance in the course of professional practice, but does not include a pharmacy.

Interested person means any person adversely affected or aggrieved by any rule or proposed rule issuable pursuant to section 201 of the Act (21 U.S.C. 811).

Inventory means all factory and branch stocks in finished form of a basic class of controlled substance manufactured or otherwise acquired by a registrant, whether in bulk, commercial containers, or contained in pharmaceutical preparations in the possession of the registrant (including stocks held by the registrant under separate registration as a manufacturer, importer, exporter, or distributor).

Isomer means:

(1) The optical isomer, except as used in § 1308.11(d) and § 1308.12(b)(4) of this chapter. As used in § 1308.11(d) of this chapter, the term "isomer" means any optical, positional, or geometric isomer. As used in § 1308.12(b)(4) of this chapter, the term "isomer" means any optical or geometric isomer;

(2) As used in § 1308.11(d) of this chapter, the term "positional isomer" means any substance possessing the same molecular formula and core structure and having the same functional group(s) and/or substituent(s) as those found in the respective Schedule I hallucinogen, attached at any position(s) on the core structure, but in such manner that no new chemical functionalities are created and no existing chemical functionalities are destroyed relative to the respective Schedule I hallucinogen. Rearrangements of alkyl moieties within or between functional group(s) or substituent(s), or divisions or combinations of alkyl moieties, that do not create new chemical functionalities or destroy existing chemical functionalities, are allowed i.e., result in compounds which are positional isomers. For purposes of this definition, the "core structure" is the parent molecule that is the common basis for the class; for example, tryptamine, phenethylamine, or ergoline. Examples of rearrangements resulting in creation and/or destruction of chemical functionalities (and therefore resulting in compounds which are not positional isomers) include, but are not limited to: Ethoxy to *alpha*-hydroxyethyl, hydroxy and methyl to methoxy, or the repositioning of a phenolic or alcoholic hydroxy group to create a hydroxyamine. Examples of rearrangements resulting in compounds which would be positional isomers include: *Tert*-butyl to *sec*-butyl, methoxy and ethyl to isopropoxy, N,N-diethyl to N-methyl-N-propyl, or *alpha*-methylamino to N-methylamino.

Label means any display of written, printed, or graphic matter placed upon the commercial container of any controlled substance by any manufacturer of such substance.

Labeling means all labels and other written, printed, or graphic matter:

(1) Upon any controlled substance or any of its commercial containers or wrappers, or

(2) Accompanying such controlled substance.

Long Term Care Facility (LTCF) means a nursing home, retirement care, mental care or other facility or institution which provides extended health care to resident patients.

Maintenance treatment means the dispensing for a period in excess of twenty-one days, of a narcotic drug or narcotic drugs in the treatment of an individual for dependence upon heroin or other morphine-like drug.

Manufacture means the producing, preparation, propagation, compounding, or processing of a drug or other substance or the packaging or repackaging of such substance, or the labeling or relabeling of the commercial container of such substance, but does not include the activities of a practitioner who, as an incident to his/her administration or dispensing such substance in the course of his/her professional practice, prepares, compounds, packages or labels such substance.

Manufacturer means a person who manufactures a drug or other substance, whether under a registration as a manufacturer or under authority of registration as a researcher or chemical analyst.

Mid-level practitioner means an individual practitioner, other than a physician, dentist, veterinarian, or podiatrist, who is licensed, registered, or otherwise permitted by the United States or the jurisdiction in which he/she practices, to dispense a controlled substance in the course of professional practice. Examples of mid-level practitioners include, but are not limited to, health care providers such as nurse practitioners, nurse midwives, nurse anesthetists, clinical nurse specialists and physician assistants who are authorized to dispense controlled substances by the State in which they practice.

Name means the official name, common or usual name, chemical name, or brand name of a substance.

Narcotic drug means any of the following whether produced directly or indirectly by extraction from substances of vegetable origin or independently by means of chemical synthesis or by a combination of extraction and chemical synthesis:

(1) Opium, opiates, derivatives of opium and opiates, including their isomers, esters, ethers, salts, and salts of isomers, esters, and ethers whenever the existence of such isomers, esters, ethers and salts is possible within the specific chemical designation. Such term does not include the isoquinoline alkaloids of opium.

(2) Poppy straw and concentrate of poppy straw.

(3) Coca leaves, except coca leaves and extracts of coca leaves from which cocaine, ecgonine and derivatives of ecgonine or their salts have been removed.

(4) Cocaine, its salts, optical and geometric isomers, and salts of isomers.

(5) Ecgonine, its derivatives, their salts, isomers and salts of isomers.

(6) Any compound, mixture, or preparation which contains any quantity of any of the substances referred to in paragraphs (1) through (5) of this definition.

Narcotic treatment program means a program engaged in maintenance and/or detoxification treatment with narcotic drugs.

Net disposal means, for a stated period, the quantity of a basic class of controlled substance distributed by the registrant to another person, plus the quantity of that basic class used by the registrant in the production of (or converted by the registrant into) another basic class of controlled substance or a noncontrolled substance, plus the quantity of that basic class otherwise disposed of by the registrant, less the quantity of that basic class returned to the registrant by any purchaser, and less the quantity of that basic class distributed by the registrant to another registered manufacturer of that basic class for purposes other than use in the production of, or conversion into, another basic class of controlled substance or a noncontrolled substance or in the manufacture of dosage forms of that basic class.

Person includes any individual, corporation, government or governmental subdivision or agency, business trust, partnership, association, or other legal entity.

Pharmacist means any pharmacist licensed by a State to dispense controlled substances, and shall include any other person (e.g., pharmacist intern) authorized by a State to dispense controlled substances under the supervision of a pharmacist licensed by such State.

Port of entry means, unless distinguished as being a foreign port of entry, any place at which a customs officer is duly authorized to accept entries of merchandise, to collect duties, and to enforce the various provisions of the customs laws of the United States (whether or not such place is a port of entry as defined in title 19 of the United States Code or its associated implementing regulations). Examples of ports of entry include, but are not limited to, places designated as ports of entry or customs stations in title 19 of the *Code of Federal Regulations* or by the governing customs authority of that area. When shipments are transported under U.S. Customs and Border Protection's immediate transportation procedures, the port of entry shall be the port of final destination.

Port of export means, unless distinguished as being a foreign port of export, any place under the control of a customs officer where goods are loaded on an aircraft, vessel or other conveyance for export outside of the United States. For goods loaded aboard an aircraft or vessel in the United States, that stops at several ports before departing the United States, the port of export is the first port where the goods were actually loaded. For goods offloaded from the original conveyance to another conveyance (even if the aircraft or vessel belongs to the same carrier) at any port subsequent to the port where the first on-loading occurred in the United States, the port where the goods were loaded onto the last conveyance before departing the United States is the port of export.

Prescription means an order for medication which is dispensed to or for an ultimate user but does not include an order for medication which is dispensed for immediate administration to the ultimate user (e.g., an order to dispense a drug to a bed patient for immediate administration in a hospital is not a prescription).

Proceeding means all actions taken for the issuance, amendment, or repeal of any rule issued pursuant to section 201 of the Act (21 U.S.C. 811), commencing with the publication by the Administrator of the proposed rule, amended rule, or repeal in the FEDERAL REGISTER.

Purchaser means any registered person entitled to obtain and execute order forms pursuant to §§1305.04 and 1305.06.

Readily retrievable means that certain records are kept by automatic data processing systems or other electronic or mechanized recordkeeping systems in such a manner that they can be separated out from all other records in a reasonable time and/or records are kept on which certain items are asterisked, redlined, or in some other manner visually identifiable apart from other items appearing on the records.

Register and *registration* refer only to registration required and permitted by sections 303 or 1007 of the Act (21 U.S.C. 823 or 957).

Registrant means any person who is registered pursuant to either section 303 or section 1008 of the Act (21 U.S.C. 823 or 958).

Return information means supplemental information required to be reported to the Administration following an import or export transaction containing the particulars of the transaction and any other information as the Administration may specify.

Reverse distribute means to acquire controlled substances from another registrant or law enforcement for the purpose of:

(1) Return to the registered manufacturer or another registrant authorized by the manufacturer to accept returns on the manufacturer's behalf; or

(2) Destruction.

Reverse distributor is a person registered with the Administration as a reverse distributor.

Supplier means any registered person entitled to fill order forms pursuant to §1305.06 of this chapter.

United States, when used in a geographic sense, means all places and waters, continental or insular, subject to the jurisdiction of the United States, which, in addition to the customs territory of the United States, include but are not limited to the U.S. Virgin Islands, Guam, American Samoa, and the Northern Mariana Islands.

[62 FR 13941, Mar. 24, 1997, as amended at 65 FR 44678, July 19, 2000; 68 FR 37409, June 24, 2003; 68 FR 41228, July 11, 2003; 70 FR 25465, May 13, 2005; 70 FR 74656, Dec. 16, 2005; 71 FR 60427, Oct. 13, 2006; 72 FR 67852, Dec. 3, 2007; 74 FR 63609, Dec. 4, 2009; 77 FR 4230, Jan. 27, 2012; 77 FR 44461, July 30, 2012; 79 FR 53559, Sept. 9, 2014; 81 FR 97018, Dec. 30, 2016]

§ 1300.02 Definitions relating to listed chemicals.

(a) Any term not defined in this part shall have the definition set forth in section 102 of the Act (21 U.S.C. 802), except that certain terms used in part 1316 of this chapter are defined at the beginning of each subpart of that part.

(b) As used in parts 1309, 1310, and 1313 of this chapter, the following terms shall have the meaning specified:

Act means the Controlled Substances Act, as amended (84 Stat. 1242; 21 U.S.C. 801) and/or the Controlled Substances

Import and Export Act, as amended (84 Stat. 1285; 21 U.S.C. 951).

Administration means the Drug Enforcement Administration.

Administrator means the Administrator of the Drug Enforcement Administration. The Administrator has been delegated authority under the Act by the Attorney General (28 CFR 0.100).

At retail, with respect to the sale or purchase of a scheduled listed chemical product, means a sale or purchase for personal use, respectively.

Broker and *trader* mean any individual, corporation, corporate division, partnership, association, or other legal entity which assists in arranging an international transaction in a listed chemical by—

(1) Negotiating contracts;

(2) Serving as an agent or intermediary; or

(3) Fulfilling a formal obligation to complete the transaction by bringing together a buyer and seller, a buyer and transporter, or a seller and transporter, or by receiving any form of compensation for so doing.

Chemical export means transferring ownership or control, or the sending or taking of threshold quantities of listed chemicals out of the United States (whether or not such sending or taking out constitutes an exportation within the meaning of the customs and related laws of the United States).

Chemical exporter is a regulated person who, as the principal party in interest in the export transaction, has the power and responsibility for determining and controlling the sending of the listed chemical out of the United States.

Chemical importer is a regulated person who, as the principal party in interest in the import transaction, has the power and responsibility for determining and controlling the bringing in or introduction of the listed chemical into the United States.

Chemical mixture means a combination of two or more chemical substances, at least one of which is not a listed chemical, except that such term does not include any combination of a listed chemical with another chemical that is present solely as an impurity or which has been created to evade the requirements of the Act.

Combination ephedrine product means a drug product containing ephedrine or its salts, optical isomers, or salts of optical isomers, and therapeutically significant quantities of another active medicinal ingredient.

Competent national authority, for purposes of importation and exportation of controlled substances and listed chemicals, means an entity lawfully entitled to authorize the import and export of controlled substances, and to regulate or enforce national controls over listed chemicals, and included as such in the directory of "Competent National Authorities Under the International Drug Control Treaties" published by the United Nations Office on Drugs and Crime.

Customs officer means either an Officer of the Customs as defined in 19 U.S.C. 1401(i) (that is, of the U.S. Customs and Border Protection), or any individual duly authorized to accept entries of merchandise, to collect duties, and to enforce the customs laws of any commonwealth, territory, or possession of the United States.

Customs territory of the United States means the several States, the District of Columbia, and Puerto Rico.

Drug product means an active ingredient in dosage form that has been approved or otherwise may be lawfully marketed under the Federal Food, Drug, and Cosmetic Act for distribution in the United States.

Encapsulating machine means any manual, semi-automatic, or fully automatic equipment which may be used to fill shells or capsules with any powdered, granular, semi-solid, or liquid material.

Established business relationship means the regulated person has imported or exported a listed chemical at least once within the past six months, or twice within the past twelve months from or to a foreign manufacturer, distributor, or end user of the chemical that has an established business with a fixed street address. A person or business that functions as a broker or intermediary is not a customer for purposes of this definition.

Established record as an importer means that the regulated person has imported a listed chemical at least once within the past six months, or twice within the past twelve months from a foreign supplier.

Export means, with respect to any article, any taking out or removal of such article from the United States (whether or not such taking out or removal constitutes an exportation within the meaning of the customs laws, export control laws enforced by other agencies, or related laws of the United States).

Hearing means any hearing held for the granting, denial, revocation, or suspension of a registration pursuant to sections 303, 304, and 1008 of the Act (21 U.S.C. 823, 824 and 958).

Import means, with respect to any article, any bringing in or introduction of such article into the customs territory of the United States from any place outside thereof (but within the United States), or into the United States from any place outside thereof (whether or not such bringing in or introduction constitutes an importation within the meaning of the tariff laws of the United States).

International transaction means a transaction involving the shipment of a listed chemical across an international border (other than a United States border) in which a broker or trader located in the United States participates.

Listed chemical means any List I chemical or List II chemical.

List I chemical means a chemical specifically designated by the Administrator in §1310.02(a) of this chapter that, in addition to legitimate uses, is used in manufacturing a controlled substance in violation of the Act and is important to the manufacture of a controlled substance.

List II chemical means a chemical, other than a List I chemical, specifically designated by the Administrator in §1310.02(b) of this chapter that, in addition to legitimate uses, is used in manufacturing a controlled substance in violation of the Act.

Mobile retail vendor means a person or entity that makes sales at retail from a stand that is intended to be temporary or is capable of being moved from one location to another, whether the stand is located within or on the premises of a fixed facility (such as a kiosk at a shopping center or an airport) or whether the stand is located on unimproved real estate (such as a lot or field leased for retail purposes).

Name means the official name, common or usual name, chemical name, or brand name of a substance.

Person includes any individual, corporation, government or governmental subdivision or agency, business trust, partnership, association, or other legal entity.

Port of entry, unless distinguished as being a foreign port of entry, means any place at which a customs officer is duly authorized to accept entries of merchandise, to collect duties, and to enforce the various provisions of the customs laws of the United States (whether or not such place is a port of entry as defined in title 19 of the United States Code or its associated implementing regulations). Examples of ports of entry include, but are not limited to, places designated as ports of entry or customs stations in title 19 of the *Code of Federal Regulations* or by the governing customs authority of that area. When shipments are transported under U.S. Customs and Border Protection immediate transportation procedures, the port of entry shall be the port of final destination.

Port of export means, unless distinguished as being a foreign port of export, any place under the control of a customs officer where goods are loaded on an aircraft, vessel or other conveyance for export outside of the United States. For goods loaded aboard an aircraft or vessel in the United States that stops at several ports before departing the United States, the port of export is the first port where the goods were loaded. For goods off-loaded from the original conveyance to another conveyance (even if the aircraft or vessel belongs to the same carrier) at any port subsequent to the port where the first on-loading occurred in the United States, the port where the goods were loaded onto the last conveyance before departing the United States is the port of export. For reporting purposes, in the case of an otherwise lawful export occurring by mail, the port of export is the place of mailing.

Readily retrievable means that certain records are kept by automatic data processing systems or other electronic or mechanized recordkeeping systems in such a manner that they can be separated out from all other records in a reasonable time and/or records are kept on which certain items are asterisked, redlined, or in some other manner visually identifiable apart from other items appearing on the records.

Register and *registration* refer only to registration required and permitted by sections 303 or 1007 of the Act (21 U.S.C. 823 or 957).

Registrant means any person who is registered pursuant to either section 303 or section 1008 of the Act (21 U.S.C. 823 or 958).

Regular customer means a person with whom the regulated person has an established business relationship for a specified listed chemical or chemicals that has been reported to the Administration subject to the criteria established in part 1313 of this chapter.

Regular importer means, with respect to a listed chemical, a person that has an established record as an importer of that listed chemical that is reported to the Administrator.

Regulated person means any individual, corporation, partnership, association, or other legal entity who manufactures, distributes, imports, or exports a listed chemical, a tableting machine, or an encapsulating machine, or who acts as a broker or trader for an international transaction involving a listed chemical, tableting machine, or encapsulating machine.

Regulated seller means a retail distributor (including a pharmacy or a mobile retail vendor), except that the term does not include an employee or agent of the distributor.

Regulated transaction means:

(1) A distribution, receipt, sale, importation, or exportation of a listed chemical, or an international transaction involving shipment of a listed chemical, or if the Administrator establishes a threshold amount for a specific listed chemical, a threshold amount as determined by the Administrator, which includes a cumulative threshold amount for multiple transactions, of a listed chemical, except that such term does not include:

(i) A domestic lawful distribution in the usual course of business between agents or employees of a single regulated person; in this context, agents or employees means individuals under the direct management and control of the regulated person;

(ii) A delivery of a listed chemical to or by a common or contract carrier for carriage in the lawful and usual course of the business of the common or contract carrier, or to or by a warehouseman for storage in the lawful and usual course of the business of the warehouseman, except that if the carriage or storage is in connection with the distribution, importation, or exportation of a listed chemical to a third person, this paragraph does not relieve a distributor, importer, or exporter from compliance with parts 1309, 1310, 1313, and 1315 of this chapter;

(iii) Any category of transaction or any category of transaction for a specific listed chemical or chemicals specified by regulation of the Administrator as excluded from this definition as unnecessary for enforcement of the Act;

(iv) Any transaction in a listed chemical that is contained in a drug other than a scheduled listed chemical product that may be marketed or distributed lawfully in the United States under the Federal Food, Drug, and Cosmetic Act, subject to paragraph (1)(v) of this definition, unless—

(A) The Administrator has determined pursuant to the criteria in §1310.10 of this chapter that the drug or group of drugs is being diverted to obtain the listed chemical for use in the illicit production of a controlled substance; and

(B) The quantity of the listed chemical contained in the drug included in the transaction or multiple transactions equals or exceeds the threshold established for that chemical;

(v) Any transaction in a scheduled listed chemical product that is a sale at retail by a regulated seller or a distributor required to submit reports under §1310.03(c) of this chapter; or

(vi) Any transaction in a chemical mixture designated in §§1310.12 and 1310.13 of this chapter that the Administrator has exempted from regulation.

(2) A distribution, importation, or exportation of a tableting machine or encapsulating machine except that such

term does not include a domestic lawful distribution in the usual course of business between agents and employees of a single regulated person; in this context, agents or employees means individuals under the direct management and control of the regulated person.

Retail distributor means a grocery store, general merchandise store, drug store, or other entity or person whose activities as a distributor relating to drug products containing pseudoephedrine or phenylpropanolamine are limited almost exclusively to sales for personal use, both in number of sales and volume of sales, either directly to walk-in customers or in face-to-face transactions by direct sales. Also for the purposes of this paragraph, a "grocery store" is an entity within Standard Industrial Classification (SIC) code 5411, a "general merchandise store" is an entity within SIC codes 5300 through 5399 and 5499, and a "drug store" is an entity within SIC code 5912.

Return information means supplemental information required to be reported to the Administration following an import or export transaction containing the particulars of the transaction and any other information as the Administration may specify.

Scheduled listed chemical product means:

(1) A product that contains ephedrine, pseudoephedrine, or phenylpropanolamine and may be marketed or distributed lawfully in the United States under the Federal Food, Drug, and Cosmetic Act as a nonprescription drug. Ephedrine, pseudoephedrine, and phenylpropanolamine include their salts, optical isomers, and salts of optical isomers.

(2) Scheduled listed chemical product does not include any product that is a controlled substance under part 1308 of this chapter. In the absence of such scheduling by the Attorney General, a chemical specified in paragraph (1) of this definition may not be considered to be a controlled substance.

Tableting machine means any manual, semi-automatic, or fully automatic equipment which may be used for the compaction or molding of powdered or granular solids, or semi-solid material, to produce coherent solid tablets.

United States, when used in a geographic sense, means all places and waters, continental or insular, subject to the jurisdiction of the United States, which, in addition to the customs territory of the United States, include but are not limited to the U.S. Virgin Islands, Guam, American Samoa, and the Northern Mariana Islands.

Valid prescription means a prescription that is issued for a legitimate medical purpose by an individual practitioner licensed by law to administer and prescribe the drugs concerned and acting in the usual course of the practitioner's professional practice.

[75 FR 16304, Mar. 31, 2010, as amended at 77 FR 4233, Jan. 27, 2012; 81 FR 97019, Dec. 30, 2016]

§ 1300.03 Definitions relating to electronic orders for controlled substances and electronic prescriptions for controlled substances.

For the purposes of this chapter, the following terms shall have the meanings specified:

Application service provider means an entity that sells electronic prescription or pharmacy applications as a hosted service, where the entity controls access to the application and maintains the software and records on its servers.

Audit trail means a record showing who has accessed an information technology application and what operations the user performed during a given period.

Authentication means verifying the identity of the user as a prerequisite to allowing access to the information application.

Authentication protocol means a well specified message exchange process that verifies possession of a token to remotely authenticate a person to an application.

Biometric authentication means authentication based on measurement of the individual's physical features or repeatable actions where those features or actions are both distinctive to the individual and measurable.

Biometric subsystem means the hardware and software used to capture, store, and compare biometric data. The biometric subsystem may be part of a larger application. The biometric subsystem is an automated system capable of:

(1) Capturing a biometric sample from an end user.

(2) Extracting and processing the biometric data from that sample.

(3) Storing the extracted information in a database.

(4) Comparing the biometric data with data contained in one or more reference databases.

(5) Determining how well the stored data matches the newly captured data and indicating whether an identification or verification of identity has been achieved.

Cache means to download and store information on a local server or hard drive.

Certificate policy means a named set of rules that sets forth the applicability of the specific digital certificate to a particular community or class of application with common security requirements.

Certificate revocation list (CRL) means a list of revoked, but unexpired certificates issued by a certification authority.

Certification authority (CA) means an organization that is responsible for verifying the identity of applicants, authorizing and issuing a digital certificate, maintaining a directory of public keys, and maintaining a Certificate Revocation List.

Certified information systems auditor (CISA) means an individual who has been certified by the Information Systems Audit and Control Association as qualified to audit information systems and who performs compliance audits as a regular ongoing business activity.

Credential means an object or data structure that authoritatively binds an identity (and optionally, additional attributes) to a token possessed and controlled by a person.

Credential service provider (CSP) means a trusted entity that issues or registers tokens and issues electronic credentials to individuals. The CSP may be an independent third party or may issue credentials for its own use.

CSOS means controlled substance ordering system.

Digital certificate means a data record that, at a minimum—

(1) Identifies the certification authority issuing it;

(2) Names or otherwise identifies the certificate holder;

(3) Contains a public key that corresponds to a private key under the sole control of the certificate holder;

(4) Identifies the operational period; and

(5) Contains a serial number and is digitally signed by the certification authority issuing it.

Digital signature means a record created when a file is algorithmically transformed into a fixed length digest that is then encrypted using an asymmetric cryptographic private key associated with a digital certificate. The combination of the encryption and algorithm transformation ensure that the signer's identity and the integrity of the file can be confirmed.

Digitally sign means to affix a digital signature to a data file.

Electronic prescription means a prescription that is generated on an electronic application and transmitted as an electronic data file.

Electronic prescription application provider means an entity that develops or markets electronic prescription software either as a stand-alone application or as a module in an electronic health record application.

Electronic signature means a method of signing an electronic message that identifies a particular person as the source of the message and indicates the person's approval of the information contained in the message.

False match rate means the rate at which an impostor's biometric is falsely accepted as being that of an authorized user. It is one of the statistics used to measure biometric performance when operating in the verification or authentication task. The false match rate is similar to the false accept (or acceptance) rate.

False non-match rate means the rate at which a genuine user's biometric is falsely rejected when the user's biometric data fail to match the enrolled data for the user. It is one of the statistics used to measure biometric performance when operating in the verification or authentication task. The false match rate is similar to the false reject (or rejection) rate, except that it does not include the rate at which a biometric system fails to acquire a biometric sample from a genuine user.

FIPS means Federal Information Processing Standards. These Federal standards, as incorporated by reference in § 1311.08 of this chapter, prescribe specific performance requirements, practices, formats, communications protocols, etc., for hardware, software, data, etc.

FIPS 140–2, as incorporated by reference in § 1311.08 of this chapter, means the National Institute of Standards and Technology publication entitled "Security Requirements for Cryptographic Modules," a Federal standard for security requirements for cryptographic modules.

FIPS 180–2, as incorporated by reference in § 1311.08 of this chapter, means the National Institute of Standards and Technology publication entitled "Secure Hash Standard," a Federal secure hash standard.

FIPS 180–3, as incorporated by reference in § 1311.08 of this chapter, means the National Institute of Standards and Technology publication entitled "Secure Hash Standard (SHS)," a Federal secure hash standard.

FIPS 186–2, as incorporated by reference in § 1311.08 of this chapter, means the National Institute of Standards and Technology publication entitled "Digital Signature Standard," a Federal standard for applications used to generate and rely upon digital signatures.

FIPS 186–3, as incorporated by reference in § 1311.08 of this chapter, means the National Institute of Standards and Technology publication entitled "Digital Signature Standard (DSS)," a Federal standard for applications used to generate and rely upon digital signatures.

Hard token means a cryptographic key stored on a special hardware device (e.g., a PDA, cell phone, smart card, USB drive, one-time password device) rather than on a general purpose computer.

Identity proofing means the process by which a credential service provider or certification authority validates sufficient information to uniquely identify a person.

Installed electronic prescription application means software that is used to create electronic prescriptions and that is installed on a practitioner's computers and servers, where access and records are controlled by the practitioner.

Installed pharmacy application means software that is used to process prescription information and that is installed on a pharmacy's computers or servers and is controlled by the pharmacy.

Intermediary means any technology system that receives and transmits an electronic prescription between the practitioner and pharmacy.

Key pair means two mathematically related keys having the properties that:

(1) One key can be used to encrypt a message that can only be decrypted using the other key; and

(2) Even knowing one key, it is computationally infeasible to discover the other key.

NIST means the National Institute of Standards and Technology.

NIST SP 800–63–1, as incorporated by reference in § 1311.08 of this chapter, means the National Institute of Standards and Technology publication entitled "Electronic Authentication Guideline," a Federal standard for electronic authentication.

NIST SP 800–76–1, as incorporated by reference in § 1311.08 of this chapter, means the National Institute of Standards and Technology publication entitled "Biometric Data Specification for Personal Identity Verification," a Federal standard for biometric data specifications for personal identity verification.

Operating point means a point chosen on a receiver operating characteristic (ROC) curve for a specific algorithm at which the biometric system is set to function. It is defined by its corresponding coordinates—a false match rate and a false non-match rate. An ROC curve shows graphically the trade-off between the principal two types of errors (false match rate and false non-match rate) of a biometric system by plotting the performance of a specific algorithm on a specific set of data.

Paper prescription means a prescription created on paper or computer generated to be printed or transmitted via facsimile that meets the requirements of part 1306 of this chapter including a manual signature.

Password means a secret, typically a character string (letters, numbers, and other symbols), that a person memorizes and uses to authenticate his identity.

PDA means a Personal Digital Assistant, a handheld computer used to manage contacts, appointments, and tasks.

Pharmacy application provider means an entity that develops or markets software that manages the receipt and processing of electronic prescriptions.

Private key means the key of a key pair that is used to create a digital signature.

Public key means the key of a key pair that is used to verify a digital signature. The public key is made available to anyone who will receive digitally signed messages from the holder of the key pair.

Public Key Infrastructure (PKI) means a structure under which a certification authority verifies the identity of applicants; issues, renews, and revokes digital certificates; maintains a registry of public keys; and maintains an up-to-date certificate revocation list.

Readily retrievable means that certain records are kept by automatic data processing applications or other electronic or mechanized recordkeeping systems in such a manner that they can be separated out from all other records in a reasonable time and/or records are kept on which certain items are asterisked, redlined, or in some other manner visually identifiable apart from other items appearing on the records.

SAS 70 Audit means a third-party audit of a technology provider that meets the American Institute of Certified Public Accountants (AICPA) Statement of Auditing Standards (SAS) 70 criteria.

Signing function means any keystroke or other action used to indicate that the practitioner has authorized for transmission and dispensing a controlled substance prescription. The signing function may occur simultaneously with or after the completion of the two-factor authentication protocol that meets the requirements of part 1311 of this chapter. The signing function may have different names (e.g., approve, sign, transmit), but it serves as the practitioner's final authorization that he intends to issue the prescription for a legitimate medical reason in the normal course of his professional practice.

SysTrust means a professional service performed by a qualified certified public accountant to evaluate one or more aspects of electronic systems.

Third-party audit means an independent review and examination of records and activities to assess the adequacy of system controls, to ensure compliance with established policies and operational procedures, and to recommend necessary changes in controls, policies, or procedures.

Token means something a person possesses and controls (typically a key or password) used to authenticate the person's identity.

Trusted agent means an entity authorized to act as a representative of a certification authority or credential service provider in confirming practitioner identification during the enrollment process.

Valid prescription means a prescription that is issued for a legitimate medical purpose by an individual practitioner licensed by law to administer and prescribe the drugs concerned and acting in the usual course of the practitioner's professional practice.

WebTrust means a professional service performed by a qualified certified public accountant to evaluate one or more aspects of Web sites.

[75 FR 16304, Mar. 31, 2010]

§ 1300.04 Definitions relating to the dispensing of controlled substances by means of the Internet.

(a) Any term not defined in this part or elsewhere in this chapter shall have the definition set forth in sections 102 and 309 of the Act (21 U.S.C. 802, 829).

(b) The term *covering practitioner* means, with respect to a patient, a practitioner who conducts a medical evaluation (other than an in-person medical evaluation) at the request of a practitioner who:

(1) Has conducted at least one in-person medical evaluation of the patient or an evaluation of the patient through

the practice of telemedicine, within the previous 24 months; and

(2) Is temporarily unavailable to conduct the evaluation of the patient.

(c) The term *deliver, distribute, or dispense by means of the Internet* refers, respectively, to any delivery, distribution, or dispensing of a controlled substance that is caused or facilitated by means of the Internet.

(d) The term *filling new prescriptions for controlled substances in Schedule III, IV, or V* means filling a prescription for an individual for a controlled substance in Schedule III, IV, or V, if:

(1) The pharmacy dispensing that prescription has previously dispensed to the patient a controlled substance other than by means of the Internet and pursuant to the valid prescription of a practitioner that meets the applicable requirements of subsections (b) and (c) of section 309 of the Act (21 U.S.C. 829) and §§ 1306.21 and 1306.22 of this chapter (for purposes of this definition, such a prescription shall be referred to as the "original prescription");

(2) The pharmacy contacts the practitioner who issued the original prescription at the request of that individual to determine whether the practitioner will authorize the issuance of a new prescription for that individual for the controlled substance described in paragraph (d)(1) of this section (*i.e.*, the same controlled substance as described in paragraph (d)(1)); and

(3) The practitioner, acting in the usual course of professional practice, determines there is a legitimate medical purpose for the issuance of the new prescription.

(e) The term *homepage* means the opening or main page or screen of the Web site of an online pharmacy that is viewable on the Internet.

(f) The term *in-person medical evaluation* means a medical evaluation that is conducted with the patient in the physical presence of the practitioner, without regard to whether portions of the evaluation are conducted by other health professionals. Nothing in this paragraph shall be construed to imply that one in-person medical evaluation demonstrates that a prescription has been issued for a legitimate medical purpose within the usual course of professional practice.

(g) The term *Internet* means collectively the myriad of computer and telecommunications facilities, including equipment and operating software, which comprise the interconnected worldwide network of networks that employ the Transmission Control Protocol/Internet Protocol, or any predecessor or successor protocol to such protocol, to communicate information of all kinds by wire or radio.

(h) The term *online pharmacy* means a person, entity, or Internet site, whether in the United States or abroad, that knowingly or intentionally delivers, distributes, or dispenses, or offers or attempts to deliver, distribute, or dispense, a controlled substance by means of the Internet. The term includes, but is not limited to, a pharmacy that has obtained a modification of its registration pursuant to §§ 1301.13 and 1301.19 of this chapter that currently authorizes it to dispense controlled substances by means of the Internet, regardless of whether the pharmacy is currently dispensing controlled substances by means of the Internet. The term does not include:

(1) Manufacturers or distributors registered under subsection (a), (b), (d), or (e) of section 303 of the Act (21 U.S.C. 823(a), (b), (d), or (e)) (§ 1301.13 of this chapter) who do not dispense controlled substances to an unregistered individual or entity;

(2) Nonpharmacy practitioners who are registered under section 303(f) of the Act (21 U.S.C. 823(f)) (§ 1301.13 of this chapter) and whose activities are authorized by that registration;

(3) Any hospital or other medical facility that is operated by an agency of the United States (including the Armed Forces), provided such hospital or other facility is registered under section 303(f) of the Act (21 U.S.C. 823(f)) (§ 1301.13 of this chapter);

(4) A health care facility owned or operated by an Indian tribe or tribal organization, only to the extent such facility is carrying out a contract or compact under the Indian Self-Determination and Education Assistance Act;

(5) Any agent or employee of any hospital or facility referred to in paragraph (h)(3) or (h)(4) of this section, provided such agent or employee is lawfully acting in the usual course of business or employment, and within the scope of the official duties of such agent or employee, with such hospital or facility, and, with respect to agents or employees of health care facilities specified in paragraph (h)(4) of this section, only to the extent such individuals are furnishing services pursuant to the contracts or compacts described in such paragraph;

(6) Mere advertisements that do not attempt to facilitate an actual transaction involving a controlled substance;

(7) A person, entity, or Internet site that is not in the United States and does not facilitate the delivery, distribution, or dispensing of a controlled substance by means of the Internet to any person in the United States;

(8) A pharmacy registered under section 303(f) of the Act (21 U.S.C. 823(f)) (§ 1301.13 of this chapter) whose dispensing of controlled substances via the Internet consists solely of:

(i) Refilling prescriptions for controlled substances in Schedule III, IV, or V, as defined in paragraph (k) of this section; or

(ii) Filling new prescriptions for controlled substances in Schedule III, IV, or V, as defined in paragraph (d) of this section;

(9)(i) Any registered pharmacy whose delivery, distribution, or dispensing of controlled substances by means of the Internet consists solely of filling prescriptions that were electronically prescribed in a manner authorized by this chapter and otherwise in compliance with the Act.

(ii) A registered pharmacy will be deemed to meet this exception if, in view of all of its activities other than those referred to in paragraph (h)(9)(i) of this section, it would fall outside the definition of an online pharmacy; or

(10)(i) Any registered pharmacy whose delivery, distribution, or dispensing of controlled substances by means of the Internet consists solely of the transmission of prescription information between a pharmacy and an automated dispensing system located in a long term care facility when the registration of the automated dispensing system is held by that pharmacy as described in §§ 1301.17 and 1301.27 and the pharmacy is otherwise complying with this chapter.

(ii) A registered pharmacy will be deemed to meet this exception if, in view of all of its activities other than those referred to in paragraph (h)(10)(i) of this section, it would fall outside the definition of an online pharmacy.

(i) Effective January 15, 2010, the term *practice of telemedicine* means the practice of medicine in accordance with applicable Federal and State laws by a practitioner (other than a pharmacist) who is at a location remote from the patient and is communicating with the patient, or health care professional who is treating the patient, using a telecommunications system referred to in section 1834(m) of the Social Security Act (42 U.S.C. 1395m(m)), which practice falls within a category listed in the following paragraphs (i)(1) through (7):

(1) *Treatment in a hospital or clinic.* The practice of telemedicine is being conducted while the patient is being treated by, and physically located in, a hospital or clinic registered under section 303(f) of the Act (21 U.S.C. 823(f)) by a practitioner acting in the usual course of professional practice, who is acting in accordance with applicable State law, and who is registered under section 303(f) of the Act (21 U.S.C. 823(f)) in the State in which the patient is located, unless the practitioner:

(i) Is exempted from such registration in all States under section 302(d) of the Act (21 U.S.C. 822(d); or

(ii) Is an employee or contractor of the Department of Veterans Affairs who is acting in the scope of such employment or contract, and registered under section 303(f) of the Act (21 U.S.C. 823(f)) in any State or is utilizing the registration of a hospital or clinic operated by the Department of Veterans Affairs registered under section 303(f);

(2) *Treatment in the physical presence of a practitioner.* The practice of telemedicine is being conducted while the patient is being treated by, and in the physical presence of, a practitioner

acting in the usual course of professional practice, who is acting in accordance with applicable State law, and who is registered under section 303(f) of the Act (21 U.S.C. 823(f)) in the State in which the patient is located, unless the practitioner:

(i) Is exempted from such registration in all States under section 302(d) of the Act (21 U.S.C. 822(d)); or

(ii) Is an employee or contractor of the Department of Veterans Affairs who is acting in the scope of such employment or contract, and registered under section 303(f) of the Act (21 U.S.C. 823(f)) in any State or is using the registration of a hospital or clinic operated by the Department of Veterans Affairs registered under section 303(f);

(3) *Indian Health Service or tribal organization.* The practice of telemedicine is being conducted by a practitioner who is an employee or contractor of the Indian Health Service, or is working for an Indian tribe or tribal organization under its contract or compact with the Indian Health Service under the Indian Self-Determination and Education Assistance Act; who is acting within the scope of the employment, contract, or compact; and who is designated as an Internet Eligible Controlled Substances Provider by the Secretary of Health and Human Services under section 311(g)(2) of the Act (21 U.S.C. 831(g)(2));

(4) *Public health emergency declared by the Secretary of Health and Human Services.* The practice of telemedicine is being conducted during a public health emergency declared by the Secretary of Health and Human Services under section 319 of the Public Health Service Act (42 U.S.C. 247d), and involves patients located in such areas, and such controlled substances, as the Secretary of Health and Human Services, with the concurrence of the Administrator, designates, provided that such designation shall not be subject to the procedures prescribed by the Administrative Procedure Act (5 U.S.C. 551–559 and 701–706);

(5) *Special registration.* The practice of telemedicine is being conducted by a practitioner who has obtained from the Administrator a special registration under section 311(h) of the Act (21 U.S.C. 831(h));

(6) *Department of Veterans Affairs medical emergency.* The practice of telemedicine is being conducted:

(i) In a medical emergency situation:

(A) That prevents the patient from being in the physical presence of a practitioner registered under section 303(f) of the Act (21 U.S.C. 823(f)) who is an employee or contractor of the Veterans Health Administration acting in the usual course of business and employment and within the scope of the official duties or contract of that employee or contractor;

(B) That prevents the patient from being physically present at a hospital or clinic operated by the Department of Veterans Affairs registered under section 303(f) of the Act (21 U.S.C. 823(f));

(C) During which the primary care practitioner of the patient or a practitioner otherwise practicing telemedicine within the meaning of this paragraph is unable to provide care or consultation; and

(D) That requires immediate intervention by a health care practitioner using controlled substances to prevent what the practitioner reasonably believes in good faith will be imminent and serious clinical consequences, such as further injury or death; and

(ii) By a practitioner that:

(A) Is an employee or contractor of the Veterans Health Administration acting within the scope of that employment or contract;

(B) Is registered under section 303(f) of the Act (21 U.S.C. 823(f)) in any State or is utilizing the registration of a hospital or clinic operated by the Department of Veterans Affairs registered under section 303(f); and

(C) Issues a controlled substance prescription in this emergency context that is limited to a maximum of a five-day supply which may not be extended or refilled; or

(7) *Other circumstances specified by regulation.* The practice of telemedicine is being conducted under any other circumstances that the Administrator and the Secretary of Health and Human Services have jointly, by regulation, determined to be consistent

with effective controls against diversion and otherwise consistent with the public health and safety.

(j) *Temporary definition of practice of telemedicine.* Prior to January 15, 2010, or as otherwise specified by regulation prior to that date, instead of the definition in paragraph (i), the term *practice of telemedicine* means the practice of medicine in accordance with applicable Federal and State laws by a practitioner (as that term is defined in section 102 of the Act (21 U.S.C. 802)) (other than a pharmacist) who is at a location remote from the patient and is communicating with the patient, or health care professional who is treating the patient, using a telecommunications system referred to in section 1834(m) of the Social Security Act (42 U.S.C. 1395m(m)), if the practitioner is using an interactive telecommunications system that satisfies the requirements of section 410.78(a)(3) of title 42, Code of Federal Regulations.

(k) The term *refilling prescriptions for controlled substances in Schedule III, IV, or V:*

(1) Means the dispensing of a controlled substance in Schedule III, IV, or V in accordance with refill instructions issued by a practitioner as part of a valid prescription that meets the requirements of subsections (b) and (c) of section 309 of the Act (21 U.S.C. 829) and §§ 1306.21 and 1306.22 of this chapter, as appropriate; and

(2) Does not include the issuance of a new prescription to an individual for a controlled substance that individual was previously prescribed.

(l)(1) The term *valid prescription* means a prescription that is issued for a legitimate medical purpose in the usual course of professional practice by:

(i) A practitioner who has conducted at least one in-person medical evaluation of the patient; or

(ii) A covering practitioner.

(2) Nothing in this paragraph (l) shall be construed to imply that one in-person medical evaluation demonstrates that a prescription has been issued for a legitimate medical purpose within the usual course of professional practice.

[74 FR 15619, Apr. 6, 2009]

§ 1300.05 Definitions relating to the disposal of controlled substances.

(a) Any term not defined in this part or elsewhere in this chapter shall have the definition set forth in section 102 of the Act (21 U.S.C. 802).

(b) As used in part 1317 of this chapter, the following terms shall have the meanings specified:

Employee means an employee as defined under the general common law of agency. Some of the factors relevant to the determination of employee status include: The hiring party's right to control the manner and means by which the product is accomplished; the skill required; the source of the instrumentalities and tools; the location of the work; the duration of the relationship between the parties; whether the hiring party has the right to assign additional projects to the hired party; the extent of the hired party's discretion over when and how long to work; the method of payment; the hired party's role in hiring and paying assistants; whether the work is part of the regular business of the hiring party; whether the hiring party is in business; the provision of employee benefits; and the tax treatment of the hired party. Other applicable factors may be considered and no one factor is dispositive. The following criteria will determine whether a person is an *employee* of a registrant for the purpose of disposal: The person is directly paid by the registrant; subject to direct oversight by the registrant; required, as a condition of employment, to follow the registrant's procedures and guidelines pertaining to the handling of controlled substances; subject to receive a performance rating or performance evaluation on a regular/routine basis from the registrant; subject to disciplinary action by the registrant; and required to render services at the registrant's registered location.

Law enforcement officer means a person who is described in paragraph (1), (2) or (3) of this definition:

(1) Meets all of the following criteria:

(i) Employee of either a law enforcement agency, or law enforcement component of a Federal agency;

(ii) Is under the direction and control of a Federal, State, tribal, or local government;

(iii) Acting in the course of his/her official duty; and

(iv) Duly sworn and given the authority by a Federal, State, tribal, or local government to carry firearms, execute and serve warrants, make arrests without warrant, and make seizures of property;

(2) Is a Veterans Health Administration (VHA) police officer authorized by the Department of Veterans Affairs to participate in collection activities conducted by the VHA; or

(3) Is a Department of Defense (DOD) police officer authorized by the DOD to participate in collection activities conducted by the DOD.

Non-retrievable means, for the purpose of destruction, the condition or state to which a controlled substance shall be rendered following a process that permanently alters that controlled substance's physical or chemical condition or state through irreversible means and thereby renders the controlled substance unavailable and unusable for all practical purposes. The process to achieve a non-retrievable condition or state may be unique to a substance's chemical or physical properties. A controlled substance is considered "non-retrievable" when it cannot be transformed to a physical or chemical condition or state as a controlled substance or controlled substance analogue. The purpose of destruction is to render the controlled substance(s) to a non-retrievable state and thus prevent diversion of any such substance to illicit purposes.

On-site means located on or at the physical premises of the registrant's registered location. A controlled substance is destroyed *on-site* when destruction occurs on the physical premises of the destroying registrant's registered location. A hospital/clinic has an *on-site* pharmacy when it has a pharmacy located on the physical premises of the registrant's registered location.

[79 FR 53560, Sept. 9, 2014]

PART 1301—REGISTRATION OF MANUFACTURERS, DISTRIBUTORS, AND DISPENSERS OF CONTROLLED SUBSTANCES

GENERAL INFORMATION

Sec.

REGISTRATION

EXCEPTIONS TO REGISTRATION AND FEES

ACTION ON APPLICATION FOR REGISTRATION: REVOCATION OR SUSPENSION OF REGISTRATION

AUTHORITY: 21 U.S.C. 821, 822, 823, 824, 831, 871(b), 875, 877, 886a, 951, 952, 956, 957, 958, 965 unless otherwise noted.

SOURCE: 36 FR 7778, Apr. 24, 1971, unless otherwise noted. Redesignated at 38 FR 26609, Sept. 24, 1973.

GENERAL INFORMATION

§ 1301.01 Scope of this part 1301.

Procedures governing the registration of manufacturers, distributors, dispensers, importers, and exporters of controlled substances pursuant to sections 301–304 and 1007–1008 of the Act (21 U.S.C. 821–824 and 957–958) are set forth generally by those sections and specifically by the sections of this part.

[62 FR 13945, Mar. 24, 1997]

§ 1301.02 Definitions.

Any term used in this part shall have the definition set forth in section 102 of the Act (21 U.S.C. 802) or part 1300 of this chapter.

[62 FR 13945, Mar. 24, 1997]

§ 1301.03 Information; special instructions.

Information regarding procedures under these rules and instructions supplementing these rules will be furnished upon request by writing to the Registration Section, Drug Enforcement Administration. See the Table of DEA Mailing Addresses in § 1321.01 of this chapter for the current mailing address.

[75 FR 10676, Mar. 9, 2010]

REGISTRATION

§ 1301.11 Persons required to register; requirement of modification of registration authorizing activity as an online pharmacy.

(a) Every person who manufactures, distributes, dispenses, imports, or exports any controlled substance or who proposes to engage in the manufacture, distribution, dispensing, importation or exportation of any controlled substance shall obtain a registration unless exempted by law or pursuant to §§ 1301.22 through 1301.26. Except as provided in paragraph (b) of this section, only persons actually engaged in such activities are required to obtain a registration; related or affiliated persons who are not engaged in such activities are not required to be registered. (For example, a stockholder or parent corporation of a corporation manufacturing controlled substances is not required to obtain a registration.)

(b) As provided in sections 303(f) and 401(h) of the Act (21 U.S.C. 823(f) and 841(h)), it is unlawful for any person who falls within the definition of "online pharmacy" (as set forth in section 102(52) of the Act (21 U.S.C. 802(52)) and § 1300.04(h) of this chapter) to deliver, distribute, or dispense a controlled substance by means of the Internet if such person is not validly registered with a modification of such registration authorizing such activity (unless such person is exempt from such modified registration requirement under the Act or this chapter). The Act further provides that the Administrator may only issue such modification of registration to a person who is registered as a pharmacy under section 303(f) of the Act (21 U.S.C. 823(f)). Accordingly, any pharmacy registered pursuant to § 1301.13 of this part that falls within the definition of an online pharmacy and proposes to dispense controlled substances by means of the Internet must obtain a modification of its registration authorizing such activity following the submission of an application in accordance with § 1301.19 of this part. This requirement does not apply to a registered pharmacy that does not fall within the definition of an online pharmacy set forth in § 1300.04(h). Under the Act, persons other than registered pharmacies are not eligible to obtain such a modification of registration but remain liable under section 401(h) of the Act (21 U.S.C. 841(h)) if they deliver, distribute, or dispense a controlled substance while acting as an online pharmacy without being validly registered with a modification authorizing such activity.

[74 FR 15621, Apr. 6, 2009]

§ 1301.12 Separate registrations for separate locations.

(a) A separate registration is required for each principal place of business or professional practice at one general physical location where controlled substances are manufactured, distributed, imported, exported, or dispensed by a person.

(b) The following locations shall be deemed not to be places where controlled substances are manufactured, distributed, or dispensed:

(1) A warehouse where controlled substances are stored by or on behalf of a registered person, unless such substances are distributed directly from such warehouse to registered locations other than the registered location from which the substances were delivered or to persons not required to register by virtue of subsection 302(c)(2) or subsection 1007(b)(1)(B) of the Act (21 U.S.C. 822(c)(2) or 957(b)(1)(B));

(2) An office used by agents of a registrant where sales of controlled substances are solicited, made, or supervised but which neither contains such substances (other than substances for display purposes or lawful distribution as samples only) nor serves as a distribution point for filling sales orders; and

(3) An office used by a practitioner (who is registered at another location in the same State in which he or she practices) where controlled substances are prescribed but neither administered nor otherwise dispensed as a regular part of the professional practice of the practitioner at such office, and where no supplies of controlled substances are maintained.

(4) A freight forwarding facility, as defined in § 1300.01 of this part, provided that the distributing registrant operating the facility has submitted written notice of intent to operate the facility by registered mail, return receipt requested (or other suitable means of documented delivery) and such notice has been approved. The notice shall be submitted to the Special Agent in Charge of the Administration's offices in both the area in which the facility is located and each area in which the distributing registrant maintains a registered location that will transfer controlled substances through the facility. The notice shall detail the registered locations that will utilize the facility, the location of the facility, the hours of operation, the individual(s) responsible for the controlled substances, the security and recordkeeping procedures that will be employed, and whether controlled substances returns will be processed through the facility. The notice must also detail what state licensing requirements apply to the facility and the registrant's actions to comply with

any such requirements. The Special Agent in Charge of the DEA Office in the area where the freight forwarding facility will be operated will provide written notice of approval or disapproval to the person within thirty days after confirmed receipt of the notice. Registrants that are currently operating freight forwarding facilities under a memorandum of understanding with the Administration must provide notice as required by this section no later than September 18, 2000 and receive written approval from the Special Agent in Charge of the DEA Office in the area in which the freight forwarding facility is operated in order to continue operation of the facility.

[62 FR 13945, Mar. 24, 1997, as amended at 65 FR 44678, July 19, 2000; 65 FR 45829, July 25, 2000; 71 FR 69480, Dec. 1, 2006; 81 FR 97019, Dec. 30, 2016]

§ 1301.13 Application for registration; time for application; expiration date; registration for independent activities; application forms, fees, contents and signature; coincident activities.

(a) Any person who is required to be registered and who is not so registered may apply for registration at any time. No person required to be registered shall engage in any activity for which registration is required until the application for registration is granted and a Certificate of Registration is issued by the Administrator to such person.

(b) Any person who is registered may apply to be reregistered not more than 60 days before the expiration date of his/her registration, except that a bulk manufacturer of Schedule I or II controlled substances or an importer of Schedule I or II controlled substances may apply to be reregistered no more than 120 days before the expiration date of their registration.

(c) At the time a manufacturer, distributor, reverse distributor, researcher, analytical lab, importer, exporter or narcotic treatment program is first registered, that business activity shall be assigned to one of twelve groups, which shall correspond to the months of the year. The expiration date of the registrations of all registrants within any group will be the last date of the month designated for that group. In assigning any of these business activities to a group, the Administration may select a group the expiration date of which is less than one year from the date such business activity was registered. If the business activity is assigned to a group which has an expiration date less than three months from the date of which the business activity is registered, the registration shall not expire until one year from that expiration date; in all other cases, the registration shall expire on the expiration date following the date on which the business activity is registered.

(d) At the time a retail pharmacy, hospital/clinic, practitioner or teaching institution is first registered, that business activity shall be assigned to one of twelve groups, which shall correspond to the months of the year. The expiration date of the registrations of all registrants within any group will be the last day of the month designated for that group. In assigning any of the above business activities to a group, the Administration may select a group the expiration date of which is not less than 28 months nor more than 39 months from the date such business activity was registered. After the initial registration period, the registration shall expire 36 months from the initial expiration date.

(e) Any person who is required to be registered and who is not so registered, shall make application for registration for one of the following groups of controlled substances activities, which are deemed to be independent of each other. Application for each registration shall be made on the indicated form, and shall be accompanied by the indicated fee. Fee payments shall be made in the form of a personal, certified, or cashier's check or money order made payable to the "Drug Enforcement Administration". The application fees are not refundable. Any person, when registered to engage in the activities described in each subparagraph in this paragraph, shall be authorized to engage in the coincident activities described without obtaining a registration to engage in such coincident activities, provided that, unless specifically exempted, he/she complies with all requirements and duties prescribed by law for persons registered to engage in such coincident activities. Any person who engages in more than one group of independent activities shall obtain a separate registration for each group of activities, except as provided in this paragraph under coincident activities. A single registration to engage in any group of independent activities listed below may include one or more controlled substances listed in the schedules authorized in that group of independent activities. A person registered to conduct research with controlled substances listed in Schedule I may conduct research with any substances listed in Schedule I for which he/she has filed and had approved a research protocol.

(1)

Business activity	Controlled substances	DEA Application forms	Application fee ($)	Registration period (years)	Coincident activities allowed
(i) Manufacturing	Schedules I–V ...	New—225 Renewal—225a.	3,047	1	Schedules I–V: May distribute that substance or class for which registration was issued; may not distribute any substance or class for which not registered. Schedules II–V: May conduct chemical analysis and preclinical research (including quality control analysis) with substances listed in those schedules for which authorization as a mfr. was issued.
(ii) Distributing	Schedules I–V ...	New—225 Renewal—225a.	1,523	1	May acquire Schedules II–V controlled substances from collectors for the purposes of destruction.
(iii) Reverse distributing.	Schedules I–V ...	New–225 Renewal–225a.	1,523	1	
(iv) Dispensing or instructing (includes Practitioner, Hospital/ Clinic, Retail Pharmacy, Central fill pharmacy, Teaching Institution).	Schedules II–V ..	New–224 Renewal–224a.	731	3	May conduct research and instructional activities with those substances for which registration was granted, except that a mid-level practitioner may conduct such research only to the extent expressly authorized under state statute. A pharmacist may manufacture an aqueous or oleaginous solution or solid dosage form containing a narcotic controlled substance in Schedule II–V in a proportion not exceeding 20% of the complete solution, compound or mixture. A retail pharmacy may perform central fill pharmacy activities.
(v) Research	Schedule I	New–225 Renewal–225a.	244	1	A researcher may manufacture or import the basic class of substance or substances for which registration was issued, provided that such manufacture or import is set forth in the protocol required in § 1301.18 and to distribute such class to persons registered or authorized to conduct research with such class of substance or registered or authorized to conduct chemical analysis with controlled substances.

Business activity	Controlled substances	DEA Application forms	Application fee ($)	Registration period (years)	Coincident activities allowed
(vi) Research	Schedules II–V ..	New–225 Renewal–225a.	244	1	May conduct chemical analysis with controlled substances in those schedules for which registration was issued; manufacture such substances if and to the extent that such manufacture is set forth in a statement filed with the application for registration or reregistration and provided that the manufacture is not for the purposes of dosage form development; import such substances for research purposes; distribute such substances to persons registered or authorized to conduct chemical analysis, instructional activities or research with such substances, and to persons exempted from registration pursuant to § 1301.24; and conduct instructional activities with controlled substances.
(vii) Narcotic Treatment Program (including compounder).	Narcotic Drugs in Schedules II–V.	New–363 Renewal–363a.	244	1	
(viii) Importing	Schedules I–V ...	New–225 Renewal–225a.	1,523	1	May distribute that substance or class for which registration was issued; may not distribute any substance or class for which not registered.
(ix) Exporting	Schedules I–V ...	New–225 Renewal–225a.	1,523	1	
(x) Chemical Analysis.	Schedules I–V ...	New–225 Renewal–225a.	244	1	May manufacture and import controlled substances for analytical or instructional activities; may distribute such substances to persons registered or authorized to conduct chemical analysis, instructional activities, or research with such substances and to persons exempted from registration pursuant to § 1301.24; may export such substances to persons in other countries performing chemical analysis or enforcing laws related to controlled substances or drugs in those countries; and may conduct instructional activities with controlled substances.

(2) DEA Forms 224, 225, and 363 may be obtained at any area office of the Administration or by writing to the Registration Section, Drug Enforcement Administration. See the Table of DEA Mailing Addresses in §1321.01 of this chapter for the current mailing address.

(3) Registrants will receive renewal notifications approximately 60 days prior to the registration expiration date. DEA Forms 224a, 225a, and 363a may be mailed, as applicable, to registrants; if any registered person does not receive such notification within 45 days before the registration expiration date, the registrant must promptly give notice of such fact and may request such forms by writing to the Registration Section, Drug Enforcement Administration.

(f) Each application for registration to handle any basic class of controlled substance listed in Schedule I (except to conduct chemical analysis with such classes), and each application for registration to manufacture a basic class of controlled substance listed in Schedule II shall include the Administration Controlled Substances Code Number, as set forth in part 1308 of this chapter, for each basic class to be covered by such registration.

(g) Each application for registration to import or export controlled substances shall include the Administration Controlled Substances Code Number, as set forth in part 1308 of this chapter, for each controlled substance whose importation or exportation is to be authorized by such registration. Registration as an importer or exporter shall not entitle a registrant to import or export any controlled substance not specified in such registration.

(h) Each application for registration to conduct research with any basic class of controlled substance listed in Schedule II shall include the Administration Controlled Substances Code Number, as set forth in part 1308 of this chapter, for each such basic class to be manufactured or imported as a coincident activity of that registration. A statement listing the quantity of each such basic class of controlled substance to be imported or manufactured during the registration period for which application is being made shall be included with each such application. For purposes of this paragraph only, manufacturing is defined as the production of a controlled substance by synthesis, extraction or by agricultural/horticultural means.

(i) Each application shall include all information called for in the form, unless the item is not applicable, in which case this fact shall be indicated.

(j) Each application, attachment, or other document filed as part of an application, shall be signed by the applicant, if an individual; by a partner of the applicant, if a partnership; or by an officer of the applicant, if a corporation, corporate division, association, trust or other entity. An applicant may authorize one or more individuals, who would not otherwise be authorized to do so, to sign applications for the applicant by filing with the Registration Unit of the Administration a power of attorney for each such individual. The power of attorney shall be signed by a person who is authorized to sign applications under this paragraph and shall contain the signature of the individual being authorized to sign applications. The power of attorney shall be valid until revoked by the applicant.

[62 FR 13946, Mar. 24, 1997, as amended at 68 FR 37409, June 24, 2003; 68 FR 41228, July 11, 2003; 68 FR 58598, Oct. 10, 2003; 71 FR 51112, Aug. 29, 2006; 74 FR 15622, Apr. 6, 2009; 75 FR 10676, Mar. 9, 2010; 77 FR 15248, Mar. 15, 2012; 79 FR 53560, Sept. 9, 2014]

§ 1301.14 Filing of application; acceptance for filing; defective applications.

(a) All applications for registration shall be submitted for filing to the Registration Unit, Drug Enforcement Administration. The appropriate registration fee and any required attachments must accompany the application. See the Table of DEA Mailing Addresses in § 1321.01 of this chapter for the current mailing address.

(b) Any person required to obtain more than one registration may submit all applications in one package. Each application must be complete and should not refer to any accompanying application for required information.

(c) Applications submitted for filing are dated upon receipt. If found to be complete, the application will be accepted for filing. Applications failing to comply with the requirements of this part will not generally be accepted for filing. In the case of minor defects as to completeness, the Administrator may accept the application for filing with a request to the applicant for additional information. A defective application will be returned to the applicant within 10 days following its receipt with a statement of the reason for not accepting the application for filing. A defective application may be corrected and resubmitted for filing at any time; the Administrator shall accept for filing any application upon resubmission by the applicant, whether complete or not.

(d) Accepting an application for filing does not preclude any subsequent request for additional information pursuant to § 1301.15 and has no bearing on whether the application will be granted.

[62 FR 13948, Mar. 24, 1997, as amended at 75 FR 10676, Mar. 9, 2010]

§ 1301.15 Additional information.

The Administrator may require an applicant to submit such documents or written statements of fact relevant to the application as he/she deems necessary to determine whether the application should be granted. The failure of the applicant to provide such documents or statements within a reasonable time after being requested to do so shall be deemed to be a waiver by the applicant of an opportunity to present such documents or facts for consideration by the Administrator in granting or denying the application.

[62 FR 13948, Mar. 24, 1997]

§ 1301.16 Amendments to and withdrawal of applications.

(a) An application may be amended or withdrawn without permission of the Administrator at any time before the date on which the applicant receives an order to show cause pursuant to § 1301.37. An application may be amended or withdrawn with permission of the Administrator at any time where good cause is shown by the applicant or where the amendment or withdrawal is in the public interest.

(b) After an application has been accepted for filing, the request by the applicant that it be returned or the failure of the applicant to respond to official correspondence regarding the application, when sent by registered or certified mail, return receipt requested, shall be deemed to be a withdrawal of the application.

[62 FR 13949, Mar. 24, 1997]

§ 1301.17 Special procedures for certain applications.

(a) If, at the time of application for registration of a new pharmacy, the pharmacy has been issued a license from the appropriate State licensing agency, the applicant may include with his/her application an affidavit as to the existence of the State license in the following form:

Affidavit for New Pharmacy

I, ________, the ________ (Title of officer, official, partner, or other position) of ________ (Corporation, partnership, or sole proprietor), doing business as ________ (Store name) at ________ (Number and Street), ________ (City) ________ (State) ________ (Zip code), hereby certify that said store was issued a pharmacy permit No. ________ by the ________ (Board of Pharmacy or Licensing Agency) of the State of ________ on ________ (Date).

This statement is submitted in order to obtain a Drug Enforcement Administration registration number. I understand that if any information is false, the Administration may immediately suspend the registration for this store and commence proceedings to revoke under 21 U.S.C. 824(a) because of the danger to public health and safety. I further understand that any false information contained in this affidavit may subject me personally and the above-named corporation/partnership/business to prosecution under 21 U.S.C. 843, the penalties for conviction of which include imprisonment for up to 4 years, a fine of not more than $30,000 or both.

____

Signature (Person who signs Application for Registration)

State of ________

County of ________

Subscribed to and sworn before me this ________ day of ________, 19____.

____

Notary Public

(b) Whenever the ownership of a pharmacy is being transferred from one person to another, if the transferee owns at least one other pharmacy licensed in the same State as the one the ownership of which is being transferred, the transferee may apply for registration prior to the date of transfer. The Administrator may register the applicant and authorize him to obtain controlled substances at the time of transfer. Such registration shall not authorize the transferee to dispense controlled substances until the pharmacy has been issued a valid State license. The transferee shall include with his/her application the following affidavit:

Affidavit for Transfer of Pharmacy

I, ________, the ________ (Title of officer, official, partner or other position) of ________ (Corporation, partnership, or sole proprietor), doing business as ________ (Store name) hereby certify:

(1) That said company was issued a pharmacy permit No. ________ by the ________ (Board of Pharmacy of Licensing Agency) of the State of ________ and a DEA Registration Number ________ for a pharmacy located at

_______________ (Number and Street) __________ (City) __________ (State) __________ (Zip Code); and

(2) That said company is acquiring the pharmacy business of ______________ (Name of Seller) doing business as______________with DEA Registration Number __________ on or about __________ (Date of Transfer) and that said company has applied (or will apply on __________ (Date) for a pharmacy permit from the board of pharmacy (or licensing agency) of the State of __________ to do business as ______________ (Store name) at ______________ (Number and Street) ______________ (City) __________ (State) __________ (Zip Code).

This statement is submitted in order to obtain a Drug Enforcement Administration registration number.

I understand that if a DEA registration number is issued, the pharmacy may acquire controlled substances but may not dispense them until a pharmacy permit or license is issued by the State board of pharmacy or licensing agency.

I understand that if any information is false, the Administration may immediately suspend the registration for this store and commence proceedings to revoke under 21 U.S.C. 824(a) because of the danger to public health and safety. I further understand that any false information contained in this affidavit may subject me personally to prosecution under 21 U.S.C. 843, the penalties for conviction of which include imprisonment for up to 4 years, a fine of not more than $30,000 or both.

____
Signature (Person who signs Application for Registration)

State of ______________________

County of ______________________

Subscribed to and sworn before me this __________ day of ______________, 19___.

____
Notary Public

(c) If at the time of application for a separate registration at a long term care facility, the retail pharmacy has been issued a license, permit, or other form of authorization from the appropriate State agency to install and operate an automated dispensing system for the dispensing of controlled substances at the long term care facility, the applicant must include with his/her application for registration (DEA Form 224) an affidavit as to the existence of the State authorization. Exact language for this affidavit may be found at the DEA Diversion Control Program Web site. The affidavit must include the following information:

(1) The name and title of the corporate officer or official signing the affidavit;

(2) The name of the corporation, partnership or sole proprietorship operating the retail pharmacy;

(3) The name and complete address (including city, state, and Zip code) of the retail pharmacy;

(4) The name and complete address (including city, state, and Zip code) of the long term care facility at which DEA registration is sought;

(5) Certification that the named retail pharmacy has been authorized by the state Board of Pharmacy or licensing agency to install and operate an automated dispensing system for the dispensing of controlled substances at the named long term care facility (including the license or permit number, if applicable);

(6) The date on which the authorization was issued;

(7) Statements attesting to the following:

(i) The affidavit is submitted to obtain a Drug Enforcement Administration registration number;

(ii) If any material information is false, the Administrator may commence proceedings to deny the application under section 304 of the Act (21 U.S.C. 824(a));

(iii) Any false or fraudulent material information contained in this affidavit may subject the person signing this affidavit and the above-named corporation/partnership/business to prosecution under section 403 of the Act (21 U.S.C. 843);

(8) Signature of the person authorized to sign the Application for Registration for the named retail pharmacy;

(9) Notarization of the affidavit.

(d) The Administrator shall follow the normal procedures for approving an application to verify the statements in the affidavit. If the statements prove to be false, the Administrator may revoke the registration on the basis of section 304(a)(1) of the Act (21 U.S.C. 824(a)(1)) and suspend the registration immediately by pending revocation on the basis of section 304(d) of the Act (21 U.S.C. 824(d)). At the same time, the

Administrator may seize and place under seal all controlled substances possessed by the applicant under section 304(f) of the Act (21 U.S.C. 824(f)). Intentional misuse of the affidavit procedure may subject the applicant to prosecution for fraud under section 403(a)(4) of the Act (21 U.S.C. 843(a)(4)), and obtaining controlled substances through registration by fraudulent means may subject the applicant to prosecution under section 403(a)(3) of the Act (21 U.S.C. 843(a)(3)). The penalties for conviction of either offense include imprisonment for up to 4 years, a fine not exceeding $30,000 or both.

[62 FR 13949, Mar. 24, 1997, as amended at 70 FR 25465, May 13, 2005]

§ 1301.18 Research protocols.

(a) A protocol to conduct research with controlled substances listed in Schedule I shall be in the following form and contain the following information where applicable:

(1) Investigator:

(i) Name, address, and DEA registration number; if any.

(ii) Institutional affiliation.

(iii) Qualifications, including a curriculum vitae and an appropriate bibliography (list of publications).

(2) Research project:

(i) Title of project.

(ii) Statement of the purpose.

(iii) Name of the controlled substances or substances involved and the amount of each needed.

(iv) Description of the research to be conducted, including the number and species of research subjects, the dosage to be administered, the route and method of administration, and the duration of the project.

(v) Location where the research will be conducted.

(vi) Statement of the security provisions for storing the controlled substances (in accordance with § 1301.75) and for dispensing the controlled substances in order to prevent diversion.

(vii) If the investigator desires to manufacture or import any controlled substance listed in paragraph (a)(2)(iii) of this section, a statement of the quantity to be manufactured or imported and the sources of the chemicals to be used or the substance to be imported.

(3) Authority:

(i) Institutional approval.

(ii) Approval of a Human Research Committee for human studies.

(iii) Indication of an approved active Notice of Claimed Investigational Exemption for a New Drug (number).

(iv) Indication of an approved funded grant (number), if any.

(b) In the case of a clinical investigation with controlled substances listed in Schedule I, the applicant shall submit three copies of a Notice of Claimed Investigational Exemption for a New Drug (IND) together with a statement of the security provisions (as proscribed in paragraph (a)(2)(vi) of this section for a research protocol) to, and have such submission approved by, the Food and Drug Administration as required in 21 U.S.C. 355(i) and § 130.3 of this title. Submission of this Notice and statement to the Food and Drug Administration shall be in lieu of a research protocol to the Administration as required in paragraph (a) of this section. The applicant, when applying for registration with the Administration, shall indicate that such notice has been submitted to the Food and Drug Administration by submitting to the Administration with his/her DEA Form 225 three copies of the following certificate:

I hereby certify that on ________________ (Date), pursuant to 21 U.S.C. 355(i) and 21 CFR 130.3, I, ________________ (Name and Address of IND Sponsor) submitted a Notice of Claimed Investigational Exemption for a New Drug (IND) to the Food and Drug Administration for:

____

(Name of Investigational Drug).

____

(Date)

____

(Signature of Applicant).

(c) In the event that the registrant desires to increase the quantity of a controlled substance used for an approved research project, he/she shall submit a request to the Registration Unit, Drug Enforcement Administration, by registered mail, return receipt requested. See the Table of DEA Mailing Addresses in § 1321.01 of this chapter for the current mailing address. The request shall contain the following information: DEA registration number;

name of the controlled substance or substances and the quantity of each authorized in the approved protocol; and the additional quantity of each desired. Upon return of the receipt, the registrant shall be authorized to purchase the additional quantity of the controlled substance or substances specified in the request. The Administration shall review the letter and forward it to the Food and Drug Administration together with the Administration comments. The Food and Drug Administration shall approve or deny the request as an amendment to the protocol and so notify the registrant. Approval of the letter by the Food and Drug Administration shall authorize the registrant to use the additional quantity of the controlled substance in the research project.

(d) In the event the registrant desires to conduct research beyond the variations provided in the registrant's approved protocol (excluding any increase in the quantity of the controlled substance requested for his/her research project as outlined in paragraph (c) of this section), he/she shall submit three copies of a supplemental protocol in accordance with paragraph (a) of this section describing the new research and omitting information in the supplemental protocol which has been stated in the original protocol. Supplemental protocols shall be processed and approved or denied in the same manner as original research protocols.

[62 FR 13949, Mar. 24, 1997, as amended at 75 FR 10676, Mar. 9, 2010]

§ 1301.19 Special requirements for online pharmacies.

(a) A pharmacy that has been issued a registration under § 1301.13 may request that the Administrator modify its registration to authorize the pharmacy to dispense controlled substances by means of the Internet as an online pharmacy. The Administrator may deny an application for a modification of registration if the Administrator determines that the issuance of a modification would be inconsistent with the public interest. In determining the public interest, the Administrator will consider the factors listed in section 303(f) of the Act (21 U.S.C. 823(f)).

(b) Each online pharmacy shall comply with the requirements of State law concerning licensure of pharmacies in each State from which it, and in each State to which it, delivers, distributes, or dispenses, or offers to deliver, distribute, or dispense controlled substances by means of the Internet.

(c) Application for a modified registration authorizing the dispensing of controlled substances by means of the Internet will be made by an online application process as specified in § 1301.13 of this part. Subsequent online pharmacy registration renewals will be accomplished by an online process.

(d) A pharmacy that seeks to discontinue its modification of registration authorizing it to dispense controlled substances by means of the Internet as an online pharmacy (but continue its business activity as a non-online pharmacy) shall so notify the Administrator by requesting to modify its registration to reflect the appropriate business activity. Once the registration has been so changed, the pharmacy may no longer dispense controlled substances by means of the Internet. A pharmacy that has so changed its registration status back to that of a non-online pharmacy remains responsible for submitting reports in accordance with § 1304.55 of this chapter with respect to any controlled substances that it dispensed while it was registered with a modification authorizing it to operate as an online pharmacy.

(e) Registrants applying for modified registrations under this section must comply with notification and reporting requirements set forth in §§ 1304.40, 1304.45, 1304.50, and 1304.55 of this chapter.

(f) No person (including a registrant) required to obtain a modification of a registration under §§ 1301.11(b) and 1301.13 of this part authorizing it to operate as an online pharmacy may engage in any activity for which such modification of registration is required until the application for such modified registration is granted and an active Certificate of Registration indicating the modification of the registration has been issued by the Administrator to such person.

[74 FR 15622, Apr. 6, 2009]

EXCEPTIONS TO REGISTRATION AND FEES

§ 1301.21 Exemption from fees.

(a) The Administrator shall exempt from payment of an application fee for registration or reregistration:

(1) Any hospital or other institution which is operated by an agency of the United States (including the U.S. Army, Navy, Marine Corps., Air Force, and Coast Guard), of any State, or any political subdivision or agency thereof.

(2) Any individual practitioner who is required to obtain an individual registration in order to carry out his or her duties as an official of an agency of the United States (including the U.S. Army, Navy, Marine Corps, Air Force, and Coast Guard), of any State, or any political subdivision or agency thereof.

(b) In order to claim exemption from payment of a registration or reregistration application fee, the registrant shall have completed the certification on the appropriate application form, wherein the registrant's superior (if the registrant is an individual) or officer (if the registrant is an agency) certifies to the status and address of the registrant and to the authority of the registrant to acquire, possess, or handle controlled substances.

(c) Exemption from payment of a registration or reregistration application fee does not relieve the registrant of any other requirements or duties prescribed by law.

[62 FR 13950, Mar. 24, 1997]

§ 1301.22 Exemption of agents and employees; affiliated practitioners.

(a) The requirement of registration is waived for any agent or employee of a person who is registered to engage in any group of independent activities, if such agent or employee is acting in the usual course of his/her business or employment.

(b) An individual practitioner who is an agent or employee of another practitioner (other than a mid-level practitioner) registered to dispense controlled substances may, when acting in the normal course of business or employment, administer or dispense (other than by issuance of prescription) controlled substances if and to the extent that such individual practitioner is authorized or permitted to do so by the jurisdiction in which he or she practices, under the registration of the employer or principal practitioner in lieu of being registered him/herself.

(c) An individual practitioner who is an agent or employee of a hospital or other institution may, when acting in the normal course of business or employment, administer, dispense, or prescribe controlled substances under the registration of the hospital or other institution which is registered in lieu of being registered him/herself, provided that:

(1) Such dispensing, administering or prescribing is done in the usual course of his/her professional practice;

(2) Such individual practitioner is authorized or permitted to do so by the jurisdiction in which he/she is practicing;

(3) The hospital or other institution by whom he/she is employed has verified that the individual practitioner is so permitted to dispense, administer, or prescribe drugs within the jurisdiction;

(4) Such individual practitioner is acting only within the scope of his/her employment in the hospital or institution;

(5) The hospital or other institution authorizes the individual practitioner to administer, dispense or prescribe under the hospital registration and designates a specific internal code number for each individual practitioner so authorized. The code number shall consist of numbers, letters, or a combination thereof and shall be a suffix to the institution's DEA registration number, preceded by a hyphen (e.g., APO123456–10 or APO123456–A12); and

(6) A current list of internal codes and the corresponding individual practitioners is kept by the hospital or other institution and is made available at all times to other registrants and law enforcement agencies upon request for the purpose of verifying the authority of the prescribing individual practitioner.

[62 FR 13950, Mar. 24, 1997]

§ 1301.23 Exemption of certain military and other personnel.

(a) The requirement of registration is waived for any official of the U.S.

Army, Navy, Marine Corps, Air Force, Coast Guard, Public Health Service, or Bureau of Prisons who is authorized to prescribe, dispense, or administer, but not to procure or purchase, controlled substances in the course of his/her official duties. Such officials shall follow procedures set forth in part 1306 of this chapter regarding prescriptions, but shall state the branch of service or agency (e.g., "U.S. Army" or "Public Health Service") and the service identification number of the issuing official in lieu of the registration number required on prescription forms. The service identification number for a Public Health Service employee is his/her Social Security identification number.

(b) The requirement of registration is waived for any official or agency of the U.S. Army, Navy, Marine Corps, Air Force, Coast Guard, or Public Health Service who or which is authorized to import or export controlled substances in the course of his/her official duties.

(c) If any official exempted by this section also engages as a private individual in any activity or group of activities for which registration is required, such official shall obtain a registration for such private activities.

[62 FR 13951, Mar. 24, 1997]

§ 1301.24 Exemption of law enforcement officials.

(a) The requirement of registration is waived for the following persons in the circumstances described in this section:

(1) Any officer or employee of the Administration, any customs officer, any officer or employee of the U.S. Food and Drug Administration, and any other Federal or Insular officer who is lawfully engaged in the enforcement of any Federal law relating to controlled substances, drugs, or customs, and is duly authorized to possess or to import or export controlled substances in the course of his/her official duties; and

(2) Any officer or employee of any State, or any political subdivision or agency thereof, who is engaged in the enforcement of any State or local law relating to controlled substances and is duly authorized to possess controlled substances in the course of his/her official duties.

(b) Any official exempted by this section may, when acting in the course of his/her official duties, procure any controlled substance in the course of an inspection, in accordance with §1316.03(d) of this chapter, or in the course of any criminal investigation involving the person from whom the substance was procured, and may possess any controlled substance and distribute any such substance to any other official who is also exempted by this section and acting in the course of his/her official duties.

(c) In order to enable law enforcement agency laboratories, including laboratories of the Administration, to obtain and transfer controlled substances for use as standards in chemical analysis, such laboratories shall obtain annually a registration to conduct chemical analysis. Such laboratories shall be exempted from payment of a fee for registration. Laboratory personnel, when acting in the scope of their official duties, are deemed to be officials exempted by this section and within the activity described in section 515(d) of the Act (21 U.S.C. 885(d)). For purposes of this paragraph, laboratory activities shall not include field or other preliminary chemical tests by officials exempted by this section.

(d) In addition to the activities authorized under a registration to conduct chemical analysis pursuant to §1301.13(e)(1)(ix), laboratories of the Administration shall be authorized to manufacture or import controlled substances for any lawful purpose, to distribute or export such substances to any person, and to import and export such substances in emergencies without regard to the requirements of part 1312 of this chapter if a report concerning the importation or exportation is made to the Drug Operations Section of the Administration within 30 days of such importation or exportation.

[62 FR 13951, Mar. 24, 1997, as amended at 81 FR 97019, Dec. 30, 2016]

§ 1301.25 Registration regarding ocean vessels, aircraft, and other entities.

(a) If acquired by and dispensed under the general supervision of a medical officer described in paragraph (b) of this section, or the master or first officer of the vessel under the circumstances described in paragraph (d) of this section, controlled substances may be held for stocking, be maintained in, and dispensed from medicine chests, first aid packets, or dispensaries:

(1) On board any vessel engaged in international trade or in trade between ports of the United States and any merchant vessel belonging to the U.S. Government;

(2) On board any aircraft operated by an air carrier under a certificate of permit issued pursuant to the Federal Aviation Act of 1958 (49 U.S.C. 1301); and

(3) In any other entity of fixed or transient location approved by the Administrator as appropriate for application of this section (e.g., emergency kits at field sites of an industrial firm).

(b) A medical officer shall be:

(1) Licensed in a state as a physician;

(2) Employed by the owner or operator of the vessel, aircraft or other entity; and

(3) Registered under the Act at either of the following locations:

(i) The principal office of the owner or operator of the vessel, aircraft or other entity or

(ii) At any other location provided that the name, address, registration number and expiration date as they appear on his/her Certificate of Registration (DEA Form 223) for this location are maintained for inspection at said principal office in a readily retrievable manner.

(c) A registered medical officer may serve as medical officer for more than one vessel, aircraft, or other entity under a single registration, unless he/she serves as medical officer for more than one owner or operator, in which case he/she shall either maintain a separate registration at the location of the principal office of each such owner or operator or utilize one or more registrations pursuant to paragraph (b)(3)(ii) of this section.

(d) If no medical officer is employed by the owner or operator of a vessel, or in the event such medical officer is not accessible and the acquisition of controlled substances is required, the master or first officer of the vessel, who shall not be registered under the Act, may purchase controlled substances from a registered manufacturer or distributor, or from an authorized pharmacy as described in paragraph (f) of this section, by following the procedure outlined below:

(1) The master or first officer of the vessel must personally appear at the vendor's place of business, present proper identification (e.g., Seaman's photographic identification card) and a written requisition for the controlled substances.

(2) The written requisition must be on the vessel's official stationery or purchase order form and must include the name and address of the vendor, the name of the controlled substance, description of the controlled substance (dosage form, strength and number or volume per container) number of containers ordered, the name of the vessel, the vessel's official number and country of registry, the owner or operator of the vessel, the port at which the vessel is located, signature of the vessel's officer who is ordering the controlled substances and the date of the requisition.

(3) The vendor may, after verifying the identification of the vessel's officer requisitioning the controlled substances, deliver the control substances to that officer. The transaction shall be documented, in triplicate, on a record of sale in a format similar to that outlined in paragraph (d)(4) of this section. The vessel's requisition shall be attached to copy 1 of the record of sale and filed with the controlled substances records of the vendor, copy 2 of the record of sale shall be furnished to the officer of the vessel and retained aboard the vessel, copy 3 of the record of sale shall be forwarded to the nearest DEA Division Office within 15 days after the end of the month in which the sale is made.

(4) The vendor's record of sale should be similar to, and must include all the information contained in, the below listed format.

SALE OF CONTROLLED SUBSTANCES TO VESSELS

(Name of registrant) ____________

(Address of registrant) ____________

(DEA registration number) ____________

Line No.	Number of packages ordered	Size of packages	Name of product	Packages distributed	Date distributed
1	....	....	....	....	....
2	....	....	....	....	....
3	....	....	....	....	....

FOOTNOTE: Line numbers may be continued according to needs of the vendor.

Number of lines completed ________
Name of vessel ________
Vessel's official number ________
Vessel's country of registry ________
Owner or operator of the vessel ________
Name and title of vessel's officer who presented the requisition ______
Signature of vessel's officer who presented the requisition ______

(e) Any medical officer described in paragraph (b) of this section shall, in addition to complying with all requirements and duties prescribed for registrants generally, prepare an annual report as of the date on which his/her registration expires, which shall give in detail an accounting for each vessel, aircraft, or other entity, and a summary accounting for all vessels, aircraft, or other entities under his/her supervision for all controlled substances purchased, dispensed or disposed of during the year. The medical officer shall maintain this report with other records required to be kept under the Act and, upon request, deliver a copy of the report to the Administration. The medical officer need not be present when controlled substances are dispensed, if the person who actually dispensed the controlled substances is responsible to the medical officer to justify his/her actions.

(f) Any registered pharmacy that wishes to distribute controlled substances pursuant to this section shall be authorized to do so, provided:

(1) The registered pharmacy notifies the nearest Division Office of the Administration of its intention to so distribute controlled substances prior to the initiation of such activity. This notification shall be by registered mail and shall contain the name, address, and registration number of the pharmacy as well as the date upon which such activity will commence; and

(2) Such activity is authorized by state law; and

(3) The total number of dosage units of all controlled substances distributed by the pharmacy during any calendar year in which the pharmacy is registered to dispense does not exceed the limitations imposed upon such distribution by § 1307.11(a)(1)(iv) and (b) of this chapter.

(g) Owners or operators of vessels, aircraft, or other entities described in this section shall not be deemed to possess or dispense any controlled substance acquired, stored and dispensed in accordance with this section. Additionally, owners or operators of vessels, aircraft, or other entities described in this section or in Article 32 of the Single Convention on Narcotic Drugs, 1961, or in Article 14 of the Convention on Psychotropic Substances, 1971, shall not be deemed to import or export any controlled substances purchased and stored in accordance with that section or applicable article.

(h) The Master of a vessel shall prepare a report for each calendar year which shall give in detail an accounting for all controlled substances purchased, dispensed, or disposed of during the year. The Master shall file this report with the medical officer employed by the owner or operator of his/her vessel, if any, or, if not, he/she shall maintain this report with other records required to be kept under the Act and, upon request, deliver a copy of the report to the Administration.

(i) Controlled substances acquired and possessed in accordance with this section shall be distributed only to persons under the general supervision of the medical officer employed by the owner or operator of the vessel, aircraft, or other entity, except in accordance with part 1317 of this chapter.

[62 FR 13951, Mar. 24, 1997, as amended at 79 FR 53561, Sept. 9, 2014; 84 FR 68342, Dec. 16, 2019]

§ 1301.26 Exemptions from import or export requirements for personal medical use.

Any individual who has in his/her possession a controlled substance listed in schedules II, III, IV, or V, which he/she has lawfully obtained for his/her personal medical use, or for administration to an animal accompanying him/her, may enter or depart the United States with such substance notwithstanding sections 1002–1005 of the Act (21 U.S.C. 952–955), provided the following conditions are met:

(a) The controlled substance is in the original container in which it was dispensed to the individual; and

(b) The individual makes a declaration to an appropriate customs officer stating:

(1) That the controlled substance is possessed for his/her personal use, or for an animal accompanying him/her; and

(2) The trade or chemical name and the symbol designating the schedule of the controlled substance if it appears on the container label, or, if such name does not appear on the label, the name and address of the pharmacy or practitioner who dispensed the substance and the prescription number.

(c) In addition to (and not in lieu of) the foregoing requirements of this section, a United States resident may import into the United States no more than 50 dosage units combined of all such controlled substances in the individual's possession that were obtained abroad for personal medical use. (For purposes of this section, a United States resident is a person whose residence (*i.e.*, place of general abode—meaning one's principal, actual dwelling place in fact, without regard to intent) is in the United States.) This 50 dosage unit limitation does not apply to controlled substances lawfully obtained in the United States pursuant to a prescription issued by a DEA registrant.

[69 FR 55347, Sept. 14, 2004, as amended at 81 FR 97019, Dec. 30, 2016]

§ 1301.27 Separate registration by retail pharmacies for installation and operation of automated dispensing systems at long term care facilities.

(a) A retail pharmacy may install and operate automated dispensing systems, as defined in § 1300.01 of this chapter, at long term care facilities, under the requirements of § 1301.17. No person other than a registered retail pharmacy may install and operate an automated dispensing system at a long term care facility.

(b) Retail pharmacies installing and operating automated dispensing systems at long term care facilities must maintain a separate registration at the location of each long term care facility at which automated dispensing systems are located. If more than one registered retail pharmacy operates automated dispensing systems at the same long term care facility, each retail pharmacy must maintain a registration at the long term care facility.

(c) A registered retail pharmacy applying for a separate registration to operate an automated dispensing system for the dispensing of controlled substances at a long term care facility is exempt from application fees for any such additional registrations.

[70 FR 25465, May 13, 2005]

§ 1301.28 Exemption from separate registration for practitioners dispensing or prescribing Schedule III, IV, or V narcotic controlled drugs approved by the Food and Drug Administration specifically for use in maintenance or detoxification treatment.

(a) An individual practitioner may dispense or prescribe Schedule III, IV, or V narcotic controlled drugs or combinations of narcotic controlled drugs which have been approved by the Food and Drug Administration (FDA) specifically for use in maintenance or detoxification treatment without obtaining the separate registration required by § 1301.13(e) if all of the following conditions are met:

(1) The individual practitioner meets the conditions specified in paragraph (b) of this section.

(2) The narcotic drugs or combination of narcotic drugs meet the conditions specified in paragraph (c) of this section.

(3) The individual practitioner is in compliance with either paragraph (d) or paragraph (e) of this section.

(b)(1) The individual practitioner must submit notification to the Secretary of Health and Human Services stating the individual practitioner's intent to dispense or prescribe narcotic drugs under paragraph (a) of this section. The notice must contain all of the following certifications:

(i) The individual practitioner is registered under § 1301.13 as an individual practitioner and is a "qualifying physician" as defined in section 303(g)(2)(G)(ii) of the Act (21 U.S.C. 823(g)(2)(G)(ii)), or during the period beginning on July 22, 2016 and ending on October 1, 2021, a "qualifying other practitioner" as defined in section 303(g)(2)(G)(iv) of Act (21 U.S.C. 823(g)(2)(G)(iv)). The Secretary of Health and Human Services may, by regulation, revise the requirements for being a qualifying other practitioner.

(ii) With respect to patients to whom the practitioner will provide such drugs or combinations of drugs, the individual practitioner has the capacity to provide directly, by referral, or in such other manner as determined by the Secretary of Health and Human Services:

(A) All drugs approved by the Food and Drug Administration for the treatment of opioid use disorder, including for maintenance, detoxification, overdose reversal, and relapse prevention; and

(B) Appropriate counseling and other appropriate ancillary services.

(iii)(A) The total number of patients to whom the individual practitioner will provide narcotic drugs or combinations of narcotic drugs under this section at any one time will not exceed the applicable number. Except as provided in paragraphs (b)(1)(iii)(B) and (C) of this section, the applicable number is 30.

(B) The applicable number is 100 if, not sooner than 1 year after the date on which the practitioner submitted the initial notification, the practitioner submits a second notification to the Secretary of Health and Human Services of the need and intent of the practitioner to treat up to 100 patients.

(C) The applicable number is 275 for a practitioner who has been approved by the Secretary of Health and Human Services under 42 CFR part 8 to treat up to 275 patients at any one time, and provided further that the practitioner has renewed such approval to the extent such renewal is required under this part of the HHS regulations.

(2) If an individual practitioner wishes to prescribe or dispense narcotic drugs pursuant to paragraph (e) of this section, the individual practitioner must provide the Secretary of Health and Human Services the following:

(i) Notification as required under paragraph (b)(1) of this section in writing, stating the individual practitioner's name and DEA registration number issued under § 1301.13.

(ii) If the individual practitioner is a member of a group practice, the names of the other individual practitioners in the group and the DEA registration numbers issued to the other individual practitioners under § 1301.13.

(c) The narcotic drugs or combination of narcotic drugs to be dispensed or prescribed under this section must meet all of the following conditions:

(1) The drugs or combination of drugs have been approved for use in "maintenance treatment" or "detoxification treatment" under the Federal Food, Drug, and Cosmetic Act or section 351 of the Public Health Service Act.

(2) The drugs or combination of drugs have not been the subject of an adverse determination by the Secretary of Health and Human Services, after consultation with the Attorney General, that the use of the drugs or combination of drugs requires additional standards respecting the qualifications of practitioners or the quantities of the drugs that may be provided for unsupervised use.

(d)(1) After receiving the notification submitted under paragraph (b) of this section, the Secretary of Health and Human Services will forward a copy of the notification to the Administrator. The Secretary of Health and Human Services will have 45 days from the date of receipt of the notification to make a determination of whether the individual practitioner involved meets all requirements for a waiver under section 303(g)(2)(B) of the Act (21 U.S.C. 823(g)(2)(B)). Health and Human Services will notify DEA of its determination regarding the individual practitioner. If the individual practitioner has the appropriate registration under § 1301.13, then the Administrator will issue the practitioner an identification number as soon as one of the following conditions occurs:

(i) The Administrator receives a positive determination from the Secretary of Health and Human Services before the conclusion of the 45-day review period, or

(ii) The 45-day review period has concluded and no determination by the Secretary of Health and Human Services has been made.

(2) If the Secretary denies certification to an individual practitioner or withdraws such certification once it is issued, then DEA will not issue the individual practitioner an identification number, or will withdraw the identification number if one has been issued.

(3) The individual practitioner must include the identification number on all records when dispensing and on all prescriptions when prescribing narcotic drugs under this section.

(e) An individual practitioner may begin to prescribe or dispense narcotic drugs to a specific individual patient under this section before receiving an identification number from the Administrator if the following conditions are met:

(1) The individual practitioner has submitted a written notification under paragraph (b) of this section in good faith to the Secretary of Health and Human Services.

(2) The individual practitioner reasonably believes that the conditions specified in paragraphs (b) and (c) of this section have been met.

(3) The individual practitioner reasonably believes that the treatment of an individual patient would be facilitated if narcotic drugs are prescribed or dispensed under this section before the sooner of:

(i) Receipt of an identification number from the Administrator, or

(ii) Expiration of the 45-day period.

(4) The individual practitioner has notified both the Secretary of Health and Human Services and the Administrator of his or her intent to begin prescribing or dispensing the narcotic drugs before expiration of the 45-day period.

(5) The Secretary has not notified the registrant that he/she is not qualified under paragraph (d) of this section.

(6) The individual practitioner has the appropriate registration under §1301.13.

(f) If an individual practitioner dispenses or prescribes Schedule III, IV, or V narcotic drugs approved by the Food and Drug Administration specifically for maintenance or detoxification treatment in violation of any of the conditions specified in paragraphs (b), (c) or (e) of this section, the Administrator may revoke the individual practitioner's registration in accordance with § 1301.36.

[70 FR 36342, June 23, 2005, as amended at 73 FR 29688, May 22, 2008; 83 FR 3074, Jan. 23, 2018]

§ 1301.29 [Reserved]

Action on Application for Registration: Revocation or Suspension of Registration

§ 1301.31 Administrative review generally.

The Administrator may inspect, or cause to be inspected, the establishment of an applicant or registrant, pursuant to subpart A of part 1316 of this chapter. The Administrator shall review the application for registration and other information gathered by the Administrator regarding an applicant in order to determine whether the applicable standards of section 303 (21 U.S.C. 823) or section 1008 (21 U.S.C. 958) of the Act have been met by the applicant.

[62 FR 13953, Mar. 24, 1997]

§ 1301.32 Action on applications for research in Schedule I substances.

(a) In the case of an application for registration to conduct research with controlled substances listed in Schedule I, the Administrator shall process the application and protocol and forward a copy of each to the Secretary of Health and Human Services (Secretary) within 7 days after receipt. The Secretary shall determine the qualifications and competency of the applicant, as well as the merits of the protocol (and shall notify the Administrator of his/her determination) within 21 days after receipt of the application and complete protocol, except that in the case of a clinical investigation, the Secretary shall have 30 days to make such determination and notify the Administrator. The Secretary, in determining the merits of the protocol, shall consult with the Administrator as to effective procedures to safeguard adequately against diversion of such controlled substances from legitimate medical or scientific use.

(b) An applicant whose protocol is defective shall be notified by the Secretary within 21 days after receipt of such protocol from the Administrator (or in the case of a clinical investigation within 30 days), and he/she shall be requested to correct the existing defects before consideration shall be given to his/her submission.

(c) If the Secretary determines the applicant qualified and competent and the research protocol meritorious, he/she shall notify the Administrator in writing of such determination. The Administrator shall issue a certificate of registration within 10 days after receipt of this notice, unless he/she determines that the certificate of registration should be denied on a ground specified in section 304(a) of the Act (21 U.S.C. 824(a)). In the case of a supplemental protocol, a replacement certificate of registration shall be issued by the Administrator.

(d) If the Secretary determines that the protocol is not meritorious and/or the applicant is not qualified or competent, he/she shall notify the Administrator in writing setting forth the reasons for such determination. If the Administrator determines that grounds exist for the denial of the application, he/she shall within 10 days issue an order to show cause pursuant to § 1301.37 and, if requested by the applicant, hold a hearing on the application pursuant to § 1301.41. If the grounds for denial of the application include a determination by the Secretary, the Secretary or his duly authorized agent shall furnish testimony and documents pertaining to his determination at such hearing.

(e) Supplemental protocols will be processed in the same manner as original research protocols. If the processing of an application or research protocol is delayed beyond the time limits imposed by this section, the applicant shall be so notified in writing.

[62 FR 13953, Mar. 24, 1997]

§ 1301.33 Application for bulk manufacture of Schedule I and II substances.

(a) In the case of an application for registration or reregistration to manufacture in bulk a basic class of controlled substance listed in Schedule I or II, the Administrator shall, upon the filing of such application, publish in the FEDERAL REGISTER a notice naming the applicant and stating that such applicant has applied to be registered as a bulk manufacturer of a basic class of narcotic or nonnarcotic controlled substance, which class shall be identified. A copy of said notice shall be mailed simultaneously to each person registered as a bulk manufacturer of that basic class and to any other applicant therefor. Any such person may, within 60 days from the date of publication of the notice in the FEDERAL REGISTER, file with the Administrator written comments on or objections to the issuance of the proposed registration.

(b) In order to provide adequate competition, the Administrator shall not be required to limit the number of manufacturers in any basic class to a number less than that consistent with maintenance of effective controls against diversion solely because a smaller number is capable of producing an adequate and uninterrupted supply.

(c) This section shall not apply to the manufacture of basic classes of controlled substances listed in Schedules I or II as an incident to research or chemical analysis as authorized in § 1301.13(e)(1).

[62 FR 13953, Mar. 24, 1997]

§ 1301.34 Application for importation of Schedule I and II substances.

(a) In the case of an application for registration or reregistration to import a controlled substance listed in Schedule I or II, under the authority of section 1002(a)(2)(B) of the Act (21 U.S.C. 952(a)(2)(B)), the Administrator shall, upon the filing of such application, publish in the FEDERAL REGISTER a notice naming the applicant and stating that such applicant has applied to be registered as an importer of a Schedule I or II controlled substance, which substance shall be identified. A copy of said notice shall be mailed simultaneously to each person registered as a bulk manufacturer of that controlled substance and to any other applicant therefor. Any such person may, within 30 days from the date of publication of the notice in the FEDERAL REGISTER, file written comments on or objections to the issuance of the proposed registration, and may, at the same time, file a written request for a hearing on the application pursuant to § 1301.43. If a hearing is requested, the Administrator shall hold a hearing on the application in accordance with § 1301.41. Notice of the hearing shall be published in the FEDERAL REGISTER, and shall be mailed simultaneously to the applicant and to all persons to whom notice of the application was mailed. Any such person may participate in the hearing by filing a notice of appearance in accordance with § 1301.43 of this chapter. Notice of the hearing shall contain a summary of all comments and objections filed regarding the application and shall state the time and place for the hearing, which shall not be less than 30 days after the date of publication of such notice in the FEDERAL REGISTER. A hearing pursuant to this section may be consolidated with a hearing held pursuant to § 1301.35 or § 1301.36 of this part.

(b) The Administrator shall register an applicant to import a controlled substance listed in Schedule I or II if he/she determines that such registration is consistent with the public interest and with U.S. obligations under international treaties, conventions, or protocols in effect on May 1, 1971. In determining the public interest, the following factors shall be considered:

(1) Maintenance of effective controls against diversion of particular controlled substances and any controlled substance in Schedule I or II compounded therefrom into other than legitimate medical, scientific research, or industrial channels, by limiting the importation and bulk manufacture of such controlled substances to a number of establishments which can produce an adequate and uninterrupted supply of these substances under adequately competitive conditions for legitimate medical, scientific, research, and industrial purposes;

(2) Compliance with applicable State and local law;

(3) Promotion of technical advances in the art of manufacturing these substances and the development of new substances;

(4) Prior conviction record of applicant under Federal and State laws relating to the manufacture, distribution, or dispensing of such substances;

(5) Past experience in the manufacture of controlled substances, and the existence in the establishment of effective control against diversion;

(6) That the applicant will be permitted to import only:

(i) Such amounts of crude opium, poppy straw, concentrate of poppy straw, and coca leaves as the Administrator finds to be necessary to provide for medical, scientific, or other legitimate purposes; or

(ii) Such amounts of any controlled substances listed in Schedule I or II as the Administrator shall find to be necessary to provide for the medical, scientific, or other legitimate needs of the United States during an emergency in which domestic supplies of such substances are found by the Administrator to be inadequate; or

(iii) Such amounts of any controlled substance listed in Schedule I or II as the Administrator shall find to be necessary to provide for the medical, scientific, or other legitimate needs of the United States in any case in which the Administrator finds that competition among domestic manufacturers of the controlled substance is inadequate and will not be rendered adequate by the registration of additional manufacturers under section 303 of the Act (21 U.S.C. 823); or

(iv) Such limited quantities of any controlled substance listed in Schedule I or II as the Administrator shall find to be necessary for scientific, analytical or research uses; and

(7) Such other factors as may be relevant to and consistent with the public health and safety.

(c) In determining whether the applicant can and will maintain effective controls against diversion within the meaning of paragraph (b) of this section, the Administrator shall consider among other factors:

(1) Compliance with the security requirements set forth in §§ 1301.71–1301.76; and

(2) Employment of security procedures to guard against in-transit losses.

(d) In determining whether competition among the domestic manufacturers of a controlled substance is adequate within the meaning of paragraphs (b)(1) and (b)(6)(iii) of this section, as well as section 1002(a)(2)(B) of the Act (21 U.S.C. 952(a)(2)(B)), the Administrator shall consider:

(1) The extent of price rigidity in the light of changes in:

(i) raw materials and other costs and

(ii) conditions of supply and demand;

(2) The extent of service and quality competition among the domestic manufacturers for shares of the domestic market including:

(i) Shifts in market shares and

(ii) Shifts in individual customers among domestic manufacturers;

(3) The existence of substantial differentials between domestic prices and the higher of prices generally prevailing in foreign markets or the prices at which the applicant for registration to import is committed to undertake to provide such products in the domestic market in conformity with the Act. In determining the existence of substantial differentials hereunder, appropriate consideration should be given to any additional costs imposed on domestic manufacturers by the requirements of the Act and such other cost-related and other factors as the Administrator may deem relevant. In no event shall an importer's offering prices in the United States be considered if they are lower than those prevailing in the foreign market or markets from which the importer is obtaining his/her supply;

(4) The existence of competitive restraints imposed upon domestic manufacturers by governmental regulations; and

(5) Such other factors as may be relevant to the determinations required under this paragraph.

(e) In considering the scope of the domestic market, consideration shall be given to substitute products which are reasonably interchangeable in terms of price, quality and use.

(f) The fact that the number of existing manufacturers is small shall not demonstrate, in and of itself, that adequate competition among them does not exist.

[62 FR 13953, Mar. 24, 1997, as amended at 81 FR 97019, Dec. 30, 2016]

§ 1301.35 Certificate of registration; denial of registration.

(a) The Administrator shall issue a Certificate of Registration (DEA Form 223) to an applicant if the issuance of registration or reregistration is required under the applicable provisions of sections 303 or 1008 of the Act (21 U.S.C. 823 and 958). In the event that the issuance of registration or reregistration is not required, the Administrator shall deny the application. Before denying any application, the Administrator shall issue an order to show cause pursuant to § 1301.37 and, if requested by the applicant, shall hold a hearing on the application pursuant to § 1301.41.

(b) If in response to a show cause order a hearing is requested by an applicant for registration or reregistration to manufacture in bulk a basic class of controlled substance listed in Schedule I or II, notice that a hearing has been requested shall be published in the FEDERAL REGISTER and shall be mailed simultaneously to the applicant and to all persons to whom notice of the application was mailed. Any person entitled to file comments or objections to the issuance of the proposed registration pursuant to § 1301.33(a) may participate in the hearing by filing notice of appearance in accordance with § 1301.43. Such persons shall have 30 days to file a notice of appearance after the date of publication of the notice of a request for a hearing in the FEDERAL REGISTER.

(c) The Certificate of Registration (DEA Form 223) shall contain the name, address, and registration number of the registrant, the activity authorized by the registration, the schedules and/or Administration Controlled Substances Code Number (as set forth in part 1308 of this chapter) of the controlled substances which the registrant is authorized to handle, the amount of fee paid (or exemption), and the expiration date of the registration. The registrant shall maintain the certificate of registration at the registered location in a readily retrievable manner and shall permit inspection of the certificate by any official, agent or employee of the Administration or of any Federal, State, or local agency engaged in enforcement of laws relating to controlled substances.

[62 FR 13954, Mar. 24, 1997]

§ 1301.36 Suspension or revocation of registration; suspension of registration pending final order; extension of registration pending final order.

(a) For any registration issued under section 303 of the Act (21 U.S.C. 823), the Administrator may:

(1) Suspend the registration pursuant to section 304(a) of the Act (21 U.S.C. 824(a)) for any period of time.

(2) Revoke the registration pursuant to section 304(a) of the Act (21 U.S.C. 824(a)).

(b) For any registration issued under section 1008 of the Act (21 U.S.C. 958), the Administrator may:

(1) Suspend the registration pursuant to section 1008(d) of the Act (21 U.S.C. 958(d)) for any period of time.

(2) Revoke the registration pursuant to section 1008(d) of the Act (21 U.S.C. 958(d)) if he/she determines that such registration is inconsistent with the public interest as defined in section 1008 or with the United States obligations under international treaties, conventions, or protocols in effect on October 12, 1984.

(c) The Administrator may limit the revocation or suspension of a registration to the particular controlled substance, or substances, with respect to which grounds for revocation or suspension exist.

(d) Before revoking or suspending any registration, the Administrator shall issue an order to show cause pursuant to § 1301.37 and, if requested by the registrant, shall hold a hearing pursuant to § 1301.41.

(e) The Administrator may suspend any registration simultaneously with or at any time subsequent to the service upon the registrant of an order to show cause why such registration should not be revoked or suspended, in any case where he/she finds that there is an imminent danger to the public health or safety. If the Administrator so suspends, he/she shall serve with the order to show cause pursuant to § 1301.37 an order of immediate suspension which shall contain a statement of his findings regarding the danger to public health or safety.

(f) Upon service of the order of the Administrator suspending or revoking registration, the registrant shall immediately deliver his/her Certificate of Registration, any order forms, and any import or export permits in his/her possession to the nearest office of the Administration. The suspension or revocation of a registration shall suspend or revoke any individual manufacturing or procurement quota fixed for the registrant pursuant to part 1303 of this chapter and any import or export permits issued to the registrant pursuant to part 1312 of this chapter. Also, upon service of the order of the Administrator revoking or suspending registration, the registrant shall, as instructed by the Administrator:

(1) Deliver all controlled substances in his/her possession to the nearest office of the Administration or to authorized agents of the Administration; or

(2) Place all controlled substances in his/her possession under seal as described in sections 304(f) or 1008(d)(6) of the Act (21 U.S.C. 824(f) or 958(d)(6)).

(g) In the event that revocation or suspension is limited to a particular controlled substance or substances, the registrant shall be given a new Certificate of Registration for all substances not affected by such revocation or suspension; no fee shall be required to be paid for the new Certificate of Registration. The registrant shall deliver the old Certificate of Registration and, if appropriate, any order forms in his/her possession to the nearest office of the Administration. The suspension or revocation of a registration, when limited to a particular basic class or classes of controlled substances, shall suspend or revoke any individual manufacturing or procurement quota fixed for the registrant for such class or classes pursuant to part 1303 of this chapter and any import or export permits issued to the registrant for such class or classes pursuant to part 1312 of this chapter. Also, upon service of the order of the Administrator revoking or suspending registration, the registrant shall, as instructed by the Administrator:

(1) Deliver to the nearest office of the Administration or to authorized agents of the Administration all of the particular controlled substance or substances affected by the revocation or suspension which are in his/her possession; or

(2) Place all of such substances under seal as described in sections 304(f) or 958(d)(6) of the Act (21 U.S.C. 824(f) or 958(d)(6)).

(h) Any suspension shall continue in effect until the conclusion of all proceedings upon the revocation or suspension, including any judicial review thereof, unless sooner withdrawn by the Administrator or dissolved by a court of competent jurisdiction. Any registrant whose registration is suspended under paragraph (e) of this section may request a hearing on the revocation or suspension of his/her registration at a time earlier than specified in the order to show cause pursuant to § 1301.37. This request shall be granted by the Administrator, who shall fix a date for such hearing as early as reasonably possible.

(i) In the event that an applicant for reregistration (who is doing business under a registration previously granted and not revoked or suspended) has applied for reregistration at least 45 days before the date on which the existing registration is due to expire, and the Administrator has issued no order on the application on the date on which the existing registration is due to expire, the existing registration of the applicant shall automatically be extended and continue in effect until the date on which the Administrator so issues his/her order. The Administrator may extend any other existing registration under the circumstances contemplated in this section even though the registrant failed to apply for reregistration at least 45 days before expiration of the existing registration, with or without request by the registrant, if the Administrator finds that such extension is not inconsistent with the public health and safety.

[62 FR 13955, Mar. 24, 1997]

§ 1301.37 Order to show cause.

(a) If, upon examination of the application for registration from any applicant and other information gathered by the Administration regarding the applicant, the Administrator is unable to make the determinations required by the applicable provisions of section 303 and/or section 1008 of the Act (21 U.S.C. 823 and 958) to register the applicant, the Administrator shall serve upon the applicant an order to show cause why the registration should not be denied.

(b) If, upon information gathered by the Administration regarding any registrant, the Administrator determines that the registration of such registrant is subject to suspension or revocation pursuant to section 304 or section 1008 of the Act (21 U.S.C. 824 and 958), the Administrator shall serve upon the registrant an order to show cause why the registration should not be revoked or suspended.

(c) The order to show cause shall call upon the applicant or registrant to appear before the Administrator at a time and place stated in the order, which shall not be less than 30 days after the date of receipt of the order. The order to show cause shall also contain a statement of the legal basis for such hearing and for the denial, revocation, or suspension of registration and a summary of the matters of fact and law asserted.

(d) Upon receipt of an order to show cause, the applicant or registrant must, if he/she desires a hearing, file a request for a hearing pursuant to § 1301.43. If a hearing is requested, the Administrator shall hold a hearing at the time and place stated in the order, pursuant to § 1301.41.

(e) When authorized by the Administrator, any agent of the Administration may serve the order to show cause.

[62 FR 13955, Mar. 24, 1997]

HEARINGS

§ 1301.41 Hearings generally.

(a) In any case where the Administrator shall hold a hearing on any registration or application therefor, the procedures for such hearing shall be governed generally by the adjudication procedures set forth in the Administrative Procedure Act (5 U.S.C. 551–559) and specifically by sections 303, 304, and 1008 of the Act (21 U.S.C. 823–824 and 958), by §§ 1301.42–1301.46 of this part, and by the procedures for administrative hearings under the Act set forth in §§ 1316.41–1316.67 of this chapter.

(b) Any hearing under this part shall be independent of, and not in lieu of, criminal prosecutions or other proceedings under the Act or any other law of the United States.

[62 FR 13956, Mar. 24, 1997]

§ 1301.42 Purpose of hearing.

If requested by a person entitled to a hearing, the Administrator shall hold a hearing for the purpose of receiving factual evidence regarding the issues involved in the denial, revocation, or suspension of any registration, and the granting of any application for registration to import or to manufacture in bulk a basic class of controlled substance listed in Schedule I or II. Extensive argument should not be offered into evidence but rather presented in opening or closing statements of counsel or in memoranda or proposed findings of fact and conclusions of law.

[62 FR 13956, Mar. 24, 1997]

§ 1301.43 Request for hearing or appearance; waiver.

(a) Any person entitled to a hearing pursuant to § 1301.32 or §§ 1301.34–1301.36 and desiring a hearing shall, within 30 days after the date of receipt of the order to show cause (or the date of publication of notice of the application for registration in the FEDERAL REGISTER in the case of § 1301.34), file with the Administrator a written request for a hearing in the form prescribed in § 1316.47 of this chapter.

(b) Any person entitled to participate in a hearing pursuant to § 1301.34 or § 1301.35(b) and desiring to do so shall, within 30 days of the date of publication of notice of the request for a hearing in the FEDERAL REGISTER, file with the Administrator a written notice of intent to participate in such hearing in the form prescribed in § 1316.48 of this chapter. Any person filing a request for a hearing need not also file a notice of appearance.

(c) Any person entitled to a hearing or to participate in a hearing pursuant to § 1301.32 or §§ 1301.34–1301.36 may, within the period permitted for filing a request for a hearing or a notice of appearance, file with the Administrator a waiver of an opportunity for a hearing or to participate in a hearing, together with a written statement regarding such person's position on the matters of fact and law involved in such hearing. Such statement, if admissible, shall be made a part of the record and shall be considered in light of the lack of opportunity for cross-examination in determining the weight to be attached to matters of fact asserted therein.

(d) If any person entitled to a hearing or to participate in a hearing pursuant to § 1301.32 or §§ 1301.34–1301.36 fails to file a request for a hearing or a notice of appearance, or if such person so files and fails to appear at the hearing, such person shall be deemed to have waived the opportunity for a hearing or to participate in the hearing, unless such person shows good cause for such failure.

(e) If all persons entitled to a hearing or to participate in a hearing waive or are deemed to waive their opportunity for the hearing or to participate in the hearing, the Administrator may cancel the hearing, if scheduled, and issue his/her final order pursuant to § 1301.46 without a hearing.

[62 FR 13956, Mar. 24, 1997]

§ 1301.44 Burden of proof.

(a) At any hearing on an application to manufacture any controlled substance listed in Schedule I or II, the applicant shall have the burden of proving that the requirements for such registration pursuant to section 303(a) of the Act (21 U.S.C. 823(a)) are satisfied. Any other person participating in the hearing pursuant to § 1301.35(b) shall have the burden of proving any propositions of fact or law asserted by such person in the hearing.

(b) At any hearing on the granting or denial of an applicant to be registered to conduct a narcotic treatment program or as a compounder, the applicant shall have the burden of proving that the requirements for each registration pursuant to section 303(g) of the Act (21 U.S.C. 823(g)) are satisfied.

(c) At any hearing on the granting or denial of an application to be registered to import or export any controlled substance listed in Schedule I or II, the applicant shall have the burden of proving that the requirements for such registration pursuant to sections 1008(a) and (d) of the Act (21 U.S.C. 958 (a) and (d)) are satisfied. Any other person participating in the hearing pursuant to §1301.34 shall have the burden of proving any propositions of fact or law asserted by him/her in the hearings.

(d) At any other hearing for the denial of a registration, the Administration shall have the burden of proving that the requirements for such registration pursuant to section 303 or section 1008(c) and (d) of the Act (21 U.S.C. 823 or 958(c) and (d)) are not satisfied.

(e) At any hearing for the revocation or suspension of a registration, the Administration shall have the burden of proving that the requirements for such revocation or suspension pursuant to section 304(a) or section 1008(d) of the Act (21 U.S.C. 824(a) or 958(d)) are satisfied.

[62 FR 13956, Mar. 24, 1997]

§ 1301.45 Time and place of hearing.

The hearing will commence at the place and time designated in the order to show cause or notice of hearing published in the FEDERAL REGISTER (unless expedited pursuant to §1301.36(h)) but thereafter it may be moved to a different place and may be continued from day to day or recessed to a later day without notice other than announcement thereof by the presiding officer at the hearing.

[62 FR 13956, Mar. 24, 1997]

§ 1301.46 Final order.

As soon as practicable after the presiding officer has certified the record to the Administrator, the Administrator shall issue his/her order on the granting, denial, revocation, or suspension of registration. In the event that an application for registration to import or to manufacture in bulk a basic class of any controlled substance listed in Schedule I or II is granted, or any application for registration is denied, or any registration is revoked or suspended, the order shall include the findings of fact and conclusions of law upon which the order is based. The order shall specify the date on which it shall take effect. The Administrator shall serve one copy of his/her order upon each party in the hearing.

[62 FR 13956, Mar. 24, 1997]

MODIFICATION, TRANSFER AND TERMINATION OF REGISTRATION

§ 1301.51 Modification in registration.

(a) Any registrant may apply to modify his/her registration to authorize the handling of additional controlled substances or to change his/her name or address by submitting a written request to the Registration Unit, Drug Enforcement Administration. See the Table of DEA Mailing Addresses in §1321.01 of this chapter for the current mailing address. Additionally, such a request may be submitted on-line at *www.DEAdiversion.usdoj.gov*.

(1) The request shall contain:

(i) The registrant's name, address, and registration number as printed on the certificate of registration;

(ii) The substances and/or schedules to be added to the registration or the new name or address; and

(iii) A signature in accordance with §1301.13(j).

(2) If the registrant is seeking to handle additional controlled substances listed in Schedule I for the purpose of research or instructional activities, the registrant shall attach three copies of a research protocol describing each research project involving the additional substances, or two copies of a statement describing the nature, extent, and duration of such instructional activities, as appropriate.

(b) Any manufacturer, distributor, reverse distributor, narcotic treatment program, hospital/clinic with an on-site pharmacy, or retail pharmacy registered pursuant to this part, may apply to modify its registration to become authorized as a collector by submitting a written request to the Registration Unit, Drug Enforcement Administration. See the Table of DEA Mailing Addresses in §1321.01 of this chapter for the current mailing address. Additionally, such request may be submitted on-line at *www.DEAdiversion.usdoj.gov*.

(1) The request shall contain:

(i) The registrant's name, address, and registration number as printed on the certificate of registration;

(ii) The method(s) of collection the registrant intends to conduct (collection receptacle and/or mail-back program); and

(iii) A signature in accordance with § 1301.13(j).

(2) If a hospital/clinic with an on-site pharmacy or retail pharmacy is applying for a modification in registration to authorize such registrant to be a collector to maintain a collection receptacle at a long-term care facility in accordance with § 1317.80 of this chapter, the request shall also include the name and physical location of each long-term care facility at which the hospital/clinic with an on-site pharmacy, or the retail pharmacy, intends to operate a collection receptacle.

(c) No fee shall be required for modification. The request for modification shall be handled in the same manner as an application for registration. If the modification of registration is approved, the Administrator shall issue a new certificate of registration (DEA Form 223) to the registrant, who shall maintain it with the old certificate of registration until expiration.

[79 FR 53561, Sept. 9, 2014]

§ 1301.52 Termination of registration; transfer of registration; distribution upon discontinuance of business.

(a) Except as provided in paragraph (b) of this section, the registration of any person, and any modifications of that registration, shall terminate, without any further action by the Administration, if and when such person dies, ceases legal existence, discontinues business or professional practice, or surrenders a registration. Any registrant who ceases legal existence or discontinues business or professional practice shall notify the Administrator promptly of such fact. In the case of a surrender, termination shall occur upon receipt by any employee of the Administration of a duly executed DEA form 104 or any signed writing indicating the desire to surrender a registration.

(b) No registration or any authority conferred thereby shall be assigned or otherwise transferred except upon such conditions as the Administration may specifically designate and then only pursuant to written consent. Any person seeking authority to transfer a registration shall submit a written request, providing full details regarding the proposed transfer of registration, to the Deputy Assistant Administrator, Office of Diversion Control, Drug Enforcement Administration. See the Table of DEA Mailing Addresses in § 1321.01 of this chapter for the current mailing address.

(c) Any registrant desiring to discontinue business activities altogether or with respect to controlled substances (without transferring such business activities to another person) shall return for cancellation his/her certificate of registration, and any unexecuted order forms in his/her possession, to the Registration Unit, Drug Enforcement Administration. See the Table of DEA Mailing Addresses in § 1321.01 of this chapter for the current mailing address. Any controlled substances in his/her possession may be disposed of in accordance with part 1317 of this chapter.

(d) Any registrant desiring to discontinue business activities altogether or with respect to controlled substance (by transferring such business activities to another person) shall submit in person or by registered or certified mail, return receipt requested, to the Special Agent in Charge in his/her area, at least 14 days in advance of the date of the proposed transfer (unless the Special Agent in Charge waives this time limitation in individual instances), the following information:

(1) The name, address, registration number, and authorized business activity of the registrant discontinuing the business (registrant-transferor);

(2) The name, address, registration number, and authorized business activity of the person acquiring the business (registrant-transferee);

(3) Whether the business activities will be continued at the location registered by the person discontinuing business, or moved to another location

(if the latter, the address of the new location should be listed);

(4) Whether the registrant-transferor has a quota to manufacture or procure any controlled substance listed in Schedule I or II (if so, the basic class or class of the substance should be indicated); and

(5) The date on which the transfer of controlled substances will occur.

(e) Unless the registrant-transferor is informed by the Special Agent in Charge, before the date on which the transfer was stated to occur, that the transfer may not occur, the registrant-transferor may distribute (without being registered to distribute) controlled substances in his/her possession to the registrant-transferee in accordance with the following:

(1) On the date of transfer of the controlled substances, a complete inventory of all controlled substances being transferred shall be taken in accordance with § 1304.11 of this chapter. This inventory shall serve as the final inventory of the registrant-transferor and the initial inventory of the registrant-transferee, and a copy of the inventory shall be included in the records of each person. It shall not be necessary to file a copy of the inventory with the Administration unless requested by the Special Agent in Charge. Transfers of any substances listed in Schedule I or II shall require the use of order forms in accordance with part 1305 of this chapter.

(2) On the date of transfer of the controlled substances, all records required to be kept by the registrant-transferor with reference to the controlled substances being transferred, under part 1304 of this chapter, shall be transferred to the registrant-transferee. Responsibility for the accuracy of records prior to the date of transfer remains with the transferor, but responsibility for custody and maintenance shall be upon the transferee.

(3) In the case of registrants required to make reports pursuant to part 1304 of this chapter, a report marked "Final" will be prepared and submitted by the registrant-transferor showing the disposition of all the controlled substances for which a report is required; no additional report will be required from him, if no further transactions involving controlled substances are consummated by him. The initial report of the registrant-transferee shall account for transactions beginning with the day next succeeding the date of discontinuance or transfer of business by the transferor-registrant and the substances transferred to him shall be reported as receipts in his/her initial report.

(f) Any registrant that has been authorized as a collector and desires to discontinue its collection of controlled substances from ultimate users shall notify the Administration of its intent by submitting a written notification to the Registration Unit, Drug Enforcement Administration. See the Table of DEA Mailing Addresses in § 1321.01 of this chapter for the current mailing address. Additionally, such notice may be submitted on-line at *www.DEAdiversion.usdoj.gov*. When ceasing collection activities of an authorized mail-back program, the registrant shall provide the Administration with the name, registered address, and registration number of the collector that will receive the remaining mail-back packages in accordance with § 1317.70(e)(3) of this chapter.

[62 FR 13957, Mar. 24, 1997, as amended at 74 FR 15623, Apr. 6, 2009; 75 FR 10676, Mar. 9, 2010; 76 FR 61564, Oct. 5, 2011; 79 FR 53561, Sept. 9, 2014]

SECURITY REQUIREMENTS

§ 1301.71 Security requirements generally.

(a) All applicants and registrants shall provide effective controls and procedures to guard against theft and diversion of controlled substances. In order to determine whether a registrant has provided effective controls against diversion, the Administrator shall use the security requirements set forth in §§ 1301.72–1301.76 as standards for the physical security controls and operating procedures necessary to prevent diversion. Materials and construction which will provide a structural equivalent to the physical security controls set forth in §§ 1301.72, 1301.73 and 1301.75 may be used in lieu of the materials and construction described in those sections.

(b) Substantial compliance with the standards set forth in §§ 1301.72–1301.76 may be deemed sufficient by the Administrator after evaluation of the overall security system and needs of the applicant or registrant. In evaluating the overall security system of a registrant or applicant, the Administrator may consider any of the following factors as he may deem relevant to the need for strict compliance with security requirements:

(1) The type of activity conducted (e.g., processing of bulk chemicals, preparing dosage forms, packaging, labeling, cooperative buying, etc.);

(2) The type and form of controlled substances handled (e.g., bulk liquids or dosage units, usable powders or nonusable powders);

(3) The quantity of controlled substances handled;

(4) The location of the premises and the relationship such location bears on security needs;

(5) The type of building construction comprising the facility and the general characteristics of the building or buildings;

(6) The type of vault, safe, and secure enclosures or other storage system (e.g., automatic storage and retrieval system) used;

(7) The type of closures on vaults, safes, and secure enclosures;

(8) The adequacy of key control systems and/or combination lock control systems;

(9) The adequacy of electric detection and alarm systems, if any including use of supervised transmittal lines and standby power sources;

(10) The extent of unsupervised public access to the facility, including the presence and characteristics of perimeter fencing, if any;

(11) The adequacy of supervision over employees having access to manufacturing and storage areas;

(12) The procedures for handling business guests, visitors, maintenance personnel, and nonemployee service personnel;

(13) The availability of local police protection or of the registrant's or applicant's security personnel;

(14) The adequacy of the registrant's or applicant's system for monitoring the receipt, manufacture, distribution, and disposition of controlled substances in its operations; and

(15) The applicability of the security requirements contained in all Federal, State, and local laws and regulations governing the management of waste.

(c) When physical security controls become inadequate as a result of a controlled substance being transferred to a different schedule, or as a result of a noncontrolled substance being listed on any schedule, or as a result of a significant increase in the quantity of controlled substances in the possession of the registrant during normal business operations, the physical security controls shall be expanded and extended accordingly. A registrant may adjust physical security controls within the requirements set forth in §§ 1301.72–1301.76 when the need for such controls decreases as a result of a controlled substance being transferred to a different schedule, or a result of a controlled substance being removed from control, or as a result of a significant decrease in the quantity of controlled substances in the possession of the registrant during normal business operations.

(d) Any registrant or applicant desiring to determine whether a proposed security system substantially complies with, or is the structural equivalent of, the requirements set forth in §§ 1301.72–1301.76 may submit any plans, blueprints, sketches or other materials regarding the proposed security system either to the Special Agent in Charge in the region in which the system will be used, or to the Regulatory Section, Drug Enforcement Administration. See the Table of DEA Mailing Addresses in § 1321.01 of this chapter for the current mailing address.

(e) Physical security controls of locations registered under the Harrison Narcotic Act or the Narcotics Manufacturing Act of 1960 on April 30, 1971, shall be deemed to comply substantially with the standards set forth in §§ 1301.72, 1301.73 and 1301.75. Any new facilities or work or storage areas constructed or utilized for controlled substances, which facilities or work or storage areas have not been previously approved by the Administration, shall not necessarily be deemed to comply substantially with the standards set forth in §§ 1301.72, 1301.73 and 1301.75, notwithstanding that such facilities or work or storage areas have physical security controls similar to those previously approved by the Administration.

(f) A collector shall not employ, as an agent or employee who has access to or influence over controlled substances acquired by collection, any person who has been convicted of any felony offense relating to controlled substances or who, at any time, had an application for registration with DEA denied, had a DEA registration revoked or suspended, or has surrendered a DEA registration for cause. For purposes of this subsection, "for cause" means in lieu of, or as a consequence of, any Federal or State administrative, civil, or criminal action resulting from an investigation of the individual's handling of controlled substances.

[36 FR 18729, Sept. 21, 1971. Redesignated at 38 FR 26609, Sept. 24, 1973, and amended at 46 FR 28841, May 29, 1981; 47 FR 41735, Sept. 22, 1982; 51 FR 5319, Feb. 13, 1986; 68 FR 41228, July 11, 2003; 75 FR 10677, Mar. 9, 2010; 79 FR 53561, Sept. 9, 2014]

§ 1301.72 Physical security controls for non-practitioners; narcotic treatment programs and compounders for narcotic treatment programs; storage areas.

(a) *Schedules I and II.* Raw material, bulk materials awaiting further processing, finished products which are controlled substances listed in Schedule I or II (except GHB that is manufactured or distributed in accordance with an exemption under section 505(i) of the Federal Food Drug and Cosmetic Act which shall be subject to the requirements of paragraph (b) of this section), and sealed mail-back packages and inner liners acquired in accordance with part 1317 of this chapter, shall be stored in one of the following secured areas:

(1) Where small quantities permit, a safe or steel cabinet;

(i) Which safe or steel cabinet shall have the following specifications or the equivalent: 30 man-minutes against surreptitious entry, 10 man-minutes against forced entry, 20 man-hours against lock manipulation, and 20 man-hours against radiological techniques;

(ii) Which safe or steel cabinet, if it weighs less than 750 pounds, is bolted or cemented to the floor or wall in such a way that it cannot be readily removed; and

(iii) Which safe or steel cabinet, if necessary, depending upon the quantities and type of controlled substances stored, is equipped with an alarm system which, upon attempted unauthorized entry, shall transmit a signal directly to a central protection company or a local or State police agency which has a legal duty to respond, or a 24-hour control station operated by the registrant, or such other protection as the Administrator may approve.

(2) A vault constructed before, or under construction on, September 1, 1971, which is of substantial construction with a steel door, combination or key lock, and an alarm system; or

(3) A vault constructed after September 1, 1971:

(i) The walls, floors, and ceilings of which vault are constructed of at least 8 inches of reinforced concrete or other substantial masonry, reinforced vertically and horizontally with ½-inch steel rods tied 6 inches on center, or the structural equivalent to such reinforced walls, floors, and ceilings;

(ii) The door and frame unit of which vault shall conform to the following specifications or the equivalent: 30 man-minutes against surreptitious entry, 10 man-minutes against forced entry, 20 man-hours against lock manipulation, and 20 man-hours against radiological techniques;

(iii) Which vault, if operations require it to remain open for frequent access, is equipped with a "day-gate" which is self-closing and self-locking, or the equivalent, for use during the hours of operation in which the vault door is open;

(iv) The walls or perimeter of which vault are equipped with an alarm, which upon unauthorized entry shall transmit a signal directly to a central station protection company, or a local or State police agency which has a legal duty to respond, or a 24-hour control station operated by the registrant, or such other protection as the Administrator may approve, and, if necessary, holdup buttons at strategic points of entry to the perimeter area of the vault;

(v) The door of which vault is equipped with contact switches; and

(vi) Which vault has one of the following: Complete electrical lacing of the walls, floor and ceilings; sensitive ultrasonic equipment within the vault; a sensitive sound accumulator system; or such other device designed to detect illegal entry as may be approved by the Administration.

(b) *Schedules III, IV and V*. Raw material, bulk materials awaiting further processing, and finished products which are controlled substances listed in Schedules III, IV, and V, and GHB when it is manufactured or distributed in accordance with an exemption under section 505(i) of the FFDCA, shall be stored in the following secure storage areas:

(1) A safe or steel cabinet as described in paragraph (a)(1) of this section;

(2) A vault as described in paragraph (a)(2) or (3) of this section equipped with an alarm system as described in paragraph (b)(4)(v) of this section;

(3) A building used for storage of Schedules III through V controlled substances with perimeter security which limits access during working hours and provides security after working hours and meets the following specifications:

(i) Has an electronic alarm system as described in paragraph (b)(4)(v) of this section,

(ii) Is equipped with self-closing, self-locking doors constructed of substantial material commensurate with the type of building construction, provided, however, a door which is kept closed and locked at all times when not in use and when in use is kept under direct observation of a responsible employee or agent of the registrant is permitted in lieu of a self-closing, self-locking door. Doors may be sliding or hinged. Regarding hinged doors, where hinges are mounted on the outside, such hinges shall be sealed, welded or otherwise constructed to inhibit removal. Locking devices for such doors shall be either of the multiple-position combination or key lock type and:

(*a*) In the case of key locks, shall require key control which limits access to a limited number of employees, or;

(*b*) In the case of combination locks, the combination shall be limited to a minimum number of employees and can be changed upon termination of employment of an employee having knowledge of the combination;

(4) A cage, located within a building on the premises, meeting the following specifications:

(i) Having walls constructed of not less than No. 10 gauge steel fabric mounted on steel posts, which posts are:

(*a*) At least one inch in diameter;

(*b*) Set in concrete or installed with lag bolts that are pinned or brazed; and

(*c*) Which are placed no more than ten feet apart with horizontal one and one-half inch reinforcements every sixty inches;

(ii) Having a mesh construction with openings of not more than two and one-half inches across the square,

(iii) Having a ceiling constructed of the same material, or in the alternative, a cage shall be erected which reaches and is securely attached to the structural ceiling of the building. A lighter gauge mesh may be used for the ceilings of large enclosed areas if walls are at least 14 feet in height,

(iv) Is equipped with a door constructed of No. 10 gauge steel fabric on a metal door frame in a metal door flange, and in all other respects conforms to all the requirements of 21 CFR 1301.72(b)(3)(ii), and

(v) Is equipped with an alarm system which upon unauthorized entry shall transmit a signal directly to a central station protection agency or a local or state police agency, each having a legal duty to respond, or to a 24-hour control station operated by the registrant, or to such other source of protection as the Administrator may approve;

(5) An enclosure of masonry or other material, approved in writing by the Administrator as providing security comparable to a cage;

(6) A building or enclosure within a building which has been inspected and approved by DEA or its predecessor agency, BND, and continues to provide adequate security against the diversion of Schedule III through V controlled substances, of which fact written acknowledgment has been made by the

Special Agent in Charge of DEA for the area in which such building or enclosure is situated;

(7) Such other secure storage areas as may be approved by the Administrator after considering the factors listed in § 1301.71(b);

(8)(i) Schedule III through V controlled substances may be stored with Schedules I and II controlled substances under security measures provided by 21 CFR 1301.72(a);

(ii) Non-controlled drugs, substances and other materials may be stored with Schedule III through V controlled substances in any of the secure storage areas required by 21 CFR 1301.72(b), provided that permission for such storage of non-controlled items is obtained in advance, in writing, from the Special Agent in Charge of DEA for the area in which such storage area is situated. Any such permission tendered must be upon the Special Agent in Charge's written determination that such non-segregated storage does not diminish security effectiveness for Schedules III through V controlled substances.

(c) *Multiple storage areas.* Where several types or classes of controlled substances are handled separately by the registrant or applicant for different purposes (e.g., returned goods, or goods in process), the controlled substances may be stored separately, provided that each storage area complies with the requirements set forth in this section.

(d) *Accessibility to storage areas.* The controlled substances storage areas shall be accessible only to an absolute minimum number of specifically authorized employees. When it is necessary for employee maintenance personnel, nonemployee maintenance personnel, business guests, or visitors to be present in or pass through controlled substances storage areas, the registrant shall provide for adequate observation of the area by an employee specifically authorized in writing.

[36 FR 18730, Sept. 21, 1971. Redesignated at 38 FR 26609, Sept. 24, 1973]

EDITORIAL NOTE: For FEDERAL REGISTER citations affecting § 1301.72, see the List of CFR Sections Affected, which appears in the Finding Aids section of the printed volume and at *www.govinfo.gov*.

§ 1301.73 Physical security controls for non-practitioners; compounders for narcotic treatment programs; manufacturing and compounding areas.

All manufacturing activities (including processing, packaging and labeling) involving controlled substances listed in any schedule and all activities of compounders shall be conducted in accordance with the following:

(a) All in-process substances shall be returned to the controlled substances storage area at the termination of the process. If the process is not terminated at the end of a workday (except where a continuous process or other normal manufacturing operation should not be interrupted), the processing area or tanks, vessels, bins or bulk containers containing such substances shall be securely locked, with adequate security for the area or building. If such security requires an alarm, such alarm, upon unauthorized entry, shall transmit a signal directly to a central station protection company, or local or state police agency which has a legal duty to respond, or a 24-hour control station operated by the registrant.

(b) Manufacturing activities with controlled substances shall be conducted in an area or areas of clearly defined limited access which is under surveillance by an employee or employees designated in writing as responsible for the area. "Limited access" may be provided, in the absence of physical dividers such as walls or partitions, by traffic control lines or restricted space designation. The employee designated as responsible for the area may be engaged in the particular manufacturing operation being conducted: *Provided*, That he is able to provide continuous surveillance of the area in order that unauthorized persons may not enter or leave the area without his knowledge.

(c) During the production of controlled substances, the manufacturing areas shall be accessible to only those employees required for efficient operation. When it is necessary for employee maintenance personnel, nonemployee maintenance personnel, business guests, or visitors to be present in or pass through manufacturing areas during production of controlled substances, the registrant shall provide for adequate observation of the area by an employee specifically authorized in writing.

[36 FR 18731, Sept. 21, 1971. Redesignated at 38 FR 26609, Sept. 24, 1973 and amended at 39 FR 37984, Oct. 25, 1974]

§ 1301.74 Other security controls for non-practitioners; narcotic treatment programs and compounders for narcotic treatment programs.

(a) Before distributing a controlled substance to any person who the registrant does not know to be registered to possess the controlled substance, the registrant shall make a good faith inquiry either with the Administration or with the appropriate State controlled substances registration agency, if any, to determine that the person is registered to possess the controlled substance.

(b) The registrant shall design and operate a system to disclose to the registrant suspicious orders of controlled substances. The registrant shall inform the Field Division Office of the Administration in his area of suspicious orders when discovered by the registrant. Suspicious orders include orders of unusual size, orders deviating substantially from a normal pattern, and orders of unusual frequency.

(c) The registrant must notify the Field Division Office of the Administration in his or her area, in writing, of any theft or significant loss of any controlled substances within one business day of discovery of the theft or loss. Unless the theft or loss occurs during an import or export transaction, the supplier is responsible for reporting all in-transit losses of controlled substances by their agent or the common or contract carrier selected pursuant to paragraph (e) of this section, within one business day of discovery of such theft or loss. In an import transaction, once a shipment has been released by the customs officer at the port of entry, the importer is responsible for reporting all in-transit losses of controlled substances by their agent or the common or contract carrier selected pursuant to paragraph (e) of this section, within one business day of discovery of such theft or loss. In an export transaction, the exporter is responsible for reporting all in-transit losses of controlled substances by their agent or the common or contract carrier selected pursuant to paragraph (e) of this section within one business day of discovery of such theft or loss, until the shipment has been released by the customs officer at the port of export. The registrant must also complete, and submit to the Field Division Office in his or her area, DEA Form 106 regarding the theft or loss. Thefts and significant losses must be reported whether or not the controlled substances are subsequently recovered or the responsible parties are identified and action taken against them. When determining whether a loss is significant, a registrant should consider, among others, the following factors:

(1) The actual quantity of controlled substances lost in relation to the type of business;

(2) The specific controlled substances lost;

(3) Whether the loss of the controlled substances can be associated with access to those controlled substances by specific individuals, or whether the loss can be attributed to unique activities that may take place involving the controlled substances;

(4) A pattern of losses over a specific time period, whether the losses appear to be random, and the results of efforts taken to resolve the losses; and, if known,

(5) Whether the specific controlled substances are likely candidates for diversion;

(6) Local trends and other indicators of the diversion potential of the missing controlled substance.

(d) The registrant shall not distribute any controlled substance listed in Schedules II through V as a complimentary sample to any potential or current customer (1) without the prior written request of the customer, (2) to be used only for satisfying the legitimate medical needs of patients of the customer, and (3) only in reasonable quantities. Such request must contain the name, address, and registration number of the customer and the name and quantity of the specific controlled substance desired. The request shall be preserved by the registrant with other records of distribution of controlled substances. In addition, the requirements of part 1305 of the chapter shall be complied with for any distribution of a controlled substance listed in Schedule II. For purposes of this paragraph, the term "customer" includes a person to whom a complimentary sample of a substance is given in order to encourage the prescribing or recommending of the substance by the person.

(e) When shipping controlled substances, a registrant is responsible for selecting common or contract carriers which provide adequate security to guard against in-transit losses. When storing controlled substances in a public warehouse, a registrant is responsible for selecting a warehouseman which will provide adequate security to guard against storage losses; wherever possible, the registrant shall store controlled substances in a public warehouse which complies with the requirements set forth in § 1301.72. In addition, the registrant shall employ precautions (e.g., assuring that shipping containers do not indicate that contents are controlled substances) to guard against storage or in-transit losses.

(f) When distributing controlled substances through agents (e.g., detailmen), a registrant is responsible for providing and requiring adequate security to guard against theft and diversion while the substances are being stored or handled by the agent or agents.

(g) Before the initial distribution of thiafentanil, carfentanil, etorphine hydrochloride and/or diprenorphine to any person, the registrant must verify that the person is authorized to handle the substance(s) by contacting the Drug Enforcement Administration.

(h) The acceptance of delivery of narcotic substances by a narcotic treatment program shall be made only by a licensed practitioner employed at the facility or other authorized individuals designated in writing. At the time of delivery, the licensed practitioner or other authorized individual designated in writing (excluding persons currently or previously dependent on narcotic drugs), shall sign for the narcotics and place his specific title (if any) on any invoice. Copies of these signed invoices shall be kept by the distributor.

(i) Narcotics dispensed or administered at a narcotic treatment program will be dispensed or administered directly to the patient by either (1) the licensed practitioner, (2) a registered nurse under the direction of the licensed practitioner, (3) a licensed practical nurse under the direction of the licensed practitioner, or (4) a pharmacist under the direction of the licensed practitioner.

(j) Persons enrolled in a narcotic treatment program will be required to wait in an area physically separated from the narcotic storage and dispensing area. This requirement will be enforced by the program physician and employees.

(k) All narcotic treatment programs must comply with standards established by the Secretary of Health and Human Services (after consultation with the Administration) respecting the quantities of narcotic drugs which may be provided to persons enrolled in a narcotic treatment program for unsupervised use.

(l) DEA may exercise discretion regarding the degree of security required in narcotic treatment programs based on such factors as the location of a program, the number of patients enrolled in a program and the number of physicians, staff members and security guards. Similarly, such factors will be taken into consideration when evaluating existing security or requiring new security at a narcotic treatment program.

(m) A reverse distributor shall not employ, as an agent or employee who has access to or influence over controlled substances, any person who has been convicted of any felony offense relating to controlled substances or who, at any time, had an application for registration with the DEA denied, had a DEA registration revoked or suspended, or has surrendered a DEA registration for cause. For purposes of this subsection, "for cause" means in lieu of, or as a consequence of, any Federal or State administrative, civil, or criminal action resulting from an investigation of the individual's handling of controlled substances.

[36 FR 7778, Apr. 24, 1971. Redesignated at 38 FR 26609, Sept. 24, 1973]

EDITORIAL NOTE: For FEDERAL REGISTER citations affecting §1301.74, see the List of CFR Sections Affected, which appears in the Finding Aids section of the printed volume and at *www.govinfo.gov*.

§ 1301.75 Physical security controls for practitioners.

(a) Controlled substances listed in Schedule I shall be stored in a securely locked, substantially constructed cabinet.

(b) Controlled substances listed in Schedules II, III, IV, and V shall be stored in a securely locked, substantially constructed cabinet. However, pharmacies and institutional practitioners may disperse such substances throughout the stock of noncontrolled substances in such a manner as to obstruct the theft or diversion of the controlled substances.

(c) Sealed mail-back packages and inner liners collected in accordance with part 1317 of this chapter shall only be stored at the registered location in a securely locked, substantially constructed cabinet or a securely locked room with controlled access, except as authorized by §1317.80(d).

(d) This section shall also apply to nonpractitioners authorized to conduct research or chemical analysis under another registration.

(e) Thiafentanil, carfentanil, etorphine hydrochloride and diprenorphine shall be stored in a safe or steel cabinet equivalent to a U.S. Government Class V security container.

[39 FR 3674, Jan. 29, 1974, as amended at 39 FR 17838, May 21, 1974; 54 FR 33674, Aug. 16, 1989; 62 FR 13957, Mar. 24, 1997; 79 FR 53562, Sept. 9, 2014; 81 FR 58839, Aug. 26, 2016]

§ 1301.76 Other security controls for practitioners.

(a) The registrant shall not employ, as an agent or employee who has access to controlled substances, any person who has been convicted of a felony offense relating to controlled substances or who, at any time, had an application for registration with the DEA denied, had a DEA registration revoked or has surrendered a DEA registration for cause. For purposes of this subsection, the term "for cause" means a surrender in lieu of, or as a consequence of, any federal or state administrative, civil or criminal action resulting from an investigation of the individual's handling of controlled substances.

(b) The registrant shall notify the Field Division Office of the Administration in his area, in writing, of the theft or significant loss of any controlled substances within one business day of discovery of such loss or theft. The registrant shall also complete, and submit to the Field Division Office in his area, DEA Form 106 regarding the loss or theft. When determining whether a loss is significant, a registrant should consider, among others, the following factors:

(1) The actual quantity of controlled substances lost in relation to the type of business;

(2) The specific controlled substances lost;

(3) Whether the loss of the controlled substances can be associated with access to those controlled substances by specific individuals, or whether the loss can be attributed to unique activities that may take place involving the controlled substances;

(4) A pattern of losses over a specific time period, whether the losses appear to be random, and the results of efforts taken to resolve the losses; and, if known,

(5) Whether the specific controlled substances are likely candidates for diversion;

(6) Local trends and other indicators of the diversion potential of the missing controlled substance.

(c) Whenever the registrant distributes a controlled substance (without being registered as a distributor as permitted in §§1301.13(e)(1), 1307.11, 1317.05, and/or 1317.10 of this chapter), he/she shall comply with the requirements imposed on non-practitioners in §1301.74(a), (b), and (e).

(d) Central fill pharmacies must comply with §1301.74(e) when selecting private, common or contract carriers to transport filled prescriptions to a retail pharmacy for delivery to the ultimate user. When central fill pharmacies contract with private, common or contract carriers to transport filled prescriptions to a retail pharmacy, the central fill pharmacy is responsible for reporting in-transit losses upon discovery of such loss by use of a DEA Form 106. Retail pharmacies must comply with § 1301.74(e) when selecting private, common or contract carriers to retrieve filled prescriptions from a central fill pharmacy. When retail pharmacies contract with private, common or contract carriers to retrieve filled prescriptions from a central fill pharmacy, the retail pharmacy is responsible for reporting in-transit losses upon discovery of such loss by use of a DEA Form 106.

[36 FR 7778, Apr. 24, 1971, as amended at 36 FR 18731, Sept. 21, 1971; 37 FR 15919, Aug. 8, 1972. Redesignated at 38 FR 26609, Sept. 24, 1973; 47 FR 41735, Sept. 22, 1982; 56 FR 36728, Aug. 1, 1991; 62 FR 13957, Mar. 24, 1997; 68 FR 37409, June 24, 2003; 70 FR 47097, Aug. 12, 2005; 79 FR 53562, Sept. 9, 2014]

§ 1301.77 Security controls for freight forwarding facilities.

(a) All Schedule II–V controlled substances that will be temporarily stored at the freight forwarding facility must be either:

(1) stored in a segregated area under constant observation by designated responsible individual(s); or

(2) stored in a secured area that meets the requirements of Section 1301.72(b) of this Part. For purposes of this requirement, a facility that may be locked down (*i.e.*, secured against physical entry in a manner consistent with requirements of Section 1301.72(b)(3)(ii) of this part) and has a monitored alarm system or is subject to continuous monitoring by security personnel will be deemed to meet the requirements of Section 1301.72(b)(3) of this Part.

(b) Access to controlled substances must be kept to an absolute minimum number of specifically authorized individuals. Non-authorized individuals may not be present in or pass through controlled substances storage areas without adequate observation provided by an individual authorized in writing by the registrant.

(c) Controlled substances being transferred through a freight forwarding facility must be packed in sealed, unmarked shipping containers.

[65 FR 44678, July 19, 2000; 65 FR 45829, July 25, 2000]

EMPLOYEE SCREENING—NON-PRACTITIONERS

§ 1301.90 Employee screening procedures.

It is the position of DEA that the obtaining of certain information by non-practitioners is vital to fairly assess the likelihood of an employee committing a drug security breach. The need to know this information is a matter of business necessity, essential to overall controlled substances security. In this regard, it is believed that conviction of crimes and unauthorized use of controlled substances are activities that are proper subjects for inquiry. It is, therefore, assumed that the following questions will become a part of an employer's comprehensive employee screening program:

Question. Within the past five years, have you been convicted of a felony, or within the past two years, of any misdemeanor or are you presently formally charged with committing a criminal offense? (Do not include any traffic violations, juvenile offenses or military convictions, except by general court-martial.) If the answer is yes, furnish details of conviction, offense, location, date and sentence.

Question. In the past three years, have you ever knowingly used any narcotics, amphetamines or barbiturates, other than those prescribed to you by a physician? If the answer is yes, furnish details.

Advice. An authorization, in writing, that allows inquiries to be made of courts and law enforcement agencies for possible pending charges or convictions must be executed by a person who is allowed to work in an area where access to controlled substances clearly exists. A person must be advised that any false information or omission of information will jeopardize his or her position with respect to employment. The application for employment should inform a person that information furnished or recovered as a result of any inquiry will not necessarily preclude employment, but will be considered as part of an overall evaluation of the person's qualifications. The maintaining of fair employment practices, the protection of the person's right of privacy, and the assurance that the results of such inquiries will be treated by the employer in confidence will be explained to the employee.

[40 FR 17143, Apr. 17, 1975]

§ 1301.91 Employee responsibility to report drug diversion.

Reports of drug diversion by fellow employees is not only a necessary part of an overall employee security program but also serves the public interest at large. It is, therefore, the position of DEA that an employee who has knowledge of drug diversion from his employer by a fellow employee has an obligation to report such information to a responsible security official of the employer. The employer shall treat such information as confidential and shall take all reasonable steps to protect the confidentiality of the information and the identity of the employee furnishing information. A failure to report information of drug diversion will be considered in determining the feasibility of continuing to allow an employee to work in a drug security area. The employer shall inform all employees concerning this policy.

[40 FR 17143, Apr. 17, 1975]

§ 1301.92 Illicit activities by employees.

It is the position of DEA that employees who possess, sell, use or divert controlled substances will subject themselves not only to State or Federal prosecution for any illicit activity, but shall also immediately become the subject of independent action regarding their continued employment. The employer will assess the seriousness of the employee's violation, the position of responsibility held by the employee, past record of employment, etc., in determining whether to suspend, transfer, terminate or take other action against the employee.

[40 FR 17143, Apr. 17, 1975]

§ 1301.93 Sources of information for employee checks.

DEA recommends that inquiries concerning employees' criminal records be made as follows:

Local inquiries. Inquiries should be made by name, date and place of birth, and other identifying information, to local courts and law enforcement agencies for records of pending charges and convictions. Local practice may require such inquiries to be made in person, rather than by mail, and a copy of an authorization from the employee may be required by certain law enforcement agencies.

DEA inquiries. Inquiries supplying identifying information should also be furnished to DEA Field Division Offices along with written consent from the concerned individual for a check of DEA files for records of convictions. The Regional check will result in a national check being made by the Field Division Office.

[40 FR 17143, Apr. 17, 1975, as amended at 47 FR 41735, Sept. 22, 1982]

PART 1302—LABELING AND PACKAGING REQUIREMENTS FOR CONTROLLED SUBSTANCES

Sec.

AUTHORITY: 21 U.S.C. 821, 825, 871(b), 958(e).

SOURCE: 36 FR 7785, Apr. 24, 1971, unless otherwise noted. Redesignated at 38 FR 26609, Sept. 24, 1973.

§ 1302.01 Scope of part 1302.

Requirements governing the labeling and packaging of controlled substances pursuant to sections 1305 and 1008(d) of the Act (21 U.S.C. 825 and 958(d)) are set forth generally by those sections and specifically by the sections of this part.

[36 FR 13386, July 21, 1971. Redesignated at 38 FR 26609, Sept. 24, 1973]

§ 1302.02 Definitions.

Any term contained in this part shall have the definition set forth in section 102 of the Act (21 U.S.C. 802) or part 1300 of this chapter.

[62 FR 13958, Mar. 24, 1997]

§ 1302.03 Symbol required; exceptions.

(a) Each commercial container of a controlled substance (except for a controlled substance excepted by the Administrator pursuant to § 1308.31 of this chapter) shall have printed on the label the symbol designating the schedule in which such controlled substance is listed. Each such commercial container, if it otherwise has no label, must bear a label complying with the requirement of this part.

(b) Each manufacturer shall print upon the labeling of each controlled substance distributed by him the symbol designating the schedule in which such controlled substance is listed.

(c) The following symbols shall designate the schedule corresponding thereto:

Schedule	
Schedule I	CI or C–I.
Schedule II	CII or C–II.
Schedule III	CIII or C–III.
Schedule IV	CIV or C–IV.
Schedule V	CV or C–V.

The word "schedule" need not be used. No distinction need be made between narcotic and nonnarcotic substances.

(d) The symbol is not required on a carton or wrapper in which a commercial container is held if the symbol is easily legible through such carton or wrapper.

(e) The symbol is not required on a commercial container too small or otherwise unable to accommodate a label, if the symbol is printed on the box or package from which the commercial container is removed upon dispensing to an ultimate user.

(f) The symbol is not required on a commercial container containing, or on the labeling of, a controlled substance being utilized in clinical research involving blind and double blind studies.

[36 FR 7785, Apr. 24, 1971, as amended at 36 FR 18731, Sept. 21, 1971. Redesignated at 38 FR 26609, Sept. 24, 1973]

§ 1302.04 Location and size of symbol on label and labeling.

The symbol shall be prominently located on the label or the labeling of the commercial container and/or the panel of the commercial container normally displayed to dispensers of any controlled substance. The symbol on labels shall be clear and large enough to afford easy identification of the schedule of the controlled substance upon inspection without removal from the dispenser's shelf. The symbol on all other labeling shall be clear and large enough to afford prompt identification of the controlled substance upon inspection of the labeling.

[62 FR 13958, Mar. 24, 1997]

§ 1302.05 Effective dates of labeling requirements.

All labels on commercial containers of, and all labeling of, a controlled substance which either is transferred to another schedule or is added to any schedule shall comply with the requirements of § 1302.03, on or before the effective date established in the final order for the transfer or addition.

[62 FR 13958, Mar. 24, 1997]

§ 1302.06 Sealing of controlled substances.

On each bottle, multiple dose vial, or other commercial container of any controlled substance, there shall be securely affixed to the stopper, cap, lid, covering, or wrapper or such container a seal to disclose upon inspection any tampering or opening of the container.

[62 FR 13958, Mar. 24, 1997]

§ 1302.07 Labeling and packaging requirements for imported and exported substances.

(a) The symbol requirements of §§ 1302.03 through 1302.05 apply to every commercial container containing, and to all labeling of, controlled substances imported into the customs territory of the United States from any place outside thereof (but within the United States), or imported into the United States from any place outside thereof.

(b) The symbol requirements of §§ 1302.03 through 1302.05 do not apply to any commercial containers containing, or any labeling of, a controlled substance intended for export.

(c) The sealing requirements of § 1302.06 apply to every bottle, multiple dose vial, or other commercial container of any controlled substance listed in schedule I or II, or any narcotic controlled substance listed in schedule

III or IV imported into the customs territory of the United States from any place outside thereof (but within the United States), or imported into the United States from any place outside thereof. The sealing requirements of §1302.06 apply to every bottle, multiple dose vial, or other commercial container of any controlled substance listed in schedule I or II, or any narcotic controlled substance listed in schedule III or IV, exported or intended for export from the United States. These sealing and labeling requirements are in addition to any sealing requirements required under applicable customs laws.

[81 FR 97020, Dec. 30, 2016]

PART 1303—QUOTAS

AUTHORITY: 21 U.S.C. 821, 826, 871(b).

GENERAL INFORMATION

§1303.01 Scope of part 1303.

Procedures governing the establishment of production and manufacturing quotas on basic classes of controlled substances listed in schedules I and II pursuant to section 306 of the Act (21 U.S.C. 826) are governed generally by that section and specifically by the sections of this part.

[36 FR 7786, Apr. 24, 1971. Redesignated at 38 FR 26609, Sept. 24, 1973]

§1303.02 Definitions.

Any term contained in this part shall have the definition set forth in section 102 of the Act (21 U.S.C. 802) or part 1300 of this chapter.

[62 FR 13958, Mar. 24, 1997]

AGGREGATE PRODUCTION AND PROCUREMENT QUOTAS

§1303.11 Aggregate production quotas.

(a) The Administrator shall determine the total quantity of each basic class of controlled substance listed in Schedule I or II necessary to be manufactured during the following calendar year to provide for the estimated medical, scientific, research and industrial needs of the United States, for lawful export requirements, and for the establishment and maintenance of reserve stocks.

(b) In making his determinations, the Administrator shall consider the following factors:

(1) Total net disposal of the class by all manufacturers during the current and 2 preceding years;

(2) Trends in the national rate of net disposal of the class;

(3) Total actual (or estimated) inventories of the class and of all substances manufactured from the class, and trends in inventory accumulation;

(4) Projected demand for such class as indicated by procurement quotas requested pursuant to §1303.12;

(5) The extent of any diversion of the controlled substance in the class;

(6) Relevant information obtained from the Department of Health and Human Services, including from the Food and Drug Administration, the

Centers for Disease Control and Prevention, and the Centers for Medicare and Medicaid Services, and relevant information obtained from the states; and

(7) Other factors affecting medical, scientific, research, and industrial needs in the United States and lawful export requirements, as the Administrator finds relevant, including changes in the currently accepted medical use in treatment with the class or the substances which are manufactured from it, the economic and physical availability of raw materials for use in manufacturing and for inventory purposes, yield and stability problems, potential disruptions to production (including possible labor strikes), and recent unforeseen emergencies such as floods and fires.

(c) The Administrator shall, on or before May 1 of each year, publish in the FEDERAL REGISTER, general notice of an aggregate production quota for any basic class determined by him under this section. A copy of said notice shall be mailed simultaneously to each person registered as a bulk manufacturer of the basic class and transmitted to each state attorney general. The Administrator shall permit any interested person to file written comments on or objections to the proposal and shall designate in the notice the time during which such filings may be made. The Administrator may, but shall not be required to, hold a public hearing on one or more issues raised by the comments and objections filed with him, except that the Administrator shall hold a hearing if he determines it is necessary to resolve an issue of material fact raised by a state objecting to the proposed quantity for the class as excessive for legitimate United States' needs. In the event the Administrator decides to hold a hearing, he shall publish notice of the hearing in the FEDERAL REGISTER, which notice shall summarize the issues to be heard and shall set the time for the hearing, which shall not be less than 30 days after the date of publication of the notice. After consideration of any comments or objections, or after a hearing if one is ordered by the Administrator, the Administrator shall issue and publish in the FEDERAL REGISTER his final order determining the aggregate production quota for the basic class of controlled substances. The order shall include the findings of fact and conclusions of law upon which the order is based. The order shall specify the date on which it shall take effect. A copy of said order shall be mailed simultaneously to each person registered as a bulk manufacturer of the basic class and transmitted to each state attorney general.

[36 FR 7786, Apr. 24, 1971, as amended at 37 FR 15919, Aug. 8, 1972. Redesignated at 38 FR 26609, Sept. 24, 1973; 77 FR 4235, Jan. 27, 2012; 83 FR 32789, July 16, 2018]

§ 1303.12 Procurement quotas.

(a) In order to determine the estimated needs for, and to insure an adequate and uninterrupted supply of, basic classes of controlled substances listed in Schedules I and II (except raw opium being imported by the registrant pursuant to an import permit) the Administrator shall issue procurement quotas authorizing persons to procure and use quantities of each basic class of such substances for the purpose of manufacturing such class into dosage forms or into other substances.

(b) Any person who is registered to manufacture controlled substances listed in any schedule and who desires to use during the next calendar year any basic class of controlled substances listed in Schedule I or II (except raw opium being imported by the registrant pursuant to an import permit) for purposes of manufacturing, shall apply on DEA Form 250 for a procurement quota for such basic class. A separate application must be made for each basic class desired to be procured or used. The applicant shall state whether he intends to manufacture the basic class himself or purchase it from another manufacturer. The applicant shall state separately each purpose for which the basic class is desired, the quantity desired for that purpose during the next calendar year, and the quantities used and estimated to be used, if any, for that purpose during the current and preceding 2 calendar years. If the purpose is to manufacture the basic class into dosage form, the applicant shall state the official name, common or usual name, chemical name, or brand name of that form. The Administrator may require additional information from an applicant which, in the Administrator's judgment, may be helpful in detecting or preventing diversion, including customer identities and amounts of the controlled substance sold to each customer.If the purpose is to manufacture another substance, the applicant shall state the official name, common or usual name, chemical name, or brand name of the substance, and, if a controlled substance listed in any schedule, the schedule number and Administration Controlled Substances Code Number, as set forth in part 1308 of this chapter, of the substance. If the purpose is to manufacture another basic class of controlled substance listed in Schedule I or II, the applicant shall also state the quantity of the other basic class which the applicant has applied to manufacture pursuant to §1303.22 and the quantity of the first basic class necessary to manufacture a specified unit of the second basic class. DEA Form 250 shall be filed on or before April 1 of the year preceding the calendar year for which the procurement quota is being applied. Copies of DEA Form 250 may be obtained from, and shall be filed with, the UN Reporting and Quota Section, Diversion Control Division. See the Table of DEA Mailing Addresses in §1321.01 of this chapter for the current mailing address.

(c) The Administrator shall, on or before July 1 of the year preceding the calendar year during which the quota shall be effective, issue to each qualified applicant a procurement quota authorizing him to procure and use:

(1) All quantities of such class necessary to manufacture all quantities of other basic classes of controlled substances listed in Schedules I and II which the applicant is authorized to manufacture pursuant to §1303.23; and

(2) Such other quantities of such class as the applicant has applied to procure and use and are consistent with his past use, his estimated needs, and the total quantity of such class that will be produced.

(d) Any person to whom a procurement quota has been issued may at any time request an adjustment in the quota by applying to the Administrator with a statement showing the need for the adjustment. Such application shall be filed with the UN Reporting and Quota Section, Diversion Control Division. See the Table of DEA Mailing Addresses in §1321.01 of this chapter for the current mailing address. The Administrator shall increase or decrease the procurement quota of such person if and to the extent that he finds, after considering the factors enumerated in paragraph (c) of this section and any occurrences since the issuance of the procurement quota, that the need justifies an adjustment.

(e) The following persons need not obtain a procurement quota:

(1) Any person who is registered to manufacture a basic class of controlled substance listed in Schedule I or II and who uses all of the quantity he manufactures in the manufacture of a substance not controlled under the Act;

(2) Any person who is registered or authorized to conduct chemical analysis with controlled substances (for controlled substances to be used in such analysis only); and

(3) Any person who is registered to conduct research with a basic class of controlled substance listed in Schedule I or II and who is authorized to manufacture a quantity of such class pursuant to §1301.13 of this chapter.

(f) Any person to whom a procurement quota has been issued, authorizing that person to procure and use a quantity of a basic class of controlled substances listed in Schedules I or II during the current calendar year, shall, at or before the time of giving an order to another manufacturer requiring the distribution of a quantity of such basic class, certify in writing to such other manufacturer that the quantity of such basic class ordered does not exceed the person's unused and available procurement quota of such basic class for the current calendar year. The written certification shall be executed by the same individual who signed the DEA Form 222 transmitting the order. Manufacturers shall not fill an order from persons required to apply for a procurement quota under paragraph (b) of this section unless the order is accompanied by a certification as required under this section. The certification required by this section shall contain the following: The date of the certification; the name and address of the bulk manufacturer to whom the certification is directed; a reference to the number of the DEA Form 222 to which the certification applies; the name of the person giving the order to which the certification applies; the name of the basic class specified in the DEA Form 222 to which the certification applies; the appropriate schedule within which is listed the basic class specified in the DEA Form 222 to which the certification applies; a statement that the quantity (expressed in grams) of the basic class specified in the DEA Form 222 to which the certification applies does not exceed the unused and available procurement quota of such basic class, issued to the person giving the order, for the current calendar year; and the signature of the individual who signed the DEA Form 222 to which the certification applies.

[36 FR 7786, Apr. 24, 1971. Redesignated at 38 FR 26609, Sept. 24, 1973]

EDITORIAL NOTE: For FEDERAL REGISTER citations affecting § 1303.12, see the List of CFR Sections Affected, which appears in the Finding Aids section of the printed volume and at *www.govinfo.gov*.

§ 1303.13 Adjustments of aggregate production quotas.

(a) The Administrator may at any time increase or reduce the aggregate production quota for a basic class of controlled substance listed in Schedule I or II which he has previously fixed pursuant to § 1303.11.

(b) In determining to adjust the aggregate production quota, the Administrator shall consider the following factors:

(1) Changes in the demand for that class, changes in the national rate of net disposal of the class, changes in the rate of net disposal of the class by registrants holding individual manufacturing quotas for that class, and changes in the extent of any diversion in the class;

(2) Whether any increased demand for that class, the national and/or individual rates of net disposal of that class are temporary, short term, or long term;

(3) Whether any increased demand for that class can be met through existing inventories, increased individual manufacturing quotas, or increased importation, without increasing the aggregate production quota, taking into account production delays and the probability that other individual manufacturing quotas may be suspended pursuant to § 1303.24(b);

(4) Whether any decreased demand for that class will result in excessive inventory accumulation by all persons registered to handle that class (including manufacturers, distributors, practitioners, importers, and exporters), notwithstanding the possibility that individual manufacturing quotas may be suspended pursuant to § 1303.24(b) or abandoned pursuant to § 1303.27;

(5) Other factors affecting medical, scientific, research, and industrial needs in the United States and lawful export requirements, as the Administrator finds relevant, including changes in the currently accepted medical use in treatment with the class or the substances which are manufactured from it, the economic and physical availability of raw materials for use in manufacturing and for inventory purposes, yield and stability problems, potential disruptions to production (including possible labor strikes), and recent unforeseen emergencies such as floods and fires.

(c) The Administrator in the event he determines to increase or reduce the aggregate production quota for a basic class of controlled substance, shall publish in the FEDERAL REGISTER general notice of an adjustment in the aggregate production quota for that class determined by him under this section. A copy of said notice shall be mailed simultaneously to each person registered as a bulk manufacturer of the basic class and transmitted to each state attorney general. The Administrator shall permit any interested person to file written comments on or objections to the proposal and shall designate in the notice the time during which such filings may be made. The Administrator may, but shall not be required to, hold a public hearing on one or more issues raised by the comments and objections filed with him, except that the Administrator shall hold a hearing if he determines it is necessary to resolve an issue of material fact raised by a state objecting to the proposed adjusted quota as excessive for legitimate United States' needs. In the event the Administrator decides to hold a hearing, he shall publish notice of the hearing in the FEDERAL REGISTER, which notice shall summarize the issues to be heard and shall set the time for the hearing, which shall not be less than 10 days after the date of publication of the notice. After consideration of any comments or objections, or after a hearing if one is ordered by the Administrator, the Administrator shall issue and publish in the FEDERAL REGISTER his final order determining the aggregate production for the basic class of controlled substance. The order shall include the findings of fact and conclusions of law upon which the order is based. The order shall specify the date on which it shall take effect. A copy of said order shall be mailed simultaneously to each person registered as a bulk manufacturer of the basic class and transmitted to each state attorney general.

[37 FR 15919, Aug. 8, 1972. Redesignated at 38 FR 26609, Sept. 24, 1973; 83 FR 32790, July 16, 2018]

INDIVIDUAL MANUFACTURING QUOTAS

§ 1303.21 Individual manufacturing quotas.

(a) The Administrator shall, on or before July 1 of each year, fix for and issue to each person who is registered to manufacture a basic class of controlled substance listed in Schedule I or II, and who applies for a manufacturing quota, an individual manufacturing quota authorizing that person to manufacture during the next calendar year a quantity of that basic class. Any manufacturing quota fixed and issued by the Administrator shall be subject to his authority to reduce or limit it at a later date pursuant to § 1303.26 and to his authority to revoke or suspend it at any time pursuant to § 1301.36 of this chapter.

(b) No individual manufacturing quota shall be required for registrants listed in § 1303.12(e).

[36 FR 7786, Apr. 24, 1971. Redesignated at 38 FR 26609, Sept. 24, 1973, as amended at 62 FR 13958, Mar. 24, 1997; 83 FR32790, July 16, 2018]

§ 1303.22 Procedure for applying for individual manufacturing quotas.

Any person who is registered to manufacture any basic class of controlled substance listed in Schedule I or II and who desires to manufacture a quantity of such class shall apply on DEA Form 189 for a manufacturing quota for such quantity of such class. Copies of DEA Form 189 may be obtained from, and shall be filed (on or before May 1 of the year preceding the calendar year for which the manufacturing quota is being applied) with, the UN Reporting and Quota Section, Diversion Control Division. See the Table of DEA Mailing Addresses in § 1321.01 of this chapter for the current mailing address. A separate application must be made for each basic class desired to be manufactured. The applicant shall state:

(a) The name and Administration Controlled Substances Code Number, as set forth in part 1308 of this chapter, of the basic class.

(b) For the basic class in each of the current and preceding 2 calendar years,

(1) The authorized individual manufacturing quota, if any;

(2) The actual or estimated quantity manufactured;

(3) The actual or estimated net disposal;

(4) The actual or estimated inventory allowance pursuant to § 1303.24; and

(5) The actual or estimated inventory as of December 31;

(c) For the basic class in the next calendar year,

(1) The desired individual manufacturing quota; and

(2) Any additional factors which the applicant finds relevant to the fixing of his individual manufacturing quota, including the trend of (and recent changes in) his and the national rates of net disposal, his production cycle and current inventory position, the economic and physical availability of raw materials for use in manufacturing and for inventory purposes, yield and

stability problems, potential disruptions to production (including possible labor strikes) and recent unforeseen emergencies such as floods and fires.

(d) The Administrator may require additional information from an applicant which, in the Administrator's judgment, may be helpful in detecting or preventing diversion, including customer identities and amounts of the controlled substance sold to each customer.

[36 FR 7786, Apr. 24, 1971, as amended at 36 FR 13386, July 21, 1971; 37 FR 15920, Aug. 8, 1972. Redesignated at 38 FR 26609, Sept. 24, 1973, and amended at 46 FR 28841, May 29, 1981; 51 FR 5319, Feb. 13, 1986; 62 FR 13958, Mar. 24, 1997; 75 FR 10677, Mar. 9, 2010; 81 FR 97020, Dec. 30, 2016; 83 FR 32790, July 16, 2018]

§ 1303.23 Procedure for fixing individual manufacturing quotas.

(a) In fixing individual manufacturing quotas for a basic class of controlled substance listed in Schedule I or II, the Administrator shall allocate to each applicant who is currently manufacturing such class a quota equal to 100 percent of the estimated net disposal of that applicant for the next calendar year, adjusted—

(1) By the amount necessary to increase or reduce the estimated inventory of the applicant on December 31 of the current year to his estimated inventory allowance for the next calendar year, pursuant to § 1303.24, and

(2) By any other factors which the Administrator deems relevant to the fixing of the individual manufacturing quota of the applicant, including the trend of (and recent changes in) his and the national rates of net disposal, his production cycle and current inventory position, the economic and physical availability of raw materials for use in manufacturing and for inventory purposes, yield and stability problems, potential disruptions to production (including possible labor strikes), the extent of any diversion of the controlled substance, and recent unforeseen emergencies such as floods and fires.

(b) In fixing individual manufacturing quotas for a basic class of controlled substance listed in Schedule I or II, the Administrator shall allocate to each applicant who is not currently manufacturing such class a quota equal to 100 percent of the reasonably estimated net disposal of that applicant for the next calendar year, as determined by the Administrator, adjusted—

(1) By the amount necessary to provide the applicant his estimated inventory allowance for the next calendar year, pursuant to § 1303.24, and

(2) By any other factors which the Administrator deems relevant to the fixing of the individual manufacturing quota of the applicant, including the trend of (and recent changes in) the national rate of net disposal, his production cycle and current inventory position, the economic and physical availability of raw materials for use in manufacturing and for inventory purposes, yield and stability problems, potential disruptions to production (including possible labor strikes), any risk of diversion of the controlled substance, and recent unforeseen emergencies such as floods and fires.

(c) The Administrator shall, on or before March 1 of each year, adjust the individual manufacturing quota allocated for that year to each applicant in paragraph (a) of this section by the amount necessary to increase or reduce the actual inventory of the applicant to December 31 of the preceding year to his estimated inventory allowance for the current calendar year, pursuant to § 1303.24.

[36 FR 7786, Apr. 24, 1971, as amended at 37 FR 15920, Aug. 8, 1972. Redesignated at 38 FR 26609, Sept. 24, 1973; 83 FR 32790, July 16, 2018]

§ 1303.24 Inventory allowance.

(a) For the purpose of determining individual manufacturing quotas pursuant to § 1303.23, each registered manufacturer shall be allowed as a part of such quota an amount sufficient to maintain an inventory equal to,

(1) For current manufacturers, 50 percent of his average estimated net disposal for the current calendar year and the last preceding calendar year; or

(2) For new manufacturers, 50 percent of his reasonably estimated net disposal for the next calendar year as determined by the Administrator.

(b) During each calendar year each registered manufacturer shall be allowed to maintain an inventory of a basic class not exceeding 65 percent of his estimated net disposal of that class for that year, as determined at the time his quota for that year was determined. At any time the inventory of a basic class held by a manufacturer exceeds 65 percent of his estimated net disposal, his quota for that class is automatically suspended and shall remain suspended until his inventory is less than 60 percent of his estimated net disposal. The Administrator may, upon application and for good cause shown, permit a manufacturer whose quota is, or is likely to be, suspended pursuant to this paragraph to continue manufacturing and to accumulate an inventory in excess of 65 percent of his estimated net disposal, upon such conditions and within such limitations as the Administrator may find necessary or desirable.

(c) If, during a calendar year, a registrant has manufactured the entire quantity of a basic class allocated to him under an individual manufacturing quota, and his inventory of that class is less than 40 percent of his estimated net disposal of that class for that year, the Administrator may, upon application pursuant to § 1303.25, increase the quota of such registrant sufficiently to allow restoration of the inventory to 50 percent of the estimated net disposal for that year.

[36 FR 7786, Apr. 24, 1971, as amended at 36 FR 13386, July 21, 1971. Redesignated at 38 FR 26609, Sept. 24, 1973]

§ 1303.25 Increase in individual manufacturing quotas.

(a) Any registrant who holds an individual manufacturing quota for a basic class of controlled substance listed in Schedule I or II may file with the Administrator an application on Administration Form 189 for an increase in such quota in order for him to meet his estimated net disposal, inventory and other requirements during the remainder of such calendar year.

(b) The Administrator, in passing upon a registrant's application for an increase in his individual manufacturing quota, shall take into consideration any occurrences since the filing of such registrant's initial quota application that may require an increased manufacturing rate by such registrant during the balance of the calendar year. In passing upon such application the Administrator may also take into consideration the amount, if any, by which his determination of the total quantity for the basic class of controlled substance to be manufactured under § 1303.11 exceeds the aggregate of all the individual manufacturing quotas for the basic class of controlled substance, and the equitable distribution of such excess among other registrants.

[36 FR 7786, Apr. 24, 1971, as amended at 36 FR 13386, July 21, 1971. Redesignated at 38 FR 26609, Sept. 24, 1973]

§ 1303.26 Reduction in individual manufacturing quotas.

The Administrator may at any time reduce an individual manufacturing quota for a basic class of controlled substance listed in Schedule I or II which he has previously fixed in order to prevent the aggregate of the individual manufacturing quotas and import permits outstanding or to be granted from exceeding the aggregate production quota which has been established for that class pursuant of § 1303.11, as adjusted pursuant to § 1303.13. If a quota assigned to a new manufacturer pursuant to § 1303.23(b), or if a quota assigned to any manufacturer is increased pursuant to § 1303.24(c), or if an import permit issued to an importer pursuant to part 1312 of this chapter, causes the total quantity of a basic class to be manufactured and imported during the year to exceed the aggregate production quota which has been established for that class pursuant to § 1303.11, as adjusted pursuant to § 1303.13, the Administrator may proportionately reduce the individual manufacturing quotas and import permits of all other registrants to keep the aggregate production quota within the limits originally established, or, alternatively, the Administrator may reduce the individual manufacturing quota of any registrant whose quota is suspended pursuant to § 1303.24(b) or § 1301.36 of this chapter, or is abandoned pursuant to § 1303.27.

[36 FR 7786, Apr. 24, 1971, as amended at 37 FR 15920, Aug. 8, 1972. Redesignated at 38 FR 26609, Sept. 24, 1973, as amended at 62 FR 13958, Mar. 24, 1997]

§ 1303.27 Abandonment of quota.

Any manufacturer assigned an individual manufacturing quota for any basic class pursuant to § 1303.23 may at any time abandon his right to manufacture all or any part of such quota by filing with the Drug & Chemical Evaluation Section a written notice of such abandonment, stating the name and Administration Controlled Substances Code Number, as set forth in part 1308 of this chapter, of the substance and the amount which he has chosen not to manufacture. The Administrator may, in his discretion, allocate such amount among the other manufacturers in proportion to their respective quotas.

[36 FR 7786, Apr. 24, 1971, as amended at 36 FR 13386, July 21, 1971. Redesignated at 38 FR 26609, Sept. 24, 1973, and amended at 46 FR 28841, May 29, 1981; 51 FR 5319, Feb. 13, 1986; 62 FR 13958, Mar. 24, 1997]

HEARINGS

§ 1303.31 Hearings generally.

(a) In any case where the Administrator shall hold a hearing regarding the determination of an aggregate production quota pursuant to § 1303.11(c), or regarding the adjustment of an aggregate production quota pursuant to § 1303.13(c), the procedures for such hearing shall be governed generally by the rule making procedures set forth in the Administrative Procedure Act (5 U.S.C. 551–559) and specifically by section 306 of the Act (21 U.S.C. 826), by §§ 1303.32–1303.37, and by the procedures for administrative hearings under the Act set forth in §§ 1316.41–1316.67 of this chapter.

(b) In any case where the Administrator shall hold a hearing regarding the issuance, adjustment, suspension, or denial of a procurement quota pursuant to § 1303.12, or the issuance, adjustment, suspension, or denial of an individual manufacturing quota pursuant to §§ 1303.21–1303.27, the procedures for such hearing shall be governed generally by the adjudication procedures set forth in the Administrative Procedures Act (5 U.S.C. 551–559) and specifically by section 306 of the Act (21 U.S.C. 826), by §§ 1303.32–1303.37, and by the procedures for administrative hearings under the Act set forth in §§ 1316.41–1316.67 of this chapter.

[36 FR 7786, Apr. 24, 1971, as amended at 37 FR 15920, Aug. 8, 1972. Redesignated at 38 FR 26609, Sept. 24, 1973]

§ 1303.32 Purpose of hearing.

(a) The Administrator may, in his sole discretion, and shall, if determined by the Administrator to be necessary under § 1303.11(c) or 1303.13(c) based on objection by a state, hold a hearing for the purpose of receiving factual evidence regarding any one or more issues (to be specified by him) involved in the determination or adjustment of any aggregate production quota.

(b) If requested by a person applying for or holding a procurement quota or an individual manufacturing quota, the Administrator shall hold a hearing for the purpose of receiving factual evidence regarding the issues involved in the issuance, adjustment, suspension, or denial of such quota to such person, but the Administrator need not hold a hearing on the suspension of a quota pursuant to § 1301.36 of this chapter separate from a hearing on the suspension of registration pursuant to those sections.

(c) Extensive argument should not be offered into evidence but rather presented in opening or closing statements of counsel or in memoranda or proposed findings of fact and conclusions of law.

[36 FR 7786, Apr. 24, 1971, as amended at 37 FR 15920, Aug. 8, 1972. Redesignated at 38 FR 26609, Sept. 24, 1973, as amended at 62 FR 13958, Mar. 24, 1997; 83 FR 32790, July 16, 2018]

§ 1303.33 Waiver or modification of rules.

The Administrator or the presiding officer (with respect to matters pending before him) may modify or waive any rule in this part by notice in advance of the hearing, if he determines that no party in the hearing will be unduly prejudiced and the ends of justice will thereby be served. Such notice of modification or waiver shall be made a part of the record of the hearing.

[36 FR 7786, Apr. 24, 1971. Redesignated at 38 FR 26609, Sept. 24, 1973]

§ 1303.34 Request for hearing or appearance; waiver.

(a) Any applicant or registrant who desires a hearing on the issuance, adjustment, suspension, or denial of his procurement and/or individual manufacturing quota shall, within 30 days after the date of receipt of the issuance, adjustment, suspension, or denial of such quota, file with the Administrator a written request for a hearing in the form prescribed in § 1316.47 of this chapter. Any interested person who desires a hearing on the determination of an aggregate production quota shall, within the time prescribed in § 1303.11(c), file with the Administrator a written request for a hearing in the form prescribed in § 1316.47 of this chapter, including in the request a statement of the grounds for a hearing.

(b) Any interested person who desires to participate in a hearing on the determination or adjustment of an aggregate production quota, which hearing is ordered by the Administrator pursuant to § 1303.11(c) or § 1303.13(c) may do so by filing with the Administrator, within 30 days of the date of publication of notice of the hearing in the FEDERAL REGISTER, a written notice of his intention to participate in such hearing in the form prescribed in § 1316.48 of this chapter.

(c) Any person entitled to a hearing or to participate in a hearing pursuant to paragraph (b) of this section, may, within the period permitted for filing a request for a hearing of notice of appearance, file with the Administrator a waiver of an opportunity for a hearing or to participate in a hearing, together with a written statement regarding his position on the matters of fact and law involved in such hearing. Such statement, if admissible, shall be made a part of the record and shall be considered in light of the lack of opportunity for cross-examination in determining the weight to be attached to matters of fact asserted therein.

(d) If any person entitled to a hearing or to participate in a hearing pursuant to paragraph (b) of this section, fails to file a request for a hearing or notice of appearance, or if he so files and fails to appear at the hearing, he shall be deemed to have waived his opportunity for the hearing or to participate in the hearing, unless he shows good cause for such failure.

(e) If all persons entitled to a hearing or to participate in a hearing waive or are deemed to waive their opportunity for the hearing or to participate in the hearing, the Administrator may cancel the hearing, if scheduled, and issue his final order pursuant to § 1303.37 without a hearing.

[36 FR 7786, Apr. 24, 1971, as amended at 36 FR 18731, Sept. 21, 1971; 37 FR 15920, Aug. 8, 1972. Redesignated at 38 FR 26609, Sept. 24, 1973]

§ 1303.35 Burden of proof.

(a) At any hearing regarding the determination or adjustment of an aggregate production quota, each interested person participating in the hearing shall have the burden of proving any propositions of fact or law asserted by him in the hearing.

(b) At any hearing regarding the issuance, adjustment, suspension, or denial of a procurement or individual manufacturing quota, the Administration shall have the burden of proving that the requirements of this part for such issuance, adjustment, suspension, or denial are satisfied.

[36 FR 7786, Apr. 24, 1971, as amended at 37 FR 15920, Aug. 8, 1972. Redesignated at 38 FR 26609, Sept. 24, 1973, as amended at 62 FR 13958, Mar. 24, 1997]

§ 1303.36 Time and place of hearing.

(a) If any applicant or registrant requests a hearing on the issuance, adjustment, suspension, or denial of his procurement and/or individual manufacturing quota pursuant to § 1303.34, the Administrator shall hold such hearing. Notice of the hearing shall be given to the applicant or registrant of the time and place at least 30 days prior to the hearing, unless the applicant or registrant waives such notice and requests the hearing be held at an earlier time, in which case the Administrator shall fix a date for such hearing as early as reasonably possible.

(b) The hearing will commence at the place and time designated in the notice given pursuant to paragraph (a) of this section or in the notice of hearing published in the FEDERAL REGISTER pursuant to § 1303.11(c) or § 1303.13 (c), but thereafter it may be moved to a different place and may be continued from day to day or recessed to a later day without notice other than announcement thereof by the presiding officer at the hearing.

[36 FR 7786, Apr. 24, 1971, as amended at 37 FR 15920, Aug. 8, 1972. Redesignated at 38 FR 26609, Sept. 24, 1973]

§ 1303.37 Final order.

As soon as practicable after the presiding officer has certified the record to the Administrator, the Administrator shall issue his order on the determination or adjustment of the aggregate production quota or on the issuance, adjustment, suspension, or denial of the procurement quota or individual manufacturing quota, as case may be. The order shall include the findings of fact and conclusions of law upon which the order is based. The order shall specify the date on which it shall take effect. The Administrator shall serve one copy of his order upon each party in the hearing.

[36 FR 7786, Apr. 24, 1971, as amended at 37 FR 15920, Aug. 8, 1972. Redesignated at 38 FR 26609, Sept. 24, 1973]

PART 1304—RECORDS AND REPORTS OF REGISTRANTS

AUTHORITY: 21 U.S.C. 821, 827, 831, 871(b), 958(e)–(g), and 965, unless otherwise noted.

GENERAL INFORMATION

§ 1304.01 Scope of part 1304.

Inventory and other records and reports required under section 307, section 311, or section 1008(e) of the Act (21 U.S.C. 827, 831, and 958(e)) shall be in accordance with, and contain the information required by, those sections and by the sections of this part.

[74 FR 15623, Apr. 6, 2009]

§ 1304.02 Definitions.

Any term contained in this part shall have the definition set forth in section 102 of the Act (21 U.S.C. 802) or § 1300.01, § 1300.03, § 1300.04, or § 1300.05 of this chapter.

[81 FR 97020, Dec. 30, 2016]

§ 1304.03 Persons required to keep records and file reports.

(a) Every registrant, including collectors, shall maintain the records and inventories and shall file the reports required by this part, except as exempted by this section. Any registrant that is authorized to conduct other activities without being registered to conduct those activities, pursuant to

§§ 1301.22(b), 1307.11, 1307.13, or part 1317 of this chapter, shall maintain the records and inventories and shall file the reports required by this part for persons registered or authorized to conduct such activities. This latter requirement should not be construed as requiring stocks of controlled substances being used in various activities under one registration to be stored separately, nor that separate records are required for each activity. The intent of the Administration is to permit the registrant to keep one set of records which are adapted by the registrant to account for controlled substances used in any activity. Also, the Administration does not wish to require separate stocks of the same substance to be purchased and stored for separate activities. Otherwise, there is no advantage gained by permitting several activities under one registration. Thus, when a researcher manufactures a controlled item, he must keep a record of the quantity manufactured; when he distributes a quantity of the item, he must use and keep invoices or order forms to document the transfer; when he imports a substance, he keeps as part of his records the documentation required of an importer; and when substances are used in chemical analysis, he need not keep a record of this because such a record would not be required of him under a registration to do chemical analysis. All of these records may be maintained in one consolidated record system. Similarly, the researcher may store all of his controlled items in one place, and every two years take inventory of all items on hand, regardless of whether the substances were manufactured by him, imported by him, or purchased domestically by him, of whether the substances will be administered to subjects, distributed to other researchers, or destroyed during chemical analysis.

(b) A registered individual practitioner is required to keep records, as described in § 1304.04, of controlled substances in Schedules II, III, IV, and V which are dispensed, other than by prescribing or administering in the lawful course of professional practice.

(c) Except as provided in § 1304.06, a registered individual practitioner is not required to keep records of controlled substances in Schedules II, III, IV, and V that are prescribed in the lawful course of professional practice, unless such substances are prescribed in the course of maintenance or detoxification treatment of an individual.

(d) A registered individual practitioner is not required to keep records of controlled substances listed in Schedules II, III, IV and V which are administered in the lawful course of professional practice unless the practitioner regularly engages in the dispensing or administering of controlled substances and charges patients, either separately or together with charges for other professional services, for substances so dispensed or administered. Records are required to be kept for controlled substances administered in the course of maintenance or detoxification treatment of an individual.

(e) Each registered mid-level practitioner shall maintain in a readily retrievable manner those documents required by the state in which he/she practices which describe the conditions and extent of his/her authorization to dispense controlled substances and shall make such documents available for inspection and copying by authorized employees of the Administration. Examples of such documentation include protocols, practice guidelines or practice agreements.

(f) Registered persons using any controlled substances while conducting preclinical research, in teaching at a registered establishment which maintains records with respect to such substances or conducting research in conformity with an exemption granted under section 505(i) or 512(j) of the Federal Food, Drug, and Cosmetic Act (21 U.S.C. 355(i) or 360b(j)) at a registered establishment which maintains records in accordance with either of those sections, are not required to keep records if he/she notifies the Administration of the name, address, and registration number of the establishment maintaining such records. This notification shall be given at the time the person applies for registration or reregistration and shall be made in the form of an attachment to the application, which shall be filed with the application.

(g) A distributing registrant who utilizes a freight forwarding facility shall maintain records to reflect transfer of controlled substances through the facility. These records must contain the date, time of transfer, number of cartons, crates, drums or other packages in which commercial containers of controlled substances are shipped and authorized signatures for each transfer. A distributing registrant may, as part of the initial request to operate a freight forwarding facility, request permission to store records at a central location. Approval of the request to maintain central records would be implicit in the approval of the request to operate the facility. Otherwise, a request to maintain records at a central location must be submitted in accordance with §1304.04 of this part. These records must be maintained for a period of two years.

(h) A person is required to keep the records and file the reports specified in §1304.06 and part 1311 of this chapter if they are either of the following:

(1) An electronic prescription application provider.

(2) An electronic pharmacy application provider.

[36 FR 7790, Apr. 24, 1971, as amended at 36 FR 18731, Sept. 21, 1971; 37 FR 15920, Aug. 8, 1972. Redesignated at 38 FR 26609, Sept. 24, 1973, and amended at 50 FR 40523, Oct. 4, 1985; 51 FR 5320, Feb. 13, 1986; 51 FR 26154, July 21, 1986; 58 FR 31175, June 1, 1993; 62 FR 13958, Mar. 24, 1997; 65 FR 44679, July 19, 2000; 75 FR 16306, Mar. 31, 2010; 77 FR 4235, Jan. 27, 2012; 79 FR 53562, Sept. 9, 2014]

§ 1304.04 Maintenance of records and inventories.

(a) Except as provided in paragraphs (a)(1) and (a)(2) of this section, every inventory and other records required to be kept under this part must be kept by the registrant and be available, for at least 2 years from the date of such inventory or records, for inspection and copying by authorized employees of the Administration.

(1) Financial and shipping records (such as invoices and packing slips but not executed order forms subject to §§1305.17 and 1305.27 of this chapter) may be kept at a central location, rather than at the registered location, if the registrant has notified the Administration of his intention to keep central records. Written notification must be submitted by registered or certified mail, return receipt requested, in triplicate, to the Special Agent in Charge of the Administration in the area in which the registrant is located. Unless the registrant is informed by the Special Agent in Charge that permission to keep central records is denied, the registrant may maintain central records commencing 14 days after receipt of his notification by the Special Agent in Charge. All notifications must include the following:

(i) The nature of the records to be kept centrally.

(ii) The exact location where the records will be kept.

(iii) The name, address, DEA registration number and type of DEA registration of the registrant whose records are being maintained centrally.

(iv) Whether central records will be maintained in a manual, or computer readable, form.

(2) A registered retail pharmacy that possesses additional registrations for automated dispensing systems at long term care facilities may keep all records required by this part for those additional registered sites at the retail pharmacy or other approved central location.

(3) A collector that is authorized to maintain a collection receptacle at a long-term care facility shall keep all records required by this part relating to those collection receptacles at the registered location, or other approved central location.

(b) All registrants that are authorized to maintain a central recordkeeping system under paragraph (a) of this section shall be subject to the following conditions:

(1) The records to be maintained at the central record location shall not include executed order forms and inventories, which shall be maintained at each registered location.

(2) If the records are kept on microfilm, computer media or in any form requiring special equipment to render the records easily readable, the registrant shall provide access to such equipment with the records. If any code system is used (other than pricing information), a key to the code shall be

provided to make the records understandable.

(3) The registrant agrees to deliver all or any part of such records to the registered location within two business days upon receipt of a written request from the Administration for such records, and if the Administration chooses to do so in lieu of requiring delivery of such records to the registered location, to allow authorized employees of the Administration to inspect such records at the central location upon request by such employees without a warrant of any kind.

(4) In the event that a registrant fails to comply with these conditions, the Special Agent in Charge may cancel such central recordkeeping authorization, and all other central recordkeeping authorizations held by the registrant without a hearing or other procedures. In the event of a cancellation of central recordkeeping authorizations under this paragraph the registrant shall, within the time specified by the Special Agent in Charge, comply with the requirements of this section that all records be kept at the registered location.

(c) Registrants need not notify the Special Agent in Charge or obtain central recordkeeping approval in order to maintain records on an in-house computer system.

(d) ARCOS participants who desire authorization to report from other than their registered locations must obtain a separate central reporting identifier. Request for central reporting identifiers will be submitted to the ARCOS Unit. See the Table of DEA Mailing Addresses in § 1321.01 of this chapter for the current mailing address.

(e) All central recordkeeping permits previously issued by the Administration expired September 30, 1980.

(f) Each registered manufacturer, distributor, importer, exporter, narcotic treatment program and compounder for narcotic treatment program shall maintain inventories and records of controlled substances as follows:

(1) Inventories and records of controlled substances listed in Schedules I and II shall be maintained separately from all of the records of the registrant; and

(2) Inventories and records of controlled substances listed in Schedules III, IV, and V shall be maintained either separately from all other records of the registrant or in such form that the information required is readily retrievable from the ordinary business records of the registrant.

(g) Each registered individual practitioner required to keep records and institutional practitioner shall maintain inventories and records of controlled substances in the manner prescribed in paragraph (f) of this section.

(h) Each registered pharmacy shall maintain the inventories and records of controlled substances as follows:

(1) Inventories and records of all controlled substances listed in Schedule I and II shall be maintained separately from all other records of the pharmacy.

(2) Paper prescriptions for Schedule II controlled substances shall be maintained at the registered location in a separate prescription file.

(3) Inventories and records of Schedules III, IV, and V controlled substances shall be maintained either separately from all other records of the pharmacy or in such form that the information required is readily retrievable from ordinary business records of the pharmacy.

(4) Paper prescriptions for Schedules III, IV, and V controlled substances shall be maintained at the registered location either in a separate prescription file for Schedules III, IV, and V controlled substances only or in such form that they are readily retrievable from the other prescription records of the pharmacy. Prescriptions will be deemed readily retrievable if, at the time they are initially filed, the face of the prescription is stamped in red ink in the lower right corner with the letter "C" no less than 1 inch high and filed either in the prescription file for controlled substances listed in Schedules I and II or in the usual consecutively numbered prescription file for noncontrolled substances. However, if a pharmacy employs a computer application for prescriptions that permits identification by prescription number and retrieval of original documents by prescriber name, patient's name, drug

dispensed, and date filled, then the requirement to mark the hard copy prescription with a red "C" is waived.

(5) Records of electronic prescriptions for controlled substances shall be maintained in an application that meets the requirements of part 1311 of this chapter. The computers on which the records are maintained may be located at another location, but the records must be readily retrievable at the registered location if requested by the Administration or other law enforcement agent. The electronic application must be capable of printing out or transferring the records in a format that is readily understandable to an Administration or other law enforcement agent at the registered location. Electronic copies of prescription records must be sortable by prescriber name, patient name, drug dispensed, and date filled.

(Authority: 21 U.S.C. 821 and 871(b); 28 CFR 0.100)

[36 FR 7790, Apr. 24, 1971, as amended at 36 FR 13386, July 21, 1971. Redesignated at 38 FR 26609, Sept. 24, 1973, and amended at 39 FR 37985, Oct. 25, 1974; 45 FR 44266, July 1, 1980; 47 FR 41735, Sept. 22, 1982; 51 FR 5320, Feb. 13, 1986; 62 FR 13959, Mar. 24, 1997; 70 FR 25466, May 13, 2005; 75 FR 10677, Mar. 9, 2010; 75 FR 16306, Mar. 31, 2010; 79 FR 53562, Sept. 9, 2014]

§ 1304.05 Records of authorized central fill pharmacies and retail pharmacies.

(a) Every retail pharmacy that utilizes the services of a central fill pharmacy must keep a record of all central fill pharmacies, including name, address and DEA number, that are authorized to fill prescriptions on its behalf. The retail pharmacy must also verify the registration for each central fill pharmacy authorized to fill prescriptions on its behalf. These records must be made available upon request for inspection by DEA.

(b) Every central fill pharmacy must keep a record of all retail pharmacies, including name, address and DEA number, for which it is authorized to fill prescriptions. The central fill pharmacy must also verify the registration for all retail pharmacies for which it is authorized to fill prescriptions. These records must be made available upon request for inspection by DEA.

[68 FR 37410, June 24, 2003]

§ 1304.06 Records and reports for electronic prescriptions.

(a) As required by § 1311.120 of this chapter, a practitioner who issues electronic prescriptions for controlled substances must use an electronic prescription application that retains the following information:

(1) The digitally signed record of the information specified in part 1306 of this chapter.

(2) The internal audit trail and any auditable event identified by the internal audit as required by § 1311.150 of this chapter.

(b) An institutional practitioner must retain a record of identity proofing and issuance of the two-factor authentication credential, where applicable, as required by § 1311.110 of this chapter.

(c) As required by § 1311.205 of this chapter, a pharmacy that processes electronic prescriptions for controlled substances must use an application that retains the following:

(1) All of the information required under § 1304.22(c) and part 1306 of this chapter.

(2) The digitally signed record of the prescription as received as required by § 1311.210 of this chapter.

(3) The internal audit trail and any auditable event identified by the internal audit as required by § 1311.215 of this chapter.

(d) A registrant and application service provider must retain a copy of any security incident report filed with the Administration pursuant to §§ 1311.150 and 1311.215 of this chapter.

(e) An electronic prescription or pharmacy application provider must retain third party audit or certification reports as required by § 1311.300 of this chapter.

(f) An application provider must retain a copy of any notification to the Administration regarding an adverse audit or certification report filed with the Administration on problems identified by the third-party audit or certification as required by § 1311.300 of this chapter.

(g) Unless otherwise specified, records and reports must be retained for two years.

[75 FR 16306, Mar. 31, 2010]

INVENTORY REQUIREMENTS

§ 1304.11 Inventory requirements.

(a) *General requirements.* Each inventory shall contain a complete and accurate record of all controlled substances on hand on the date the inventory is taken, and shall be maintained in written, typewritten, or printed form at the registered location. An inventory taken by use of an oral recording device must be promptly transcribed. Controlled substances shall be deemed to be "on hand" if they are in the possession of or under the control of the registrant, including substances returned by a customer, ordered by a customer but not yet invoiced, stored in a warehouse on behalf of the registrant, and substances in the possession of employees of the registrant and intended for distribution as complimentary samples. A separate inventory shall be made for each registered location and each independent activity registered, except as provided in paragraph (e)(4) of this section. In the event controlled substances in the possession or under the control of the registrant are stored at a location for which he/she is not registered, the substances shall be included in the inventory of the registered location to which they are subject to control or to which the person possessing the substance is responsible. The inventory may be taken either as of opening of business or as of the close of business on the inventory date and it shall be indicated on the inventory.

(b) *Initial inventory date.* Every person required to keep records shall take an inventory of all stocks of controlled substances on hand on the date he/she first engages in the manufacture, distribution, or dispensing of controlled substances, in accordance with paragraph (e) of this section as applicable. In the event a person commences business with no controlled substances on hand, he/she shall record this fact as the initial inventory.

(c) *Biennial inventory date.* After the initial inventory is taken, the registrant shall take a new inventory of all stocks of controlled substances on hand at least every two years. The biennial inventory may be taken on any date which is within two years of the previous biennial inventory date.

(d) *Inventory date for newly controlled substances.* On the effective date of a rule by the Administrator pursuant to §§ 1308.45, 1308.46, or 1308.47 of this chapter adding a substance to any schedule of controlled substances, which substance was, immediately prior to that date, not listed on any such schedule, every registrant required to keep records who possesses that substance shall take an inventory of all stocks of the substance on hand. Thereafter, such substance shall be included in each inventory made by the registrant pursuant to paragraph (c) of this section.

(e) *Inventories of manufacturers, distributors, registrants that reverse distribute, importers, exporters, chemical analysts, dispensers, researchers, and collectors.* Each person registered or authorized (by §§ 1301.13, 1307.11, 1307.13, or part 1317 of this chapter) to manufacture, distribute, reverse distribute, dispense, import, export, conduct research or chemical analysis with controlled substances, or collect controlled substances from ultimate users, and required to keep records pursuant to § 1304.03 shall include in the inventory the information listed below.

(1) *Inventories of manufacturers.* Each person registered or authorized to manufacture controlled substances shall include the following information in the inventory:

(i) For each controlled substance in bulk form to be used in (or capable of use in) the manufacture of the same or other controlled or non-controlled substances in finished form, the inventory shall include:

(A) The name of the substance and

(B) The total quantity of the substance to the nearest metric unit weight consistent with unit size.

(ii) For each controlled substance in the process of manufacture on the inventory date, the inventory shall include:

(A) The name of the substance;

(B) The quantity of the substance in each batch and/or stage of manufacture, identified by the batch number or other appropriate identifying number; and

(C) The physical form which the substance is to take upon completion of the manufacturing process (e.g., granulations, tablets, capsules, or solutions), identified by the batch number or other appropriate identifying number, and if possible the finished form of the substance (e.g., 10-milligram tablet or 10-milligram concentration per fluid ounce or milliliter) and the number or volume thereof.

(iii) For each controlled substance in finished form the inventory shall include:

(A) The name of the substance;

(B) Each finished form of the substance (e.g., 10-milligram tablet or 10-milligram concentration per fluid ounce or milliliter);

(C) The number of units or volume of each finished form in each commercial container (e.g., 100-tablet bottle or 3-milliliter vial); and

(D) The number of commercial containers of each such finished form (e.g. four 100-tablet bottles or six 3-milliliter vials).

(iv) For each controlled substance not included in paragraphs (e)(1) (i), (ii) or (iii) of this section (e.g., damaged, defective or impure substances awaiting disposal, substances held for quality control purposes, or substances maintained for extemporaneous compoundings) the inventories shall include:

(A) The name of the substance;

(B) The total quantity of the substance to the nearest metric unit weight or the total number of units of finished form; and

(C) The reason for the substance being maintained by the registrant and whether such substance is capable of use in the manufacture of any controlled substance in finished form.

(2) *Inventories of distributors.* Each person registered or authorized to distribute controlled substances shall include in the inventory the same information required of manufacturers pursuant to paragraphs (e)(1)(iii) and (iv) of this section.

(3) *Inventories of registrants that reverse distribute.* Each person registered or authorized to reverse distribute controlled substances shall include in the inventory, the following information:

(i) The name of the substance, and

(ii) The total quantity of the substance:

(A) For controlled substances in bulk form, to the nearest metric unit weight consistent with unit size;

(B) For each controlled substance in finished form: Each finished form of the substance (e.g., 10-milligram tablet or 10-milligram concentration per fluid ounce or milliliter); the number of units or volume of each finished form in each commercial container (e.g., 100-tablet bottle or 3-milliliter vial); and the number of commercial containers of each such finished form (e.g., four 100-tablet bottles or six 3-milliliter vials); and

(C) For controlled substances in a commercial container, carton, crate, drum, or other receptacle that has been opened: If the substance is listed in Schedule I or II, make an exact count or measure of the contents; or if the substance is listed in Schedule III, IV, or V, make an estimated count or measure of the contents, unless the container holds more than 1,000 tablets or capsules in which case an exact count of the contents shall be made; or

(iii) For controlled substances acquired from collectors and law enforcement: The number and size (e.g., five 10-gallon liners, etc.) of sealed inner liners on hand, or

(iv) For controlled substances acquired from law enforcement: the number of sealed mail-back packages on hand.

(4) *Inventories of importers and exporters.* Each person registered or authorized to import or export controlled substances shall include in the inventory the same information required of manufacturers pursuant to paragraphs (e)(1) (iii) and (iv) of this section. Each such person who is also registered as a manufacturer or as a distributor shall include in his/her inventory as an importer or exporter only those stocks of controlled substances that are actually separated from his stocks as a manufacturer or as a distributor (e.g., in transit or in storage for shipment).

(5) *Inventories of chemical analysts.* Each person registered or authorized to

conduct chemical analysis with controlled substances shall include in his inventory the same information required of manufacturers pursuant to paragraphs (e)(1) (iii) and (iv) of this section as to substances which have been manufactured, imported, or received by such person. If less than 1 kilogram of any controlled substance (other than a hallucinogenic controlled substance listed in Schedule I), or less than 20 grams of a hallucinogenic substance listed in Schedule I (other than lysergic acid diethylamide), or less than 0.5 gram of lysergic acid diethylamide, is on hand at the time of inventory, that substance need not be included in the inventory. Laboratories of the Administration may possess up to 150 grams of any hallucinogenic substance in Schedule I without regard to a need for an inventory of those substances. No inventory is required of known or suspected controlled substances received as evidentiary materials for analysis.

(6) *Inventories of dispensers and researchers*. Each person registered or authorized to dispense or conduct research with controlled substances shall include in the inventory the same information required of manufacturers pursuant to paragraphs (e)(1)(iii) and (iv) of this section. In determining the number of units of each finished form of a controlled substance in a commercial container that has been opened, the dispenser or researcher shall do as follows:

(i) If the substance is listed in Schedules I or II, make an exact count or measure of the contents; or

(ii) If the substance is listed in Schedule III, IV, or V, make an estimated count or measure of the contents, unless the container holds more than 1,000 tablets or capsules in which case he/she must make an exact count of the contents.

(7) *Inventories of collectors*. Each registrant authorized to collect controlled substances from ultimate users shall include in the inventory the following information:

(i) For registrants authorized to collect through a mail-back program, the record shall include the following information about each unused mail-back package and each returned mail-back package on hand awaiting destruction:

(A) The date of the inventory;

(B) The number of mail-back packages; and

(C) The unique identification number of each package on hand, whether unused or awaiting destruction.

(ii) For registrants authorized to collect through a collection receptacle, the record shall include the following information about each unused inner liner on hand and each sealed inner liner on hand awaiting destruction:

(A) The date of the inventory;

(B) The number and size of inner liners (e.g., five 10-gallon liners, etc.);

(C) The unique identification number of each inner liner.

[62 FR 13959, Mar. 24, 1997, as amended at 68 FR 41228, July 11, 2003; 79 FR 53562, Sept. 9, 2014]

CONTINUING RECORDS

§ 1304.21 General requirements for continuing records.

(a) Every registrant required to keep records pursuant to § 1304.03 shall maintain, on a current basis, a complete and accurate record of each substance manufactured, imported, received, sold, delivered, exported, or otherwise disposed of by him/her, and each inner liner, sealed inner liner, and unused and returned mail-back package, except that no registrant shall be required to maintain a perpetual inventory.

(b) Separate records shall be maintained by a registrant for each registered location except as provided in § 1304.04 (a). In the event controlled substances are in the possession or under the control of a registrant at a location for which he is not registered, the substances shall be included in the records of the registered location to which they are subject to control or to which the person possessing the substance is responsible.

(c) Separate records shall be maintained by a registrant for each independent activity and collection activity for which he/she is registered or authorized, except as provided in § 1304.22(d).

(d) In recording dates of receipt, distribution, other transfers, or destruction, the date on which the controlled substances are actually received, distributed, otherwise transferred, or destroyed will be used as the date of receipt, distribution, transfer, or destruction (*e.g.*, invoices or packing slips, or DEA Form 41). In maintaining records concerning imports and exports, the registrant must record the anticipated date of release by a customs official for permit applications and declarations and the date on which the controlled substances are released by a customs officer at the port of entry or port of export for return information.

(e) *Record of destruction.* In addition to any other recordkeeping requirements, any registered person that destroys a controlled substance pursuant to § 1317.95(d), or causes the destruction of a controlled substance pursuant to § 1317.95(c), shall maintain a record of destruction on a DEA Form 41. The records shall be complete and accurate, and include the name and signature of the two employees who witnessed the destruction. Except, destruction of a controlled substance dispensed by a practitioner for immediate administration at the practitioner's registered location, when the substance is not fully exhausted (e.g., some of the substance remains in a vial, tube, or syringe after administration but cannot or may not be further utilized), shall be properly recorded in accordance with § 1304.22(c), and such record need not be maintained on a DEA Form 41.

[36 FR 7792, Apr. 24, 1971, as amended at 36 FR 13386, July 21, 1971. Redesignated at 38 FR 26609, Sept. 24, 1973, as amended at 62 FR 13960, Mar. 24, 1997; 79 FR 53563, Sept. 9, 2014; 81 FR 97020, Dec. 30, 2016]

§ 1304.22 Records for manufacturers, distributors, dispensers, researchers, importers, exporters, registrants that reverse distribute, and collectors.

Each person registered or authorized (by §§ 1301.13(e), 1307.11, 1307.13, or part 1317 of this chapter) to manufacture, distribute, dispense, import, export, reverse distribute, destroy, conduct research with controlled substances, or collect controlled substances from ultimate users, shall maintain records with the information listed in paragraphs (a) through (f) of this section.

(a) *Records for manufacturers.* Each person registered or authorized to manufacture controlled substances shall maintain records with the following information:

(1) For each controlled substance in bulk form to be used in, or capable of use in, or being used in, the manufacture of the same or other controlled or noncontrolled substances in finished form,

(i) The name of the substance;

(ii) The quantity manufactured in bulk form by the registrant, including the date, quantity and batch or other identifying number of each batch manufactured;

(iii) The quantity received from other persons, including the date and quantity of each receipt and the name, address, and registration number of the other person from whom the substance was received;

(iv) The quantity imported directly by the registrant (under a registration as an importer) for use in manufacture by him/her, including the date, quantity, and import permit or declaration number for each importation;

(v) The quantity used to manufacture the same substance in finished form, including:

(A) The date and batch or other identifying number of each manufacture;

(B) The quantity used in the manufacture;

(C) The finished form (e.g., 10-milligram tablets or 10-milligram concentration per fluid ounce or milliliter);

(D) The number of units of finished form manufactured;

(E) The quantity used in quality control;

(F) The quantity lost during manufacturing and the causes therefore, if known;

(G) The total quantity of the substance contained in the finished form;

(H) The theoretical and actual yields; and

(I) Such other information as is necessary to account for all controlled substances used in the manufacturing process;

(vi) The quantity used to manufacture other controlled and noncontrolled substances, including the name of each substance manufactured and the information required in paragraph (a)(1)(v) of this section;

(vii) The quantity distributed in bulk form to other persons, including the date and quantity of each distribution and the name, address, and registration number of each person to whom a distribution was made;

(viii) The quantity exported directly by the registrant (under a registration as an exporter), including the date, quantity, and export permit or declaration number of each exportation;

(ix) The quantity distributed or disposed of in any other manner by the registrant (e.g., by distribution of complimentary samples or by destruction), including the date and manner of distribution or disposal, the name, address, and registration number of the person to whom distributed, and the quantity distributed or disposed; and

(x) The originals of all written certifications of available procurement quotas submitted by other persons (as required by § 1303.12(f) of this chapter) relating to each order requiring the distribution of a basic class of controlled substance listed in Schedule I or II.

(2) For each controlled substance in finished form,

(i) The name of the substance;

(ii) Each finished form (e.g., 10-milligram tablet or 10-milligram concentration per fluid ounce or milliliter) and the number of units or volume of finished form in each commercial container (e.g., 100-tablet bottle or 3-milliliter vial);

(iii) The number of containers of each such commercial finished form manufactured from bulk form by the registrant, including the information required pursuant to paragraph (a)(1)(v) of this section;

(iv) The number of units of finished forms and/or commercial containers acquired from other persons, including the date of and number of units and/or commercial containers in each acquisition to inventory and the name, address, and registration number of the person from whom the units were acquired;

(v) The number of units of finished forms and/or commercial containers imported directly by the person (under a registration or authorization to import), including the date of, the number of units and/or commercial containers in, and the import permit or declaration number for, each importation;

(vi) The number of units and/or commercial containers manufactured by the registrant from units in finished form received from others or imported, including:

(A) The date and batch or other identifying number of each manufacture;

(B) The operation performed (e.g., repackaging or relabeling);

(C) The number of units of finished form used in the manufacture, the number manufactured and the number lost during manufacture, with the causes for such losses, if known; and

(D) Such other information as is necessary to account for all controlled substances used in the manufacturing process;

(vii) The number of commercial containers distributed to other persons, including the date of and number of containers in each reduction from inventory, and the name, address, and registration number of the person to whom the containers were distributed;

(viii) The number of commercial containers exported directly by the registrant (under a registration as an exporter), including the date, number of containers and export permit or declaration number for each exportation; and

(ix) The number of units of finished forms and/or commercial containers distributed or disposed of in any other manner by the registrant (e.g., by distribution of complimentary samples or by destruction), including the date and manner of distribution or disposal, the name, address, and registration number of the person to whom distributed, and the quantity in finished form distributed or disposed.

(b) *Records for distributors.* Except as provided in paragraph (e) of this section, each person registered or authorized to distribute controlled substances shall maintain records with the same information required of manufacturers pursuant to paragraphs (a)(2)(i), (ii), (iv), (v), (vii), (viii) and (ix) of this section.

(c) *Records for dispensers and researchers.* Each person registered or authorized to dispense or conduct research with controlled substances shall maintain records with the same information required of manufacturers pursuant to paragraph (a)(2)(i), (ii), (iv), (vii), and (ix) of this section. In addition, records shall be maintained of the number of units or volume of such finished form dispensed, including the name and address of the person to whom it was dispensed, the date of dispensing, the number of units or volume dispensed, and the written or typewritten name or initials of the individual who dispensed or administered the substance on behalf of the dispenser. In addition to the requirements of this paragraph, practitioners dispensing gamma-hydroxybutyric acid under a prescription must also comply with § 1304.26.

(d) *Records for importers and exporters.* Each person registered or authorized to import or export controlled substances shall maintain records with the same information required of manufacturers pursuant to paragraphs (a)(2) (i), (iv), (v) and (vii) of this section. In addition, the quantity disposed of in any other manner by the registrant (except quantities used in manufacturing by an importer under a registration as a manufacturer), which quantities are to be recorded pursuant to paragraphs (a)(1) (iv) and (v) of this section; and the quantity (or number of units or volume in finished form) exported, including the date, quantity (or number of units or volume), and the export permit or declaration number for each exportation, but excluding all quantities (and number of units and volumes) manufactured by an exporter under a registration as a manufacturer, which quantities (and numbers of units and volumes) are to be recorded pursuant to paragraphs (a)(1)(xiii) or (a)(2)(xiii) of this section.

(e) *Records for registrants that reverse distribute.* Each person registered or authorized to reverse distribute controlled substances shall maintain records with the following information for each controlled substance:

(1) For controlled substances acquired for the purpose of return or recall to the manufacturer or another registrant authorized by the manufacturer to accept returns on the manufacturer's behalf pursuant to part 1317 of this chapter:

(i) The date of receipt; the name and quantity of each controlled substance received; the name, address, and registration number of the person from whom the substance was received; and the reason for return (e.g., recall or return); and

(ii) The date of return to the manufacturer or other registrant authorized by the manufacturer to accept returns on the manufacturer's behalf; the name and quantity of each controlled substance returned; the name, address, and registration number of the person from whom the substance was received; the name, address, and registration number of the registrant to whom the substance was returned; and the method of return (e.g., common or contract carrier).

(2) For controlled substances acquired from registrant inventory for destruction pursuant to § 1317.05(a)(2), (b)(2), and (b)(4) of this chapter:

(i) The date of receipt; the name and quantity of each controlled substance received; and the name, address, and registration number of the person from whom the substance was received; and

(ii) The date, place, and method of destruction; the name and quantity of each controlled substance destroyed; the name, address, and registration number of the person from whom the substance was received; and the name and signatures of the two employees of the registrant that witnessed the destruction.

(3) The total quantity of each controlled substance shall be recorded in accordance with the following:

(i) For controlled substances in bulk form: To the nearest metric unit weight or volume consistent with unit size;

(ii) For controlled substances in finished form: Each finished form (e.g., 10-milligram tablet or 10-milligram concentration per fluid ounce or milliliter); the number of units or volume of finished form in each commercial container (e.g., 100-tablet bottle or 3-milliliter vial); and the number of commercial containers of each such finished form (e.g., four 100-tablet bottles or six 3-milliliter vials); and

(iii) For controlled substances in a commercial container, carton, crate, drum, or other receptacle that has been opened: If the substance is listed in Schedule I or II make an exact count or measure of the contents; or if the substance is listed in Schedule III, IV, or V, make an estimated count or measure of the contents, unless the container holds more than 1,000 tablets or capsules in which case an exact count of the contents shall be made.

(4) For each sealed inner liner acquired from collectors or law enforcement and each sealed mail-back package acquired from law enforcement pursuant to §1317.55 of this chapter:

(i) The number of sealed inner liners acquired from other persons, including the date of acquisition, the number and, for sealed inner liners the size (e.g., five 10-gallon liners, etc.), of all sealed inner liners and mail-back packages acquired to inventory, the unique identification number of each sealed inner liner and mail-back package, and the name, address, and, for registrants, the registration number of the person from whom the sealed inner liners and mail-back packages were received, and

(ii) The date, place, and method of destruction; the number of sealed inner liners and mail-back packages destroyed; the name, address, and, for registrants, the registration number of the person from whom the sealed inner liners and mail-back packages were received; the number and, for sealed inner liners the size (e.g., five 10-gallon liners, etc.), of all sealed inner liners and mail-back packages destroyed; the unique identification number of each sealed inner liner and sealed mail-back package destroyed; and the name and signatures of the two employees of the registrant that witnessed the destruction.

(5) For all records, the record of receipt shall be maintained together with the corresponding record of return or destruction (DEA Form 41).

(f) *Records for collectors.* Each person registered or authorized to collect controlled substances from ultimate users shall maintain the following records:

(1) Mail-Back Packages:

(i) For unused packages that the collector makes available to ultimate users and other authorized non-registrants at the collector's registered address: The date made available, the number of packages, and the unique identification number of each package;

(ii) For unused packages provided to a third party to make available to ultimate users and other authorized non-registrants: The name of the third party and physical address of the location receiving the unused packages, date sent, and the number of unused packages sent with the corresponding unique identification numbers;

(iii) For sealed mail-back packages received by the collector: Date of receipt and the unique identification number on the individual package; and

(iv) For sealed mail-back packages destroyed on-site by the collector: Number of sealed mail-back packages destroyed, the date and method of destruction, the unique identification number of each mail-back package destroyed, and the names and signatures of the two employees of the registrant who witnessed the destruction.

(2) Collection receptacle inner liners:

(i) Date each unused inner liner acquired, unique identification number and size (e.g., 5-gallon, 10-gallon, etc.) of each unused inner liner acquired;

(ii) Date each inner liner is installed, the address of the location where each inner liner is installed, the unique identification number and size (e.g., 5-gallon, 10-gallon, etc.) of each installed inner liner, the registration number of the collector, and the names and signatures of the two employees that witnessed each installation;

(iii) Date each inner liner is removed and sealed, the address of the location from which each inner liner is removed, the unique identification number and size (e.g., 5-gallon, 10-gallon, etc.) of each inner liner removed, the registration number of the collector, and the names and signatures of the two employees that witnessed each removal;

(iv) Date each sealed inner liner is transferred to storage, the unique identification number and size (e.g., 5-gallon, 10-gallon, etc.) of each sealed inner liner stored, and the names and signatures of the two employees that transferred each sealed inner liner to storage;

(v) Date each sealed inner liner is transferred for destruction, the address and registration number of the reverse distributor or distributor to whom each sealed inner liner was transferred, the unique identification number and the size (e.g., 5-gallon, 10-gallon, etc.) of each sealed inner liner transferred, and the names and signatures of the two employees that transferred each sealed inner liner to the reverse distributor or distributor; and

(vi) For sealed inner liners destroyed on-site by the collector: The same information required of reverse distributors in paragraph (e)(4)(ii) of this section.

[62 FR 13960, Mar. 24, 1997, as amended at 68 FR 41229, July 11, 2003; 70 FR 293, Jan. 4, 2005; 79 FR 53564, Sept. 9, 2014]

§ 1304.23 Records for chemical analysts.

(a) Each person registered or authorized (by § 1301.22(b) of this chapter) to conduct chemical analysis with controlled substances shall maintain records with the following information (to the extent known and reasonably ascertainable by him) for each controlled substance:

(1) The name of the substance;

(2) The form or forms in which the substance is received, imported, or manufactured by the registrant (e.g., powder, granulation, tablet, capsule, or solution) and the concentration of the substance in such form (e.g., C.P., U.S.P., N.F., 10-milligram tablet or 10-milligram concentration per milliliter);

(3) The total number of the forms received, imported or manufactured (e.g., 100 tablets, thirty 1-milliliter vials, or 10 grams of powder), including the date and quantity of each receipt, importation, or manufacture and the name, address, and registration number, if any, of the person from whom the substance was received;

(4) The quantity distributed, exported, or destroyed in any manner by the registrant (except quantities used in chemical analysis or other laboratory work), including the date and manner of distribution, exportation, or destruction, and the name, address, and registration number, if any, of each person to whom the substance was distributed or exported.

(b) Records of controlled substances used in chemical analysis or other laboratory work are not required.

(c) Records relating to known or suspected controlled substances received as evidentiary material for analysis are not required under paragraph (a) of this section.

[36 FR 7793, Apr. 24, 1971, as amended at 36 FR 13386, July 21, 1971; 36 FR 18732, Sept. 21, 1971. Redesignated at 38 FR 26609, Sept. 24, 1973, and further redesignated at 62 FR 13961, Mar. 24, 1997]

§ 1304.24 Records for maintenance treatment programs and detoxification treatment programs.

(a) Each person registered or authorized (by § 1301.22 of this chapter) to maintain and/or detoxify controlled substance users in a narcotic treatment program shall maintain records with the following information for each narcotic controlled substance:

(1) Name of substance;

(2) Strength of substance;

(3) Dosage form;

(4) Date dispensed;

(5) Adequate identification of patient (consumer);

(6) Amount consumed;

(7) Amount and dosage form taken home by patient; and

(8) Dispenser's initials.

(b) The records required by paragraph (a) of this section will be maintained in a dispensing log at the narcotic treatment program site and will be maintained in compliance with § 1304.22 without reference to § 1304.03.

(c) All sites which compound a bulk narcotic solution from bulk narcotic powder to liquid for on-site use must keep a separate batch record of the compounding.

(d) Records of identity, diagnosis, prognosis, or treatment of any patients which are maintained in connection with the performance of a narcotic treatment program shall be confidential, except that such records may be disclosed for purposes and under the circumstances authorized by part 310 and 42 CFR part 2.

[39 FR 37985, Oct. 25, 1974. Redesignated and amended at 62 FR 13961, Mar. 24, 1997]

§ 1304.25 Records for treatment programs that compound narcotics for treatment programs and other locations.

Each person registered or authorized by § 1301.22 of this chapter to compound narcotic drugs for off-site use in a narcotic treatment program shall maintain records which include the following information for each narcotic drug:

(a) For each narcotic controlled substance in bulk form to be used in, or capable of use in, or being used in, the compounding of the same or other noncontrolled substances in finished form:

(1) The name of the substance;

(2) The quantity compounded in bulk form by the registrant, including the date, quantity and batch or other identifying number of each batch compounded;

(3) The quantity received from other persons, including the date and quantity of each receipt and the name, address and registration number of the other person from whom the substance was received;

(4) The quantity imported directly by the registrant (under a registration as an importer) for use in compounding by him, including the date, quantity and import permit or declaration number of each importation;

(5) The quantity used to compound the same substance in finished form, including:

(i) The date and batch or other identifying number of each compounding;

(ii) The quantity used in the compound;

(iii) The finished form (e.g., 10-milligram tablets or 10-milligram concentration per fluid ounce or milliliter;

(iv) The number of units of finished form compounded;

(v) The quantity used in quality control;

(vi) The quantity lost during compounding and the causes therefore, if known;

(vii) The total quantity of the substance contained in the finished form;

(viii) The theoretical and actual yields; and

(ix) Such other information as is necessary to account for all controlled substances used in the compounding process;

(6) The quantity used to manufacture other controlled and non-controlled substances; including the name of each substance manufactured and the information required in paragraph (a)(5) of this section;

(7) The quantity distributed in bulk form to other programs, including the date and quantity of each distribution and the name, address and registration number of each program to whom a distribution was made;

(8) The quantity exported directly by the registrant (under a registration as an exporter), including the date, quantity, and export permit or declaration number of each exploration; and

(9) The quantity disposed of by destruction, including the reason, date, and manner of destruction.

(b) For each narcotic controlled substance in finished form:

(1) The name of the substance;

(2) Each finished form (e.g., 10-milligram tablet or 10 milligram concentration per fluid ounce or milliliter) and the number of units or volume or finished form in each commercial container (e.g., 100-tablet bottle or 3-milliliter vial);

(3) The number of containers of each such commercial finished form compounded from bulk form by the registrant, including the information required pursuant to paragraph (a)(5) of this section;

(4) The number of units of finished forms and/or commercial containers received from other persons, including the date of and number of units and/or commercial containers in each receipt and the name, address and registration number of the person from whom the units were received;

(5) The number of units of finished forms and/or commercial containers imported directly by the person (under a registration or authorization to import), including the date of, the number of units and/or commercial containers in, and the import permit or declaration number for, each importation;

(6) The number of units and/or commercial containers compounded by the registrant from units in finished form received from others or imported, including:

(i) The date and batch or other identifying number of each compounding;

(ii) The operation performed (e.g., repackaging or relabeling);

(iii) The number of units of finished form used in the compound, the number compounded and the number lost during compounding, with the causes for such losses, if known; and

(iv) Such other information as is necessary to account for all controlled substances used in the compounding process;

(7) The number of containers distributed to other programs, including the date, the number of containers in each distribution, and the name, address and registration number of the program to whom the containers were distributed;

(8) The number of commercial containers exported directly by the registrant (under a registration as an exporter), including the date, number of containers and export permit or declaration number for each exportation; and

(9) The number of units of finished forms and/or commercial containers destroyed in any manner by the registrant, including the reason, date, and manner of destruction.

[39 FR 37985, Oct. 25, 1974. Redesignated at 62 FR 13961, Mar. 24, 1997; 79 FR 53564, Sept. 9, 2014]

§ 1304.26 Additional recordkeeping requirements applicable to drug products containing gamma-hydroxybutyric acid.

In addition to the recordkeeping requirements for dispensers and researchers provided in § 1304.22, practitioners dispensing gamma-hydroxybutyric acid that is manufactured or distributed in accordance with an application under section 505 of the Federal Food, Drug, and Cosmetic Act must maintain and make available for inspection and copying by the Attorney General, all of the following information for each prescription:

(a) Name of the prescribing practitioner.

(b) Prescribing practitioner's Federal and State registration numbers, with the expiration dates of these registrations.

(c) Verification that the prescribing practitioner possesses the appropriate registration to prescribe this controlled substance.

(d) Patient's name and address.

(e) Patient's insurance provider, if available.

[70 FR 293, Jan. 4, 2005]

REPORTS

§ 1304.31 Reports from manufacturers importing narcotic raw material.

(a) Every manufacturer which imports or manufactures from narcotic raw material (opium, poppy straw, and concentrate of poppy straw) shall submit information which accounts for the importation and for all manufacturing operations performed between importation and the production in bulk or finished marketable products, standardized in accordance with the U.S. Pharmacopeia, National Formulary or other recognized medical standards. Reports shall be signed by the authorized official and submitted quarterly on company letterhead to the UN Reporting and Quota Section, Diversion Control Division, on or before the 15th day of the month immediately following the period for which it is submitted. See the Table of DEA Mailing Addresses in § 1321.01 of this chapter for the current mailing address.

(b) The following information shall be submitted for each type of narcotic raw material (quantities are expressed as grams of anhydrous morphine alkaloid):

(1) Beginning inventory;

(2) Gains on reweighing;

(3) Imports;

(4) Other receipts;

(5) Quantity put into process;

(6) Losses on reweighing;

(7) Other dispositions and

(8) Ending inventory.

(c) The following information shall be submitted for each narcotic raw material derivative including morphine, codeine, thebaine, oxycodone, hydrocodone, medicinal opium, manufacturing opium, crude alkaloids and other derivatives (quantities are expressed as grams of anhydrous base or anhydrous morphine alkaloid for manufacturing opium and medicinal opium):

(1) Beginning inventory;

(2) Gains on reweighing;

(3) Quantity extracted from narcotic raw material;

(4) Quantity produced/manufactured/synthesized;

(5) Quantity sold;

(6) Quantity returned to conversion processes for reworking;

(7) Quantity used for conversion;

(8) Quantity placed in process;

(9) Other dispositions;

(10) Losses on reweighing and

(11) Ending inventory.

(d) The following information shall be submitted for importation of each narcotic raw material:

(1) Import permit number;

(2) Date shipment arrived at the United States port of entry;

(3) Actual quantity shipped;

(4) Assay (percent) of morphine, codeine and thebaine and

(5) Quantity shipped, expressed as anhydrous morphine alkaloid.

(e) Upon importation of crude opium, samples will be selected and assays made by the importing manufacturer in the manner and according to the method specified in the U.S. Pharmacopoeia. Where final assay data is not determined at the time of rendering report, the report shall be made on the basis of the best data available, subject to adjustment, and the necessary adjusting entries shall be made on the next report.

(f) Where factory procedure is such that partial withdrawals of opium are made from individual containers, there shall be attached to each container a stock record card on which shall be kept a complete record of all withdrawals therefrom.

(g) All in-process inventories should be expressed in terms of end-products and not precursors. Once precursor material has been changed or placed into process for the manufacture of a specified end-product, it must no longer be accounted for as precursor stocks available for conversion or use, but rather as end-product in-process inventories.

[62 FR 13961, Mar. 24, 1997, as amended at 75 FR 10677, Mar. 9, 2010; 81 FR 97020, Dec. 30, 2016]

§ 1304.32 Reports of manufacturers importing coca leaves.

(a) Every manufacturer importing or manufacturing from raw coca leaves shall submit information accounting for the importation and for all manufacturing operations performed between the importation and the manufacture of bulk or finished products standardized in accordance with U.S. Pharmacopoeia, National Formulary, or other recognized standards. The reports shall be submitted quarterly on company letterhead to the UN Reporting and Quota Section, Diversion Control Division, on or before the 15th day of the month immediately following the period for which it is submitted. See the Table of DEA Mailing Addresses in § 1321.01 of this chapter for the current mailing address.

(b) The following information shall be submitted for raw coca leaf, ecgonine, ecgonine for conversion or further manufacture, benzoylecgonine, manufacturing coca extracts (list for tinctures and extracts; and others separately), other crude alkaloids and other derivatives (quantities should be reported as grams of actual quantity involved and the cocaine alkaloid content or equivalency):

(1) Beginning inventory;

(2) Imports;

(3) Gains on reweighing;

(4) Quantity purchased;

(5) Quantity produced;

(6) Other receipts;

(7) Quantity returned to processes for reworking;

(8) Material used in purification for sale;

(9) Material used for manufacture or production;

(10) Losses on reweighing;

(11) Material used for conversion;

(12) Other dispositions and

(13) Ending inventory.

(c) The following information shall be submitted for importation of coca leaves:

(1) Import permit number;

(2) Date the shipment arrived at the United States port of entry;

(3) Actual quantity shipped;

(4) Assay (percent) of cocaine alkaloid and

(5) Total cocaine alkaloid content.

(d) Upon importation of coca leaves, samples will be selected and assays made by the importing manufacturer in accordance with recognized chemical procedures. These assays shall form the basis of accounting for such coca leaves, which shall be accounted for in terms of their cocaine alkaloid content or equivalency or their total anhydrous coca alkaloid content. Where final assay data is not determined at the time of submission, the report shall be made on the basis of the best data available, subject to adjustment, and the necessary adjusting entries shall be made on the next report.

(e) Where factory procedure is such that partial withdrawals of medicinal coca leaves are made from individual containers, there shall be attached to the container a stock record card on which shall be kept a complete record of withdrawals therefrom.

(f) All in-process inventories should be expressed in terms of end-products and not precursors. Once precursor material has been changed or placed into process for the manufacture of a specified end-product, it must no longer be accounted for as precursor stocks available for conversion or use, but rather as end-product in-process inventories.

[62 FR 13962, Mar. 24, 1997, as amended at 75 FR 10678, Mar. 9, 2010; 81 FR 97020, Dec. 30, 2016]

§ 1304.33 Reports to Automation of Reports and Consolidated Orders System (ARCOS).

(a) *Reports generally.* All reports required by this section shall be filed with the Pharmaceutical Investigations Section, Diversion Control Division, Drug Enforcement Administration on DEA Form 333, or on media which contains the data required by DEA Form 333 and which is acceptable to the Administration. See the Table of DEA Mailing Addresses in § 1321.01 of this chapter for the current mailing address.

(b) *Frequency of reports.* Acquisition/Distribution transaction reports shall be filed every quarter not later than the 15th day of the month succeeding the quarter for which it is submitted; except that a registrant may be given permission to file more frequently (but not more frequently than monthly), depending on the number of transactions being reported each time by that registrant. Inventories shall provide data on the stocks of each reported controlled substance on hand as of the close of business on December 31 of each year, indicating whether the substance is in storage or in process of manufacturing. These reports shall be filed not later than January 15 of the following year. Manufacturing transaction reports shall be filed annually for each calendar year not later than January 15 of the following year, except that a registrant may be given permission to file more frequently (but not more frequently than quarterly).

(c) *Persons reporting.* For controlled substances in Schedules I, II, narcotic controlled substances in Schedule III, and gamma-hydroxybutyric acid drug product controlled substances in Schedule III, each person who is registered to manufacture in bulk or dosage form, or to package, repackage, label or relabel, and each person who is registered to distribute, including each person who is registered to reverse distribute, shall report acquisition/distribution transactions. In addition to reporting acquisition/distribution transactions, each person who is registered to manufacture controlled substances in bulk or dosage form shall report manufacturing transactions on controlled substances in Schedules I and II, each narcotic controlled substance listed in Schedules III, IV, and V, gamma-hydroxybutyric acid drug product controlled substances in Schedule III, and on each psychotropic controlled substance listed in Schedules III and IV as identified in paragraph (d) of this section.

(d) *Substances covered.* (1) Manufacturing and acquisition/distribution transaction reports shall include data on each controlled substance listed in Schedules I and II, on each narcotic controlled substance listed in Schedule III (but not on any material, compound, mixture or preparation containing a quantity of a substance having a stimulant effect on the central nervous system, which material, compound, mixture or preparation is listed in Schedule III or on any narcotic controlled substance listed in Schedule V), and on gamma-hydroxybutyric acid drug products listed in Schedule III. Additionally, reports on manufacturing transactions shall include the following psychotropic controlled substances listed in Schedules III and IV:

(i) Schedule III

(A) Benzphetamine;

(B) Cyclobarbital;

(C) Methyprylon; and

(D) Phendimetrazine.

(ii) Schedule IV

(A) Barbital;

(B) Diethylpropion (Amfepramone);

(C) Ethchlorvynol;

(D) Ethinamate;

(E) Lefetamine (SPA);

(F) Mazindol;

(G) Meprobamate;

(H) Methylphenobarbital;

(I) Phenobarbital;

(J) Phentermine; and

(K) Pipradrol.

(2) Data shall be presented in such a manner as to identify the particular form, strength, and trade name, if any, of the product containing the controlled substancefor which the report is being made. For this purpose, persons filing reports shall utilize the National Drug Code Number assigned to the product under the National Drug Code System of the Food and Drug Administration.

(e) *Transactions reported.* Acquisition/distribution transaction reports shall provide data on each acquisition to inventory (identifying whether it is, e.g., by purchase or transfer, return from a customer, or supply by the Federal Government) and each reduction from inventory (identifying whether it is, e.g., by sale or transfer, theft, destruction or seizure by Government agencies). Manufacturing reports shall provide data on material manufactured, manufacture from other material, use in manufacturing other material and use in producing dosage forms.

(f) *Exceptions.* (1) A registered institutional practitioner that repackages or relabels exclusively for distribution or that distributes exclusively to (for dispensing by) agents, employees, or affiliated institutional practitioners of the registrant may be exempted from filing reports under this section by applying to the Pharmaceutical Investigations Section, Diversion Control Division, Drug Enforcement Administration. See the Table of DEA Mailing Addresses in § 1321.01 of this chapter for the current mailing address.

(2) Registrants that acquire recalled controlled substances from ultimate users pursuant to § 1317.85 of this chapter may report as a single transaction all recalled controlled substances of the same name and finished form (e.g., all 10-milligram tablets or all 5-milligram concentration per fluid ounce or milliliter) received from ultimate users for the purpose of reporting acquisition transactions.

(g) *Exemptions.* (1) Collectors that acquire controlled substances from ultimate users are exempt from the ARCOS reporting requirements only with respect to controlled substances collected through mail-back programs and collection receptacles for the purpose of disposal.

(2) Reverse distributors and distributors that acquire controlled substances pursuant to § 1317.55(a) or (b) of this chapter are exempt from the ARCOS reporting requirements in this section with regard to any controlled substances acquired pursuant to § 1317.55(a) or (b) of this chapter.

(Approved by the Office of Management and Budget under control number 1117–0003)

[62 FR 13962, Mar. 24, 1997, as amended at 68 FR 41229, July 11, 2003; 70 FR 294, Jan. 4, 2005; 75 FR 10678, Mar. 9, 2010; 79 FR 53564, Sept. 9, 2014; 81 FR 97020, Dec. 30, 2016]

ONLINE PHARMACIES

§ 1304.40 Notification by online pharmacies.

(a) Thirty days prior to offering a controlled substance for sale, delivery, distribution, or dispensing by means of the Internet, an online pharmacy shall:

(1) Notify the Administrator of its intent to do so by submitting an application for a modified registration in accordance with §§ 1301.13 and 1301.19 of this chapter, with such application containing the information required by this section; and

(2) Notify the State boards of pharmacy in any States in which the online pharmacy offers to sell, deliver, distribute, or dispense controlled substances.

(b) The following information must be included in the notification submitted under paragraph (a) of this section:

(1) The pharmacy's Internet Pharmacy Site Disclosure information required to be posted on the homepage of the online pharmacy's Internet site under section 311(c) of the Act (21 U.S.C. 831(c)) and § 1304.45 of this part.

(2) Certification that the information disclosed on its Internet site under the Internet Pharmacy Site Disclosure is true and accurate. The statement shall be in a form similar to the following: "The above-named pharmacy, a DEA registrant, certifies, under penalty of perjury, that the information contained in this statement is true and accurate."

(3) Each Internet site address utilized by the online pharmacy and a certification that the online pharmacy shall notify the Administrator of any change in any such Internet address at least 30 days in advance. In the event that a pharmacy delivers, distributes, or dispenses controlled substances pursuant to orders made on, through, or on behalf of, more than one Web site, the pharmacy shall provide, for purposes of complying with this paragraph, the Internet site address of each such site.

(4) The DEA registration numbers of:

(i) Every pharmacy that delivers, distributes, or dispenses controlled substances pursuant to orders made on, through, or on behalf of, each Web site referred to in paragraph (b)(3) of this section; and

(ii) Every practitioner who has a contractual relationship to provide medical evaluations or issue prescriptions for controlled substances, through referrals from the Web site or at the request of the owner or operator of the Web site, or any employee or agent thereof.

(c) An online pharmacy that is in operation at the time Public Law 110–425 becomes effective (April 13, 2009) must make the notifications required in this section on or before May 13, 2009. However, in accordance with section 401(h) of the Act (21 U.S.C. 841(h)), as of April 13, 2009, it is unlawful for any online pharmacy to deliver, distribute, or dispense a controlled substance by means of the Internet unless such online pharmacy is validly registered with a modification of such registration authorizing such activity.

(d) On and after the date an online pharmacy makes the notifications required under this section, each online pharmacy shall display on the homepage of its Internet site, a declaration that it has made such notifications to the Administrator in the following form: "In accordance with the Controlled Substances Act and the DEA regulations, this online pharmacy has made the notifications to the DEA Administrator required by 21 U.S.C. 831 and 21 CFR 1304.40."

(e)(1) Except as provided in paragraphs (e)(2) and (e)(3) of this section, if any of the information required to be submitted under this section changes after the online pharmacy submits the notification to the Administrator, the online pharmacy shall notify the Administrator of the updated information no later than 30 days before the change becomes effective via the online process.

(2) If a pharmacy referred to in paragraph (b)(4)(i) of this section ceases to deliver, distribute, or dispense controlled substances pursuant to orders made on, through, or on behalf of, each Web site referred to in paragraph (b)(3) of this section, the online pharmacy shall notify the Administrator no later than 30 days after the change becomes effective via the online process.

(3) If a practitioner referred to in paragraph (b)(4)(ii) of this section ceases to have a contractual relationship with the online pharmacy, the online pharmacy shall notify the Administrator no later than 30 days after the change becomes effective via the online process.

[74 FR 15623, Apr. 6, 2009]

§ 1304.45 Internet Web site disclosure requirements.

(a) Each online pharmacy shall display, at all times and in a visible and clear manner, on its homepage a statement that it complies with the requirements of section 311 of the Act (21 U.S.C. 831) with respect to the delivery or sale or offer for sale of controlled substances. This statement must include the name of the pharmacy as it appears on the DEA Certificate of Registration.

(b) Each online pharmacy shall clearly display the following information on the homepage of each Internet site it operates, or on a page directly linked to the homepage. If the information is displayed on a page directly linked to the homepage, that link on the homepage must be visible and clear. The information must be displayed for each pharmacy that delivers, distributes, or dispenses controlled substances pursuant to orders made on, through, or on behalf of that Web site.

(1) The name and address of the pharmacy as it appears on the pharmacy's DEA Certificate of Registration.

(2) The pharmacy's telephone number and e-mail address.

(3) The name, professional degree, and States of licensure of the pharmacist-in-charge, and a telephone number at which the pharmacist-in-charge can be contacted.

(4) A list of the States in which the pharmacy is licensed to dispense controlled substances.

(5) A certification that the pharmacy is registered under part 1301 of this chapter with a modification of its registration authorizing it to deliver, distribute, or dispense controlled substances by means of the Internet.

(6) The name, address, telephone number, professional degree, and States of licensure with State license number of any practitioner who has a contractual relationship to provide medical evaluations or issue prescriptions for controlled substances, through referrals from the Web site or at the request of the owner or operator of the Web site, or any employee or agent thereof.

(7) The following statement: "This online pharmacy is obligated to comply fully with the Controlled Substances Act and DEA regulations. As part of this obligation, this online pharmacy has obtained a modified DEA registration authorizing it to operate as an online pharmacy. In addition, this online pharmacy will only dispense a controlled substance to a person who has a valid prescription issued for a legitimate medical purpose based upon a medical relationship with a prescribing practitioner. This includes at least one prior in-person medical evaluation in accordance with section 309 of the Controlled Substances Act (21 U.S.C. 829) or a medical evaluation via telemedicine in accordance with section 102(54) of the Controlled Substances Act (21 U.S.C. 802(54))."

[74 FR 15623, Apr. 6, 2009]

§ 1304.50 Disclosure requirements for Web sites of nonpharmacy practitioners that dispense controlled substances by means of the Internet.

For a Web site to identify itself as being exempt from the definition of an online pharmacy by virtue of section 102(52)(B)(ii) of the Act (21 U.S.C. 802(52)(B)(ii)) and § 1300.04(h)(2) of this chapter, the Web site shall post in a visible and clear manner on its homepage, or on a page directly linked thereto in which the hyperlink is also visible and clear on the homepage, a list of the DEA-registered nonpharmacy practitioners who are affiliated with the Web site. Any nonpharmacy practitioner affiliated with such a Web site is responsible for compliance with this section. An institutional practitioner that otherwise complies with the requirements of the Act and this chapter will be deemed to meet the requirements of this section if, in lieu of posting the names of each affiliated individual practitioner, it posts its name (as it appears on its Certificate of Registration) in a visible and clear manner on its homepage and in a manner that identifies itself as being responsible for the operation of the Web site.

[74 FR 15623, Apr. 6, 2009]

§ 1304.55 Reports by online pharmacies.

(a) Each online pharmacy shall report to the Administrator the total quantity of each controlled substance that the pharmacy has dispensed each calendar month. The report must include the total quantity of such dispensing by any means, regardless of whether the controlled substances are dispensed by means of the Internet. Thus, such reporting shall include all controlled substances dispensed via Internet transactions, mail-order transactions, face-to-face transactions, or any other means. However, the pharmacy is not required to describe in its report to the Administrator such means of dispensing. Such reporting is required for every calendar month in which the total quantity of controlled substances dispensed by the pharmacy meets or exceeds one of the following thresholds:

(1) 100 or more prescriptions for controlled substances filled; or

(2) 5,000 or more dosage units dispensed of all controlled substances combined.

(b) Each online pharmacy shall report a negative response if, during a given calendar month, its total dispensing of controlled substances falls below both of the thresholds in paragraph (a) of this section.

(c) The reporting requirements of this section apply to every pharmacy that, at any time during a calendar month, holds a modified registration authorizing it to operate as an online pharmacy, regardless of whether the online pharmacy dispenses any controlled substances by means of the Internet during the month.

(d) Reports will be submitted to DEA electronically via online reporting, electronic file upload, or other means as approved by DEA.

(e) Reports shall be filed every month not later than the fifteenth day of the month succeeding the month for which they are submitted.

(f) An online pharmacy filing a report under paragraph (a) of this section shall utilize the National Drug Code number assigned to the product under the National Drug Code System of the Food and Drug Administration, and indicate the total number of dosage units dispensed for each such National Drug Code number.

(g) Records required to be kept under this section must be kept by the registrant for at least two years from the date of such records. The information shall be readily retrievable from the ordinary business records of the registrant and available for inspection and copying by authorized employees of the Administration.

[74 FR 15623, Apr. 6, 2009]

PART 1305—ORDERS FOR SCHEDULE I AND II CONTROLLED SUBSTANCES

Subpart A—General Requirements

Sec.

Subpart B—DEA Form 222

Subpart C—Electronic Orders

AUTHORITY: 21 U.S.C. 821, 828, 871(b), unless otherwise noted.

SOURCE: 70 FR 16911, Apr. 1, 2005, unless otherwise noted.

Subpart A—General Requirements

§ 1305.01 Scope of part 1305.

Procedures governing the issuance, use, and preservation of orders for Schedule I and II controlled substances are set forth generally by section 308 of the Act (21 U.S.C. 828) and specifically by the sections of this part.

§ 1305.02 Definitions.

Any term contained in this part shall have the definition set forth in the Act or part 1300 of this chapter.

§ 1305.03 Distributions requiring a Form 222 or a digitally signed electronic order.

Either a DEA Form 222 or its electronic equivalent as set forth in subpart C of this part and Part 1311 of this chapter is required for each distribution of a Schedule I or II controlled substance except for the following:

(a) Distributions to persons exempted from registration under Part 1301 of this chapter.

(b) Exports from the United States that conform with the requirements of the Act.

(c) Deliveries to a registered analytical laboratory or its agent approved by DEA.

(d) Delivery from a central fill pharmacy, as defined in § 1300.01 of this chapter, to a retail pharmacy.

(e) Deliveries to an authorized DEA registrant by an ultimate user, a long-term care facility on behalf of an ultimate user who resides or has resided at that facility, or a person authorized to dispose of the ultimate user decedent's property.

(f) Distributions to reverse distributors and distributors by collectors and law enforcement pursuant to § 1317.55 of this chapter.

(g) Deliveries of controlled substances from ultimate users for the purpose of recalls pursuant to § 1317.85 of this chapter.

[70 FR 16911, Apr. 1, 2005, as amended at 77 FR 4235, Jan. 27, 2012; 79 FR 53564, Sept. 9, 2014]

§ 1305.04 Persons entitled to order Schedule I and II controlled substances.

(a) Only persons who are registered with DEA under section 303 of the Act (21 U.S.C. 823) to handle Schedule I or II controlled substances, and persons who are registered with DEA under section 1008 of the Act (21 U.S.C. 958) to export these substances may obtain and use DEA Form 222 (order forms) or issue electronic orders for these substances. Persons not registered to handle Schedule I or II controlled substances and persons registered only to import controlled substances are not entitled to obtain Form 222 or issue electronic orders for these substances.

(b) An order for Schedule I or II controlled substances may be executed only on behalf of the registrant named on the order and only if his or her registration for the substances being purchased has not expired or been revoked or suspended.

§ 1305.05 Power of attorney.

(a) A registrant may authorize one or more individuals, whether or not located at his or her registered location, to issue orders for Schedule I and II controlled substances on the registrant's behalf by executing a power of attorney for each such individual, if the power of attorney is retained in the files, with executed Forms 222 where applicable, for the same period as any order bearing the signature of the attorney. The power of attorney must be available for inspection together with other order records.

(b) A registrant may revoke any power of attorney at any time by executing a notice of revocation.

(c) The power of attorney and notice of revocation must be similar to the following format:

Power of Attorney for DEA Forms 222 and Electronic Orders

____
(Name of registrant)

____
(Address of registrant)

____
(DEA registration number)

I, _______ (name of person granting power), the undersigned, who am authorized to sign the current application for registration of the above-named registrant under the Controlled Substances Act or Controlled Substances Import and Export Act, have made, constituted, and appointed, and by these presents, do make, constitute, and appoint _______ (name of attorney-in-fact), my true and lawful attorney for me in my name, place, and stead, to execute applications for Forms 222 and to sign orders for Schedule I and II controlled substances, whether these orders be on Form 222 or electronic, in accordance with 21 U.S.C. 828 and Part 1305 of Title 21 of the Code of Federal Regulations. I hereby ratify and confirm all that said attorney must lawfully do or cause to be done by virtue hereof.

____
(Signature of person granting power)

I, _______ (name of attorney-in-fact), hereby affirm that I am the person named herein as attorney-in-fact and that the signature affixed hereto is my signature.

(signature of attorney-in-fact)

Witnesses:

1. __________

2. __________

Signed and dated on the _______ day of _______, (year), at _______ .

Notice of Revocation

The foregoing power of attorney is hereby revoked by the undersigned, who is authorized to sign the current application for registration of the above-named registrant under the Controlled Substances Act or the Controlled Substances Import and Export Act. Written notice of this revocation has been given to the attorney-in-fact _______ this same day.

____
(Signature of person revoking power)

Witnesses:

1. __________

2. __________

Signed and dated on the ______ day of ______, (year), at ______.

(d) A power of attorney must be executed by:

(1) The registrant, if an individual; a partner of the registrant, if a partnership; or an officer of the registrant, if a corporation, corporate division, association, trust or other entity;

(2) The person to whom the power of attorney is being granted; and

(3) Two witnesses.

(e) A power of attorney must be revoked by the person who signed the most recent application for DEA registration or reregistration, and two witnesses.

(f) A power of attorney executed under this section may be signed electronically, by any or all of the persons required to sign.

[70 FR 16911, Apr. 1, 2005, as amended at 84 FR 51374, Sept. 30, 2019]

§ 1305.06 Persons entitled to fill orders for Schedule I and II controlled substances.

An order for Schedule I and II controlled substances, whether on a DEA Form 222 or an electronic order, may be filled only by a person registered with DEA as a manufacturer or distributor of controlled substances listed in Schedule I or II pursuant to section 303 of the Act (21 U.S.C. 823) or as an importer of such substances pursuant to section 1008 of the Act (21 U.S.C. 958), except for the following:

(a) A person registered with DEA to dispense the substances, or to export the substances, if he/she is discontinuing business or if his/her registration is expiring without reregistration, may dispose of any Schedule I or II controlled substances in his/her possession with a DEA Form 222 or an electronic order in accordance with § 1301.52 of this chapter.

(b) A purchaser who has obtained any Schedule I or II controlled substance by either a DEA Form 222 or an electronic order may return the substance to the supplier of the substance with either a DEA Form 222 or an electronic order from the supplier.

(c) A person registered to dispense Schedule II substances may distribute the substances to another dispenser with either a DEA Form 222 or an electronic order only in the circumstances described in § 1307.11 of this chapter.

(d) A person registered or authorized to conduct chemical analysis or research with controlled substances may distribute a Schedule I or II controlled substance to another person registered or authorized to conduct chemical analysis, instructional activities, or research with the substances with either a DEA Form 222 or an electronic order, if the distribution is for the purpose of furthering the chemical analysis, instructional activities, or research.

(e) A person registered as a compounder of narcotic substances for use at off-site locations in conjunction with a narcotic treatment program at the compounding location, who is authorized to handle Schedule II narcotics, is authorized to fill either a DEA Form 222 or an electronic order for distribution of narcotic drugs to off-site narcotic treatment programs only.

§ 1305.07 Special procedure for filling certain orders.

A supplier of thiafentanil, carfentanil, etorphine hydrochloride, or diprenorphine, if he or she determines that the purchaser is a veterinarian engaged in zoo and exotic animal practice, wildlife management programs, or research, and is authorized by the Administrator to handle these substances, may fill the order in accordance with the procedures set forth in § 1305.17 except that:

(a) A DEA Form 222 or an electronic order for thiafentanil, carfentanil, etorphine hydrochloride, and diprenorphine must contain only these substances in reasonable quantities.

(b) The substances must be shipped, under secure conditions using substantial packaging material with no markings on the outside that would indicate the content, only to the purchaser's registered location.

[70 FR 16911, Apr. 1, 2005, as amended at 81 FR 58839, Aug. 26, 2016]

Subpart B—DEA Form 222

§ 1305.11 Procedure for obtaining DEA Forms 222.

(a) DEA Forms 222 are issued in mailing envelopes containing a predetermined number of forms based on the business activity of the registrant, each form consisting of one single-sheet. A limit, which is based on the business activity of the registrant, will be imposed on the number of DEA Forms 222 that will be furnished upon a requisition for order forms unless additional forms are specifically requested and a reasonable need for such additional forms is shown.

(b) Any person with an active registration that is authorized to order schedule I and II controlled substances is entitled to obtain a DEA Form 222, which will be supplied at any time after the DEA registration is granted. Any person holding a registration authorizing the person to obtain a DEA Form 222 may requisition the forms through a DEA secured network connection or by contacting any Division Office or the Registration Section of the Administration through the customer service center.

(c) Each requisition must show the name, address, and registration number of the registrant and the number of DEA Forms 222 desired.

(d) DEA Forms 222 will have an order form number and be issued with the name, address and registration number of the registrant, the authorized activity, and schedules of the registrant. This information cannot be altered or changed by the registrant; the registrant must report any errors to the local Division Office or the Registration Section of the Administration to modify the registration.

[84 FR 51374, Sept. 30, 2019]

§ 1305.12 Procedure for executing DEA Forms 222.

(a) A purchaser must prepare and execute a DEA Form 222 by use of a typewriter, computer printer, pen, or indelible pencil.

(b) Only one item may be entered on each numbered line. An item must consist of one or more commercial or bulk containers of the same finished or bulk form and quantity of the same substance. The number of lines completed must be noted on that form at the bottom of the form, in the space provided. DEA Forms 222 for carfentanil, etorphine hydrochloride, and diprenorphine must contain only these substances.

(c) The name and address of the supplier from whom the controlled substances are being ordered must be entered on the form. Only one supplier may be listed on any form.

(d) Each DEA Form 222 must be signed and dated by a person authorized to sign an application for registration or a person granted power of attorney to sign a Form 222 under § 1305.05. The name of the purchaser, if different from the individual signing the DEA Form 222, must also be inserted in the signature space.

(e) Unexecuted DEA Forms 222 may be kept and may be executed at a location other than the registered location printed on the form, provided that all unexecuted forms are delivered promptly to the registered location upon an inspection of the location by any officer authorized to make inspections, or to enforce, any Federal, State, or local law regarding controlled substances.

[70 FR 16911, Apr. 1, 2005, as amended at 84 FR 51374, Sept. 30, 2019]

§1305.13 Procedure for filling DEA Forms 222.

(a) A purchaser must make a copy of the original DEA Form 222 for its records and then submit the original to the supplier. The copy retained by the purchaser may be in paper or electronic form.

(b) A supplier may fill the order, if possible and if the supplier desires to do so, and must record on the original DEA Form 222 its DEA registration number and the number of commercial or bulk containers furnished on each item and the date on which the containers are shipped to the purchaser. If an order cannot be filled in its entirety, it may be filled in part and the balance supplied by additional shipments within 60 days following the date of the DEA Form 222. No DEA Form 222 is valid more than 60 days after its execution by the purchaser, except as specified in paragraph (f) of this section.

(c) The controlled substances must be shipped only to the purchaser and the location printed by the Administration on the DEA Form 222, except as specified in paragraph (f) of this section.

(d) The supplier must retain the original DEA Form 222 for the supplier's files in accordance with §1305.17(c). Any supplier who is not required to report acquisition/disposition transactions to the Automation of Reports and Consolidated Orders System (ARCOS) under §1304.33(c) (such as a practitioner) must make and submit a copy of the original DEA Form 222 to DEA, either by mail to the Registration Section, or by email to *DEA.Orderforms@usdoj.gov*. The copy must be forwarded at the close of the month during which the order is filled. If an order is filled by partial shipments, the copy must be forwarded at the close of the month during which the final shipment is made or the 60-day validity period expires.

(e) The purchaser must record on its copy of the DEA Form 222 the number of commercial or bulk containers furnished on each item and the dates on which the containers are received by the purchaser.

(f) DEA Forms 222 submitted by registered procurement officers of the Defense Supply Center of the Defense Logistics Agency for delivery to armed services establishments within the United States may be shipped to locations other than the location printed on the DEA Form 222, and in partial shipments at different times not to exceed six months from the date of the order, as designated by the procurement officer when submitting the order.

[70 FR 16911, Apr. 1, 2005, as amended at 84 FR 51374, Sept. 30, 2019]

§1305.14 Procedure for endorsing DEA Forms 222.

(a) A DEA Form 222, made out to any supplier who cannot fill all or a part of the order within the time limitation set forth in §1305.13, may be endorsed to another supplier for filling. The endorsement must be made only by the supplier to whom the DEA Form 222 was first made, must state (in the spaces provided in Part 3 on the original DEA Form 222) the DEA number of the second supplier, and must be signed and dated by a person authorized to obtain and execute DEA Forms 222 on behalf of the first supplier. The first supplier may not fill any part of an order on an endorsed form. The second supplier may fill the order, if possible and if the supplier desires to do so, in accordance with §1305.13(b), (c), and (d), including shipping all substances directly to the purchaser.

(b) Distributions made on endorsed DEA Forms 222 must be reported by the second supplier in the same manner as all other distributions.

[70 FR 16911, Apr. 1, 2005, as amended at 84 FR 51375, Sept. 30, 2019]

§ 1305.15 Unaccepted and defective DEA Forms 222.

(a) A DEA Form 222 must not be filled if either of the following apply:

(1) The order is not complete, legible, or properly prepared, executed, or endorsed.

(2) The order shows any alteration, erasure, or change of any description.

(b) If a DEA Form 222 cannot be filled for any reason under this section, the supplier must return the original DEA Form 222 to the purchaser with a statement as to the reason (*e.g.*, illegible or altered).

(c) A supplier may for any reason refuse to accept any order and if a supplier refuses to accept the order, a statement that the order is not accepted is sufficient for purposes of this paragraph.

(d) When a purchaser receives an unaccepted order, the original DEA Form 222 and the statement must be retained in the files of the purchaser in accordance with § 1305.17. A defective DEA Form 222 may not be corrected; it must be replaced by a new DEA Form 222 for the order to be filled.

[70 FR 16911, Apr. 1, 2005, as amended at 84 FR 51375, Sept. 30, 2019]

§ 1305.16 Lost and stolen DEA Forms 222.

(a) If a purchaser ascertains that an unfilled DEA Form 222 has been lost, the purchaser must execute another and attach a statement containing the order form number and date of the lost form, and stating that the goods covered by the first DEA Form 222 were not received through loss of that DEA Form 222. A copy of the second form and a copy of the statement must be retained with a copy of the DEA Form 222 first executed. A copy of the statement must be attached to a copy of the second DEA Form 222 sent to the supplier. If the first DEA Form 222 is subsequently received by the supplier to whom it was directed, the supplier must mark upon the face "Not accepted" and return the original DEA Form 222 to the purchaser, who must attach it to the statement.

(b) Whenever any used or unused DEA Forms 222 are stolen or lost (other than in the course of transmission) by any purchaser or supplier, the purchaser or supplier must immediately upon discovery of the theft or loss, report the theft or loss to the Special Agent in Charge of the Drug Enforcement Administration in the Divisional Office responsible for the area in which the registrant is located, stating the serial number of each form stolen or lost.

(c) If the theft or loss includes any original DEA Forms 222 received from purchasers and the supplier is unable to state the serial numbers of the DEA Forms 222, the supplier must report the date or approximate date of receipt and the names and addresses of the purchasers.

(d) If any DEA Forms 222 are lost or stolen, and the purchaser is unable to state the order form numbers of the DEA Forms 222, the purchaser must report, in lieu of numbers of the forms, the date or approximate date of issuance.

(e) If any unused DEA Form 222 reported stolen or lost is subsequently recovered or found, the Special Agent in Charge of the Drug Enforcement Administration in the Divisional Office responsible for the area in which the registrant is located must immediately be notified.

[70 FR 16911, Apr. 1, 2005, as amended at 84 FR 51375, Sept. 30, 2019]

§ 1305.17 Preservation of DEA Forms 222.

(a) The purchaser must retain a copy of each executed DEA Form 222 and all copies of unaccepted or defective forms with each statement attached.

(b) The supplier must retain the original of each DEA Form 222 that it has filled.

(c) DEA Forms 222 must be maintained separately from all other records of the registrant. DEA Forms 222 are required to be kept available for inspection for a period of two years. If a purchaser has several registered locations, the purchaser must retain a copy of the executed DEA Form 222 and any attached statements or other related documents (not including unexecuted DEA Forms 222, which may be kept elsewhere under § 1305.12(e)), at the registered location printed on the DEA Form 222.

(d) The supplier of thiafentanil, carfentanil, etorphine hydrochloride, and diprenorphine must maintain DEA Forms 222 for these substances separately from all other DEA Forms 222 and records required to be maintained by the registrant.

(e) Electronic copies of DEA Forms 222 will be deemed to be maintained separately from all other records of the registrant, for the purposes of this section, if such copies are readily retrievable separately from all other records. Electronic copies of DEA Forms 222 may be stored on a system at a location different from the registered location, provided such copies are readily retrievable at the registered location.

[70 FR 16911, Apr. 1, 2005, as amended at 81 FR 58839, Aug. 26, 2016; 84 FR 51375, Sept. 30, 2019]

§ 1305.18 Return of unused DEA Forms 222.

If the registration of any purchaser terminates (because the purchaser dies, ceases legal existence, discontinues business or professional practice, or changes the name or address as shown on the purchaser's registration) or is suspended or revoked under § 1301.36 of this chapter for all Schedule I and II controlled substances for which the purchaser is registered, the purchaser must return all unused DEA Forms 222 to the Registration Section.

[84 FR 51375, Sept. 30, 2019]

§ 1305.19 Cancellation and voiding of DEA Forms 222.

(a) A purchaser may cancel part or all of an order on a DEA Form 222 by notifying the supplier in writing of the cancellation. The supplier must indicate the cancellation on the original DEA Form 222 sent by the purchaser by drawing a line through the canceled items and printing "canceled" in the space provided for the number of items shipped.

(b) A supplier may void part or all of an order on a DEA Form 222 by notifying the purchaser in writing of the voiding. The supplier must indicate the voiding in the manner prescribed for cancellation in paragraph (a) of this section.

[70 FR 16911, Apr. 1, 2005, as amended at 84 FR 51375, Sept. 30, 2019]

§ 1305.20 Transition provisions allowing continued use of existing stocks of triplicate DEA Forms 222.

Registrants may continue to use existing stocks of the triplicate DEA Form 222 until October 30, 2021. In any case, as soon as a registrant's supply of triplicate DEA Forms 222 is exhausted, the registrant must use the new single-sheet DEA Form 222. The provisions of this part are applicable to the use of triplicate forms, except for the specific rules as provided in this section.

(a) *Procedure for obtaining triplicate DEA Forms 222.* The DEA will no longer issue triplicate forms. Triplicate DEA Forms 222 will not be accepted after October 30, 2021.

(b) *Procedure for executing triplicate DEA Forms 222.* (1) A purchaser must prepare and execute a triplicate DEA Form 222 simultaneously by means of interleaved carbon sheets that are part of the triplicate DEA Form 222. Triplicate DEA Form 222 must be prepared by use of a typewriter, pen, or indelible pencil.

(2) Only one item may be entered on each numbered line. An item must consist of one or more commercial or bulk containers of the same finished or bulk form and quantity of the same substance. The number of lines completed must be noted on that form at the bottom of the form, in the space provided. Triplicate DEA Forms 222 for carfentanil, etorphine hydrochloride, and diprenorphine must contain only these substances.

(3) The name and address of the supplier from whom the controlled substances are being ordered must be entered on the form. Only one supplier may be listed on any form.

(4) Each triplicate DEA Form 222 must be signed and dated by a person authorized to sign an application for registration or a person granted power of attorney to sign a DEA Form 222 under § 1305.05. The name of the purchaser, if different from the individual signing the DEA Form 222, must also be inserted in the signature space.

(5) Unexecuted DEA Forms 222 may be kept and may be executed at a location other than the registered location printed on the form, provided that all unexecuted forms are delivered promptly to the registered location upon an inspection of the location by any officer authorized to make inspections, or to enforce, any Federal, State, or local law regarding controlled substances.

(c) *Procedure for filling triplicate DEA Forms 222.* (1) A purchaser must submit Copy 1 and Copy 2 of the triplicate DEA Form 222 to the supplier and retain Copy 3 in the purchaser's files.

(2) A supplier may fill the order, if possible and if the supplier desires to do so, and must record on Copies 1 and 2 the number of commercial or bulk containers furnished on each item and the date on which the containers are shipped to the purchaser. If an order cannot be filled in its entirety, it may be filled in part and the balance supplied by additional shipments within 60 days following the date of the triplicate DEA Form 222. No triplicate DEA Form 222 is valid more than 60 days after its execution by the purchaser, except as specified in paragraph (c)(6) of this section.

(3) The controlled substances must be shipped only to the purchaser and the location printed by the Administration on the triplicate DEA Form 222, except as specified in paragraph (c)(6) of this section.

(4) The supplier must retain Copy 1 of the triplicate DEA Form 222 for his or her files in accordance with paragraph (g)(3) of this section and forward Copy 2 to the Special Agent in Charge of the Drug Enforcement Administration in the area in which the supplier is located. Copy 2 must be forwarded at the close of the month during which the order is filled. If an order is filled by partial shipments, Copy 2 must be forwarded at the close of the month during which the final shipment is made or the 60-day validity period expires.

(5) The purchaser must record on Copy 3 of the triplicate DEA Form 222 the number of commercial or bulk containers furnished on each item and the dates on which the containers are received by the purchaser.

(6) DEA triplicate Forms 222 submitted by registered procurement officers of the Defense Supply Center of the Defense Logistics Agency for delivery to armed services establishments within the United States may be shipped to locations other than the location printed on the triplicate DEA Form 222, and in partial shipments at different times not to exceed six months from the date of the order, as designated by the procurement officer when submitting the order.

(d) *Procedure for endorsing triplicate DEA Forms 222.* (1) A triplicate DEA Form 222, made out to any supplier who cannot fill all or a part of the order within the time limitation set forth in paragraph (c) of this section, may be endorsed to another supplier for filling. The endorsement must be made only by the supplier to whom the triplicate DEA Form 222 was first made, must state (in the spaces provided on the reverse sides of Copies 1 and 2 of the triplicate DEA Form 222) the name and address of the second supplier, and must be signed by a person authorized to obtain and execute triplicate DEA Forms 222 on behalf of the first supplier. The first supplier may not fill any part of an order on an endorsed form. The second supplier may fill the order, if possible and if the supplier desires to do so, in accordance with paragraphs (c)(2) through (4) of this section, including shipping all substances directly to the purchaser.

(2) Distributions made on endorsed triplicate DEA Forms 222 must be reported by the second supplier in the same manner as all other distributions.

(e) *Unaccepted and defective triplicate DEA Forms 222.* (1) A triplicate DEA Form 222 must not be filled if either of the following apply:

(i) The order is not complete, legible, or properly prepared, executed, or endorsed.

(ii) The order shows any alteration, erasure, or change of any description.

(2) If a triplicate DEA Form 222 cannot be filled for any reason under this section, the supplier must return Copies 1 and 2 to the purchaser with a statement as to the reason (*e.g.* illegible or altered).

(3) A supplier may for any reason refuse to accept any order and if a supplier refuses to accept the order, a statement that the order is not accepted is sufficient for purposes of this paragraph.

(4) When a purchaser receives an unaccepted order, Copies 1 and 2 of the triplicate DEA Form 222 and the statement must be attached to Copy 3 and retained in the files of the purchaser in accordance with paragraph (g) of this section. A defective triplicate DEA Form 222 may not be corrected; it must be replaced by a new triplicate DEA Form 222 for the order to be filled.

(f) *Lost and stolen triplicate DEA Forms 222.* (1) If a purchaser ascertains that an unfilled triplicate DEA Form 222 has been lost, the purchaser must execute another in triplicate and attach a statement containing the serial number and date of the lost form, and stating that the goods covered by the first triplicate DEA Form 222 were not received through loss of that triplicate DEA Form 222. Copy 3 of the second form and a copy of the statement must be retained with Copy 3 of the triplicate DEA Form 222 first executed. A copy of the statement must be attached to Copies 1 and 2 of the second triplicate DEA Form 222 sent to the supplier. If the first triplicate DEA Form 222 is subsequently received by the supplier to whom it was directed, the supplier must mark upon the face "Not accepted" and return Copies 1 and 2 to the purchaser, who must attach it to Copy 3 and the statement. However, if the registrant no longer can use triplicate forms, then the registrant shall proceed by issuing a new single-sheet form in accordance with § 1305.16.

(2) Whenever any used or unused triplicate DEA Forms 222 are stolen or lost (other than in the course of transmission) by any purchaser or supplier, the purchaser or supplier must immediately upon discovery of the theft or loss, report the theft or loss to the Special Agent in Charge of the Drug Enforcement Administration in the Divisional Office responsible for the area in which the registrant is located, stating the serial number of each form stolen or lost.

(3) If the theft or loss includes any original triplicate DEA Forms 222 received from purchasers and the supplier is unable to state the serial numbers of the triplicate DEA Forms 222, the supplier must report the date or approximate date of receipt and the names and addresses of the purchasers.

(4) If an entire book of triplicate DEA Forms 222 is lost or stolen, and the purchaser is unable to state the serial numbers of the triplicate DEA Forms 222 in the book, the purchaser must report, in lieu of the numbers of the forms contained in the book, the date or approximate date of issuance.

(5) If any unused triplicate DEA Form 222 reported stolen or lost is subsequently recovered or found, the Special Agent in Charge of the Drug Enforcement Administration in the Divisional Office responsible for the area in which the registrant is located must immediately be notified.

(g) *Preservation of triplicate DEA Forms 222.* (1) The purchaser must retain Copy 3 of each executed triplicate DEA Form 222 and all copies of unaccepted or defective forms with each statement attached.

(2) The supplier must retain Copy 1 of each triplicate DEA Form 222 that it has filled.

(3) Triplicate DEA Forms 222 must be maintained separately from all other records of the registrant. Triplicate DEA Forms 222 are required to be kept available for inspection for a period of two years. If a purchaser has several registered locations, the purchaser must retain Copy 3 of the executed triplicate DEA Form 222 and any attached statements or other related documents (not including unexecuted triplicate DEA Forms 222, which may be kept elsewhere under paragraph (b)(5) of this section), at the registered location printed on the triplicate DEA Form 222.

(4) The supplier of thiafentanil, carfentanil, etorphine hydrochloride, and diprenorphine must maintain triplicate DEA Forms 222 for these substances separately from all other DEA triplicate Forms 222 and records required to be maintained by the registrant.

(h) *Return of unused triplicate DEA Forms 222.* If the registration of any purchaser terminates (because the purchaser dies, ceases legal existence, discontinues business or professional practice, or changes the name or address as shown on the purchaser's registration) or is suspended or revoked under § 1301.36 of this chapter for all schedule I and II controlled substances for which the purchaser is registered, the purchaser must return all unused triplicate DEA Forms 222 to the Registration Section.

(i) *Cancellation and voiding of triplicate DEA Forms 222.* (1) A purchaser may cancel part or all of an order on a triplicate DEA Form 222 by notifying the supplier in writing of the cancellation. The supplier must indicate the cancellation on Copies 1 and 2 of the triplicate DEA Form 222 by drawing a line through the canceled items and printing "canceled" in the space provided for the number of items shipped.

(2) A supplier may void part or all of an order on a triplicate DEA Form 222 by notifying the purchaser in writing of the voiding. The supplier must indicate the voiding in the manner prescribed for cancellation in paragraph (i)(1) of this section.

[84 FR 51375, Sept. 30, 2019]

Subpart C—Electronic Orders

§ 1305.21 Requirements for electronic orders.

(a) To be valid, the purchaser must sign an electronic order for a Schedule I or II controlled substance with a digital signature issued to the purchaser, or the purchaser's agent, by DEA as provided in part 1311 of this chapter.

(b) The following data fields must be included on an electronic order for Schedule I and II controlled substances:

(1) A unique number the purchaser assigns to track the order. The number must be in the following 9-character format: the last two digits of the year, X, and six characters as selected by the purchaser.

(2) The purchaser's DEA registration number.

(3) The name of the supplier.

(4) The complete address of the supplier (may be completed by either the purchaser or the supplier).

(5) The supplier's DEA registration number (may be completed by either the purchaser or the supplier).

(6) The date the order is signed.

(7) The name (including strength where appropriate) of the controlled substance product or the National Drug Code (NDC) number (the NDC number may be completed by either the purchaser or the supplier).

(8) The quantity in a single package or container.

(9) The number of packages or containers of each item ordered.

(c) An electronic order may include controlled substances that are not in schedules I and II and non-controlled substances.

§ 1305.22 Procedure for filling electronic orders.

(a) A purchaser must submit the order to a specific supplier. The supplier may initially process the order (e.g., entry of the order into the computer system, billing functions, inventory identification, etc.) centrally at any location, regardless of the location's registration with DEA. Following centralized processing, the supplier may distribute the order to one or more registered locations maintained by the supplier for filling. The registrant must maintain control of the processing of the order at all times.

(b) A supplier may fill the order for a Schedule I or II controlled substance, if possible and if the supplier desires to do so and is authorized to do so under § 1305.06.

(c) A supplier must do the following before filling the order:

(1) Verify the integrity of the signature and the order by using software that complies with Part 1311 of this chapter to validate the order.

(2) Verify that the digital certificate has not expired.

(3) Check the validity of the certificate holder's certificate by checking the Certificate Revocation List. The supplier may cache the Certificate Revocation List until it expires.

(4) Verify the registrant's eligibility to order the controlled substances by checking the certificate extension data.

(d) The supplier must retain an electronic record of every order, and, linked to each order, a record of the number of commercial or bulk containers furnished on each item and the date on which the supplier shipped the containers to the purchaser. The linked record must also include any data on the original order that the supplier completes. Software used to handle digitally signed orders must comply with part 1311 of this chapter.

(e) If an order cannot be filled in its entirety, a supplier may fill it in part and supply the balance by additional shipments within 60 days following the date of the order. No order is valid more than 60 days after its execution by the purchaser, except as specified in paragraph (h) of this section.

(f) A supplier must ship the controlled substances to the registered location associated with the digital certificate used to sign the order, except as specified in paragraph (h) of this section.

(g) When a purchaser receives a shipment, the purchaser must create a record of the quantity of each item received and the date received. The record must be electronically linked to the original order and archived.

(h) Registered procurement officers of the Defense Supply Center of the Defense Logistics Agency may order controlled substances for delivery to armed services establishments within the United States. These orders may be shipped to locations other than the registered location, and in partial shipments at different times not to exceed six months from the date of the order, as designated by the procurement officer when submitting the order.

§ 1305.23 Endorsing electronic orders.

A supplier may not endorse an electronic order to another supplier to fill.

§ 1305.24 Central processing of orders.

(a) A supplier that has one or more registered locations and maintains a central processing computer system in which orders are stored may have one or more of the supplier's registered locations fill an electronic order if the supplier does the following:

(1) Assigns each item on the order to a specific registered location for filling.

(2) Creates a record linked to the central file noting both which items a location filled and the location identity.

(3) Ensures that no item is filled by more than one location.

(4) Maintains the original order with all linked records on the central computer system.

(b) A company that has central processing of orders must assign responsibility for filling parts of orders only to registered locations that the company owns and operates.

§ 1305.25 Unaccepted and defective electronic orders.

(a) No electronic order may be filled if:

(1) The required data fields have not been completed.

(2) The order is not signed using a digital certificate issued by DEA.

(3) The digital certificate used had expired or had been revoked prior to signature.

(4) The purchaser's public key will not validate the digital signature.

(5) The validation of the order shows that the order is invalid for any reason.

(b) If an order cannot be filled for any reason under this section, the supplier must notify the purchaser and provide a statement as to the reason (e.g., improperly prepared or altered). A supplier may, for any reason, refuse to accept any order, and if a supplier refuses to accept the order, a statement that the order is not accepted is sufficient for purposes of this paragraph.

(c) When a purchaser receives an unaccepted electronic order from the supplier, the purchaser must electronically link the statement of nonacceptance to the original order. The original order and the statement must be retained in accordance with § 1305.27.

(d) Neither a purchaser nor a supplier may correct a defective order; the purchaser must issue a new order for the order to be filled.

§ 1305.26 Lost electronic orders.

(a) If a purchaser determines that an unfilled electronic order has been lost before or after receipt, the purchaser must provide, to the supplier, a signed statement containing the unique tracking number and date of the lost order and stating that the goods covered by the first order were not received through loss of that order.

(b) If the purchaser executes an order to replace the lost order, the purchaser must electronically link an electronic record of the second order and a copy of the statement with the record of the first order and retain them.

(c) If the supplier to whom the order was directed subsequently receives the first order, the supplier must indicate that it is "Not Accepted" and return it to the purchaser. The purchaser must link the returned order to the record of that order and the statement.

§ 1305.27 Preservation of electronic orders.

(a) A purchaser must, for each order filled, retain the original signed order and all linked records for that order for two years. The purchaser must also retain all copies of each unaccepted or defective order and each linked statement.

(b) A supplier must retain each original order filled and the linked records for two years.

(c) If electronic order records are maintained on a central server, the records must be readily retrievable at the registered location.

§ 1305.28 Canceling and voiding electronic orders.

(a) A supplier may void all or part of an electronic order by notifying the purchaser of the voiding. If the entire order is voided, the supplier must make an electronic copy of the order, indicate on the copy "Void," and return it to the purchaser. The supplier is not required to retain a record of orders that are not filled.

(b) The purchaser must retain an electronic copy of the voided order.

(c) To partially void an order, the supplier must indicate in the linked record that nothing was shipped for each item voided.

§ 1305.29 Reporting to DEA.

A supplier must, for each electronic order filled, forward either a copy of the electronic order or an electronic report of the order in a format that DEA specifies to DEA within two business days.

PART 1306—PRESCRIPTIONS

GENERAL INFORMATION

AUTHORITY: 21 U.S.C. 821, 829, 831, 871(b), unless otherwise noted.

SOURCE: 36 FR 7799, Apr. 24, 1971; 36 FR 13386, July 21, 1971, unless otherwise noted. Redesignated at 38 FR 26609, Sept. 24, 1973.

GENERAL INFORMATION

§ 1306.01 Scope of part 1306.

Rules governing the issuance, filling and filing of prescriptions pursuant to section 309 of the Act (21 U.S.C. 829) are set forth generally in that section and specifically by the sections of this part.

§ 1306.02 Definitions.

Any term contained in this part shall have the definition set forth in section 102 of the Act (21 U.S.C. 802) or part 1300 of this chapter.

[62 FR 13964, Mar. 24, 1997]

§ 1306.03 Persons entitled to issue prescriptions.

(a) A prescription for a controlled substance may be issued only by an individual practitioner who is:

(1) Authorized to prescribe controlled substances by the jurisdiction in which he is licensed to practice his profession and

(2) Either registered or exempted from registration pursuant to §§ 1301.22(c) and 1301.23 of this chapter.

(b) A prescription issued by an individual practitioner may be communicated to a pharmacist by an employee or agent of the individual practitioner.

[36 FR 7799, Apr. 24, 1971, as amended at 36 FR 18732, Sept. 21, 1971. Redesignated at 38 FR 26609, Sept. 24, 1973, as amended at 62 FR 13966, Mar. 24, 1997]

§ 1306.04 Purpose of issue of prescription.

(a) A prescription for a controlled substance to be effective must be issued for a legitimate medical purpose by an individual practitioner acting in the usual course of his professional practice. The responsibility for the proper prescribing and dispensing of controlled substances is upon the prescribing practitioner, but a corresponding responsibility rests with the pharmacist who fills the prescription. An order purporting to be a prescription issued not in the usual course of professional treatment or in legitimate and authorized research is not a prescription within the meaning and intent of section 309 of the Act (21 U.S.C. 829) and the person knowingly filling such a purported prescription, as well as the person issuing it, shall be subject to the penalties provided for violations of the provisions of law relating to controlled substances.

(b) A prescription may not be issued in order for an individual practitioner to obtain controlled substances for supplying the individual practitioner for the purpose of general dispensing to patients.

(c) A prescription may not be issued for "detoxification treatment" or "maintenance treatment," unless the prescription is for a Schedule III, IV, or V narcotic drug approved by the Food and Drug Administration specifically for use in maintenance or detoxification treatment and the practitioner is in compliance with requirements in § 1301.28 of this chapter.

[36 FR 7799, Apr. 24, 1971. Redesignated at 38 FR 26609, Sept. 24, 1973, and amended at 39 FR 37986, Oct. 25, 1974; 70 FR 36343, June 23, 2005]

§ 1306.05 Manner of issuance of prescriptions.

(a) All prescriptions for controlled substances shall be dated as of, and signed on, the day when issued and shall bear the full name and address of the patient, the drug name, strength, dosage form, quantity prescribed, directions for use, and the name, address and registration number of the practitioner.

(b) A prescription for a Schedule III, IV, or V narcotic drug approved by FDA specifically for "detoxification treatment" or "maintenance treatment" must include the identification number issued by the Administrator under § 1301.28(d) of this chapter or a written notice stating that the practitioner is acting under the good faith exception of § 1301.28(e) of this chapter.

(c) Where a prescription is for gamma-hydroxybutyric acid, the practitioner shall note on the face of the prescription the medical need of the patient for the prescription.

(d) A practitioner may sign a paper prescription in the same manner as he would sign a check or legal document (e.g., J.H. Smith or John H. Smith). Where an oral order is not permitted, paper prescriptions shall be written with ink or indelible pencil, typewriter, or printed on a computer printer and shall be manually signed by the practitioner. A computer-generated prescription that is printed out or faxed by the practitioner must be manually signed.

(e) Electronic prescriptions shall be created and signed using an application that meets the requirements of part 1311 of this chapter.

(f) A prescription may be prepared by the secretary or agent for the signature of a practitioner, but the prescribing practitioner is responsible in case the prescription does not conform in all essential respects to the law and regulations. A corresponding liability rests upon the pharmacist, including a pharmacist employed by a central fill pharmacy, who fills a prescription not prepared in the form prescribed by DEA regulations.

(g) An individual practitioner exempted from registration under § 1301.22(c) of this chapter shall include on all prescriptions issued by him the registration number of the hospital or other institution and the special internal code number assigned to him by the hospital or other institution as provided in § 1301.22(c) of this chapter, in lieu of the registration number of the practitioner required by this section. Each paper prescription shall have the name of the practitioner stamped, typed, or handprinted on it, as well as the signature of the practitioner.

(h) An official exempted from registration under § 1301.23(a) of this chapter must include on all prescriptions issued by him his branch of service or agency (e.g., "U.S. Army" or "Public Health Service") and his service identification number, in lieu of the registration number of the practitioner required by this section. The service identification number for a Public Health Service employee is his Social Security identification number. Each paper prescription shall have the name of the officer stamped, typed, or handprinted on it, as well as the signature of the officer.

[75 FR 16307, Mar. 31, 2010]

§ 1306.06 Persons entitled to fill prescriptions.

A prescription for a controlled substance may only be filled by a pharmacist, acting in the usual course of his professional practice and either registered individually or employed in a registered pharmacy, a registered central fill pharmacy, or registered institutional practitioner.

[68 FR 37410, June 24, 2003, as amended at 70 FR 36343, June 23, 2005]

§ 1306.07 Administering or dispensing of narcotic drugs.

(a) A practitioner may administer or dispense directly (but not prescribe) a narcotic drug listed in any schedule to a narcotic dependant person for the purpose of maintenance or detoxification treatment if the practitioner meets both of the following conditions:

(1) The practitioner is separately registered with DEA as a narcotic treatment program.

(2) The practitioner is in compliance with DEA regulations regarding treatment qualifications, security, records, and unsupervised use of the drugs pursuant to the Act.

(b) Nothing in this section shall prohibit a physician who is not specifically registered to conduct a narcotic treatment program from administering (but not prescribing) narcotic drugs to a person for the purpose of relieving acute withdrawal symptoms when necessary while arrangements are being made for referral for treatment. Not more than one day's medication may be administered to the person or for the person's use at one time. Such emergency treatment may be carried out for not more than three days and may not be renewed or extended.

(c) This section is not intended to impose any limitations on a physician or authorized hospital staff to administer or dispense narcotic drugs in a hospital to maintain or detoxify a person as an incidental adjunct to medical or surgical treatment of conditions other than addiction, or to administer or dispense narcotic drugs to persons with intractable pain in which no relief or cure is possible or none has been found after reasonable efforts.

(d) A practitioner may administer or dispense (including prescribe) any Schedule III, IV, or V narcotic drug approved by the Food and Drug Administration specifically for use in maintenance or detoxification treatment to a narcotic dependent person if the practitioner complies with the requirements of § 1301.28 of this chapter.

[39 FR 37986, Oct. 25, 1974, as amended at 70 FR 36344, June 23, 2005]

§ 1306.08 Electronic prescriptions.

(a) An individual practitioner may sign and transmit electronic prescriptions for controlled substances provided the practitioner meets all of the following requirements:

(1) The practitioner must comply with all other requirements for issuing controlled substance prescriptions in this part;

(2) The practitioner must use an application that meets the requirements of part 1311 of this chapter; and

(3) The practitioner must comply with the requirements for practitioners in part 1311 of this chapter.

(b) A pharmacy may fill an electronically transmitted prescription for a controlled substance provided the pharmacy complies with all other requirements for filling controlled substance prescriptions in this part and with the requirements of part 1311 of this chapter.

(c) To annotate an electronic prescription, a pharmacist must include all of the information that this part requires in the prescription record.

(d) If the content of any of the information required under § 1306.05 for a controlled substance prescription is altered during the transmission, the prescription is deemed to be invalid and the pharmacy may not dispense the controlled substance.

[75 FR 16307, Mar. 31, 2010]

§ 1306.09 Prescription requirements for online pharmacies.

(a) No controlled substance that is a prescription drug may be delivered, distributed, or dispensed by means of the Internet without a valid prescription.

(b) In accordance with the Act, it is unlawful for any person to knowingly or intentionally fill a prescription for a controlled substance that was issued in a manner that constitutes dispensing by means of the Internet unless such person is a pharmacist who is acting in the usual course of his professional practice and is acting on behalf of a pharmacy whose registration has been modified under sections 1301.13 and 1301.19 of this chapter to authorize it to operate as an online pharmacy.

(c) Any online pharmacy that participates in the transfer between pharmacies of prescription information must do so in accordance with the requirements of §§ 1306.15 and 1306.25 of this part.

[74 FR 15624, Apr. 6, 2009]

Controlled Substances Listed in Schedule II

§ 1306.11 Requirement of prescription.

(a) A pharmacist may dispense directly a controlled substance listed in Schedule II that is a prescription drug as determined under section 503 of the Federal Food, Drug, and Cosmetic Act (21 U.S.C. 353(b)) only pursuant to a written prescription signed by the practitioner, except as provided in paragraph (d) of this section. A paper prescription for a Schedule II controlled substance may be transmitted by the practitioner or the practitioner's agent to a pharmacy via facsimile equipment, provided that the original manually signed prescription is presented to the pharmacist for review prior to the actual dispensing of the controlled substance, except as noted in paragraph (e), (f), or (g) of this section. The original prescription shall be maintained in accordance with § 1304.04(h) of this chapter.

(b) An individual practitioner may administer or dispense directly a controlled substance listed in Schedule II in the course of his professional practice without a prescription, subject to § 1306.07.

(c) An institutional practitioner may administer or dispense directly (but not prescribe) a controlled substance listed in Schedule II only pursuant to a written prescription signed by the prescribing individual practitioner or to an order for medication made by an individual practitioner that is dispensed for immediate administration to the ultimate user.

(d) In the case of an emergency situation, as defined by the Secretary in § 290.10 of this title, a pharmacist may dispense a controlled substance listed in Schedule II upon receiving oral authorization of a prescribing individual practitioner, provided that:

(1) The quantity prescribed and dispensed is limited to the amount adequate to treat the patient during the emergency period (dispensing beyond the emergency period must be pursuant to a paper or electronic prescription signed by the prescribing individual practitioner);

(2) The prescription shall be immediately reduced to writing by the pharmacist and shall contain all information required in § 1306.05, except for the signature of the prescribing individual practitioner;

(3) If the prescribing individual practitioner is not known to the pharmacist, he must make a reasonable effort to determine that the oral authorization came from a registered individual practitioner, which may include a callback to the prescribing individual practitioner using his phone number as listed in the telephone directory and/or other good faith efforts to insure his identity; and

(4) Within 7 days after authorizing an emergency oral prescription, the prescribing individual practitioner shall cause a written prescription for the emergency quantity prescribed to be delivered to the dispensing pharmacist. In addition to conforming to the requirements of § 1306.05, the prescription shall have written on its face "Authorization for Emergency Dispensing," and the date of the oral order. The paper prescription may be delivered to the pharmacist in person or by mail, but if delivered by mail it must be postmarked within the 7-day period. Upon receipt, the dispensing pharmacist must attach this paper prescription to the oral emergency prescription that had earlier been reduced to writing. For electronic prescriptions, the pharmacist must annotate the record of the electronic prescription with the original authorization and date of the oral order. The pharmacist must notify the nearest office of the Administration if the prescribing individual practitioner fails to deliver a written prescription to him; failure of the pharmacist to do so shall void the authority conferred by this paragraph to dispense without a written prescription of a prescribing individual practitioner.

(5) Central fill pharmacies shall not be authorized under this paragraph to prepare prescriptions for a controlled substance listed in Schedule II upon receiving an oral authorization from a retail pharmacist or an individual practitioner.

(e) A prescription prepared in accordance with § 1306.05 written for a Schedule II narcotic substance to be compounded for the direct administration to a patient by parenteral, intravenous, intramuscular, subcutaneous or intraspinal infusion may be transmitted by the practitioner or the practitioner's agent to the pharmacy by facsimile. The facsimile serves as the original written prescription for purposes of this paragraph (e) and it shall be maintained in accordance with § 1304.04(h) of this chapter.

(f) A prescription prepared in accordance with § 1306.05 written for Schedule II substance for a resident of a Long Term Care Facility may be transmitted by the practitioner or the practitioner's agent to the dispensing pharmacy by facsimile. The facsimile serves as the original written prescription for purposes of this paragraph (f) and it shall be maintained in accordance with § 1304.04(h).

(g) A prescription prepared in accordance with § 1306.05 written for a Schedule II narcotic substance for a patient enrolled in a hospice care program certified and/or paid for by Medicare under Title XVIII or a hospice program which is licensed by the state may be transmitted by the practitioner or the practitioner's agent to the dispensing pharmacy by facsimile. The practitioner or the practitioner's agent will note on the prescription that the patient is a hospice patient. The facsimile serves as the original written prescription for purposes of this paragraph (g) and it shall be maintained in accordance with § 1304.04(h).

[36 FR 7799, Apr. 24, 1971, as amended at 36 FR 18733, Sept. 21, 1971. Redesignated at 38 FR 26609, Sept. 24, 1973 and amended at 53 FR 4964, Feb. 19, 1988; 59 FR 26111, May 19, 1994; 59 FR 30832, June 15, 1994; 62 FR 13964, Mar. 24, 1997; 65 FR 45713, July 25, 2000; 68 FR 37410, June 24, 2003; 75 FR 16307, Mar. 31, 2010]

§ 1306.12 Refilling prescriptions; issuance of multiple prescriptions.

(a) The refilling of a prescription for a controlled substance listed in Schedule II is prohibited.

(b)(1) An individual practitioner may issue multiple prescriptions authorizing the patient to receive a total of up to a 90-day supply of a Schedule II controlled substance provided the following conditions are met:

(i) Each separate prescription is issued for a legitimate medical purpose by an individual practitioner acting in the usual course of professional practice;

(ii) The individual practitioner provides written instructions on each prescription (other than the first prescription, if the prescribing practitioner intends for that prescription to be filled immediately) indicating the earliest date on which a pharmacy may fill each prescription;

(iii) The individual practitioner concludes that providing the patient with multiple prescriptions in this manner does not create an undue risk of diversion or abuse;

(iv) The issuance of multiple prescriptions as described in this section is permissible under the applicable state laws; and

(v) The individual practitioner complies fully with all other applicable requirements under the Act and these regulations as well as any additional requirements under state law.

(2) Nothing in this paragraph (b) shall be construed as mandating or encouraging individual practitioners to issue multiple prescriptions or to see their patients only once every 90 days when prescribing Schedule II controlled substances. Rather, individual practitioners must determine on their own, based on sound medical judgment, and in accordance with established medical standards, whether it is appropriate to issue multiple prescriptions and how often to see their patients when doing so.

[72 FR 64929, Nov. 19, 2007]

§ 1306.13 Partial filling of prescriptions.

(a) The partial filling of a prescription for a controlled substance listed in Schedule II is permissible if the pharmacist is unable to supply the full quantity called for in a written or emergency oral prescription and he makes a notation of the quantity supplied on the face of the written prescription, written record of the emergency oral prescription, or in the electronic prescription record. The remaining portion of the prescription may be filled within 72 hours of the first partial filling; however, if the remaining portion is not or cannot be filled within the 72-hour period, the pharmacist shall notify the prescribing individual practitioner. No further quantity may be supplied beyond 72 hours without a new prescription.

(b) A prescription for a Schedule II controlled substance written for a patient in a Long Term Care Facility (LTCF) or for a patient with a medical diagnosis documenting a terminal illness may be filled in partial quantities to include individual dosage units. If there is any question whether a patient may be classified as having a terminal illness, the pharmacist must contact the practitioner prior to partially filling the prescription. Both the pharmacist and the prescribing practitioner have a corresponding responsibility to assure that the controlled substance is for a terminally ill patient. The pharmacist must record on the prescription whether the patient is "terminally ill" or an "LTCF patient." A prescription that is partially filled and does not contain the notation "terminally ill" or "LTCF patient" shall be deemed to have been filled in violation of the Act. For each partial filling, the dispensing pharmacist shall record on the back of the prescription (or on another appropriate record, uniformly maintained, and readily retrievable) the date of the partial filling, quantity dispensed, remaining quantity authorized to be dispensed, and the identification of the dispensing pharmacist. The total quantity of Schedule II controlled substances dispensed in all partial fillings must not exceed the total quantity prescribed. Schedule II prescriptions for patients in a LTCF or patients with a medical diagnosis documenting a terminal illness shall be valid for a period not to exceed 60 days from the issue date unless sooner terminated by the discontinuance of medication.

(c) Information pertaining to current Schedule II prescriptions for patients in a LTCF or for patients with a medical diagnosis documenting a terminal illness may be maintained in a computerized system if this system has the capability to permit:

(1) Output (display or printout) of the original prescription number, date of issue, identification of prescribing individual practitioner, identification of patient, address of the LTCF or address of the hospital or residence of the patient, identification of medication authorized (to include dosage, form, strength and quantity), listing of the partial fillings that have been dispensed under each prescription and the information required in § 1306.13(b).

(2) Immediate (real time) updating of the prescription record each time a partial filling of the prescription is conducted.

(3) Retrieval of partially filled Schedule II prescription information is the same as required by § 1306.22(b) (4) and (5) for Schedule III and IV prescription refill information.

(Authority: 21 U.S.C. 801, *et seq.*)

[36 FR 7799, Apr. 24, 1971. Redesignated at 38 FR 26609, Sept. 24, 1973, and amended at 45 FR 54330, July 15, 1980; 56 FR 25027, June 3, 1991; 62 FR 13965, Mar. 24, 1997; 75 FR 16308, Mar. 31, 2010]

§ 1306.14 Labeling of substances and filling of prescriptions.

(a) The pharmacist filling a written or emergency oral prescription for a controlled substance listed in Schedule II shall affix to the package a label showing date of filling, the pharmacy name and address, the serial number of the prescription, the name of the patient, the name of the prescribing practitioner, and directions for use and cautionary statements, if any, contained in such prescription or required by law.

(b) If the prescription is filled at a central fill pharmacy, the central fill pharmacy shall affix to the package a label showing the retail pharmacy name and address and a unique identifier, (*i.e.* the central fill pharmacy's DEA registration number) indicating that the prescription was filled at the central fill pharmacy, in addition to the information required under paragraph (a) of this section.

(c) The requirements of paragraph (a) of this section do not apply when a controlled substance listed in Schedule II is prescribed for administration to an ultimate user who is institutionalized: *Provided*, That:

(1) Not more than 7-day supply of the controlled substance listed in Schedule II is dispensed at one time;

(2) The controlled substance listed in Schedule II is not in the possession of the ultimate user prior to the administration;

(3) The institution maintains appropriate safeguards and records regarding the proper administration, control, dispensing, and storage of the controlled substance listed in Schedule II; and

(4) The system employed by the pharmacist in filling a prescription is adequate to identify the supplier, the product, and the patient, and to set forth the directions for use and cautionary statements, if any, contained in the prescription or required by law.

(d) All written prescriptions and written records of emergency oral prescriptions shall be kept in accordance with requirements of § 1304.04(h) of this chapter.

(e) Where a prescription that has been prepared in accordance with section 1306.12(b) contains instructions from the prescribing practitioner indicating that the prescription shall not be filled until a certain date, no pharmacist may fill the prescription before that date.

[36 FR 13368, July 21, 1971, as amended at 37 FR 15921, Aug. 8, 1972. Redesignated at 38 FR 26609, Sept. 24, 1973, as amended at 62 FR 13965, Mar. 24, 1997; 68 FR 37410, June 24, 2003; 72 FR 64930, Nov. 19, 2007]

§ 1306.15 Provision of prescription information between retail pharmacies and central fill pharmacies for prescriptions of Schedule II controlled substances.

Prescription information may be provided to an authorized central fill pharmacy by a retail pharmacy for dispensing purposes. The following requirements shall also apply:

(a) Prescriptions for controlled substances listed in Schedule II may be transmitted electronically from a retail pharmacy to a central fill pharmacy including via facsimile. The retail pharmacy transmitting the prescription information must:

(1) Write the words "CENTRAL FILL" on the face of the original paper prescription and record the name, address, and DEA registration number of the central fill pharmacy to which the prescription has been transmitted, the name of the retail pharmacy pharmacist transmitting the prescription, and the date of transmittal. For electronic prescriptions the name, address, and DEA registration number of the central fill pharmacy to which the prescription has been transmitted, the name of the retail pharmacy pharmacist transmitting the prescription, and the date of transmittal must be added to the electronic prescription record.

(2) Ensure that all information required to be on a prescription pursuant to Section 1306.05 of this part is transmitted to the central fill pharmacy (either on the face of the prescription or in the electronic transmission of information);

(3) Maintain the original prescription for a period of two years from the date the prescription was filled;

(4) Keep a record of receipt of the filled prescription, including the date of receipt, the method of delivery (private, common or contract carrier) and the name of the retail pharmacy employee accepting delivery.

(b) The central fill pharmacy receiving the transmitted prescription must:

(1) Keep a copy of the prescription (if sent via facsimile) or an electronic record of all the information transmitted by the retail pharmacy, including the name, address, and DEA registration number of the retail pharmacy transmitting the prescription;

(2) Keep a record of the date of receipt of the transmitted prescription, the name of the pharmacist filling the prescription, and the date of filling of the prescription;

(3) Keep a record of the date the filled prescription was delivered to the retail pharmacy and the method of delivery (*i.e.* private, common or contract carrier).

[68 FR 37410, June 24, 2003, as amended at 75 FR 16308, Mar. 31, 2010]

CONTROLLED SUBSTANCES LISTED IN SCHEDULES III, IV, AND V

§ 1306.21 Requirement of prescription.

(a) A pharmacist may dispense directly a controlled substance listed in Schedule III, IV, or V that is a prescription drug as determined under section 503(b) of the Federal Food, Drug, and Cosmetic Act (21 U.S.C. 353(b)) only pursuant to either a paper prescription signed by a practitioner, a facsimile of a signed paper prescription transmitted by the practitioner or the practitioner's agent to the pharmacy, an electronic prescription that meets the requirements of this part and part 1311 of this chapter, or an oral prescription made by an individual practitioner and promptly reduced to writing by the pharmacist containing all information required in §1306.05, except for the signature of the practitioner.

(b) An individual practitioner may administer or dispense directly a controlled substance listed in Schedule III, IV, or V in the course of his/her professional practice without a prescription, subject to §1306.07.

(c) An institutional practitioner may administer or dispense directly (but not prescribe) a controlled substance listed in Schedule III, IV, or V only pursuant to a paper prescription signed by an individual practitioner, a facsimile of a paper prescription or order for medication transmitted by the practitioner or the practitioner's agent to the institutional practitioner-pharmacist, an electronic prescription that meets the requirements of this part and part 1311 of this chapter, or an oral prescription made by an individual practitioner and promptly reduced to writing by the pharmacist (containing all information required in §1306.05 except for the signature of the individual practitioner), or pursuant to an order for medication made by an individual practitioner that is dispensed for immediate administration to the ultimate user, subject to §1306.07.

[62 FR 13965, Mar. 24, 1997, as amended at 75 FR 16308, Mar. 31, 2010]

§ 1306.22 Refilling of prescriptions.

(a) No prescription for a controlled substance listed in Schedule III or IV shall be filled or refilled more than six months after the date on which such prescription was issued. No prescription for a controlled substance listed in Schedule III or IV authorized to be refilled may be refilled more than five times.

(b) Each refilling of a prescription shall be entered on the back of the prescription or on another appropriate document or electronic prescription record. If entered on another document, such as a medication record, or electronic prescription record, the document or record must be uniformly maintained and readily retrievable.

(c) The following information must be retrievable by the prescription number:

(1) The name and dosage form of the controlled substance.

(2) The date filled or refilled.

(3) The quantity dispensed.

(4) The initials of the dispensing pharmacist for each refill.

(5) The total number of refills for that prescription.

(d) If the pharmacist merely initials and dates the back of the prescription or annotates the electronic prescription record, it shall be deemed that the full face amount of the prescription has been dispensed.

(e) The prescribing practitioner may authorize additional refills of Schedule III or IV controlled substances on the original prescription through an oral refill authorization transmitted to the pharmacist provided the following conditions are met:

(1) The total quantity authorized, including the amount of the original prescription, does not exceed five refills nor extend beyond six months from the date of issue of the original prescription.

(2) The pharmacist obtaining the oral authorization records on the reverse of the original paper prescription or annotates the electronic prescription record with the date, quantity of refill, number of additional refills authorized, and initials the paper prescription or annotates the electronic prescription record showing who received the authorization from the prescribing practitioner who issued the original prescription.

(3) The quantity of each additional refill authorized is equal to or less than the quantity authorized for the initial filling of the original prescription.

(4) The prescribing practitioner must execute a new and separate prescription for any additional quantities beyond the five-refill, six-month limitation.

(f) As an alternative to the procedures provided by paragraphs (a) through (e) of this section, a computer application may be used for the storage and retrieval of refill information for original paper prescription orders for controlled substances in Schedule III and IV, subject to the following conditions:

(1) Any such proposed computerized application must provide online retrieval (via computer monitor or hard-copy printout) of original prescription order information for those prescription orders that are currently authorized for refilling. This shall include, but is not limited to, data such as the original prescription number; date of issuance of the original prescription order by the practitioner; full name and address of the patient; name, address, and DEA registration number of the practitioner; and the name, strength, dosage form, quantity of the controlled substance prescribed (and quantity dispensed if different from the quantity prescribed), and the total number of refills authorized by the prescribing practitioner.

(2) Any such proposed computerized application must also provide online retrieval (via computer monitor or hard-copy printout) of the current refill history for Schedule III or IV controlled substance prescription orders (those authorized for refill during the past six months). This refill history shall include, but is not limited to, the name of the controlled substance, the date of refill, the quantity dispensed, the identification code, or name or initials of the dispensing pharmacist for each refill and the total number of refills dispensed to date for that prescription order.

(3) Documentation of the fact that the refill information entered into the

computer each time a pharmacist refills an original paper, fax, or oral prescription order for a Schedule III or IV controlled substance is correct must be provided by the individual pharmacist who makes use of such an application. If such an application provides a hard-copy printout of each day's controlled substance prescription order refill data, that printout shall be verified, dated, and signed by the individual pharmacist who refilled such a prescription order. The individual pharmacist must verify that the data indicated are correct and then sign this document in the same manner as he would sign a check or legal document (e.g., J.H. Smith, or John H. Smith). This document shall be maintained in a separate file at that pharmacy for a period of two years from the dispensing date. This printout of the day's controlled substance prescription order refill data must be provided to each pharmacy using such a computerized application within 72 hours of the date on which the refill was dispensed. It must be verified and signed by each pharmacist who is involved with such dispensing. In lieu of such a printout, the pharmacy shall maintain a bound log book, or separate file, in which each individual pharmacist involved in such dispensing shall sign a statement (in the manner previously described) each day, attesting to the fact that the refill information entered into the computer that day has been reviewed by him and is correct as shown. Such a book or file must be maintained at the pharmacy employing such an application for a period of two years after the date of dispensing the appropriately authorized refill.

(4) Any such computerized application shall have the capability of producing a printout of any refill data that the user pharmacy is responsible for maintaining under the Act and its implementing regulations. For example, this would include a refill-by-refill audit trail for any specified strength and dosage form of any controlled substance (by either brand or generic name or both). Such a printout must include name of the prescribing practitioner, name and address of the patient, quantity dispensed on each refill, date of dispensing for each refill, name or identification code of the dispensing pharmacist, and the number of the original prescription order. In any computerized application employed by a user pharmacy the central recordkeeping location must be capable of sending the printout to the pharmacy within 48 hours, and if a DEA Special Agent or Diversion Investigator requests a copy of such printout from the user pharmacy, it must, if requested to do so by the Agent or Investigator, verify the printout transmittal capability of its application by documentation (e.g., postmark).

(5) In the event that a pharmacy which employs such a computerized application experiences system downtime, the pharmacy must have an auxiliary procedure which will be used for documentation of refills of Schedule III and IV controlled substance prescription orders. This auxiliary procedure must ensure that refills are authorized by the original prescription order, that the maximum number of refills has not been exceeded, and that all of the appropriate data are retained for online data entry as soon as the computer system is available for use again.

(g) When filing refill information for original paper, fax, or oral prescription orders for Schedule III or IV controlled substances, a pharmacy may use only one of the two applications described in paragraphs (a) through (e) or (f) of this section.

(h) When filing refill information for electronic prescriptions, a pharmacy must use an application that meets the requirements of part 1311 of this chapter.

[75 FR 16308, Mar. 31, 2010]

§ 1306.23 Partial filling of prescriptions.

The partial filling of a prescription for a controlled substance listed in Schedule III, IV, or V is permissible, provided that:

(a) Each partial filling is recorded in the same manner as a refilling,

(b) The total quantity dispensed in all partial fillings does not exceed the total quantity prescribed, and

(c) No dispensing occurs after 6 months after the date on which the prescription was issued.

[36 FR 18733, Sept. 21, 1971. Redesignated at 38 FR 26609, Sept. 24, 1973, and amended at 51 FR 5320, Feb. 13, 1986; 62 FR 13965, Mar. 24, 1997]

§ 1306.24 Labeling of substances and filling of prescriptions.

(a) The pharmacist filling a prescription for a controlled substance listed in Schedule III, IV, or V shall affix to the package a label showing the pharmacy name and address, the serial number and date of initial filling, the name of the patient, the name of the practitioner issuing the prescription, and directions for use and cautionary statements, if any, contained in such prescription as required by law.

(b) If the prescription is filled at a central fill pharmacy, the central fill pharmacy shall affix to the package a label showing the retail pharmacy name and address and a unique identifier, (*i.e.* the central fill pharmacy's DEA registration number) indicating that the prescription was filled at the central fill pharmacy, in addition to the information required under paragraph (a) of this section.

(c) The requirements of paragraph (a) of this section do not apply when a controlled substance listed in Schedule III, IV, or V is prescribed for administration to an ultimate user who is institutionalized: Provided, That:

(1) Not more than a 34-day supply or 100 dosage units, whichever is less, of the controlled substance listed in Schedule III, IV, or V is dispensed at one time;

(2) The controlled substance listed in Schedule III, IV, or V is not in the possession of the ultimate user prior to administration;

(3) The institution maintains appropriate safeguards and records the proper administration, control, dispensing, and storage of the controlled substance listed in Schedule III, IV, or V; and

(4) The system employed by the pharmacist in filling a prescription is adequate to identify the supplier, the product and the patient, and to set forth the directions for use and cautionary statements, if any, contained in the prescription or required by law.

(d) All prescriptions for controlled substances listed in Schedules III, IV, and V shall be kept in accordance with § 1304.04(h) of this chapter.

[62 FR 13965, Mar. 24, 1997, as amended at 68 FR 37411, June 24, 2003]

§ 1306.25 Transfer between pharmacies of prescription information for Schedules III, IV, and V controlled substances for refill purposes.

(a) The transfer of original prescription information for a controlled substance listed in Schedule III, IV, or V for the purpose of refill dispensing is permissible between pharmacies on a one-time basis only. However, pharmacies electronically sharing a real-time, online database may transfer up to the maximum refills permitted by law and the prescriber's authorization.

(b) Transfers are subject to the following requirements:

(1) The transfer must be communicated directly between two licensed pharmacists.

(2) The transferring pharmacist must do the following:

(i) Write the word "VOID" on the face of the invalidated prescription; for electronic prescriptions, information that the prescription has been transferred must be added to the prescription record.

(ii) Record on the reverse of the invalidated prescription the name, address, and DEA registration number of the pharmacy to which it was transferred and the name of the pharmacist receiving the prescription information; for electronic prescriptions, such information must be added to the prescription record.

(iii) Record the date of the transfer and the name of the pharmacist transferring the information.

(3) For paper prescriptions and prescriptions received orally and reduced to writing by the pharmacist pursuant to § 1306.21(a), the pharmacist receiving the transferred prescription information must write the word "transfer" on the face of the transferred prescription and reduce to writing all information required to be on a prescription pursuant to § 1306.05 and include:

(i) Date of issuance of original prescription.

(ii) Original number of refills authorized on original prescription.

(iii) Date of original dispensing.

(iv) Number of valid refills remaining and date(s) and locations of previous refill(s).

(v) Pharmacy's name, address, DEA registration number, and prescription number from which the prescription information was transferred.

(vi) Name of pharmacist who transferred the prescription.

(vii) Pharmacy's name, address, DEA registration number, and prescription number from which the prescription was originally filled.

(4) For electronic prescriptions being transferred electronically, the transferring pharmacist must provide the receiving pharmacist with the following information in addition to the original electronic prescription data:

(i) The date of the original dispensing.

(ii) The number of refills remaining and the date(s) and locations of previous refills.

(iii) The transferring pharmacy's name, address, DEA registration number, and prescription number for each dispensing.

(iv) The name of the pharmacist transferring the prescription.

(v) The name, address, DEA registration number, and prescription number from the pharmacy that originally filled the prescription, if different.

(5) The pharmacist receiving a transferred electronic prescription must create an electronic record for the prescription that includes the receiving pharmacist's name and all of the information transferred with the prescription under paragraph (b)(4) of this section.

(c) The original and transferred prescription(s) must be maintained for a period of two years from the date of last refill.

(d) Pharmacies electronically accessing the same prescription record must satisfy all information requirements of a manual mode for prescription transferal.

(e) The procedure allowing the transfer of prescription information for refill purposes is permissible only if allowable under existing State or other applicable law.

[75 FR 16309, Mar. 31, 2010]

§ 1306.26 Dispensing without prescription.

A controlled substance listed in Schedules II, III, IV, or V which is not a prescription drug as determined under the Federal Food, Drug, and Cosmetic Act, may be dispensed by a pharmacist without a prescription to a purchaser at retail, provided that:

(a) Such dispensing is made only by a pharmacist (as defined in part 1300 of this chapter), and not by a nonpharmacist employee even if under the supervision of a pharmacist (although after the pharmacist has fulfilled his professional and legal responsibilities set forth in this section, the actual cash, credit transaction, or delivery, may be completed by a nonpharmacist);

(b) Not more than 240 cc. (8 ounces) of any such controlled substance containing opium, nor more than 120 cc. (4 ounces) of any other such controlled substance nor more than 48 dosage units of any such controlled substance containing opium, nor more than 24 dosage units of any other such controlled substance may be dispensed at retail to the same purchaser in any given 48-hour period;

(c) The purchaser is at least 18 years of age;

(d) The pharmacist requires every purchaser of a controlled substance under this section not known to him to furnish suitable identification (including proof of age where appropriate);

(e) A bound record book for dispensing of controlled substances under this section is maintained by the pharmacist, which book shall contain the name and address of the purchaser, the name and quantity of controlled substance purchased, the date of each purchase, and the name or initials of the pharmacist who dispensed the substance to the purchaser (the book shall be maintained in accordance with the recordkeeping requirement of § 1304.04 of this chapter); and

(f) A prescription is not required for distribution or dispensing of the substance pursuant to any other Federal, State or local law.

(g) Central fill pharmacies may not dispense controlled substances to a purchaser at retail pursuant to this section.

[36 FR 7799, Apr. 24, 1971, as amended at 36 FR 18733, Sept. 21, 1971. Redesignated at 38 FR 26609, Sept. 24, 1973, and further redesignated and amended at 62 FR 13966, Mar. 24, 1997; 68 FR 37411, June 24, 2003]

§ 1306.27 Provision of prescription information between retail pharmacies and central fill pharmacies for initial and refill prescriptions of Schedule III, IV, or V controlled substances.

Prescription information may be provided to an authorized central fill pharmacy by a retail pharmacy for dispensing purposes. The following requirements shall also apply:

(a) Prescriptions for controlled substances listed in Schedule III, IV or V may be transmitted electronically from a retail pharmacy to a central fill pharmacy including via facsimile. The retail pharmacy transmitting the prescription information must:

(1) Write the word "CENTRAL FILL" on the face of the original prescription and record the name, address, and DEA registration number of the central fill pharmacy to which the prescription has been transmitted and the name of the retail pharmacy pharmacist transmitting the prescription, and the date of transmittal;

(2) Ensure that all information required to be on a prescription pursuant to § 1306.05 of this part is transmitted to the central fill pharmacy (either on the face of the prescription or in the electronic transmission of information);

(3) Indicate in the information transmitted the number of refills already dispensed and the number of refills remaining;

(4) Maintain the original prescription for a period of two years from the date the prescription was last refilled;

(5) Keep a record of receipt of the filled prescription, including the date of receipt, the method of delivery (private, common or contract carrier) and the name of the retail pharmacy employee accepting delivery.

(b) The central fill pharmacy receiving the transmitted prescription must:

(1) Keep a copy of the prescription (if sent via facsimile) or an electronic record of all the information transmitted by the retail pharmacy, including the name, address, and DEA registration number of the retail pharmacy transmitting the prescription;

(2) Keep a record of the date of receipt of the transmitted prescription, the name of the licensed pharmacist filling the prescription, and dates of filling or refilling of the prescription;

(3) Keep a record of the date the filled prescription was delivered to the retail pharmacy and the method of delivery (*i.e.* private, common or contract carrier).

[68 FR 37411, June 24, 2003]

PART 1307—MISCELLANEOUS

AUTHORITY: 21 U.S.C. 821, 822(d), 871(b), unless otherwise noted.

SOURCE: 36 FR 7801, Apr. 24, 1971, unless otherwise noted. Redesignated at 38 FR 26609, Sept. 24, 1973.

GENERAL INFORMATION

§ 1307.01 Definitions.

Any term contained in this part shall have the definition set forth in section 102 of the Act (21 U.S.C. 802) or part 1300 of this chapter.

[62 FR 13966, Mar. 24, 1997]

§ 1307.02 Application of State law and other Federal law.

Nothing in this chapter shall be construed as authorizing or permitting any person to do any act which such person is not authorized or permitted to do under other Federal laws or obligations under international treaties, conventions or protocols, or under the law of the State in which he/she desires to do such act nor shall compliance with such parts be construed as compliance with other Federal or State laws unless expressly provided in such other laws.

[62 FR 13966, Mar. 24, 1997]

§ 1307.03 Exceptions to regulations.

Any person may apply for an exception to the application of any provision of this chapter by filing a written request with the Office of Diversion Control, Drug Enforcement Administration, stating the reasons for such exception. See the Table of DEA Mailing Addresses in § 1321.01 of this chapter for the current mailing address. The Administrator may grant an exception in his discretion, but in no case shall he/she be required to grant an exception to any person which is otherwise required by law or the regulations cited in this section.

[75 FR 10678, Mar. 9, 2010]

SPECIAL EXCEPTIONS FOR MANUFACTURE AND DISTRIBUTION OF CONTROLLED SUBSTANCES

§ 1307.11 Distribution by dispenser to another practitioner.

(a) A practitioner who is registered to dispense a controlled substance may distribute (without being registered to distribute) a quantity of such substance to—

(1) Another practitioner for the purpose of general dispensing by the practitioner to patients, provided that—

(i) The practitioner to whom the controlled substance is to be distributed is registered under the Act to dispense that controlled substance;

(ii) The distribution is recorded by the distributing practitioner in accordance with § 1304.22(c) of this chapter and by the receiving practitioner in accordance with § 1304.22(c) of this chapter;

(iii) If the substance is listed in Schedule I or II, an order form is used as required in part 1305 of this chapter; and

(iv) The total number of dosage units of all controlled substances distributed by the practitioner pursuant to this section and § 1301.25 of this chapter during each calendar year in which the practitioner is registered to dispense does not exceed 5 percent of the total number of dosage units of all controlled substances distributed and dispensed by the practitioner during the same calendar year.

(2) [Reserved]

(b) If, during any calendar year in which the practitioner is registered to dispense, the practitioner has reason to believe that the total number of dosage units of all controlled substances which will be distributed by him pursuant to paragraph (a)(1) of this section and § 1301.25 of this chapter will exceed 5 percent of this total number of dosage units of all controlled substances distributed and dispensed by him during that calendar year, the practitioner shall obtain a registration to distribute controlled substances.

(c) The distributions that a registered retail pharmacy makes to automated dispensing systems at long term care facilities for which the retail pharmacy also holds registrations do not count toward the 5 percent limit in paragraphs (a)(1)(iv) and (b) of this section.

[68 FR 41229, July 11, 2003, as amended at 70 FR 25466, May 13, 2005; 79 FR 53565, Sept. 9, 2014]

§ 1307.13 Incidental manufacture of controlled substances.

Any registered manufacturer who, incidentally but necessarily, manufactures a controlled substance as a result of the manufacture of a controlled substance or basic class of controlled substance for which he is registered and has been issued an individual manufacturing quota pursuant to part 1303 of this chapter (if such substance or class is listed in Schedule I or II) shall be exempt from the requirement of registration pursuant to part 1301 of this chapter and, if such incidentally manufactured substance is listed in Schedule I or II, shall be exempt from the requirement of an individual manufacturing quota pursuant to part 1303 of this chapter, if such substances are disposed of in accordance with part 1317 of this chapter.

[79 FR 53565, Sept. 9, 2014]

DISPOSAL OF CONTROLLED SUBSTANCES

§ 1307.22 Delivery of surrendered and forfeited controlled substances.

Any controlled substance surrendered by delivery to the Administration under part 1317 of this chapter or forfeited pursuant to section 511 of the Act (21 U.S.C. 881) may be delivered to any department, bureau, or other agency of the United States or of any State upon proper application addressed to the Office of Diversion Control, Drug Enforcement Administration. See the Table of DEA Mailing Addresses in § 1321.01 of this chapter for the current mailing address. The application shall show the name, address, and official title of the person or agency to whom the controlled drugs are to be delivered, including the name and quantity of the substances desired and the purpose for which intended. The delivery of such controlled drugs shall be ordered by the Administrator, if, in his opinion, there exists a medical or scientific need therefor.

[75 FR 10678, Mar. 9, 2010, as amended at 79 FR 53565, Sept. 9, 2014]

SPECIAL EXEMPT PERSONS

§ 1307.31 Native American Church.

The listing of peyote as a controlled substance in Schedule I does not apply to the nondrug use of peyote in bona fide religious ceremonies of the Native American Church, and members of the Native American Church so using peyote are exempt from registration. Any person who manufactures peyote for or distributes peyote to the Native American Church, however, is required to obtain registration annually and to comply with all other requirements of law.

PART 1308—SCHEDULES OF CONTROLLED SUBSTANCES

AUTHORITY: 21 U.S.C. 811, 812, 871(b), 956(b), unless otherwise noted.

SOURCE: 38 FR 8254, Mar. 30, 1973, unless otherwise noted. Redesignated at 38 FR 26609, Sept. 24, 1973.

GENERAL INFORMATION

§ 1308.01 Scope of this part.

Schedules of controlled substances established by section 202 of the Act (21 U.S.C. 812) and nonnarcotic substances, chemical preparations, veterinary anabolic steroid implant products, prescription products, anabolic steroid products, and cannabis plant material and products made therefrom that contain tetrahydrocannabinols excluded pursuant to section 201 of the Act (21 U.S.C. 811), as they are changed, updated, and republished from time to time, are set forth in this part.

[81 FR 97021, Dec. 30, 2016]

§ 1308.02 Definitions.

Any term contained in this part shall have the definition set forth in section 102 of the Act (21 U.S.C. 802) or part 1300 of this chapter.

[62 FR 13967, Mar. 24, 1997]

§ 1308.03 Administration Controlled Substances Code Number.

(a) Each controlled substance, or basic class thereof, has been assigned an "Administration Controlled Substances Code Number" for purposes of identification of the substances or class on certain Certificates of Registration issued by the Administration pursuant to §§ 1301.35 of this chapter and on certain order forms issued by the Administration pursuant to § 1305.05(d) of this chapter. Applicants for procurement and/or individual manufacturing quotas must include the appropriate code number on the application as required in §§ 1303.12(b) and 1303.22(a) of this chapter. Applicants for import and export permits must include the appropriate code number on the application as required in §§ 1312.12(a) and 1312.22(a) of this chapter. Authorized registrants who desire to import or export a controlled substance for which an import or export permit is not required must include the appropriate Administration Controlled Substances Code Number beneath or beside the name of each controlled substance listed on the DEA Form 236 (Controlled Substance Import/Export Declaration) which is executed for such importation or exportation as required in §§ 1312.18(c) and 1312.27(b) of this chapter.

(b) Except as stated in paragraph (a) of this section, no applicant or registrant is required to use the Administration Controlled Substances Code Number for any purpose.

[38 FR 8254, Mar. 30, 1973. Redesignated at 38 FR 26609, Sept. 24, 1973 and amended at 51 FR 15318, Apr. 23, 1986; 62 FR 13968, Mar. 24, 1997]

SCHEDULES

§ 1308.11 Schedule I.

(a) Schedule I shall consist of the drugs and other substances, by whatever official name, common or usual name, chemical name, or brand name designated, listed in this section. Each drug or substance has been assigned the DEA Controlled Substances Code Number set forth opposite it.

(b) *Opiates.* Unless specifically excepted or unless listed in another schedule, any of the following opiates, including their isomers, esters, ethers, salts, and salts of isomers, esters and ethers, whenever the existence of such isomers, esters, ethers and salts is possible within the specific chemical designation (for purposes of 3-methylthiofentanyl only, the term isomer includes the optical and geometric isomers):

(1) Acetyl-alpha-methylfentanyl (*N*-[1-(1-methyl-2-phenethyl)-4-piperidinyl]-*N*-phenylacetamide)	9815
(2) Acetylmethadol	9601
(3) Acetyl fentanyl (*N*-(1-phenethylpiperidin-4-yl)-*N*-phenylacetamide)	9821
(4) Acryl fentanyl (*N*-(1-phenethylpiperidin-4-yl)-*N*-phenylacrylamide; other name: acryloylfentanyl)	9811
(5) AH-7921 (3,4-dichloro-*N*-[(1-dimethylamino) cyclohexylmethyl]benzamide	9551
(6) Allylprodine	9602

(7) Alphacetylmethadol (except levo-alphacetylmethadol also known as levo-alpha-acetylmethadol, levomethadyl acetate, or LAAM) ... 9603
(8) Alphameprodine ... 9604
(9) Alphamethadol ... 9605
(10) Alpha-methylfentanyl (N-[1-(alpha-methyl-beta-phenyl)ethyl-4-piperidyl] propionanilide; 1-(1-methyl-2-phenylethyl)-4-(N-propanilido) piperidine) ... 9814
(11) Alpha-methylthiofentanyl (*N*-[1-methyl-2-(2-thienyl)ethyl-4-piperidinyl]-*N*-phenylpropanamide) ... 9832
(12) Benzethidine ... 9606
(13) Betacetylmethadol ... 9607
(14) Beta-hydroxyfentanyl (*N*-[1-(2-hydroxy-2-phenethyl)-4-piperidinyl]-*N*-phenylpropanamide) ... 9830
(15) Beta-hydroxy-3-methylfentanyl (other name: N-[1-(2-hydroxy-2-phenethyl)-3-methyl-4-piperidinyl]-N-phenylpropanamide ... 9831
(16) *N*-[1-[2-hydroxy-2-(thiophen-2-yl)ethyl]piperidin-4-yl]-*N*-phenylpropionamide (Other name: *beta*-Hydroxythiofentanyl) ... 9836
(17) Betameprodine ... 9608
(18) Betamethadol ... 9609
(19) Betaprodine ... 9611
(20) Butyryl fentanyl (N-(1-phenethylpiperidin-4-yl)-N-phenylbutyramide) ... 9822
(21) Clonitazene ... 9612
(22) Cyclopropyl fentanyl (*N*-(1-phenethylpiperidin-4-yl)-*N*-phenylcyclopropanecarboxamide) ... 9845
(23) Dextromoramide ... 9613
(24) Diampromide ... 9615
(25) Diethylthiambutene ... 9616
(26) Difenoxin ... 9168
(27) Dimenoxadol ... 9617
(28) Dimepheptanol ... 9618
(29) Dimethylthiambutene ... 9619
(30) Dioxaphetyl butyrate ... 9621
(31) Dipipanone ... 9622
(32) Ethylmethylthiambutene ... 9623
(33) Etonitazene ... 9624
(34) Etoxeridine ... 9625
(35) 4-Fluoroisobutyryl fentanyl (*N*-(4-fluorophenyl)-*N*-(1-phenethylpiperidin-4-yl)isobutyramide; other name: *para*-fluoroisobutyryl fentanyl) ... 9824
(36) Furanyl fentanyl (*N*-(1-phenethylpiperidin-4-yl)-*N*-phenylfuran-2-carboxamide) ... 9834
(37) Furethidine ... 9626
(38) Hydroxypethidine ... 9627
(39) Ketobemidone ... 9628
(40) Levomoramide ... 9629
(41) Levophenacylmorphan ... 9631
(42) Methoxyacetyl fentanyl (2-methoxy-*N*-(1-phenethylpiperidin-4-yl)-*N*-phenylacetamide) ... 9825
(43) 3-Methylfentanyl (*N*-[3-methyl-1-(2-phenylethyl)-4-piperidyl]-*N*-phenylpropanamide) ... 9813
(44) 3-methylthiofentanyl (*N*-[(3-methyl-1-(2-thienyl)ethyl-4-piperidinyl]-*N*-phenylpropanamide) ... 9833
(45) Morpheridine ... 9632
(46) MPPP (1-methyl-4-phenyl-4-propionoxypiperidine) ... 9661
(47) MT–45 (1-cyclohexyl-4-(1,2-diphenylethyl)piperazine) ... (9560)
(48) Noracymethadol ... 9633
(49) Norlevorphanol ... 9634
(50) Normethadone ... 9635
(51) Norpipanone ... 9636
(52) Ocfentanil (*N*-(2-fluorophenyl)-2-methoxy-*N*-(1-phenethylpiperidin-4-yl)acetamide) ... 9838
(53) *ortho*-Fluorofentanyl (*N*-(2-fluorophenyl)-*N*-(1-phenethylpiperidin-4-yl)propionamide); other name: 2-fluorofentanyl) ... 9816
(54) *para*-Fluorobutyryl fentanyl (*N*-(4-fluorophenyl)-*N*-(1-phenethylpiperidin-4-yl)butyramide) ... 9823
(55) Para-fluorofentanyl (*N*-(4-fluorophenyl)-*N*-[1-(2-phenethyl)-4-piperidinyl] propanamide ... 9812
(56) PEPAP (1-(-2-phenethyl)-4-phenyl-4-acetoxypiperidine ... 9663
(57) Phenadoxone ... 9637
(58) Phenampromide ... 9638
(59) Phenomorphan ... 9647
(60) Phenoperidine ... 9641
(61) Piritramide ... 9642

(62) Proheptazine 9643
(63) Properidine 9644
(64) Propiram 9649
(65) Racemoramide 9645
(66) Tetrahydrofuranyl fentanyl (*N*-(1-phenethylpiperidin-4-yl)-*N*-phenyltetrahydrofuran-2-carboxamide) 9843
(67) Thiofentanyl (*N*-phenyl-*N*-[1-(2-thienyl)ethyl-4-piperidinyl]-propanamide 9835
(68) Tilidine 9750
(69) Trimeperidine 9646
(70) U–47700 (3,4-Dichloro-N-[2-(dimethylamino)cyclohexyl]-N-methylbenzamide) 9547

(c) *Opium derivatives*. Unless specifically excepted or unless listed in another schedule, any of the following opium derivatives, its salts, isomers, and salts of isomers whenever the existence of such salts, isomers, and salts of isomers is possible within the specific chemical designation:

(1) Acetorphine 9319
(2) Acetyldihydrocodeine 9051
(3) Benzylmorphine 9052
(4) Codeine methylbromide 9070
(5) Codeine-N-Oxide 9053
(6) Cyprenorphine 9054
(7) Desomorphine 9055
(8) Dihydromorphine 9145
(9) Drotebanol 9335
(10) Etorphine (except hydrochloride salt) 9056
(11) Heroin 9200
(12) Hydromorphinol 9301
(13) Methyldesorphine 9302
(14) Methyldihydromorphine 9304
(15) Morphine methylbromide .. 9305
(16) Morphine methylsulfonate 9306
(17) Morphine-N-Oxide 9307
(18) Myrophine 9308
(19) Nicocodeine 9309
(20) Nicomorphine 9312
(21) Normorphine 9313
(22) Pholcodine 9314
(23) Thebacon 9315

(d) *Hallucinogenic substances*. Unless specifically excepted or unless listed in another schedule, any material, compound, mixture, or preparation, which contains any quantity of the following hallucinogenic substances, or which contains any of its salts, isomers, and salts of isomers whenever the existence of such salts, isomers, and salts of isomers is possible within the specific chemical designation (for purposes of this paragraph only, the term "isomer" includes the optical, position and geometric isomers):

(1) Alpha-ethyltryptamine 7249
Some trade or other names: etryptamine; Monase; α-ethyl-1H-indole-3-ethanamine; 3-(2-aminobutyl) indole; α-ET; and AET.
(2) 4-bromo-2,5-dimethoxy-amphetamine 7391
Some trade or other names: 4-bromo-2,5-dimethoxy-α-methylphenethylamine; 4-bromo-2,5-DMA
(3) 4-Bromo-2,5-dimethoxyphenethylamine 7392
Some trade or other names: 2-(4-bromo-2,5-dimethoxyphenyl)-1-aminoethane; alpha-desmethyl DOB; 2C-B, Nexus.
(4) 2,5-dimethoxyamphetamine 7396
Some trade or other names: 2,5-dimethoxy-α-methylphenethylamine; 2,5-DMA
(5) 2,5-dimethoxy-4-ethylamphet-amine 7399
Some trade or other names: DOET
(6) 2,5-dimethoxy-4-(n)-propylthiophenethylamine (other name: 2C–T–7) 7348
(7) 4-methoxyamphetamine 7411
Some trade or other names: 4-methoxy-α-methylphenethylamine; paramethoxyamphetamine, PMA
(8) 5-methoxy-3,4-methylenedioxy-amphetamine 7401
(9) 4-methyl-2,5-dimethoxy-amphetamine 7395
Some trade and other names: 4-methyl-2,5-dimethoxy-α-methylphenethylamine; "DOM"; and "STP"
(10) 3,4-methylenedioxy amphetamine 7400
(11) 3,4-methylenedioxymethamphetamine (MDMA) 7405

(12) 3,4-methylenedioxy-N-ethylamphetamine (also known as N-ethyl-alpha-methyl-3,4(methylenedioxy)-phenethylamine, N-ethyl MDA, MDE, MDEA 7404

(13) N-hydroxy-3,4-methylenedioxyamphetamine (also known as N-hydroxy-alpha-methyl-3,4(methylenedioxy)-phenethylamine, and N-hydroxy MDA 7402

(14) 3,4,5-trimethoxy amphetamine 7390

(15) 5-methoxy-N,N-dimethyltryptamine Some trade or other names: 5-methoxy-3-[2-(dimethylamino)ethyl]indole; 5-MeO-DMT 7431

(16) Alpha-methyltryptamine (other name: AMT) 7432

(17) Bufotenine 7433

Some trade and other names: 3-(β-Dimethylaminoethyl)-5-hydroxyindole; 3-(2-dimethylaminoethyl)-5-indolol; N, N-dimethylserotonin; 5-hydroxy-N,N-dimethyltryptamine; mappine

(18) Diethyltryptamine 7434

Some trade and other names: N,N-Diethyltryptamine; DET

(19) Dimethyltryptamine 7435

Some trade or other names: DMT

(20) 5-methoxy-N,N-diisopropyltryptamine (other name: 5-MeO-DIPT) 7439

(21) Ibogaine 7260

Some trade and other names: 7-Ethyl-6,6β,7,8,9,10,12,13-octahydro-2-methoxy-6,9-methano-5H-pyrido [1′, 2′:1,2] azepino [5,4-b] indole; Tabernanthe iboga

(22) Lysergic acid diethylamide 7315

(23) Marihuana 7360

(24) Mescaline 7381

(25) Parahexyl—7374; some trade or other names: 3-Hexyl-1-hydroxy-7,8,9,10-tetrahydro-6,6,9-trimethyl-6H-dibenzo[b,d]pyran; Synhexyl.

(26) Peyote 7415

Meaning all parts of the plant presently classified botanically as *Lophophora williamsii Lemaire*, whether growing or not, the seeds thereof, any extract from any part of such plant, and every compound, manufacture, salts, derivative, mixture, or preparation of such plant, its seeds or extracts

(Interprets 21 USC 812(c), Schedule I(c) (12))

(27) N-ethyl-3-piperidyl benzilate 7482

(28) N-methyl-3-piperidyl benzilate 7484

(29) Psilocybin 7437

(30) Psilocyn 7438

(31) Tetrahydrocannabinols 7370

Meaning tetrahydrocannabinols naturally contained in a plant of the genus Cannabis (cannabis plant), as well as synthetic equivalents of the substances contained in the cannabis plant, or in the resinous extractives of such plant, and/or synthetic substances, derivatives, and their isomers with similar chemical structure and pharmacological activity to those substances contained in the plant, such as the following:

1 cis or trans tetrahydrocannabinol, and their optical isomers

6 cis or trans tetrahydrocannabinol, and their optical isomers

3, 4 cis or trans tetrahydrocannabinol, and its optical isomers

(Since nomenclature of these substances is not internationally standardized, compounds of these structures, regardless of numerical designation of atomic positions covered.)

(32) Ethylamine analog of phencyclidine 7455

Some trade or other names: N-ethyl-1-phenylcyclohexylamine, (1-phenylcyclohexyl)ethylamine, N-(1-phenylcyclohexyl)ethylamine, cyclohexamine, PCE

(33) Pyrrolidine analog of phencyclidine 7458

Some trade or other names: 1-(1-phenylcyclohexyl)-pyrrolidine, PCPy, PHP

(34) Thiophene analog of phencyclidine 7470

Some trade or other names: 1-[1-(2-thienyl)-cyclohexyl]-piperidine, 2-thienylanalog of phencyclidine, TPCP, TCP

(35) 1-[1-(2-thienyl)cyclohexyl]pyrrolidine 7473

Some other names: TCPy

(36) 4-methylmethcathinone (Mephedrone) 1248

(37) 3,4-methylenedioxypyrovalerone (MDPV) 7535

(38) 2-(2,5-Dimethoxy-4-ethylphenyl)ethanamine (2C–E) 7509

(39) 2-(2,5-Dimethoxy-4-methylphenyl)ethanamine (2C–D) 7508

(40) 2-(4-Chloro-2,5-dimethoxyphenyl)ethanamine (2C–C) 7519

(41) 2-(4-Iodo-2,5-dimethoxyphenyl)ethanamine (2C–I) 7518

(42) 2-[4-(Ethylthio)-2,5-dimethoxyphenyl]ethanamine (2C–T–2) 7385

(43) 2-[4-(Isopropylthio)-2,5-dimethoxyphenyl]ethanamine (2C–T–4) 7532

(44) 2-(2,5-Dimethoxyphenyl)ethanamine (2C–H) 7517

(45) 2-(2,5-Dimethoxy-4-nitro-phenyl)ethanamine (2C–N) 7521

(46) 2-(2,5-Dimethoxy-4-(n)-propylphenyl)ethanamine (2C–P) 7524

(47) 3,4-Methylenedioxy-N-methylcathinone (Methylone) 7540

(48) (1-pentyl-1*H*-indol-3-yl)(2,2,3,3-tetramethylcyclopropyl)methanone (UR-144) .... (7144)

(49) [1-(5-fluoro-pentyl)-1*H*-indol-3-yl](2,2,3,3-tetramethylcyclopropyl)methanone (5-fluoro-UR-144, XLR11) .... (7011)

(50) *N*-(1-adamantyl)-1-pentyl-1*H*-indazole-3-carboxamide (APINACA, AKB48) .... (7048)

(51) quinolin-8-yl 1-pentyl-1*H*-indole-3-carboxylate (PB-22; QUPIC) .... (7222)

(52) quinolin-8-yl 1-(5-fluoropentyl)-1*H*-indole-3-carboxylate (5-fluoro-PB-22; 5F-PB-22) .... (7225)

(53) *N*-(1-amino-3-methyl-1-oxobutan-2-yl)-1-(4-fluorobenzyl)-1*H*-indazole-3-carboxamide (AB-FUBINACA) .... (7012)

(54) *N*-(1-amino-3,3-dimethyl-1-oxobutan-2-yl)-1-pentyl-1*H*-indazole-3-carboxamide (ADB-PINACA) .... (7035)

(55) 2-(4-iodo-2,5-dimethoxyphenyl)-*N*-(2-methoxybenzyl)ethanamine (25I-NBOMe, 2C-I-NBOMe) .... (7538)

(56) 2-(4-chloro-2,5-dimethoxyphenyl)-*N*-(2-methoxybenzyl)ethanamine (25C-NBOMe, 2C-C-NBOMe) ... (7537)

(57) 2-(4-bromo-2,5-dimethoxyphenyl)-*N*-(2-methoxybenzyl)ethanamine (25B-NBOMe, 2C-B-NBOMe) ... (7536)

(58) Marihuana Extract—Meaning an extract containing one or more cannabinoids that has been derived from any plant of the genus Cannabis, other than the separated resin (whether crude or purified) obtained from the plant (7350)

(59) 4-methyl-*N*-ethylcathinone (4-MEC) .... (1249)

(60) 4-methyl-*alpha*-pyrrolidinopropiophenone (4-MePPP) .... (7498)

(61) *alpha*-pyrrolidinopentiophenone (α-PVP) .... (7545)

(62) 1-(1,3-benzodioxol-5-yl)-2-(methylamino)butan-1-one (butylone, bk-MBDB) .... (7541)

(63) 2-(methylamino)-1-phenylpentan-1-one (pentedrone) .... (1246)

(64) 1-(1,3-benzodioxol-5-yl)-2-(methylamino)pentan-1-one (pentylone, bk-MBDP) .... (7542)

(65) 4-fluoro-*N*-methylcathinone (4-FMC; flephedrone) .... (1238)

(66) 3-fluoro-*N*-methylcathinone (3-FMC) .... (1233)

(67) 1-(naphthalen-2-yl)-2-(pyrrolidin-1-yl)pentan-1-one (naphyrone) .... (1258)

(68) *alpha*-pyrrolidinobutiophenone (α-PBP) .... (7546)

(69) *N*-(1-amino-3-methyl-1-oxobutan-2-yl)-1-(cyclohexylmethyl)-1*H*-indazole-3-carboxamide (AB-CHMINACA) .... (7031)

(70) *N*-(1-amino-3-methyl-1-oxobutan-2-yl)-1-pentyl-1*H*-indazole-3-carboxamide (AB-PINACA) .... (7023)

(71) [1-(5-fluoropentyl)-1*H*-indazol-3-yl](naphthalen-1-yl)methanone (THJ-2201) .... (7024)

(72) *N*-(1-amino-3,3-dimethyl-1-oxobutan-2-yl)-1-(cyclohexylmethyl)-1*H*-indazole-3-carboxamide (MAB-CHMINACA; ADB-CHMINACA) .... (7032)

(73) methyl 2-(1-(5-fluoropentyl)-1*H*-indazole-3-carboxamido)-3,3-dimethylbutanoate (Other names: 5F-ADB; 5F-MDMB-PINACA) 7034

(74) methyl 2-(1-(5-fluoropentyl)-1*H*-indazole-3-carboxamido)-3-methylbutanoate (Other names: 5F-AMB) 7033

(75) *N*-(adamantan-1-yl)-1-(5-fluoropentyl)-1*H*-indazole-3-carboxamide (Other names: 5F-APINACA, 5F-AKB48) 7049

(76) *N*-(1-amino-3,3-dimethyl-1-oxobutan-2-yl)-1-(4-fluorobenzyl)-1*H*-indazole-3-carboxamide (Other names: ADB-FUBINACA) 7010

(77) methyl 2-(1-(cyclohexylmethyl)-1*H*-indole-3-carboxamido)-3,3-dimethylbutanoate (Other names: MDMB-CHMICA, MMB-CHMINACA) 7042

(78) methyl 2-(1-(4-fluorobenzyl)-1*H*-indazole-3-carboxamido)-3,3-dimethylbutanoate (Other names: MDMB-FUBINACA) ... 7020

(79) methyl 2-(1-(4-fluorobenzyl)-1*H*-indazole-3-carboxamido)-3-methylbutanoate, (FUB–AMB, MMB–FUBINACA, AMB–FUBINACA) .... (7021)

(e) *Depressants.* Unless specifically excepted or unless listed in another schedule, any material, compound, mixture, or preparation which contains any quantity of the following substances having a depressant effect on the central nervous system, including its salts, isomers, and salts of isomers whenever the existence of such salts, isomers, and salts of isomers is possible within the specific chemical designation:

(1) gamma-hydroxybutyric acid (some other names include GHB; gamma-hydroxybutyrate; 4-hydroxybutyrate; 4-hydroxybutanoic acid; sodium oxybate; sodium oxybutyrate) 2010
(2) Mecloqualone 2572
(3) Methaqualone 2565

(f) *Stimulants.* Unless specifically excepted or unless listed in another schedule, any material, compound, mixture, or preparation which contains any quantity of the following substances having a stimulant effect on the central nervous system, including its salts, isomers, and salts of isomers:

(1) Aminorex (Some other names: aminoxaphen; 2-amino-5-phenyl-2-oxazoline; or 4,5-dihydro-5-phenly-2-oxazolamine) 1585
(2) N-Benzylpiperazine (some other names: BZP, 1-benzylpiperazine) 7493
(3) Cathinone 1235
Some trade or other names: 2-amino-1-phenyl-1-propanone, alpha-aminopropiophenone, 2-aminopropiophenone, and norephedrone
(4) Fenethylline 1503
(5) Methcathinone (Some other names: 2-(methylamino)-propiophenone; alpha-(methylamino)propiophenone; 2-(methylamino)-1-phenylpropan-1-one; alpha-*N*-methylaminopropiophenone; monomethylpropion; ephedrone; *N*-methylcathinone; methylcathinone; AL–464; AL–422; AL–463 and UR1432), its salts, optical isomers and salts of optical isomers 1237
(6) (±)*cis*-4-methylaminorex ((±)*cis*-4,5-dihydro-4-methyl-5-phenyl-2-oxazolamine) 1590
(7) N-ethylamphetamine 1475
(8) *N,N*-dimethylamphetamine (also known as *N,N*-alpha-trimethyl-benzeneethanamine; *N,N*-alpha-trimethylphenethylamine) 1480

(g) *Cannabimimetic agents.* Unless specifically exempted or unless listed in another schedule, any material, compound, mixture, or preparation which contains any quantity of the following substances, or which contains their salts, isomers, and salts of isomers whenever the existence of such salts, isomers, and salts of isomers is possible within the specific chemical designation:

(1) 5-(1,1-dimethylheptyl)-2-[(1R,3S)-3-hydroxycyclohexyl]-phenol (CP–47,497) 7297
(2) 5-(1,1-dimethyloctyl)-2-[(1R,3S)-3-hydroxycyclohexyl]-phenol (cannabicyclohexanol or CP–47,497 C8-homolog) 7298
(3) 1-pentyl-3-(1-naphthoyl)indole (JWH–018 and AM678) 7118
(4) 1-butyl-3-(1-naphthoyl)indole (JWH–073) 7173
(5) 1-hexyl-3-(1-naphthoyl)indole (JWH–019) 7019
(6) 1-[2-(4-morpholinyl)ethyl]-3-(1-naphthoyl)indole (JWH–200) 7200
(7) 1-pentyl-3-(2-methoxyphenylacetyl)indole (JWH–250) 6250

(8) 1-pentyl-3-[1-(4-methoxynaphthoyl)]indole (JWH–081) 7081

(9) 1-pentyl-3-(4-methyl-1-naphthoyl)indole (JWH–122) 7122

(10) 1-pentyl-3-(4-chloro-1-naphthoyl)indole (JWH–398) 7398

(11) 1-(5-fluoropentyl)-3-(1-naphthoyl)indole (AM2201) 7201

(12) 1-(5-fluoropentyl)-3-(2-iodobenzoyl)indole (AM694) ... 7694

(13) 1-pentyl-3-[(4-methoxy)-benzoyl]indole (SR–19 and RCS–4) 7104

(14) 1-cyclohexylethyl-3-(2-methoxyphenylacetyl)indole 7008 (SR–18 and RCS–8) 7008

(15) 1-pentyl-3-(2-chlorophenylacetyl)indole (JWH–203) 7203

(h) *Temporary listing of substances subject to emergency scheduling.* Any material, compound, mixture or preparation which contains any quantity of the following substances:

(1)–(17) [Reserved].

(18) [Reserved].

(19) [Reserved].

(20) [Reserved].

(21) [Reserved].

(22) [Reserved].

(23) *N*-(1-phenethylpiperidin-4-yl)-*N*-phenylpentanamide, its isomers, esters, ethers, salts and salts of isomers, esters and ethers (Other name: Valeryl fentanyl) .... (9840)

(24) [Reserved].

(25) *N*-(4-methoxyphenyl)-*N*-(1-phenethylpiperidin-4-yl)butyramide, its isomers, esters, ethers, salts and salts of isomers, esters and ethers (Other name: *para*-methoxybutyryl fentanyl) ... (9837)

(26) *N*-(4-chlorophenyl)-*N*-(1-phenethylpiperidin-4-yl)isobutyramide, its isomers, esters, ethers, salts and salts of isomers, esters and ethers (Other name: *para*-chloroisobutyryl fentanyl) .... (9826)

(27) *N*-(1-phenethylpiperidin-4-yl)-*N*-phenylisobutyramide, its isomers, esters, ethers, salts and salts of isomers, esters and ethers (Other name: isobutyryl fentanyl) .. (9827)

(28) *N*-(1-phenethylpiperidin-4-yl)-*N*-phenylcyclopentanecarboxamide, its isomers, esters, ethers, salts and salts of isomers, esters and ethers (Other name: cyclopentyl fentanyl) .... (9847)

(29) [Reserved].

(30) [Reserved].

(31) Naphthalen-1-yl 1-(5-fluoropentyl)-1*H*-indole-3-carboxylate, its optical, positional, and geometric isomers, salts and salts of isomers (Other names: NM2201; CBL2201) .... (7221)

(32) *N*-(1-amino-3-methyl-1-oxobutan-2-yl)-1-(5-fluoropentyl)-1*H*-indazole-3-carboxamide, its optical, positional, and geometric isomers, salts and salts of isomers (Other names: 5F-AB-PINACA) .... (7025)

(33) 1-(4-cyanobutyl)-*N*-(2-phenylpropan-2-yl)-1*H*-indazole-3-carboxamide, its optical, positional, and geometric isomers, salts and salts of isomers (Other names: 4-CN-CUMYL-BUTINACA; 4-cyano-CUMYL-BUTINACA; 4-CN-CUMYL BINACA; CUMYL-4CN-BINACA; SGT-78) .... (7089)

(34) methyl 2-(1-(cyclohexylmethyl)-1*H*-indole-3-carboxamido)-3-methylbutanoate, its optical, positional, and geometric isomers, salts and salts of isomers (Other names: MMB-CHMICA, AMB-CHMICA) .... (7044)

(35) 1-(5-fluoropentyl)-*N*-(2-phenylpropan-2-yl)-1*H*-pyrrolo[2,3-b]pyridine-3-carboxamide, its optical, positional, and geometric isomers, salts and salts of isomers (Other names: 5F-CUMYL-P7AICA) .... (7085)

(36) *N*-Ethylpentylone, its optical, positional, and geometric isomers, salts and salts of isomers (Other names: ephylone, 1-(1,3-benzodioxol-5-yl)-2-(ethylamino)-pentan-1-one) (7543)

(37) ethyl 2-(1-(5-fluoropentyl)-1*H*-indazole-3-carboxamido)-3,3-dimethylbutanoate, its optical, positional, and geometric isomers, salts and salts of isomers (trivial name: 5F-EDMB-PINACA) ... 7036

(38) methyl 2-(1-(5-fluoropentyl)-1*H*-indole-3-carboxamido)-3,3-dimethylbutanoate, its optical, positional, and geometric isomers, salts and salts of isomers (trivial name: 5F-MDMB-PICA) 7041

(39) *N*-(adamantan-1-yl)-1-(4-fluorobenzyl)-1*H*-indazole-3-carboxamide, its optical, positional, and geometric isomers, salts and salts of isomers (trivial names: FUB-AKB48; FUB-APINACA; AKB48 N-(4-FLUOROBENZYL)) 7047

(40) 1-(5-fluoropentyl)-*N*-(2-phenylpropan-2-yl)-1*H*-indazole-3-carboxamide, its optical, positional, and geometric isomers, salts and salts of isomers (trivial names: 5F-CUMYL-PINACA; SGT-25) 7083

(41) (1-(4-fluorobenzyl)-1*H*-indol-3-yl)(2,2,3,3-tetramethylcyclopropyl) methanone, its optical, positional, and geometric isomers, salts and salts of isomers (trivial name: FUB-144) 7014

(42) *N*-Ethylhexedrone, its optical, positional, and geometric isomers, salts and salts of isomers (Other name: 2-(ethylamino)-1-phenylhexan-1-one) 7246

(43) *alpha*-Pyrrolidinohexanophenone, its optical, positional, and geometric isomers, salts and salts of isomers (Other names: α-PHP; *alpha*-pyrrolidinohexiophenone; 1-phenyl-2-(pyrrolidin-1-yl)hexan-1-one) 7544

(44) 4-Methyl-*alpha*-ethylaminopentiophenone, its optical, positional, and geometric isomers, salts and salts of isomers (Other names: 4–MEAP; 2-(ethylamino)-1-(4-methylphenyl)pentan-1-one) 7245

(45) 4′-Methyl-*alpha*-pyrrolidinohexiophenone, its optical, positional, and geometric isomers, salts and salts of isomers (Other names: MPHP; 4′-methyl-*alpha*-pyrrolidinohexanophenone; 1-(4-methylphenyl)-2-(pyrrolidin-1-yl)hexan-1-one) 7446

(46) *alpha*-Pyrrolidinoheptaphenone, its optical, positional, and geometric isomers, salts and salts of isomers (Other names: PV8; 1-phenyl-2-(pyrrolidin-1-yl)heptan-1-one) 7548

(47) 4′-Chloro-*alpha*-pyrrolidinovalerophenone, its optical, positional, and geometric isomers, salts and salts of isomers (Other names: 4-chloro-α-PVP; 4′-chloro-*alpha*-pyrrolidinopentiophenone; 1-(4-chlorophenyl)-2-(pyrrolidin-1-yl)pentan-1-one) 7443

[39 FR 22141, June 20, 1974]

EDITORIAL NOTE: For FEDERAL REGISTER citations affecting § 1308.11, see the List of CFR Sections Affected, which appears in the Finding Aids section of the printed volume and at *www.govinfo.gov*.

EFFECTIVE DATE NOTES: 1. At 83 FR 31882, July 10, 2018, § 1308.11 was amended by adding paragraphs (h)(31) through (h)(35) effective July 10, 2018 through July 10, 2020.

2. At 83 FR 44478, Aug. 31, 2018, § 1308.11 was amended by adding paragraph (h)(36) effective Aug. 31, 2018 through Aug. 31, 2020.

3. At 84 FR 13796, Apr. 10, 2019,§ 1308.11 was amended by extending the order at 82 FR 17119, Apr. 10, 2017, is effective Apr. 10, 2019 and will expire on Apr. 10, 2020.

4. At 84 FR 15511, Apr. 16, 2019, § 1308.11 was amended by adding paragraphs (h)(37) through (h)(41) effective Apr. 16, 2019 through Apr. 16, 2021.

5. At 84 FR 34297, July 17, 2019, § 1308.11 was amended by adding paragraphs (h)(42) through (h)(47) effective July 18, 2019 through July 18, 2021.

6. At 85 FR 5322, Jan. 30, 2020, § 1308.11 was amended by extending the order at 83 FR 4580, Feb. 1, 2018, is effective Feb. 1, 2020 and expires Feb. 1. 2021.

§ 1308.12 Schedule II.

(a) Schedule II shall consist of the drugs and other substances, by whatever official name, common or usual name, chemical name, or brand name designated, listed in this section. Each drug or substance has been assigned the Controlled Substances Code Number set forth opposite it.

(b) *Substances, vegetable origin or chemical synthesis.* Unless specifically excepted or unless listed in another schedule, any of the following substances whether produced directly or indirectly by extraction from substances of vegetable origin, or independently by means of chemical synthesis, or by a combination of extraction and chemical synthesis:

(1) Opium and opiate, and any salt, compound, derivative, or preparation of opium or opiate excluding apomorphine, thebaine-derived butorphanol, dextrorphan, nalbuphine, naldemedine, nalmefene, naloxegol, naloxone, 6β-naltrexol and naltrexone, and their respective salts, but including the following:

(i) Codeine	9050
(ii) Dihydroetorphine	9334
(iii) Ethylmorphine	9190
(iv) Etorphine hydrochloride	9059
(v) Granulated opium	9640
(vi) Hydrocodone	9193
(vii) Hydromorphone	9150
(viii) Metopon	9260
(ix) Morphine	9300
(x) Noroxymorphone	9668
(xi) Opium extracts	9610
(xii) Opium fluid	9620
(xiii) Oripavine	9330
(xiv) Oxycodone	9143
(xv) Oxymorphone	9652
(xvi) Powdered opium	9639
(xvii) Raw opium	9600
(xviii) Thebaine	9333
(xix) Tincture of opium	9630

(2) Any salt, compound, derivative, or preparation thereof which is chemically equivalent or identical with any of the substances referred to in paragraph (b) (1) of this section, except that these substances shall not include the isoquinoline alkaloids of opium.

(3) Opium poppy and poppy straw.

(4) Coca leaves (9040) and any salt, compound, derivative or preparation of coca leaves (including cocaine (9041) and ecgonine (9180) and their salts, isomers, derivatives and salts of isomers and derivatives), and any salt, compound, derivative, or preparation thereof which is chemically equivalent or identical with any of these substances, except that the substances shall not include:

(i) Decocainized coca leaves or extraction of coca leaves, which extractions do not contain cocaine or ecgonine; or

(ii) [^{123}I]ioflupane.

(5) Concentrate of poppy straw (the crude extract of poppy straw in either liquid, solid or powder form which contains the phenanthrene alkaloids of the opium poppy), 9670.

(c) *Opiates.* Unless specifically excepted or unless in another schedule any of the following opiates, including its isomers, esters, ethers, salts and salts of isomers, esters and ethers whenever the existence of such isomers, esters, ethers, and salts is possible within the specific chemical designation, dextrorphan and levopropoxyphene excepted:

(1) Alfentanil	9737
(2) Alphaprodine	9010
(3) Anileridine	9020
(4) Bezitramide	9800
(5) Bulk dextropropoxyphene (non-dosage forms)	9273
(6) Carfentanil	9743
(7) Dihydrocodeine	9120
(8) Diphenoxylate	9170
(9) Fentanyl	9801
(10) Isomethadone	9226
(11) Levo-alphacetylmethadol	9648

[Some other names: levo-alpha-acetylmethadol, levomethadyl acetate, LAAM]

(12) Levomethorphan	9210
(13) Levorphanol	9220
(14) Metazocine	9240
(15) Methadone	9250
(16) Methadone-Intermediate, 4-cyano-2-dimethylamino-4,4-diphenyl butane	9254
(17) Moramide-Intermediate, 2-methyl-3-morpholino-1, 1-diphenylpropane-carboxylic acid	9802
(18) Pethidine (meperidine)	9230
(19) Pethidine-Intermediate-A, 4-cyano-1-methyl-4-phenylpiperidine	9232
(20) Pethidine-Intermediate-B, ethyl-4-phenylpiperidine-4-carboxylate	9233
(21) Pethidine-Intermediate-C, 1-methyl-4-phenylpiperidine-4-carboxylic acid	9234
(22) Phenazocine	9715
(23) Piminodine	9730
(24) Racemethorphan	9732
(25) Racemorphan	9733
(26) Remifentanil	9739
(27) Sufentanil	9740
(28) Tapentadol	9780
(29) Thiafentanil	9729

(d) *Stimulants*. Unless specifically excepted or unless listed in another schedule, any material, compound, mixture, or preparation which contains any quantity of the following substances having a stimulant effect on the central nervous system:

(1) Amphetamine, its salts, optical isomers, and salts of its optical isomers	1100
(2) Methamphetamine, its salts, isomers, and salts of its isomers	1105
(3) Phenmetrazine and its salts	1631
(4) Methylphenidate	1724
(5) Lisdexamfetamine, its salts, isomers, and salts of its isomers	1205.

(e) *Depressants*. Unless specifically excepted or unless listed in another schedule, any material, compound, mixture, or preparation which contains any quantity of the following substances having a depressant effect on the central nervous system, including its salts, isomers, and salts of isomers whenever the existence of such salts, isomers, and salts of isomers is possible within the specific chemical designation:

(1) Amobarbital	2125
(2) Glutethimide	2550
(3) Pentobarbital	2270
(4) Phencyclidine	7471
(5) Secobarbital	2315

(f) *Hallucinogenic substances*.

(1) Nabilone	7379
[Another name for nabilone: (±)-*trans*-3-(1,1-dimethylheptyl)-6,6a,7,8,10,10a-hexahydro-1-hydroxy-6,6-dimethyl-9H-dibenzo[b,d]pyran-9-one]	
(2) Dronabinol [(-)-delta-9-*trans* tetrahydrocannabinol] in an oral solution in a drug product approved for marketing by the U.S. Food and Drug Administration	(7365)

(g) *Immediate precursors*. Unless specifically excepted or unless listed in another schedule, any material, compound, mixture, or preparation which contains any quantity of the following substances:

(1) Immediate precursor to amphetamine and methamphetamine:

(i) Phenylacetone	8501
Some trade or other names: phenyl-2-propanone; P2P; benzyl methyl ketone; methyl benzyl ketone;	

(2) Immediate precursors to phencyclidine (PCP):

(i) 1-phenylcyclohexylamine	7460
(ii) 1-piperidinocyclohexanecarbonitrile (PCC)	8603

(3) Immediate precursor to fentanyl:

(i) 4-anilino-N-phenethylpiperidine (ANPP)	8333
(ii) [Reserved].	

[39 FR 22142, June 20, 1974]

EDITORIAL NOTE: For FEDERAL REGISTER citations affecting § 1308.12, see the List of CFR Sections Affected, which appears in the Finding Aids section of the printed volume and at *www.govinfo.gov*.

§ 1308.13 Schedule III.

(a) Schedule III shall consist of the drugs and other substances, by whatever official name, common or usual name, chemical name, or brand name designated, listed in this section. Each drug or substance has been assigned the DEA Controlled Substances Code Number set forth opposite it.

(b) *Stimulants.* Unless specifically excepted or unless listed in another schedule, any material, compound, mixture, or preparation which contains any quantity of the following substances having a stimulant effect on the central nervous system, including its salts, isomers (whether optical, positional, or geometric), and salts of such isomers whenever the existence of such salts, isomers, and salts of isomers is possible within the specific chemical designation:

(1) Those compounds, mixtures, or preparations in dosage unit form containing any stimulant substances listed in schedule II which compounds, mixtures, or preparations were listed on August 25, 1971, as excepted compounds under §1308.32, and any other drug of the quantitative composition shown in that list for those drugs or which is the same except that it contains a lesser quantity of controlled substances 1405
(2) Benzphetamine 1228
(3) Chlorphentermine 1645
(4) Clortermine 1647
(5) Phendimetrazine 1615

(c) *Depressants.* Unless specifically excepted or unless listed in another schedule, any material, compound, mixture, or preparation which contains any quantity of the following substances having a depressant effect on the central nervous system:

(1) Any compound, mixture or preparation containing:
(i) Amobarbital 2126
(ii) Secobarbital 2316
(iii) Pentobarbital 2271
or any salt thereof and one or more other active medicinal ingredients which are not listed in any schedule.
(2) Any suppository dosage form containing:
(i) Amobarbital 2126
(ii) Secobarbital 2316
(iii) Pentobarbital 2271
or any salt of any of these drugs and approved by the Food and Drug Administration for marketing only as a suppository.
(3) Any substance which contains any quantity of a derivative of barbituric acid or any salt thereof 2100
(4) Chlorhexadol 2510
(5) Embutramide 2020
(6) Any drug product containing gamma hydroxybutyric acid, including its salts, isomers, and salts of isomers, for which an application is approved under section 505 of the Federal Food, Drug, and Cosmetic Act 2012
(7) Ketamine, its salts, isomers, and salts of isomers 7285
[Some other names for ketamine: (±)-2-(2-chlorophenyl)-2-(methylamino)-cyclohexanone]
(8) Lysergic acid 7300
(9) Lysergic acid amide 7310
(10) Methyprylon 2575
(11) Perampanel, and its salts, isomers, and salts of isomers .. 2261
(12) Sulfondiethylmethane 2600
(13) Sulfonethylmethane 2605
(14) Sulfonmethane 2610
(15) Tiletamine and zolazepam or any salt thereof 7295
Some trade or other names for a tiletamine-zolazepam combination product:
Telazol.
Some trade or other names for tiletamine:
2-(ethylamino)-2-(2-thienyl)-cyclohexanone.

Some trade or other names for zolazepam:
4-(2-fluorophenyl)-6,8-dihydro-1,3,8-trimethylpyrazolo-[3,4-*e*] [1,4]-diazepin-7(1*H*)-one, flupyrazapon.

(d) Nalorphine 9400.

(e) *Narcotic drugs.* Unless specifically excepted or unless listed in another schedule:

(1) Any material, compound, mixture, or preparation containing any of the following narcotic drugs, or their salts calculated as the free anhydrous base or alkaloid, in limited quantities as set forth below:

(i) Not more than 1.8 grams of codeine per 100 milliliters or not more than 90 milligrams per dosage unit, with an equal or greater quantity of an isoquinoline alkaloid of opium 9803

(ii) Not more than 1.8 grams of codeine per 100 milliliters or not more than 90 milligrams per dosage unit, with one or more active, nonnarcotic ingredients in recognized therapeutic amounts ... 9804

(iii) Not more than 1.8 grams of dihydrocodeine per 100 milliliters or not more than 90 milligrams per dosage unit, with one or more active nonnarcotic ingredients in recognized therapeutic amounts 9807

(iv) Not more than 300 milligrams of ethylmorphine per 100 milliliters or not more than 15 milligrams per dosage unit, with one or more active, nonnarcotic ingredients in recognized therapeutic amounts 9808

(v) Not more than 500 milligrams of opium per 100 milliliters or per 100 grams or not more than 25 milligrams per dosage unit, with one or more active, nonnarcotic ingredients in recognized therapeutic amounts ... 9809

(vi) Not more than 50 milligrams of morphine per 100 milliliters or per 100 grams, with one or more active, nonnarcotic ingredients in recognized therapeutic amounts ... 9810

(2) Any material, compound, mixture, or preparation containing any of the following narcotic drugs or their salts, as set forth below:

(i) Buprenorphine 9064

(ii) [Reserved] ....

(f) *Anabolic Steroids.* Unless specifically excepted or unless listed in another schedule, any material, compound, mixture or preparation containing any quantity of the following substances, including its salts, esters and ethers:

(1) Anabolic steroids (see § 1300.01 of this chapter)—4000

(2) [Reserved]

(g) *Hallucinogenic substances.* (1) Dronabinol (synthetic) in sesame oil and encapsulated in a soft gelatin capsule in a U.S. Food and Drug Administration approved product—7369.

[Some other names for dronabinol: (6a*R*-*trans*)-6a,7,8,10a-tetrahydro-6,6,9-trimethyl-3-pentyl-6*H*-dibenzo [*b*,*d*]pyran-1-ol] or (-)-delta-9-(*trans*)-tetrahydrocannabinol]

(2) [Reserved]

[39 FR 22142, June 20, 1974]

EDITORIAL NOTE: For FEDERAL REGISTER citations affecting § 1308.13, see the List of CFR Sections Affected, which appears in the Finding Aids section of the printed volume and at *www.govinfo.gov*.

§ 1308.14 Schedule IV.

(a) Schedule IV shall consist of the drugs and other substances, by whatever official name, common or usual name, chemical name, or brand name designated, listed in this section. Each drug or substance has been assigned the DEA Controlled Substances Code Number set forth opposite it.

(b) *Narcotic drugs.* Unless specifically excepted or unless listed in another schedule, any material, compound, mixture, or preparation containing any of the following narcotic drugs, or their salts calculated as the free anhydrous base or alkaloid, in limited quantities as set forth below:

(1) Not more than 1 milligram of difenoxin and not less than 25 micrograms of atropine sulfate per dosage unit 9167
(2) Dextropropoxyphene (alpha-(+)-4-dimethylamino-1,2-diphenyl-3-methyl-2-propionoxybutane) 9278
(3) 2-[(dimethylamino)methyl]-1-(3-methoxyphenyl)cyclohexanol, its salts, optical and geometric isomers and salts of these isomers (including tramadol) 9752

(c) *Depressants.* Unless specifically excepted or unless listed in another schedule, any material, compound, mixture, or preparation which contains any quantity of the following substances, including its salts, isomers, and salts of isomers whenever the existence of such salts, isomers, and salts of isomers is possible within the specific chemical designation:

(1) Alfaxalone 2731
(2) Alprazolam 2882
(3) Barbital 2145
(4) Brexanolone 2400
(5) Bromazepam 2748
(6) Camazepam 2749
(7) Carisoprodol 8192
(8) Chloral betaine 2460
(9) Chloral hydrate 2465
(10) Chlordiazepoxide 2744
(11) Clobazam 2751
(12) Clonazepam 2737
(13) Clorazepate 2768
(14) Clotiazepam 2752
(15) Cloxazolam 2753
(16) Delorazepam 2754
(17) Diazepam 2765
(18) Dichloralphenazone 2467
(19) Estazolam 2756
(20) Ethchlorvynol 2540
(21) Ethinamate 2545
(22) Ethyl loflazepate 2758
(23) Fludiazepam 2759
(24) Flunitrazepam 2763
(25) Flurazepam 2767
(26) Fospropofol 2138
(27) Halazepam 2762
(28) Haloxazolam 2771
(29) Ketazolam 2772
(30) Loprazolam 2773
(31) Lorazepam 2885
(32) Lormetazepam 2774
(33) Mebutamate 2800
(34) Medazepam 2836
(35) Meprobamate 2820
(36) Methohexital 2264
(37) Methylphenobarbital (mephobarbital) 2250
(38) Midazolam 2884
(39) Nimetazepam 2837
(40) Nitrazepam 2834
(41) Nordiazepam 2838
(42) Oxazepam 2835
(43) Oxazolam 2839
(44) Paraldehyde 2585
(45) Petrichloral 2591
(46) Phenobarbital 2285
(47) Pinazepam 2883
(48) Prazepam 2764
(49) Quazepam 2881
(50) Suvorexant 2223
(51) Temazepam 2925
(52) Tetrazepam 2886
(53) Triazolam 2887
(54) Zaleplon 2781
(55) Zolpidem 2783
(56) Zopiclone 2784

(d) *Fenfluramine.* Any material, compound, mixture, or preparation which contains any quantity of the following substances, including its salts, isomers (whether optical, position, or geometric), and salts of such isomers, whenever the existence of such salts, isomers, and salts of isomers is possible:

(1) Fenfluramine 1670

(e) *Lorcaserin.* Any material, compound, mixture, or preparation which contains any quantity of the following substances, including its salts, isomers, and salts of such isomers, whenever the existence of such salts, isomers, and salts of isomers is possible:

(1) Lorcaserin 1625

(f) *Stimulants.* Unless specifically excepted or unless listed in another schedule, any material, compound, mixture, or preparation which contains any quantity of the following substances having a stimulant effect on the central nervous system, including its salts, isomers and salts of isomers:

(1) Cathine ((+)-norpseudoephedrine) 1230
(2) Diethylpropion 1610
(3) Fencamfamin 1760
(4) Fenproporex 1575
(5) Mazindol 1605
(6) Mefenorex 1580
(7)Modafinil 1680
(8) Pemoline (including organometallic complexes and chelates thereof) 1530
(9) Phentermine 1640
(10) Pipradrol 1750
(11) Sibutramine 1675
(12) Solriamfetol (2-amino-3-phenylpropyl carbamate; benzenepropanol, beta-amino-, carbamate (ester)) 1650
(13) SPA ((-)-1-dimethylamino-1,2-diphenylethane) 1635

(g) *Other substances.* Unless specifically excepted or unless listed in another schedule, any material, compound, mixture or preparation which contains any quantity of the following substances, including its salts:

(1) Pentazocine 9709
(2) Butorphanol (including its optical isomers) 9720
(3) Eluxadoline (5-[[[(2*S*)-2-amino-3-[4-aminocarbonyl)-2,6-dimethylphenyl]-1-oxopropyl][(1*S*)-1-(4-phenyl-1*H*-imidazol-2-yl)ethyl]amino]methyl]-2-methoxybenzoic acid) (including its optical isomers) and its salts, isomers, and salts of isomers (9725)..

[39 FR 22143, June 20, 1974]

EDITORIAL NOTE: For FEDERAL REGISTER citations affecting § 1308.14, see the List of CFR Sections Affected, which appears in the Finding Aids section of the printed volume and at *www.govinfo.gov*.

§ 1308.15 Schedule V.

(a) Schedule V shall consist of the drugs and other substances, by whatever official name, common or usual name, chemical name, or brand name designated, listed in this section.

(b) *Narcotic drugs.* Unless specifically excepted or unless listed in another schedule, any material, compound, mixture, or preparation containing any of the following narcotic drugs and their salts, as set forth below:

(1) [Reserved]

(c) *Narcotic drugs containing non-narcotic active medicinal ingredients.* Any compound, mixture, or preparation containing any of the following narcotic drugs, or their salts calculated as the free anhydrous base or alkaloid, in limited quantities as set forth below, which shall include one or more non-narcotic active medicinal ingredients in sufficient proportion to confer upon the compound, mixture, or preparation valuable medicinal qualities other than those possessed by narcotic drugs alone:

(1) Not more than 200 milligrams of codeine per 100 milliliters or per 100 grams.

(2) Not more than 100 milligrams of dihydrocodeine per 100 milliliters or per 100 grams.

(3) Not more than 100 milligrams of ethylmorphine per 100 milliliters or per 100 grams.

(4) Not more than 2.5 milligrams of diphenoxylate and not less than 25 micrograms of atropine sulfate per dosage unit.

(5) Not more than 100 milligrams of opium per 100 milliliters or per 100 grams.

(6) Not more than 0.5 milligram of difenoxin and not less than 25 micrograms of atropine sulfate per dosage unit.

(d) *Stimulants.* Unless specifically exempted or excluded or unless listed in another schedule, any material, compound, mixture, or preparation which contains any quantity of the following substances having a stimulant effect on the central nervous system, including its salts, isomers and salts of isomers:

(1) Pyrovalerone .... 1485.
(2) [Reserved].

(e) *Depressants.* Unless specifically exempted or excluded or unless listed in another schedule, any material, compound, mixture, or preparation which contains any quantity of the following substances having a depressant effect on the central nervous system, including its salts:

(1) Brivaracetam ((2S)-2-[(4R)-2-oxo-4-propylpyrrolidin-1-yl] butanamide) (also referred to as BRV; UCB–34714; Briviact) (including its salts) 2710

(2) Cenobamate ([(1R)-1-(2-chlorophenyl)-2-(tetrazol-2-yl)ethyl] carbamate; 2*H*-tetrazole-2-ethanol, alpha-(2-chlorophenyl)-, carbamate (ester), (alpha*R*)-; carbamic acid (*R*)-(+)-1-(2-chlorophenyl)-2-(2*H*-tetrazol-2-yl)ethyl ester) 2720

(3) Ezogabine [N-[2-amino-4-(4-fluorobenzylamino)-phenyl]-carbamic acid ethyl ester] 2779

(4) Lacosamide [(*R*)-2-acetoamido-*N*-benzyl-3-methoxy-propionamide] 2746

(5) Lasmiditan [2,4,6-trifluoro-*N*-(6-(1-methylpiperidine-4-carbonyl)pyridine-2-yl-benzamide] 2790

(6) Pregabalin [(S)-3-(aminomethyl)-5-methylhexanoic acid] 2782

(f) *Approved cannabidiol drugs.* (1) A drug product in finished dosage formulation that has been approved by the U.S. Food and Drug Administration that contains cannabidiol (2-[1R-3-methyl-6R-(1-methylethenyl)-2-cyclohexen-1-yl]-5-pentyl-1,3-benzenediol) derived from cannabis and no more than 0.1 percent (w/w) residual tetrahydrocannabinols 7367

(2) [Reserved]

[39 FR 22143, June 20, 1974, as amended at 43 FR 38383, Aug. 28, 1978; 44 FR 40888, July 13, 1979; 47 FR 49841, Nov. 3, 1982; 50 FR 8108, Feb. 28, 1985; 52 FR 5952, Feb. 27, 1987; 53 FR 10870, Apr. 4, 1988; 56 FR 61372, Dec. 3, 1991; 67 FR 62370, Oct. 7, 2002; 70 FR 43635, July 28, 2005; 74 FR 23790, May 21, 2009; 76 FR 77899, Dec. 15, 2011; 81 FR 29491, May 12, 2016; 83 FR 48953, Sept 28, 2018; 85 FR 5562, Jan. 31, 2020; 85 FR 13746, Mar. 10, 2020]

EXCLUDED NONNARCOTIC SUBSTANCES

§ 1308.21 Application for exclusion of a nonnarcotic substance.

(a) Any person seeking to have any nonnarcotic drug that may, under the Federal Food, Drug, and Cosmetic Act (21 U.S.C. 301), be lawfully sold over the counter without a prescription, excluded from any schedule, pursuant to section 201(g)(1) of the Act (21 U.S.C. 811(g)(1)), may apply to the Drug and Chemical Evaluation Section, Diversion Control Division, Drug Enforcement Administration. See the Table of DEA Mailing Addresses in § 1321.01 of this chapter for the current mailing address.

(b) An application for an exclusion under this section shall contain the following information:

(1) The name and address of the applicant;

(2) The name of the substance for which exclusion is sought; and

(3) The complete quantitative composition of the substance.

(c) Within a reasonable period of time after the receipt of an application for an exclusion under this section, the Administrator shall notify the applicant of his acceptance or nonacceptance of his application, and if not accepted, the reason therefore. The Administrator need not accept an application for filing if any of the requirements prescribed in paragraph (b) of this section is lacking or is not set forth as to be readily understood. If the applicant desires, he may amend the application to meet the requirements of paragraph (b) of this section. If the application is accepted for filing, the Administrator shall issue and publish in the FEDERAL REGISTER his order on the application, which shall include a reference to the legal authority under which the order is issued and the findings of fact and conclusions of law upon which the order is based. This order shall specify the date on which it shall take effect. The Administrator shall permit any interested person to file written comments on or objections to the order within 60 days of the date of publication of his order in the FEDERAL REGISTER. If any such comments or objections raise significant issues regarding any finding of fact or conclusion of law upon which the order is based, the Administrator shall immediately suspend the effectiveness of the order until he may reconsider the application in light of the comments and objections filed. Thereafter, the Administrator shall reinstate, revoke, or amend his original order as he determines appropriate.

(d) The Administrator may at any time revoke any exclusion granted pursuant to section 201(g) of the Act (21 U.S.C. 811(g)) by following the procedures set forth in paragraph (c) of this section for handling an application for an exclusion which has been accepted for filing.

[38 FR 8254, Mar. 30, 1973, as amended at 70 FR 74657, Dec. 16, 2005; 75 FR 10678, Mar. 9, 2010; 81 FR 97021, Dec. 30, 2016]

§ 1308.22 Excluded substances.

The following nonnarcotic substances which may, under the Federal Food, Drug, and Cosmetic Act (21 U.S.C. 301), be lawfully sold over the counter without a prescription, are excluded from all schedules pursuant to section 201(g) (1) of the Act (21 U.S.C. 811(g) (1)):

EXCLUDED NONNARCOTIC PRODUCTS

Company	Trade name	NDC code	Form	Controlled substance	(mg or mg/ml)
Aphena Pharma Solutions—New York, LLC.	Nasal Decongestant Inhaler/Vapor Inhaler.		IN	Levmetamfetamine (l-Desoxyephedrine).	50.00
Bioline Laboratories	Theophed	00719–1945	TB	Phenobarbital	8.00
Goldline Laboratories	Guiaphed Elixir	00182–1377	EL	Phenobarbital	4.00
Goldline Laboratories	Tedrigen Tablets	00182–0134	TB	Phenobarbital	8.00
Hawthorne Products Inc	Choate's Leg Freeze		LQ	Chloral hydrate	246.67
Parke-Davis & Co	Tedral	00071–0230	TB	Phenobarbital	8.00
Parke-Davis & Co	Tedral Elixir	00071–0242	EX	Phenobarbital	40.00
Parke-Davis & Co	Tedral S.A.	00071–0231	TB	Phenobarbital	8.00
Parke-Davis & Co	Tedral Suspension	00071–0237	SU	Phenobarbital	80.00
Parmed Pharmacy	Asma-Ese	00349–2018	TB	Phenobarbital	8.10
Procter & Gamble Co., The	Vicks VapoInhaler	37000–686–01	IN	Levmetamfetamine (*l*-Desoxyephedrine).	50.00
Rondex Labs	Azma-Aids	00367–3153	TB	Phenobarbital	8.00
Smith Kline Consumer	Benzedrex	49692–0928	IN	Propylhexedrine	250.00
Sterling Drug, Inc	Bronkolixir	00057–1004	EL	Phenobarbital	0.80
Sterling Drug, Inc	Bronkotabs	00057–1005	TB	Phenobarbital	8.00
White Hall Labs	Primatene (P-tablets)	00573–2940	TB	Phenobarbital	8.00

[38 FR 8255, Mar. 30, 1973. Redesignated at 38 FR 26609, Sept. 24, 1973, and amended at 41 FR 16553, Apr. 20, 1976; 41 FR 53477, Dec. 7, 1976; 46 FR 51603, Oct. 21, 1981; 47 FR 45867, Oct. 14, 1982; 54 FR 2100, Jan. 19, 1989; 55 FR 12162, Mar. 30, 1990; 62 FR 13968, Mar. 24, 1997; 74 FR 44283, Aug. 28, 2009; 80 FR 65634, 65637, Oct. 27, 2015; 81 FR 6453, Feb. 8, 2016]

EXEMPT CHEMICAL PREPARATIONS

§ 1308.23 Exemption of certain chemical preparations; application.

(a) The Administrator may, by regulation, exempt from the application of all or any part of the Act any chemical preparation or mixture containing one or more controlled substances listed in any schedule, which preparation or mixture is intended for laboratory, industrial, educational, or special research purposes and not for general administration to a human being or other animal, if the preparation or mixture either:

(1) Contains no narcotic controlled substance and is packaged in such a form or concentration that the packaged quantity does not present any significant potential for abuse (the type of packaging and the history of abuse of the same or similar preparations may be considered in determining the potential for abuse of the preparation or mixture); or

(2) Contains either a narcotic or nonnarcotic controlled substance and one or more adulterating or denaturing agents in such a manner, combination, quantity, proportion, or concentration, that the preparation or mixture does not present any potential for abuse. If the preparation or mixture contains a narcotic controlled substance, the preparation or mixture must be formulated in such a manner that it incorporates methods of denaturing or other means so that the preparation or mixture is not liable to be abused or have

ill effects, if abused, and so that the narcotic substance cannot in practice be removed.

(b) Any person seeking to have any preparation or mixture containing a controlled substance and one or more noncontrolled substances exempted from the application of all or any part of the Act, pursuant to paragraph (a) of this section, may apply to the Drug and Chemical Evaluation Section, Diversion Control Division, Drug Enforcement Administration. See the Table of DEA Mailing Addresses in § 1321.01 of this chapter for the current mailing address.

(c) An application for an exemption under this section shall contain the following information:

(1) The name, address, and registration number, if any, of the applicant;

(2) The name, address, and registration number, if any, of the manufacturer or importer of the preparation or mixture, if not the applicant;

(3) The exact trade name or other designation of the preparation or mixture;

(4) The complete qualitative and quantitative composition of the preparation or mixture (including all active and inactive ingredients and all controlled and noncontrolled substances);

(5) The form of the immediate container in which the preparation or mixture will be distributed with sufficient descriptive detail to identify the preparation or mixture (e.g., bottle, packet, vial, soft plastic pillow, agar gel plate, etc.);

(6) The dimensions or capacity of the immediate container of the preparation or mixture;

(7) The label and labeling, as defined in part 1300 of this chapter, of the immediate container and the commercial containers, if any, of the preparation or mixture;

(8) A brief statement of the facts which the applicant believes justify the granting of an exemption under this paragraph, including information on the use to which the preparation or mixture will be put;

(9) The date of the application; and

(10) Which of the information submitted on the application, if any, is deemed by the applicant to be a trade secret or otherwise confidential and entitled to protection under subsection 402(a)(8) of the Act (21 U.S.C. 842(a) (8)) or any other law restricting public disclosure of information.

(d) The Administrator may require the applicant to submit such documents or written statements of fact relevant to the application as he deems necessary to determine whether the application should be granted.

(e) Within a reasonable period of time after the receipt of an application for an exemption under this section, the Administrator shall notify the applicant of his acceptance or nonacceptance of his application, and if not accepted, the reason therefor. The Administrator need not accept an application for filing if any of the requirements prescribed in paragraph (c) or requested pursuant to paragraph (d) is lacking or is not set forth as to be readily understood. If the applicant desires, he may amend the application to meet the requirements of paragraphs (c) and (d) of this section. If the application is accepted for filing, the Administrator shall issue and publish in the FEDERAL REGISTER his order on the application, which shall include a reference to the legal authority under which the order is based. This order shall specify the date on which it shall take effect. The Administrator shall permit any interested person to file written comments on or objections to the order within 60 days of the date of publication of his order in the FEDERAL REGISTER. If any such comments or objections raise significant issues regarding any finding of fact or conclusion of law upon which the order is based, the Administrator shall immediately suspend the effectiveness of the order until he may reconsider the application in light of the comments and objections filed. Thereafter, the Administrator shall reinstate, revoke, or amend his original order as he determines appropriate.

(f) The Administrator may at any time revoke or modify any exemption granted pursuant to this section by following the procedures set forth in paragraph (e) of this section for handling an application for an exemption which has been accepted for filing. The Administrator may also modify or revoke the criteria by which exemptions are granted (and thereby modify or revoke all preparations and mixtures granted under the old criteria) and modify the scope of exemptions at any time.

[38 FR 8254, Mar. 30, 1973. Redesignated at 38 FR 26609, Sept. 24, 1973, and amended at 46 FR 28841, May 29, 1981; 62 FR 13968, Mar. 24, 1997; 75 FR 10678, Mar. 9, 2010; 81 FR 97021, Dec. 30, 2016]

§ 1308.24 Exempt chemical preparations.

(a) The chemical preparations and mixtures approved pursuant to § 1308.23 are exempt from application of sections 302, 303, 305, 306, 307, 308, 309, 1002, 1003 and 1004 of the Act (21 U.S.C. 822–823, 825–829, 952–954) and § 1301.74 of this chapter, to the extent described in paragraphs (b) to (h) of this section. Substances set forth in paragraph (j) of this section shall be exempt from the application of sections 305, 306, 307, 308, 309, 1002, 1003 and 1004 of the Act (21 U.S.C. 825–829, 952–954) and §§ 1301.71–1301.73 and 1301.74 (a), (b), (d), (e) and (f) of this chapter to the extent as hereinafter may be provided.

(b) Registration and security: Any person who manufactures an exempt chemical preparation or mixture must be registered under the Act and comply with all relevant security requirements regarding controlled substances being used in the manufacturing process until the preparation or mixture is in the form described in paragraph (i) of this section. Any other person who handles an exempt chemical preparation after it is in the form described in paragraph (i) of this section is not required to be registered under the Act to handle that preparation, and the preparation is not required to be stored in accordance with security requirements regarding controlled substances.

(c) Labeling: In lieu of the requirements set forth in part 1302 of this chapter, the label and the labeling of an exempt chemical preparation must be prominently marked with its full trade name or other description and the name of the manufacturer or supplier as set forth in paragraph (i) of this section, in such a way that the product can be readily identified as an exempt chemical preparation. The label and labeling must also include in a prominent manner the statement "For industrial use only" or "For chemical use only" or "For in vitro use only—not for human or animal use" or "Diagnostic reagent—for professional use only" or a comparable statement warning the person reading it that human or animal use is not intended. The symbol designating the schedule of the controlled substance is not required on either the label or the labeling of the exempt chemical preparation, nor is it necessary to list all ingredients of the preparation.

(d) *Records and reports:* Any person who manufactures an exempt chemical preparation or mixture must keep complete and accurate records and file all reports required under part 1304 of this chapter regarding all controlled substances being used in the manufacturing process until the preparation or mixture is in the form described in paragraph (i) of this section. In lieu of records and reports required under part 1304 of this chapter regarding exempt chemical preparations, the manufacturer need only record the name, address, and registration number, if any, of each person to whom the manufacturer distributes any exempt chemical preparation. Each importer or exporter of an exempt narcotic chemical preparation must submit a semiannual report of the total quantity of each substance imported or exported in each calendar half-year within 30 days of the close of the period to the Drug and Chemical Evaluation Section, Drug Enforcement Administration. See the Table of DEA Mailing Addresses in § 1321.01 of this chapter for the current mailing address. Any other person who handles an exempt chemical preparation after it is in the form described in paragraph (i) of this section is not required to maintain records or file reports.

(e) Quotas, order forms, prescriptions, import, export, and transshipment requirements: Once an exempt chemical preparation is in the form described in paragraph (i) of this section, the requirements regarding quotas, order forms, prescriptions, import permits and declarations, export permit and declarations, and transshipment and intransit permits and declarations do not apply. These requirements do apply, however, to any controlled substances used in manufacturing the exempt chemical preparation before it is in the form described in paragraph (i) of this section.

(f) Criminal penalties: No exemption granted pursuant to § 1308.23 affects the criminal liability for illegal manufacture, distribution, or possession of controlled substances contained in the exempt chemical preparation. Distribution, possession, and use of an exempt chemical preparation are lawful for registrants and nonregistrants only as long as such distribution, possession, or use is intended for laboratory, industrial, or educational purposes and not for immediate or subsequent administration to a human being or other animal.

(g) Bulk materials: For materials exempted in bulk quantities, the Administrator may prescribe requirements other than those set forth in paragraphs (b) through (e) of this section on a case-by-case basis.

(h) Changes in chemical preparations: Any change in the quantitative or qualitative composition of the preparation or mixture after the date of application, or change in the trade name or other designation of the preparation or mixture, set forth in paragraph (i) of this section, requires a new application for exemption.

(i) A listing of exempt chemical preparations may be obtained by submitting a written request to the Drug and Chemical Evaluation Section, Drug Enforcement Administration. See the Table of DEA Mailing Addresses in § 1321.01 of this chapter for the current mailing address.

(j) The following substances are designated as exempt chemical preparations for the purposes set forth in this section.

(1) *Chloral.* When packaged in a sealed, oxygen-free environment, under nitrogen pressure, safeguarded against exposure to the air.

(2) *Emit*[R] *Phenobarbital Enzyme Reagent B.* In one liter quantities each with a 5 ml. retention sample for repackaging as an exempt chemical preparation only.

[38 FR 8255, Mar. 30, 1973]

EDITORIAL NOTE: For FEDERAL REGISTER citations affecting § 1308.24, see the List of CFR Sections Affected, which appears in the Finding Aids section of the printed volume and at *www.govinfo.gov.*

EXCLUDED VETERINARY ANABOLIC STEROID IMPLANT PRODUCTS

§ 1308.25 Exclusion of a veterinary anabolic steroid implant product; application.

(a) Any person seeking to have any anabolic steroid product, which is expressly intended for administration through implants to cattle or other nonhuman species and which has been approved by the Secretary of Health and Human Services for such administration, identified as being excluded from any schedule, pursuant to section 102(41)(B)(i) of the Act (21 U.S.C. 802(41)(B)(i)), may apply to the Drug and Chemical Evaluation Section, Diversion Control Division, Drug Enforcement Administration . See the Table of DEA Mailing Addresses in § 1321.01 of this chapter for the current mailing address.

(b) An application for any exclusion under this section shall be submitted in triplicate and contain the following information:

(1) The name and address of the applicant;

(2) The name of the product;

(3) The chemical structural formula or description for any anabolic steroid contained in the product;

(4) A complete description of dosage and quantitative composition of the dosage form;.

(5) The conditions of use including whether or not Federal law restricts this product to use by or on the order of a licensed veterinarian;

(6) A description of the delivery system in which the dosage form will be distributed with sufficient detail to identify the product (e.g. 20 cartridge brown plastic belt);

(7) The label and labeling of the immediate container and the commercial containers, if any, of the product;.

(8) The name and address of the manufacturer of the dosage form if different from that of the applicant; and

(9) Evidence that the product has been approved by the Secretary of Health and Human Services for administration through implant to cattle or other nonhuman species.

(c) Within a reasonable period of time after the receipt of an application for an exclusion under this section, the Administrator shall notify the applicant of his acceptance or nonacceptance of the application, and if not accepted, the reason therefore. The Administrator need not accept an application for filing if any of the requirements prescribed in paragraph (b) of this section is lacking or is not set forth as to be readily understood. The applicant may amend the application to meet the requirements of paragraph (b) of this section. If the application is accepted for filing, the Administrator shall issue and have published in the FEDERAL REGISTER his order on the application, which shall include a reference to the legal authority under which the order is issued and the findings of fact and conclusions of law upon which the order is based. This order shall specify the date on which it will take effect. The Administrator shall permit any interested person to file written comments on or objections to the order within 60 days of the date of publication in the FEDERAL REGISTER. If any such comments or objections raise significant issues regarding any finding of fact or conclusion of law upon which the order is based, the Administrator shall immediately suspend the effectiveness of the order until he may reconsider the application in light of the comments and objections filed. Thereafter, the Administrator shall reinstate, revoke, or amend his original order as he determines appropriate.

(d) The Administrator may at any time revoke or modify any designation of excluded status granted pursuant to this section by following the procedures set forth in paragraph (c) of this section for handling an application for an exclusion which has been accepted for filing.

[56 FR 42936, Aug. 30, 1991, as amended at 75 FR 10679, Mar. 9, 2010; 81 FR 97021, Dec. 30, 2016]

§ 1308.26 Excluded veterinary anabolic steroid implant products.

(a) Products containing an anabolic steroid, that are expressly intended for administration through implants to cattle or other nonhuman species and which have been approved by the Secretary of Health and Human Services for such administration are excluded from all schedules pursuant to section 102(41)(B)(i) of the Act (21 U.S.C. 802(41)(B)(i)). A listing of the excluded products may be obtained by submitting a written request to the Drug and Chemical Evaluation Section, Drug Enforcement Administration. See the Table of DEA Mailing Addresses in § 1321.01 of this chapter for the current mailing address.

(b) In accordance with section 102(41)(B)(ii) of the Act (21 U.S.C. 802(41)(B)(ii)) if any person prescribes, dispenses, or distributes a product listed in paragraph (a) of this section for human use, such person shall be considered to have prescribed, dispensed, or distributed an anabolic steroid within the meaning of section 102(41)(A) of the Act (21 U.S.C. 802(41)(A)).

[56 FR 42936, Aug. 30, 1991, as amended at 57 FR 19534, May 7, 1992; 58 FR 15088, Mar. 19, 1993; 62 FR 13967, Mar. 24, 1997; 75 FR 10679, Mar. 9, 2010]

EXEMPTED PRESCRIPTION PRODUCTS

§ 1308.31 Application for exemption of a nonnarcotic prescription product.

(a) Any person seeking to have any compound, mixture, or preparation containing any nonnarcotic controlled substance listed in § 1308.12(e), or in § 1308.13(b) or (c), or in § 1308.14, or in § 1308.15, exempted from application of all or any part of the Act pursuant to section 201(g)(3)(A), of the Act (21 U.S.C. 811(g)(3)(A)) may apply to the Drug and Chemical Evaluation Section, Diversion Control Division, Drug Enforcement Administration. See the Table of DEA Mailing Addresses in § 1321.01 of this chapter for the current mailing address.

(b) An application for an exemption under this section shall contain the following information:

(1) The complete quantitative composition of the dosage form.

(2) Description of the unit dosage form together with complete labeling.

(3) A summary of the pharmacology of the product including animal investigations and clinical evaluations and studies, with emphasis on the psychic and/or physiological dependence liability (this must be done for each of the

active ingredients separately and for the combination product).

(4) Details of synergisms and antagonisms among ingredients.

(5) Deterrent effects of the noncontrolled ingredients.

(6) Complete copies of all literature in support of claims.

(7) Reported instances of abuse.

(8) Reported and anticipated adverse effects.

(9) Number of dosage units produced for the past 2 years.

(c) Within a reasonable period of time after the receipt of an application for an exemption under this section, the Administrator shall notify the applicant of his acceptance or non-acceptance of the application, and if not accepted, the reason therefor. The Administrator need not accept an application for filing if any of the requirements prescribed in paragraph (b) of this section is lacking or is not set forth so as to be readily understood. If the applicant desires, he may amend the application to meet the requirements of paragraph (b) of this section. If accepted for filing, the Administrator shall publish in the FEDERAL REGISTER general notice of this proposed rulemaking in granting or denying the application. Such notice shall include a reference to the legal authority under which the rule is proposed, a statement of the proposed rule granting or denying an exemption, and, in the discretion of the Administrator, a summary of the subjects and issues involved. The Administrator shall permit any interested person to file written comments on or objections to the proposal and shall designate in the notice of proposed rule making the time during which such filings may be made. After consideration of the application and any comments on or objections to his proposed rulemaking, the Administrator shall issue and publish in the FEDERAL REGISTER his final order on the application, which shall set forth the findings of fact and conclusions of law upon which the order is based. This order shall specify the date on which it shall take effect, which shall not be less than 30 days from the date of publication in the FEDERAL REGISTER unless the Administrator finds that conditions of public health or safety necessitate an earlier effective date, in which event the Administrator shall specify in the order his findings as to such conditions.

(d) The Administrator may revoke any exemption granted pursuant to section 201(g)(3)(A) of the Act (21 U.S.C. 811(g)(3)(A)) by following the procedures set forth in paragraph (c) of this section for handling an application for an exemption which has been accepted for filing.

[38 FR 8254, Mar. 30, 1973. Redesignated at 38 FR 26609, Sept. 24, 1973, as amended at 44 FR 18968, Mar. 30, 1979; 52 FR 9803, Mar. 27, 1987; 75 FR 10679, Mar. 9, 2010; 81 FR 97021, Dec. 30, 2016]

§ 1308.32 Exempted prescription products.

The compounds, mixtures, or preparations that contain a nonnarcotic controlled substance listed in § 1308.12(e) or in § 1308.13(b) or (c) or in § 1308.14 or in § 1308.15 listed in the Table of Exempted Prescription Products have been exempted by the Administrator from the application of sections 302 through 305, 307 through 309, and 1002 through 1004 of the Act (21 U.S.C. 822–825, 827–829, and 952–954) and §§ 1301.13, 1301.22, and §§ 1301.71 through 1301.76 of this chapter for administrative purposes only. An exception to the above is that those products containing butalbital shall not be exempt from the requirement of 21 U.S.C. 952–954 concerning importation, exportation, transshipment and in-transit shipment of controlled substances. Any deviation from the quantitative composition of any of the listed drugs shall require a petition of exemption in order for the product to be exempted. A listing of the Exempted Prescription Products may be obtained by submitting a written request to the Drug and Chemical Evaluation Section, Drug Enforcement Administration. See the Table of DEA Mailing Addresses in § 1321.01 of this chapter for the current mailing address.

[75 FR 10679, Mar. 9, 2010]

EXEMPT ANABOLIC STEROID PRODUCTS

§ 1308.33 Exemption of certain anabolic steroid products; application.

(a) The Administrator, upon the recommendation of Secretary of Health and Human Services, may, by regulation, exempt from the application of all or any part of the Act any compound, mixture, or preparation containing an anabolic steroid as defined in part 1300 of this chapter, which is intended for administration to a human being or animal, if, because of its concentration, preparation, formulation, or delivery system, it has no significant potential for abuse.

(b) Any person seeking to have any compound, mixture, or preparation containing an anabolic steroid as defined in part 1300 of this chapter exempted from the application of all or any part of the Act, pursuant to paragraph (a) of this section, may apply to the Drug and Chemical Evaluation Section, Diversion Control Division, Drug Enforcement Administration. See the Table of DEA Mailing Addresses in § 1321.01 of this chapter for the current mailing address.

(c) An application for an exemption under this section shall be submitted in triplicate and contain the following information:

(1) The name and address of the applicant;

(2) The name of the product;

(3) The chemical structural formula or description for any anabolic steroid contained in the product;

(4) The complete description of dosage and quantitative composition of the dosage form;

(5) A description of the delivery system, if applicable;

(6) The indications and conditions for use in which species, including whether or not this product is a prescription drug;

(7) Information to facilitate identification of the dosage form, such as shape, color, coating, and scoring;

(8) The label and labeling of the immediate container and the commercial containers, if any, of the product;

(9) The units in which the dosage form is ordinarily available; and

(10) The facts which the applicant believes justify:

(i) A determination that the product has no significant potential for abuse and

(ii) a granting of an exemption under this section.

(d) Within a reasonable period of time after the receipt of the application for an exemption under this section, the Administrator shall notify the applicant of his acceptance or nonacceptance of the application, and if not accepted, the reason therefor. The Administrator need not accept an application for filing if any of the requirements prescribed in paragraph (c) of this section is lacking or is not set forth so as to be readily understood. The applicant may amend the application to meet the requirements of paragraph (c) of this section. If accepted for filing, the Administrator will request from the Secretary for Health and Human Services his recommendation, as to whether such product which contains an anabolic steroid should be considered for exemption from certain portions of the Controlled Substances Act. On receipt of the recommendation of the Secretary, the Administrator shall make a determination as to whether the evidence submitted or otherwise available sufficiently establishes that the product possesses no significant potential for abuse. The Administrator shall issue and publish in the FEDERAL REGISTER his order on the application, which shall include a reference to the legal authority under which the order is issued, and the findings of fact and conclusions of law upon which the order is based. This order shall specify the date on which it will take effect. The Administrator shall permit any interested person to file written comments on or objections to the order within 60 days of the date of publication of his order in the FEDERAL REGISTER. If any such comments or objections raise significant issues regarding any finding of fact or conclusion of law upon which the order is based, the Administrator shall immediately suspend the effectiveness of the order until he may reconsider the application in light of the comments and objections filed. Thereafter, the Administrator shall reinstate, revoke, or amend his original order as he determines appropriate.

(e) The Administrator may revoke any exemption granted pursuant to section 1903(a) of Public Law 101–647 by following the procedures set forth in paragraph (d) of this section for handling an application for an exemption which has been accepted for filing.

[56 FR 42936, Aug. 30, 1991; 57 FR 10815, Mar. 31, 1992, as amended at 62 FR 13968, Mar. 24, 1997; 70 FR 74657, Dec. 16, 2005; 75 FR 10679, Mar. 9, 2010; 81 FR 97021, Dec. 30, 2016]

§ 1308.34 Exempt anabolic steroid products.

The list of compounds, mixtures, or preparations that contain an anabolic steroid that have been exempted by the Administrator from application of sections 302 through 309 and 1002 through 1004 of the Act (21 U.S.C. 822–829 and 952–954) and §§ 1301.13, 1301.22, and 1301.71 through 1301.76 of this chapter for administrative purposes only may be obtained by submitting a written request to the Drug and Chemical Evaluation Section, Drug Enforcement Administration. See the Table of DEA Mailing Addresses in § 1321.01 of this chapter for the current mailing address.

[75 FR 10679, Mar. 9, 2010]

Exempt Cannabis Plant Material, and Products Made Therefrom, that Contain Tetrahydrocannabinols

§ 1308.35 Exemption of certain cannabis plant material, and products made therefrom, that contain tetrahydrocannabinols.

(a) Any processed plant material or animal feed mixture containing any amount of tetrahydrocannabinols (THC) that is both:

(1) Made from any portion of a plant of the genus Cannabis excluded from the definition of marijuana under the Act [i.e., the mature stalks of such plant, fiber produced from such stalks, oil or cake made from the seeds of such plant, any other compound, manufacture, salt, derivative, mixture, or preparation of such mature stalks (except the resin extracted therefrom), fiber, oil, or cake, or the sterilized seed of such plant which is incapable of germination] and

(2) Not used, or intended for use, for human consumption, has been exempted by the Administrator from the application of the Act and this chapter.

(b) As used in this section, the following terms shall have the meanings specified:

(1) The term *processed plant material* means cannabis plant material that has been subject to industrial processes, or mixed with other ingredients, such that it cannot readily be converted into any form that can be used for human consumption.

(2) The term *animal feed mixture* means sterilized cannabis seeds mixed with other ingredients (not derived from the cannabis plant) in a formulation that is designed, marketed, and distributed for animal consumption (and not for human consumption).

(3) The term *used for human consumption* means either:

(i) Ingested orally or

(ii) Applied by any means such that THC enters the human body.

(4) The term *intended for use for human consumption* means any of the following:

(i) Designed by the manufacturer for human consumption;

(ii) Marketed for human consumption; or

(iii) Distributed, exported, or imported, with the intent that it be used for human consumption.

(c) In any proceeding arising under the Act or this chapter, the burden of going forward with the evidence that a material, compound, mixture, or preparation containing THC is exempt from control pursuant to this section shall be upon the person claiming such exemption, as set forth in section 515(a)(1) of the Act (21 U.S.C. 885(a)(1)). In order to meet this burden with respect to a product or plant material that has not been expressly exempted from control by the Administrator pursuant to § 1308.23, the person claiming the exemption must present rigorous scientific evidence, including well-documented scientific studies by experts trained and qualified to evaluate the effects of drugs on humans.

[66 FR 51544, Oct. 9, 2001]

HEARINGS

§ 1308.41 Hearings generally.

In any case where the Administrator shall hold a hearing on the issuance, amendment, or repeal of rules pursuant to section 201 of the Act, the procedures for such hearing and accompanying proceedings shall be governed generally by the rulemaking procedures set forth in the Administrative Procedure Act (5 U.S.C. 551–559) and specifically by section 201 of the Act (21 U.S.C. 811), by §§ 1308.42–1308.51, and by §§ 1316.41–1316.67 of this chapter.

§ 1308.42 Purpose of hearing.

If requested by any interested person after proceedings are initiated pursuant to § 1308.43, the Administrator shall hold a hearing for the purpose of receiving factual evidence and expert opinion regarding the issues involved in the issuance, amendment or repeal of a rule issuable pursuant to section 201(a) of the Act (21 U.S.C. 811(a)). Extensive argument should not be offered into evidence but rather presented in opening or closing statements of counsel or in memoranda or proposed findings of fact and conclusions of law. Additional information relating to hearings to include waivers or modification of rules, request for hearing, burden of proof, time and place, and final order are set forth in part 1316 of this chapter.

[62 FR 13968, Mar. 24, 1997]

§ 1308.43 Initiation of proceedings for rulemaking.

(a) Any interested person may submit a petition to initiate proceedings for the issuance, amendment, or repeal of any rule or regulation issuable pursuant to the provisions of section 201 of the Act.

(b) Petitions shall be submitted in quintuplicate to the Administrator. See the Table of DEA Mailing Addresses in § 1321.01 of this chapter for the current mailing address. Petitions shall be in the following form:

________________ (Date)

Administrator, Drug Enforcement Administration __________ (Mailing Address)

Dear Sir: The undersigned ____________ hereby petitions the Administrator to initiate proceedings for the issuance (amendment or repeal) of a rule or regulation pursuant to section 201 of the Controlled Substances Act.

Attached hereto and constituting a part of this petition are the following:

(A) The proposed rule in the form proposed by the petitioner. (If the petitioner seeks the amendment or repeal of an existing rule, the existing rule, together with a reference to the section in the Code of Federal Regulations where it appears, should be included.)

(B) A statement of the grounds which the petitioner relies for the issuance (amendment or repeal) of the rule. (Such grounds shall include a reasonably concise statement of the facts relied upon by the petitioner, including a summary of any relevant medical or scientific evidence known to the petitioner.)

All notices to be sent regarding this petition should be addressed to:

________________ (Name)
________________ (Street Address)
________________ (City and State)

Respectfully yours,

________________ (Signature of petitioner)

(c) Within a reasonable period of time after the receipt of a petition, the Administrator shall notify the petitioner of his acceptance or nonacceptance of the petition, and if not accepted, the reason therefor. The Administrator need not accept a petition for filing if any of the requirements prescribed in paragraph (b) of this section is lacking or is not set forth so as to be readily understood. If the petitioner desires, he may amend the petition to meet the requirements of paragraph (b) of this section. If accepted for filing, a petition may be denied by the Administrator within a reasonable period of time thereafter if he finds the grounds upon which the petitioner relies are not sufficient to justify the initiation of proceedings.

(d) The Administrator shall, before initiating proceedings for the issuance, amendment, or repeal of any rule either to control a drug or other substance, or to transfer a drug or other substance from one schedule to another, or to remove a drug or other substance entirely from the schedules, and after gathering the necessary data, request from the Secretary a scientific and medical evaluation and the Secretary's recommendations as to whether such drug or other substance should be so controlled, transferred, or removed as a controlled substance. The recommendations of the Secretary to the Administrator shall be binding on the Administrator as to such scientific and medical matters, and if the Secretary recommends that a drug or other substance not be controlled, the Administrator shall not control that drug or other substance.

(e) If the Administrator determines that the scientific and medical evaluation and recommendations of the Secretary and all other relevant data constitute substantial evidence of potential for abuse such as to warrant control or additional control over the drug or other substance, or substantial evidence that the drug or other substances should be subjected to lesser control or removed entirely from the schedules, he shall initiate proceedings for control, transfer, or removal as the case may be.

(f) If and when the Administrator determines to initiate proceedings, he shall publish in the FEDERAL REGISTER general notice of any proposed rule making to issue, amend, or repeal any rule pursuant to section 201 of the Act. Such published notice shall include a statement of the time, place, and nature of any hearings on the proposal in the event a hearing is requested pursuant to § 1308.44. Such hearings may not be commenced until after the expiration of at least 30 days from the date the general notice is published in the FEDERAL REGISTER. Such published notice shall also include a reference to the legal authority under which the rule is proposed, a statement of the proposed rule, and, in the discretion of the Administrator, a summary of the subjects and issues involved.

(g) The Administrator may permit any interested persons to file written comments on or objections to the proposal and shall designate in the notice of proposed rule making the time during which such filings may be made.

[38 FR 8254, Mar. 30, 1973. Redesignated at 38 FR 26609, Sept. 24, 1973, and further redesignated and amended at 62 FR 13968, Mar. 24, 1997; 75 FR 10679, Mar. 9, 2010]

§ 1308.44 Request for hearing or appearance; waiver.

(a) Any interested person desiring a hearing on a proposed rulemaking, shall, within 30 days after the date of publication of notice of the proposed rulemaking in the FEDERAL REGISTER, file with the Administrator a written request for a hearing in the form prescribed in § 1316.47 of this chapter.

(b) Any interested person desiring to participate in a hearing pursuant to § 1308.41 shall, within 30 days after the date of publication of the notice of hearing in the FEDERAL REGISTER, file with the Administrator a written notice of his intention to participate in such hearing in the form prescribed in § 1316.48 of this chapter. Any person filing a request for a hearing need not also file a notice of appearance; the request for a hearing shall be deemed to be a notice of appearance.

(c) Any interested person may, within the period permitted for filing a request for a hearing, file with the Administrator a waiver of an opportunity for a hearing or to participate in a hearing, together with a written statement regarding his position on the matters of fact and law involved in such hearing. Such statement, if admissible, shall be made a part of the record and shall be considered in light of the lack of opportunity for cross-examination in determining the weight to be attached to matters of fact asserted therein.

(d) If any interested person fails to file a request for a hearing; or if he so files and fails to appear at the hearing, he shall be deemed to have waived his opportunity for the hearing or to participate in the hearing, unless he shows good cause for such failure.

(e) If all interested persons waive or are deemed to waive their opportunity for the hearing or to participate in the hearing, the Administrator may cancel the hearing, if scheduled, and issue his final order pursuant to § 1308.45 without a hearing.

[38 FR 8254, Mar. 30, 1973. Redesignated at 38 FR 26609, Sept. 24, 1973, and further redesignated and amended at 62 FR 13968, Mar. 24, 1997]

§ 1308.45 Final order.

As soon as practicable after the presiding officer has certified the record to the Administrator, the Administrator shall cause to be published in the FEDERAL REGISTER his order in the proceeding, which shall set forth the final rule and the findings of fact and conclusions of law upon which the rule is based. This order shall specify the date on which it shall take effect, which shall not be less than 30 days from the date of publication in the FEDERAL REGISTER unless the Administrator finds that conditions of public health or safety necessitate an earlier effective date, in which event the Administrator shall specify in the order his findings as to such conditions.

[38 FR 8254, Mar. 30, 1973. Redesignated at 38 FR 26609, Sept. 24, 1973, and further redesignated at 62 FR 13968, Mar. 24, 1997]

§ 1308.46 Control required under international treaty.

Pursuant to section 201(d) of the Act (21 U.S.C. 811(d)), where control of a substance is required by U.S. obligations under international treaties, conventions, or protocols in effect on May 1, 1971, the Administrator shall issue and publish in the FEDERAL REGISTER an order controlling such substance under the schedule he deems most appropriate to carry out obligations. Issuance of such an order shall be without regard to the findings required by subsections 201(a) or 202(b) of the Act (21 U.S.C. 811(a) or 812(b)) and without regard to the procedures prescribed by § 1308.41 or subsections 201 (a) and (b) of the Act (21 U.S.C. 811 (a) and (b)). An order controlling a substance shall become effective 30 days from the date of publication in the FEDERAL REGISTER, unless the Administrator finds that conditions of public health or safety necessitate an earlier effective date, in which event the Administrator shall specify in the order his findings as to such conditions.

[38 FR 8254, Mar. 30, 1973. Redesignated at 38 FR 26609, Sept. 24, 1973, and further redesignated at 62 FR 13968, Mar. 24, 1997]

§ 1308.47 Control of immediate precursors.

Pursuant to section 201(e) of the Act (21 U.S.C. 811(e)), the Administrator may, without regard to the findings required by subsection 201(a) or 202 (b) of the Act (21 U.S.C. 811(a) or 812(b)) and without regard to the procedures prescribed by § 1308.41 or subsections 201 (a) and (b) of the Act (21 U.S.C. 811(a) and (b)), issue and publish in the FEDERAL REGISTER an order controlling an immediate precursor. The order shall designate the schedule in which the immediate precursor is to be placed, which shall be the same schedule in which the controlled substance of which it is an immediate precursor is placed or any other schedule with a higher numerical designation. An order controlling an immediate precursor shall become effective 30 days from the date of publication in the FEDERAL REGISTER, unless the Administrator finds that conditions of public health or safety necessitate an earlier effective date, in which event the Administrator shall specify in the order his findings as to such conditions.

[38 FR 8254, Mar. 30, 1973. Redesignated at 38 FR 26609, Sept. 24, 1973, and further redesignated at 62 FR 13968, Mar. 24, 1997]

§ 1308.49 Temporary scheduling.

(a) Pursuant to 21 U.S.C. 811(h) and without regard to the requirements of 21 U.S.C. 811(b) relating to the scientific and medical evaluation of the Secretary of Health and Human Services, the Drug Enforcement Administration may place a substance into Schedule I on a temporary basis, if it determines that such action is necessary to avoid an imminent hazard to the public safety. An order issued under this section may not be effective before the expiration of 30 calendar days from:

(1) The date of publication by the Administration of a notice in the FEDERAL REGISTER of its intention to issue such order and the grounds upon which such order is to be issued; and

(2) The date the Administration has transmitted notification to the Secretary of Health and Human Services of the Administration's intention to issue such order.

(b) An order issued under this section will be vacated upon the conclusion of a subsequent rulemaking proceeding initiated under section 201(a) (21 U.S.C. 811(a)) with respect to such substance or at the end of two years from the effective date of the order scheduling the substance, except that during the pendency of proceedings under section 201(a) (21 U.S.C. 811(a)) with respect to the substance, the Administration may extend the temporary scheduling for up to one year.

[81 FR 97021, Dec. 30, 2016]

PART 1309—REGISTRATION OF MANUFACTURERS, DISTRIBUTORS, IMPORTERS AND EXPORTERS OF LIST I CHEMICALS

AUTHORITY: 21 U.S.C. 802, 821, 822, 823, 824, 830, 871(b), 875, 877, 886a, 952, 953, 957, 958.

SOURCE: 60 FR 32454, June 22, 1995, unless otherwise noted.

GENERAL INFORMATION

§ 1309.01 Scope of part 1309.

Procedures governing the registration of manufacturers, distributors, importers and exporters of List I chemicals pursuant to Sections 102, 302, 303, 1007 and 1008 of the Act (21 U.S.C. 802, 822, 823, 957 and 958) are set forth generally by those sections and specifically by the sections of this part.

§ 1309.02 Definitions.

Any term used in this part shall have the definition set forth in section 102 of the Act (21 U.S.C. 802) or part 1300 of this chapter.

[62 FR 13968, Mar. 24, 1997]

§ 1309.03 Information; special instructions.

Information regarding procedures under these rules and instructions supplementing these rules will be furnished upon request by writing to the Registration Section, Drug Enforcement Administration. See the Table of DEA Mailing Addresses in § 1321.01 of this chapter for the current mailing address.

[75 FR 10680, Mar. 9, 2010]

FEES FOR REGISTRATION AND REREGISTRATION

§ 1309.11 Fee amounts.

(a) For each application for registration or reregistration to manufacture the applicant shall pay an annual fee of $3,047.

(b) For each application for registration or reregistration to distribute, import, or export a List I chemical, the applicant shall pay an annual fee of $1,523.

[77 FR 15250, Mar. 15, 2012]

§ 1309.12 Time and method of payment; refund.

(a) For each application for registration or reregistration to manufacture, distribute, import, or export, the applicant shall pay the fee when the application for registration or reregistration is submitted for filing.

(b) Payments should be made in the form of a credit card; a personal, certified, or cashier's check; or a money order made payable to "Drug Enforcement Administration." Payments made in the form of stamps, foreign currency, or third party endorsed checks will not be accepted. These application fees are not refundable.

[75 FR 4980, Feb. 1, 2010]

REQUIREMENTS FOR REGISTRATION

§ 1309.21 Persons required to register.

(a) Unless exempted by law or under §§ 1309.24 through 1309.26 or §§ 1310.12 through 1310.13 of this chapter, the following persons must annually obtain a registration specific to the List I chemicals to be handled:

(1) Every person who manufactures or imports or proposes to manufacture or import a List I chemical or a drug product containing ephedrine, pseudoephedrine, or phenylpropanolamine.

(2) Every person who distributes or exports or proposes to distribute or export any List I chemical, other than those List I chemicals contained in a product exempted under paragraph (1)(iv) of the definition of regulated transaction in § 1300.02 of this chapter.

(b) Only persons actually engaged in the activities are required to obtain a registration; related or affiliated persons who are not engaged in the activities are not required to be registered. (For example, a stockholder or parent corporation of a corporation distributing List I chemicals is not required to obtain a registration.)

(c) The registration requirements are summarized in the following table:

SUMMARY OF REGISTRATION REQUIREMENTS AND LIMITATIONS

Business activity	Chemicals	DEA Forms	Application fee	Registration period (years)	Coincident activities allowed
Manufacturing ...	List I	New–510	$3,047	1	May distribute that chemical for which registration was issued; may not distribute any chemical for which not registered.
	Drug products containing ephedrine, pseudoephedrine, phenylpropanolamine.	Renewal–510a.	3,047		
Distributing	List I	New–510	1,523	1	
	Scheduled listed chemical products.	Renewal–510a.	1,523		
Importing	List I	New–510	1,523	1	May distribute that chemical for which registration was issued; may not distribute any chemical for which not registered.
	Drug Products containing ephedrine, pseudoephedrine, phenylpropanolamine.	Renewal–510a.	1,523		
Exporting	List I	New–510	1,523	1	
	Scheduled listed chemical products.	Renewal–510a.	1,523		

[75 FR 4980, Feb. 1, 2010, as amended at 77 FR 4236, Jan. 27, 2012; 77 FR 15250, Mar. 15, 2012]

§ 1309.22 Separate registration for independent activities.

(a) The following groups of activities are deemed to be independent of each other:

(1) Manufacturing of List I chemicals or drug products containing ephedrine, pseudoephedrine, or phenylpropanolamine.

(2) Distributing of List I chemicals and scheduled listed chemical products.

(3) Importing List I chemicals or drug products containing ephedrine, pseudoephedrine, or phenylpropanolamine.

(4) Exporting List I chemicals and scheduled listed chemical products.

(b) Except as provided in paragraphs (c) and (d) of this section, every person who engages in more than one group of independent activities must obtain a separate registration for each group of activities, unless otherwise exempted by the Act or §§ 1309.24 through 1309.26.

(c) A person registered to import any List I chemical shall be authorized to distribute that List I chemical after importation, but no other chemical that the person is not registered to import.

(d) A person registered to manufacture any List I chemical shall be authorized to distribute that List I chemical after manufacture, but no other chemical that the person is not registered to manufacture.

[75 FR 4981, Feb. 1, 2010]

§ 1309.23 Separate registration for separate locations.

(a) A separate registration is required for each principal place of business at one general physical location where List I chemicals are manufactured, distributed, imported, or exported by a person.

(b) The following locations shall be deemed to be places not subject to the registration requirement:

(1) A warehouse where List I chemicals are stored by or on behalf of a registered person, unless such chemicals are distributed directly from such warehouse to locations other than the registered location from which the chemicals were originally delivered; and

(2) An office used by agents of a registrant where sales of List I chemicals are solicited, made, or supervised but which neither contains such chemicals (other than chemicals for display purposes) nor serves as a distribution point for filling sales orders.

[60 FR 32454, June 22, 1995, as amended at 75 FR 4981, Feb. 1, 2010]

§ 1309.24 Waiver of registration requirement for certain activities.

(a) The requirement of registration is waived for any agent or employee of a person who is registered to engage in any group of independent activities, if the agent or employee is acting in the usual course of his or her business or employment.

(b) The requirement of registration is waived for any person who manufactures or distributes a scheduled listed chemical product or other product containing a List I chemical that is described and included in paragraph (1)(iv) of the definition of regulated transaction in § 1300.02 of this chapter, if that person is registered with the Administration to engage in the same activity with a controlled substance.

(c) The requirement of registration is waived for any person who imports or exports a scheduled listed chemical product or other product containing a List I chemical that is described and included in paragraph (1)(iv) of the definition of regulated transaction in § 1300.02 of this chapter, if that person is registered with the Administration to engage in the same activity with a controlled substance.

(d) The requirement of registration is waived for any person who only distributes a prescription drug product containing a List I chemical that is regulated pursuant to paragraph (1)(iv) of the definition of regulated transaction in § 1300.02 of this chapter.

(e) The requirement of registration is waived for any person whose activities with respect to List I chemicals are limited to the distribution of red phosphorus, white phosphorus, or hypophosphorous acid (and its salts) to another location operated by the same firm solely for internal end-use, or an EPA or State licensed waste treatment or disposal firm for the purpose of waste disposal.

(f) The requirement of registration is waived for any person whose distribution of red phosphorus or white phosphorus is limited solely to residual quantities of chemical returned to the producer, in reusable rail cars and intermodal tank containers which conform to International Standards Organization specifications (with capacities greater than or equal to 2,500 gallons in a single container).

(g) The requirement of registration is waived for any person whose activities with respect to List I chemicals are limited solely to the distribution of Lugol's Solution (consisting of 5 percent iodine and 10 percent potassium iodide in an aqueous solution) in original manufacturer's packaging of one fluid ounce (30 ml) or less.

(h) The requirement of registration is waived for any manufacturer of a List I chemical, if that chemical is produced solely for internal consumption by the manufacturer and there is no subsequent distribution or exportation of the List I chemical.

(i) If any person exempted under paragraph (b), (c), (d), (e), or (f) of this section also engages in the distribution, importation, or exportation of a List I chemical, other than as described in such paragraph, the person shall obtain a registration for the activities, as required by § 1309.21.

(j) The Administrator may, upon finding that continuation of the waiver would not be in the public interest, suspend or revoke a waiver granted under paragraph (b), (c), (d), (e), or (f) of this section pursuant to the procedures set forth in §§ 1309.43 through 1309.46 and §§ 1309.51 through 1309.55. In considering the revocation or suspension of a person's waiver granted pursuant to paragraph (b) or (c) of this section, the Administrator shall also consider whether action to revoke or suspend the person's controlled substance registration pursuant to section 304 of the Act (21 U.S.C. 824) is warranted.

(k) Any person exempted from the registration requirement under this section must comply with the security requirements set forth in §§ 1309.71 through 1309.73 and the recordkeeping and reporting requirements set forth under Parts 1310, 1313, 1314, and 1315 of this chapter.

[75 FR 4981, Feb. 1, 2010, as amended at 77 FR 4236, Jan. 25, 2012]

§ 1309.25 Temporary exemption from registration for chemical registration applicants.

(a) Each person required by section 302 of the Act (21 U.S.C. 822) to obtain a registration to distribute, import, or export a combination ephedrine product is temporarily exempted from the registration requirement, provided that the person submits a proper application for registration on or before July 12, 1997. The exemption will remain in effect for each person who has made such application until the Administration has approved or denied that application. This exemption applies only to registration; all other chemical control requirements set forth in this part 1309 and parts 1310, and 1313 of this chapter remain in full force and effect.

(b) Each person required by section 302 of the Act (21 U.S.C. 822) to obtain a registration to distribute, import, or export a pseudoephedrine or phenylpropanolamine drug product is temporarily exempted from the registration requirement, provided that the person submits a proper application for registration on or before October 3, 1997. The exemption will remain in effect for each person who has made such application until the Administration has approved or denied that application. This exemption applies only to registration; all other chemical control requirements set forth in this part 1309 and parts 1310 and 1313 of this chapter remain in full force and effect.

(c) Each person required by sections 302 or 1007 of the Act (21 U.S.C. 822 or 957) to obtain a registration to manufacture or import prescription drug products containing ephedrine, pseudoephedrine, or phenylpropanolamine is temporarily exempted from the registration requirement, provided that the person submits a proper application for registration on or before March 3, 2010. The exemption will remain in effect for each person who has made such application until the Administration has approved or denied the application. This exemption applies only to registration; all other chemical control requirements set forth in this part and parts 1310, 1313, and 1315 of this chapter remain in full force and effect.

[67 FR 14860, Mar. 28, 2002, as amended at 75 FR 4982, Feb. 1, 2010]

§ 1309.26 Exemption of law enforcement officials.

(a) The requirement of registration is waived for the following persons in the circumstances described in this section:

(1) Any officer or employee of the Administration, any customs officer, any officer or employee of the U.S. Food and Drug Administration, and any Federal or Insular officer who is lawfully engaged in the enforcement of any federal law relating to listed chemicals, controlled substances, drugs, or customs, and is duly authorized to possess and distribute List I chemicals in the course of his/her official duties; and

(2) Any officer or employee of any State, or any political subdivision or agency thereof, who is engaged in the enforcement of any State or local law relating to listed chemicals and controlled substances and is duly authorized to possess and distribute List I chemicals in the course of his official duties.

(b) Any official exempted by this section may, when acting in the course of official duties, possess any List I chemical and distribute any such chemical to any other official who is also exempted by this section and acting in the course of official duties.

[60 FR 32454, June 22, 1995, as amended at 81 FR 97021, Dec. 30, 2016]

Application for Registration

§ 1309.31 Time for application for registration; expiration date.

(a) Any person who is required to be registered and who is not so registered may apply for registration at any time. No person required to be registered shall engage in any activity for which registration is required until the application for registration is approved and a Certificate of Registration is issued by the Administrator to such person.

(b) Any person who is registered may apply to be reregistered not more than 60 days before the expiration date of his registration.

(c) At the time a person is first registered, that person shall be assigned to one of twelve groups, which shall correspond to the months of the year. The expiration date of the registrations of all registrants within any group will be the last day of the month designated for that group. In assigning any of the above persons to a group, the Administration may select a group the expiration date of which is less than one year from the date such business activity was registered. If the person is assigned to a group which has an expiration date less than eleven months from the date of which the person is registered, the registration shall not expire until one year from that expiration date; in all other cases, the registration shall expire on the expiration date following the date on which the person is registered.

§ 1309.32 Application forms; contents; signature.

(a) Any person who is required to be registered pursuant to § 1309.21 and is not so registered, shall apply on DEA Form 510.

(b) Any person who is registered pursuant to Section 1309.21, shall apply for reregistration on DEA Form 510a.

(c) DEA Form 510 may be obtained at any divisional office of the Administration or by writing to the Registration Section, Drug Enforcement Administration. See the Table of DEA Mailing Addresses in § 1321.01 of this chapter for the current mailing address. DEA Form 510a will be mailed to each List I chemical registrant approximately 60 days before the expiration date of his or her registration; if any registered person does not receive such forms within 45 days before the expiration date of the registration, notice must be promptly given of such fact and DEA Form 510a must be requested by writing to the Registration Section of the Administration at the foregoing address.

(d) Each application for registration must include the Administration Chemical Code Number, as set forth in § 1310.02 of this chapter, for each List I chemical to be manufactured, distributed, imported, or exported.

(e) Registration shall not entitle a person to engage in any activity with any List I chemical not specified in his or her application.

(f) Each application shall include all information called for in the form, unless the item is not applicable, in which case this fact shall be indicated.

(g) Each application, attachment, or other document filed as part of an application, shall be signed by the applicant, if an individual; by a partner of the applicant, if a partnership; or by an officer of the applicant, if a corporation, corporate division, association, trust or other entity. An applicant may authorize one or more individuals, who would not otherwise be authorized to do so, to sign applications for the applicant by filing with the application or other document a power of attorney for each such individual. The power of attorney shall be signed by a person who is authorized to sign applications under this paragraph and shall contain the signature of the individual being authorized to sign the application or other document. The power of attorney shall be valid until revoked by the applicant.

[60 FR 32454, June 22, 1995, as amended at 75 FR 10680, Mar. 9, 2010; 81 FR 97021, Dec. 30, 2016]

§ 1309.33 Filing of application; joint filings.

(a) All applications for registration shall be submitted for filing to the Registration Section, Drug Enforcement Administration. See the Table of DEA Mailing Addresses in § 1321.01 of this chapter for the current mailing address. The appropriate registration fee and any required attachments must accompany the application.

(b) Any person required to obtain more than one registration may submit all applications in one package. Each application must be complete and must not refer to any accompanying application for required information.

[60 FR 32454, June 22, 1995, as amended at 75 FR 10680, Mar. 9, 2010]

§ 1309.34 Acceptance for filing; defective applications.

(a) Applications submitted for filing are dated upon receipt. If found to be complete, the application will be accepted for filing. Applications failing to comply with the requirements of this part will not generally be accepted for filing. In the case of minor defects as to completeness, the Administrator may accept the application for filing with a request to the applicant for additional information. A defective application will be returned to the applicant within 10 days of receipt with a statement of the reason for not accepting the application for filing. A defective application may be corrected and resubmitted for filing at any time.

(b) Accepting an application for filing does not preclude any subsequent request for additional information pursuant to § 1309.35 and has no bearing on whether the application will be granted.

§ 1309.35 Additional information.

The Administrator may require an applicant to submit such documents or written statements of fact relevant to the application as he deems necessary to determine whether the application should be granted. The failure of the applicant to provide such documents or statements within a reasonable time after being requested to do so shall be deemed to be a waiver by the applicant of an opportunity to present such documents or facts for consideration by the Administrator in granting or denying the application.

§ 1309.36 Amendments to and withdrawals of applications.

(a) An application may be amended or withdrawn without permission of the Administration at any time before the date on which the applicant receives an order to show cause pursuant to § 1309.46. An application may be amended or withdrawn with permission of the Administrator at any time where good cause is shown by the applicant or where the amendment or withdrawal is in the public interest.

(b) After an application has been accepted for filing, the request by the applicant that it be returned or the failure of the applicant to respond to official correspondence regarding the application, including a request that the applicant submit the required fee, when sent by registered or certified mail, return receipt requested, shall be deemed to be a withdrawal of the application.

ACTION ON APPLICATIONS FOR REGISTRATION: REVOCATION OR SUSPENSION OF REGISTRATION

§ 1309.41 Administrative review generally.

The Administrator may inspect, or cause to be inspected, the establishment of an applicant or registrant, pursuant to subpart A of part 1316 of this chapter. The Administrator shall review the application for registration and other information gathered by the Administrator regarding an applicant in order to determine whether the applicable standards of Section 303 of the Act (21 U.S.C. 823) have been met by the applicant.

§ 1309.42 Certificate of registration; denial of registration.

(a) The Administrator shall issue a Certificate of Registration (DEA Form 511) to an applicant if the issuance of registration or reregistration is required under the applicable provisions of section 303 of the Act (21 U.S.C. 823). In the event that the issuance of registration or reregistration is not required, the Administrator shall deny the application. Before denying any application, the Administrator shall issue an order to show cause pursuant to Section 1309.46 and, if requested by the applicant, shall hold a hearing on the application pursuant to § 1309.51.

(b) The Certificate of Registration (DEA Form 511) shall contain the name, address, and registration number of the registrant, the activity authorized by the registration, the amount of fee paid, and the expiration date of the registration. The registrant shall maintain the certificate of registration at the registered location in a readily retrievable manner and shall permit inspection of the certificate by any official, agent or employee of the Administration or of any Federal, State, or local agency engaged in enforcement of laws relating to List I chemicals or controlled substances.

§ 1309.43 Suspension or revocation of registration.

(a) The Administrator may suspend any registration pursuant to section 304(a) of the Act (21 U.S.C. 824(a)) for any period of time he determines.

(b) The Administrator may revoke any registration pursuant to section 304(a) of the Act (21 U.S.C. 824(a)).

(c) Before revoking or suspending any registration, the Administrator shall issue an order to show cause pursuant to Section 1309.46 and, if requested by the registrant, shall hold a hearing pursuant to Section 1309.51. Notwithstanding the requirements of this Section, however, the Administrator may suspend any registration pending a final order pursuant to § 1309.44.

(d) Upon service of the order of the Administrator suspending or revoking registration, the registrant shall immediately deliver his or her Certificate of Registration to the nearest office of the Administration. Also, upon service of the order of the Administrator revoking or suspending registration, the registrant shall, as instructed by the Administrator:

(1) Deliver all List I chemicals in his or her possession that were obtained under the authority of a registration or an exemption from registration granted by the Administrator by regulation, to the nearest office of the Administration or to authorized agents of the Administration; or

(2) Place all such List I chemicals in his or her possession under seal as described in section 304(f) of the Act (21 U.S.C. 824(f)).

(e) In the event that revocation or suspension is limited to a particular chemical or chemicals, the registrant shall be given a new Certificate of Registration for all substances not affected by such revocation or suspension; no fee shall be required for the new Certificate of Registration. The registrant shall deliver the old Certificate of Registration to the nearest office of the Administration. Also, upon service of the order of the Administrator revoking or suspending registration with respect to a particular chemical or chemicals, the registrant shall, as instructed by the Administrator:

(1) Deliver to the nearest office of the Administration or to authorized agents of the Administration all of the particular chemical or chemicals in his or her possession that were obtained under the authority of a registration or an exemption from registration granted by the Administrator by regulation, which are affected by the revocation or suspension; or

(2) Place all of such chemicals under seal as described in section 304(f) of the Act (21 U.S.C. 824(f)).

[60 FR 32454, June 22, 1995, as amended at 62 FR 5916, Feb. 10, 1997]

§ 1309.44 Suspension of registration pending final order.

(a) The Administrator may suspend any registration simultaneously with or at any time subsequent to the service upon the registrant of an order to show cause why such registration should not be revoked or suspended, in any case where he finds that there is an imminent danger to the public health or safety. If the Administrator so suspends, he shall serve with the order to show cause pursuant to § 1309.46 an order of immediate suspension that shall contain a statement of his findings regarding the danger to public health or safety.

(b) Upon service of the order of immediate suspension, the registrant shall promptly return his Certificate of Registration to the nearest office of the Administration. Also, upon service of the order of immediate suspension, the registrant shall, as instructed by the Administrator:

(1) Deliver to the nearest office of the Administration or to authorized agents of the Administration all of the particular chemical or chemicals in his or her possession that were obtained under the authority of a registration or an exemption from registration granted by the Administrator by regulation, which are affected by the revocation or suspension; or

(2) Place all of such chemicals under seal as described in section 304(f) of the Act (21 U.S.C. 824(f)).

(c) Any suspension shall continue in effect until the conclusion of all proceedings upon the revocation or suspension, including any judicial review thereof, unless sooner withdrawn by the Administrator or dissolved by a court of competent jurisdiction. Any registrant whose registration is suspended under this section may request a hearing on the revocation or suspension of his registration at a time earlier than specified in the order to show cause pursuant to Section 1309.46, which request shall be granted by the Administrator, who shall fix a date for such hearing as early as reasonably possible.

[60 FR 32454, June 22, 1995, as amended at 62 FR 5916, Feb. 10, 1997]

§ 1309.45 Extension of registration pending final order.

In the event that an applicant for reregistration (who is doing business under a registration previously granted and not revoked or suspended) has applied for reregistration at least 45 days before the date on which the existing registration is due to expire, and the Administrator has issued no order on the application on the date on which the existing registration is due to expire, the existing registration of the applicant shall automatically be extended and continue in effect until the date on which the Administrator so issues his order. The Administrator may extend any other existing registration under the circumstances contemplated in this section even though the registrant failed to apply for reregistration at least 45 days before expiration of the existing registration, with or without request by the registrant, if the Administrator finds that such extension is not inconsistent with the public health and safety.

§ 1309.46 Order to show cause.

(a) If, upon examination of the application for registration from any applicant and other information gathered by the Administration regarding the applicant, the Administrator is unable to make the determinations required by the applicable provisions of section 303 of the Act (21 U.S.C. 823) to register the applicant, the Administrator shall serve upon the applicant an order to show cause why the application for registration should not be denied.

(b) If, upon information gathered by the Administration regarding any registrant, the Administrator determines that the registration of such registrant is subject to suspension or revocation pursuant to section 304 of the Act (21 U.S.C. 824), the Administrator shall serve upon the registrant an order to show cause why the registration should not be revoked or suspended.

(c) The order to show cause shall call upon the applicant or registrant to appear before the Administrator at a time and place stated in the order, which shall not be less than 30 days after the date of receipt of the order. The order to show cause shall also contain a statement of the legal basis for such hearing and for the denial, revocation, or suspension of registration and a summary of the matters of fact and law asserted.

(d) Upon Receipt of an order to show cause, the applicant or registrant must, if he desires a hearing, file a request for a hearing pursuant to §1309.53. If a hearing is requested, the Administrator shall hold a hearing at the time and place stated in the order, pursuant to §1309.51.

(e) When authorized by the Administrator, any agent of the Administration may serve the order to show cause.

[60 FR 32454, June 22, 1995, as amended at 81 FR 97021, Dec. 30, 2016]

HEARINGS

§ 1309.51 Hearings generally.

(a) In any case where the Administrator shall hold a hearing on any registration or application therefore, the procedures for such hearing shall be governed generally by the adjudication procedures set forth in the Administrative Procedure Act (5 U.S.C. 551–559) and specifically by sections 303 and 304 of the Act (21 U.S.C. 823–824), by §§1309.52 through 1309.55, and by the procedures for administrative hearings under the Act set forth in §§1316.41 through 1316.67 of this chapter.

(b) Any hearing under this part shall be independent of, and not in lieu of, criminal prosecutions or other proceedings under the Act or any other law of the United States.

[60 FR 32454, June 22, 1995, as amended at 81 FR 97021, Dec. 30, 2016]

§ 1309.52 Purpose of hearing.

If requested by a person entitled to a hearing, the Administrator shall hold a hearing for the purpose of receiving factual evidence regarding the issues involved in the denial, revocation, or suspension of any registration. Extensive argument should not be offered into evidence but rather presented in opening or closing statements of counsel or in memoranda or proposed findings of fact and conclusions of law.

§ 1309.53 Request for hearing or appearance; waiver.

(a) Any person entitled to a hearing pursuant to §§1309.42 and 1309.43 and desiring a hearing shall, within 30 days after the date of receipt of the order to show cause, file with the Administrator a written request for a hearing in the form prescribed in §1316.47 of this chapter.

(b) Any person entitled to a hearing pursuant to §§1309.42 and 1309.43 may, within the period permitted for filing a request for a hearing, file with the Administrator a waiver of an opportunity for a hearing, together with a written statement regarding his position on the matters of fact and law involved in such hearing. Such statement, if admissible, shall be made a part of the record and shall be considered in light of the lack of opportunity for cross-examination in determining the weight to be attached to matters of fact asserted therein.

(c) If any person entitled to a hearing pursuant to §§1309.42 and 1309.43 fails to file a request for a hearing, or if he so files and fails to appear at the hearing, he shall be deemed to have waived his opportunity for the hearing, unless he shows good cause for such failure.

(d) If any person entitled to a hearing waives or is deemed to waive his or her opportunity for the hearing, the Administrator may cancel the hearing, if scheduled, and issue his final order pursuant to §1309.57 without a hearing.

[60 FR 32454, June 22, 1995. Redesignated at 62 FR 13968, Mar. 24, 1997]

§ 1309.54 Burden of proof.

(a) At any hearing for the denial of a registration, the Administration shall have the burden of proving that the requirements for such registration pursuant to section 303 of the Act (21 U.S.C. 823) are not satisfied.

(b) At any hearing for the revocation or suspension of a registration, the Administration shall have the burden of proving that the requirements for such revocation or suspension pursuant to section 304(a) of the Act (21 U.S.C. 824(a)) are satisfied.

[60 FR 32454, June 22, 1995. Redesignated at 62 FR 13968, Mar. 24, 1997]

§ 1309.55 Time and place of hearing.

The hearing will commence at the place and time designated in the order to show cause or notice of hearing published in the FEDERAL REGISTER (unless expedited pursuant to Section 1309.44(c)) but thereafter it may be moved to a different place and may be continued from day to day or recessed to a later day without notice other than announcement thereof by the presiding officer at the hearing.

[60 FR 32454, June 22, 1995. Redesignated at 62 FR 13968, Mar. 24, 1997]

MODIFICATION, TRANSFER AND TERMINATION OF REGISTRATION

§ 1309.61 Modification in registration.

Any registrant may apply to modify his or her registration to authorize the handling of additional List I chemicals or to change his or her name or address, by submitting a letter of request to the Registration Section, Drug Enforcement Administration. See the Table of DEA Mailing Addresses in § 1321.01 of this chapter for the current mailing address. The letter shall contain the registrant's name, address, and registration number as printed on the certificate of registration, and the List I chemicals to be added to his registration or the new name or address and shall be signed in accordance with § 1309.32(g). No fee shall be required to be paid for the modification. The request for modification shall be handled in the same manner as an application for registration. If the modification in registration is approved, the Administrator shall issue a new certificate of registration (DEA Form 511) to the registrant, who shall maintain it with the old certificate of registration until expiration.

[75 FR 10680, Mar. 9, 2010]

§ 1309.62 Termination of registration.

(a) The registration of any person shall terminate, without any further action by the Administration, if and when such person dies, ceases legal existence, discontinues business or professional practice, or surrenders a registration. Any registrant who ceases legal existence or discontinues business or professional practice shall promptly notify the Special Agent in Charge of the Administration in the area in which the person is located of such fact and seek authority and instructions to dispose of any List I chemicals obtained under the authority of that registration. Any registrant who ceases legal existence or discontinues business or professional practice or wishes to surrender a registration shall notify the Special Agent in Charge of the Administration in the area in which the person is located of such fact and seek authority and instructions to dispose of any List I chemicals obtained under the authority of that registration.

(b) The Special Agent in Charge shall authorize and instruct the person to dispose of the List I chemical in one of the following manners:

(1) By transfer to person registered under the Act and authorized to possess the substances;

(2) By delivery to an agent of the Administration or to the nearest office of the Administration;

(3) By such other means as the Special Agent in Charge may determine to assure that the substance does not become available to unauthorized persons.

[60 FR 32454, June 22, 1995, as amended at 62 FR 5916, Feb. 10, 1997; 76 FR 61564, Oct. 5, 2011; 77 FR 4236, Jan. 27, 2012]

§ 1309.63 Transfer of registration.

No registration or any authority conferred thereby shall be assigned or otherwise transferred except upon such conditions as the Administrator may specifically designate and then only pursuant to his written consent.

SECURITY REQUIREMENTS

§ 1309.71 General security requirements.

(a) All applicants and registrants must provide effective controls and procedures to guard against theft and diversion of List I chemicals. Chemicals must be stored in containers sealed in such a manner as to indicate any attempts at tampering with the container. Where chemicals cannot be stored in sealed containers, access to the chemicals should be controlled through physical means or through human or electronic monitoring.

(b) In evaluating the effectiveness of security controls and procedures, the Administrator shall consider the following factors:

(1) The type, form, and quantity of List I chemicals handled;

(2) The location of the premises and the relationship such location bears on the security needs;

(3) The type of building construction comprising the facility and the general characteristics of the building or buildings;

(4) The availability of electronic detection and alarm systems;

(5) The extent of unsupervised public access to the facility;

(6) The adequacy of supervision over employees having access to List I chemicals;

(7) The procedures for handling business guests, visitors, maintenance personnel, and nonemployee service personnel in areas where List I chemicals are processed or stored; and

(8) The adequacy of the registrant's or applicant's systems for monitoring the receipt, distribution, and disposition of List I chemicals in its operations.

(c) Any registrant or applicant desiring to determine whether a proposed system of security controls and procedures is adequate may submit materials and plans regarding the proposed security controls and procedures either to the Special Agent in Charge in the region in which the security controls and procedures will be used, or to the Regulatory Section, Drug Enforcement Administration. See the Table of DEA Mailing Addresses in § 1321.01 of this chapter for the current mailing address.

[60 FR 32454, June 22, 1995, as amended at 62 FR 13968, Mar. 24, 1997; 67 FR 14861, Mar. 28, 2002; 71 FR 56023, Sept. 26, 2006; 75 FR 10680, Mar. 9, 2010; 81 FR 97021, Dec. 30, 2016]

§ 1309.72 Felony conviction; employer responsibilities.

(a) The registrant shall exercise caution in the consideration of employment of persons who will have access to listed chemicals, who have been convicted of a felony offense relating to controlled substances or listed chemicals, or who have, at any time, had an application for registration with the DEA denied, had a DEA registration revoked, or surrendered a DEA registration for cause. (For purposes of this subsection, the term "for cause" means a surrender in lieu of, or as a consequence of, any Federal or State administrative, civil or criminal action resulting from an investigation of the individual's handling of controlled substances or listed chemicals.) The registrant should be aware of the circumstances regarding the action against the potential employee and the rehabilitative efforts following the action. The registrant shall assess the risks involved in employing such persons, including the potential for action against the registrant pursuant to § 1309.43, If such person is found to have diverted listed chemicals, and, in the event of employment, shall institute procedures to limit the potential for diversion of List I chemicals.

(b) It is the position of DEA that employees who possess, sell, use or divert listed chemicals or controlled substances will subject themselves not only to State or Federal prosecution for any illicit activity, but shall also immediately become the subject of independent action regarding their continued employment. The employer will assess the seriousness of the employee's violation, the position of responsibility held by the employee, past record of employment, etc., in determining whether to suspend, transfer, terminate or take other action against the employee.

§ 1309.73 Employee responsibility to report diversion.

Reports of listed chemical diversion by fellow employees is not only a necessary part of an overall employee security program but also serves the public interest at large. It is, therefore, the position of DEA that an employee who has knowledge of diversion from his employer by a fellow employee has an obligation to report such information to a responsible security official of the employer. The employer shall treat such information as confidential and shall take all reasonable steps to protect the confidentiality of the information and the identity of the employee furnishing information. A failure to report information of chemical diversion will be considered in determining the feasibility of continuing to allow an employee to work in an area with access to chemicals. The employer shall inform all employees concerning this policy.

PART 1310—RECORDS AND REPORTS OF LISTED CHEMICALS AND CERTAIN MACHINES; IMPORTATION AND EXPORTATION OF CERTAIN MACHINES

AUTHORITY: 21 U.S.C. 802, 827(h), 830, 871(b) 890.

SOURCE: 54 FR 31665, Aug. 1, 1989, unless otherwise noted.

§ 1310.01 Definitions.

Any term used in this part shall have the definition set forth in section 102 of the Act (21 U.S.C. 802) or part 1300 of this chapter.

[62 FR 13968, Mar. 24, 1997]

§ 1310.02 Substances covered.

The following chemicals have been specifically designated by the Administrator of the Drug Enforcement Administration as the listed chemicals subject to the provisions of this part and parts 1309 and 1313 of this chapter. Each chemical has been assigned the DEA Chemical Code Number set forth opposite it.

(a) List I chemicals

(1) Alpha-phenylacetoacetonitrile and its salts, optical isomers, and salts of optical isomers (APAAN)	8512
(2) Anthranilic acid, its esters, and its salts	8530
(3) Benzyl cyanide	8735
(4) Ephedrine, its salts, optical isomers, and salts of optical isomers	8113
(5) Ergonovine and its salts	8675
(6) Ergotamine and its salts	8676
(7) N-Acetylanthranilic acid, its esters, and its salts	8522
(8) Norpseudoephedrine, its salts, optical isomers, and salts of optical isomers	8317
(9) Phenylacetic acid, its esters, and its salts	8791
(10) Phenylpropanolamine, its salts, optical isomers, and salts of optical isomers	1225
(11) Piperidine and its salts	2704
(12) Pseudoephedrine, its salts, optical isomers, and salts of optical isomers	8112
(13) 3,4-Methylenedioxyphenyl-2-propanone	8502
(14) Methylamine and its salts	8520
(15) Ethylamine and its salts	8678
(16) Propionic anhydride	8328
(17) Isosafrole	8704

(18) Safrole 8323
(19) Piperonal 8750
(20) N-Methylephedrine, its salts, optical isomers, and salts of optical isomers (N-Methylephedrine) 8115
(21) N-Methylpseudoephedrine, its salts, optical isomers, and salts of optical isomers 8119
(22) Hydriodic Acid 6695
(23) Benzaldehyde 8256
(24) Nitroethane 6724
(25) Gamma-Butyrolactone (Other names include: GBL; Dihydro-2 (3H)-furanone; 1,2-Butanolide; 1,4-Butanolide; 4-Hydroxybutanoic acid lactone; gamma-hydroxybutyric acid lactone) 2011
(26) Red phosphorus 6795
(27) White phosphorus (Other names: Yellow Phosphorus) 6796
(28) Hypophosphorous acid and its salts (Including ammonium hypophosphite, calcium hypophosphite, iron hypophosphite, potassium hypophosphite, manganese hypophosphite, magnesium hypophosphite and sodium hypophosphite) 6797
(29) N-phenethyl-4-piperidone (NPP) 8332
(30) Iodine 6699
(31) Ergocristine and its salts 8612

(b) List II chemicals:

(1) Acetic anhydride 8519
(2) Acetone 6532
(3) Benzyl chloride 8570
(4) Ethyl ether 6584
(5) Potassium permanganate 6579
(6) 2-Butanone (or Methyl Ethyl Ketone or MEK) 6714
(7) Toluene 6594
(8) Hydrochloric acid (including anhydrous hydrogen chloride) 6545
(9) Sulfuric acid 6552
(10) Methyl Isobutyl Ketone (MIBK) 6715
(11) Sodium Permanganate 6588

(c) The Administrator may add or delete a substance as a listed chemical by publishing a final rule in the FEDERAL REGISTER following a proposal which shall be published at least 30 days prior to the final rule.

(d) Any person may petition the Administrator to have any substance added or deleted from paragraphs (a) or (b) of this section.

(e) Any petition under this section shall contain the following information:

(1) The name and address of the petitioner;

(2) The name of the chemical to which the petition pertains;

(3) The name and address of the manufacturer(s) of the chemical (if known);

(4) A complete statement of the facts which the petitioner believes justifies the addition or deletion of the substance from paragraphs (a) or (b) of this section;

(5) The date of the petition.

(f) The Administrator may require the petitioner to submit such documents or written statements of fact relevant to the petition as he deems necessary in making a determination.

(g) Within a reasonable period of time after the receipt of the petition, the Administrator shall notify the petitioner of his decision and the reason therefor. The Administrator need not accept a petition if any of the requirements prescribed in paragraph (e) of this section or requested pursuant to paragraph (f) of this section are lacking or are not clearly set forth as to be readily understood. If the petitioner desires, he may amend and resubmit the petition to meet the requirements of paragraphs (e) and (f) of this section.

(h) If a petition is granted or the Administrator, upon his own motion, proposes to add or delete substances as listed chemicals as set forth in paragraph (c) of this section, he shall issue and publish in the FEDERAL REGISTER a proposal to add or delete a substance as a listed chemical. The Administrator shall permit any interested person to file written comments regarding the proposal within 30 days of the date of publication of his order in the FEDERAL REGISTER. The Administrator will consider any comments filed by interested persons and publish a final rule in accordance with his decision in the matter.

[54 FR 31665, Aug. 1, 1989, as amended at 56 FR 48733, Sept. 26, 1991; 57 FR 43615, Sept. 22, 1992; 60 FR 19510, Apr. 19, 1995; 60 FR 32460, June 22, 1995; 62 FR 5917, Feb. 10, 1997; 65 FR 21647, Apr. 24, 2000; 65 FR 47316, Aug. 2, 2000; 66 FR 52675, Oct. 17, 2001; 71 FR 60826, Oct. 17, 2006; 72 FR 20046, Apr. 23, 2007; 72 FR 35391, July 2, 2007; 72 FR 40238, July 24, 2007; 76 FR 17781, Mar. 31, 2011; 82 FR 32460, July 14, 2017]

§ 1310.03 Persons required to keep records and file reports.

(a) Each regulated person who engages in a regulated transaction involving a listed chemical, a tableting machine, or an encapsulating machine shall keep a record of the transaction as specified by § 1310.04 and file reports as specified by § 1310.05. However, a non-regulated person who acquires listed chemicals for internal consumption or "end use" and becomes a regulated person by virtue of infrequent or rare distribution of a listed chemical from inventory, shall not be required to maintain receipt records of listed chemicals under this section.

(b) Each regulated person who manufactures a List I or List II chemical shall file reports regarding such manufacture as specified in § 1310.05.

(c)(1) Each regulated person who engages in a transaction with a nonregulated person which:

(i) Involves ephedrine, pseudoephedrine, phenylpropanolamine, or gamma hydroxybutyric acid (including drug products containing these chemicals or controlled substance); and

(ii) Uses or attempts to use the U.S. Postal Service or any private or commercial carrier must, on a monthly basis, report to the Administration each such transaction conducted during the previous month as specified in §§ 1310.05(e) and 1310.06(k) on DEA Form 453 through the DEA Diversion Control Division secure network application.

(2) Each regulated person who engages in an export transaction which:

(i) Involves ephedrine, pseudoephedrine, phenylpropanolamine, or gamma hydroxybutyric acid (including drug products containing these chemicals or controlled substance); and

(ii) Uses or attempts to use the U.S. Postal Service or any private or commercial carrier must, on a monthly basis, report each such transaction conducted during the previous month as specified in §§ 1310.05(e) and 1310.06(k) on DEA Form 453 through the DEA Diversion Control Division secure network application.

[54 FR 31665, Aug. 1, 1989, as amended at 56 FR 8277, Feb. 28, 1991; 61 FR 14023, Mar. 29, 1996; 67 FR 14861, Mar. 28, 2002; 68 FR 57804, Oct. 7, 2003; 70 FR 294, Jan. 4, 2005; 81 FR 97022, Dec. 30, 2016]

§ 1310.04 Maintenance of records.

(a) Every record required to be kept subject to § 1310.03 for a List I chemical, a tableting machine, or an encapsulating machine shall be kept by the regulated person for 2 years after the date of the transaction.

(b) Every record required to be kept subject to Section 1310.03 for List II chemical shall be kept by the regulated person for two years after the date of the transaction.

(c) A record under this section shall be kept at the regulated person's place of business where the transaction occurred, except that records may be kept at a single, central location of the regulated person if the regulated person has notified the Administration of the intention to do so. Written notification must be submitted by registered or certified mail, return receipt requested, to the Special Agent in Charge of the DEA Divisional Office for the area in which the records are required to be kept.

(d) The records required to be kept under this section shall be readily retrievable and available for inspection and copying by authorized employees of the Administration under the provisions of 21 U.S.C. 880.

(e) The regulated person with more than one place of business where records are required to be kept shall devise a system to detect any party purchasing from several individual locations of the regulated person thereby seeking to avoid the application of the cumulative threshold or evading the requirements of the Act.

(f) For those listed chemicals for which thresholds have been established, the quantitative threshold or the cumulative amount for multiple transactions within a calendar month, to be utilized in determining whether a receipt, sale, importation or exportation is a regulated transaction is as follows:

(1) List I chemicals:

(i) Except as provided in paragraph (f)(1)(ii) of this section, the following thresholds have been established for List I chemicals.

Code	Chemical	Threshold by base weight
8522	N-Acetylanthranilic acid, its esters, and its salts	40 kilograms.
8530	Anthranilic acid, its esters, and its salts	30 kilograms.
8256	Benzaldehyde	4 kilograms.
8735	Benzyl cyanide	1 kilogram.
8675	Ergonovine and its salts	10 grams.
8676	Ergotamine and its salts	20 grams.
8678	Ethylamine and its salts	1 kilogram.
6695	Hydriodic acid	1.7 kilograms (or 1 liter by volume).
8704	Isosafrole	4 kilograms.
8520	Methylamine and its salts	1 kilogram.
8502	3,4–Methylenedioxyphenyl-2-propanone	4 kilograms.
8115	N–Methylephedrine, its salts, optical isomers, and salts of optical isomers.	1 kilogram.
8119	N–Methylpseudoephedrine, its salts, optical isomers, and salts of optical isomers.	1 kilogram.
6724	Nitroethane	2.5 kilograms.
8317	Norpseudoephedrine, its salts, optical isomers, and salts of optical isomers.	2.5 kilograms.
8791	Phenylacetic acid, its esters, and its salts	1 kilogram.
2704	Piperidine and its salts	500 grams.
8750	Piperonal (also called heliotropine)	4 kilograms.
8328	Propionic anhydride	1 gram.
8323	Safrole	4 kilograms.

(ii) For List I chemicals that are contained in scheduled listed chemical products as defined in § 1300.02 of this chapter, the thresholds established in paragraph (g) of this section apply only to non-retail distribution, import, and export. Sales of these products at retail are subject to the requirements of part 1314 of this chapter.

(2) List II Chemicals:

(i) Imports and Exports

Chemical	Threshold by volume	Threshold by weight
(A) Acetic anhydride	250 gallons	1,023 kilograms.
(B) Acetone	500 gallons	1,500 kilograms.
(C) Benzyl chloride	N/A	4 kilograms.
(D) Ethyl ether	500 gallons	1,364 kilograms.
(E) Potassium permanganate	N/A	500 kilograms.
(F) 2-Butanone (MEK)	500 gallons	1,455 kilograms.
(G) Toluene	500 gallons	1,591 kilograms.
(H) Sodium permanganate	N/A	500 kilograms

(ii) Domestic Sales

Chemical	Threshold by volume	Threshold by weight
(A) Acetic anhydride	250 gallons	1,023 kilograms.
(B) Acetone	50 gallons	150 kilograms.
(C) Benzyl chloride	N/A	1 kilogram.
(D) Ethyl ether	50 gallons	135.8 kilograms.
(E) Potassium permanganate	N/A	55 kilograms.
(F) 2-Butanone (MEK)	50 gallons	145 kilograms.
(G) Toluene	50 gallons	159 kilograms.
(H) Anhydrous Hydrogen chloride	N/A	0.0 kilograms.
(I) Sodium permanganate	N/A	55 kilograms

(iii) The cumulative threshold is not applicable to domestic sales of Acetone, 2-Butanone (MEK), and Toluene.

(iv) Exports, Transshipments and International Transactions to Designated Countries as Set Forth in § 1310.08(b).

Chemical	Threshold by volume	Threshold by weight
(A) Hydrochloric acid	50 gallons	
(*1*) Anhydrous Hydrogen chloride.	....	27 kilograms.
(B) Sulfuric acid	50 gallons	

(v) Export and International Transactions to Designated Countries, and Importations for Transshipment or Transfer to Designated Countries

Chemical	Threshold by volume	Threshold by weight
(A) Methyl Isobutyl Ketone (MIBK).	500 gallons	1523 kilograms.
(B) Reserved.		

(g) For listed chemicals for which no thresholds have been established, the size of the transaction is not a factor in determining whether the transaction meets the definition of a regulated transaction as set forth in § 1300.02 of this chapter. All such transactions, regardless of size, are subject to recordkeeping and reporting requirements as set forth in this part and notification provisions as set forth in part 1313 of this chapter.

(1) Listed chemicals for which no thresholds have been established:

(i) Alpha-phenylacetoacetonitrile and its salts, optical isomers, and salts of optical isomers (APAAN)

(ii) Ephedrine, its salts, optical isomers, and salts of optical isomers;

(iii) Ergocristine and its salts

(iv) Gamma-Butyrolactone (Other names include: GBL; Dihydro-2(3H)-furanone; 1,2-Butanolide; 1,4-Butanolide; 4-Hydroxybutanoic acid lactone; gamma-hydroxybutyric acid lactone)

(v) Hypophosphorous acid and its salts (including ammonium hypophosphite, calcium hypophosphite, iron hypophosphite, potassium hypophosphite, manganese hypophosphite, magnesium hypophosphite, and sodium hypophosphite)

(vi) Iodine

(vii) N-phenethyl-4-piperidone (NPP)

(viii) Pseudoephedrine, its salts, optical isomers, and salts of optical isomers

(ix) Phenylpropanolamine, its salts, optical isomers, and salts of optical isomers

(x) Red phosphorus

(xi) White phosphorus (Other names: Yellow Phosphorus)

(2) [Reserved]

(h) The thresholds and conditions in paragraphs (f) and (g) of this section will apply to transactions involving regulated chemical mixtures. For purposes of determining whether the weight or volume of a chemical mixture meets or exceeds the applicable quantitative threshold, the following rules apply:

(1) For chemical mixtures containing List I chemicals or List II chemicals other than those in paragraph (h)(2) of this section, the threshold is determined by the weight of the listed chemical in the chemical mixture.

(2) For the List II chemicals acetone, ethyl ether, 2-butanone, toluene, and methyl isobutyl ketone, the threshold is determined by the weight of the entire chemical mixture.

(3) If two or more listed chemicals are present in a chemical mixture, and the quantity of any of these chemicals equals or exceeds the threshold applicable to that chemical, then the transaction is regulated.

[54 FR 31665, Aug. 1, 1989]

EDITORIAL NOTE: For FEDERAL REGISTER citations affecting § 1310.04, see the List of CFR Sections Affected, which appears in the Finding Aids section of the printed volume and at *www.govinfo.gov*.

§ 1310.05 Reports.

(a)(1) Each regulated person must report to the Special Agent in Charge of the DEA Divisional Office for the area in which the regulated person making the report is located any regulated transaction involving an extraordinary quantity of a listed chemical, an uncommon method of payment or delivery, or any other circumstance that the regulated person believes may indicate that the listed chemical will be used in violation of this part. The regulated person will orally report to the

Special Agent in Charge of the DEA Divisional Office at the earliest practicable opportunity after the regulated person becomes aware of the circumstances involved and as much in advance of the conclusion of the transaction as possible. The regulated person must file a written report of the transaction(s) with the Special Agent in Charge of the DEA Divisional Office as set forth in § 1310.06 within 15 calendar days after the regulated person becomes aware of the circumstances of the event.

(2) Each regulated person must report to the Special Agent in Charge of the DEA Divisional Office for the area in which the regulated person making the report is located any proposed regulated transaction with a person whose description or other identifying characteristic the Administration has previously furnished to the regulated person. The regulated person will orally report to the Special Agent in Charge of the DEA Divisional Office at the earliest practicable opportunity after the regulated person becomes aware of the circumstances involved. A transaction may not be completed with a person whose description or identifying characteristic has previously been furnished to the regulated person by the Administration unless the transaction is approved by the Administration.

(b)(1) Each regulated person must report to the Special Agent in Charge of the DEA Divisional Office for the area in which the regulated person making the report is located any unusual or excessive loss or disappearance of a listed chemical under the control of the regulated person. The regulated person will orally report to the Special Agent in Charge of the DEA Divisional Office at the earliest practicable opportunity after the regulated person becomes aware of the circumstances involved. Unless the loss or disappearance occurs during an import or export transaction, the supplier is responsible for reporting all in-transit losses of any listed chemical by their agent or the common or contract carrier. In an import transaction, once a shipment has been released by the customs officer at the port of entry, the importer is responsible for reporting all in-transit losses of any listed chemical by their agent or the common or contract carrier. In an export transaction, the exporter is responsible for reporting all in-transit losses of any listed chemical by their agent or the common or contract carrier until the shipment has been released by the customs officer at the port of export. The regulated person must also file a complete and accurate DEA Form 107, in accordance with § 1310.06(d), with the Administration through the DEA Diversion Control Division secure network application within 15 calendar days after becoming aware of the circumstances requiring the report. Unusual or excessive losses or disappearances must be reported whether or not the listed chemical is subsequently recovered or the responsible parties are identified and action taken against them. When determining whether a loss or disappearance of a listed chemical was unusual or excessive, the regulated persons should consider, among others, the following factors:

(i) The actual quantity of a listed chemical;

(ii) The specific listed chemical involved;

(iii) Whether the loss or disappearance of the listed chemical can be associated with access to those listed chemicals by specific individuals, or whether the loss or disappearance can be attributed to unique activities that may take place involving the listed chemical; and

(iv) A pattern of losses or disappearances over a specific time period, whether the losses or disappearances appear to be random, and the result of efforts taken to resolve the losses.

(v) If known, the regulated person should also consider whether the specific listed chemical was a likely candidate for diversion as well as local trends and other indicators of the diversion potential of the listed chemical.

(2) Each regulated person must orally report any domestic regulated transaction in a tableting machine or an encapsulating machine to the Special Agent in Charge of the DEA Divisional Office for the area in which the regulated person making the report is located when the order is placed with the seller. The regulated person also must

file a report of the transaction (on DEA Form 452) with the Administration through the DEA Diversion Control Division secure network application within 15 calendar days after the order has been shipped by the seller. A report (DEA Form 452) may list more than one machine for a single transaction. Upon receipt and review, the Administration will assign a completed report a transaction identification number. The report will not be deemed filed until a transaction identification number has been issued by the Administration.

(c) *Imports and exports of tableting machines and encapsulating machines.* (1) Each regulated person who imports or exports a tableting machine, or encapsulating machine, must file a report of such importation or exportation on DEA Form 452 with the Administration through the DEA Diversion Control Division secure network application, at least 15 calendar days before the anticipated arrival at the port of entry or port of export. In order to facilitate the importation or exportation of any tableting machine or encapsulating machine and implement the purpose of the Act, regulated persons may report to the Administration as far in advance as possible. A separate report (DEA Form 452) must be filed for each shipment, in accordance with §1310.06(e). Upon receipt and review, the Administration will assign a completed report a transaction identification number. The report will not be deemed filed until a transaction identification number has been issued by the Administration. The importer or exporter may only proceed with the transaction once the transaction identification number has been issued. Any tableting machine or encapsulating machine may be imported or exported if that machine is needed for medical, commercial, scientific, or other legitimate uses. However, an importation or exportation of a tableting machine or encapsulating machine may not be completed with a person whose description or identifying characteristic has previously been furnished to the regulated person by the Administration unless the transaction is approved by the Administration.

(2) *Denied release at the port of entry.* In the event that a shipment of tableting or encapsulating machine(s) has been denied release by a customs officer at the port of entry for any reason, the importer who attempted to import the shipment must, within 5 business days of the denial, report to the Administration that the shipment was denied, the basis for denial, and such other information as is required by §1310.06(g). Such report must be transmitted to the Administration through the DEA Diversion Control Division secure network application. Upon the importer's report of a denied entry, DEA will assign the report a transaction identification number and the original import notification will be void and of no effect. No shipment of tableting machines or encapsulating machines denied entry for any reason will be allowed entry without a subsequent refiling of an amended DEA Form 452 by the regulated person. In such circumstances, the regulated person may proceed with the release of the tableting machines or encapsulating machines upon receipt of a transaction identification number for the refiled and amended DEA Form 452 without regard to the 15-day advance filing requirement in paragraph (c)(1) of this section, so long as the article is otherwise cleared for entry under U.S. customs laws.

(d) Each regulated bulk manufacturer of a listed chemical must submit manufacturing, inventory and use data on an annual basis as set forth in §1310.06(j). This data must be submitted annually to the Drug and Chemical Evaluation Section, Diversion Control Division, Drug Enforcement Administration, on or before the 15th day of March of the year immediately following the calendar year for which submitted. See the Table of DEA Mailing Addresses in §1321.01 of this chapter for the current mailing address. A business entity which manufactures a listed chemical may elect to report separately by individual location or report as an aggregate amount for the entire business entity provided that they inform the DEA of which method they will use. This reporting requirement does not apply to drugs or other products that are exempted under paragraph (1)(iv) or (v) of the definition of regulated transaction in §1300.02 of this chapter except as set forth in §1310.06(i)(5). Bulk manufacturers that produce a listed chemical solely for internal consumption are not required to report for that listed chemical. For purposes of these reporting requirements, internal consumption consists of any quantity of a listed chemical otherwise not available for further resale or distribution. Internal consumption includes (but is not limited to) quantities used for quality control testing, quantities consumed in-house, or production losses. Internal consumption does not include the quantities of a listed chemical consumed in the production of exempted products. If an existing standard industry report contains the information required in §1310.06(j) and such information is separate or readily retrievable from the report, that report may be submitted in satisfaction of this requirement. Each report must be submitted to the DEA under company letterhead and signed by an appropriate, responsible official. For purposes of this paragraph (d) only, the term regulated bulk manufacturer of a listed chemical means a person who manufactures a listed chemical by means of chemical synthesis or by extraction from other substances. The term bulk manufacturer does not include persons whose sole activity consists of the repackaging or relabeling of listed chemical products or the manufacture of drug dosage forms of products which contain a listed chemical.

(e) Each regulated person required to report pursuant to §1310.03(c) must file a report containing the transaction identification number for each such transaction (if the regulated person is required to obtain a transaction identification number under part 1313of this chapter) and information set forth in §1310.06(k), on or before the 15th day of each month following the month in which the distributions took place.

(f) Except as provided in paragraph (g) of this section, the following distributions to nonregulated persons, and the following export transactions, are not subject to the reporting requirements in §1310.03(c):

(1) Distributions of sample packages of drug products when those packages contain not more than two solid dosage units or the equivalent of two dosage units in liquid form, not to exceed 10 milliliters of liquid per package, and not more than one package is distributed to an individual or residential address in any 30-day period.

(2) Distributions of drug products by retail distributors that may not include face-to-face transactions to the extent that such distributions are consistent with the activities authorized for a retail distributor as defined in §1300.02 of this chapter, except that this paragraph does not apply to sales of scheduled listed chemical products at retail.

(3) Distributions of drug products to a resident of a long term care facility or distributions of drug products to a long term care facility for dispensing to or for use by a resident of that facility.

(4) Distributions of drug products in accordance with a valid prescription.

(5) Exports which have been reported to the Administrator under §§1313.31 and 1313.32 of this chapter or which are subject to a waiver granted under §1313.21 of this chapter.

(g) The Administrator may revoke any or all of the exemptions listed in paragraph (f) of this section for an individual regulated person if the Administrator finds that drug products distributed by the regulated person are being used in violation of the regulations in this chapter or the Controlled Substances Act. The Administrator will notify the regulated person of the revocation, as provided in §1313.41(a) of this chapter. The revocation will be effective upon receipt of the notice by the person. The regulated person has the right to an expedited hearing regarding the revocation, as provided in §1313.56(a) of this chapter.

[54 FR 31665, Aug. 1, 1989, as amended at 57 FR 2461, Jan. 22, 1992; 61 FR 14024, Mar. 29, 1996; 61 FR 17958, Apr. 23, 1996; 62 FR 13968, Mar. 24, 1997; 67 FR 14862, Mar. 28, 2002; 67 FR 49569, July 31, 2002; 68 FR 57804, Oct. 7, 2003; 71 FR 56024, Sept. 26, 2006; 75 FR 10680, Mar. 9, 2010; 77 FR 4236, Jan. 27, 2012; 81 FR 97022, Dec. 30, 2016]

§ 1310.06 Content of records and reports.

(a) Each record required by §1310.03(a) must include the following:

(1) The name/business name, address/business address, and contact information (*e.g.*, telephone number(s), email address (es), etc.), and, if required, DEA registration number of each party to the regulated transaction.

(2) The date of the regulated transaction.

(3) The quantity, chemical name, and, if applicable, National Drug Code (NDC) number. If NDC number is not applicable, the form of packaging of the listed chemical or a description of the tableting machine or encapsulating machine (including make, model, serial number, if any, and whether the machine is manual or electric).

(4) The method of transfer (company truck, picked up by customer, etc.).

(5) The type of identification used by the purchaser and any unique number on that identification.

(b) For purposes of this section, normal business records will be considered adequate if they contain the information listed in paragraph (a) of this section and are readily retrievable from other business records of the regulated person. For prescription drug products, prescription and hospital records kept in the normal course of medical treatment will be considered adequate for satisfying the requirements of paragraph (a) of this section with respect to dispensing to patients, and records required to be maintained pursuant to the U.S. Food and Drug Administration regulations relating to the distribution of prescription drugs, as set forth in 21 CFR part 205, will be considered adequate for satisfying the requirements of paragraph (a) of this section with respect to distributions.

(c)(1) Each report required by §1310.05(a) must include the information as specified by paragraph (a) of this section, the basis for making the report, and, where obtainable, the registration number of the other party, if such party is registered. A report of an uncommon method of payment or delivery submitted in accordance with §1310.05(a)(1) must also include a reason why the method of payment or delivery was uncommon.

(2) A suggested format for the reports in §1310.05(a)(1) is provided below:

Shipping Address (if different than purchaser Address):

Street ____________

City ____________

State ____________

Zip ____________

Date of Shipment ____________

Description of Listed Chemical:

Chemical Name ____________

Quantity ____________

National Drug Code (NDC) Number(s), or Form(s) of Packaging ____________

Other:

The basis (*i.e.*, reason) for making the report: ____________

Any additional pertinent information: ______

(d) Each report of an unusual or excessive loss or disappearance of a listed chemical required by §1310.05(b)(1) (on DEA Form 107), must include the following information:

(1) The name/business name, address/business address, and contact information (*e.g.*, telephone number(s), email address (es), etc.), and, if applicable, DEA registration number of each party to the regulated transaction.

(2) The date (or estimated date) on which unusual or excessive loss or disappearance occurred, and the actual date on which the unusual or excessive loss or disappearance was discovered by the regulated person.

(3) The quantity, chemical name, and National Drug Code (NDC) number, if applicable or if not the form of packaging of the listed chemical.

(4) The type of business conducted by the regulated person, (*e.g.*, grocery store, pharmacy/drug store, discount department store, warehouse club or superstore, convenience store, specialty food store, gas station, mobile retail vendor, mail-order, etc.) if the regulated person is not a DEA registrant.

(e)(1) Each report of an importation of a tableting machine or an encapsulating machine required by §1310.05(c)(1) (on DEA Form 452) must include the following information:

(i) The name/business name, address/business address, and contact information (*e.g.*, telephone number(s), email address(es), etc.) of the regulated person; the name/business name, address/business address, and contact information (*e.g.*, telephone number(s), email address(es), etc.) of the import broker or forwarding agent, if any;

(ii) A description of each machine (including make, model, serial number, if any, and whether the machine is manual or electric) and the number of machines being received;

(iii) The anticipated date of arrival at the port of entry, and the anticipated port of entry;

(iv) The name/business name, address/business address, and contact information (*e.g.*, telephone number(s), email address(es), etc.) of the consignor in the foreign country of exportation;

(v) The intended medical, commercial, scientific, or other legitimate use of the machine; and

(vi) Any proposed changes in identifying information of the imported machines (*e.g.*, name, brand, serial number, if any, etc.) that will take place after importation.

(2) Each report of an exportation of a tableting machine or an encapsulating machine required by § 1310.05(c)(1) (on DEA Form 452) must include the following information:

(i) The name/business name, address/business address, and contact information (*e.g.*, telephone number(s), email address(es), etc.) of the regulated person; the name/business name, address/business address, and contact information (*e.g.*, telephone number(s), email address(es), etc.) of the export broker (if applicable);

(ii) A description of each machine (including make, model, serial number, if any, and whether the machine is manual or electric) and the number of machines being received;

(iii) The anticipated date of arrival at the port of export, the foreign port and country of entry; and

(iv) The name/business name, address/business address, and contact information (*e.g.*, telephone number(s), email address(es), etc.) of the consignee in the country where the shipment is destined; the name(s)/business name(s) and address(es)/business address(es), and contact information (*e.g.*, telephone number(s), email address(es), etc.) of the intermediate consignee(s) (if any).

(f) Each report of a domestic regulated transaction in a tableting machine or encapsulating machine required by § 1310.05(b)(2) (on DEA Form 452) must include the following information:

(1) The name/business name, address/business address, and contact information (*e.g.*, telephone number(s), email address(es), etc.) of the regulated person; the name/business name, address/business address, and contact information (*e.g.*, telephone number(s), email address(es), etc.) of the purchaser;

(2) A description of each machine (including make, model, serial number, if any, and whether the machine is manual or electric) and the number of machines being received; and

(3) Any changes made by the regulated person in identifying information of the machines (*e.g.*, name, brand, serial number, etc.).

(g) Each report of a denied release by a customs officer at the port of entry of a tableting machine or an encapsulating machine required by § 1310.05(c)(2) must include the following information: the quantity of machines denied release; a concise description of the machines denied release; the date on which release was denied; the port where the denial of release was issued from; and the basis for the denial.

(h) *Return information.* (1) Within 30 calendar days after actual receipt of a tableting or encapsulating machine, or within 10 calendar days after receipt of a written request by the Administration to the importer, whichever is sooner, the importer must file a report with the Administration (on DEA Form 452) specifying the particulars of the transaction utilizing the DEA Diversion Control Division secure network application. This report must include the following information: The date on which a customs officer at the port of entry released the machine(s); the date on which the machine(s) arrived at the final destination; the port of entry where the machine(s) were actually released by a customs officer; the actual quantity of machines released by a customs officer; the actual quantity of machines that arrived at the final destination; a description of each tableting or encapsulating machine imported (including make, model, and serial number, if any); any changes in identifying information of the imported machines (*e.g.*, name, brand, serial number, if any, etc.) that will take place after importation; and any other information as the Administration may from time to time specify. Upon receipt and review, the Administration will assign a transaction identification number to a completed report. The report will not be deemed filed until the Administration has issued a transaction identification number. A single return declaration may include the particulars of both the importation and distribution. For DEA reporting purposes, import responsibilities are concluded upon the receipt of the machines by the importer. Once machines are received by the importer, domestic transaction reporting requirements commence. Distributions of tableting and encapsulating machines from the importer to their customers must be reported as domestic regulated transactions in accordance with § 1310.05(b)(2).

(2) Within 30 calendar days after the tableting or encapsulating machine is released by a customs officer at the port of export, or within 10 calendar days after receipt of a written request by the Administration to the exporter, whichever is sooner, the exporter must file a report with the Administration (on DEA Form 452) through the DEA Diversion Control Division secure network application specifying the particulars of the transaction. This report must include the following information: The date on which the machine(s) was (were) released by a customs officer at the port of export; the actual quantity of machines released; a description of each tableting or encapsulating machine released (including make, model, serial number, if any, and whether the machine is manual or electric); and any other information as the Administration may from time to time specify.

(i) Declared exports of machines which are refused, rejected, or otherwise deemed undeliverable may be returned to the U.S. exporter of record. A brief written report outlining the circumstances must be filed with the Administration through the DEA Diversion Control Division secure network application, following the return at the earliest practicable opportunity after the regulated person becomes aware of the circumstances involved. This provision does not apply to shipments that have cleared foreign customs, been delivered, and accepted by the foreign consignee. Returns to third parties in the United States will be regarded as imports.

(j) Each annual report required by § 1310.05(d) must provide the following information for each listed chemical manufactured:

(1) The name/business name, address/business address, and contact information (*e.g.*, telephone number(s), email address(es), etc.) and chemical registration number (if any) of the manufacturer.

(2) The aggregate quantity of each listed chemical that the company manufactured during the preceding calendar year.

(3) The year-end inventory of each listed chemical as of the close of business on the 31st day of December of each year. (For each listed chemical, if the prior period's ending inventory has not previously been reported to DEA, this report should also detail the beginning inventory for the period.) For purposes of this requirement, inventory shall reflect the quantity of listed chemicals, whether in bulk or non-exempt product form, held in storage for later distribution. Inventory does not include waste material for destruction, material stored as an in-process intermediate or other in-process material.

(4) The aggregate quantity of each listed chemical used for internal consumption during the preceding calendar year, unless the chemical is produced solely for internal consumption.

(5) The aggregate quantity of each listed chemical manufactured which becomes a component of a product exempted from paragraph (1)(iv) or (v) of the definition of regulated transaction in § 1300.02 of this chapter during the preceding calendar year.

(6) Data shall identify the specific isomer, salt or ester when applicable but quantitative data shall be reported as anhydrous base or acid in kilogram units of measure.

(k) Each monthly report required by §§ 1310.03(c) and 1310.05(e) (on DEA Form 453) must provide the following information for each transaction:

(1) Supplier name/business name, address/business address, and contact information (*e.g.*, telephone number(s),

email address(es), etc.) and registration number.

(2) Purchaser's name/business name, address/business address, and contact information (*e.g.*, telephone number(s), email address(es), etc.).

(3) Name/business name, address/business address shipped to (if different from purchaser's name/address).

(4) Chemical name, National Drug Code (NDC) number, if applicable, and total amount shipped.

(5) Date of shipment.

(6) Product name (if drug product).

(7) Dosage form (if drug product) (*e.g.*, pill, tablet, liquid).

(8) Dosage strength (if drug product) (*e.g.*, 30mg, 60mg, per dose etc.).

(9) Number of dosage units (if drug product) (*e.g.*, 100 doses per package).

(10) Package type (if drug product) (*e.g.*, bottle, blister pack, etc.).

(11) Number of packages (if drug product) (*e.g.*, 10 bottles).

(12) Lot number (if drug product).

(l) Information provided in reports required by § 1310.05(e) which is exempt from disclosure under section 552(a) of title 5, by reason of section 552(b)(6) of title 5, will be provided the same protections from disclosure as are provided in section 310(c) of the Act (21 U.S.C. 830(c)) for confidential business information.

[81 FR 97023, Dec. 30, 2016]

§ 1310.07 Proof of identity.

(a) Each regulated person who engages in a regulated transaction must identify the other party to the transaction. For domestic transaction, this shall be accomplished by having the other party present documents which would verify the identity, or registration status if a registrant, of the other party to the regulated person at the time the order is placed. For export transactions, this shall be accomplished by good faith inquiry through reasonably available research documents or publicly available information which would indicate the existence of the foreign customer. No proof of identity is required for foreign suppliers.

(b) The regulated person must verify the existence and apparent validity of a business entity ordering a listed chemical, tableting machine or encapsulating machine. For domestic transactions, this may be accomplished by such methods as checking the telephone directory, the local credit bureau, the local Chamber of Commerce or the local Better Business Bureau, or, if the business entity is a registrant, by verification of the registration. For export transactions, a good faith inquiry to verify the existence and apparent validity of a foreign business entity may be accomplished by such methods as verifying the business telephone listing through international telephone information, the firm's listing in international or foreign national chemical directories or other commerce directories or trade publications, confirmation through foreign subsidiaries of the U.S. regulated person, verification through the country of destination's embassy Commercial Attache, or official documents provided by the purchaser which confirm the existence and apparent validity of the business entity.

(c) When transacting business with a new representative of a firm, the regulated person must verify the claimed agency status of the representative.

(d) For sales to individuals or cash purchasers, the type of documents and other evidence of proof must consist of at least a signature of the purchaser, a driver's license and one other form of identification. Any exports to individuals or exports paid in cash are suspect and should be handled as such. For such exports, the regulated person shall diligently obtain from the purchaser or independently seek to confirm clear documentation which proves the person is properly identified such as through foreign identity documents, driver's license, passport information and photograph, etc. Any regulated person who fails to adequately prove the identity of the other party to the transaction may be subject to the specific penalties provided for violations of law related to regulated transactions in listed chemicals.

(e) For a new customer who is not an individual or cash customer, the regulated person shall establish the identity of the authorized purchasing agent or agents and have on file that person's signature, electronic password, or other identification. Once the authorized purchasing agent has been established, the agent list may be updated annually rather than on each order. The regulated person must ensure that shipments are not made unless the order is placed by an authorized agent of record.

(f) With respect to electronic orders, the identity of the purchaser shall consist of a computer password, identification number or some other means of identification consistent with electronic orders and with § 1310.07(e).

[54 FR 31665, Aug. 1, 1989, as amended at 60 FR 32461, June 22, 1995]

§ 1310.08 Excluded transactions.

Pursuant to 21 U.S.C. 802(39)(A)(iii), regulation of the following transactions has been determined to be unnecessary for the enforcement of the Chemical Diversion and Trafficking Act and, therefore, they have been excluded from the definitions of regulated transactions:

(a) Domestic and import transactions of hydrochloric and sulfuric acids but not including anhydrous hydrogen chloride.

(b) Exports, transshipments, and international transactions of hydrochloric (including anhydrous hydrogen chloride) and sulfuric acids, except for exports, transshipments and international transactions to the following countries:

(1) Argentina
(2) Bolivia
(3) Brazil
(4) Chile
(5) Colombia
(6) Ecuador
(7) French Guiana
(8) Guyana
(9) Panama
(10) Paraguay
(11) Peru
(12) Suriname
(13) Uruguay
(14) Venezuela

(c) Domestic transactions of Methyl Isobutyl Ketone (MIBK).

(d) Import transactions of Methyl Isobutyl Ketone (MIBK) destined for the United States.

(e) Export transactions, international transactions, and import transactions for transshipment or transfer of Methyl Isobutyl Ketone (MIBK) destined for Canada or any country outside of the Western Hemisphere.

(f) Domestic and international transactions of Lugol's Solution (consisting of 5 percent iodine and 10 percent potassium iodide in an aqueous solution) in original manufacturer's packaging of one-fluid-ounce (30 milliliters) or less, and no greater than one package per transaction.

(g) Import transactions of anhydrous hydrogen chloride.

(h) Domestic distribution of anhydrous hydrogen chloride weighing 12,000 pounds (net weight) or more in a single container.

(i) Domestic distribution of anhydrous hydrogen chloride by pipeline.

(j) Domestic and international return shipments of reusable containers from customer to producer containing residual quantities of red phosphorus or white phosphorus in rail cars and intermodal tank containers which conform to International Standards Organization specifications (with capacities greater than or equal to 2,500 gallons in a single container).

(k) Domestic, import, and export distributions of gamma-butyrolactone weighing 4,000 kilograms (net weight) or more in a single container.

(l) Domestic and import transactions in chemical mixtures that contain acetone, ethyl ether, 2-butanone, and/or toluene, unless regulated because of being formulated with other List I or List II chemical(s) above the concentration limit.

[57 FR 43615, Sept. 22, 1992, as amended at 60 FR 19510, Apr. 19, 1995; 60 FR 32461, June 22, 1995; 62 FR 13968, Mar. 24, 1997; 65 FR 47316, Aug. 2, 2000; 66 FR 52675, Oct. 17, 2001; 68 FR 37414, June 24, 2003; 68 FR 53292, Sept. 10, 2003; 69 FR 74971, Dec. 15, 2004; 72 FR 10928, Mar. 12, 2007; 72 FR 35931, July 2, 2007]

§ 1310.09 Temporary exemption from registration.

(a) Each person required by section 302 of the act (21 U.S.C. 822) to obtain a registration to distribute, import, or export a combination ephedrine product is temporarily exempted from the registration requirement, provided that the person submits a proper application for registration on or before

July 12, 1997. The exemption will remain in effect for each person who has made such application until the Administration has approved or denied that application. This exemption applies only to registration; all other chemical control requirements set forth in parts 1309, 1310, and 1313 of this chapter remain in full force and effect.

(b) Each person required by section 302 of the Act (21 U.S.C. 822) to obtain a registration to distribute, import, or export a drug product that contains pseudoephedrine or phenylpropanolamine that is regulated pursuant to paragraph (1)(iv) of the definition of regulated transaction in § 1300.02 of this chapter is temporarily exempted from the registration requirement, provided that the person submits a proper application for registration on or before December 3, 1997.The exemption will remain in effect for each person who has made such application until the Administration has approved or denied that application. This exemption applies only to registration; all other chemical control requirements set forth in parts 1309, 1310, and 1313 of this chapter remain in full force and effect.

(c) Each person required by section 302 of the act (21 U.S.C. 822) to obtain a registration to distribute, import, or export GBL is temporarily exempted from the registration requirement, provided that the DEA receives a proper application for registration on or before July 24, 2000. The exemption will remain in effect for each person who has made such application until the Administration has approved or denied that application. This exemption applies only to registration; all other chemical control requirements set forth in parts 1309, 1310, and 1313 of this chapter remain in full force and effect.

(d) Each person required by section 302 of the Act (21 U.S.C. 822) to obtain a registration to distribute, import, or export the List I chemicals red phosphorus, white phosphorus, and hypophosphorous acid (and its salts), is temporarily exempted from the registration requirement, provided that the person submits a proper application for registration on or before December 17, 2001. The exemption will remain in effect for each person who has made such application until the Administration has approved or denied that application. This exemption applies only to registration; all other chemical control requirements set forth in parts 1309, 1310, and 1313 of this chapter remain in full force and effect.

(e) Each person required by section 302 of the Act (21 U.S.C. 822) to obtain a registration to distribute, import, or export regulated chemical mixtures which contain ephedrine, N-methylephedrine, N-methylpseudoephedrine, norpseudoephedrine, phenylpropanolamine, and/or pseudoephedrine, pursuant to §§ 1310.12 and 1310.13, is temporarily exempted from the registration requirement, provided that DEA receives a proper application for registration or application for exemption on or before June 30, 2003. The exemption will remain in effect for each person who has made such application until the Administration has approved or denied that application. This exemption applies only to registration; all other chemical control requirements set forth in parts 1309, 1310, and 1313 of this chapter remain in full force and effect. Any person who distributes, imports or exports a chemical mixture whose application for exemption is subsequently denied by DEA must obtain a registration with DEA. A temporary exemption from the registration requirement will also be provided for these persons, provided that DEA receives a properly completed application for registration on or before 30 days following the date of official DEA notification that the application for exemption has not been approved. The temporary exemption for such persons will remain in effect until DEA takes final action on their registration application.

(f) Except for chemical mixtures containing the listed chemicals in paragraph (e) of this section, each person required by section 302 of the Act (21 U.S.C. 822) to obtain a registration to distribute, import, or export regulated chemical mixtures, pursuant to §§ 1310.12 and 1310.13, is temporarily exempted from the registration requirement, provided that DEA receives a proper application for registration or application for exemption on or before February 14, 2005. The exemption will remain in effect for each person who has made such application until the Administration has approved or denied that application. This exemption applies only to registration; all other chemical control requirements set forth in parts 1309, 1310, and 1313 of this chapter remain in full force and effect.

(g) Any person who distributes, imports, or exports a chemical mixture whose application for exemption is subsequently denied by DEA must obtain a registration with DEA. A temporary exemption from the registration requirement will also be provided for these persons, provided that DEA receives a properly completed application for registration on or before 30 days following the date of official DEA notification that the application for exemption has not been approved. The temporary exemption for such persons will remain in effect until DEA takes final action on their registration application.

(h) Each person required under 21 U.S.C. 822 and 21 U.S.C. 957 to obtain a registration to manufacture, distribute, import, or export regulated N-phenethyl-4-piperidone (NPP), including regulated chemical mixtures pursuant to § 1310.12, is temporarily exempted from the registration requirement, provided that DEA receives a proper application for registration or application for exemption for a chemical mixture containing NPP pursuant to § 1310.13 on or before June 22, 2007. The exemption will remain in effect for each person who has made such application until the Administration has approved or denied that application. This exemption applies only to registration; all other chemical control requirements set forth in the Act and parts 1309, 1310, 1313, and 1316 of this chapter remain in full force and effect. Any person who manufactures, distributes, imports or exports a chemical mixture containing N-phenethyl-4-piperidone (NPP) whose application for exemption is subsequently denied by DEA must obtain a registration with DEA. A temporary exemption from the registration requirement will also be provided for those persons whose application for exemption are denied, provided that DEA receives a properly completed application for registration on or before 30 days following the date of official DEA notification that the application for exemption has been denied. The temporary exemption for such persons will remain in effect until DEA takes final action on their registration application.

(i) Each person required by section 302 of the Act (21 U.S.C. 822) to obtain a registration to manufacture, distribute, import, or export regulated iodine, including regulated iodine chemical mixtures pursuant to §§ 1310.12 and 1310.13, is temporarily exempted from the registration requirement, provided that the Administration receives a proper application for registration or application for exemption for a chemical mixture containing iodine on or before August 31, 2007. The exemption will remain in effect for each person who has made such application until the Administration has approved or denied that application. This exemption applies only to registration; all other chemical control requirements set forth in the Act and parts 1309, 1310, and 1313 of this chapter remain in full force and effect. Any person who distributes, imports, or exports a chemical mixture containing iodine whose application for exemption is subsequently denied by the Administration must obtain a registration with the Administration. A temporary exemption from the registration requirement will also be provided for these persons, provided that the Administration receives a properly completed application for registration on or before 30 days following the date of official Administration notification that the application for exemption has not been approved. The temporary exemption for such persons will remain in effect until the Administration takes final action on their registration application.

(j) Each person required by section 302 of the Act (21 U.S.C. 822) to obtain a registration to manufacture, distribute, import, or export regulated chemical mixtures which contain ephedrine, and/or pseudoephedrine, pursuant to Sections 1310.12 and 1310.13, is temporarily exempted from the registration requirement, provided that DEA receives a properly completed application for registration or application for exemption on or before August

24, 2007. The exemption will remain in effect for each person who has made such application until the Administration has approved or denied that application. This exemption applies only to registration; all other chemical control requirements set forth in parts 1309, 1310, 1313, and 1315 of this chapter remain in full force and effect. Any person who manufactures, distributes, imports, or exports a chemical mixture whose application for exemption is subsequently denied by DEA must obtain a registration with DEA. A temporary exemption from the registration requirement will also be provided for these persons, provided that DEA receives a properly completed application for registration on or before 30 days following the date of official DEA notification that the application for exemption has not been approved. The temporary exemption for such persons will remain in effect until DEA takes final action on their registration application.

(k)(1) Each person required by sections 302 or 1007 of the Act (21 U.S.C. 822, 957) to obtain a registration to manufacture, distribute, import, or export regulated GBL-containing chemical mixtures, pursuant to sections 1310.12 and 1310.13, is temporarily exempted from the registration requirement, provided that DEA receives a properly completed application for registration or application for exemption on or before July 29, 2010. The exemption will remain in effect for each person who has made such application until the Administration has approved or denied that application. This exemption applies only to registration; all other chemical control requirements set forth in parts 1309, 1310, and 1313 of this chapter remain in full force and effect.

(2) Any person who manufactures, distributes, imports or exports a GBL-containing chemical mixture whose application for exemption is subsequently denied by DEA must obtain a registration with DEA. A temporary exemption from the registration requirement will also be provided for those persons whose applications for exemption are denied, provided that DEA receives a properly completed application for registration on or before 30 days following the date of official DEA notification that the application for exemption has been denied. The temporary exemption for such persons will remain in effect until DEA takes final action on their registration application.

(l)(1) Each person required under sections 302 and 1007 of the Act (21 U.S.C. 822, 957) to obtain a registration to manufacture, distribute, import, or export regulated ergocristine and its salts, including regulated chemical mixtures pursuant to § 1310.12, is temporarily exempted from the registration requirement, provided that DEA receives a properly completed application for registration or application for exemption for a chemical mixture containing ergocristine and its salts pursuant to § 1310.13 on or before May 2, 2011. The exemption will remain in effect for each person who has made such application until the Administration has approved or denied that application. This exemption applies only to registration; all other chemical control requirements set forth in the Act and parts 1309, 1310, 1313, and 1316 of this chapter remain in full force and effect.

(2) Any person who manufactures, distributes, imports, or exports a chemical mixture containing ergocristine and its salts whose application for exemption is subsequently denied by DEA must obtain a registration with DEA. A temporary exemption from the registration requirement will also be provided for those persons whose applications for exemption are denied, provided that DEA receives a properly completed application for registration on or before 30 days following the date of official DEA notification that the application for exemption has been denied. The temporary exemption for such persons will remain in effect until DEA takes final action on their registration application.

(m)(1) Each person required by Sections 302 or 1007 of the Act (21 U.S.C. 822, 957) to obtain a registration to manufacture, distribute, import, or export regulated chemical mixtures which contain red phosphorus, white phosphorus, hypophosphorous acid (and its salts), pursuant to §§ 1310.12 and 1310.13, is temporarily exempted from the registration requirement, provided that DEA receives a properly completed application for registration or application for exemption on or before July 5, 2011. The exemption will remain in effect for each person who has made such application until the Administration has approved or denied that application. This exemption applies only to registration; all other chemical control requirements set forth in parts 1309, 1310, and 1313 of this chapter remain in full force and effect.

(2) Any person who manufactures, distributes, imports, or exports a chemical mixture which contains red phosphorus, white phosphorus, hypophosphorous acid (and its salts) whose application for exemption is subsequently denied by DEA must obtain a registration with DEA. A temporary exemption from the registration requirement will also be provided for those persons whose applications are denied, provided that DEA receives a properly completed application for registration on or before 30 days following the date of official DEA notification that the application for exemption has not been approved. The temporary exemption for such persons will remain in effect until DEA takes final action on their registration application.

(n)(1) Each person required under sections 302 and 1007 of the Act (21 U.S.C. 822, 957) to obtain a registration to manufacture, distribute, import, or export regulated alpha-phenylacetoacetonitrile (APAAN) and its salts, optical isomers, and salts of optical isomers, including regulated chemical mixtures pursuant to § 1310.12, is temporarily exempted from the registration requirement, provided that the DEA receives a properly completed application for registration or application for exemption for a chemical mixture containing alpha-phenylacetoacetonitrile (APAAN) and its salts, optical isomers, and salts of optical isomers, pursuant to § 1310.13 on or before August 14, 2017. The exemption will remain in effect for each person who has made such application until the Administration has approved or denied that application. This exemption applies only to registration; all other chemical control requirements set forth in the Act and parts 1309, 1310, 1313, and 1316 of this chapter remain in full force and effect.

(2) Any person who manufactures, distributes, imports or exports a chemical mixture containing alpha-phenylacetoacetonitrile (APAAN) and its salts, optical isomers, and salts of optical isomers whose application for exemption is subsequently denied by the DEA must obtain a registration with the DEA. A temporary exemption from the registration requirement will also be provided for those persons whose applications for exemption are denied, provided that the DEA receives a properly completed application for registration on or before 30 days following the date of official DEA notification that the application for exemption has been denied. The temporary exemption for such persons will remain in effect until the DEA takes final action on their registration application.

[62 FR 27693, May 21, 1997, as amended at 62 FR 53960, Oct. 17, 1997; 65 FR 21647, Apr. 24, 2000; 66 FR 52675, Oct. 17, 2001; 68 FR 23203, May 1, 2003; 69 FR 74971, Dec. 15, 2004; 72 FR 20046, Apr. 23, 2007; 72 FR 35931, July 2, 2007; 72 FR 40239, July 24, 2007; 72 FR 40744, July 25, 2007; 75 FR 37306, June 29, 2010; 76 FR 17781, Mar. 31, 2011; 76 FR 31829, June 2, 2011; 77 FR 4237, Jan. 27, 2012; 82 FR 32460, July 14, 2017]

§ 1310.10 Removal of the exemption of drugs distributed under the Federal Food, Drug and Cosmetic Act.

(a) The Administrator may remove from exemption under paragraph (1)(iv) of the definition of regulated transaction in § 1300.02 of this chapter any drug or group of drugs that the Administrator finds is being diverted to obtain a listed chemical for use in the illicit production of a controlled substance. In removing a drug or group of drugs from the exemption the Administrator shall consider:

(1) The scope, duration, and significance of the diversion;

(2) Whether the drug or group of drugs is formulated in such a way that it cannot be easily used in the illicit production of a controlled substance; and

(3) Whether the listed chemical can be readily recovered from the drug or group of drugs.

(b) Upon determining that a drug or group of drugs should be removed from the exemption under paragraph (a) of this section, the Administrator shall issue and publish in the FEDERAL REGISTER his proposal to remove the drug or group of drugs from the exemption, which shall include a reference to the legal authority under which the proposal is based. The Administrator shall permit any interested person to file written comments on or objections to the proposal. After considering any comments or objections filed, the Administrator shall publish in the FEDERAL REGISTER his final order.

(c) The Administrator shall limit the removal of a drug or group of drugs from exemption under paragraph (a) of this section to the most identifiable type of the drug or group of drugs for which evidence of diversion exists unless there is evidence, based on the pattern of diversion and other relevant factors, that the diversion will not be limited to that particular drug or group of drugs.

(d) Any manufacturer seeking reinstatement of a particular drug product that has been removed from an exemption may apply to the Administrator for reinstatement of the exemption for that particular drug product on the grounds that the particular drug product is manufactured and distributed in a manner that prevents diversion. In determining whether the exemption should be reinstated the Administrator shall consider:

(1) The package sizes and manner of packaging of the drug product;

(2) The manner of distribution and advertising of the drug product;

(3) Evidence of diversion of the drug product;

(4) Any actions taken by the manufacturer to prevent diversion of the drug product; and

(5) Such other factors as are relevant to and consistent with the public health and safety, including the factors described in paragraph (a) of this section as applied to the drug product.

(e) Within a reasonable period of time after receipt of the application for reinstatement of the exemption, the Administrator shall notify the applicant of his acceptance or non-acceptance of his application, and if not accepted, the reason therefor. If the application is accepted for filing, the Administrator shall issue and publish in the FEDERAL REGISTER his order on the reinstatement of the exemption for the particular drug product, which shall include a reference to the legal authority under which the order is based. This order shall specify the date on which it shall take effect. The Administrator shall permit any interested person to file written comments on or objections to the order. If any such comments raise significant issues regarding any finding of fact or conclusion of law upon which the order is based, the Administrator shall immediately suspend the effectiveness of the order until he may reconsider the application in light of the comments and objections filed. Thereafter, the Administrator shall reinstate, revoke, or amend his original order as he determines appropriate.

(f) Unless the Administrator has evidence that the drug product is being diverted, as determined by applying the factors set forth in paragraph (a) of this section, and the Administrator so notifies the applicant, transactions involving a specific drug product will not be considered regulated transactions during the following periods:

(1) While a bonafide application for reinstatement of exemption under paragraph (d) of this section for the specific drug product is pending resolution, provided that the application for reinstatement is filed not later than 60 days after the publication of the final order removing the exemption; and

(2) For a period of 60 days following the Administrator's denial of an application for reinstatement.

(g) An order published by the Administrator in the FEDERAL REGISTER, pursuant to paragraph (e) of this section, to reinstate an exemption may be modified or revoked with respect to a particular drug product upon a finding that:

(1) Applying the factors set forth in paragraph (a) of this section to the particular drug product, the drug product is being diverted; or

(2) There is a significant change in the data that led to the issuance of the final rule.

[60 FR 32461, June 22, 1995, as amended at 62 FR 13968, Mar. 24, 1997; 67 FR 14862, Mar. 28, 2002; 75 FR 38922, July 7, 2010; 77 FR 4237, Jan. 27, 2012]

§1310.11 Reinstatement of exemption for drug products distributed under the Food, Drug and Cosmetic Act.

(a) The Administrator has reinstated the exemption for the drug products listed in paragraph (e) of this section from application of sections 302, 303, 310, 1007, and 1008 of the Act (21 U.S.C. 822–823, 830, and 957–958), to the extent described in paragraphs (b), (c), and (d) of this section.

(b) No reinstated exemption granted pursuant to 1310.10 affects the criminal liability for illegal possession or distribution of listed chemicals contained in the exempt drug product.

(c) Changes in exempt drug product compositions: Any change in the quantitative or qualitative composition, trade name or other designation of an exempt drug product listed in paragraph (d) requires a new application for reinstatement of the exemption.

(d) The following drug products, in the form and quantity listed in the application submitted (indicated as the "date") are designated as reinstated exempt drug products for the purposes set forth in this section:

EXEMPT DRUG PRODUCTS

Supplier	Product name	Form	Date
[Reserved]	....	....	

[60 FR 32462, June 22, 1995]

§1310.12 Exempt chemical mixtures.

(a) The chemical mixtures meeting the criteria in paragraphs (c) or (d) of this section are exempted by the Administrator from application of sections 302, 303, 310, 1007, 1008, and 1018 of the Act (21 U.S.C. 822, 823, 830, 957, 958, and 971) to the extent described in paragraphs (b) and (c) of this section.

(b) No exemption granted pursuant to this §1310.12 or §1310.13 affects the criminal liability for illegal possession, distribution, exportation, or importation of listed chemicals contained in the exempt chemical mixture or the civil liability for unlawful acts related to exempt chemical mixtures, including distribution in violation of 21 U.S.C. 842(a)(11).

(c) Mixtures containing a listed chemical in concentrations equal to or less than those specified in the "Table of Concentration Limits" are designated as exempt chemical mixtures for the purpose set forth in this section. The concentration is determined for liquid-liquid mixtures by using the volume or weight and for mixtures containing solids or gases by using the unit of weight.

TABLE OF CONCENTRATION LIMITS

	DEA chemical code number	Concentration	Special conditions
List I Chemicals			
N-Acetylanthranilic acid, its salts and esters.	8522	20% by Weight	Concentration based on any combination of N-acetylanthranilic acid and its salts and esters.
Alpha-phenylacetoacetonitrile, and its salts, optical isomers, and salts of optical isomers. (APAAN).	8512	Not exempt at any concentration.	Chemical mixtures containing any amount of APAAN are not exempt.
Anthranilic acid, and its salts and esters.	8530	50% by Weight	Concentration is based on any combination of anthranilic acid and its salts and esters.
Benzaldehyde	8256	50% by Weight or Volume.	
Benzyl cyanide	8570	20% by Weight or Volume.	
Ephedrine, its salts, optical isomers, and salts of optical isomers.	8113	Not exempt at any concentration.	Chemical mixtures containing any amount of ephedrine and/or pseudoephedrine, and their salts, optical isomers and salts of optical isomers are not exempt due to concentration, unless otherwise exempted.
Ergocristine and its salts	8612	Not exempt at any concentration.	Chemical mixtures containing any amount of ergocristine and its salts are not exempt.
Ergonovine and its salts	8675	Not exempt at any concentration.	Chemical mixtures containing any amount of ergonovine, including its salts, are not exempt.
Ergotamine and its salts	8676	Not exempt at any concentration.	Chemical mixtures containing amount of any ergotamine, including its salts, are not exempt.

TABLE OF CONCENTRATION LIMITS—Continued

	DEA chemical code number	Concentration	Special conditions
Ethylamine and its salts	8678	20% by Weight or Volume	Ethylamine or its salts in an inert carrier solvent is not considered a mixture. Concentration is based on ethylamine in the mixture and not the combination of ethylamine and carrier solvent, if any.
Gamma-Butyrolactone	2011	70% by weight or volume.	
Hydriodic acid	6695	20% by Weight or Volume.	
Hypophosphorous acid and its salts.	6797	30% by weight if a solid, weight or volume if a liquid.	The weight is determined by measuring the mass of hypophosphorous acid and its salts in the mixture, the concentration limit is calculated by summing the concentrations of all forms of hypophosphorous acid and its salts in the mixture. The Administration does not consider a chemical mixture to mean the combination of a listed chemical and an inert carrier. Therefore, any solution consisting of hypophosphorous acid (and its salts), dispersed in water, alcohol, or another inert carrier, is not considered a chemical mixture and is therefore subject to chemical regulatory controls at all concentrations.
Iodine	6699	2.2	Calculated as weight/volume (w/v).
Isosafrole	8704	20% by Weight or Volume	Concentration in a mixture cannot exceed 20% if taken alone or in any combination with safrole.
Methylamine and its salts	8520	20% by Weight	Methylamine or its salts in an inert carrier solvent is not considered a mixture. Weight is based on methylamine in the mixture and not the combined weight of carrier solvent, if any.
3,4-Methylenedioxyphenyl-2-propanone.	8502	20% by Weight.	
N-Methylephedrine, its salts, optical isomers, and salts of optical isomers.	8115	0.1% by Weight	Concentration based on any combination of salts N-methylephedrine, N-methylpseudoephedrine and their salts, optical isomers and salts of optical isomers.
N-Methylpseudoephedrine, its salts, optical isomers, and salts of optical isomers.	8119	0.1% by Weight	Concentration based on any combination of N-methylpseudoephedrine, N-methylephedrine, and their salts, optical isomers and salts of optical isomers.
Nitroethane	6724	20% by Weight or Volume.	
Norpseudoephedrine, its salts, optical isomers, and salts of optical isomers.	8317	0.6% by Weight	Concentration based on any combination of norpseudoephedrine, phenylpropanolamine and their salts, optical isomers and salts of optical isomers.
N-phenethyl-4-piperidone (NPP).	8332	Not exempt at any concentration.	Chemical mixtures containing any amount of NPP are not exempt.
Phenylacetic acid, and its salts and esters.	8791	40% by Weight	Concentration is based on any combination of phenylacetic acid and its salts and esters.
Phenylpropanolamine, its salts, optical isomers, and salts of optical isomers.	1225	0.6% by Weight	Concentration based on any combination of phenylpropanolamine, norpseudoephedrine and their salts, optical isomers and salts of optical isomers.
Piperidine, and its salts	2704	20% by Weight or Volume	Concentration based on any combination of piperidine and its salts. Concentration based on weight if a solid, weight or volume if a liquid.
Piperonal	8750	20% by Weight or Volume.	
Propionic anhydride	8328	20% by Weight or Volume.	
Pseudoephedrine, its salts, optical isomers, and salts of optical isomers.	8112	Not exempt at any concentration.	Chemical mixtures containing any amount of ephedrine and/or pseudoephedrine, and their salts, optical isomers and salts of optical isomers are not exempt due to concentration, unless otherwise exempted.
Red Phosphorus	6795	80% by weight.	
Safrole	8323	20% by Volume	Concentration in a mixture cannot exceed 20% if taken alone or in any combination with isosafrole.
White phosphorus	6796	Not exempt at any concentration.	Chemical mixtures containing any amount of white phosphorus are not exempt due to concentration, unless otherwise exempted.
List II Chemicals			
Acetic Anhydride	8519	20% by Weight or Volume.	

TABLE OF CONCENTRATION LIMITS—Continued

	DEA chemical code number	Concentration	Special conditions
Acetone	6532	35% by Weight or Volume	Exports only; Limit applies to acetone or any combination of acetone, ethyl ether, 2-butanone, methyl isobutyl ketone, and toluene if present in the mixture by summing the concentrations for each chemical.
Benzyl chloride	8568	20% by Weight or Volume.	
2-butanone	6714	35% by Weight or Volume	Exports only; Limit applies to 2-butanone or any combination of acetone, ethyl ether, 2-butanone, methyl isobutyl ketone, and toluene if present in the mixture by summing the concentrations for each chemical.
Ethyl ether	6584	35% by Weight or Volume	Exports only; Limit applies to ethyl ether or any combination of acetone, ethyl ether, 2-butanone, methyl isobutyl ketone, and toluene if present in the mixture by summing the concentrations for each chemical.
Hydrochloric acid	6545	20% by Weight or Volume	Hydrogen chloride in an inert carrier solvent, such as aqueous or alcoholic solutions, is not considered a mixture. Weight is based on hydrogen chloride in the mixture and not the combined weight of the carrier solvent, if any.
Methyl isobutyl ketone	6715	35% by Weight or Volume	Exports only pursuant to §1310.08; Limit applies to methyl isobutyl ketone or any combination of acetone, ethyl ether, 2-butanone, methyl isobutyl ketone, and toluene if present in the mixture by summing the concentrations for each chemical.
Potassium permanganate	6579	15% by Weight.	
Sodium Permanganate	6588	15% by Weight.	
Sulfuric acid	6552	20% by Weight or Volume	Sulfuric acid in an inert carrier solvent, such as aqueous or alcoholic solutions, is not considered a mixture. Weight is based on sulfuric acid in the mixture and not the combined weight of the carrier solvent, if any.
Toluene	594	35% by Weight or Volume	Exports only; Limit applies to toluene or any combination of acetone, ethyl ether, 2-butanone, methyl isobutyl ketone, and toluene if present in the mixture by summing the concentrations for each chemical.

(d) The following categories of chemical mixtures are automatically exempt from the provisions of the Controlled Substances Act as described in paragraph (a) of this section:

(1) Chemical mixtures that are distributed directly to an incinerator for destruction or directly to an authorized waste recycler or reprocessor where such distributions are documented on United States Environmental Protection Agency Form 8700–22; persons distributing the mixture to the incinerator or recycler must maintain and make available to agents of the Administration, upon request, such documentation for a period of no less than two years.

(2) Completely formulated paints and coatings: Completely formulated paints and coatings are only those formulations that contain all of the components of the paint or coating for use in the final application without the need to add any additional substances except a thinner if needed in certain cases. A completely formulated paint or coating is defined as any clear or pigmented liquid, liquefiable or mastic composition designed for application to a substrate in a thin layer that is converted to a clear or opaque solid protective, decorative, or functional adherent film after application. Included in this category are clear coats, topcoats, primers, varnishes, sealers, adhesives, lacquers, stains, shellacs, inks, temporary protective coatings and film-forming agents.

(3) Iodine products classified as iodophors that exist as an iodine complex to include poloxamer-iodine complex, polyvinyl pyrrolidone-iodine complex (*i.e.*, povidone-iodine), undecoylium chloride iodine,

nonylphenoxypoly (ethyleneoxy) ethanol-iodine complex, iodine complex with phosphate ester of alkylaryloxy polyethylene glycol, and iodine complex with ammonium ether sulfate/polyoxyethylene sorbitan monolaurate.

(4) Iodine products that consist of organically bound iodine (a non-ionic complex) (e.g., iopamidol, iohexol, and amiodarone.)

(e) The Administrator may, at any time, terminate or modify the exemption for any chemical mixture which has been granted an exemption pursuant to the concentration limits as specified in paragraph (c) of this section or pursuant to the category exemption as specified in paragraph (d) of this section. In terminating or modifying an exemption, the Administrator shall issue, and publish in the FEDERAL REGISTER, notification of the removal of an exemption for a product or group of products for which evidence of diversion has been found, as well as the date on which the termination of exemption shall take effect. The Administrator shall permit any interested party to file written comments on or objections to the order within 60 days of the date of publication of the order in the FEDERAL REGISTER. If any such comments or objections raise significant issues regarding any finding of fact or conclusion of law upon which the order is based, the Administrator shall immediately suspend the effectiveness of the order until he may reconsider the order in light of comments and objections filed. Thereafter, the Administrator shall reinstate, terminate, or amend the original order as determined appropriate.

(f) The Administrator may modify any part of the criteria for exemption as specified in paragraphs (c) and (d) of this section upon evidence of diversion or attempted diversion. In doing so, the Administrator shall issue and publish a Notice of Proposed Rulemaking in the FEDERAL REGISTER. The Administrator shall permit any interested persons to file written comments on or objections to the proposal. After considering any comments or objections filed, the Administrator shall publish in the FEDERAL REGISTER a final order.

[68 FR 23204, May 1, 2003, as amended at 69 FR 74971, Dec. 15, 2004; 71 FR 60826, Oct. 17, 2006; 72 FR 20047, Apr. 23, 2007; 72 FR 35931, July 2, 2007; 72 FR 40745, July 25, 2007; 75 FR 37306, June 29, 2010; 76 FR 17781, Mar. 31, 2011; 76 FR 31830, June 2, 2011; 82 FR 32460, July 14, 2017]

§ 1310.13 Exemption of chemical mixtures; application.

(a) The Administrator may, by publication of a Final Rule in the FEDERAL REGISTER, exempt from the application of all or any part of the Act a chemical mixture consisting of two or more chemical components, at least one of which is not a List I or List II chemical, if:

(1) The mixture is formulated in such a way that it cannot be easily used in the illicit production of a controlled substance; and

(2) The listed chemical or chemicals contained in the chemical mixture cannot be readily recovered.

(b) Any manufacturer seeking an exemption for a chemical mixture, not exempt under § 1310.12, from the application of all or any part of the Act, may apply to the Drug and Chemical Evaluation Section, Diversion Control Division, Drug Enforcement Administration. See the Table of DEA Mailing Addresses in § 1321.01 of this chapter for the current mailing address.

(c) An application for exemption under this section shall contain the following information:

(1) The name, address, and registration number, if any, of the applicant;

(2) The date of the application;

(3) The exact trade name(s) of the applicant's chemical mixture and:

(i) If the applicant formulates or manufactures the chemical mixture for other entities, the exact trade names of the chemical mixtures and the names of the entities for which the chemical mixtures were prepared; and

(ii) If a group of mixtures (e.g. formulations having identical function and containing the same listed chemical(s)), the information required in paragraph (c)(3)(i) of this section and a brief narrative of their use.

(4) (i) The complete qualitative and quantitative composition of the chemical mixture (including all listed and all non-listed chemicals); or

(ii) If a group of mixtures, the concentration range for the listed chemical and a listing of all non-listed chemicals with respective concentration ranges.

(5) (i) The chemical and physical properties of the mixture and how they differ from the properties of the listed chemical or chemicals; and

(ii) If a group of mixtures, how the group's properties differ from the properties of the listed chemical.

(6) A statement that the applicant believes justifies an exemption for the chemical mixture or group of mixtures. The statement must explain how the chemical mixture(s) meets the exemption criteria set forth in paragraph (a) of this section.

(7) A statement that the applicant accepts the right of the Administrator to terminate exemption from regulation for the chemical mixture(s) granted exemption under this section.

(8) The identification of any information on the application that is considered by the applicant to be a trade secret or confidential and entitled to protection under U.S. laws restricting the public disclosure of such information.

(d) The Administrator may require the applicant to submit such additional documents or written statements of fact relevant to the application that he deems necessary for determining if the application should be granted.

(e) Within a reasonable period of time after the receipt of an application for an exemption under this section, the Administrator will notify the applicant in writing of the acceptance or rejection of the application for filing. If the application is not accepted for filing, an explanation will be provided. The Administrator is not required to accept an application if any information required pursuant to paragraph (c) of this section or requested pursuant to paragraph (d) of this section is lacking or not readily understood. The applicant may, however, amend the application to meet the requirements of paragraphs (c) and (d) of this section. If the exemption is subsequently granted, the applicant shall again be notified in writing and the Administrator shall issue, and publish in the FEDERAL REGISTER, an order on the application. This order shall specify the date on which it shall take effect. The Administrator shall permit any interested person to file written comments on or objections to the order. If any comments or objections raise significant issues regarding any findings of fact or conclusions of law upon which the order is based, the Administrator may suspend the effectiveness of the order until he has reconsidered the application in light of the comments and objections filed. Thereafter, the Administrator shall reinstate, terminate, or amend the original order as deemed appropriate.

(f) The Administrator may, at any time, terminate or modify an exemption for any product pursuant to paragraph (e) of this section. In terminating or modifying an exemption, the Administrator shall issue, and publish in the FEDERAL REGISTER, notification of the removal of an exempt product or group of exempt products for which evidence of diversion has been found. This order shall specify the date on which the termination of exemption shall take effect. The Administrator shall permit any interested party to file written comments on or objections to the order within 60 days of the date of publication of the order in the FEDERAL REGISTER. If any such comments or objections raise significant issues regarding any finding of fact or conclusion of law upon which the order is based, the Administrator may suspend the effectiveness of the order until he has reconsidered the order in light of comments and objections filed. Thereafter, the Administrator shall reinstate, terminate, or amend the original order as determined appropriate.

(g) A manufacturer of an exempted chemical mixture shall notify DEA in writing, of any change in the quantitative or qualitative composition of a chemical mixture that has been granted an exemption by application. Changes include those greater than the range of concentration given in the application or that remove non-listed chemical(s) given in the application as part of the formulation. A new application will be required only if reformulation results in a new product having a different commercial application or can no longer be defined as part of a group of exempted chemicals. DEA must be notified of reformulation at least 30 days in advance of marketing the reformulated mixture. For a change in name or other designation, code, or any identifier, a written notification is required. DEA must be notified of any changes at least 60 days in advance of the effective date for the change.

(h) Each manufacturer seeking exemption must apply for such an exemption. A formulation granted exemption by publication in the FEDERAL REGISTER will not be exempted for all manufacturers.

(i) The following chemical mixtures, in the form and quantity listed in the application submitted (indicated as the "date") are designated as exempt chemical mixtures for the purposes set forth in this section and are exempted by the Administrator from application of Sections 302, 303, 310, 1007, 1008, and 1018 of the Act (21 U.S.C. 822, 823, 830, 957, 958, and 971):

TABLE 1 TO PARAGRAPH (i)—EXEMPT CHEMICAL MIXTURES

Manufacturer	Product name [1]	Form	Date
Cerilliant Corporation	1R,2S(-)-Ephedrine hydrochloride 1.0 mg/ml as free base in one of: 1,2-dimethoxyethane, acetonitrile, acetonitrile: water (≥50% acetonitrile), dimethylformamide, ethylene glycol, isopropanol, methanol, methanol/water (50:50), methanol/dimethyl sulfoxide (80:20), methylene chloride, or tetrahydrofuran.	Liquid	8/2/2007
Cerilliant Corporation	1S,2R(+)-Ephedrine-D_3 hydrochloride 0.1 mg/ml as free base in one of: 1,2-dimethoxyethane, acetonitrile, acetonitrile: water (≥50% acetonitrile), dimethylformamide, ethylene glycol, isopropanol, methanol, methanol/water (50:50), methanol/dimethyl sulfoxide (80:20), methylene chloride, or tetrahydrofuran.	Liquid	8/2/2007
Cerilliant Corporation	1S,2R(+)-Ephedrine-D_3 hydrochloride 1.0 mg/ml as free base in one of: 1,2-dimethoxyethane, acetonitrile, acetonitrile: water (≥50% acetonitrile), dimethylformamide, ethylene glycol, isopropanol, methanol, methanol/water (50:50), methanol/dimethyl sulfoxide (80:20), methylene chloride, or tetrahydrofuran.	Liquid	8/2/2007
Cerilliant Corporation	1S,2R(+)-Ephedrine hydrochloride 1.0 mg/ml as free base in one of: 1,2-dimethoxyethane, acetonitrile, acetonitrile: water (≥50% acetonitrile), dimethylformamide, ethylene glycol, isopropanol, methanol, methanol/water (50:50), methanol/dimethyl sulfoxide (80:20), methylene chloride, or tetrahydrofuran.	Liquid	8/2/2007
Cerilliant Corporation	Pseudoephedrine-D_3 hydrochloride 0.1 mg/ml as free base in one of: 1,2-dimethoxyethane, acetonitrile, acetonitrile: water (≥50% acetonitrile), dimethylformamide, ethylene glycol, isopropanol, methanol, methanol/water (50:50), methanol/dimethyl sulfoxide (80:20), methylene chloride, or tetrahydrofuran.	Liquid	8/2/2007
Cerilliant Corporation	R,R(-)-Pseudoephedrine 1.0 mg/ml as free base in one of: 1,2-dimethoxyethane, acetonitrile, acetonitrile: water (≥50% acetonitrile), dimethylformamide, ethylene glycol, isopropanol, methanol, methanol/water (50:50), methanol/dimethyl sulfoxide (80:20) methylene chloride, or tetrahydrofuran.	Liquid	8/2/2007
Cerilliant Corporation	S,S(+)-Pseudoephedrine 1.0 mg/ml as free base in one of: 1,2-dimethoxyethane, acetonitrile, acetonitrile: water (≥50% acetonitrile), dimethylformamide, ethylene glycol, isopropanol, methanol, methanol/water (50:50), methanol/dimethyl sulfoxide (80:20), methylene chloride, or tetrahydrofuran.	Liquid	8/2/2007
E.I. DuPont deNemours & Co.	RC–5156	Liquid	4/22/2005
E.I. DuPont deNemours & Co.	VH–6037	Liquid	4/22/2005
GFS Chemicals	WaterMark® Karl-Fisher Reagent, Pyridine-Free Single Solution, 5 mg/ml.	Liquid	11/26/2018
GFS Chemicals	WaterMark® Karl-Fisher Reagent, 5 mg/ml Single Solution NON–HAZ	Liquid	11/26/2018
GFS Chemicals	WaterMark® Karl-Fisher Reagent, Pyridine-Free Single Solution, 2 mg/ml.	Liquid	11/26/2018
GFS Chemicals	WaterMark® Karl-Fisher Reagent, 2 mg/ml Single Solution NON–HAZ	Liquid	11/26/2018
GFS Chemicals	WaterMark® Karl-Fisher Reagent, 5 mg/ml, Stabilized, Pyridine-Based	Liquid	11/26/2018
Hawthorne Products, Inc.	Sole Pack Hoof Dressing	Paste	8/14/2007
Hawthorne Products, Inc.	Sole Pack Hoof Packing	Paste	8/14/2007
Lord Corporation	Chemlok TS701–52	Liquid	05/03/2018
Lord Corporation	Chemlok TS701–53	Liquid	05/03/2018

TABLE 1 TO PARAGRAPH (i)—EXEMPT CHEMICAL MIXTURES—Continued

Manufacturer	Product name[1]	Form	Date
Quality Assurance Service Corporation.	10 to 1000 nanograms per milliliter of ephedrine in blood, serum, or urine.	Liquid	9/26/2007
Quality Assurance Service Corporation.	10 to 1000 nanograms per milliliter of pseudoephedrine in blood, serum, or urine.	Liquid	9/26/2007
Quality Assurance Service Corporation.	10 to 1000 nanograms per milliliter of phenylpropanolamine in blood, serum, or urine.	Liquid	9/26/2007
Reichhold, Inc	Beckosol® 12021–00 AA–200, IA–441, P531–T	Liquid	5/05/2005
Reichhold, Inc	Urotuf® L06–30S, F78–50T	Liquid	5/05/2005
Reichhold, Inc	Beckosol AA–220	Liquid	6/14/2005
Sigma-Aldrich	Hydranal®-Composite 1	Liquid	5/29/2013
Sigma-Aldrich	Hydranal®-Composite 2	Liquid	5/29/2013
Sigma-Aldrich	Hydranal®-Composite 5K	Liquid	5/29/2013
Sigma-Aldrich	Hydranal®-Composite 5	Liquid	5/29/2013
Standard Homeopathic Co.	Baby Cough Syrup	Liquid	9/28/2012
Standard Homeopathic Co.	Defend Cough & Cold Night	Liquid	9/28/2012
Standard Homeopathic Co.	Defend Cough & Cold	Liquid	9/28/2012
Standard Homeopathic Co.	Diarrex	Liquid	9/28/2012
Waterbury Companies, Inc.	Waterbury 332500	Liquid	4/11/2005
Waterbury Companies, Inc.	Waterbury 332762	Liquid	4/11/2005
Waterbury Companies, Inc.	Waterbury 332400	Liquid	4/11/2005
Waterbury Companies, Inc.	Waterbury 346201	Liquid	4/11/2005

[1] Designate product line if a group.

[68 FR 23204, May 1, 2003, as amended at 75 FR 10681, Mar. 9, 2010; 75 FR 53869, Sept. 2, 2010; 76 FR 31830, June 2, 2011; 81 FR 97025, Dec. 30, 2016; 85 FR 4586, Jan. 27, 2020]

§1310.14 Removal of exemption from definition of regulated transaction.

The Administrator finds that the following drugs or groups of drugs are being diverted to obtain a listed chemical for use in the illicit production of a controlled substance and removes the drugs or groups of drugs from exemption under paragraph (1)(iv) of the definition of regulated transaction in §1300.02 of this chapter pursuant to the criteria listed in §1310.10 of this part:

(a) Nonprescription drugs containing ephedrine, its salts, optical isomers, and salts of optical isomers.

(b) Nonprescription drugs containing phenylpropanolamine, its salts, optical isomers, and salts of optical isomers.

(c) Nonprescription drugs containing pseudoephedrine, its salts, optical isomers, and salts of optical isomers.

[75 FR 38922, July 7, 2010, as amended at 77 FR 4237, Jan. 27, 2012]

§1310.16 Exemptions for certain scheduled listed chemical products.

(a) Upon the application of a manufacturer of a scheduled listed chemical product, the Administrator may by regulation provide that the product is exempt from part 1314 of this chapter if the Administrator determines that the product cannot be used in the illicit manufacture of a controlled substance.

(b) An application for an exemption under this section must contain all of the following information:

(1) The name and address of the applicant.

(2) The exact trade name of the scheduled listed chemical product for which exemption is sought.

(3) The complete quantitative and qualitative composition of the drug product.

(4) A brief statement of the facts that the applicant believes justify the granting of an exemption under this section.

(5) Certification by the applicant that the product may be lawfully marketed or distributed under the Federal, Food, Drug, and Cosmetic Act.

(6) The identification of any information on the application that is considered by the applicant to be a trade secret or confidential and entitled to protection under U.S. laws restricting the public disclosure of such information by government employees.

(c) The Administrator may require the applicant to submit additional documents or written statements of fact relevant to the application that he deems necessary for determining if the application should be granted.

(d) Within a reasonable period of time after the receipt of a completed application for an exemption under this section, the Administrator shall notify the applicant of acceptance or non-acceptance of the application. If the application is not accepted, an explanation will be provided. The Administrator is not required to accept an application if any of the information required in paragraph (b) of this section or requested under paragraph (c) of this section is lacking or not readily understood. The applicant may, however, amend the application to meet the requirements of paragraphs (b) and (c) of this section.

(e) If the application is accepted for filing, the Administrator shall issue and publish in the FEDERAL REGISTER an order on the application, which shall include a reference to the legal authority under which the order is based. This order shall specify the date on which it shall take effect.

(f) The Administrator shall permit any interested person to file written comments on or objections to the order. If any comments or objections raise significant issues regarding any findings of fact or conclusions of law upon which the order is based, the Administrator shall immediately suspend the effectiveness of the order until he may reconsider the application in light of the comments and objections filed. Thereafter, the Administrator shall reinstate, revoke, or amend the original order as deemed appropriate.

[71 FR 56024, Sept. 26, 2006]

§ 1310.21 Sale by Federal departments or agencies of chemicals which could be used to manufacture controlled substances.

(a) A Federal department or agency may not sell from the stocks of the department or agency any chemical which, as determined by the Administrator of the Drug Enforcement Administration, could be used in the manufacture of a controlled substance, unless the Administrator certifies in writing to the head of the department or agency that there is no reasonable cause to believe that the sale of the specific chemical to a specific person would result in the illegal manufacture of a controlled substance. For purposes of this requirement, reasonable cause to believe means that the Administration has knowledge of facts which would cause a reasonable person to reasonably conclude that a chemical would be diverted to the illegal manufacture of a controlled substance.

(b) A Federal department or agency must request certification by submitting a written request to the Administrator, Drug Enforcement Administration. See the Table of DEA Mailing Addresses in § 1321.01 of this chapter for the current mailing address. A request for certification may be transmitted directly to the Office of Diversion Control, Drug Enforcement Administration, through electronic facsimile media. A request for certification must be submitted no later than fifteen calendar days before the proposed sale is to take place. In order to facilitate the sale of chemicals from Federal departments' or agencies' stocks, Federal departments or agencies may wish to submit requests as far in advance of the fifteen calendar days as possible. The written notification of the proposed sale must include:

(1) The name and amount of the chemical to be sold;

(2) The name and address of the prospective bidder;

(3) The name and address of the prospective end-user, in cases where a sale is being brokered;

(4) Point(s) of contact for the prospective bidder and, where appropriate, prospective end-user; and

(5) The end use of the chemical.

(c) Within fifteen calendar days of receipt of a request for certification, the Administrator will certify in writing to the head of the Federal department or agency that there is, or is not, reasonable cause to believe that the sale of the specific chemical to the specific bidder and end-user would result in the illegal manufacture of a controlled substance. In making this determination, the following factors must be considered:

(1) Past experience of the prospective bidder or end-user in the maintenance of effective controls against diversion of listed chemicals into other than legitimate medical, scientific, and industrial channels;

(2) Compliance of the prospective bidder or end-user with applicable Federal, state and local law;

(3) Prior conviction record of the prospective bidder or end-user relating to listed chemicals or controlled substances under Federal or state laws; and

(4) Such other factors as may be relevant to and consistent with the public health and safety.

(d) If the Administrator certifies to the head of a Federal department or agency that there is no reasonable cause to believe that the sale of a specific chemical to a prospective bidder and end-user will result in the illegal manufacture of a controlled substance, that certification will be effective for one year from the date of issuance with respect to further sales of the same chemical to the same prospective bidder and end-user, unless the Administrator notifies the head of the Federal department or agency in writing that the certification is withdrawn. If the certification is withdrawn, DEA will also provide written notice to the bidder and end-user, which will contain a statement of the legal and factual basis for this determination.

(e) If the Administrator determines there is reasonable cause to believe the sale of the specific chemical to a specific bidder and end-user would result in the illegal manufacture of a controlled substance, DEA will provide written notice to the head of a Federal department or agency refusing to certify the proposed sale under the authority of 21 U.S.C. 890. DEA also will provide, within fifteen calendar days of receiving a request for certification from a Federal department or agency, the same written notice to the prospective bidder and end-user, and this notice also will contain a statement of the legal and factual basis for the refusal of certification. The prospective bidder and end-user may, within thirty calendar days of receipt of notification of the refusal, submit written comments or written objections to the Administrator's refusal. At the same time, the prospective bidder and end-user also may provide supporting documentation to contest the Administrator's refusal. If such written comments or written objections raise issues regarding any finding of fact or conclusion of law upon which the refusal is based, the Administrator will reconsider the refusal of the proposed sale in light of the written comments or written objections filed. Thereafter, within a reasonable time, the Administrator will withdraw or affirm the original refusal of certification as he determines appropriate. The Administrator will provide written reasons for any affirmation of the original refusal. Such affirmation of the original refusal will constitute a final decision for purposes of judicial review under 21 U.S.C. 877.

(f) If the Administrator determines there is reasonable cause to believe that an existing certification should be withdrawn, DEA will provide written notice to the head of a Federal department or agency of such withdrawal under the authority of 21 U.S.C. 890. DEA also will provide, within fifteen calendar days of withdrawal of an existing certification, the same written notice to the bidder and end-user, and this notice also will contain a statement of the legal and factual basis for the withdrawal. The bidder and end-user may, within thirty calendar days of receipt of notification of the withdrawal of the existing certification, submit written comments or written objections to the Administrator's withdrawal. At the same time, the bidder and end-user also may provide supporting documentation to contest the Administrator's withdrawal. If such written comments or written objections raise issues regarding any finding of fact or conclusion of law upon which the withdrawal of the existing certification is based, the Administrator will reconsider the withdrawal of the existing certification in light of the written comments or written objections filed. Thereafter, within a reasonable time, the Administrator will withdraw or affirm the original withdrawal of the existing certification as he determines appropriate. The Administrator will provide written reasons for any affirmation of the original withdrawal of the existing certification. Such affirmation of the original withdrawal of the existing certification will constitute a final decision for purposes of judicial review under 21 U.S.C. 877.

[68 FR 62737, Nov. 6, 2003, as amended at 75 FR 10681, Mar. 9, 2010]

PART 1311—REQUIREMENTS FOR ELECTRONIC ORDERS AND PRESCRIPTIONS

Subpart A—General

Sec.

Subpart B—Obtaining and Using Digital Certificates for Electronic Orders

Subpart C—Electronic Prescriptions

AUTHORITY: 21 U.S.C. 821, 828, 829, 871(b), 958(e), 965, unless otherwise noted.

SOURCE: 70 FR 16915, Apr. 1, 2005, unless otherwise noted.

Subpart A—General

§ 1311.01 Scope.

This part sets forth the rules governing the creation, transmission, and storage of electronic orders and prescriptions.

[75 FR 16310, Mar. 31, 2010]

§ 1311.02 Definitions.

Any term contained in this part shall have the definition set forth in section 102 of the Act (21 U.S.C. 802) or part 1300 of this chapter.

[75 FR 16310, Mar. 31, 2010]

§ 1311.05 Standards for technologies for electronic transmission of orders.

(a) A registrant or a person with power of attorney to sign orders for Schedule I and II controlled substances may use any technology to sign and electronically transmit orders if the technology provides all of the following:

(1) *Authentication:* The system must enable a recipient to positively verify the signer without direct communication with the signer and subsequently demonstrate to a third party, if needed, that the sender's identity was properly verified.

(2) *Nonrepudiation:* The system must ensure that strong and substantial evidence is available to the recipient of the sender's identity, sufficient to prevent the sender from successfully denying having sent the data. This criterion includes the ability of a third party to verify the origin of the document.

(3) *Message integrity:* The system must ensure that the recipient, or a third party, can determine whether the contents of the document have been altered during transmission or after receipt.

(b) DEA has identified the following means of electronically signing and transmitting order forms as meeting all of the standards set forth in paragraph (a) of this section.

(1) Digital signatures using Public Key Infrastructure (PKI) technology.

(2) [Reserved]

§ 1311.08 Incorporation by reference.

(a) These incorporations by reference were approved by the Director of the Federal Register in accordance with 5 U.S.C. 552(a) and 1 CFR part 51. Copies may be inspected at the Drug Enforcement Administration, 600 Army Navy Drive, Arlington, VA 22202 or at the National Archives and Records Administration (NARA). For information on the availability of this material at the Drug Enforcement Administration, call (202) 307–1000. For information on the availability of this material at NARA, call (202) 741–6030 or go to: *http://www.archives.gov/federal_register/code_of_federal_regulations/ibr_locations.html.*

(b) These standards are available from the National Institute of Standards and Technology, Computer Security Division, Information Technology Laboratory, National Institute of Standards and Technology, 100 Bureau Drive, Gaithersburg, MD 20899–8930, (301) 975–6478 or TTY (301) 975–8295, *inquiries@nist.gov*, and are available at *http://csrc.nist.gov/.* The following standards are incorporated by reference:

(1) Federal Information Processing Standard Publication (FIPS PUB) 140–2, Change Notices (12–03–2002), Security Requirements for Cryptographic Modules, May 25, 2001 (FIPS 140–2) including Annexes A through D; incorporation by reference approved for §§ 1311.30(b), 1311.55(b), 1311.115(b), 1311.120(b), 1311.205(b).

(i) *Annex A:* Approved Security Functions for FIPS PUB 140–2, Security Requirements for Cryptographic Modules, September 23, 2004.

(ii) *Annex B:* Approved Protection Profiles for FIPS PUB 140–2, Security Requirements for Cryptographic Modules, November 4, 2004.

(iii) *Annex C:* Approved Random Number Generators for FIPS PUB 140–2, Security Requirements for Cryptographic Modules, January 31, 2005.

(iv) *Annex D:* Approved Key Establishment Techniques for FIPS PUB 140–2, Security Requirements for Cryptographic Modules, February 23, 2004.

(2) Federal Information Processing Standard Publication (FIPS PUB) 180–2, Secure Hash Standard, August 1, 2002, as amended by change notice 1, February 25, 2004 (FIPS 180–2); incorporation by reference approved for §§ 1311.30(b) and 1311.55(b).

(3) Federal Information Processing Standard Publication (FIPS PUB) 180–3, Secure Hash Standard (SHS), October 2008 (FIPS 180–3); incorporation by reference approved for §§ 1311.120(b) and 1311.205(b).

(4) Federal Information Processing Standard Publication (FIPS PUB) 186–2, Digital Signature Standard, January 27, 2000, as amended by Change Notice 1, October 5, 2001 (FIPS 186–2); incorporation by reference approved for §§ 1311.30(b) and 1311.55(b).

(5) Federal Information Processing Standard Publication (FIPS PUB) 186–3, Digital Signature Standard (DSS),

June 2009 (FIPS 186–3); incorporation by reference approved for §§ 1311.120(b), 1311.205(b), and 1311.210(c).

(6) Draft NIST Special Publication 800–63–1, Electronic Authentication Guideline, December 8, 2008 (NIST SP 800–63–1); Burr, W. et al.; incorporation by reference approved for § 1311.105(a).

(7) NIST Special Publication 800–76–1, Biometric Data Specification for Personal Identity Verification, January 2007 (NIST SP 800–76–1); Wilson, C. et al.; incorporation by reference approved for § 1311.116(d).

[75 FR 16310, Mar. 31, 2010]

Subpart B—Obtaining and Using Digital Certificates for Electronic Orders

§ 1311.10 Eligibility to obtain a CSOS digital certificate.

The following persons are eligible to obtain a CSOS digital certificate from the DEA Certification Authority to sign electronic orders for controlled substances.

(a) The person who signed the most recent DEA registration application or renewal application and a person authorized to sign a registration application.

(b) A person granted power of attorney by a DEA registrant to sign orders for one or more schedules of controlled substances.

§ 1311.15 Limitations on CSOS digital certificates.

(a) A CSOS digital certificate issued by the DEA Certification Authority will authorize the certificate holder to sign orders for only those schedules of controlled substances covered by the registration under which the certificate is issued.

(b) When a registrant, in a power of attorney letter, limits a certificate applicant to a subset of the registrant's authorized schedules, the registrant is responsible for ensuring that the certificate holder signs orders only for that subset of schedules.

§ 1311.20 Coordinators for CSOS digital certificate holders.

(a) Each registrant, regardless of number of digital certificates issued, must designate one or more responsible persons to serve as that registrant's CSOS coordinator regarding issues pertaining to issuance of, revocation of, and changes to digital certificates issued under that registrant's DEA registration. While the coordinator will be the main point of contact between one or more DEA registered locations and the CSOS Certification Authority, all digital certificate activities are the responsibility of the registrant with whom the digital certificate is associated. Even when an individual registrant, *i.e.*, an individual practitioner, is applying for a digital certificate to order controlled substances a CSOS Coordinator must be designated; though in such a case, the individual practitioner may also serve as the coordinator.

(b) Once designated, coordinators must identify themselves, on a one-time basis, to the Certification Authority. If a designated coordinator changes, the Certification Authority must be notified of the change and the new responsibilities assumed by each of the registrant's coordinators, if applicable. Coordinators must complete the application that the DEA Certification Authority provides and submit the following:

(1) Two copies of identification, one of which must be a government-issued photographic identification.

(2) A copy of each current DEA Certificate of Registration (DEA form 223) for each registered location for which the coordinator will be responsible or, if the applicant (or their employer) has not been issued a DEA registration, a copy of each application for registration of the applicant or the applicant's employer.

(3) The applicant must have the completed application notarized and forward the completed application and accompanying documentation to the DEA Certification Authority.

(c) Coordinators will communicate with the Certification Authority regarding digital certificate applications, renewals and revocations. For applicants applying for a digital certificate from the DEA Certification Authority, and for applicants applying for a power of attorney digital certificate for a

DEA registrant, the registrant's Coordinator must verify the applicant's identity, review the application package, and submit the completed package to the Certification Authority.

§1311.25 Requirements for obtaining a CSOS digital certificate.

(a) To obtain a certificate to use for signing electronic orders for controlled substances, a registrant or person with power of attorney for a registrant must complete the application that the DEA Certification Authority provides and submit the following:

(1) Two copies of identification, one of which must be a government-issued photographic identification.

(2) A current listing of DEA registrations for which the individual has authority to sign controlled substances orders.

(3) A copy of the power of attorney from the registrant, if applicable.

(4) An acknowledgment that the applicant has read and understands the Subscriber Agreement and agrees to the statement of subscriber obligations that DEA provides.

(b) The applicant must provide the completed application to the registrant's coordinator for CSOS digital certificate holders who will review the application and submit the completed application and accompanying documentation to the DEA Certification Authority.

(c) When the Certification Authority approves the application, it will send the applicant a one-time use reference number and access code, via separate channels, and information on how to use them. Using this information, the applicant must then electronically submit a request for certification of the public digital signature key. After the request is approved, the Certification Authority will provide the applicant with the signed public key certificate.

(d) Once the applicant has generated the key pair, the Certification Authority must prove that the user has possession of the key. For public keys, the corresponding private key must be used to sign the certificate request. Verification of the signature using the public key in the request will serve as proof of possession of the private key.

§1311.30 Requirements for storing and using a private key for digitally signing orders.

(a) Only the certificate holder may access or use his or her digital certificate and private key.

(b) The certificate holder must provide FIPS-approved secure storage for the private key, as discussed by FIPS 140–2, 180–2, 186–2, and accompanying change notices and annexes, as incorporated by reference in §1311.08.

(c) A certificate holder must ensure that no one else uses the private key. While the private key is activated, the certificate holder must prevent unauthorized use of that private key.

(d) A certificate holder must not make back-up copies of the private key.

(e) The certificate holder must report the loss, theft, or compromise of the private key or the password, via a revocation request, to the Certification Authority within 24 hours of substantiation of the loss, theft, or compromise. Upon receipt and verification of a signed revocation request, the Certification Authority will revoke the certificate. The certificate holder must apply for a new certificate under the requirements of §1311.25.

§1311.35 Number of CSOS digital certificates needed.

A purchaser of Schedule I and II controlled substances must obtain a separate CSOS certificate for each registered location for which the purchaser will order these controlled substances.

§1311.40 Renewal of CSOS digital certificates.

(a) A CSOS certificate holder must generate a new key pair and obtain a new CSOS digital certificate when the registrant's DEA registration expires or whenever the information on which the certificate is based changes. This information includes the registered name and address, the subscriber's name, and the schedules the registrant is authorized to handle. A CSOS certificate will expire on the date on which the DEA registration on which the certificate is based expires.

(b) The Certification Authority will notify each CSOS certificate holder 45 days in advance of the expiration of the certificate holder's CSOS digital certificate.

(c) If a CSOS certificate holder applies for a renewal before the certificate expires, the certificate holder may renew electronically twice. For every third renewal, the CSOS certificate holder must submit a new application and documentation, as provided in § 1311.25.

(d) If a CSOS certificate expires before the holder applies for a renewal, the certificate holder must submit a new application and documentation, as provided in § 1311.25.

§ 1311.45 Requirements for registrants that allow powers of attorney to obtain CSOS digital certificates under their DEA registration.

(a) A registrant that grants power of attorney must report to the DEA Certification Authority within 6 hours of either of the following (advance notice may be provided, where applicable):

(1) The person with power of attorney has left the employ of the institution.

(2) The person with power of attorney has had his or her privileges revoked.

(b) A registrant must maintain a record that lists each person granted power of attorney to sign controlled substances orders.

§ 1311.50 Requirements for recipients of digitally signed orders.

(a) The recipient of a digitally signed order must do the following before filling the order:

(1) Verify the integrity of the signature and the order by having the system validate the order.

(2) Verify that the certificate holder's CSOS digital certificate has not expired by checking the expiration date against the date the order was signed.

(3) Check the validity of the certificate holder's certificate by checking the Certificate Revocation List.

(4) Check the certificate extension data to determine whether the sender has the authority to order the controlled substance.

(b) A recipient may cache Certificate Revocation Lists for use until they expire.

§ 1311.55 Requirements for systems used to process digitally signed orders.

(a) A CSOS certificate holder and recipient of an electronic order may use any system to write, track, or maintain orders provided that the system has been enabled to process digitally signed documents and that it meets the requirements of paragraph (b) or (c) of this section.

(b) A system used to digitally sign Schedule I or II orders must meet the following requirements:

(1) The cryptographic module must be FIPS 140–2, Level 1 validated, as incorporated by reference in § 1311.08.

(2) The digital signature system and hash function must be compliant with FIPS 186–2 and FIPS 180–2, as incorporated by reference in § 1311.08.

(3) The private key must be stored on a FIPS 140–2 Level 1 validated cryptographic module using a FIPS-approved encryption algorithm, as incorporated by reference in § 1311.08.

(4) The system must use either a user identification and password combination or biometric authentication to access the private key. Activation data must not be displayed as they are entered.

(5) The system must set a 10-minute inactivity time period after which the certificate holder must reauthenticate the password to access the private key.

(6) For software implementations, when the signing module is deactivated, the system must clear the plain text private key from the system memory to prevent the unauthorized access to, or use of, the private key.

(7) The system must be able to digitally sign and transmit an order.

(8) The system must have a time system that is within five minutes of the official National Institute of Standards and Technology time source.

(9) The system must archive the digitally signed orders and any other records required in part 1305 of this chapter, including any linked data.

(10) The system must create an order that includes all data fields listed under § 1305.21(b) of this chapter.

(c) A system used to receive, verify, and create linked records for orders signed with a CSOS digital certificate must meet the following requirements:

(1) The cryptographic module must be FIPS 140–2, Level 1 validated, as incorporated by reference in § 1311.08.

(2) The digital signature system and hash function must be compliant with FIPS 186–2 and FIPS 180–2, as incorporated by reference in § 1311.08.

(3) The system must determine that an order has not been altered during transmission. The system must invalidate any order that has been altered.

(4) The system must validate the digital signature using the signer's public key. The system must invalidate any order in which the digital signature cannot be validated.

(5) The system must validate that the DEA registration number contained in the body of the order corresponds to the registration number associated with the specific certificate by separately generating the hash value of the registration number and certificate subject distinguished name serial number and comparing that hash value to the hash value contained in the certificate extension for the DEA registration number. If the hash values are not equal the system must invalidate the order.

(6) The system must check the Certificate Revocation List automatically and invalidate any order with a certificate listed on the Certificate Revocation List.

(7) The system must check the validity of the certificate and the Certification Authority certificate and invalidate any order that fails these validity checks.

(8) The system must have a time system that is within five minutes of the official National Institute of Standards and Technology time source.

(9) The system must check the substances ordered against the schedules that the registrant is allowed to order and invalidate any order that includes substances the registrant is not allowed to order.

(10) The system must ensure that an invalid finding cannot be bypassed or ignored and the order filled.

(11) The system must archive the order and associate with it the digital certificate received with the order.

(12) If a registrant sends reports on orders to DEA, the system must create a report in the format DEA specifies, as provided in § 1305.29 of this chapter.

(d) For systems used to process CSOS orders, the system developer or vendor must have an initial independent third-party audit of the system and an additional independent third-party audit whenever the signing or verifying functionality is changed to determine whether it correctly performs the functions listed under paragraphs (b) and (c) of this section. The system developer must retain the most recent audit results and retain the results of any other audits of the software completed within the previous two years.

§ 1311.60 Recordkeeping.

(a) A supplier and purchaser must maintain records of CSOS electronic orders and any linked records for two years. Records may be maintained electronically. Records regarding controlled substances that are maintained electronically must be readily retrievable from all other records.

(b) Electronic records must be easily readable or easily rendered into a format that a person can read. They must be made available to the Administration upon request.

(c) CSOS certificate holders must maintain a copy of the subscriber agreement that the Certification Authority provides for the life of the certificate.

Subpart C—Electronic Prescriptions

SOURCE: 75 FR 16310, Mar. 31, 2010, unless otherwise noted.

§ 1311.100 General.

(a) This subpart addresses the requirements that must be met to issue and process Schedule II, III, IV, and V controlled substance prescriptions electronically.

(b) A practitioner may issue a prescription for a Schedule II, III, IV, or V controlled substance electronically if all of the following conditions are met:

(1) The practitioner is registered as an individual practitioner or exempt from the requirement of registration under part 1301 of this chapter and is authorized under the registration or

exemption to dispense the controlled substance;

(2) The practitioner uses an electronic prescription application that meets all of the applicable requirements of this subpart; and

(3) The prescription is otherwise in conformity with the requirements of the Act and this chapter.

(c) An electronic prescription for a Schedule II, III, IV, or V controlled substance created using an electronic prescription application that does not meet the requirements of this subpart is not a valid prescription, as that term is defined in § 1300.03 of this chapter.

(d) A controlled substance prescription created using an electronic prescription application that meets the requirements of this subpart is not a valid prescription if any of the functions required under this subpart were disabled when the prescription was indicated as ready for signature and signed.

(e) A registered pharmacy may process electronic prescriptions for controlled substances only if all of the following conditions are met:

(1) The pharmacy uses a pharmacy application that meets all of the applicable requirements of this subpart; and

(2) The prescription is otherwise in conformity with the requirements of the Act and this chapter.

(f) Nothing in this part alters the responsibilities of the practitioner and pharmacy, specified in part 1306 of this chapter, to ensure the validity of a controlled substance prescription.

§ 1311.102 Practitioner responsibilities.

(a) The practitioner must retain sole possession of the hard token, where applicable, and must not share the password or other knowledge factor, or biometric information, with any other person. The practitioner must not allow any other person to use the token or enter the knowledge factor or other identification means to sign prescriptions for controlled substances. Failure by the practitioner to secure the hard token, knowledge factor, or biometric information may provide a basis for revocation or suspension of registration pursuant to section 304(a)(4) of the Act (21 U.S.C. 824(a)(4)).

(b) The practitioner must notify the individuals designated under § 1311.125 or § 1311.130 within one business day of discovery that the hard token has been lost, stolen, or compromised or the authentication protocol has been otherwise compromised. A practitioner who fails to comply with this provision may be held responsible for any controlled substance prescriptions written using his two-factor authentication credential.

(c) If the practitioner is notified by an intermediary or pharmacy that an electronic prescription was not successfully delivered, as provided in § 1311.170, he must ensure that any paper or oral prescription (where permitted) issued as a replacement of the original electronic prescription indicates that the prescription was originally transmitted electronically to a particular pharmacy and that the transmission failed.

(d) Before initially using an electronic prescription application to sign and transmit controlled substance prescriptions, the practitioner must determine that the third-party auditor or certification organization has found that the electronic prescription application records, stores, and transmits the following accurately and consistently:

(1) The information required for a prescription under § 1306.05(a) of this chapter.

(2) The indication of signing as required by § 1311.120(b)(17) or the digital signature created by the practitioner's private key.

(3) The number of refills as required by § 1306.22 of this chapter.

(e) If the third-party auditor or certification organization has found that an electronic prescription application does not accurately and consistently record, store, and transmit other information required for prescriptions under this chapter, the practitioner must not create, sign, and transmit electronic prescriptions for controlled substances that are subject to the additional information requirements.

(f) The practitioner must not use the electronic prescription application to sign and transmit electronic controlled substance prescriptions if any of the functions of the application required by this subpart have been disabled or appear to be functioning improperly.

(g) If an electronic prescription application provider notifies an individual practitioner that a third-party audit or certification report indicates that the application or the application provider no longer meets the requirements of this part or notifies him that the application provider has identified an issue that makes the application non-compliant, the practitioner must do the following:

(1) Immediately cease to issue electronic controlled substance prescriptions using the application.

(2) Ensure, for an installed electronic prescription application at an individual practitioner's practice, that the individuals designated under § 1311.125 terminate access for signing controlled substance prescriptions.

(h) If an electronic prescription application provider notifies an institutional practitioner that a third-party audit or certification report indicates that the application or the application provider no longer meets the requirements of this part or notifies it that the application provider has identified an issue that makes the application non-compliant, the institutional practitioner must ensure that the individuals designated under § 1311.130 terminate access for signing controlled substance prescriptions.

(i) An individual practitioner or institutional practitioner that receives a notification that the electronic prescription application is not in compliance with the requirements of this part must not use the application to issue electronic controlled substance prescriptions until it is notified that the application is again compliant and all relevant updates to the application have been installed.

(j) The practitioner must notify both the individuals designated under § 1311.125 or § 1311.130 and the Administration within one business day of discovery that one or more prescriptions that were issued under a DEA registration held by that practitioner were prescriptions the practitioner had not signed or were not consistent with the prescriptions he signed.

(k) The practitioner has the same responsibilities when issuing prescriptions for controlled substances via electronic means as when issuing a paper or oral prescription. Nothing in this subpart relieves a practitioner of his responsibility to dispense controlled substances only for a legitimate medical purpose while acting in the usual course of his professional practice. If an agent enters information at the practitioner's direction prior to the practitioner reviewing and approving the information and signing and authorizing the transmission of that information, the practitioner is responsible in case the prescription does not conform in all essential respects to the law and regulations.

§ 1311.105 Requirements for obtaining an authentication credential—Individual practitioners.

(a) An individual practitioner must obtain a two-factor authentication credential from one of the following:

(1) A credential service provider that has been approved by the General Services Administration Office of Technology Strategy/Division of Identity Management to conduct identity proofing that meets the requirements of Assurance Level 3 or above as specified in NIST SP 800–63–1 as incorporated by reference in § 1311.08.

(2) For digital certificates, a certification authority that is cross-certified with the Federal Bridge certification authority and that operates at a Federal Bridge Certification Authority basic assurance level or above.

(b) The practitioner must submit identity proofing information to the credential service provider or certification authority as specified by the credential service provider or certification authority.

(c) The credential service provider or certification authority must issue the authentication credential using two channels (e.g., e-mail, mail, or telephone call). If one of the factors used in the authentication protocol is a biometric, or if the practitioner has a hard token that is being enabled to sign controlled substances prescriptions, the credential service provider or certification authority must issue two pieces of information used to generate or activate the authentication credential using two channels.

§ 1311.110 Requirements for obtaining an authentication credential—Individual practitioners eligible to use an electronic prescription application of an institutional practitioner.

(a) For any registrant or person exempted from the requirement of registration under § 1301.22(c) of this chapter who is eligible to use the institutional practitioner's electronic prescription application to sign prescriptions for controlled substances, the entity within a DEA-registered institutional practitioner that grants that individual practitioner privileges at the institutional practitioner (e.g., a hospital credentialing office) may conduct identity proofing and authorize the issuance of the authentication credential. That entity must do the following:

(1) Ensure that photographic identification issued by the Federal Government or a State government matches the person presenting the identification.

(2) Ensure that the individual practitioner's State authorization to practice and, where applicable, State authorization to prescribe controlled substances, is current and in good standing.

(3) Either ensure that the individual practitioner's DEA registration is current and in good standing or ensure that the institutional practitioner has granted the individual practitioner exempt from the requirement of registration under § 1301.22 of this chapter privileges to prescribe controlled substances using the institutional practitioner's DEA registration number.

(4) If the individual practitioner is an employee of a health care facility that is operated by the Department of Veterans Affairs, confirm that the individual practitioner has been duly appointed to practice at that facility by the Secretary of the Department of Veterans Affairs pursuant to 38 U.S.C. 7401–7408.

(5) If the individual practitioner is working at a health care facility operated by the Department of Veterans Affairs on a contractual basis pursuant to 38 U.S.C. 8153 and, in the performance of his duties, prescribes controlled substances, confirm that the individual practitioner meets the criteria for eligibility for appointment under 38 U.S.C. 7401–7408 and is prescribing controlled substances under the registration of such facility.

(b) An institutional practitioner that elects to conduct identity proofing must provide authorization to issue the authentication credentials to a separate entity within the institutional practitioner or to an outside credential Service provider or certification authority that meets the requirements of § 1311.105(a).

(c) When an institutional practitioner is conducting identity proofing and submitting information to a credential service provider or certification authority to authorize the issuance of authentication credentials, the institutional practitioner must meet any requirements that the credential service provider or certification authority imposes on entities that serve as trusted agents.

(d) An institutional practitioner that elects to conduct identity proofing and authorize the issuance of the authentication credential as provided in paragraphs (a) through (c) of this section must do so in a manner consistent with the institutional practitioner's general obligation to maintain effective controls against diversion. Failure to meet this obligation may result in remedial action consistent with § 1301.36 of this chapter.

(e) An institutional practitioner that elects to conduct identity proofing must retain a record of the identity-proofing. An institutional practitioner that elects to issue the two-factor authentication credential must retain a record of the issuance of the credential.

§ 1311.115 Additional requirements for two-factor authentication.

(a) To sign a controlled substance prescription, the electronic prescription application must require the practitioner to authenticate to the application using an authentication protocol that uses two of the following three factors:

(1) Something only the practitioner knows, such as a password or response to a challenge question.

(2) Something the practitioner is, biometric data such as a fingerprint or iris scan.

(3) Something the practitioner has, a device (hard token) separate from the

computer to which the practitioner is gaining access.

(b) If one factor is a hard token, it must be separate from the computer to which it is gaining access and must meet at least the criteria of FIPS 140–2 Security Level 1, as incorporated by reference in § 1311.08, for cryptographic modules or one-time-password devices.

(c) If one factor is a biometric, the biometric subsystem must comply with the requirements of § 1311.116.

§ 1311.116 Additional requirements for biometrics.

(a) If one of the factors used to authenticate to the electronic prescription application is a biometric as described in § 1311.115, it must comply with the following requirements.

(b) The biometric subsystem must operate at a false match rate of 0.001 or lower.

(c) The biometric subsystem must use matching software that has demonstrated performance at the operating point corresponding with the false match rate described in paragraph (b) of this section, or a lower false match rate. Testing to demonstrate performance must be conducted by the National Institute of Standards and Technology or another DEA-approved government or nongovernment laboratory. Such testing must comply with the requirements of paragraph (h) of this section.

(d) The biometric subsystem must conform to Personal Identity Verification authentication biometric acquisition specifications, pursuant to NIST SP 800–76–1 as incorporated by reference in § 1311.08, if they exist for the biometric modality of choice.

(e) The biometric subsystem must either be co-located with a computer or PDA that the practitioner uses to issue electronic prescriptions for controlled substances, where the computer or PDA is located in a known, controlled location, or be built directly into the practitioner's computer or PDA that he uses to issue electronic prescriptions for controlled substances.

(f) The biometric subsystem must store device ID data at enrollment (*i.e.*, biometric registration) with the biometric data and verify the device ID at the time of authentication to the electronic prescription application.

(g) The biometric subsystem must protect the biometric data (raw data or templates), match results, and/or nonmatch results when authentication is not local. If sent over an open network, biometric data (raw data or templates), match results, and/or non-match results must be:

(1) Cryptographically source authenticated;

(2) Combined with a random challenge, a nonce, or a time stamp to prevent replay;

(3) Cryptographically protected for integrity and confidentiality; and

(4) Sent only to authorized systems.

(h) Testing of the biometric subsystem must have the following characteristics:

(1) The test is conducted by a laboratory that does not have an interest in the outcome (positive or negative) of performance of a submission or biometric.

(2) Test data are sequestered.

(3) Algorithms are provided to the testing laboratory (as opposed to scores or other information).

(4) The operating point(s) corresponding with the false match rate described in paragraph (b) of this section, or a lower false match rate, is tested so that there is at least 95% confidence that the false match and nonmatch rates are equal to or less than the observed value.

(5) Results of the testing are made publicly available.

§ 1311.120 Electronic prescription application requirements.

(a) A practitioner may only use an electronic prescription application that meets the requirements in paragraph (b) of this section to issue electronic controlled substance prescriptions.

(b) The electronic prescription application must meet the requirements of this subpart including the following:

(1) The electronic prescription application must do the following:

(i) Link each registrant, by name, to at least one DEA registration number.

(ii) Link each practitioner exempt from registration under § 1301.22(c) of this chapter to the institutional practitioner's DEA registration number and the specific internal code number required under § 1301.22(c)(5) of this chapter.

(2) The electronic prescription application must be capable of the setting of logical access controls to limit permissions for the following functions:

(i) Indication that a prescription is ready for signing and signing controlled substance prescriptions.

(ii) Creating, updating, and executing the logical access controls for the functions specified in paragraph (b)(2)(i) of this section.

(3) Logical access controls must be set by individual user name or role. If the application sets logical access control by role, it must not allow an individual to be assigned the role of registrant unless that individual is linked to at least one DEA registration number as provided in paragraph (b)(1) of this section.

(4) The application must require that the setting and changing of logical access controls specified under paragraph (b)(2) of this section involve the actions of two individuals as specified in §§ 1311.125 or 1311.130. Except for institutional practitioners, a practitioner authorized to sign controlled substance prescriptions must approve logical access control entries.

(5) The electronic prescription application must accept two-factor authentication that meets the requirements of § 1311.115 and require its use for signing controlled substance prescriptions and for approving data that set or change logical access controls related to reviewing and signing controlled substance prescriptions.

(6) The electronic prescription application must be capable of recording all of the applicable information required in part 1306 of this chapter for the controlled substance prescription.

(7) If a practitioner has more than one DEA registration number, the electronic prescription application must require the practitioner or his agent to select the DEA registration number to be included on the prescription.

(8) The electronic prescription application must have a time application that is within five minutes of the official National Institute of Standards and Technology time source.

(9) The electronic prescription application must present for the practitioner's review and approval all of the following data for each controlled substance prescription:

(i) The date of issuance.

(ii) The full name of the patient.

(iii) The drug name.

(iv) The dosage strength and form, quantity prescribed, and directions for use.

(v) The number of refills authorized, if applicable, for prescriptions for Schedule III, IV, and V controlled substances.

(vi) For prescriptions written in accordance with the requirements of § 1306.12(b) of this chapter, the earliest date on which a pharmacy may fill each prescription.

(vii) The name, address, and DEA registration number of the prescribing practitioner.

(viii) The statement required under § 1311.140(a)(3).

(10) The electronic prescription application must require the prescribing practitioner to indicate that each controlled substance prescription is ready for signing. The electronic prescription application must not permit alteration of the DEA elements after the practitioner has indicated that a controlled substance prescription is ready to be signed without requiring another review and indication of readiness for signing. Any controlled substance prescription not indicated as ready to be signed shall not be signed or transmitted.

(11) While the information required by paragraph (b)(9) of this section and the statement required by § 1311.140(a)(3) remain displayed, the electronic prescription application must prompt the prescribing practitioner to authenticate to the application, using two-factor authentication, as specified in § 1311.140(a)(4), which will constitute the signing of the prescription by the practitioner for purposes of § 1306.05(a) and (e) of this chapter.

(12) The electronic prescription application must not permit a practitioner other than the prescribing practitioner whose DEA number (or institutional

practitioner DEA number and extension data for the individual practitioner) is listed on the prescription as the prescribing practitioner and who has indicated that the prescription is ready to be signed to sign the prescription.

(13) Where a practitioner seeks to prescribe more than one controlled substance at one time for a particular patient, the electronic prescription application may allow the practitioner to sign multiple prescriptions for a single patient at one time using a single invocation of the two-factor authentication protocol provided the following has occurred: The practitioner has individually indicated that each controlled substance prescription is ready to be signed while the information required by paragraph (b)(9) of this section for each such prescription is displayed along with the statement required by § 1311.140(a)(3).

(14) The electronic prescription application must time and date stamp the prescription when the signing function is used.

(15) When the practitioner uses his two-factor authentication credential as specified in § 1311.140(a)(4), the electronic prescription application must digitally sign at least the information required by part 1306 of this chapter and electronically archive the digitally signed record. If the practitioner signs the prescription with his own private key, as provided in § 1311.145, the electronic prescription application must electronically archive a copy of the digitally signed record, but need not apply the application's digital signature to the record.

(16) The digital signature functionality must meet the following requirements:

(i) The cryptographic module used to digitally sign the data elements required by part 1306 of this chapter must be at least FIPS 140–2 Security Level 1 validated. FIPS 140–2 is incorporated by reference in § 1311.08.

(ii) The digital signature application and hash function must comply with FIPS 186–3 and FIPS 180–3, as incorporated by reference in § 1311.08.

(iii) The electronic prescription application's private key must be stored encrypted on a FIPS 140–2 Security Level 1 or higher validated cryptographic module using a FIPS-approved encryption algorithm. FIPS 140–2 is incorporated by reference in § 1311.08.

(iv) For software implementations, when the signing module is deactivated, the application must clear the plain text password from the application memory to prevent the unauthorized access to, or use of, the private key.

(17) Unless the digital signature created by an individual practitioner's private key is being transmitted to the pharmacy with the prescription, the electronic prescription application must include in the data file transmitted an indication that the prescription was signed by the prescribing practitioner.

(18) The electronic prescription application must not transmit a controlled substance prescription unless the signing function described in § 1311.140(a)(4) has been used.

(19) The electronic prescription application must not allow alteration of any of the information required by part 1306 of this chapter after the prescription has been digitally signed. Any alteration of the information required by part 1306 of this chapter after the prescription is digitally signed must cancel the prescription.

(20) The electronic prescription application must not allow transmission of a prescription that has been printed.

(21) The electronic prescription application must allow printing of a prescription after transmission only if the printed prescription is clearly labeled as a copy not for dispensing. The electronic prescription application may allow printing of prescription information if clearly labeled as being for informational purposes. The electronic prescription application may transfer such prescription information to medical records.

(22) If the transmission of an electronic prescription fails, the electronic prescription application may print the prescription. The prescription must indicate that it was originally transmitted electronically to, and provide the name of, a specific pharmacy, the date and time of transmission, and that the electronic transmission failed.

(23) The electronic prescription application must maintain an audit trail of all actions related to the following:

(i) The creation, alteration, indication of readiness for signing, signing, transmission, or deletion of a controlled substance prescription.

(ii) Any setting or changing of logical access control permissions related to the issuance of controlled substance prescriptions.

(iii) Notification of a failed transmission.

(iv) Auditable events as specified in §1311.150.

(24) The electronic prescription application must record within each audit record the following information:

(i) The date and time of the event.

(ii) The type of event.

(iii) The identity of the person taking the action, where applicable.

(iv) The outcome of the event (success or failure).

(25) The electronic prescription application must conduct internal audits and generate reports on any of the events specified in §1311.150 in a format that is readable by the practitioner. Such internal audits may be automated and need not require human intervention to be conducted.

(26) The electronic prescription application must protect the stored audit records from unauthorized deletion. The electronic prescription application shall prevent modifications to the audit records.

(27) The electronic prescription application must do the following:

(i) Generate a log of all controlled substance prescriptions issued by a practitioner during the previous calendar month and provide the log to the practitioner no later than seven calendar days after that month.

(ii) Be capable of generating a log of all controlled substance prescriptions issued by a practitioner for a period specified by the practitioner upon request. Prescription information available from which to generate the log must span at least the previous two years.

(iii) Archive all logs generated.

(iv) Ensure that all logs are easily readable or easily rendered into a format that a person can read.

(v) Ensure that all logs are sortable by patient name, drug name, and date of issuance of the prescription.

(28) Where the electronic prescription application is required by this part to archive or otherwise maintain records, it must retain such records electronically for two years from the date of the record's creation and comply with all other requirements of §1311.305.

§1311.125 Requirements for establishing logical access control—Individual practitioner.

(a) At each registered location where one or more individual practitioners wish to use an electronic prescription application meeting the requirements of this subpart to issue controlled substance prescriptions, the registrant(s) must designate at least two individuals to manage access control to the application. At least one of the designated individuals must be a registrant who is authorized to issue controlled substance prescriptions and who has obtained a two-factor authentication credential as provided in §1311.105.

(b) At least one of the individuals designated under paragraph (a) of this section must verify that the DEA registration and State authorization(s) to practice and, where applicable, State authorization(s) to dispense controlled substances of each registrant being granted permission to sign electronic prescriptions for controlled substances are current and in good standing.

(c) After one individual designated under paragraph (a) of this section enters data that grants permission for individual practitioners to have access to the prescription functions that indicate readiness for signature and signing or revokes such authorization, a second individual designated under paragraph (a) of this section must use his two-factor authentication credential to satisfy the logical access controls. The second individual must be a DEA registrant.

(d) A registrant's permission to indicate that controlled substances prescriptions are ready to be signed and to sign controlled substance prescriptions must be revoked whenever any of the following occurs, on the date the occurrence is discovered:

(1) A hard token or any other authentication factor required by the two-factor authentication protocol is lost, stolen, or compromised. Such access must be terminated immediately upon receiving notification from the individual practitioner.

(2) The individual practitioner's DEA registration expires, unless the registration has been renewed.

(3) The individual practitioner's DEA registration is terminated, revoked, or suspended.

(4) The individual practitioner is no longer authorized to use the electronic prescription application (e.g., when the individual practitioner leaves the practice).

§ 1311.130 Requirements for establishing logical access control—Institutional practitioner.

(a) The entity within an institutional practitioner that conducts the identity proofing under § 1311.110 must develop a list of individual practitioners who are permitted to use the institutional practitioner's electronic prescription application to indicate that controlled substances prescriptions are ready to be signed and to sign controlled substance prescriptions. The list must be approved by two individuals.

(b) After the list is approved, it must be sent to a separate entity within the institutional practitioner that enters permissions for logical access controls into the application. The institutional practitioner must authorize at least two individuals or a role filled by at least two individuals to enter the logical access control data. One individual in the separate entity must authenticate to the application and enter the data to grant permissions to individual practitioners to indicate that controlled substances prescriptions are ready to be signed and to sign controlled substance prescriptions. A second individual must authenticate to the application to execute the logical access controls.

(c) The institutional practitioner must retain a record of the individuals or roles that are authorized to conduct identity proofing and logical access control data entry and execution.

(d) Permission to indicate that controlled substances prescriptions are ready to be signed and to sign controlled substance prescriptions must be revoked whenever any of the following occurs, on the date the occurrence is discovered:

(1) An individual practitioner's hard token or any other authentication factor required by the practitioner's two-factor authentication protocol is lost, stolen, or compromised. Such access must be terminated immediately upon receiving notification from the individual practitioner.

(2) The institutional practitioner's or, where applicable, individual practitioner's DEA registration expires, unless the registration has been renewed.

(3) The institutional practitioner's or, where applicable, individual practitioner's DEA registration is terminated, revoked, or suspended.

(4) An individual practitioner is no longer authorized to use the institutional practitioner's electronic prescription application (e.g., when the individual practitioner is no longer associated with the institutional practitioner.)

§ 1311.135 Requirements for creating a controlled substance prescription.

(a) The electronic prescription application may allow the registrant or his agent to enter data for a controlled substance prescription, provided that only the registrant may sign the prescription in accordance with §§ 1311.120(b)(11) and 1311.140.

(b) If a practitioner holds multiple DEA registrations, the practitioner or his agent must select the appropriate registration number for the prescription being issued in accordance with the requirements of § 1301.12 of this chapter.

(c) If required by State law, a supervisor's name and DEA number may be listed on a prescription, provided the prescription clearly indicates who is the supervisor and who is the prescribing practitioner.

§ 1311.140 Requirements for signing a controlled substance prescription.

(a) For a practitioner to sign an electronic prescription for a controlled substance the following must occur:

(1) The practitioner must access a list of one or more controlled substance prescriptions for a single patient. The list must display the information required by § 1311.120(b)(9).

(2) The practitioner must indicate the prescriptions that are ready to be signed.

(3) While the prescription information required in § 1311.120(b)(9) is displayed, the following statement or its substantial equivalent is displayed: "By completing the two-factor authentication protocol at this time, you are legally signing the prescription(s) and authorizing the transmission of the above information to the pharmacy for dispensing. The two-factor authentication protocol may only be completed by the practitioner whose name and DEA registration number appear above."

(4) While the prescription information required in § 1311.120(b)(9) and the statement required by paragraph (a)(3) of this section remain displayed, the practitioner must be prompted to complete the two-factor authentication protocol.

(5) The completion by the practitioner of the two-factor authentication protocol in the manner provided in paragraph (a)(4) of this section will constitute the signing of the prescription by the practitioner for purposes of § 1306.05(a) and (e) of this chapter.

(6) Except as provided under § 1311.145, the practitioner's completion of the two-factor authentication protocol must cause the application to digitally sign and electronically archive the information required under part 1306 of this chapter.

(b) The electronic prescription application must clearly label as the signing function the function that prompts the practitioner to execute the two-factor authentication protocol using his credential.

(c) Any prescription not signed in the manner required by this section shall not be transmitted.

§ 1311.145 Digitally signing the prescription with the individual practitioner's private key.

(a) An individual practitioner who has obtained a digital certificate as provided in § 1311.105 may digitally sign a controlled substance prescription using the private key associated with his digital certificate.

(b) The electronic prescription application must require the individual practitioner to complete a two-factor authentication protocol as specified in § 1311.140(a)(4) to use his private key.

(c) The electronic prescription application must digitally sign at least all information required under part 1306 of this chapter.

(d) The electronic prescription application must electronically archive the digitally signed record.

(e) A prescription that is digitally signed with a practitioner's private key may be transmitted to a pharmacy without the digital signature.

(f) If the electronic prescription is transmitted without the digital signature, the electronic prescription application must check the certificate revocation list of the certification authority that issued the practitioner's digital certificate. If the digital certificate is not valid, the electronic prescription application must not transmit the prescription. The certificate revocation list may be cached until the certification authority issues a new certificate revocation list.

(g) When the individual practitioner digitally signs a controlled substance prescription with the private key associated with his own digital certificate obtained as provided under § 1311.105, the electronic prescription application is not required to digitally sign the prescription using the application's private key.

§ 1311.150 Additional requirements for internal application audits.

(a) The application provider must establish and implement a list of auditable events. Auditable events must, at a minimum, include the following:

(1) Attempted unauthorized access to the electronic prescription application, or successful unauthorized access where the determination of such is feasible.

(2) Attempted unauthorized modification or destruction of any information or records required by this part, or successful unauthorized modification or destruction of any information or

records required by this part where the determination of such is feasible.

(3) Interference with application operations of the prescription application.

(4) Any setting of or change to logical access controls related to the issuance of controlled substance prescriptions.

(5) Attempted or successful interference with audit trail functions.

(6) For application service providers, attempted or successful creation, modification, or destruction of controlled substance prescriptions or logical access controls related to controlled substance prescriptions by any agent or employee of the application service provider.

(b) The electronic prescription application must analyze the audit trail at least once every calendar day and generate an incident report that identifies each auditable event.

(c) Any person designated to set logical access controls under §§ 1311.125 or 1311.130 must determine whether any identified auditable event represents a security incident that compromised or could have compromised the integrity of the prescription records. Any such incidents must be reported to the electronic prescription application provider and the Administration within one business day.

§ 1311.170 Transmission requirements.

(a) The electronic prescription application must transmit the electronic prescription as soon as possible after signature by the practitioner.

(b) The electronic prescription application may print a prescription that has been transmitted only if an intermediary or the designated pharmacy notifies a practitioner that an electronic prescription was not successfully delivered to the designated pharmacy. If this occurs, the electronic prescription application may print the prescription for the practitioner's manual signature. The printed prescription must include information noting that the prescription was originally transmitted electronically to [name of the specific pharmacy] on [date/time] and that transmission failed.

(c) The electronic prescription application may print copies of the transmitted prescription if they are clearly labeled: "Copy only—not valid for dispensing." Data on the prescription may be electronically transferred to medical records, and a list of prescriptions written may be printed for patients if the list indicates that it is for informational purposes only and not for dispensing.

(d) The electronic prescription application must not allow the transmission of an electronic prescription if an original prescription was printed prior to attempted transmission.

(e) The contents of the prescription required by part 1306 of this chapter must not be altered during transmission between the practitioner and pharmacy. Any change to the content during transmission, including truncation or removal of data, will render the electronic prescription invalid. The electronic prescription data may be converted from one software version to another between the electronic prescription application and the pharmacy application; conversion includes altering the structure of fields or machine language so that the receiving pharmacy application can read the prescription and import the data.

(f) An electronic prescription must be transmitted from the practitioner to the pharmacy in its electronic form. At no time may an intermediary convert an electronic prescription to another form (e.g., facsimile) for transmission.

§ 1311.200 Pharmacy responsibilities.

(a) Before initially using a pharmacy application to process controlled substance prescriptions, the pharmacy must determine that the third-party auditor or certification organization has found that the pharmacy application does the following accurately and consistently:

(1) Import, store, and display the information required for prescriptions under § 1306.05(a) of this chapter.

(2) Import, store, and display the indication of signing as required by § 1311.120(b)(17).

(3) Import, store, and display the number of refills as required by § 1306.22 of this chapter.

(4) Import, store, and verify the practitioner's digital signature, as provided in § 1311.210(c), where applicable.

(b) If the third-party auditor or certification organization has found that a pharmacy application does not accurately and consistently import, store, and display other information required for prescriptions under this chapter, the pharmacy must not process electronic prescriptions for controlled substances that are subject to the additional information requirements.

(c) If a pharmacy application provider notifies a pharmacy that a third-party audit or certification report indicates that the application or the application provider no longer meets the requirements of this part or notifies it that the application provider has identified an issue that makes the application non-compliant, the pharmacy must immediately cease to process controlled substance prescriptions using the application.

(d) A pharmacy that receives a notification that the pharmacy application is not in compliance with the requirements of this part must not use the application to process controlled substance prescriptions until it is notified that the application is again compliant and all relevant updates to the application have been installed.

(e) The pharmacy must determine which employees are authorized to enter information regarding the dispensing of controlled substance prescriptions and annotate or alter records of these prescriptions (to the extent such alterations are permitted under this chapter). The pharmacy must ensure that logical access controls in the pharmacy application are set so that only such employees are granted access to perform these functions.

(f) When a pharmacist fills a prescription in a manner that would require, under part 1306 of this chapter, the pharmacist to make a notation on the prescription if the prescription were a paper prescription, the pharmacist must make the same notation electronically when filling an electronic prescription and retain the annotation electronically in the prescription record or in linked files. When a prescription is received electronically, the prescription and all required annotations must be retained electronically.

(g) When a pharmacist receives a paper or oral prescription that indicates that it was originally transmitted electronically to the pharmacy, the pharmacist must check its records to ensure that the electronic version was not received and the prescription dispensed. If both prescriptions were received, the pharmacist must mark one as void.

(h) When a pharmacist receives a paper or oral prescription that indicates that it was originally transmitted electronically to another pharmacy, the pharmacist must check with that pharmacy to determine whether the prescription was received and dispensed. If the pharmacy that received the original electronic prescription had not dispensed the prescription, that pharmacy must mark the electronic version as void or canceled. If the pharmacy that received the original electronic prescription dispensed the prescription, the pharmacy with the paper version must not dispense the paper prescription and must mark the prescription as void.

(i) Nothing in this part relieves a pharmacy and pharmacist of the responsibility to dispense controlled substances only pursuant to a prescription issued for a legitimate medical purpose by a practitioner acting in the usual course of professional practice.

§ 1311.205 Pharmacy application requirements.

(a) The pharmacy may only use a pharmacy application that meets the requirements in paragraph (b) of this section to process electronic controlled substance prescriptions.

(b) The pharmacy application must meet the following requirements:

(1) The pharmacy application must be capable of setting logical access controls to limit access for the following functions:

(i) Annotation, alteration, or deletion of prescription information.

(ii) Setting and changing the logical access controls.

(2) Logical access controls must be set by individual user name or role.

(3) The pharmacy application must digitally sign and archive a prescription on receipt or be capable of receiving and archiving a digitally signed record.

(4) For pharmacy applications that digitally sign prescription records upon receipt, the digital signature functionality must meet the following requirements:

(i) The cryptographic module used to digitally sign the data elements required by part 1306 of this chapter must be at least FIPS 140–2 Security Level 1 validated. FIPS 140–2 is incorporated by reference in § 1311.08.

(ii) The digital signature application and hash function must comply with FIPS 186–3 and FIPS 180–3, as incorporated by reference in § 1311.08.

(iii) The pharmacy application's private key must be stored encrypted on a FIPS 140–2 Security Level 1 or higher validated cryptographic module using a FIPS-approved encryption algorithm. FIPS 140–2 is incorporated by reference in § 1311.08.

(iv) For software implementations, when the signing module is deactivated, the pharmacy application must clear the plain text password from the application memory to prevent the unauthorized access to, or use of, the private key.

(v) The pharmacy application must have a time application that is within five minutes of the official National Institute of Standards and Technology time source.

(5) The pharmacy application must verify a practitioner's digital signature (if the pharmacy application accepts prescriptions that were digitally signed with an individual practitioner's private key and transmitted with the digital signature).

(6) If the prescription received by the pharmacy application has not been digitally signed by the practitioner and transmitted with the digital signature, the pharmacy application must either:

(i) Verify that the practitioner signed the prescription by checking the data field that indicates the prescription was signed; or

(ii) Display the field for the pharmacist's verification.

(7) The pharmacy application must read and retain the full DEA number including the specific internal code number assigned to individual practitioners authorized to prescribe controlled substances by the hospital or other institution as provided in § 1301.22(c) of this chapter.

(8) The pharmacy application must read and store, and be capable of displaying, all information required by part 1306 of this chapter.

(9) The pharmacy application must read and store in full the information required under § 1306.05(a) of this chapter. The pharmacy application must either verify that such information is present or must display the information for the pharmacist's verification.

(10) The pharmacy application must provide for the following information to be added or linked to each electronic controlled substance prescription record for each dispensing:

(i) Number of units or volume of drug dispensed.

(ii) Date dispensed.

(iii) Name or initials of the person who dispensed the prescription.

(11) The pharmacy application must be capable of retrieving controlled substance prescriptions by practitioner name, patient name, drug name, and date dispensed.

(12) The pharmacy application must allow downloading of prescription data into a database or spreadsheet that is readable and sortable.

(13) The pharmacy application must maintain an audit trail of all actions related to the following:

(i) The receipt, annotation, alteration, or deletion of a controlled substance prescription.

(ii) Any setting or changing of logical access control permissions related to the dispensing of controlled substance prescriptions.

(iii) Auditable events as specified in § 1311.215.

(14) The pharmacy application must record within each audit record the following information:

(i) The date and time of the event.

(ii) The type of event.

(iii) The identity of the person taking the action, where applicable.

(iv) The outcome of the event (success or failure).

(15) The pharmacy application must conduct internal audits and generate

reports on any of the events specified in § 1311.215 in a format that is readable by the pharmacist. Such an internal audit may be automated and need not require human intervention to be conducted.

(16) The pharmacy application must protect the stored audit records from unauthorized deletion. The pharmacy application shall prevent modifications to the audit records.

(17) The pharmacy application must back up the controlled substance prescription records daily.

(18) The pharmacy application must retain all archived records electronically for at least two years from the date of their receipt or creation and comply with all other requirements of § 1311.305.

§ 1311.210 Archiving the initial record.

(a) Except as provided in paragraph (c) of this section, a copy of each electronic controlled substance prescription record that a pharmacy receives must be digitally signed by one of the following:

(1) The last intermediary transmitting the record to the pharmacy must digitally sign the prescription immediately prior to transmission to the pharmacy.

(2) The first pharmacy application that receives the electronic prescription must digitally sign the prescription immediately on receipt.

(b) If the last intermediary digitally signs the record, it must forward the digitally signed copy to the pharmacy.

(c) If a pharmacy receives a digitally signed prescription that includes the individual practitioner's digital signature, the pharmacy application must do the following:

(1) Verify the digital signature as provided in FIPS 186–3, as incorporated by reference in § 1311.08.

(2) Check the validity of the certificate holder's digital certificate by checking the certificate revocation list. The pharmacy may cache the CRL until it expires.

(3) Archive the digitally signed record. The pharmacy record must retain an indication that the prescription was verified upon receipt. No additional digital signature is required.

§ 1311.215 Internal audit trail.

(a) The pharmacy application provider must establish and implement a list of auditable events. The auditable events must, at a minimum, include the following:

(1) Attempted unauthorized access to the pharmacy application, or successful unauthorized access to the pharmacy application where the determination of such is feasible.

(2) Attempted or successful unauthorized modification or destruction of any information or records required by this part, or successful unauthorized modification or destruction of any information or records required by this part where the determination of such is feasible.

(3) Interference with application operations of the pharmacy application.

(4) Any setting of or change to logical access controls related to the dispensing of controlled substance prescriptions.

(5) Attempted or successful interference with audit trail functions.

(6) For application service providers, attempted or successful annotation, alteration, or destruction of controlled substance prescriptions or logical access controls related to controlled substance prescriptions by any agent or employee of the application service provider.

(b) The pharmacy application must analyze the audit trail at least once every calendar day and generate an incident report that identifies each auditable event.

(c) The pharmacy must determine whether any identified auditable event represents a security incident that compromised or could have compromised the integrity of the prescription records. Any such incidents must be reported to the pharmacy application service provider, if applicable, and the Administration within one business day.

§ 1311.300 Application provider requirements—Third-party audits or certifications.

(a) Except as provided in paragraph (e) of this section, the application provider of an electronic prescription application or a pharmacy application must have a third-party audit of the application that determines that the application meets the requirements of this part at each of the following times:

(1) Before the application may be used to create, sign, transmit, or process controlled substance prescriptions.

(2) Whenever a functionality related to controlled substance prescription requirements is altered or every two years, whichever occurs first.

(b) The third-party audit must be conducted by one of the following:

(1) A person qualified to conduct a SysTrust, WebTrust, or SAS 70 audit.

(2) A Certified Information System Auditor who performs compliance audits as a regular ongoing business activity.

(c) An audit for installed applications must address processing integrity and determine that the application meets the requirements of this part.

(d) An audit for application service providers must address processing integrity and physical security and determine that the application meets the requirements of this part.

(e) If a certifying organization whose certification process has been approved by DEA verifies and certifies that an electronic prescription or pharmacy application meets the requirements of this part, certification by that organization may be used as an alternative to the audit requirements of paragraphs (b) through (d) of this section, provided that the certification that determines that the application meets the requirements of this part occurs at each of the following times:

(1) Before the application may be used to create, sign, transmit, or process controlled substance prescriptions.

(2) Whenever a functionality related to controlled substance prescription requirements is altered or every two years, whichever occurs first.

(f) The application provider must make the audit or certification report available to any practitioner or pharmacy that uses the application or is considering use of the application. The electronic prescription or pharmacy application provider must retain the most recent audit or certification results and retain the results of any other audits or certifications of the application completed within the previous two years.

(g) Except as provided in paragraphs (h) and (i) of this section, if the third-party auditor or certification organization finds that the application does not meet one or more of the requirements of this part, the application must not be used to create, sign, transmit, or process electronic controlled substance prescriptions. The application provider must notify registrants within five business days of the issuance of the audit or certification report that they should not use the application for controlled substance prescriptions. The application provider must also notify the Administration of the adverse audit or certification report and provide the report to the Administration within one business day of issuance.

(h) For electronic prescription applications, the third-party auditor or certification organization must make the following determinations:

(1) If the information required in § 1306.05(a) of this chapter, the indication that the prescription was signed as required by § 1311.120(b)(17) or the digital signature created by the practitioner's private key, if transmitted, and the number of refills as required by § 1306.22 of this chapter, cannot be consistently and accurately recorded, stored, and transmitted, the third-party auditor or certification organization must indicate that the application does not meet the requirements of this part.

(2) If other information required under this chapter cannot be consistently and accurately recorded, stored, and transmitted, the third-party auditor or certification organization must indicate that the application has failed to meet the requirements for the specific information and should not be used to create, sign, and transmit prescriptions that require the additional information.

(i) For pharmacy applications, the third-party auditor or certification organization must make the following determinations:

(1) If the information required in § 1306.05(a) of this chapter, the indication that the prescription was signed as required by § 1311.205(b)(6), and the number of refills as required by § 1306.22

of this chapter, cannot be consistently and accurately imported, stored, and displayed, the third-party auditor or certification organization must indicate that the application does not meet the requirements of this part.

(2) If the pharmacy application accepts prescriptions with the practitioner's digital signature, the third-party auditor or certification organization must indicate that the application does not meet the requirements of this part if the application does not consistently and accurately import, store, and verify the digital signature.

(3) If other information required under this chapter cannot be consistently and accurately imported, stored, and displayed, the third-party auditor or certification organization must indicate that the application has failed to meet the requirements for the specific information and should not be used to process electronic prescriptions that require the additional information.

§ 1311.302 Additional application provider requirements.

(a) If an application provider identifies or is made aware of any issue with its application that make the application non-compliant with the requirements of this part, the application provider must notify practitioners or pharmacies that use the application as soon as feasible, but no later than five business days after discovery, that the application should not be used to issue or process electronic controlled substance prescriptions.

(b) When providing practitioners or pharmacies with updates to any issue that makes the application non-compliant with the requirements of this part, the application provider must indicate that the updates must be installed before the practitioner or pharmacy may use the application to issue or process electronic controlled substance prescriptions.

§ 1311.305 Recordkeeping.

(a) If a prescription is created, signed, transmitted, and received electronically, all records related to that prescription must be retained electronically.

(b) Records required by this subpart must be maintained electronically for two years from the date of their creation or receipt. This record retention requirement shall not pre-empt any longer period of retention which may be required now or in the future, by any other Federal or State law or regulation, applicable to practitioners, pharmacists, or pharmacies.

(c) Records regarding controlled substances prescriptions must be readily retrievable from all other records. Electronic records must be easily readable or easily rendered into a format that a person can read.

(d) Records required by this part must be made available to the Administration upon request.

(e) If an application service provider ceases to provide an electronic prescription application or an electronic pharmacy application or if a registrant ceases to use an application service provider, the application service provider must transfer any records subject to this part to the registrant in a format that the registrant's applications are capable of retrieving, displaying, and printing in a readable format.

(f) If a registrant changes application providers, the registrant must ensure that any records subject to this part are migrated to the new application or are stored in a format that can be retrieved, displayed, and printed in a readable format.

(g) If a registrant transfers its electronic prescription files to another registrant, both registrants must ensure that the records are migrated to the new application or are stored in a format that can be retrieved, displayed, and printed in a readable format.

(h) Digitally signed prescription records must be transferred or migrated with the digital signature.

PART 1312—IMPORTATION AND EXPORTATION OF CONTROLLED SUBSTANCES

Sec.

AUTHORITY: 21 U.S.C. 821, 871(b), 952, 953, 954, 957, 958.

SOURCE: 36 FR 7815, Apr. 24, 1971, unless otherwise noted. Redesignated at 38 FR 26609, Sept. 24, 1973.

§ 1312.01 Scope of part 1312.

Procedures governing the importation, exportation, transshipment and intransit shipment of controlled substances pursuant to section 1002, 1003, and 1004 of the Act (21 U.S.C. 952, 953, and 954) are governed generally by those sections and specifically by the sections of this part.

§ 1312.02 Definitions.

Any term contained in this part shall have the definition set forth in section 102 of the Act (21 U.S.C. 802) or part 1300 of this chapter.

[62 FR 13969, Mar. 24, 1997]

§ 1312.03 Forms applicable to this part.

Form	Access/ submission
DEA Form 35, Permit to Import	electronic.
DEA Form 36, Permit to Export	electronic.
DEA Form 161, Application for Permit to Export Controlled Substances	electronic.
DEA Form 161R, Application for Permit to Export Controlled Substances For Subsequent Reexport	electronic.
DEA Form 161R–EEA, Application for Permit to Export Controlled Substances for Subsequent Reexport Among Members of the European Economic Area.	electronic.
DEA Form 236, Controlled Substances Import/Export Declaration	electronic.
DEA Form 357, Application for Permit to Import Controlled Substances for Domestic And/Or Scientific Purposes.	electronic.

[81 FR 97025, Dec. 30, 2016]

IMPORTATION OF CONTROLLED SUBSTANCES

§ 1312.11 Requirement of authorization to import.

(a) No person shall import, or cause to be imported, into the customs territory of the United States from any place outside thereof (but within the United States), or into the United States from any place outside thereof, any controlled substances listed in Schedule I or II, or any narcotic controlled substance listed in Schedule III, IV, or V, or any non-narcotic controlled substance listed in Schedule III which the Administrator has specifically designated by regulation in § 1312.30 or any non-narcotic controlled substance listed in Schedule IV or V which is also listed in Schedule I or II of the Convention on Psychotropic Substances, 1971, unless and until such person is properly registered under the Act (or, in accordance with part 1301 of this chapter, exempt from registration) and the Administration has issued him or her a permit to do so in accordance with § 1312.13.

(b) No person shall import, or cause to be imported, into the customs territory of the United States from any place outside thereof (but within the United States), or into the United States from any place outside thereof, any non-narcotic controlled substance listed in Schedule III, IV, or V, excluding those described in paragraph (a) of this section, unless and until such person is properly registered under the Act (or, in accordance with part 1301 of this chapter, exempt from registration) and has filed an import declaration to do so in accordance with § 1312.18.

(c) A separate permit or declaration is required for each shipment of a controlled substance to be imported.

[81 FR 97026, Dec. 30, 2016]

§ 1312.12 Application for import permit; return information.

(a) Registered importers, other registrants authorized to import as a coincident activity of their registrations, and persons who in accordance with part 1301 of this chapter are exempt from registration, seeking to import a controlled substance in schedule I or II; any narcotic drug in schedule III, IV, or V; any non-narcotic drug in schedule III that has been specifically designated by regulation in § 1312.30; or any non-narcotic substance listed in schedule IV or V that is also listed in schedule I or II of the Convention on Psychotropic Substances, 1971, must submit an application for a permit to import controlled substances on DEA Form 357. All applications and supporting materials must be submitted to the Administration through the DEA Diversion Control Division secure network application. The application must be signed and dated by the importer and must contain the importer's registered address to which the controlled substances will be imported.

(b) The applicant must include on the DEA Form 357 the registration number of the importer and a detailed description of each controlled substance to be imported including the drug name, dosage form, National Drug Code (NDC) number, the Administration Controlled Substance Code Number as set forth in part 1308 of this chapter, the number and size of the packages or containers, the name and quantity of the controlled substance contained in any finished dosage units, and the quantity of any controlled substance (expressed in anhydrous acid, base or alkaloid) given in kilograms or parts thereof. The application must also include the following:

(1) The name/business name, address/business address, contact information (*e.g.*, telephone number(s), email address(es), etc.), and business of the consignor, if known at the time the application is submitted, but if unknown at that time, the fact should be indicated and the name and address afterwards furnished to the Administration as soon as ascertained by the importer;

(2) The foreign port and country of initial exportation (*i.e.*, the place where the article will begin its journey of exportation to the United States);

(3) The port of entry into the United States;

(4) The latest date said shipment will leave said foreign port or country;

(5) The stock on hand of the controlled substance desired to be imported;

(6) The name of the importing carrier or vessel (if known), or if unknown it should be stated whether the shipment will be made by express, freight, or otherwise, imports of controlled substances in Schedules I or II and narcotic drugs in Schedules III, IV, or V by mail being prohibited);

(7) The total tentative allotment to the importer of such controlled substance for the current calendar year; and

(8) The total number of kilograms of said allotment for which permits have previously been issued and the total quantity of controlled substance actually imported during the current year to date.

(c) If desired, alternative foreign ports of exportation within the same country may be indicated upon the application (*e.g.*, 1. Kolkata, 2. Mumbai). If a permit is issued pursuant to such application, it will bear the names of the two ports in the order given in the application and will authorize shipment from either port. Alternative ports in different countries will not be authorized in the same permit.

(d) *Return information.* Within 30 calendar days after actual receipt of a controlled substance at the importer's registered location, or within 10 calendar days after receipt of a written request by the Administration to the importer, whichever is sooner, the importer must file a report with the Administration through the DEA Diversion Control Division secure network application specifying the particulars of the transaction. This report must include the following information: The date the controlled substance was released by a customs officer at the port of entry; the date on which the controlled substance arrived at the registered location; the actual quantity of the controlled substance released by a customs officer at the port of entry; and the actual quantity of the controlled substance that arrived at the registered location. Upon receipt and review, the Administration will assign a transaction identification number to a completed report. The report will not be deemed filed until the Administration has issued a transaction identification number.

(e) *Denied release at the port of entry.* In the event that a shipment of controlled substances has been denied release by a customs officer at the port of entry for any reason, the importer who attempted to have the shipment released must, within 5 business days of the denial, report to the Administration that the shipment was denied and the reason for denial. Such report must be transmitted to the Administration through the DEA Diversion Control Division secure network application. This report must include the following information: The quantity of the controlled substance denied release; the date on which release was denied; and the basis for the denied release. Upon the importer's report of a denied release at the port of entry, the DEA will assign the report a transaction identification number and the import permit will be void and of no effect. No shipment of controlled substances denied release for any reason will be allowed to be released into the United States unless the importer submits a new DEA Form 357 and the Administration issues a new import permit.

[81 FR 97026, Dec. 30, 2016]

§1312.13 Issuance of import permit.

(a) The Administrator may authorize importation of any controlled substance listed in Schedule I or II or any narcotic drug listed in Schedule III, IV, or V if he finds:

(1) That the substance is crude opium, poppy straw, concentrate of poppy straw, or coca leaves, in such quantity as the Administrator finds necessary to provide for medical, scientific, or other legitimate purposes;

(2) That the substance is necessary to provide for medical and scientific needs or other legitimate needs of the United States during an emergency where domestic supplies of such substance or drug are found to be inadequate, or in any case in which the Administrator finds that competition among domestic manufacturers of the controlled substance is inadequate and will not be rendered adequate by the registration of additional manufacturers under section 303 of the Controlled Substances Act (21 U.S.C. 823); or

(3) That the domestic supply of any controlled substance is inadequate for scientific studies, and that the importation of that substance for scientific purposes is only for delivery to officials of the United Nations, of the United States, or of any State, or to any person registered or exempted from registration under sections 1007 and 1008 of the Act (21 U.S.C. 957 and 958).

(4) That the importation of the controlled substance is for ballistics or other analytical or scientific purposes, and that the importation of that substance is only for delivery to officials of the United Nations, of the United States, or of any State, or to any person registered or exempted from registration under sections 1007 and 1008 of the Act (21 U.S.C. 957 and 958).

(b) The Administrator may require that such non-narcotic controlled substances in Schedule III as he shall designate by regulation in §1312.30 of this part be imported only pursuant to the issuance of an import permit. The Administrator may authorize the importation of such substances if he finds that the substance is being imported for medical, scientific or other legitimate uses.

(c) If a non-narcotic substance listed in Schedule IV or V is also listed in Schedule I or II of the Convention on Psychotropic Substances, 1971, it shall be imported only pursuant to the issuance of an import permit. The Administrator may authorize the importation of such substances if it is found that the substance is being imported for medical, scientific or other legitimate uses.

(d) The Administrator may require an applicant to submit such documents or written statements of fact relevant to the application as he deems necessary to determine whether the application should be granted. The failure of the applicant to provide such documents or statements within a reasonable time after being requested to do so shall be deemed to be a waiver by the applicant of an opportunity to present such documents or facts for consideration by the Administrator in granting or denying the application.

(e) If an importation is approved, the Administrator will issue an import permit bearing his or her signature or that of his or her delegate. Each permit will be assigned a unique permit number. A permit must not be altered or changed by any person after being signed. Any change or alteration upon the face of any permit after it has been signed renders it void and of no effect. Permits are not transferable. The Administrator or his/her delegate will date and certify on each permit that the importer named therein is thereby permitted as a registrant under the Act, to import, through the port of entry named, one shipment of not to exceed the specified quantity of the named controlled substances, shipment to be made before a specified date. Only one shipment may be made on a single import permit. A single import permit shall authorize a quantity of goods to be imported/exported at one place, at one time, for delivery to one consignee, on a single conveyance, at one place, on one bill of lading, air waybill, or commercial loading document; a single permit shall not authorize a quantity of goods to be imported/exported if the goods are divided onto two or more conveyances. The permit must state that the Administration is satisfied that the consignment proposed to be imported is required for legitimate purposes.

(f) Notwithstanding paragraphs (a)(1) and (a)(2) of this section, the Administrator shall permit, pursuant to section 1002(a)(1) or 1002(a)(2)(A) of the Act (21 U.S.C. 952(a)(1) or (a)(2)(A)), the importation of approved narcotic raw material (opium, poppy straw and concentrate of poppy straw) having as its source:

(1) Turkey,

(2) India,

(3) Spain,

(4) France,

(5) Poland,

(6) Hungary, and

(7) Australia.

(g) At least eighty (80) percent of the narcotic raw material imported into the United States shall have as its original source Turkey and India. Except under conditions of insufficient supplies of narcotic raw materials, not more than twenty (20) percent of the narcotic raw material imported into the United States annually shall have as its source Spain, France, Poland, Hungary and Australia.

[36 FR 23624, Dec. 11, 1971, as amended at 37 FR 15923, Aug. 8, 1972. Redesignated at 38 FR 26609, Sept. 24, 1973, and amended at 46 FR 41776, Aug. 18, 1981; 52 FR 17289, May 7, 1987; 73 FR 6851, Feb. 6, 2008; 81 FR 97027, Dec. 30, 2016]

§ 1312.14 Distribution of import permits.

The Administration shall transmit the import permit to the competent national authority of the exporting country and shall make an official record of the import permit available to the importer through secure electronic means. The importer, or their agent, must submit an official record of the import permit and/or required data concerning the import transaction to a customs officer at the port of entry in compliance with all import control requirements of agencies with import control authorities under the Act or statutory authority other than the Controlled Substances Import and Export Act. The importer must maintain an official record of the import permit (available from the DEA Diversion Control Division secure network application after issuance) in accordance with part 1304 of this chapter as the record of authority for the importation and shall transmit an official record of the permit to the foreign exporter. If required by the foreign competent national authority, the importer shall ensure that an official record of the import permit is provided (*e.g.*, by transmitting an official record of the permit to the foreign exporter who shall transmit such record to the competent national authority of the exporting county). The importer must ensure that an official record of the permit accompanies the shipment of controlled substances to its final destination, the registered location of the importer (*i.e.*, drop shipments are prohibited).

[81 FR 97027, Dec. 30, 2016]

§ 1312.15 Shipments in greater or less amount than authorized.

(a) If the shipment made under an import permit is greater than the maximum amount authorized to be imported under the permit, as determined at the weighing by the District Director of the U.S. Customs and Border Protection or customs service of an Insular Area, such difference shall be seized subject to forfeiture, pending an explanation; except that shipments of substances exceeding the maximum authorized amount by less than 1 percent may be released to the importer upon the filing by him of an amended import permit in accordance with § 1312.16(a). If the substance is included in Schedule I, it will be summarily forfeited to the Government.

(b) If the shipment made under the permit is less than the maximum amount authorized to be imported under the permit as determined at the weighing by the District Director of the U.S. Customs and Border Protection or customs service of an Insular Area, such difference, when ascertained by the Administration, shall be recredited to the tentative allotment against which the quantity covered by the permit was charged, and the balance of any such tentative allotment with any such recredits will remain available to the importer to whom made (unless previously revoked in whole or in part), for importations pursuant to any permit or permits as are requested and issued during the remainder of the calendar year to which the allotment is applicable. No permit shall be issued for importation of a quantity of controlled substances as a charge against the tentative allotment for a given calendar year, after the close of such calendar year, unless the Administrator decides to make an exception for good cause shown.

[36 FR 7815, Apr. 24, 1971. Redesignated at 38 FR 26609, Sept. 24, 1973, and amended at 46 FR 28841, May 29, 1981; 81 FR 97027, Dec. 30, 2016]

§ 1312.16 Amendment, cancellation, expiration of import permit.

(a) Importers may only request that an import permit or application for an import permit be amended in accordance with paragraphs (a)(1) through (7) of this section. Requests for an amendment must be submitted through the DEA Diversion Control Division secure network application. Except as provided in paragraph (a)(5) of this section and § 1312.15(a), importers must submit all requests for an amendment at least one full business day in advance of the date of release by a customs officer. Importers must specifically request that an amendment be made; supplementary information submitted by an importer through the DEA Diversion Control Division secure network application will not automatically trigger the amendment process. While the request for an amendment is being reviewed by the Administration, the original permit will be temporarily stayed and may not be used to authorize entry of a shipment of controlled substances. If the importer's request for an amendment to an issued permit is granted by the Administration, the Administration will immediately cancel the original permit and re-issue the permit, as amended, with a revised permit number. The DEA and importer will distribute the amended permit in accordance with § 1312.14. If a request for an amendment is denied by the Administration, the temporary stay will be lifted; once lifted, the originally issued permit may immediately be used to authorize entry of a shipment in accordance with the terms of the permit, subject to the shipment being compliant with all other applicable laws.

(1) An importer may request that an import permit or application for a permit be amended to change the National Drug Control number, description of the packaging, or trade name of the product, so long as the description is for the same basic class of controlled substance as in the original permit.

(2) An importer may request that an import permit or application for a permit be amended to change the proposed port of entry, the date of release by a customs officer, or the method of transport.

(3) An importer may request that an import permit or application for a permit be amended to change the justification provided as to why an import shipment is needed to meet the legitimate scientific or medical needs of the United States.

(4) An importer may request that an import permit or application for a permit be amended to change any registrant notes.

(5) Prior to departure of the shipment from its original foreign location, an importer may request that an import permit or application for a permit be amended to increase the total base weight of a controlled substance. At the U.S. port of entry, an importer may request that an import permit be amended in accordance with § 1312.15(a). Importers are not required to amend an import permit for the sole purpose of decreasing the total base weight of a controlled substance authorized to be imported. However, the balance of any unimported authorized quantity of controlled substances on an import permit is void upon entry of a shipment on the issued permit or upon expiration of the unused permit in accordance with paragraph (b) of this section, whichever is sooner. Other than for an amendment to an import permit under § 1312.15(a), importers must submit a request for an amendment to increase the total base weight of a controlled substance at least three business days in advance of the date of release by a customs officer.

(6) An importer may request that an import permit be amended to remove a controlled substance from the permit. However, an importer may not amend an import permit to add or replace a controlled substance/Administration controlled substance code number to the item(s) to be imported. Importers who desire to import a different controlled substance than that contained on their issued import permit or permit application must submit a request for the permit or permit application to be canceled and request a new permit in accordance with § 1312.12.

(7) An importer may not amend the importer's name (as it appears on their DEA certificate of registration) or the name of the foreign exporter as provided in the DEA Form 357. Importers who need to make any changes to any of these fields must submit a request for the permit or permit application to be canceled and request a new permit in accordance with § 1312.12.

(b) An import permit will be void and of no effect after the expiration date specified therein, and in no event will the date be more than 180 calendar days after the date the permit is issued. Amended import permits will retain the original expiration date.

(c) An import permit may be canceled after being issued, at the request of the importer submitted to the Administration through the DEA Diversion Control Division secure network application, provided that no shipment has been made thereunder.

Nothing in this part will affect the right, hereby reserved by the Administration, to cancel a permit at any time for proper cause.

[81 FR 97027, Dec. 30, 2016]

§ 1312.17 Special report from importers.

Whenever requested by the Administrator, importers shall render to him not later than 30 days after receipt of the request therefor a statement under oath of the stocks of controlled substances on hand as of the date specified by the Administrator in his request, and, if desired by the Administrator, an estimate of the probable requirements for legitimate uses of the importer for any subsequent period that may be designated by the Administrator. In lieu of any special statement that may be considered necessary, the Administrator may accept the figures given upon the reports subsequent by said importer under part 1304 of this chapter.

[36 FR 7815, Apr. 24, 1971. Redesignated at 38 FR 26609, Sept. 24, 1973, as amended at 62 FR 13969, Mar. 24, 1997]

§ 1312.18 Import declaration.

(a) Any non-narcotic controlled substance listed in Schedule III, IV, or V, not subject to the requirement of an import permit pursuant to § 1312.13 (b) or (c) of this chapter, may be imported if that substance is needed for medical, scientific or other legitimate uses in the United States, and will be imported pursuant to a controlled substances import declaration.

(b) Any person registered or authorized to import and seeking to import any non-narcotic controlled substance listed in Schedules III, IV, or V which is not subject to the requirement of an import permit as described in paragraph (a) of this section, must file a controlled substances import declaration (DEA Form 236) with the Administration through the DEA Diversion Control Division secure network application not later than 15 calendar days prior to the anticipated date of release by a customs officer and distribute an official record of the declaration as hereinafter directed in § 1312.19. The declaration must be signed and dated by the importer and must specify the address of the final destination for the shipment, which must be the importer's registered location. Upon receipt and review, the Administration will assign a transaction identification number to each completed declaration. The import declaration is not deemed filed, and therefore is not valid, until the Administration has issued a transaction identification number. The importer may only proceed with the import transaction once the transaction identification number has been issued.

(c) DEA Form 236 must include the following information:

(1) The name, address, and registration number of the importer; and the name and address and registration number of the import broker, if any; and

(2) A complete description of the controlled substances to be imported, including drug name, dosage form, National Drug Code (NDC) number, the Administration Controlled Substances Code Number as set forth in part 1308 of this chapter, the number and size of packages or containers, the name and quantity of the controlled substance contained in any finished dosage units, and the net quantity of any controlled substance (expressed in anhydrous acid, base, or alkaloid) given in kilograms or parts thereof; and

(3) The anticipated date of release by a customs officer at the port of entry, the foreign port and country of exportation to the United States, the port of entry, and the name, address, and registration number of the recipient in the United States; and

(4) The name and address of the consignor in the foreign country of exportation, and any registration or license numbers if the consignor is required to have such numbers either by the country of exportation or under U.S. law.

(d) Notwithstanding the time limitations included in paragraph (b) of this section, an applicant may obtain a special waiver of these time limitations in emergency or unusual instances, provided that a specific confirmation is received from the Administrator or his delegate advising the registrant to proceed pursuant to the special waiver.

(e) *Return information*. Within 30 calendar days after actual receipt of a controlled substance at the importer's registered location, or within 10 calendar days after receipt of a written request by the Administration to the importer, whichever is sooner, the importer must file a report with the Administration through the DEA Diversion Control Division secure network application specifying the particulars of the transaction. This report must include the following information: The date on which the controlled substance was released by a customs officer at the port of entry; the date on which the controlled substance arrived at the registered location; the actual quantity of the controlled substance released by a customs officer at the port of entry; the actual quantity of the controlled substance that arrived at the registered location; and the actual port of entry. Upon receipt and review, the Administration will assign a transaction identification number to a completed report. The report will not be deemed filed until the Administration has issued a transaction identification number.

(f) An importer may amend an import declaration in the same circumstances in which an importer may request amendment to an import permit, as set forth in § 1312.16(a)(1) through (7). Amendments to declarations must be submitted through the DEA Diversion Control Division secure network application. Except as provided in §§ 1312.16(a)(5) and 1312.15(a), importers must submit all amendments at least one full business day in advance of the date of release by a customs officer. Importers must specifically note that an amendment is being made; supplementary information submitted by an importer through the DEA Diversion Control Division secure network application will not automatically be considered an amendment. While the amendment is being processed by the Administration, the original declaration will be temporarily stayed and may not be used to authorize release of a shipment of controlled substances. Upon receipt and review, the Administration will assign each completed amendment a transaction identification number. The amendment will not be deemed filed until the Administration issues a transaction identification number. The DEA and importer will distribute the amended declaration in accordance with § 1312.19. A filed amendment will not change the date that the declaration becomes void and of no effect pursuant to paragraph (g) of this section.

(g) An import declaration may be canceled after being filed with the Administration, at the request of the importer by the importer submitting to the Administration the request through the DEA Diversion Control Division secure network application, provided that no shipment has been made thereunder. Import declarations shall become void and of no effect 180 calendar days after the date the declaration is deemed filed with the Administration.

(h) *Denied release at the port of entry.* In the event that a shipment of controlled substances has been denied release by a customs officer at the port of entry for any reason, the importer who attempted to have the shipment released, within 5 business days of the denial, report to the Administration that the shipment was denied release and the reason for denial. Such report must be transmitted to the Administration through the DEA Diversion Control Division secure network application. This report must include the following information: The quantity of the controlled substance denied release; the date on which release was denied; and the basis for the denied release. Upon the importer's report of a denied release, the DEA will assign the report a transaction identification number and the import declaration will become void and of no effect. No shipment of controlled substances denied release for any reason will be allowed to be released into the United States until the importer has filed a new import declaration and the Administration has issued a new transaction identification number.

[36 FR 7815, Apr. 24, 1971, as amended at 37 FR 15923, Aug. 8, 1972. Redesignated at 38 FR 26609, Sept. 24, 1973, and amended at 45 FR 74715, Nov. 12, 1980; 51 FR 5319, Feb. 13, 1986; 52 FR 17290, May 7, 1987; 62 FR 13969, Mar. 24, 1997; 75 FR 10682, Mar. 9, 2010; 77 FR 4237, Jan. 27, 2012; 81 FR 97028, Dec. 30, 2016]

§ 1312.19 Distribution of import declaration.

The importer must furnish an official record of the declaration (available through the DEA Diversion Control Division secure network application after the Administration issues a transaction identification number) to the foreign shipper. The foreign shipper must submit an official record of the declaration to the competent national authority of the exporting country, if required as a prerequisite to export authorization. The importer, or their agent, must submit an official record of the declaration and/or required data concerning the import transaction to a customs officer at the port of entry in compliance with all import control requirements of agencies with import control authorities under the Act or statutory authority other than the Controlled Substances Import and Export Act. The importer must ensure that an official record of the declaration accompanies the shipment to its final destination, which must only be the registered location of the importer (*i.e.*, drop shipments are prohibited). The importer must maintain an official record of the declaration in accordance with part 1304 of this chapter.

[81 FR 97029, Dec. 30, 2016]

EXPORTATION OF CONTROLLED SUBSTANCES

§ 1312.21 Requirement of authorization to export.

(a) No person shall in any manner export, or cause to be exported, from the United States any controlled substance listed in Schedule I or II, or any narcotic controlled substance listed in Schedule III or IV, or any non-narcotic controlled substance in Schedule III which the Administrator has specifically designated by regulation in § 1312.30 or any non-narcotic controlled substance in Schedule IV or V which is also listed in Schedule I or II of the Convention on Psychotropic Substances, 1971, unless and until such person is properly registered under the Act (or, in accordance with part 1301 of this chapter, exempt from registration) and the Administrator has issued him or her a permit to do so in accordance with § 1312.23.

(b) No person shall in any manner export, or cause to be exported, from the United States any non-narcotic controlled substance listed in Schedule III, IV, or V, excluding those described in paragraph (a) of this section, or any narcotic controlled substance listed in Schedule V, unless and until such person is properly registered under the Act (or, in accordance with part 1301 of this chapter, exempt from registration) and has furnished an export declaration as provided by section 1003 of the Act (21 U.S.C. 953(e)) to the Administration in accordance with § 1312.28.

(c) A separate permit or declaration is required for each shipment of controlled substance to be exported.

[81 FR 97029, Dec. 30, 2016]

§ 1312.22 Application for export or reexport permit; return information.

(a) Registered exporters, and persons who in accordance with part 1301 of this chapter are exempt from registration, seeking to export controlled substances must submit an application for a permit to export controlled substances on DEA Form 161. Registered exporters, and persons who in accordance with part 1301 of this chapter are exempt from registration, seeking to reexport controlled substances must submit an application for a permit to reexport controlled substances on DEA Form 161R or DEA Form 161R–EEA, whichever applies. All applications and supporting materials must be submitted to the Administration through the DEA Diversion Control Division secure network application. The application must be signed and dated by the exporter and contain the exporter's registered address from which the controlled substances will be exported. Controlled substances may not be exported until a permit number has been issued.

(b) Exports of controlled substances by mail are prohibited.

(c) *Applications.* (1) Except as provided in paragraph (c)(2) of this section, each application for a permit to export or reexport must include the following information:

(i) The exporter's name/business name, address/business address, and contact information (*e.g.*, telephone number(s), email address (es), etc.);

(ii) The exporter's registration number, address, and contact information (*e.g.*, telephone number(s), etc.) from which the controlled substances will be exported;

(iii) A detailed description of each controlled substance to be exported including the drug name, dosage form, National Drug Code (NDC) number, Administration Controlled Substance Code Number as set forth in part 1308 of this chapter, the number and size of the packages or containers, the name and quantity of the controlled substance contained in any finished dosage units, and the quantity of any controlled substance (expressed in anhydrous acid, base, or alkaloid) given in kilograms or parts thereof;

(iv) The name/business name, address/business address, contact information (*e.g.*, telephone number(s), email address(es), etc.) and business of the consignee in the first country (the country to which the controlled substance is exported from the United

States), foreign port and country of entry/first country of entry, the port of export, the anticipated date of release by a customs officer at the port of export, the name of the exporting carrier or vessel (if known), or if unknown it should be stated whether the shipment will be made by express, freight, or otherwise), the date and number, if any, of the supporting foreign import license or permit accompanying the application, and the authority by whom such foreign license or permit was issued; and

(v) An affidavit that the packages or containers are labeled in conformance with obligations of the United States under international treaties, conventions, or protocols in effect at the time of the export or reexport. The affidavit shall further state that to the best of the affiant's knowledge and belief, the controlled substances therein are to be applied exclusively to medical or scientific uses within the country to which exported, will not be reexported therefrom and that there is an actual need for the controlled substance for medical or scientific uses within such country, unless the application is submitted for reexport in accordance with paragraphs (f), (g), and (h) of this section. In the case of exportation of crude cocaine, the affidavit may state that to the best of affiant's knowledge and belief, the controlled substances will be processed within the country to which exported, either for medical or scientific use within that country or for reexportation in accordance with the laws of that country to another for medical or scientific use within that country.

(2) With respect to reexports among members of the European Economic Area in accordance with section 1003(f) of the Act (21 U.S.C. 953(f)), the requirements of paragraph (c)(1) of this section shall apply only with respect to the export from the United States to the first country and not to any subsequent export from that country to another country of the European Economic Area.

(d)(1) Except as provided in paragraph (d)(2) of this section, the applicant must also submit with the application any import license or permit or a certified copy of any such license or permit issued by the competent national authority in the country of destination, or other documentary evidence deemed adequate by the Administration, showing: That the merchandise is consigned to an authorized permittee; that it is to be applied exclusively to medical or scientific use within the country of destination; that it will not be reexported from such country (unless the application is submitted for reexport in accordance with paragraphs (f), (g), and (h) of this section); and that there is an actual need for the controlled substance for medical or scientific use within such country or countries. If the import license or permit, or the certified copy of such, is not written in English or bilingual with another language and English, the registrant must also submit with their application a certified translation of the permit or license. For purposes of this requirement, certified translation means that the translator has signed the translation legally attesting the accuracy of the translation. (In the case of exportation of bulk coca leaf alkaloid, the applicant need only include with the application the material outlined in paragraph (c) of this section.)

(2) With respect to reexports among members of the European Economic Area in accordance with section 1003(f) of the Act (21 U.S.C. 953(f)), the requirements of paragraph (d)(1) of this section shall apply only with respect to the export from the United States to the first country and not to any subsequent export from that country to another country of the European Economic Area.

(e) *Return information for exports (on a DEA Form 161).* Within 30 calendar days after the controlled substance is released by a customs officer at the port of export, or within 10 calendar days after receipt of a written request by the Administration to the exporter, whichever is sooner, the exporter must report to the Administration through the DEA Diversion Control Division secure network application the particulars of the transaction. This report must include the following information: The date on which the controlled substance left the registered location;

the date on which the controlled substance was released by a customs officer at the port of export; the actual quantity of controlled substance that left the registered location; and the actual quantity of the controlled substance released by a customs officer at the port of export; the actual port of export, and any other information as the Administration may from time to time specify. Upon receipt and review, the Administration will assign a transaction identification number to a completed report. The report will not be deemed filed until the Administration has issued a transaction identification number.

(f) *Reexports outside of the European Economic Area.* Except as provided in paragraph (g) of this section, the Administration may authorize any controlled substance listed in Schedule I or II, or any narcotic drug listed in Schedule III or IV, to be exported from the United States to a country for subsequent export from that country to another country, if each of the following conditions is met, in accordance with section 1003(f) of the Act (21 U.S.C. 953(f)):

(1) Both the country to which the controlled substance is exported from the United States (referred to in this section as the "first country") and the country to which the controlled substance is exported from the first country (referred to in this section as the "second country") are parties to the Single Convention on Narcotic Drugs, 1961, and the Convention on Psychotropic Substances, 1971;

(2) The first country and the second country have each instituted and maintain, in conformity with such Conventions, a system of controls of imports of controlled substances which the Administration deems adequate;

(3) With respect to the first country, the controlled substance is consigned to a holder of such permits or licenses as may be required under the laws of such country, and a permit or license to import the controlled substance has been issued by the country;

(4) With respect to the second country, substantial evidence is furnished to the Administration by the applicant for the export permit that—

(i) The controlled substance is to be consigned to a holder of such permits or licenses as may be required under the laws of such country, and a permit or license to import the controlled substance is to be issued by the country; and

(ii) The controlled substance is to be applied exclusively to medical, scientific, or other legitimate uses within the country;

(5) The controlled substance will not be exported from the second country;

(6) The exporter has complied with paragraph (h) of this section and a permit to export the controlled substance from the United States has been issued by the Administration; and

(7) *Return information for reexports outside of the European Economic Area (on DEA Form 161R)*—(i) *Return information for export from the United States, for reexport.* Within 30 calendar days after the controlled substance is released by a customs officer at the port of export the exporter must file a report with the Administration through the DEA Diversion Control Division secure network application specifying the particulars of the transaction. This report must include the following information: The date on which the controlled substance left the registered location; the date on which the controlled substance was released by a customs officer at the port of export; the actual quantity of controlled substance released by a customs officer at the port of export; and the actual port of export. Upon receipt and review, the Administration will assign a completed report a transaction identification number. The report will not be deemed filed until the Administration has issued a transaction identification number. In determining whether the exporter has complied with the requirement to file within 30 calendar days, the report shall be deemed filed on the first date on which a complete report is filed.

(ii) *Return information for export from a first country that is or is not a member of the European Economic Area to a country outside of the European Economic Area; return information for export from a first country that is not a member of the European Economic Area to a member of the European Economic Area.*

Within 30 calendar days after the controlled substance is exported from the first country to the second country the exporter must file a report with the Administration through the DEA Diversion Control Division secure network application specifying the particulars of the export from the first country. If the permit issued by the Administration authorized the reexport of a controlled substance from the first country to more than one second country, a report for each individual reexport is required. These reports must include the following information: Name of second country; actual quantity of controlled substance shipped; and the date shipped from the first country, the actual port from which the controlled substances were shipped from the first country. Upon receipt and review, the Administration will assign each completed report a transaction identification number. The report will not be deemed filed until the Administration has issued a transaction identification number.

(g) *Reexports among members of the European Economic Area (on DEA Form 161R–EEA).* The Administration may authorize any controlled substance listed in Schedule I or II, or any narcotic drug listed in Schedule III or IV, to be exported from the United States to a country of the European Economic Area for subsequent export from that country to another country of the European Economic Area, if the following conditions and the conditions of paragraphs (f)(1) through (4) and (6) of this section are met, in accordance with section 1003(f) of the Act (21 U.S.C. 953(f)):

(1)(i) The controlled substance will not be exported from the second country, except that the controlled substance may be exported from a second country that is a member of the European Economic Area to another country that is a member of the European Economic Area, provided that the first country is also a member of the European Economic Area; and

(ii) Subsequent to any reexportation described in paragraph (g)(1)(i) of this section, a controlled substance may continue to be exported from any country that is a member of the European Economic Area to any other such country, if—

(A) The conditions applicable with respect to the first country under paragraphs (f)(1) through (4) and (6) of this section and paragraph (g)(2) are met with respect to each subsequent country from which the controlled substance is exported pursuant to this paragraph (g); and

(B) The conditions applicable with respect to the second country under paragraphs (f)(1) through (4) and (6) of this section and paragraph (g)(2) of this section are met with respect to each subsequent country to which the controlled substance is exported pursuant to this paragraph (g).

(2) *Return information for reexports among members of the European Economic Area*—(i) *Return information for export from the United States, for reexport among members of the European Economic Area.* Exporters must comply with the return reporting requirements of paragraph (f)(7)(i) of this section.

(ii) *Reexports among members of the European Economic Area.* Within 30 calendar days after the controlled substance is exported from the first country to the second country, and within 30 calendar days of each subsequent reexport within the European Economic Area, if any, the U.S. exporter must file a report with the Administration through the DEA Diversion Control Division secure network application specifying the particulars of the export. These reports must include the name of country to which the controlled substance was reexported, *i.e.*, another member of the European Economic Area; the actual quantity of controlled substance shipped; the date shipped from the first country, the name/business name, address/business address, contact information (*e.g.*, telephone number(s), email address(es), etc.) and business of the consignee; and the name/business name, address/business address, contact information (*e.g.*, telephone number(s), email address(es), etc.) and business of the exporter. Upon receipt and review, the Administration will assign each completed report a transaction identification number. The report will not be deemed filed until the Administration has issued a transaction identification number.

(h) Where a person is seeking to export a controlled substance for reexport outside of the European Economic Area in accordance with paragraph (f) of this section, the requirements of paragraphs (h)(1) through (7) of this section shall apply in addition to (and not in lieu of) the requirements of paragraphs (a) through (d) of this section. Where a person is seeking to export a controlled substance for reexport among members of the European Economic Area in accordance with paragraph (g) of this section, the requirements of paragraph (h)(4) of this section shall apply in addition to (and not in lieu of) the requirements of paragraphs (a) through (d) of this section.

(1) Bulk substances will not be reexported in the same form as exported from the United States, *i.e.*, the material must undergo further manufacturing process. This further manufactured material may only be reexported to a second country.

(2) Finished dosage units, if reexported, must be in a commercial package, properly sealed and labeled for legitimate medical use in the second country.

(3) Any proposed reexportation must be made known to the Administration at the time the initial DEA Form 161R is submitted. In addition, the following information must also be provided where indicated on the form:

(i) Whether the drug or preparation will be reexported in bulk or finished dosage units;

(ii) The product name, dosage strength, commercial package size, and quantity; and

(iii) The name of consignee, complete address, and expected shipment date, as well as the name and address of the ultimate consignee in the second country.

(4) The application must contain an affidavit that the consignee in the second country, and any country of subsequent reexport within the European Economic Area, is authorized under the laws and regulations of the second and/or subsequent country to receive the controlled substances. The affidavit must also contain the following statements, in addition to the statements required under paragraph (c) of this section:

(i) That the packages are labeled in conformance with the obligations of the United States under the Single Convention on Narcotic Drugs, 1961, the Convention on Psychotropic Substances, 1971, and any amendments to such treaties in effect;

(ii) That the controlled substances are to be applied exclusively to medical or scientific uses within the second country, or country of subsequent reexport within the European Economic Area;

(iii) That the controlled substances will not be further reexported from the second country except as provided by paragraph (f) of section 1003 of the Act (21 U.S.C. 953(f)); and

(iv) That there is an actual need for the controlled substances for medical or scientific uses within the second country, or country of subsequent reexport within the European Economic Area.

(5) If the applicant proposes that the shipment of controlled substances will be separated into parts after it arrives in the first country and then reexported to more than one second country, the applicant must so indicate on the DEA Form 161R and provide all the information required in this section for each second country.

(6) Except in the case of reexports among countries of the European Economic Area in accordance with section 1003(f) of the Act (21 U.S.C. 953(f)), the controlled substance will be reexported from the first country to the second country (or second countries) no later than 180 calendar days after the controlled substance was released by a customs officer from the United States.

(7) Shipments that have been exported from the United States and are refused by the consignee in either the first or second country, or subsequent member of the European Economic Area, or are otherwise unacceptable or undeliverable, may be returned to the registered exporter in the United States upon authorization of the Administration. In these circumstances, the exporter in the United States must submit a written request for the return of the controlled substances to the United States with a brief summary of

the facts that warrant the return, along with a completed DEA Form 357 through the DEA Diversion Control Division secure network application. The Administration will evaluate the request after considering all the facts as well as the exporter's registration status with the Administration. If the exporter provides sufficient justification, the Administration may issue an import permit for the return of these drugs, and the exporter may then obtain an export permit from the country of original importation. The substance may not be returned to the United States until after a permit has been issued by the Administration.

(i) In considering whether to grant an application for a permit under paragraphs (f), (g), and (h) of this section, the Administration shall consider whether the applicant has previously obtained such a permit and, if so, whether the applicant complied fully with the requirements of this section with respect to that previous permit.

(j) *Denied release at the port of export.* In the event that a shipment of controlled substances has been denied release by a customs officer at the port export from the United States for any reason, the exporter who attempted to have the shipment released must, within 5 business days of the denial, report to the Administration that the shipment was denied release and the reason for denial. Such report must be transmitted to the Administration through the DEA Diversion Control Division secure network application. This report must include the following information: The quantity of the controlled substance denied release; the date on which release was denied; the basis for the denied release, the port from which the denial was issued, and any other information as the Administration may from time to time specify. Upon the exporter's report of a denied release, DEA will assign the report a transaction identification number and the export permit will be void and of no effect. No shipment of controlled substances denied release for any reason will be allowed to be released from the United States unless the exporter submits a new DEA Form 161, 161R, or 161R–EEA, as appropriate, and the Administration issues a new export permit.

[81 FR 97029, Dec. 30, 2016]

§ 1312.23 Issuance of export permit.

(a) The Administrator may authorize exportation of any controlled substance listed in Schedule I or II or any narcotic controlled substance listed in Schedule III or IV if he finds that such exportation is permitted by subsections 1003(a), (b), (c), (d), or (f) of the Act (21 U.S.C. 953(a), (b), (c), (d), or (f).

(b) The Administrator may require that such non-narcotic controlled substances in Schedule III as shall be designated by regulation in § 1312.30 of this part be exported only pursuant to the issuance of an export permit. The Administrator may authorize the exportation of such substances if he finds that such exportation is permitted by section 1003(e) of the Act (21 U.S.C. 953(e)).

(c) If a non-narcotic substance listed in Schedule IV or V is also listed in Schedule I or II of the Convention on Psychotropic Substances, it shall be exported only pursuant to the issuance of an export permit. The Administrator may authorize the exportation of such substances if he finds that such exportation is permitted by section 1003(e) of the Act (21 U.S.C. 953(e)).

(d) The Administrator may require an applicant to submit such documents or written statements of fact relevant to the application as he deems necessary to determine whether the application should be granted. The failure of the applicant to provide such documents or statements within a reasonable time after being requested to do so shall be deemed to be a waiver by the applicant of an opportunity to present such documents or facts for consideration by the Administrator in granting or denying the application.

(e) If an exportation is approved, the Administrator shall issue an export permit bearing his or her signature or that of his or her delegate. Each permit will be assigned a permit number that is a unique, randomly generated identifier. A permit shall not be altered or changed by any person after being signed. Any change or alteration upon the face of any permit after it has been signed renders it void and of no effect.

Permits are not transferable. The Administrator or his/her delegate shall date and certify on each permit that the exporter named therein is thereby permitted as a registrant under the Act, to export, through the port of export named, one shipment of not to exceed the specified quantity of the named controlled substances, shipment to be made before a specified date. Only one shipment may be made on a single export permit. A single export permit shall authorize a quantity of goods to be exported at one place, at one time, for delivery to one consignee, on a single conveyance, at one place, on one bill of lading, air waybill, or commercial loading document; a single permit shall not authorize a quantity of goods to be exported if the goods are divided onto two or more conveyances. Each export permit shall be predicated upon, *inter alia,* an import certificate or other documentary evidence issued by a foreign competent national authority.

(f) No export permit shall be issued for the exportation, or reexportation, of any controlled substance to any country when the Administration has information to show that the estimates or assessments submitted with respect to that country for the current period, under the Single Convention on Narcotic Drugs, 1961, or the Convention on Psychotropic Substances, 1971, have been, or, considering the quantity proposed to be imported, will be exceeded. If it shall appear through subsequent advice received from the International Narcotics Control Board of the United Nations that the estimates or assessments of the country of destination have been adjusted to permit further importation of the controlled substance, an export permit may then be issued if otherwise permissible.

[36 FR 23625, Dec. 11, 1971, as amended at 37 FR 15923, Aug. 8, 1972. Redesignated at 38 FR 26609, Sept. 24, 1973, and amended at 52 FR 17290, May 7, 1987; 72 FR 72929, Dec. 26, 2007; 81 FR 97032, Dec. 30, 2016]

§ 1312.24 Distribution of export permit.

The Administration shall transmit the export permit to the competent national authority of the importing country and shall make available to the exporter an official record of the export permit through secure electronic means. The exporter, or their agent, must submit an official record of the export permit and/or required data concerning the export transaction to a customs officer at the port of export in compliance with all export control requirements of agencies with export control authorities under the Act or statutory authority other than the Controlled Substances Import and Export Act. The exporter must maintain an official record of the export permit (available from the secure network application on the DEA Diversion Control Division Web site after the Administration issues a transaction identification number) in accordance with part 1304 of this chapter as the record of authority for the exportation and shall transmit an official record of the export permit to the foreign importer. The exporter must ensure that an official record of the permit accompanies the shipment to its final destination. No shipment of controlled substances denied release for any reason shall be allowed to be released from the United States without subsequent authorization from the Administration.

[81 FR 97032, Dec. 30, 2016]

§ 1312.25 Amendment, cancellation, expiration of export permit.

(a) Exporters may only request that an export permit or application for an export permit be amended in accordance with paragraphs (a)(1) through (7) of this section. Requests for an amendment must be submitted through the DEA Diversion Control Division secure network application. Except as provided in paragraph (a)(5) of this section exporters must submit all requests for an amendment at least one full business day in advance of the date of release from the port of export. Exporters must specifically request that an amendment be made; supplementary information submitted by an exporter through the DEA Diversion Control Division secure network application will not automatically trigger the amendment process. While the request for an amendment is being reviewed by the Administration, the original permit will be temporarily stayed and may not be used to authorize release of a shipment of controlled substances. If the exporter's request for an amendment to an issued permit is granted by the Administration, the Administration will immediately cancel the original permit and re-issue the permit, as amended, with a revised permit number. The DEA and exporter will distribute the amended permit in accordance with § 1312.24. If a request for an amendment is denied by the Administration, the temporary stay will be lifted; once lifted, the originally issued permit may immediately be used to authorize release of a shipment in accordance with the terms of the permit.

(1) An exporter may request that an export permit or application for a permit be amended to change the National Drug Control number, description of the packaging, or trade name of the product, so long as the description is for the same basic class of controlled substance as in the original permit.

(2) An exporter may request that an export permit or application for a permit be amended to change the proposed port of export, the anticipated date of release by a customs officer, or the method of transport.

(3) An exporter may request that an export permit or application for a permit be amended to change the justification provided as to why an export shipment is needed to meet the legitimate scientific or medical needs of the country of import.

(4) An exporter may request that an export permit or application for a permit be amended to change any registrant notes.

(5) Prior to departure of the shipment from the exporter's registered location, an exporter may request that an export permit or application for a permit be amended to increase the total base weight of a controlled substance. However, the total base weight or the strength of the product (if listed) of a controlled substance may not exceed that permitted for import as indicated on the import permit from the foreign competent national authority. Exporters are not required to amend an export permit for the sole purpose of decreasing the total base weight of a controlled substance authorized to be exported. However, the balance of any unexported authorized quantity of controlled substances on an export permit is void upon release of a shipment on the issued permit or upon expiration of the unused permit in accordance with paragraph (b) of this section, whichever is sooner. Exporters must submit a request for an amendment to increase the total base weight of a controlled substance at least three business days in advance of the date of release from the port of export.

(6) An exporter may request that an export permit be amended to remove a controlled substance from the permit. However, an exporter may not amend an export permit to add or replace a controlled substance to the item(s) to be exported. Exporters who desire to export a different controlled substance than that contained on their issued export permit or permit application must submit a request for the permit or permit application to be canceled and request a new permit in accordance with § 1312.22.

(7) An exporter may not amend the exporter's name (as it appears on their DEA certificate of registration), the name of the foreign importer(s), or the foreign permit information as provided in the DEA Form 161, 161R, or 161R–EEA. Exporters who need to make any changes to any of these fields must submit a request for the permit or permit application to be canceled and request a new permit in accordance with § 1312.22.

(b) An export permit will be void and of no effect after the date specified therein, which date must conform to the expiration date specified in the supporting import certificate or other documentary evidence upon which the export permit is founded, but in no event will the date be more than 180 calendar days after the date the permit is issued.

(c) An export permit may be canceled after being issued, at the request of the exporter submitted to the Administration through the DEA Diversion Control Division secure network application, provided that no shipment has been made thereunder. Nothing in this part will affect the right, hereby reserved by the Administration, to cancel an export permit at any time for proper cause.

[81 FR 97032, Dec. 30, 2016]

§ 1312.26 Records required of exporter.

In addition to any other records required by this chapter, the exporter must keep a record of any serial numbers that might appear on packages of narcotic drugs in quantities of one ounce or more in such a manner as will identify the foreign consignee, along with an official record of the export permit, in accordance with part 1304 of this chapter.

[81 FR 97033, Dec. 30, 2016]

§ 1312.27 Export/reexport declaration.

(a) Any person registered or authorized to export and seeking to export any non-narcotic controlled substance listed in Schedule III, IV, or V, which is not subject to the requirement of an export permit pursuant to § 1312.23(b) or (c), or any person registered or authorized to export and seeking to export any controlled substance in Schedule V, must file a controlled substances export declaration (DEA Form 236) with the Administration through the DEA Diversion Control Division secure network application not less than 15 calendar days prior to the anticipated date of release by a customs officer at the port of export, and distribute an official record of the declaration as hereinafter directed in § 1312.28. The declaration must be signed and dated by the exporter and must contain the address of the registered location from which the substances will be shipped for exportation. Upon receipt and review, the Administration will issue a completed declaration a transaction identification number. The export declaration is not deemed filed, and therefore not valid, until the Administration has issued a transaction identification number. The exporter may only proceed with the export transaction once the transaction identification number has been issued.

(b)(1) DEA Form 236 must include the following information:

(i) The name/business name, address/business address, contact information (*e.g.*, telephone number(s), email address(es), etc.), and registration number, if any, of the exporter; and the name/business name, address/business address, contact information (*e.g.*, telephone number(s), email address(es), etc.), and registration number of the export broker, if any.

(ii) A detailed description of each controlled substance to be exported including the drug name, dosage form, National Drug Code (NDC) number, Administration Controlled Substance Code Number as set forth in part 1308 of this chapter, the number and size of the packages or containers, the name and quantity of the controlled substance contained in any finished dosage units, and the quantity of any controlled substance (expressed in anhydrous acid, base, or alkaloid) given in kilograms or parts thereof.

(iii) The anticipated date of release by a customs officer at the port of export, the port of export, the foreign port and country of entry, the carriers and shippers involved, method of shipment, the name of the vessel if applicable, and the name, address, and registration number, if any, of any forwarding agent utilized.

(iv) The name/business name, address/business address, and contact information (*e.g.*, telephone number(s), email address(es), etc.) of the consignee in the country of destination, and any registration or license number if the consignee is required to have such numbers either by the country of destination or under United States law. In addition, documentation must be provided to show that:

(A) The consignee is authorized under the laws and regulations of the country of destination to receive the controlled substances; and

(B) The substance is being imported for consumption within the importing country to satisfy medical, scientific or other legitimate purposes.

(v) The reexport of non-narcotic controlled substances in Schedules III and IV, and controlled substances in Schedule V is not permitted under the authority of 21 U.S.C. 953(e), except as provided below and in paragraph (b)(1)(vi) of this section:

(A) Bulk substances will not be reexported in the same form as exported from the United States, *i.e.*, the material must undergo further manufacturing process. This further manufactured material may only be reexported to a country of ultimate consumption.

(B) Finished dosage units, if reexported, will be in a commercial package, properly sealed and labeled for legitimate medical use in the country of destination.

(C) Any reexportation be made known to DEA at the time the initial DEA Form 236, Controlled Substances Import/Export Declaration is completed, by checking the box marked "other" on the certification. The following information will be furnished in the remarks section:

(*1*) Indicate "for reexport".

(*2*) Indicate if reexport is bulk or finished dosage units.

(*3*) Indicate product name, dosage strength, commercial package size, and quantity.

(*4*) Indicate name of consignee, complete address, and expected shipment date, as well as, the name and address of the ultimate consignee in the country to where the substances will be reexported.

(*5*) A statement that the consignee in the country of ultimate destination is authorized under the laws and regulations of the country of ultimate destination to receive the controlled substances.

(D) Shipments that have been exported from the United States and are refused by the consignee in either the first or second country, or subsequent member of the European Economic Area, or are otherwise unacceptable or undeliverable, may be returned to the registered exporter in the United States upon authorization of the Administration. In this circumstance, the exporter in the United States must file a written request for reexport, along with a completed DEA Form 236, with the Administration through the DEA Diversion Control Division secure network application. A brief summary of the facts that warrant the return of the substance to the United States along with an authorization from the country of export must be included with the request. DEA will evaluate the request after considering all the facts as well as the exporter's registration status with DEA. The substance may be returned to the United States only after affirmative authorization is issued in writing by DEA.

(vi) The reexport of non-narcotic controlled substances in Schedules III and IV, and controlled substances in Schedule V is permitted among members of the European Economic Area only as provided below:

(A) The controlled substance will not be exported from the second country or a subsequent country, except that the controlled substance may be exported from a second country or a subsequent country that is a member of the European Economic Area to another country that is a member of the European Economic Area, provided that the first country is also a member of the European Economic Area; each country is a party to the Convention on Psychotropic Substances, 1971, as amended; and each country has instituted and maintains, in conformity with such Convention, a system of controls of imports of controlled substances which the Attorney General deems adequate.

(B) Each shipment of finished dosage units, if reexported, must be in a commercial package, properly sealed and labeled for legitimate medical use in the country of destination.

(C) Any reexportation must be made known to DEA at the time the initial DEA Form 236, Controlled Substances Import/Export Declaration is completed, by checking the box marked "other" on the certification. In addition to the requirements of paragraph (b) of this section, the following information will be furnished in the remarks section:

(*1*) Indicate "for reexport among members of the European Economic Area".

(*2*) Indicate if reexport is bulk or finished dosage units.

(*3*) Indicate product name, dosage strength, commercial package size, and quantity.

(*4*) Indicate the name/business name, address/business address, contact information (*e.g.*, telephone number(s), email address(es) and business of the consignee in the first country).

(*5*) A statement that the consignee in the second country, and any subsequent consignee within the European

Economic Area, is authorized under the laws and regulations of the second and/or subsequent country to receive the controlled substances.

(2) With respect to reexports among members of the European Economic Area, the requirements of paragraph (b)(1) of this section shall apply only with respect to the export from the United States to the first country and not to any subsequent export from that country to another country of the European Economic Area.

(c) Notwithstanding the time limitations included in paragraph (a) of this section, a registrant may obtain a special waiver of these time limitations in emergency or unusual instances; provided that a specific confirmation is received from the Administrator or his delegate advising the registrant to proceed pursuant to the special waiver.

(d) *Return information*—(1) *Return information for exports.* Within 30 calendar days after the controlled substance is released by a customs officer at the port of export, or within 10 calendar days after receipt of a written request by the Administration to the exporter, whichever is sooner, the exporter must file a report with the Administration through the DEA Diversion Control Division secure network application specifying the particulars of the transaction. This report must include the following information: The date on which the controlled substance left the registered location; the date on which the controlled substance was released by a customs officer; the actual quantity of the controlled substance that left the registered location; and the actual quantity of the controlled substance released by a customs officer at the port of export; the actual port of export. Upon receipt and review, the Administration will assign a completed report a transaction identification number. The report will not be deemed filed until the Administration has issued a transaction identification number.

(2) *Return information for reexports outside of the European Economic Area*—(i) *Return information for export from the United States, for reexport.* Within 30 calendar days after the controlled substance is released by a customs officer at the port of export the exporter must file a report with the Administration through the DEA Diversion Control Division secure network application specifying the particulars of the transaction. This report must include the following information: The date on which the controlled substance left the registered location; the date on which the controlled substance was released by a customs officer at the port of export; the actual quantity of controlled substance released by a customs officer at the port of export; and the actual port of export. Upon receipt and review, the Administration will assign a completed report a transaction identification number. The report will not be deemed filed until the Administration has issued a transaction identification number.

(ii) *Return information for export from a first country that is or is not a member of the European Economic Area to a country outside of the European Economic Area; return information for export from a first country that is not a member of the European Economic Area to a member of the European Economic Area.* Within 30 calendar days after the controlled substance is exported from the first country to the second country the exporter must file a report with the Administration through the DEA Diversion Control Division secure network application specifying the particulars of the export from the first country. If the permit issued by the Administration authorized the reexport of a controlled substance from the first country to more than one second country, a report for each individual reexport is required. These reports must include the following information: Name of second country; actual quantity of controlled substance shipped; the date shipped from the first country; and the actual port from which the controlled substances were shipped from the first country. Upon receipt and review, the Administration will assign each completed report a transaction identification number. The report will not be deemed filed until the Administration has issued a transaction identification number.

(3) *Reexports among members of the European Economic Area*—(i) *Return information for exports from the United States,*

for reexport among members of the European Economic Area. Exporters must comply with the return reporting requirements of paragraph (d)(2)(i) of this section.

(ii) *Reexports among members of the European Economic Area.* Within 30 calendar days after the controlled substance is exported from the first country to the second country, and within 30 calendar days of each subsequent reexport within the European Economic Area, if any, the exporter must file a report with the Administration through the DEA Diversion Control Division secure network application specifying the particulars of the export. These reports must include the name of country to which the controlled substance was reexported to another member of the European Economic Area; the actual quantity of controlled substance shipped; the date shipped from the first country, the name/business name, address/business address, contact information (*e.g.*, telephone number(s), email address(es), etc.) and business of the consignee; and the name/business name, address/business address, contact information (*e.g.*, telephone number(s), email address(es), etc.) and business of the exporter. Upon receipt and review, the Administration will assign each completed report a transaction identification number. The report will not be deemed filed until the Administration has issued a transaction identification number.

(e) An exporter may amend an export declaration in the same circumstances in which an exporter may request amendment to an export permit, as set forth in §1312.25(a)(1) through (7). Amendments to declarations must be submitted through the DEA Diversion Control Division secure network application. Except as provided in §1312.25(a)(5) exporters must submit all amendments at least one full business day in advance of the date of release by a customs officer. Exporters must specifically note that an amendment is being made; supplementary information submitted by an exporter through the DEA Diversion Control Division secure network application will not automatically be considered an amendment. Upon receipt and review, the Administration will assign each completed amendment a transaction identification number. The amendment will not be deemed filed until the Administration issues a transaction identification number. The DEA and the exporter will distribute the amended declaration in accordance with §1312.28. A filed amendment will not change the date that the declaration becomes void and of no effect in accordance with paragraph (f) of this section.

(f) An export declaration may be canceled after being filed with the Administration, at the request of the exporter, provided no shipment has been made thereunder. Export declarations shall become void and of no effect 180 calendar days after the date the declaration is deemed filed with the Administration.

(g) *Denied release at the port of export.* In the event that a shipment of controlled substances has been denied release by a customs officer at the port of export for any reason, the exporter who attempted to have the shipment released must, within 5 business days of the denial, report to the Administration that the shipment was denied release and the reason for denial. Such report must be transmitted to the Administration through the DEA Diversion Control Division secure network application. This report must include the following information: The quantity of the controlled substance denied release; the date on which release was denied; and the basis for the denied release. Upon the exporter's report of a denied release, DEA will assign the report a transaction identification number and the export declaration will be void and of no effect. No shipment of controlled substances denied release for any reason will be allowed to be released unless the exporter files a new declaration and the Administration issues a new transaction identification number.

[36 FR 7815, Apr. 24, 1971, as amended at 37 FR 15923, Aug. 8, 1972. Redesignated at 38 FR 26609, Sept. 24, 1973, and amended at 45 FR 74715, Nov. 12, 1980; 51 FR 5319, Feb. 13, 1986; 52 FR 17290, May 7, 1987; 62 FR 13969, Mar. 24, 1997; 75 FR 10683, Mar. 9, 2010; 81 FR 97033, Dec. 30, 2016]

§ 1312.28 Distribution of export declaration.

(a) The exporter must ensure that an official record of the export declaration (available from the DEA Diversion Control Division secure network application after the Administration issues a transaction identification number) accompanies the shipment of controlled substances to its destination.

(b) The exporter, or their agent, must submit an official record of the export declaration and/or required data concerning the export transaction to a customs officer at the port of export in compliance with all export control requirements of agencies with export control authorities under the Act or statutory authority other than the Controlled Substances Import and Export Act.

(c) The exporter must maintain an official record of the export declaration and return information (both available from the Diversion Control Division secure network application after the Administration issues a transaction identification number) required pursuant to § 1312.27(d) as his or her record of authority for the exportation, in accordance with part 1304 of this chapter.

[81 FR 97035, Dec. 30, 2016]

§ 1312.29 Domestic release prohibited.

An exporter or a forwarding agent acting for an exporter must either deliver the controlled substances to the port or border, or deliver the controlled substances to a bonded carrier approved by the consignor for delivery to the port or border, and may not, under any other circumstances, release a shipment of controlled substances to anyone, including the foreign consignee or his agent, within the United States.

§ 1312.30 Schedule III, IV, and V non-narcotic controlled substances requiring an import and export permit.

The following Schedule III, IV, and V non-narcotic controlled substances have been specifically designated by the Administrator of the Drug Enforcement Administration as requiring import and export permits pursuant to sections 201(d)(1), 1002(b)(2), and 1003(e)(3) of the Act (21 U.S.C. 811(d)(1), 952(b)(2), and 953(e)(3)):

(a) Dronabinol (synthetic) in sesame oil and encapsulated in a soft gelatin capsule in a U.S. Food and Drug Administration approved product.

(b) A drug product in finished dosage formulation that has been approved by the U.S. Food and Drug Administration that contains cannabidiol (2-[1R-3-methyl-6R-(1-methylethenyl)-2-cyclohexen-1-yl]-5-pentyl-1,3-benzenediol) derived from cannabis and no more than 0.1 percent (w/w) residual tetrahydrocannabinols.

[52 FR 17291, May 7, 1987, as amended at 64 FR 35930, July 2, 1999; 83 FR 48953, Sept. 28, 2018]

Transshipment and In-Transit Shipment of Controlled Substances

§ 1312.31 Schedule I: Application for prior written approval.

(a) A controlled substance listed in schedule I may be imported into the United States for transshipment, or may be transferred or transshipped within the United States for immediate exportation, provided that:

(1) The controlled substance is necessary for scientific, medical, or other legitimate purposes in the country of destination, and

(2) A transshipment permit has been issued by the Administrator.

(b) An application for a transshipment permit must be submitted to the Regulatory Section, Diversion Control Division, Drug Enforcement Administration, at least 30 calendar days, or in the case of an emergency as soon as is practicable, prior to the expected date of arrival at the first port in the United States. See the Table of DEA Mailing Addresses in § 1321.01 of this chapter for the current mailing address. A separate permit is required for each shipment of controlled substance to be imported, transferred, or transshipped. Each application must contain the following:

(1) The date of execution;

(2) The identification and description of the controlled substance;

(3) The net quantity thereof;

(4) The number and size of the controlled substance containers;

(5) The name, address, and business of the foreign exporter;

(6) The foreign port of exportation;

(7) The approximate date of exportation;

(8) The identification of the exporting carrier;

(9) The name, address and business of the importer, transferor, or transshipper;

(10) The registration number, if any, of the importer, transferor or transshipper;

(11) The U.S. port of entry;

(12) The approximate date of entry;

(13) The name, address and business of the consignee at the foreign port of entry;

(14) The shipping route from the U.S. port of exportation to the foreign port of entry;

(15) The approximate date of receipt by the consignee at the foreign port of entry; and

(16) The signature of the importer, transferor or transshipper, or his agent accompanied by the agent's title.

(c) An application shall be accompanied by an export license, permit, or a certified copy of the export license, permit, or other authorization, issued by a competent authority of the country of origin (or other documentary evidence deemed adequate by the Administrator).

(d) An application shall be accompanied by an import license or permit or a certified copy of such license or permit issued by a competent authority of the country of destination (or other documentary evidence deemed adequate by the Administrator), indicating that the controlled substance:

(1) Is to be applied exclusively to scientific, medical or other legitimate uses within the country of destination;

(2) Will not be exported from such country;

(3) Is needed therein because there is an actual shortage thereof and a demand therefor for scientific, medical or other legitimate uses within such country; and

(4) If the import license or permit, or the certified copy of such, is not written in English or bilingual with another language and English, the application must include a certified translation of the permit or license. For purposes of this requirement, certified translation means that the translator has signed the translation legally attesting the accuracy of the translation.

(e) Verification by an American consular officer of the signatures on a foreign import license or permit shall be required, if such license or permit does not bear the seal of the authority signing them.

(f) The Administrator may require an applicant to submit such documents or written statements of fact relevant to the application as he deems necessary to determine whether the application should be granted. The failure of the applicant to provide such documents or statements within a reasonable time after being requested to do so shall be deemed to be a waiver by the applicant of an opportunity to present such documents or facts for consideration by the Administrator in granting or denying the application.

(g) The Administrator shall, within 21 days from the date of receipt of the application, either grant or deny the application. The applicant shall be accorded an opportunity to amend the application, with the Administrator either granting or denying the amended application within 7 days of its receipt. If the Administrator does not grant or deny the application within 21 days of its receipt, or in the case of an amended application, within 7 days of its receipt, the application shall be deemed approved and the applicant may proceed.

[36 FR 7815, Apr. 24, 1971, as amended at 37 FR 15923, Aug. 8, 1972. Redesignated at 38 FR 26609, Sept. 24, 1973, and further amended at 45 FR 74715, Nov. 12, 1980; 51 FR 5319, Feb. 13, 1986; 53 FR 48244, Nov. 30, 1988; 62 FR 13969, Mar. 24, 1997; 75 FR 10683, Mar. 9, 2010; 81 FR 97035, Dec. 30, 2016]

§ 1312.32 Schedules II, III, IV: Advance notice.

(a) A controlled substance listed in Schedules II, III, or IV may be imported into the United States for transshipment, or may be transferred or transshipped within the United States for immediate exportation, provided that written notice is submitted to the Regulatory Section, Diversion Control Division, Drug Enforcement Administration, at least 15 calendar days prior to the expected date of date of arrival at the first port in the United States. See the Table of DEA mailing Addresses in § 1321.01 of this chapter for the current mailing addresses.

(b) A separate advance notice is required for each shipment of controlled substance to be imported, transferred, or transshipped. Each advance notice must contain those items required by § 1312.31(b) and (c). If the export license, permit, or other authorization, issued by a competent national authority of the country of origin, is not written in English or bilingual with another language and English, the notice must be accompanied by a certified translation of the export license, permit, or other authorization. For purposes of this requirement, certified translation means that the translator has signed the translation legally attesting the accuracy of the translation.

[81 FR 97036, Dec. 30, 2016]

HEARINGS

§ 1312.41 Hearings generally.

(a) In any case where the Administrator shall hold a hearing regarding the denial of an application for an import, export or transshipment permit, the procedures for such hearing shall be governed generally by the adjudication procedures set forth in the Administrative Procedure Act (5 U.S.C. 551–559) and specifically by sections 1002 and 1003 of the Act (21 U.S.C. 952 and 953), by §§ 1312.42–1312.47, and by the procedures for administrative hearings under the Act set forth in §§ 1316.41–1316.67 of this chapter.

(b) [Reserved]

[36 FR 23625, Dec. 11, 1971, as amended at 37 FR 15923, Aug. 8, 1972. Redesignated at 38 FR 26609, Sept. 24, 1973]

§ 1312.42 Purpose of hearing.

(a) If requested by a person applying for an import, export, or transshipment permit, the Administrator shall hold a hearing for the purpose of receiving factual evidence regarding the issues involved in the issuance or denial of such permit to such person.

(b) Extensive argument should not be offered into evidence but rather presented in opening or closing statements of counsel or in memoranda or proposed findings of fact and conclusions of law.

[36 FR 23625, Dec. 11, 1971, as amended at 37 FR 15923, Aug. 8, 1972. Redesignated at 38 FR 26609, Sept. 24, 1973]

§ 1312.43 Waiver or modification of rules.

The Administrator of the presiding officer (with respect to matters pending before him) may modify or waive any rule in this part by notice in advance of the hearing, if he determines that no party in the hearing will be unduly prejudiced and the ends of justice will thereby be served. Such notice of modification or waiver shall be made a part of the record of the hearing.

[36 FR 23625, Dec. 11, 1971. Redesignated at 38 FR 26609, Sept. 24, 1973]

§ 1312.44 Request for hearing or appearance; waiver.

(a) Any applicant entitled to a hearing pursuant to § 1312.42 and who desires a hearing on the denial of his application for an import, export, or transshipment permit shall, within 30 days after the date of receipt of the denial of his application, file with the Administrator a written request for a hearing in the form prescribed in § 1316.47 of this chapter.

(b) Any applicant entitled to a hearing pursuant to § 1312.42 may, within the period permitted for filing a request for a hearing, file with the Administrator a waiver of an opportunity for a hearing, together with a written statement regarding his position on the matters of fact and law involved in such hearing. Such statement, if admissible, shall be made a part of the record and shall be considered in light of the lack of opportunity for cross-examination in determining the weight to be attached to matters of fact asserted therein.

(c) If any applicant entitled to a hearing pursuant to § 1312.42 fails to appear at the hearing, he shall be deemed to have waived his opportunity for the hearing unless he shows good cause for such failure.

(d) If the applicant waives or is deemed to have waived this opportunity for the hearing, the Administrator may cancel the hearing, if scheduled, and issue his final order pursuant to § 1312.47 without a hearing.

[37 FR 15923, Aug. 8, 1972. Redesignated at 38 FR 26609, Sept. 24, 1973]

§ 1312.45 Burden of proof.

At any hearing on the denial of an application for an import, export, or transshipment permit, the Administrator shall have the burden of proving that the requirements for such permit pursuant to sections 1002, 1003, and 1004 of the Act (21 U.S.C. 952, 953, and 954) are not satisfied.

[37 FR 15924, Aug. 8, 1972. Redesignated at 38 FR 26609, Sept. 24, 1973]

§ 1312.46 Time and place of hearing.

(a) If any applicant for an import, export, or transshipment permit requests a hearing on the issuance or denial of his application, the Administrator shall hold such hearing. Notice of the hearing shall be given to the applicant of the time and place at least 30 days prior to the hearing, unless the applicant waives such notice and requests the hearing be held at an earlier time, in which case the Administrator shall fix a date for such hearing as early as reasonably possible.

(b) The hearing will commence at the place and time designated in the notice given pursuant to paragraph (a) of this section but thereafter it may be moved to a different place and may be continued from day to day or recessed to a later day without notice other than announcement thereof by the presiding officer at the hearing.

[37 FR 15924, Aug. 8, 1972. Redesignated at 38 FR 26609, Sept. 24, 1973]

§ 1312.47 Final order.

As soon as practicable after the presiding officer has certified the record to the Administrator, the Administrator shall issue his order on the issuance or denial of the application for and import, export, or transshipment permit. The order shall include the findings of fact and conclusions of law upon which the order is based. The Administrator shall serve one copy of his order upon the applicant.

[37 FR 15924, Aug. 8, 1972. Redesignated at 38 FR 26609, Sept. 24, 1973]

PART 1313—IMPORTATION AND EXPORTATION OF LIST I AND LIST II CHEMICALS

Sec.

AUTHORITY: 21 U.S.C. 802, 830, 871(b), 971.

SOURCE: 54 FR 31665, Aug. 1, 1989, unless otherwise noted.

§1313.01 Scope.

Procedures governing the importation, exportation, transshipment and in-transit shipment of listed chemicals pursuant to section 1018 of the Act (21 U.S.C. 971) are governed generally by that section and specifically by the sections of this part.

[54 FR 31665, Aug. 1, 1989, as amended at 60 FR 32465, June 22, 1995]

§1313.02 Definitions.

Any term used in this part shall have the definition set forth in section 102 of the Act (21 U.S.C. 802) or part 1300 of this chapter.

[62 FR 13969, Mar. 24, 1997]

§1313.03 Forms applicable to this part.

Form	Access/ submission
DEA Form 486, Import/Export Declaration for List I and List II Chemicals.	electronic.
DEA Form 486A Import Declaration for ephedrine, pseudoephedrine, and phenylpropanolamine (including drug products containing these chemicals).	electronic.

[81 FR 97036, Dec. 30, 2016]

§1313.05 Requirements for an established business relationship.

To document that an importer or exporter has an established business relationship with a customer, the importer or exporter must provide the Administrator with the following information in accordance with the waiver of 15-day advance notice requirements of §1313.15 or §1313.24:

(a) The name and street address of the chemical importer or exporter and of each regular customer;

(b) The telephone number, contact person, and where available, the facsimile number for the chemical importer or exporter and for each regular customer;

(c) The nature of the regular customer's business (*i.e.*, importer, exporter, distributor, manufacturer, etc.), and if known, the use to which the listed chemical or chemicals will be applied;

(d) The duration of the business relationship;

(e) The frequency and number of transactions occurring during the preceding 12-month period;

(f) The amounts and the listed chemical or chemicals involved in regulated transactions between the chemical importer or exporter and regular customer;

(g) The method of delivery (direct shipment or through a broker or forwarding agent); and

(h) Other information that the chemical importer or exporter considers relevant for determining whether a customer is a regular customer.

[72 FR 17407, Apr. 9, 2007]

§1313.08 Requirements for establishing a record as an importer.

To establish a record as an importer, the regulated person must provide the Administrator with the following information in accordance with the waiver of the 15-day advance notice requirements of §1313.15:

(a) The name, DEA registration number (where applicable), street address, telephone number, and, where available, the facsimile number of the regulated person and of each foreign supplier; and

(b) The frequency and number of transactions occurring during the preceding 12 month period.

[72 FR 17407, Apr. 9, 2007]

Importation of Listed Chemicals

§1313.12 Notification prior to import.

(a) Each regulated person who seeks to import a listed chemical that meets or exceeds the threshold quantities identified in §1310.04(f) of this chapter or is a listed chemical for which no threshold has been established as identified in §1310.04(g) of this chapter, must notify the Administration of the intended import by filing an import declaration (on DEA Form 486/486A) not later than 15 calendar days before the date of release by a customs officer at the port of entry. Regulated persons who seek to import a listed chemical below the threshold quantities identified in §1310.04(f) are not required to file an import declaration in advance of the release by a customs officer.

(b) A complete and accurate declaration (DEA Form 486/486A) must be filed with the Administration through the DEA Diversion Control Division secure network application not later than 15 calendar days prior to the date of release by a customs officer at the port of entry. The declaration must be signed and dated by the importer and must contain the address of the final destination for the shipment, which for List I chemicals must be a registered location of the importer. Upon receipt and review, the Administration will assign a transaction identification number to each completed declaration. The 15 calendar days shall begin on the date that the regulated person submits a completed declaration, without regard to the date that the Administration assigns a transaction identification number. Listed chemicals meeting or exceeding the threshold quantities identified in § 1310.04(f) of this chapter or for which no threshold has been established may not be imported until a transaction identification number has been issued.

(c) The 15-calendar-day advance notification requirement for listed chemical imports may be waived, in whole or in part, for the following:

(1) Any importation that meets both of the following requirements:

(i) The regulated person has satisfied the requirements for reporting to the Administration as a regular importer of the listed chemicals.

(ii) The importer intends to transfer the listed chemicals to a person who is a regular customer for the chemical, as defined in § 1300.02 of this chapter.

(2) A specific listed chemical, as set forth in paragraph (f) of this section, for which the Administrator determines that advance notification is not necessary for effective chemical diversion control.

(d) For imports meeting the requirements of paragraph (c)(1) of this section, the declaration (DEA Form 486/486A) must be filed with the Administration through the DEA Diversion Control Division secure network application at least three business days before the date of release by a customs officer at the port of entry. The declaration must be signed and dated by the importer and must contain the address of the final destination for the shipment, which must be a registered location of the importer (for List I chemicals). Upon receipt and review, the Administration will assign a transaction identification number to each completed declaration. The importer may proceed with the import transaction only once the transaction identification number has been issued.

(e) For importations where advance notification is waived pursuant to paragraph (c)(2) of this section no DEA Form 486 is required; however, the regulated person must submit quarterly reports to the Regulatory Section, Diversion Control Division, Drug Enforcement Administration, not later than the 15th day of the month following the end of each quarter. See the Table of DEA Mailing Addresses in § 1321.01 of this chapter for the current mailing address. The report shall contain the following information regarding each individual importation:

(1) The name of the listed chemical;

(2) The quantity and date imported;

(3) The name and full business address of the supplier;

(4) The foreign port of embarkation; and

(5) The port of entry.

(f) The 15 day advance notification requirement set forth in paragraph (a) has been waived for imports of the following listed chemicals:

(1) Acetone.

(2) 2-Butanone (or Methyl Ethyl Ketone or MEK).

(3) Toluene.

[54 FR 31665, Aug. 1, 1989, as amended at 59 FR 51367, Oct. 11, 1994; 60 FR 32464, June 22, 1995; 66 FR 46520, Sept. 6, 2001; 67 FR 49569, July 31, 2002; 72 FR 17407, Apr. 9, 2007; 75 FR 10683, Mar. 9, 2010; 77 FR 4237, Jan. 27, 2012; 81 FR 97036, Dec. 30, 2016]

§ 1313.13 Requirements of import declaration.

(a) Any List I or List II chemical listed in § 1310.02 of this chapter may be imported if that chemical is necessary for medical, commercial, scientific, or other legitimate uses within the United States. Chemical importations into the United States for immediate transfer/transshipment outside the United States must comply with the procedures set forth in §1313.31 and all other applicable laws.

(b) The DEA Form 486/486A must include the following information:

(1) The name/business name, address/business address, and contact information (*e.g.*, telephone number(s), email address(es), etc.) of the chemical importer; the name/business name, address/business address, and contact information (*e.g.*, telephone number(s), email address(es), etc.) of the broker or forwarding agent (if any); and

(2) The name and description of each listed chemical as it appears on the label or container, the name of each chemical as it is designated in §1310.02 of this chapter, the size or weight of container, the number of containers, the net weight of each listed chemical given in kilograms or parts thereof, and the gross weight of the shipment given in kilograms or parts thereof; and

(3) The date of release by a customs officer at the port of entry, the foreign port and country of export, and the port of entry; and

(4) The name/business name, address/business address, and contact information (*e.g.*, telephone number(s), email address(es), etc.) of the consignor in the foreign country of exportation; and

(5) The name/business name, address/business address, and contact information (*e.g.*, telephone number(s), email address(es), etc.) of the person or persons to whom the importer intends to transfer the listed chemical and the quantity to be transferred to each transferee.

(c) Any regulated person importing ephedrine, pseudoephedrine, or phenylpropanolamine must submit, on the import declaration (DEA Form 486A), all information known to the importer on the chain of distribution of the chemical from the manufacturer to the importer. Ephedrine, pseudoephedrine, or phenylpropanolamine include each of the salts, optical isomers, and salts of optical isomers of the chemical.

(d) Import declarations shall become void and of no effect 180 calendar days after the date the declaration is deemed filed with the Administration.

[81 FR 97036, Dec. 30, 2016]

§ 1313.14 Disposition of import declaration.

The importer, or their agent, must submit an official record of the import declaration and/or required data concerning the import transaction to a customs officer at the port of entry in compliance with all import control requirements of agencies with import control authorities under the Act or statutory authority other than the Controlled Substances Import and Export Act. For List I chemicals, the final destination of the import transaction must only be the registered location of the importer (*i.e.*, drop shipments are prohibited). A regulated person must maintain an official record of the declaration (available from the DEA Diversion Control Division secure network application after the Administration issues a transaction identification number) in accordance with part 1310 of this chapter as the record of the import. Official records of import declarations involving listed chemicals must be retained for two years.

[81 FR 97037, Dec. 30, 2016]

§ 1313.15 Qualification of regular importers.

(a) Each regulated person seeking designation as a "regular importer" shall provide, by certified mail return receipt requested, to the Administration such information as is required under §1313.08 documenting their status as a regular importer.

(b) Each regulated person making application under paragraph (a) of this section shall be considered a "regular importer" 30 calendar days after receipt of the application by the Administration, as indicated on the return receipt, unless the regulated person is otherwise notified in writing by the Administration.

(c) The Administrator, may, at any time, disqualify a regulated person's status as a regular importer on the grounds that the chemical being imported may be diverted to the clandestine manufacture of a controlled substance.

(d) Unless the Administration notifies the chemical importer to the contrary, the qualification of a regular importer of any one of these three chemicals, acetone, 2-Butanone (MEK), or toluene, qualifies that importer as a regular importer of all three of these chemicals.

(e) All chemical importers shall be required to file a DEA Form 486 as required by Section 1313.12.

[60 FR 32464, June 22, 1995, as amended at 62 FR 13969, Mar. 24, 1997; 72 FR 17407, Apr. 9, 2007; 81 FR 97037, Dec. 30, 2016]

§ 1313.16 Updated notice for change in circumstances.

(a) In the case of a notice under § 1313.12(a) submitted by a regulated person, if the transferee identified in the notice is not a regular customer, the importer may not transfer the listed chemical until after the expiration of the 15-day period beginning on the date on which the notice is submitted to the Administration.

(b) After a notice under § 1313.12(a) or (d) is submitted to the Administration, if circumstances change and the importer will not be transferring the listed chemical to the transferee identified in the notice, or will be transferring a greater quantity of the chemical than specified in the notice, the importer must update the notice to identify the most recent prospective transferee or the most recent quantity or both (as the case may be) and may not transfer the listed chemical until after the expiration of the 15 calendar day period beginning on the date on which the update is filed with the Administration, or, if the import is being made by a regular importer or intended for transfer to a regular customer, three business days. The preceding sentence applies with respect to changing circumstances regarding a transferee or quantity identified in an update to the same extent and in the same manner as the sentence applies with respect to changing circumstances regarding a transferee or quantity identified in the original notice under § 1313.12(a) or (d). Amended declarations must be submitted to the Administration through the DEA Diversion Control Division secure network application. The amendment must be signed and dated by the importer. Upon receipt and review, the Administration will assign each completed amendment a transaction identification number. Such shipment of listed chemicals may not be imported into the United States until the transaction identification number has been issued.

(c) In the case of a transfer of a listed chemical that is subject to a 15-day restriction, the transferee involved shall, upon the expiration of the 15-day period, be considered to qualify as a regular customer, unless the Administration otherwise notifies the importer involved in writing.

(d) With respect to a transfer of a listed chemical with which a notice or update referred to in § 1313.12(a) or (d) is concerned:

(1) The Administration—

(i) May, in accordance with the same procedures as apply under §§ 1313.51 through 1313.57, order the suspension of the transfer of the listed chemical by the importer involved, except for a transfer to a regular customer, on the ground that the chemical may be diverted to the clandestine manufacture of a controlled substance (without regard to the form of the chemical that may be diverted, including the diversion of a finished drug product to be manufactured from bulk chemicals to be transferred), subject to the Administration ordering the suspension before the expiration of the 15-day period with respect to the importation (in any case in which such a period applies); and

(ii) May, for purposes of this paragraph (d), disqualify a regular customer on that ground.

(2) From and after the time when the Administration provides written notice of the order under paragraph (d)(1)(i) of this section (including a statement of the legal and factual basis for the order) to the importer, the importer may not carry out the transfer.

(e) For purposes of this section:

(1) The term *transfer*, with respect to a listed chemical, includes the sale of the chemical.

(2) The term *transferee* means a person to whom an importer transfers a listed chemical.

[72 FR 17407, Apr. 9, 2007, as amended at 81 FR 97037, Dec. 30, 2016]

§1313.17 Return declaration for imports.

(a) *Return information.* Within 30 calendar days after actual receipt of a listed chemical at the importer's registered location or place of business if not required to be registered, the importer must file a report with the Administration through the DEA Diversion Control Division secure network application specifying the particulars of the transaction. This report must include the following information: The date on which the listed chemical was released by a customs officer at the port of entry; the date on which the listed chemical arrived at the importer's registered location or place of business; the actual quantity of the listed chemical released; the actual quantity of the listed chemical that arrived at the importer's location; the date of any subsequent transfer; a description of the subsequent transfer, including the actual quantity transferred, chemical, container, and name of transferees; the actual port of entry; and any other information as the Administration may specify. A single report may include the particulars of both the importation and distribution. If the importer has not distributed all chemicals imported by the end of the initial 30 calendar day period, the importer must file supplemental reports not later than 30 calendar days from the date of any further distribution, until the distribution or other disposition of all chemicals imported under the import declaration or any amendment or other update is accounted for. Upon receipt and review, the Administration will assign each completed report a transaction identification number. In determining whether the importer has complied with the requirement to file within 30 calendar days, the report shall be deemed filed on the first date on which a complete report is filed.

(b) If an importation for which a DEA Form 486/486A has been filed fails to take place, the importer must report to the Administration that the importation did not occur through the DEA Diversion Control Division secure network application.

(c) *Denied release at the port of entry.* In the event that a shipment of listed chemicals has been denied release by a customs officer at the port of entry for any reason, the importer who attempted to have the shipment released, within 5 business days of the denial, report to the Administration that the shipment was denied release and the reason for denial. Such report must be transmitted to the Administration through the DEA Diversion Control Division secure network application. This report must include the following information: The quantity of the listed chemical denied release; the date on which release was denied; and the basis for the denied release. Upon the importer's report of a denied release, the DEA will assign the report a transaction identification number and the import declaration will be void and of no effect. No shipment of listed chemicals denied release for any reason will be allowed entry into the United States without a subsequent refiling of an import declaration. Following such refiling the importer may request release of the listed chemicals immediately after receipt of a transaction identification number without regard to the 15 day advance filing requirement in §1313.12(b).

[81 FR 97037, Dec. 30, 2016]

Exportation of Listed Chemicals

§1313.21 Notification prior to export.

(a) Each regulated person who seeks to export a listed chemical that meets or exceeds the threshold quantities identified in §1310.04(f) of this chapter, or is a listed chemical for which no threshold has been established as identified in §1310.04(g) of this chapter, must notify the Administration of the intended export by filing an export declaration (DEA Form 486) not later than 15 calendar days before the date of release by a customs officer at the port of export. Regulated persons who seek to export a listed chemical below the threshold quantities identified in §1310.04(f) are not required to file an export declaration in advance of the export.

(b) A complete and accurate declaration (DEA Form 486) must be filed with the Administration through the DEA

Diversion Control Division secure network application not later than 15 calendar days prior to the date of release by a customs officer at the port of export. The declaration must be signed and dated by the exporter and must contain the address from which the listed chemicals will be shipped for exportation. Upon receipt and review, the Administration will assign a transaction identification number to each completed declaration. The 15 calendar days shall begin on the date that the regulated person files a completed declaration without regard to the date that the Administration assigns a transaction identification number. Exporters may not request release of a listed chemical until a transaction identification number has been issued.

(c) The 15 calendar day advance notification requirement for listed chemical exports may be waived, in whole or in part, for:

(1) Any regulated person who has satisfied the requirements of § 1313.24 for reporting to the Administration an established business relationship, as defined in § 1300.02 of this chapter, with a foreign customer.

(2) A specific listed chemical to a specified country, as set forth in paragraph (f) of this section, for which the Administrator determines that advance notification is not necessary for effective chemical diversion control.

(d) For exports meeting the requirements of paragraph (c)(1) of this section, the declaration (DEA Form 486) must be filed with the Administration through the DEA Diversion Control Division secure network application at least three business days before the date of release by a customs officer. The declaration must be signed and dated by the exporter and must contain the address from which the listed chemicals will be shipped for exportation. Upon receipt and review, the Administration will assign a transaction identification number to each completed declaration. The exporter may only proceed with the export transaction once the transaction identification number has been issued.

(e) For exportations where advance notification is waived pursuant to paragraph (c)(2) of this section no DEA Form 486 is required; however, the regulated person must submit quarterly reports with the Regulatory Section, Diversion Control Division, Drug Enforcement Administration, not later than the 15th day of the month following the end of each quarter. See the Table of DEA Mailing Addresses in § 1321.01 of this chapter for the current mailing address. Such report shall contain the following information regarding each individual exportation:

(1) The name of the listed chemical;

(2) The quantity and date exported;

(3) The name and full business address of the foreign customer;

(4) The port of embarkation; and

(5) The foreign port of entry.

(f) The 15 day advance notification requirement set forth in paragraph (a) of this section has been waived for exports of the following listed chemicals to the following countries:

Name of Chemical	Country
[Reserved]	

(g) No person shall export or cause to be exported any listed chemical, knowing or having reasonable cause to believe the export is in violation of the laws of the country to which the chemical is exported or the chemical will be used to manufacture a controlled substance in violation of the Act or the laws of the country to which the chemical is exported. The Administration will publish a notice of foreign import restrictions for listed chemicals of which DEA has knowledge as provided in § 1313.25.

(h) Export declarations shall become void and of no effect 180 calendar days after the date the declaration is deemed filed with the Administration.

[54 FR 31665, Aug. 1, 1989, as amended at 59 FR 51367, Oct. 11, 1994; 60 FR 32464, June 22, 1995; 62 FR 13969, Mar. 24, 1997; 66 FR 46520, Sept. 6, 2001; 67 FR 49569, July 31, 2002; 75 FR 10683, Mar. 9, 2010; 77 FR 4237, Jan. 27, 2012; 81 FR 97038, Dec. 30, 2016]

§ 1313.22 Export declaration.

(a) Any List I or List II chemical listed in § 1310.02 of this chapter which meets or exceeds the quantitative threshold criteria established in § 1310.04(f) of this chapter or is a listed chemical for which no threshold has been established as identified in

§ 1310.04(g) of this chapter, may be exported if that chemical is needed for medical, commercial, scientific, or other legitimate uses.

(b) The export declaration (DEA Form 486) must include all the following information:

(1) The name/business name, address/business address, and contact information (*e.g.*, telephone number(s), email address(es), etc.) of the chemical exporter; the name/business name, address/business address, and contact information (*e.g.*, telephone number(s), email address(es), etc.) of the export broker, if any;

(2) The name and description of each listed chemical as it appears on the label or container, the name of each listed chemical as it is designated in § 1310.02 of this chapter, the size or weight of container, the number of containers, the net weight of each listed chemical given in kilograms or parts thereof, and the gross weight of the shipment given in kilograms or parts thereof;

(3) The anticipated date of release by a customs officer at the port of export, the port of export, and the foreign port and country of entry; and

(4) The name/business name, address/business address, and contact information (*e.g.*, telephone number(s), email address(es), etc.) of the consignee in the country where the chemical shipment is destined; the name(s) and address(es) of any intermediate consignee(s); and a copy of the foreign permit, license or registration issued by the competent national authority of the consignee and any intermediate consignees.

(c) Declared exports of listed chemicals which are refused, rejected, or otherwise deemed undeliverable by the foreign competent national authority may be returned to the U.S. chemical exporter of record. The regulated person must provide notification through the DEA Diversion Control Division secure network application (this does not require a DEA Form 486) outlining the circumstances within a reasonable time following the return. Upon receipt and review, the Administration will assign the completed notice a transaction identification number. The notice will not be deemed filed until the Administration issues a transaction identification number. Listed chemicals so returned may not be reexported until the exporter has filed a new DEA Form 486 and the Administration has issued a new transaction identification number. This provision does not apply to shipments that have cleared foreign customs, been delivered, and accepted by the foreign consignee. Returns to third parties in the United States will be regarded as imports.

[81 FR 97038, Dec. 30, 2016]

§ 1313.23 Disposition of export declaration.

The exporter, or their agent, must submit an official record of the export declaration and/or required data concerning the export transaction to a customs officer at the port of export in compliance with all export control requirements of agencies with export control authorities under the Act or statutory authority other than the Controlled Substances Import and Export Act. An official record of the declaration (available from the DEA Diversion Control Division secure network application after the Administration issues a transaction identification number) must be maintained by the chemical exporter as the official record of the export in accordance with part 1310 of this chapter. Export declarations involving a listed chemical must be retained for two years.

[81 FR 97038, Dec. 30, 2016]

§ 1313.24 Waiver of 15-day advance notice for chemical exporters.

(a) Each regulated person shall provide to the Administration the identity and information listed in the definition of established business relationship in § 1300.02 of this chapter for an established business relationship with a foreign customer not later than August 31, 1989.

(b) Not later than October 31, 1989, each regular customer so identified in notifications made under § 1313.24(a) shall be a regular customer for purposes of waiving the 15-day advance notice requirement, unless the regulated person is otherwise notified in writing by the Administration.

(c) Each foreign customer identified on an initial DEA Form 486 submitted after the effective date of the implementation of part 1313 shall, after the expiration of the 15-day period, qualify as a regular customer, unless the Administration otherwise notifies the regulated person in writing.

(d) Unless the Administration notifies the chemical exporter to the contrary, the qualification of a regular customer for any one of these three chemicals, acetone, 2-Butanone (MEK), or toluene, qualifies that customer as a regular customer for all three of these chemicals.

(e) The Administrator may notify any chemical exporter that a regular customer has been disqualified or that a new customer for whom a notification has been submitted is not to be accorded the status of a regular customer. In the event of a disqualification of an established regular customer, the chemical exporter will be notified in writing of the reasons for such action.

[54 FR 31665, Aug. 1, 1989, as amended at 56 FR 55077, Oct. 24, 1991; 62 FR 13969, Mar. 24, 1997; 75 FR 10684, Mar. 9, 2010; 77 FR 4237, Jan. 27, 2012]

§ 1313.25 Foreign import restrictions.

Any export from the United States in violation of the law of the country to which the chemical is exported is subject to the penalties of Title 21 United States Code 960(d).

§ 1313.26 Updated notice for change in circumstances.

(a) In the case of a notice under §1313.21(a) submitted by a regulated person, if the transferee identified in the notice, *i.e.*, the foreign importer, is not a regular customer, the regulated person may not transfer the listed chemical until after the expiration of the 15-day period beginning on the date on which the notice is submitted to the Administration.

(b) After a notice under §1313.21(a) is submitted to the Administration, if circumstances change and the exporter will not be transferring the listed chemical to the transferee identified in the notice, or will be transferring a greater quantity of the chemical than specified in the notice, the exporter must update the notice to identify the most recent prospective transferee or the most recent quantity or both (as the case may be). The exporter may not transfer the listed chemical until after the expiration of the 15 calendar day period beginning on the date on which the update is filed with the Administration. Except, if the listed chemical is intended for transfer to a regular customer, the exporter may not transfer the listed chemical until after the expiration of three business days. The preceding sentence applies with respect to changing circumstances regarding a transferee or quantity identified in an update to the same extent and in the same manner as the sentence applies with respect to changing circumstances regarding a transferee or quantity identified in the original notice under paragraph (a) of this section. Amended declarations must be submitted to the Administration through the DEA Diversion Control Division secure network application. The amendment must be signed and dated by the exporter. Upon receipt and review, the Administration will assign each completed amendment a transaction identification number. The amendment will not be deemed filed until the Administration issues a transaction identification number.

(c) In the case of a transfer of a listed chemical that is subject to a 15-day restriction, the transferee involved shall, upon the expiration of the 15-day period, be considered to qualify as a regular customer, unless the Administration otherwise notifies the exporter involved in writing.

(d) With respect to a transfer of a listed chemical with which a notice or update referred to in §1313.21(a) is concerned:

(1) The Administration—

(i) May, in accordance with the same procedures as apply under §§1313.51 through 1313.57, order the suspension of the transfer of the listed chemical by the exporter involved, except for a transfer to a regular customer, on the ground that the chemical may be diverted to the clandestine manufacture of a controlled substance (without regard to the form of the chemical that may be diverted, including the diversion of a finished drug product to be manufactured from bulk chemicals to be transferred), subject to the Administration ordering the suspension before the expiration of the 15-day period with respect to the exportation (in any case in which such a period applies); and

(ii) May, for purposes of this paragraph (d), disqualify a regular customer on that ground.

(2) From and after the time when the Administration provides written notice of the order under paragraph (d)(1)(i) of this section (including a statement of the legal and factual basis for the order) to the exporter, the exporter may not carry out the transfer.

(e) For purposes of this section:

(1) The term *transfer,* with respect to a listed chemical, includes the sale of the chemical.

(2) The term *transferee* means a person to whom an exporter transfers a listed chemical.

[72 FR 17408, Apr. 9, 2007, as amended at 81 FR 97039, Dec. 30, 2016]

§ 1313.27 Return declaration for exports.

(a) *Return information.* Within 30 calendar days after a listed chemical is released by a customs officer at the port of export, the exporter must file a report with the Administration through the DEA Diversion Control Division secure network application specifying the particulars of the transaction. This report must include the following information: The date on which the listed chemical left the registered location or place of business; the date on which the listed chemical was released by a customs officer at the port of export; the actual quantity of listed chemical that left the registered location or place of business; the actual quantity of the listed chemical released by a customs officer at the port of export; chemical; container; name of transferees; and any other information as the Administration may specify. Upon receipt and review, the Administration will assign a completed report a transaction identification number. The report will not be deemed filed until the Administration has issued a transaction identification number. In determining whether the exporter has complied with the requirement to file within 30 calendar days, the report shall be deemed filed on the first date on which a complete report is filed.

(b) If an exportation for which a DEA Form 486 has been filed fails to take place, the exporter must report to the Administration that the exportation did not occur through the DEA Diversion Control Division secure network application.

(c) *Denied release at the port of export.* In the event that a shipment of listed chemicals has been denied release by a customs officer at the port of export for any reason, the exporter who attempted to have the shipment released must, within 5 business days of the denial, report to the Administration that the shipment was denied release and the reason for denial. Such report must be transmitted to the Administration through the DEA Diversion Control Division secure network application. This report must include the following information: The quantity of the listed chemicals denied release; the date on which release was denied; and the basis for the denied release. Upon the exporter's report of a denied release, DEA will assign the report a transaction identification number and the export declaration will be void and of no effect. No shipment of listed chemicals denied release for any reason will be allowed to be released from the United States without a subsequent refiling of a complete and accurate export declaration. Following such refiling, the exporter may request the release of the listed chemicals immediately after receipt of a transaction identification number without regard to the 15 day advance filing required by § 1313.21(b).

[81 FR 97039, Dec. 30, 2016]

TRANSSHIPMENTS, IN-TRANSIT SHIPMENTS AND INTERNATIONAL TRANSACTIONS INVOLVING LISTED CHEMICALS

§ 1313.31 Advance notice of importation for transshipment or transfer.

(a) A quantity of a chemical listed in § 1310.02 of this chapter that meets or exceeds the threshold reporting requirements found in § 1310.04(f) of this chapter may be imported into the United States for transshipment, or may be transferred or transshipped within the United States for immediate exportation, provided that advance notice is given to the Administration.

(b) Advance notification must be provided to the Regulatory Section, Diversion Control Division, Drug Enforcement Administration, not later than 15 calendar days prior to the proposed date the listed chemical will transship or transfer through the United States. See the Table of DEA Mailing Addresses in § 1321.01 of this chapter for the current mailing address. A separate notification is required for each shipment of listed chemicals to be transferred or transshipped. The written notification (not a DEA Form 486) must contain the following information:

(1) The date the notice was executed;

(2) The complete name and description of the listed chemical as it appears on the label or container.

(3) The name of the listed chemical as designated by § 1310.02 of this chapter.

(4) The number of containers and the size or weight of the container for each listed item;

(5) The net weight of each listed chemical given in kilograms or parts thereof;

(6) The gross weight of the shipment given in kilograms or parts thereof;

(7) The name/business name, address/business address, and contact information (*e.g.*, telephone number(s), email address(es), etc.) and type of business of the foreign exporter;

(8) The foreign port and country of export;

(9) The approximate date of exportation;

(10) The complete identification of the exporting carrier;

(11) The name, address, business, telephone number, and, where available, the facsimile number of the importer, transferor, or transshipper;

(12) The U.S. port of entry;

(13) The approximate date of entry;

(14) The name/business name, address/business address, and contact information (*e.g.*, telephone number(s), email address(es), etc.) and type of business of the consignee at the foreign port or country of entry;

(15) The shipping route from the U.S. port of export to the foreign port or country of entry at final destination;

(16) The approximate date of receipt by the consignee at the foreign port of entry; and

(17) The signature of the importer, transferor or transshipper, or his agent, accompanied by the agent's title.

(c) Unless notified to the contrary prior to the expected date of delivery, the importation for transshipment or transfer is considered approved.

(d) No waiver of the 15-day advance notice will be given for imports of listed chemicals in quantities meeting or exceeding threshold quantities for transshipment or transfer outside the United States.

[54 FR 31665, Aug. 1, 1989, as amended at 67 FR 49569, July 31, 2002; 75 FR 10684, Mar. 9, 2010; 77 FR 4237, Jan. 27, 2012; 81 FR 97039, Dec. 30, 2016]

§ 1313.32 Notification of international transactions.

(a) A broker or trader must notify the Administration prior to an international transaction involving a listed chemical which meets or exceeds the threshold quantities identified in § 1310.04(f) of this chapter or is a listed chemical for which no threshold has been established as identified in § 1310.04(g) of this chapter, in which the broker or trader participates. Notification must be made not later than 15 calendar days before the transaction is to take place. In order to facilitate an international transaction involving listed chemicals and implement the purpose of the Act, regulated persons may wish to provide advance notification to the Administration as far in advance of the 15 calendar days as possible.

(b) A completed DEA Form 486 must be submitted to the Administration through the DEA Diversion Control Division secure network application, not later than 15 calendar days prior to the international transaction. The DEA Form 486 must be signed and dated by the broker or trader. Upon receipt and review, the Administration will assign a transaction identification number to each completed notification. A notification is not deemed filed, and therefore is not valid, until the Administration assigns the notification a transaction identification number. An international transaction may not take place until after a transaction identification number has been assigned and the expiration of the 15 calendar day period beginning on the date on which the broker or trader submits a complete notification to the Administration.

(c) No person shall serve as a broker or trader for an international transaction involving a listed chemical knowing or having reasonable cause to believe that the transaction is in violation of the laws of the country to which the chemical is exported or the chemical will be used to manufacture a controlled substance in violation of the laws of the country to which the chemical is exported. The Administration will publish a notice of foreign import restrictions for listed chemicals of which DEA has knowledge as provided in § 1313.25.

(d) After a notice under paragraph (a) of this section is submitted to the Administration, if circumstances change and the broker or trader will not be transferring the listed chemical to the transferee identified in the notice, or will be transferring a greater quantity of the chemical than specified in the notice, the broker or trader must amend the notice through the DEA Diversion Control Division secure network application to identify the most recent prospective transferee or the most recent quantity or both (as applicable) and may not transfer the listed chemical until after the expiration of the 15 calendar day period beginning on the date on which the update is submitted to the Administration. The preceding sentence applies with respect to changing circumstances regarding a transferee or quantity identified in an amendment to the same extent and in the same manner as the sentence applies with respect to changing circumstances regarding a transferee or quantity identified in the original notice under paragraph (a) of this section.

(e) For purposes of this section:

(1) The term *transfer*, with respect to a listed chemical, includes the sale of the chemical.

(2) The term *transferee* means a person to whom an exporter transfers a listed chemical.

[81 FR 97039, Dec. 30, 2016]

§ 1313.33 Contents of an international transaction declaration.

(a) An international transaction involving a chemical listed in § 1310.02 of this chapter which meets the threshold criteria established in § 1310.04 of this chapter may be arranged by a broker or trader if the chemical is needed for medical, commercial, scientific, or other legitimate uses.

(b) Any broker or trader who desires to arrange an international transaction, defined in 21 U.S.C. 802(42), involving a listed chemical which meets the threshold criteria set forth in § 1310.04 of this chapter must notify the Administration through the procedures outlined in § 1313.32(b).

(c) The DEA Form 486 must include:

(1) The name/business name, address/business address, and contact information (*e.g.*, telephone number(s), email address(es), etc.) of the chemical exporter; the name/business name, address/business address, and contact information (*e.g.*, telephone number(s), email address(es), etc.) of the chemical importer;

(2) The name and description of each listed chemical as it appears on the label or container, the name of each listed chemical as it is designated in § 1310.02 of this chapter, the size or weight of container, the number of containers, the net weight of each listed chemical given in kilograms or parts thereof, and the gross weight of the shipment given in kilograms or parts thereof;

(3) The anticipated date of release at the foreign port of export, the anticipated foreign port and country of export, and the foreign port and country of entry; and

(4) The name/business name, address/business address, and contact information (*e.g.*, telephone number(s), email address(es), etc.) of the consignee in

the country where the chemical shipment is destined; the name(s) and address(es) of any intermediate consignee(s).

[60 FR 32465, June 22, 1995, as amended at 77 FR 4238, Jan. 27, 2012; 81 FR 97040, Dec. 30, 2016]

§ 1313.34 Disposition of the international transaction declaration.

The broker or trader must retain an official record of the declaration (DEA Form 486) (available from the DEA Diversion Control Division secure network application after the Administration issues a transaction identification number) as the official record of the international transaction. In accordance with part 1310 of this chapter, declarations involving listed chemicals must be retained for two years.

[81 FR 97040, Dec. 30, 2016]

§ 1313.35 Return declaration or amendment to Form 486 for international transactions.

(a) Within 30 calendar days after an international transaction is completed, the broker or trader must file a report with the Administration through the DEA Diversion Control Division secure network application about the particulars of the transaction. This report must include the following information: The date(s) on which the listed chemical was released by the foreign customs officer(s) at the port(s); the actual quantity of listed chemical that left the country of export; the actual quantity of the listed chemical released by a customs officer at the port of entry; chemical; container; name of transferees; and the transaction identification and any other information as the Administration may specify. Upon receipt and review, the Administration will assign a completed report a transaction identification number. The report will not be deemed filed until the Administration has issued a transaction identification number.

(b) If an international transaction for which a DEA Form 486 has been filed fails to take place, the broker or trader must report to the Administration that the international transaction did not occur utilizing the DEA Diversion Control Division secure network application as soon as the broker or trader becomes aware of the circumstances.

[81 FR 97040, Dec. 30, 2016]

§ 1313.41 Suspension of shipments.

(a) The Administrator may suspend any importation or exportation of a chemical listed in § 1310.02 of this chapter based on evidence that the chemical proposed to be imported or exported may be diverted to the clandestine manufacture of a controlled substance. If the Administrator so suspends, he shall provide written notice of such suspension to the regulated person. Such notice shall contain a statement of the legal and factual basis for the order.

(b) Upon service of the order of suspension, the regulated person to whom the order applies under paragraph (a) of this section must, if he desires a hearing, file a written request for a hearing pursuant to §§ 1313.51–1313.57.

§ 1313.42 Prohibition of shipments from certain foreign sources.

(a) If the Administrator determines that a foreign manufacturer or distributor of ephedrine, pseudoephedrine, or phenylpropanolamine has refused to cooperate with a request by the Administrator for information known to the manufacturer or distributor on the distribution of the chemical, including sales, the Administrator may issue an order prohibiting the importation of the chemical in any case where the manufacturer or distributor is part of the chain of distribution.

(b) Not later than 60 days prior to issuing the order to prohibit importation, the Administrator shall publish in the FEDERAL REGISTER a notice of intent to issue the order. During the 60-day period, imports from the foreign manufacturer or distributor may not be restricted under this section.

[75 FR 10172, Mar. 5, 2010]

HEARINGS

§ 1313.51 Hearings generally.

In any case where a regulated person requests a hearing regarding the suspension of a shipment of a listed chemical, the procedures for such hearing shall be governed generally by the procedures set forth in the Administrative Procedure Act (5 U.S.C. 551–559) and specifically by section 6053 of the Chemical Diversion and Trafficking Act (Pub. L. 100–690), by 21 CFR 1313.52–1313.57, and by the procedures for administrative hearings under the Controlled Substances Act set forth in §§1316.41–1316.67 of this chapter.

§1313.52 Purpose of hearing.

If requested by a person entitled to a hearing, the Administrator shall cause a hearing to be held for the purpose of receiving factual evidence regarding the issues involved in the suspension of shipments within 45 days of the date of the request, unless the requesting party requests an extension of time.

§1313.53 Waiver of modification of rules.

The Administrator or the presiding officer (with respect to matters pending before him) may modify or waive any rule in this part by notice in advance of the hearing, if he determines that no party in the hearing will be unduly prejudiced and the ends of justice will thereby be served. Such notice of modification or waiver shall be made a part of the record of the hearing.

§1313.54 Request for hearing.

(a) Any person entitled to a hearing pursuant to §1313.52 and desiring a hearing shall, within 30 days after receipt of the notice to suspend the shipment, file with the Administrator a written request for a hearing in the form prescribed in §1316.47 of this chapter.

(b) If any person entitled to a hearing or to participate in a hearing pursuant to §1313.41 fails to file a request for a hearing or a notice of appearance, or if he so files and fails to appear at the hearing, he shall be deemed to have waived his opportunity for the hearing or to participate in the hearing, unless he shows good cause for such failure.

(c) If all persons entitled to a hearing or to participate in a hearing waive or are deemed to waive their opportunity for the hearing or to participate in the hearing, the Administrator may cancel the hearing, if scheduled, and issue his final order pursuant to §1313.57.

§1313.55 Burden of proof.

At any hearing regarding the suspension of shipments, the Agency shall have the burden of proving that the requirements of this part for such suspension are satisfied.

§1313.56 Time and place of hearing.

(a) If any regulated person requests a hearing on the suspension of shipments, a hearing will be scheduled no later than 45 days after the request is made, unless the regulated person requests an extension to this date.

(b) The hearing will commence at the place and time designated in the notice given pursuant to paragraph (a) of this section but thereafter it may be moved to a different place and may be continued from day to day or recessed to a later day without notice other than announcement thereof by the presiding officer at the hearing.

§1313.57 Final order.

As soon as practicable after the presiding officer has certified the record to the Administrator, the Administrator shall issue his order regarding the suspension of shipment. The order shall include the findings of fact and conclusions of law upon which the order is based. The Administrator shall serve one copy of his order upon each party in the hearing.

PART 1314—RETAIL SALE OF SCHEDULED LISTED CHEMICAL PRODUCTS

Subpart A—General

Subpart B—Sales by Regulated Sellers

Subpart C—Mail-Order Sales

Subpart D—Order To Show Cause

AUTHORITY: 21 U.S.C. 802, 830, 842, 871(b), 875, 877, 886a.

SOURCE: 71 FR 56024, Sept. 26, 2006, unless otherwise noted.

Subpart A—General

§ 1314.01 Scope.

This part specifies the requirements for retail sales of scheduled listed chemical products to individuals for personal use.

§ 1314.02 Applicability.

(a) This part applies to the following regulated persons who sell scheduled listed chemical products for personal use:

(1) Regulated sellers of scheduled listed chemical products sold at retail for personal use through face-to-face sales at stores or mobile retail vendors.

(2) Regulated persons who engage in a transaction with a non-regulated person and who ship the products to the non-regulated person by the U.S. Postal Service or by private or common carriers.

(b) The requirements in subpart A apply to all regulated persons subject to this part. The requirements in subpart B apply to regulated sellers as defined in § 1300.02 of this chapter. The requirements in subpart C apply to regulated persons who ship the products to the customer by the U.S. Postal Service or by private or common carriers.

§ 1314.03 Definitions.

As used in this part, the term "mail-order sale" means a retail sale of scheduled listed chemical products for personal use where a regulated person uses or attempts to use the U.S. Postal Service or any private or commercial carrier to deliver the product to the customer. Mail-order sale includes purchase orders submitted by phone, mail, fax, Internet, or any method other than face-to-face transaction.

§ 1314.05 Requirements regarding packaging of nonliquid forms.

A regulated seller or mail order distributor may not sell a scheduled listed chemical product in nonliquid form (including gel caps) unless the product is packaged either in blister packs, with each blister containing no more than two dosage units or, if blister packs are technically infeasible, in unit dose packets or pouches.

§ 1314.10 Effect on State laws.

Nothing in this part preempts State law on the same subject matter unless there is a positive conflict between this part and a State law so that the two cannot consistently stand together.

§ 1314.15 Loss reporting.

(a) Each regulated person must report to the Special Agent in Charge of the DEA Divisional Office for the area in which the regulated person making the report is located, any unusual or excessive loss or disappearance of a scheduled listed chemical product under the control of the regulated person. The regulated person responsible for reporting a loss in-transit is the supplier.

(b) Each report submitted under paragraph (a) of this section must, whenever possible, be made orally to the DEA Divisional Office for the area in which the regulated person making the report is located at the earliest practicable opportunity after the regulated person becomes aware of the circumstances involved.

(c) Written reports of losses must be filed within 15 days after the regulated person becomes aware of the circumstances of the event.

(d) A report submitted under this section must include a description of the circumstances of the loss (in-transit, theft from premises, *etc.*).

(e) A suggested format for the report is provided below:

Regulated Person

Registration number (if applicable) ______
Name ______
Business address ______
City ______
State ______
Zip ______
Business phone ______
Date of loss ______
Type of loss ______
Description of circumstances ______

Subpart B—Sales by Regulated Sellers

§ 1314.20 Restrictions on sales quantity.

(a) Without regard to the number of transactions, a regulated seller (including a mobile retail vendor) may not in a single calendar day sell any purchaser more than 3.6 grams of ephedrine base, 3.6 grams of pseudoephedrine base, or 3.6 grams of phenylpropanolamine base in scheduled listed chemical products.

(b) A mobile retail vendor may not in any 30-day period sell an individual purchaser more than 7.5 grams of ephedrine base, 7.5 grams of pseudoephedrine base, or 7.5 grams of phenylpropanolamine base in scheduled listed chemical products.

§ 1314.25 Requirements for retail transactions.

(a) Each regulated seller must ensure that sales of a scheduled listed chemical product at retail are made in accordance with this section and § 1314.20.

(b) The regulated seller must place the product so that customers do not have direct access to the product before the sale is made (in this paragraph referred to as "behind-the-counter" placement). For purposes of this paragraph, a behind-the-counter placement of a product includes circumstances in which the product is stored in a locked cabinet that is located in an area of the facility where customers do have direct access. Mobile retail vendors must place the product in a locked cabinet.

(c) The regulated seller must deliver the product directly into the custody of the purchaser.

§ 1314.30 Recordkeeping for retail transactions.

(a) Except for purchase by an individual of a single sales package containing not more than 60 milligrams of pseudoephedrine, the regulated seller must maintain, in accordance with criteria issued by the Administrator, a written or electronic list of each scheduled listed chemical product sale that identifies the products by name, the quantity sold, the names and addresses of the purchasers, and the dates and times of the sales (referred to as the "logbook").

(b) The regulated seller must not sell a scheduled listed chemical product at retail unless the sale is made in accordance with the following:

(1) The purchaser presents an identification card that provides a photograph and is issued by a State or the Federal Government, or a document that, with respect to identification, is considered acceptable for purposes of 8 CFR 274a.2(b)(1)(v)(A) and 274a.2(b)(1)(v)(B).

(2) The purchaser signs the logbook as follows:

(i) For written logbooks, enters in the logbook his name, address, and the date and time of the sale.

(ii) For electronic logbooks, provides a signature using one of the following means:

(A) Signing a device presented by the seller that captures signatures in an electronic format. The device must display the warning notice in paragraph (d) of this section. Any device used must preserve each signature in a manner that clearly links that signature to the other electronically captured logbook information relating to the prospective purchaser providing that signature.

(B) Signing a bound paper book.

(*1*) The bound paper book must include, for such purchaser, either—

(*i*) A printed sticker affixed to the bound paper book at the time of sale that either displays the name of each product sold, the quantity sold, the name and address of the purchaser, and the date and time of the sale, or a unique identifier which can be linked to that electronic information, or

(*ii*) A unique identifier that can be linked to that information and that is written into the book by the seller at the time of sale.

(*2*) The purchaser must sign adjacent to the printed sticker or written unique identifier related to that sale. The bound paper book must display the warning notice in paragraph (d) of this section.

(C) Signing a printed document that includes, for the purchaser, the name of each product sold, the quantity sold, the name and address of the purchaser, and the date and time of the sale. The document must be printed by the seller at the time of the sale. The document must contain a clearly identified signature line for a purchaser to sign. The printed document must display the warning notice in paragraph (d) of this section. Each signed document must be inserted into a binder or other secure means of document storage immediately after the purchaser signs the document.

(3) The regulated seller must enter in the logbook the name of the product and the quantity sold. Examples of methods of recording the quantity sold include the weight of the product per package and number of packages of each chemical, the cumulative weight of the product for each chemical, or quantity of product by Universal Product Code. These examples do not exclude other methods of displaying the quantity sold. Such information may be captured through electronic means, including through electronic data capture through bar code reader or similar technology. Such electronic records must be provided pursuant to paragraph (g) of this section in a human readable form such that the requirements of paragraph (a) of this section are satisfied.

(c) The logbook maintained by the seller must include the prospective purchaser's name, address, and the date and time of the sale, as follows:

(1) If the purchaser enters the information, the seller must determine that the name entered in the logbook corresponds to the name provided on the identification and that the date and time entered are correct.

(2) If the seller enters the information, the prospective purchaser must verify that the information is correct.

(3) Such information may be captured through electronic means, including through electronic data capture through bar code reader or similar technology.

(d) The regulated seller must include in the written or electronic logbook or display by the logbook, the following notice:

WARNING: Section 1001 of Title 18, United States Code, states that whoever, with respect to the logbook, knowingly and willfully falsifies, conceals, or covers up by any trick, scheme, or device a material fact, or makes any materially false, fictitious, or fraudulent statement or representation, or makes or uses any false writing or document knowing the same to contain any materially false, fictitious, or fraudulent statement or entry, shall be fined not more than $250,000 if an individual or $500,000 if an organization, imprisoned not more than five years, or both.

(e) The regulated seller must maintain each entry in the written or electronic logbook for not fewer than two years after the date on which the entry is made.

(f) A record under this section must be kept at the regulated seller's place of business where the transaction occurred, except that records may be kept at a single, central location of the regulated seller if the regulated seller has notified the Administration of the intention to do so. Written notification must be submitted by registered or certified mail, return receipt requested, to the Special Agent in Charge of the DEA Divisional Office for the area in which the records are required to be kept.

(g) The records required to be kept under this section must be readily retrievable and available for inspection and copying by authorized employees of the Administration under the provisions of section 510 of the Act (21 U.S.C. 880).

(h) A record developed and maintained to comply with a State law may be used to meet the requirements of this section if the record includes the information specified in this section.

[76 FR 74698, Dec. 1, 2011]

§ 1314.35 Training of sales personnel.

Each regulated seller must ensure that its sales of a scheduled listed chemical product at retail are made in accordance with the following:

(a) In the case of individuals who are responsible for delivering the products into the custody of purchasers or who deal directly with purchasers by obtaining payments for the products, the regulated seller has submitted to the Administration a self-certification that all such individuals have, in accordance with criteria issued by the Administration, undergone training provided by the regulated seller to ensure that the individuals understand the requirements that apply under this part.

(b) The regulated seller maintains a copy of each self-certification and all records demonstrating that individuals referred to in paragraph (a) of this section have undergone the training.

§ 1314.40 Self-certification.

(a) A regulated seller must submit to the Administration the self-certification referred to in § 1314.35(a) in order to sell any scheduled listed chemical product. The certification is not effective for purposes of this section unless, in addition to provisions regarding the training of individuals referred to in § 1314.35(a), the certification includes a statement that the regulated seller understands each of the requirements that apply under this part and agrees to comply with the requirements.

(b) When a regulated seller files the initial self-certification, the Administration will assign the regulated seller to one of twelve groups. The expiration date of the self-certification for all regulated sellers in any group will be the last day of the month designated for that group. In assigning a regulated seller to a group, the Administration may select a group with an expiration date that is not less than 12 months or more than 23 months from the date of the self-certification. After the initial certification period, the regulated seller must update the self-certifications annually.

(c) The regulated seller must provide a separate certification for each place of business at which the regulated seller sells scheduled listed chemical products at retail.

§ 1314.42 Self-certification fee; time and method of fee payment.

(a) A regulated seller must pay a fee for each self-certification. For each initial application to self-certify, and for the renewal of each existing self-certification, a regulated seller shall pay a fee of $21.

(b) The fee for self-certification shall be waived for any person holding a current, DEA registration in good standing as a pharmacy to dispense controlled substances.

(c) A regulated seller shall pay the fee at the time of self-certification.

(d) Payment shall be made by credit card.

(e) The self-certification fee is not refundable.

[73 FR 79323, Dec. 29, 2008]

§ 1314.45 Privacy protections.

To protect the privacy of individuals who purchase scheduled listed chemical products, the disclosure of information in logbooks under § 1314.30 is restricted as follows:

(a) The information shall be disclosed as appropriate to the Administration and to State and local law enforcement agencies.

(b) The information in the logbooks shall not be accessed, used, or shared for any purpose other than to ensure compliance with this title or to facilitate a product recall to protect public health and safety.

(c) A regulated seller who in good faith releases information in a logbook to Federal, State, or local law enforcement authorities is immune from civil liability for the release unless the release constitutes gross negligence or intentional, wanton, or willful misconduct.

[71 FR 56024, Sept. 26, 2006, as amended at 77 FR 4238, Jan. 27, 2012]

§ 1314.50 Employment measures.

A regulated seller may take reasonable measures to guard against employing individuals who may present a risk with respect to the theft and diversion of scheduled listed chemical products, which may include, notwithstanding State law, asking applicants for employment whether they have been convicted of any crime involving or related to such products or controlled substances.

Subpart C—Mail-Order Sales

§ 1314.100 Sales limits for mail-order sales.

(a) Each regulated person who makes a sale at retail of a scheduled listed chemical product and is required under § 1310.03(c) of this chapter to submit a report of the sales transaction to the Administration may not in a single calendar day sell to any purchaser more than 3.6 grams of ephedrine base, 3.6 grams of pseudoephedrine base, or 3.6 grams of phenylpropanolamine base in scheduled listed chemical products.

(b) Each regulated person who makes a sale at retail of a scheduled listed chemical product and is required under § 1310.03(c) of this chapter to submit a report of the sales transaction to the Administration may not in any 30-day period sell to an individual purchaser more than 7.5 grams of ephedrine base, 7.5 grams of pseudoephedrine base, or 7.5 grams of phenylpropanolamine base in scheduled listed chemical products.

§ 1314.101 Training of sales personnel.

Each regulated person who makes a sale at retail of a scheduled listed chemical product and is required under § 1310.03(c) of this chapter to submit a report of the sales transaction to the Administration must ensure that its sales of a scheduled listed chemical product at retail are made in accordance with the following:

(a) In the case of individuals who are responsible for preparing and packaging scheduled listed chemical products for delivery to purchasers through the Postal Service or any private or commercial carrier or who deal either directly or indirectly with purchasers by obtaining payments for the products, the regulated person has submitted to the Administration a self-certification that all such individuals have, in accordance with criteria issued by the Administration, undergone training provided by the regulated person to ensure that the individuals understand the requirements that apply under this part.

(b) The regulated person maintains a copy of each self-certification and all records demonstrating that individuals referred to in paragraph (a) of this section have undergone the training.

[76 FR 20523, Apr. 13, 2011]

§ 1314.102 Self-certification.

(a) A regulated person who makes a sale at retail of a scheduled listed chemical product and is required under § 1310.03 of this chapter to submit a report of the sales transaction to the Attorney General must submit to the Administration the self-certification referred to in § 1314.101(a) in order to sell any scheduled listed chemical product. The certification is not effective for purposes of this section unless, in addition to provisions regarding the training of individuals referred to in § 1314.101(a), the certification includes a statement that the regulated person understands each of the requirements that apply in this part and agrees to comply with the requirements.

(b) When a regulated person files the initial self-certification, the Administration will assign the regulated person to one of twelve groups. The expiration date of the self-certification for all regulated persons in any group will be the last day of the month designated for that group. In assigning a regulated person to a group, the Administration may select a group with an expiration date that is not less than 12 months or more than 23 months from the date of self-certification. After the initial certification period, the regulated person must update the self-certification annually.

(c) The regulated person who makes a sale at retail of a scheduled listed chemical product and is required under § 1310.03 of this chapter to submit a report of the sales transaction to the Attorney General must provide a separate certification for each place of business at which the regulated person sells scheduled listed chemical products at retail.

[76 FR 20523, Apr. 13, 2011]

§1314.103 Self-certification fee; time and method of fee payment.

(a) Each regulated person who makes a sale at retail of a scheduled listed chemical product and is required under §1310.03 of this chapter to submit a report of the sales transaction to the Administration must pay a fee for each self-certification. For each initial application to self-certify, and for the renewal of each existing self-certification, a regulated seller shall pay a fee of $21.

(b) The fee for self-certification shall be waived for any person holding a current, DEA registration in good standing as a pharmacy to dispense controlled substances.

(c) A regulated person shall pay the fee at the time of self-certification.

(d) Payment shall be made by credit card.

(e) The self-certification fee is not refundable.

[76 FR 20523, Apr. 13, 2011]

§1314.105 Verification of identity for mail-order sales.

(a) Each regulated person who makes a sale at retail of a scheduled listed chemical product and is required under §1310.03(c) of this chapter to submit a report of the sales transaction to the Administration must, prior to shipping the product, receive from the purchaser a copy of an identification card that provides a photograph and is issued by a State or the Federal Government, or a document that, with respect to identification, is considered acceptable for purposes of 8 CFR 274a.2(b)(1)(v)(A) and 274a.2(b)(1)(v)(B). Prior to shipping the product, the regulated person must determine that the name and address on the identification correspond to the name and address provided by the purchaser as part of the sales transaction. If the regulated person cannot verify the identities of both the purchaser and the recipient, the person may not ship the scheduled listed chemical product.

(b) If the product is being shipped to a third party, the regulated person must comply with the requirements of paragraph (a) to verify that both the purchaser and the person to whom the product is being shipped live at the addresses provided. If the regulated person cannot verify the identities of both the purchaser and the recipient, the person may not ship the scheduled listed chemical product.

§1314.110 Reports for mail-order sales.

(a) Each regulated person required to report under §1310.03(c) of this chapter must either:

(1) Submit a written report, containing the information set forth in paragraph (b) of this section, on or before the 15th day of each month following the month in which the distributions took place. The report must be submitted under company letterhead, signed by the person authorized to sign on behalf of the regulated seller, to the Regulatory Section, Diversion Control Division, Drug Enforcement Administration (see the Table of DEA Mailing Addresses in §1321.01 of this chapter for the current mailing address); or

(2) Upon request to and approval by the Administration, submit the report in electronic form, either via computer disk or direct electronic data transmission, in such form as the Administration shall direct. Requests to submit reports in electronic form should be submitted to the Regulatory Section, Diversion Control Division, Drug Enforcement Administration. See the Table of DEA Mailing Addresses in §1321.01 of this chapter for the current mailing address.

(b) Each monthly report must provide the following information for each distribution:

(1) Supplier name and registration number;

(2) Purchaser's name and address;

(3) Name/address shipped to (if different from purchaser's name/address);

(4) Method used to verify the identity of the purchaser and, where applicable, person to whom product is shipped;

(5) Name of the chemical contained in the scheduled listed chemical product and total quantity shipped (e.g. pseudoephedrine, 3 grams);

(6) Date of shipment;

(7) Product name;

(8) Dosage form (e.g., tablet, liquid);

(9) Dosage strength (e.g., 30mg, 60mg, per dose etc.);

(10) Number of dosage units (e.g., 100 doses per package);

(11) Package type (blister pack, etc.);

(12) Number of packages;

(13) Lot number.

[71 FR 56024, Sept. 26, 2006, as amended at 75 FR 10684, Mar. 9, 2010; 81 FR 97040, Dec. 30, 2016]

§ 1314.115 Distributions not subject to reporting requirements.

(a) The following distributions to nonregulated persons are not subject to the reporting requirements in § 1314.110:

(1) Distributions of sample packages when those packages contain not more than two solid dosage units or the equivalent of two dosage units in liquid form, not to exceed 10 milliliters of liquid per package, and not more than one package is distributed to an individual or residential address in any 30-day period.

(2) Distributions by retail distributors that may not include face-to-face transactions to the extent that such distributions are consistent with the activities authorized for a retail distributor as specified in the definition of retail distributor in § 1300.02 of this chapter, except that this paragraph (a)(2) does not apply to sales of scheduled listed chemical products at retail.

(3) Distributions to a resident of a long term care facility or distributions to a long term care facility for dispensing to or for use by a resident of that facility.

(4) Distributions in accordance with a valid prescription.

(b) The Administrator may revoke any or all of the exemptions listed in paragraph (a) of this section for an individual regulated person if the Administrator finds that drug products distributed by the regulated person are being used in violation of the regulations in this chapter or the Controlled Substances Act.

[[71 FR 56024, Sept. 26, 2006, as amended at 77 FR 4238, Jan. 27, 2012]

Subpart D—Order to Show Cause

§ 1314.150 Order To show cause.

(a) If, upon information gathered by the Administration regarding any regulated seller or a distributor required to submit reports under § 1310.03(c) of this chapter, the Administrator determines that a regulated seller or distributor required to submit reports under § 1310.03(c) of this chapter has sold a scheduled listed chemical product in violation of Section 402 of the Act (21 U.S.C. 842(a)(12) or (13)), the Administrator will serve upon the regulated seller or distributor an order to show cause why the regulated seller or distributor should not be prohibited from selling scheduled listed chemical products.

(b) The order to show cause shall call upon the regulated seller or distributor to appear before the Administrator at a time and place stated in the order, which shall not be less than 30 days after the date of receipt of the order. The order to show cause shall also contain a statement of the legal basis for such hearing and for the prohibition and a summary of the matters of fact and law asserted.

(c) Upon receipt of an order to show cause, the regulated seller or distributor must, if he desires a hearing, file a request for a hearing as specified in subpart D of part 1316 of this chapter. If a hearing is requested, the Administrator shall hold a hearing at the time and place stated in the order, as provided in part 1316 of this chapter.

(d) When authorized by the Administrator, any agent of the Administration may serve the order to show cause.

§ 1314.155 Suspension pending final order.

(a) The Administrator may suspend the right to sell scheduled listed chemical products simultaneously with, or at any time subsequent to, the service upon the seller or distributor required to file reports under § 1310.03(c) of this chapter of an order to show cause why the regulated seller or distributor should not be prohibited from selling scheduled listed chemical products, in any case where he finds that there is an imminent danger to the public health or safety. If the Administrator so suspends, he shall serve with the order to show cause under § 1314.150 an order of immediate suspension that shall contain a statement of his findings regarding the danger to public health or safety.

(b) Upon service of the order of immediate suspension, the regulated seller or distributor shall, as instructed by the Administrator:

(1) Deliver to the nearest office of the Administration or to authorized agents of the Administration all of the scheduled listed chemical products in his or her possession; or

(2) Place all of the scheduled listed chemical products under seal as described in Section 304 of the Act (21 U.S.C. 824(f)).

(c) Any suspension shall continue in effect until the conclusion of all proceedings upon the prohibition, including any judicial review, unless sooner withdrawn by the Administrator or dissolved by a court of competent jurisdiction. Any regulated seller or distributor whose right to sell scheduled listed chemical products is suspended under this section may request a hearing on the suspension at a time earlier than specified in the order to show cause under § 1314.150, which request shall be granted by the Administrator, who shall fix a date for such hearing as early as reasonably possible.

PART 1315—IMPORTATION AND PRODUCTION QUOTAS FOR EPHEDRINE, PSEUDOEPHEDRINE, AND PHENYLPROPANOLAMINE

Subpart A—General Information

Subpart B—Assessment of Annual Needs

Subpart C—Individual Manufacturing Quotas

Subpart D—Procurement and Import Quotas

Subpart E—Hearings

AUTHORITY: 21 U.S.C. 802, 821, 826, 871(b), 952.

SOURCE: 72 FR 37448, July 10, 2007, unless otherwise noted.

EDITORIAL NOTE: Nomenclature changes to part appear at 82 FR 97041, Dec. 30, 2016.

Subpart A—General Information

§ 1315.01 Scope.

This part specifies procedures governing the establishment of an assessment of annual needs, procurement and manufacturing quotas pursuant to section 306 of the Act (21 U.S.C. 826), and import quotas pursuant to section 1002 of the Act (21 U.S.C. 952) for ephedrine, pseudoephedrine, and phenylpropanolamine.

§ 1315.02 Definitions.

(a) Except as specified in paragraphs (b) and (c) of this section, any term contained in this part shall have the definition set forth in section 102 of the Act (21 U.S.C. 802) or part 1300 of this chapter.

(b) The term *net disposal* means, for a stated period, the sum of paragraphs (b)(1) through (b)(3) of this section minus the sum of paragraphs (b)(4) and (b)(5) of this section:

(1) The quantity of ephedrine, pseudoephedrine, or phenylpropanolamine distributed by the registrant to another person.

(2) The quantity of that chemical used by the registrant in the production of (or converted by the registrant into) another chemical or product.

(3) The quantity of that chemical otherwise disposed of by the registrant.

(4) The quantity of that chemical returned to the registrant by any purchaser.

(5) The quantity of that chemical distributed by the registrant to a registered manufacturer of that chemical for purposes other than use in the production of, or conversion into, another chemical or in the manufacture of dosage forms of that chemical.

(c) Ephedrine, pseudoephedrine, and phenylpropanolamine include their salts, optical isomers, and salts of optical isomers.

§ 1315.03 Personal use exemption.

A person need not register as an importer, file an import declaration, and obtain an import quota if both of the following conditions are met:

(a) The person purchases scheduled listed chemical products at retail and imports them for personal use, by means of shipping through any private or commercial carrier or the Postal Service.

(b) In any 30-day period, the person imports no more than 7.5 grams of ephedrine base, 7.5 grams of pseudoephedrine base, and 7.5 grams of phenylpropanolamine base in scheduled listed chemical products.

§ 1315.05 Applicability.

This part applies to all of the following:

(a) Persons registered to manufacture (including repackaging or relabeling) or to import ephedrine, pseudoephedrine, or phenylpropanolamine as bulk chemicals.

(b) Persons registered to manufacture (including repackaging or relabeling) or to import prescription and over-the-counter drug products containing ephedrine, pseudoephedrine, or phenylpropanolamine that may be lawfully marketed and distributed in the United States under the Federal Food, Drug, and Cosmetic Act.

Subpart B—Assessment of Annual Needs

§ 1315.11 Assessment of annual needs.

(a) The Administrator shall determine the total quantity of ephedrine, pseudoephedrine, and phenylpropanolamine, including drug products containing ephedrine, pseudoephedrine, and phenylpropanolamine, necessary to be manufactured and imported during the following calendar year to provide for the estimated medical, scientific, research, and industrial needs of the United States, for lawful export requirements, and for the establishment and maintenance of reserve stocks.

(b) In making his determinations, the Administrator shall consider the following factors:

(1) Total net disposal of the chemical by all manufacturers and importers during the current and 2 preceding years;

(2) Trends in the national rate of net disposal of each chemical;

(3) Total actual (or estimated) inventories of the chemical and of all substances manufactured from the chemical, and trends in inventory accumulation;

(4) Projected demand for each chemical as indicated by procurement and import quotas requested pursuant to § 1315.32; and

(5) Other factors affecting medical, scientific, research, and industrial needs in the United States, lawful export requirements, and the establishment and maintenance of reserve stocks, as the Administrator finds relevant, including changes in the currently accepted medical use in treatment with the chemicals or the substances which are manufactured from them, the economic and physical availability of raw materials for use in manufacturing and for inventory purposes, yield and stability problems, potential disruptions to production (including possible labor strikes), and recent unforeseen emergencies such as floods and fires.

(c) The Administrator shall, on or before May 1 of each year, publish in the FEDERAL REGISTER, general notice of an assessment of annual needs for ephedrine, pseudoephedrine, and phenylpropanolamine determined by him under this section. A notice of the publication shall be mailed simultaneously to each person registered to manufacture or import the chemical.

(d) The Administrator shall permit any interested person to file written comments on or objections to the proposed assessment of annual needs and shall designate in the notice the time during which the filings may be made.

(e) The Administrator may, but is not required to, hold a public hearing on one or more issues raised by the comments and objections filed with him. In the event the Administrator decides to hold such a hearing, he shall publish a notice of the hearing in the FEDERAL REGISTER. The notice shall summarize the issues to be heard and set the time for the hearing, which shall not be less than 30 days after the date of publication of the notice.

(f) After consideration of any comments or objections, or after a hearing if one is ordered by the Administrator, the Administrator shall issue and publish in the FEDERAL REGISTER the final order determining the assessment of annual needs for the chemicals. The order shall include the findings of fact and conclusions of law upon which the order is based. The order shall specify the date on which it shall take effect. A notice of the publication shall be mailed simultaneously to each person registered as a manufacturer or importer of the chemical.

§ 1315.13 Adjustments of the assessment of annual needs.

(a) The Administrator may at any time increase or reduce the assessment of annual needs for ephedrine, pseudoephedrine, or phenylpropanolamine that has been previously fixed pursuant to § 1315.11.

(b) In determining to adjust the assessment of annual needs, the Administrator shall consider the following factors:

(1) Changes in the demand for that chemical, changes in the national rate of net disposal of the chemical, and changes in the rate of net disposal of the chemical by registrants holding individual manufacturing or import quotas for that chemical;

(2) Whether any increased demand for that chemical, the national and/or changes in individual rates of net disposal of that chemical are temporary, short term, or long term;

(3) Whether any increased demand for that chemical can be met through existing inventories, increased individual manufacturing quotas, or increased importation, without increasing the assessment of annual needs, taking into account production delays and the probability that other individual manufacturing quotas may be suspended pursuant to § 1315.24(b);

(4) Whether any decreased demand for that chemical will result in excessive inventory accumulation by all persons registered to handle that chemical (including manufacturers, distributors, importers, and exporters), notwithstanding the possibility that individual manufacturing quotas may be suspended pursuant to § 1315.24(b) or abandoned pursuant to § 1315.27;

(5) Other factors affecting medical, scientific, research, industrial, and importation needs in the United States, lawful export requirements, and reserve stocks, as the Administrator finds relevant, including changes in the currently accepted medical use in treatment with the chemical or the substances that are manufactured from it, the economic and physical availability of raw materials for use in manufacturing and for inventory purposes, yield and stability problems, potential disruptions to production (including possible labor strikes), and recent unforeseen emergencies such as floods and fires.

(c) In the event that the Administrator determines to increase or reduce the assessment of annual needs for a chemical, the Administrator shall publish in the FEDERAL REGISTER general notice of an adjustment in the assessment of annual needs for that chemical as determined under this section. A notice of the publication shall be mailed simultaneously to each person registered as a manufacturer or importer of the chemical.

(d) The Administrator shall permit any interested person to file written comments on or objections to the proposal and shall designate in the notice the time during which such filings may be made.

(e) The Administrator may, but is not required to, hold a public hearing on one or more issues raised by the comments and objections filed with him. In the event the Administrator decides to hold such a hearing, he shall publish a notice of the hearing in the FEDERAL REGISTER. The notice shall summarize the issues to be heard and set the time for the hearing, which shall not be less than 10 days after the date of publication of the notice.

(f) After consideration of any comments or objections, or after a hearing if one is ordered by the Administrator, the Administrator shall issue and publish in the FEDERAL REGISTER the final order determining the assessment of annual needs for the chemical. The order shall include the findings of fact and conclusions of law upon which the order is based. The order shall specify the date on which it shall take effect. A notice of the publication shall be mailed simultaneously to each person registered as a manufacturer or importer of the chemical.

Subpart C—Individual Manufacturing Quotas

§ 1315.21 Individual manufacturing quotas.

The Administrator shall, on or before July 1 of each year, fix for and issue to each person registered to manufacture in bulk ephedrine, pseudoephedrine, or phenylpropanolamine who applies for a manufacturing quota an individual manufacturing quota authorizing that person to manufacture during the next calendar year a quantity of that chemical. Any manufacturing quota fixed and issued by the Administrator is subject to his authority to reduce or limit it at a later date pursuant to § 1315.26 and to his authority to revoke or suspend it at any time pursuant to §§ 1301.36, 1309.43, 1309.44, or 1309.45 of this chapter.

§ 1315.22 Procedure for applying for individual manufacturing quotas.

Any person who is registered to manufacture ephedrine, pseudoephedrine, or phenylpropanolamine and who desires to manufacture a quantity of the chemical must apply on DEA Form 189 for a manufacturing quota for the quantity of the chemical. Copies of DEA Form 189 may be obtained from the Office of Diversion Control Web site, and must be filed (on or before April 1 of the year preceding the calendar year for which the manufacturing quota is being applied) with the UN Reporting & Quota Section, Diversion Control Division, Drug Enforcement Administration. See the Table of DEA Mailing Addresses in § 1321.01 of this chapter for the current mailing address. A separate application must be made for each chemical desired to be manufactured. The applicant must state the following:

(a) The name and DEA Chemical Code Number, as set forth in part 1310 of this chapter, of the chemical.

(b) For the chemical in each of the current and preceding 2 calendar years,

(1) The authorized individual manufacturing quota, if any;

(2) The actual or estimated quantity manufactured;

(3) The actual or estimated net disposal;

(4) The actual or estimated inventory allowance pursuant to § 1315.24; and

(5) The actual or estimated inventory as of December 31.

(c) For the chemical in the next calendar year,

(1) The desired individual manufacturing quota; and

(2) Any additional factors that the applicant finds relevant to the fixing of the individual manufacturing quota, including any of the following:

(i) The trend of (and recent changes in) the applicant's and the national rates of net disposal.

(ii) The applicant's production cycle and current inventory position.

(iii) The economic and physical availability of raw materials for use in manufacturing and for inventory purposes.

(iv) Yield and stability problems.

(v) Potential disruptions to production (including possible labor strikes).

(vi) Recent unforeseen emergencies such as floods and fires.

[72 FR 37448, July 10, 2007, as amended at 73 FR 73555, Dec. 3, 2008; 75 FR 10684, Mar. 9, 2010]

§ 1315.23 Procedure for fixing individual manufacturing quotas.

(a) In fixing individual manufacturing quotas for ephedrine, pseudoephedrine, and phenylpropanolamine, the Administrator shall allocate to each applicant who is currently manufacturing the chemical a quota equal to 100 percent of the estimated net disposal of that applicant for the next calendar year, adjusted—

(1) By the amount necessary to increase or reduce the estimated inventory of the applicant on December 31 of the current year to his estimated inventory allowance for the next calendar year, pursuant to § 1315.24, and

(2) By any other factors which the Administrator deems relevant to the fixing of the individual manufacturing quota of the applicant, including:

(i) The trend of (and recent changes in) the applicant's and the national rates of net disposal,

(ii) The applicant's production cycle and current inventory position,

(iii) The economic and physical availability of raw materials for use in manufacturing and for inventory purposes,

(iv) Yield and stability problems,

(v) Potential disruptions to production (including possible labor strikes), and

(vi) Recent unforeseen emergencies such as floods and fires.

(b) In fixing individual manufacturing quotas for a chemical, the Administrator shall allocate to each applicant who is not currently manufacturing the chemical a quota equal to 100 percent of the reasonably estimated net disposal of that applicant for the next calendar year, as determined by the Administrator, adjusted—

(1) By the amount necessary to provide the applicant his estimated inventory allowance for the next calendar year, pursuant to § 1315.24; and

(2) By any other factors which the Administrator deems relevant to the fixing of the individual manufacturing quota of the applicant, including any of the following:

(i) The trend of (and recent changes in) the national rate of net disposal.

(ii) The applicant's production cycle and current inventory position.

(iii) The economic and physical availability of raw materials for use in manufacturing and for inventory purposes.

(iv) Yield and stability problems.

(v) Potential disruptions to production (including possible labor strikes).

(vi) Recent unforeseen emergencies such as floods and fires.

(c) On or before March 1 of each year the Administrator shall adjust the individual manufacturing quota allocated for that year to each applicant in paragraph (a) of this section by the amount necessary to increase or reduce the actual inventory of the applicant to December 31 of the preceding year to his estimated inventory allowance for the current calendar year, pursuant to § 1315.24.

§ 1315.24 Inventory allowance.

(a) For the purpose of determining individual manufacturing quotas pursuant to § 1315.23, each registered manufacturer shall be allowed as a part of the quota an amount sufficient to maintain an inventory equal to either of the following:

(1) For current manufacturers, 50 percent of his average estimated net disposal for the current calendar year and the last preceding calendar year; or

(2) For new manufacturers, 50 percent of his reasonably estimated net disposal for the next calendar year as determined by the Administrator.

(b) During each calendar year each registered manufacturer shall be allowed to maintain an inventory of a chemical not exceeding 65 percent of his estimated net disposal of that chemical for that year, as determined at the time his quota for that year was determined. At any time the inventory of a chemical held by a manufacturer exceeds 65 percent of his estimated net disposal, his quota for that chemical is automatically suspended and shall remain suspended until his inventory is less than 60 percent of his estimated net disposal. The Administrator may, upon application and for good cause shown, permit a manufacturer whose quota is, or is likely to be, suspended under this paragraph to continue manufacturing and to accumulate an inventory in excess of 65 percent of his estimated net disposal, upon such conditions and within such limitations as the Administrator may find necessary or desirable.

(c) If, during a calendar year, a registrant has manufactured the entire quantity of a chemical allocated to him under an individual manufacturing quota, and his inventory of that chemical is less than 40 percent of his estimated net disposal of that chemical for that year, the Administrator may, upon application pursuant to § 1315.25, increase the quota of such registrant sufficiently to allow restoration of the inventory to 50 percent of the estimated net disposal for that year.

§ 1315.25 Increase in individual manufacturing quotas.

(a) Any registrant who holds an individual manufacturing quota for a chemical may file with the Administrator an application on DEA Form 189 for an increase in the registrant's quota to meet the registrant's estimated net disposal, inventory, and other requirements during the remainder of that calendar year.

(b) The Administrator, in passing upon a registrant's application for an increase in the individual manufacturing quota, shall take into consideration any occurrences since the filing of the registrant's initial quota application that may require an increased manufacturing rate by the registrant during the balance of the calendar year. In passing upon the application the Administrator may also take into consideration the amount, if any, by which his determination of the total quantity for the chemical to be manufactured under § 1315.11 exceeds the aggregate of all the individual manufacturing quotas for the chemical, and the equitable distribution of such excess among other registrants.

§ 1315.26 Reduction in individual manufacturing quotas.

The Administrator may at any time reduce an individual manufacturing quota for a chemical that he has previously fixed to prevent the aggregate of the individual manufacturing quotas and import quotas outstanding or to be granted from exceeding the assessment of annual needs that has been established for that chemical pursuant to § 1315.11, as adjusted pursuant to § 1315.13. If a quota assigned to a new manufacturer pursuant to § 1315.23(b), or if a quota assigned to any manufacturer is increased pursuant to § 1315.24(c), or if an import quota issued to an importer pursuant to § 1315.34, causes the total quantity of a chemical to be manufactured and imported during the year to exceed the assessment of annual needs that has been established for that chemical pursuant to § 1315.11, as adjusted pursuant to § 1315.13, the Administrator may proportionately reduce the individual manufacturing quotas and import quotas of all other registrants to keep the assessment of annual needs within the limits originally established, or, alternatively, the Administrator may reduce the individual manufacturing quota of any registrant whose quota is suspended pursuant to § 1315.24(b) or §§ 1301.36, 1309.43, 1309.44, or 1309.45 of this chapter or is abandoned pursuant to § 1315.27.

§ 1315.27 Abandonment of quota.

Any manufacturer assigned an individual manufacturing quota for a chemical pursuant to § 1315.23 may at any time abandon his right to manufacture all or any part of the quota by filing with the UN Reporting & Quota Section, Diversion Control Division, Drug Enforcement Administration a written notice of the abandonment, stating the name and DEA Chemical Code Number, as set forth in part 1310 of this chapter, of the chemical and the amount which he has chosen not to manufacture. The Administrator may, in his discretion, allocate the amount among the other manufacturers in proportion to their respective quotas.

Subpart D—Procurement and Import Quotas

§ 1315.30 Procurement and import quotas.

(a) To determine the estimated needs for, and to insure an adequate and uninterrupted supply of, ephedrine, pseudoephedrine, and phenylpropanolamine the Administrator shall issue procurement and import quotas.

(b) A procurement quota authorizes a registered manufacturer to procure and use quantities of each chemical for the following purposes:

(1) Manufacturing the bulk chemical into dosage forms.

(2) Manufacturing the bulk chemical into other substances.

(3) Repackaging or relabeling the chemical or dosage forms.

(c) An import quota authorizes a registered importer to import quantities of the chemical for the following purposes:

(1) Distribution of the chemical to a registered manufacturer that has a procurement quota for the chemical.

(2) Other distribution of the chemical consistent with the legitimate medical and scientific needs of the United States.

§ 1315.32 Obtaining a procurement quota.

(a) Any person who is registered to manufacture ephedrine, pseudoephedrine, or phenylpropanolamine, or whose requirement of registration is waived pursuant to § 1309.24 of this chapter, and who desires to use during the next calendar year any ephedrine, pseudoephedrine, or phenylpropanolamine for purposes of manufacturing (including repackaging or relabeling), must apply on DEA Form 250 for a procurement quota for the chemical. A separate application must be made for each chemical desired to be procured or used.

(b) The applicant must state separately all of the following:

(1) Each purpose for which the chemical is desired.

(2) The quantity desired for each purpose during the next calendar year.

(3) The quantities used and estimated to be used, if any, for that purpose during the current and preceding 2 calendar years.

(c) If the purpose is to manufacture the chemical into dosage form, the applicant must state the official name, common or usual name, chemical name, or brand name of that form. If the dosage form produced is a controlled substance listed in any schedule, the applicant must also state the schedule number and National Drug Code Number, of the substance.

(d) If the purpose is to manufacture another chemical, the applicant must state the official name, common or usual name, chemical name, or brand name of the substance and the DEA Chemical Code Number, as set forth in part 1310 of this chapter.

(e) DEA Form 250 must be filed on or before April 1 of the year preceding the calendar year for which the procurement quota is being applied. Copies of DEA Form 250 may be obtained from the Office of Diversion Control Web site, and must be filed with the UN Reporting & Quota Section, Diversion Control Division, Drug Enforcement Administration. See the Table of DEA Mailing Addresses in § 1321.01 of this chapter for the current mailing address.

(f) The Administrator shall, on or before July 1 of the year preceding the calendar year during which the quota shall be effective, issue to each qualified applicant a procurement quota authorizing him to procure and use:

(1) All quantities of the chemical necessary to manufacture products that the applicant is authorized to manufacture pursuant to § 1315.23; and

(2) Such other quantities of the chemical as the applicant has applied to procure and use and are consistent with his past use, his estimated needs, and the total quantity of the chemical that will be produced.

(g) Any person to whom a procurement quota has been issued may at any time request an adjustment in the quota by applying to the Administrator with a statement showing the need for the adjustment. The application must be filed with the UN Reporting & Quota Section, Diversion Control Division, Drug Enforcement Administration. See the Table of DEA Mailing Addresses in § 1321.01 of this chapter for the current mailing address. The Administrator shall increase or decrease the procurement quota of the person if and to the extent that he finds, after considering the factors enumerated in paragraph (f) of this section and any occurrences since the issuance of the procurement quota, that the need justifies an adjustment.

(h) Any person to whom a procurement quota has been issued, authorizing that person to procure and use a quantity of ephedrine, pseudoephedrine, or phenylpropanolamine during the current calendar year, must, at or before the time of placing an order with another manufacturer or importer requiring the distribution of a quantity of the chemical, certify in writing to the other registrant that the quantity of ephedrine, pseudoephedrine, or phenylpropanolamine ordered does not exceed the person's unused and available procurement quota of the chemical for the current calendar year. The written certification must be executed by a person authorized to sign the registration application pursuant to § 1301.13 or § 1309.32(g) of this chapter or by a person granted power of attorney under § 1315.33 to sign the certifications. A copy of such certification must be retained by the person procuring the quantity of ephedrine, pseudoephedrine, or phenylpropanolamine for two years from the date of the certification. Registrants must not fill an order from persons required to apply for a procurement quota under paragraph (b) of this section unless the order is accompanied by a certification as required under this section.

(i) The certification required by paragraph (h) of this section must contain all of the following:

(1) The date of the certification.

(2) The name and address of the registrant to whom the certification is directed.

(3) A reference to the purchase order number to which the certification applies.

(4) The name of the person giving the order to which the certification applies.

(5) The name of the chemical to which the certification applies.

(6) A statement that the quantity (expressed in grams) of the chemical to which the certification applies does not exceed the unused and available procurement quota of the chemical, issued to the person giving the order, for the current calendar year.

(7) The signature of the individual authorized to sign a certification as provided in paragraph (h) of this section.

[72 FR 37448, July 10, 2007, as amended at 73 FR 73555, Dec. 3, 2008; 75 FR 10684, Mar. 9, 2010]

§ 1315.33 Power of attorney.

(a) A registrant may authorize one or more individuals, whether or not located at his registered location, to sign certifications required under § 1315.32(h) on the registrant's behalf by executing a power of attorney for each such individual. The registrant shall retain the power of attorney in the files, with certifications required by § 1315.32(h), for the same period as any certification bearing the signature of the attorney. The power of attorney must be available for inspection together with other certification records.

(b) A registrant may revoke any power of attorney at any time by executing a notice of revocation.

(c) The power of attorney and notice of revocation must be similar to the following format:

Power of Attorney for certifications of quota for procurement of ephedrine, pseudoephedrine, and phenylpropanolamine

__________ (Name of registrant)
__________ (Address of registrant)
__________ (DEA registration number)

I, __________ (name of person granting power), the undersigned, who am authorized to sign the current application for registration of the above-named registrant under the Controlled Substances Act or Controlled Substances Import and Export Act, have made, constituted, and appointed, and by these presents, do make, constitute, and appoint __________ (name of attorney-in-fact), my true and lawful attorney for me in my name, place, and stead, to sign certifications of quota for procurement of ephedrine, pseudoephedrine, and phenylpropanolamine in accordance with Part 1315 of Title 21 of the Code of Federal Regulations. I hereby ratify and confirm all that said attorney must lawfully do or cause to be done by virtue hereof.

____

(Signature of person granting power)

I, __________ (name of attorney-in-fact), hereby affirm that I am the person named herein as attorney-in-fact and that the signature affixed hereto is my signature.

(Signature of attorney-in-fact)

Witnesses:

1. __________
2. __________

Signed and dated on the ____ day of __, (year), at __________.

Notice of Revocation

The foregoing power of attorney is hereby revoked by the undersigned, who is authorized to sign the current application for registration of the above-named registrant under the Controlled Substances Act or the Controlled Substances Import and Export Act. Written notice of this revocation has been given to the attorney-in-fact ________ this same day.

____

(Signature of person revoking power)

Witnesses:

1. ________

2. ________

Signed and dated on the ____ day of __, (year), at ________.

(d) A power of attorney must be executed by the person who signed the most recent application for DEA registration or reregistration; the person to whom the power of attorney is being granted; and two witnesses.

(e) A power of attorney must be revoked by the person who signed the most recent application for DEA registration or reregistration, and two witnesses.

[73 FR 73555, Dec. 3, 2008]

§ 1315.34 Obtaining an import quota.

(a) Any person who is registered to import ephedrine, pseudoephedrine, or phenylpropanolamine, or whose requirement of registration is waived pursuant to § 1309.24(c) of this chapter, and who desires to import during the next calendar year any ephedrine, pseudoephedrine, or phenylpropanolamine or drug products containing these chemicals, must apply on DEA Form 488 for an import quota for the chemical. A separate application must be made for each chemical desired to be imported.

(b) The applicant must provide the following information in the application:

(1) The applicant's name and DEA registration number.

(2) The name and address of a contact person and contact information (telephone number, fax number, e-mail address).

(3) Name of the chemical and DEA Chemical Code number.

(4) Type of product (bulk or finished dosage forms).

(5) For finished dosage forms, the official name, common or usual name, chemical name, or brand name, NDC number, and the authority to market the drug product under the Federal Food, Drug and Cosmetic Act of each form to be imported.

(6) The amount requested expressed in terms of base.

(7) For the current and preceding two calendar years, expressed in terms of base:

(i) Distribution/Sales—name, address, and registration number (if applicable) of each customer and the amount sold.

(ii) Inventory as of December 31 (each form—bulk, in-process, finished dosage form).

(iii) Acquisition—imports.

(c) For each form of the chemical (bulk or dosage unit), the applicant must state the quantity desired for import during the next calendar year.

(d) DEA Form 488 must be filed on or before April 1 of the year preceding the calendar year for which the import quota is being applied. Copies of DEA Form 488 may be obtained from the Office of Diversion Control Web site, and must be filed with the UN Reporting & Quota Section, Diversion Control Division, Drug Enforcement Administration . See the Table of DEA Mailing Addresses in § 1321.01 of this chapter for the current mailing address.

(e) The Administrator may at his discretion request additional information from an applicant.

(f) On or before July 1 of the year preceding the calendar year during which the quota shall be effective, the Administrator shall issue to each qualified applicant an import quota authorizing him to import:

(1) All quantities of the chemical necessary to manufacture products that registered manufacturers are authorized to manufacture pursuant to § 1315.23; and

(2) Such other quantities of the chemical that the applicant has applied to import and that are consistent with his past imports, the estimated medical, scientific, and industrial needs of the United States, the establishment and maintenance of reserve

stocks, and the total quantity of the chemical that will be produced.

[72 FR 37448, July 10, 2007, as amended at 75 FR 10684, Mar. 9, 2010]

§ 1315.36 Amending an import quota.

(a) An import quota authorizes the registered importer to import up to the set quantity of ephedrine, pseudoephedrine, or phenylpropanolamine and distribute the chemical or drug products on the DEA Form 488. An importer must apply to change the quantity to be imported.

(b) Any person to whom an import quota has been issued may at any time request an increase in the quota quantity by applying to the Administrator with a statement showing the need for the adjustment. The application must be filed with the UN Reporting & Quota Section, Diversion Control Division, Drug Enforcement Administration. See the Table of DEA Mailing Addresses in § 1321.01 of this chapter for the current mailing address. The Administrator may increase the import quota of the person if and to the extent that he determines that the approval is necessary to provide for medical, scientific, or other legitimate purposes regarding the chemical. The Administrator shall specify a period of time for which the approval is in effect or shall provide that the approval is in effect until the Administrator notifies the applicant in writing that the approval is terminated.

(c) With respect to the application under paragraph (b) of this section, the Administrator shall approve or deny the application within 60 days of receiving the application. If the Administrator does not approve or deny the application within 60 days of receiving it, the application is deemed to be approved and the approval remains in effect until the Administrator notifies the applicant in writing that the approval is terminated.

[72 FR 37448, July 10, 2007, as amended at 75 FR 10685, Mar. 9, 2010]

Subpart E—Hearings

§ 1315.50 Hearings generally.

The procedures for the hearing related to assessment of annual needs or to the issuance, adjustment, suspension, or denial of a manufacturing, procurement, or import quota are governed generally by the adjudication procedures set forth in the Administrative Procedure Act (5 U.S.C. 551–559) and specifically by section 1002 of the Act (21 U.S.C. 952), by §§ 1315.52 through 1315.62 of this part, and by the procedures for administrative hearings under the Act set forth in §§ 1316.41 through 1316.67 of this chapter.

§ 1315.52 Purpose of hearing.

(a) The Administrator may, in his sole discretion, hold a hearing for the purpose of receiving factual evidence regarding any one or more issues (to be specified by him) involved in the determination or adjustment of any assessment of national needs.

(b) If requested by a person applying for or holding a procurement, import, or individual manufacturing quota, the Administrator shall hold a hearing for the purpose of receiving factual evidence regarding the issues involved in the issuance, adjustment, suspension, or denial of the quota to the person, but the Administrator need not hold a hearing on suspension of a quota under § 1301.36 or § 1309.43 of this chapter separate from a hearing on the suspension of registration under that section.

(c) Extensive argument should not be offered into evidence, but rather presented in opening or closing statements of counsel or in memoranda or proposed findings of fact and conclusions of law.

§ 1315.54 Waiver or modification of rules.

The Administrator or the presiding officer (with respect to matters pending before him) may modify or waive any rule in this part by notice in advance of the hearing, if he determines that no party in the hearing will be unduly prejudiced and the ends of justice will thereby be served. Such notice of modification or waiver shall be made a part of the record of the hearing.

§ 1315.56 Request for hearing or appearance; waiver.

(a) Any applicant or registrant entitled to a hearing under § 1315.52 and who desires a hearing on the issuance, adjustment, suspension or denial of a procurement, import, or individual manufacturing quota must, within 30 days after the date of receipt of the issuance, adjustment, suspension or denial of the application, file with the Administrator a written request for a hearing in the form prescribed in § 1316.47 of this chapter.

(b) Any interested person who desires a hearing on the determination of an assessment of annual needs must, within the time prescribed in § 1315.11(c), file with the Administrator a written request for a hearing in the form prescribed in § 1316.47 of this chapter, including in the request a statement of the grounds for the hearing.

(c) Any interested person who desires to participate in a hearing on the determination or adjustment of an assessment of annual needs, which hearing is ordered by the Administrator under § 1315.11(c) or § 1315.13(c), may do so by filing with the Administrator, within 30 days of the date of publication of notice of the hearing in the FEDERAL REGISTER, a written notice of his intention to participate in the hearing in the form prescribed in § 1316.48 of this chapter.

(d) Any person entitled to a hearing under § 1315.52 or entitled to participate in a hearing under paragraph (c) of this section may, within the period permitted for filing a request for a hearing or notice of appearance, file with the Administrator a waiver of an opportunity for a hearing, together with a written statement regarding his position on the matters of fact and law involved in such hearing. The statement, if admissible, shall be made a part of the record and shall be considered in light of the lack of opportunity for cross-examination in determining the weight to be attached to matters of fact asserted.

(e) If any person entitled to a hearing under § 1315.52 or entitled to participate in a hearing under paragraph (c) of this section fails to file a request for a hearing or notice of appearance or if he so files and fails to appear at the hearing, he shall be deemed to have waived his opportunity for the hearing unless he shows good cause for such failure.

(f) If all persons entitled to a hearing or to participate in a hearing waive or are deemed to waive their opportunity for the hearing or to participate in the hearing, the Administrator may cancel the hearing, if scheduled, and issue his final order under § 1315.62 without a hearing.

§ 1315.58 Burden of proof.

(a) At any hearing regarding the determination or adjustment of an assessment of annual needs each interested person participating in the hearing shall have the burden of proving any propositions of fact or law asserted by him in the hearing.

(b) At any hearing regarding the issuance, adjustment, suspension, or denial of a procurement, import, or individual manufacturing quota, the Administration shall have the burden of proving that the requirements of this part for such issuance, adjustment, suspension, or denial are satisfied.

§ 1315.60 Time and place of hearing.

(a) If any applicant or registrant requests a hearing on the issuance, adjustment, suspension, or denial of his procurement, import, or individual manufacturing quota under § 1315.54, the Administrator shall hold a hearing.

(b) Notice of the hearing shall be given to the applicant or registrant of the time and place at least 30 days prior to the hearing, unless the applicant or registrant waives such notice and requests the hearing be held at an earlier time, in which case the Administrator shall fix a date for such hearing as early as reasonably possible.

(c) The hearing shall commence at the place and time designated in the notice given under paragraph (b) of this section or in the notice of hearing published in the FEDERAL REGISTER pursuant to § 1315.11(c) or § 1315.13(c), but thereafter it may be moved to a different place and may be continued from day to day or recessed to a later day without notice other than announcement by the presiding officer at the hearing.

§ 1315.62 Final order.

As soon as practicable after the presiding officer has certified the record to the Administrator, the Administrator shall issue his order on the determination or adjustment of the assessment of annual needs or on the issuance, adjustment, suspension, or denial of the procurement, import, or individual manufacturing quota, as the case may be. The order shall include the findings of fact and conclusions of law upon which the order is based. The order shall specify the date on which it shall take effect. The Administrator shall serve one copy of his order upon each party in the hearing.

PART 1316—ADMINISTRATIVE FUNCTIONS, PRACTICES, AND PROCEDURES

Subpart A—Administrative Inspections

Subpart B—Protection of Researchers and Research Subjects

Subpart C—Enforcement Proceedings

Subpart D—Administrative Hearings

SOURCE: 36 FR 7820, Apr. 24, 1971, unless otherwise noted. Redesignated at 38 FR 26609, Sept. 24, 1973.

Subpart A—Administrative Inspections

AUTHORITY: 21 U.S.C. 822(f), 830(a), 871(b), 880, 958(f), 965.

§ 1316.01 Scope of subpart A.

Procedures regarding administrative inspections and warrants pursuant to sections 302(f), 510, 1008(d), and 1015 of the Act (21 U.S.C. 822(f), 880, 958(d), and 965) are governed generally by those sections and specifically by the sections of this subpart.

§ 1316.02 Definitions.

As used in this subpart, the following terms shall have the meanings specified:

(a) The term *Act* means the Controlled Substances Act (84 Stat. 1242; 21 U.S.C. 801) and/or the Controlled Substances Import and Export Act (84 Stat. 1285; 21 U.S.C. 951).

(b) The term *Administration* means the Drug Enforcement Administration.

(c) The term *controlled premises* means—

(1) Places where original or other records or documents required under the Act are kept or required to be kept, and

(2) Places, including factories, warehouses, or other establishments and conveyances, where persons registered under the Act or exempted from registration under the Act, or regulated persons may lawfully hold, manufacture, or distribute, dispense, administer, or otherwise dispose of controlled substances or listed chemicals or where records relating to those activities are maintained.

(d) The term *Administrator* means the Administrator of the Administration. The Administrator has been delegated authority under the Act by the Attorney General (28 CFR 0.100).

(e) The term *inspector* means an officer or employee of the Administration authorized by the Administrator to make inspections under the Act.

(f) The term *register* and *registration* refer to registration required and permitted by sections 303 and 1008 of the Act (21 U.S.C. 823 and 958).

(g) Any term not defined in this part shall have the definition set forth in section 102 of the Act (21 U.S.C. 802) or part 1300 of this chapter.

[36 FR 7820, Apr. 24, 1971. Redesignated at 38 FR 26609, Sept. 24, 1973, as amended at 60 FR 32465, June 22, 1995; 60 FR 36334, July 14, 1995; 62 FR 13969, Mar. 24, 1997]

§ 1316.03 Authority to make inspections.

In carrying out his functions under the Act, the Administrator, through his inspectors, is authorized in accordance with sections 510 and 1015 of the Act (21 U.S.C. 880 and 965) to enter controlled premises and conduct administrative inspections thereof, for the purpose of:

(a) Inspecting, copying, and verifying the correctness of records, reports, or other documents required to be kept or made under the Act and regulations promulgated under the Act, including, but not limited to, inventory and other records required to be kept pursuant to part 1304 of this chapter, order form records required to be kept pursuant to part 1305 of this chapter, prescription and distribution records required to be kept pursuant to part 1306 of this chapter, records of listed chemicals, tableting machines, and encapsulating machines required to be kept pursuant to part 1310 of this chapter, import/export records of listed chemicals required to be kept pursuant to part 1313 of this chapter, shipping records identifying the name of each carrier used and the date and quantity of each shipment, and storage records identifying the name of each warehouse used and the date and quantity of each storage.

(b) Inspecting within reasonable limits and to a reasonable manner all pertinent equipment, finished and unfinished controlled substances, listed chemicals, and other substances or materials, containers, and labeling found at the controlled premises relating to this Act;

(c) Making a physical inventory of all controlled substances and listed chemicals on-hand at the premises;

(d) Collecting samples of controlled substances or listed chemicals (in the event any samples are collected during an inspection, the inspector shall issue a receipt for such samples on DEA Form 400 to the owner, operator, or agent in charge of the premises);

(e) Checking of records and information on distribution of controlled substances or listed chemicals by the registrant or regulated person (*i.e.*, has the distribution of controlled substances or listed chemicals increased markedly within the past year, and if so why);

(f) Except as provided in § 1316.04, all other things therein (including records, files, papers, processes, controls and facilities) appropriate for verification of the records, reports, documents referred to above or otherwise bearing on the provisions of the Act and the regulations thereunder.

[36 FR 7820, Apr. 24, 1971. Redesignated at 38 FR 26609, Sept. 24, 1973, and amended at 51 FR 5319, Feb. 13, 1986; 55 FR 50827, Dec. 11, 1990; 60 FR 32465, June 22, 1995; 77 FR 4238, Jan. 27, 2012]

§ 1316.04 Exclusion from inspection.

(a) Unless the owner, operator or agent in charge of the controlled premises so consents in writing, no inspection authorized by these regulations shall extend to:

(1) Financial data:

(2) Sales data other than shipping data; or

(3) Pricing data.

(b) [Reserved]

§ 1316.05 Entry.

An inspection shall be carried out by an inspector. Any such inspector, upon (a) stating his purpose and (b) presenting to the owner, operator or agent in charge of the premises to be inspected (1) appropriate credentials, and (2) written notice of his inspection authority under § 1316.06 of this chapter, and (c) receiving informed consent under § 1316.08 or through the use of administrative warrant issued under §§ 1316.09–1316.13, shall have the right to enter such premises and conduct inspections at reasonable times and in a reasonable manner.

[36 FR 7820, Apr. 24, 1971, as amended at 36 FR 13387, July 21, 1971. Redesignated at 38 FR 26609, Sept. 24, 1973; 62 FR 13970, Mar. 24, 1997]

§ 1316.06 Notice of inspection.

The notice of inspection (DEA (or DNB) Form 82) shall contain:

(a) The name and title of the owner, operator, or agent in charge of the controlled premises;

(b) The controlled premises name;

(c) The address of the controlled premises to be inspected;

(d) The date and time of the inspection;

(e) A statement that a notice of inspection is given pursuant to section 510 of the Act (21 U.S.C. 880);

(f) A reproduction of the pertinent parts of section 510 of the Act; and

(g) The signature of the inspector.

§ 1316.07 Requirement for administrative inspection warrant; exceptions.

In all cases where an inspection is contemplated, an administrative inspection warrant is required pursuant to section 510 of the Act (21 U.S.C. 880), except that such warrant shall not be required for establishments applying for initial registration under the Act, for the inspection of books and records pursuant to an administrative subpoena issued in accordance with section 506 of the Act (21 U.S.C. 876) nor for entries in administrative inspections (including seizures of property):

(a) With the consent of the owner, operator, or agent in charge of the controlled premises as set forth in § 1316.08;

(b) In situations presenting imminent danger to health or safety;

(c) In situations involving inspection of conveyances where there is reasonable cause to obtain a warrant;

(d) In any other exceptional or emergency circumstance or time or opportunity to apply for a warrant is lacking; or

(e) In any other situations where a warrant is not constitutionally required.

§ 1316.08 Consent to inspection.

(a) An administrative inspection warrant shall not be required if informed consent is obtained from the owner, operator, or agent in charge of the controlled premises to be inspected.

(b) Wherever possible, informed consent shall consist of a written statement signed by the owner, operator, or agent in charge of the premises to be inspected and witnessed by two persons. The written consent shall contain the following information:

(1) That he (the owner, operator, or agent in charge of the premises) has been informed of his constitutional right not to have an administrative inspection made without an administrative inspection warrant;

(2) That he has right to refuse to consent to such an inspection;

(3) That anything of an incriminating nature which may be found may be seized and used against him in a criminal prosecution;

(4) That he has been presented with a notice of inspection as set forth in § 1316.06;

(5) That the consent is given by him is voluntary and without threats of any kind; and

(6) That he may withdraw his consent at any time during the course of inspection.

(c) The written consent shall be produced in duplicate and be distributed as follows:

(1) The original will be retained by the inspector; and

(2) The duplicate will be given to the person inspected.

[36 FR 7820, Apr. 24, 1971, as amended at 37 FR 15924, Aug. 8, 1972. Redesignated at 38 FR 26609, Sept. 24, 1973]

§ 1316.09 Application for administrative inspection warrant.

(a) An administrative inspection warrant application shall be submitted to any judge of the United States or of a State court of record, or any United States magistrate and shall contain the following information:

(1) The name and address of the controlled premises to be inspected;

(2) A statement of statutory authority for the administrative inspection warrant, and that the fact that the particular inspection in question is designed to insure compliance with the Act and the regulations promulgated thereunder;

(3) A statement relating to the nature and extent of the administrative inspection, including, where necessary, a request to seize specified items and/or to collect samples of finished or unfinished controlled substances or listed chemicals;

(4) A statement that the establishment either:

(i) Has not been previously inspected, or

(ii) Was last inspected on a particular date.

(b) The application shall be submitted under oath to an appropriate judge or magistrate.

[36 FR 7820, Apr. 24, 1971, as amended at 36 FR 13387, July 21, 1971. Redesignated at 38 FR 26609, Sept. 24, 1973; 60 FR 32466, June 22, 1995]

§ 1316.10 Administrative probable cause.

If the judge or magistrate is satisfied that "administrative probable cause," as defined in section 510(d)(1) of the Act (21 U.S.C. 880(d)(1)) exists, he shall issue an administrative warrant. Administrative probable cause shall not mean criminal probable cause as defined by Federal statute or case law.

§ 1316.11 Execution of warrants.

An administrative inspection warrant shall be executed and returned as required by, and any inventory or seizure made shall comply with the requirements of, section 510(d)(3) of the Act (21 U.S.C. 880(d)(3)). The inspection shall begin as soon as is practicable after the issuance of the administrative inspection warrant and shall be completed with reasonable promptness. The inspection shall be conducted during regular business hours and shall be completed in a reasonable manner.

§ 1316.12 Refusal to allow inspection with an administrative warrant.

If a registrant or any person subject to the Act refuses to permit execution of an administrative warrant or impedes the inspector in the execution of that warrant, he shall be advised that such refusal or action constitutes a violation of section 402(a)(6) of the Act (21 U.S.C. 842(a)(6)). If he persists and the circumstances warrant, he shall be arrested and the inspection shall commence or continue.

[36 FR 7820, Apr. 24, 1971. Redesignated at 38 FR 26609, Sept. 24, 1973, as amended at 62 FR 13970, Mar. 24, 1997]

§ 1316.13 Frequency of administrative inspections.

Except where circumstances otherwise dictate, it is the intent of the Administration to inspect all manufacturers of controlled substances listed in Schedules I and II and distributors of controlled substances listed in Schedule I once each year. Distributors of controlled substances listed in Schedules II through V and manufacturers of controlled substances listed in Schedules III through V shall be inspected as circumstances may require, based in part on the registrant's history of compliance with the requirements of this chapter and maintenance of effective controls and procedures to guard against the diversion of controlled substances.

[62 FR 13969, Mar. 24, 1997]

Subpart B—Protection of Researchers and Research Subjects

AUTHORITY: 21 U.S.C. 830, 871(b).

§ 1316.21 Definitions.

As used in this part, the following terms shall have the meanings specified:

(a) The term *investigative personnel* includes managers, Diversion Investigators, attorneys, analysts and support personnel employed by the Drug Enforcement Administration who are involved in the processing, reviewing and analyzing of declarations and other relevant documents or data relative to regulated transactions or are involved in conducting investigations initiated pursuant to the receipt of such declarations, documents or data.

(b) The term *law enforcement personnel* means Special Agents employed by the Drug Enforcement Administration who, in the course of their official duties, gain knowledge of information which is confidential under such section.

[54 FR 31670, Aug. 1, 1989]

§ 1316.22 Exemption.

(a) Any person who is aggrieved by a disclosure of information in violation of subsection (c)(1) of Section 310 of the Controlled Substances Act (21 U.S.C. 830) may bring a civil action against the violator for appropriate relief.

(b) Notwithstanding the provision of paragraph (a), a civil action may not be brought under such paragraph against investigative or law enforcement personnel of the Drug Enforcement Administration.

[54 FR 31670, Aug. 1, 1989]

§ 1316.23 Confidentiality of identity of research subjects.

(a) Any person conducting a bona fide research project directly related to the enforcement of the laws under the jurisdiction of the Attorney General concerning drugs or other substances which are or may be subject to control under the Controlled Substances Act (84 Stat. 1242; 21 U.S.C. 801) who intends to maintain the confidentiality of the identity of those persons who are the subjects of such research may petition the Administrator of the Drug Enforcement Administration for a grant of confidentiality: *Providing*, That:

(1) The Attorney General is authorized to carry out such research under the provisions of Section 502(a) (2–6) of the Controlled Substances Act of 1970 (21 U.S.C. 872(a) (2–6)); and the research is being conducted with funds provided in whole or part by the Department of Justice; or

(2) The research is of a nature that the Attorney General would be authorized to carry out under the provisions of Section 502(a) (2–6) of the Controlled Substances Act (21 U.S.C. 872(a) (2–6), and is being conducted with funds provided from sources outside the Department of Justice.

(b) All petitions for Grants of Confidentiality shall be addressed to the Administrator, Drug Enforcement Administration (see the Table of DEA Mailing Addresses in § 1321.01 of this chapter for the current mailing address):

(1) A statement as to whether the research protocol requires the manufacture, production, import, export, distribution, dispensing, administration, or possession of controlled substances, and if so the researcher's registration number or a statement that an application for such registration has been submitted to DEA;

(2) The location of the research project;

(3) The qualifications of the principal investigator;

(4) A general description of the research or a copy of the research protocol;

(5) The source of funding for the research project;

(6) A statement as to the risks posed to the research subjects by the research procedures and what protection will be afforded to the research subjects;

(7) A statement as to the risks posed to society in general by the research procedures and what measures will be taken to protect the interests of society;

(8) A specific request to withhold the names and/or any other identifying

characteristics of the research subjects; and

(9) Statements establishing that a grant of confidentiality is necessary to the successful completion of the research project.

(c) The grant of confidentiality of identity of research subjects shall consist of a letter issued by the Administrator, which shall include:

(1) The researcher's name and address.

(2) The researcher's registration number, if applicable.

(3) The title and purpose of the research.

(4) The location of the research project.

(5) An authorization for all persons engaged in the research to withhold the names and identifying characteristics of persons who are the subjects of such research, stating that persons who obtain this authorization may not be compelled in any Federal, State, or local civil, criminal, administrative, legislative, or other proceeding to identify the subjects of such research for which this authorization was obtained.

(6) The limits of this authorization, if any.

(7) A statement to the effect that the grant of confidentiality of identity of research subjects shall be perpetual but shall pertain only to the subjects of the research described in the research protocol, the description of the research submitted to DEA, or as otherwise established by DEA.

(d) Within 30 days of the date of completion of the research project, the researcher shall so notify the Administrator. The Administrator shall issue another letter including the information required in paragraph (c) of this section and stating the starting and finishing dates of the research for which the confidentiality of identity of research subjects was granted; upon receipt of this letter, the research shall return the original letter of exemption.

[42 FR 54946, Oct. 12, 1977. Redesignated at 54 FR 31670, Aug. 1, 1989, as amended at 62 FR 13970, Mar. 24, 1997; 75 FR 10685, Mar. 9, 2010]

§ 1316.24 Exemption from prosecution for researchers.

(a) Upon registration of an individual to engage in research in controlled substances under the Controlled Substances Act (84 Stat. 1242; 21 U.S.C. 801), the Administrator of the Drug Enforcement Administration, on his own motion or upon request in writing from the Secretary or from the researcher or researching practitioner, may exempt the registrant when acting within the scope of his registration, from prosecution under Federal, State, or local laws for offenses relating to possession, distribution or dispensing of those controlled substances within the scope of his exemption. However, this exemption does not diminish any requirement of compliance with the Federal Food, Drug and Cosmetic Act (21 U.S.C. 301).

(b) All petitions for Grants of Exemption from Prosecution for the Researcher shall be addressed to the Administrator, Drug Enforcement Administration, (see the Table of DEA Mailing Addresses in § 1321.01 of this chapter for the current mailing address) and shall contain the following:

(1) The researcher's registration number if any, for the project;

(2) The location of the research project;

(3) The qualifications of the principal investigator;

(4) A general description of the research or a copy of the research protocol;

(5) The source of funding for the research project;

(6) A statement as to the risks posed to the research subjects by the research procedures and what protection will be afforded to the research subjects;

(7) A statement as to the risks posed to society in general by the research procedures and what measures will be taken to protect the interests of society;

(8) A specific request for exemption from prosecution by Federal, State, or local authorities for offenses related to the possession, distribution, and dispensing of controlled substances in accord with the procedures described in the research protocol;

(9) A statement establishing that a grant of exemption from prosecution is necessary to the successful completion of the research project.

(c) Any researcher or practitioner proposing to engage in research requesting both exemption from prosecution and confidentiality of identity of research subjects may submit a single petition incorporating the information required in §§ 1316.23(b) and 1316.24(b).

(d) The exemption shall consist of a letter issued by the Administrator, which shall include:

(1) The researcher's name and address;

(2) The researcher's registration number for the research project;

(3) The location of the research project;

(4) A concise statement of the scope of the researcher's registration;

(5) Any limits of the exemption; and

(6) A statement that the exemption shall apply to all acts done in the scope of the exemption while the exemption is in effect. The exemption shall remain in effect until completion of the research project or until the registration of the researcher is either revoked or suspended or his renewal of registration is denied. However, the protection afforded by the grant of exemption from prosecution during the research period shall be perpetual.

(e) Within 30 days of the date of completion of the research project, the researcher shall so notify the Administrator. The Administrator shall issue another letter including the information required in paragraph (d) of this section and stating the date of which the period of exemption concluded; upon receipt of this letter the researcher shall return the original letter of exemption.

[42 FR 54946, Oct. 12, 1977. Redesignated at 54 FR 31670, Aug. 1, 1989, as amended at 62 FR 13970, Mar. 24, 1997; 75 FR 10685, Mar. 9, 2010]

Subpart C—Enforcement Proceedings

AUTHORITY: 21 U.S.C. 871(b), 883.

§ 1316.31 Authority for enforcement proceeding.

A hearing may be ordered or granted by any Special Agent in Charge of the Drug Enforcement Administration, at his discretion, to permit any person against whom criminal and/or civil action is contemplated under the Controlled Substances Act (84 Stat. 1242; 21 U.S.C. 801) or the Controlled Substances Import and Export Act (84 Stat. 1285; 21 U.S.C. 951) an opportunity to present his views and his proposals for bringing his alleged violations into compliance with the law. Such hearing will also permit him to show cause why prosecution should not be instituted, or to present his views on the contemplated proceeding.

[36 FR 7820, Apr. 24, 1971. Redesignated at 38 FR 26609, Sept. 24, 1973, and amended at 47 FR 41735, Sept. 22, 1982]

§ 1316.32 Notice of proceeding; time and place.

Appropriate notice designating the time and place for the hearing shall be given to the person. Upon request, timely and properly made, by the person to whom notice has been given, the time or place of the hearing, or both, may be changed if the request states reasonable grounds for such change. Such request shall be addressed to the Special Agent in Charge who issued the notice.

[36 FR 7820, Apr. 24, 1971. Redesignated at 38 FR 26609, Sept. 24, 1973, and amended at 47 FR 41735, Sept. 22, 1982]

§ 1316.33 Conduct of proceeding.

Presentation of views at a hearing under this subpart shall be private and informal. The views presented shall be confined to matters relevant to bringing violations into compliance with the Act or to other contemplated proceedings under the Act. These views may be presented orally or in writing by the person to whom the notice was given, or by his authorized representative.

§ 1316.34 Records of proceeding.

A formal record, either verbatim or summarized, of the hearing may be made at the discretion of the Special Agent in Charge. If a verbatim record is to be made, the person attending the hearing will be so advised prior to the start of the hearing.

[37 FR 15924, Aug. 8, 1972. Redesignated at 38 FR 26609, Sept. 24, 1973, and amended at 47 FR 41735, Sept. 22, 1982]

Subpart D—Administrative Hearings

AUTHORITY: 21 U.S.C. 811, 812, 871(b), 875, 958(d), 965.

§ 1316.41 Scope of subpart D.

Procedures in any administrative hearing held under the Act are governed generally by the rule making and/or adjudication procedures set forth in the Administrative Procedure Act (5 U.S.C. 551–559) and specifically by the procedures set forth in this subpart, except where more specific regulations (set forth in §§ 1301.51–1301.57, §§ 1303.31–1303.37, §§ 1308.41–1308.51, §§ 1311.51–1311.53, §§ 1312.41–1312.47, §§ 1313.51–1313.57, or §§ 1315.50–1315.62) apply.

[73 FR 73556, Dec. 3, 2008]

§ 1316.42 Definitions.

As used in this subpart, the following terms shall have the meanings specified:

(a) The term *Act* means the Controlled Substances Act (84 Stat. 1242; 21 U.S.C. 801) and/or the Controlled Substances Import and Export Act (84 Stat. 1285; 21 U.S.C. 951).

(b) The term *Administrator* means the Administrator of the Administration. The Administrator has been delegated authority under the Act by the Attorney General (28 CFR 0.100).

(c) The term *hearing* means any hearing held pursuant to the Act.

(d) The term *Hearing Clerk* means the hearing clerk of the Administration.

(e) The term *person* includes an individual, corporation, government or governmental subdivision or agency, business trust, partnership, association or other legal entity.

(f) The term *presiding officer* means an administrative law judge qualified and appointed as provided in the Administrative Procedure Act (5 U.S.C. 556).

(g) The term *proceeding* means all actions involving a hearing, commencing with the publication by the Administrator of the notice of proposed rulemaking or the issuance of an order to show cause.

(h) Any term not defined in this part shall have the definition set forth in section 102 of the Act (21 U.S.C. 802) or part 1300 of this chapter.

[36 FR 7820, Apr. 24, 1971, as amended at 38 FR 757, Jan. 4, 1973. Redesignated at 38 FR 26609, Sept. 24, 1973, as amended at 62 FR 13969, Mar. 24, 1997; 77 FR 4238, Jan. 27, 2012]

§ 1316.43 Information; special instructions.

Information regarding procedure under these rules and instructions supplementing these rules in special instances will be furnished by the Hearing Clerk upon request.

§ 1316.44 Waiver or modification of rules.

The Administrator or the presiding officer (with respect to matters pending before him) may modify or waive any rule in this subpart by notice in advance of the hearing, if he determines that no party in the hearing will be unduly prejudiced and the ends of justice will thereby be served. Such notice of modification or waiver shall be made a part of the record of the hearing.

§ 1316.45 Filings; address; hours.

Documents required or permitted to be filed in, and correspondence relating to, hearings governed by the regulations in this chapter shall be filed with the Hearing Clerk, Drug Enforcement Administration. See the Table of DEA Mailing Addresses in § 1321.01 of this chapter for the current mailing address. This office is open Monday through Friday from 8:30 a.m. to 5 p.m. eastern standard or daylight saving time, whichever is effective in the District of Columbia at the time, except on national legal holidays. Documents shall be dated and deemed filed upon receipt by the Hearing Clerk.

[75 FR 10685, Mar. 9, 2010]

§ 1316.46 Inspection of record.

(a) The record bearing on any proceeding, except for material described in subsection (b) of this section, shall be available for inspection and copying by any person entitled to participate in such proceeding, during office hours in the office of the Hearing Clerk, Drug Enforcement Administration. See the Table of DEA Mailing Addresses in

§ 1321.01 of this chapter for the current mailing address.

(b) The following material shall not be available for inspection as part of the record:

(1) A research protocol filed with an application for registration to conduct research with controlled substances listed in Schedule I, pursuant to § 1301.32 (a)(6) of this chapter, if the applicant requests that the protocol be kept confidential;

(2) An outline of a production or manufacturing process filed with an application for registration to manufacture a new narcotic controlled substance, pursuant to § 1301.33 of this chapter, if the applicant requests that the outline be kept confidential;

(3) Any confidential or trade secret information disclosed in conjunction with an application for registration, or in reports filed while registered, or acquired in the course of an investigation, entitled to protection under subsection 402(a) (8) of the Act (21 U.S.C. 842(a) (8)) or any other law restricting public disclosure of information; and

(4) Any material contained in any investigatory report, memorandum, or file, or case report compiled by the Administration.

[36 FR 7820, Apr. 24, 1971. Redesignated at 38 FR 26609, Sept. 24, 1973, as amended at 62 FR 13970, Mar. 24, 1997; 75 FR 10645, Mar. 9, 2010]

§ 1316.47 Request for hearing.

(a) Any person entitled to a hearing and desiring a hearing shall, within the period permitted for filing, file a request for a hearing and/or an answer that complies with the following format (see the Table of DEA Mailing Addresses in § 1321.01 of this chapter for the current mailing address):

(Date) __________
Drug Enforcement Administration, Attn: Hearing Clerk/OALJ

(Mailing Address) __________
Subject: Request for Hearing

Dear Sir:

The undersigned __________ (Name of the Person) hereby requests a hearing in the matter of: __________ (Identification of the proceeding).

(A) (State with particularity the interest of the person in the proceeding.)

(B) (State with particularity the objections or issues, if any, concerning which the person desires to be heard.)

(C) (State briefly the position of the person with regard to the particular objections or issues.)

All notices to be sent pursuant to the proceeding should be addressed to:

(Name) __________
(Street Address) __________
(City and State) __________

Respectfully yours,
(Signature of Person) __________

(b) The Administrative Law Judge, upon request and showing of good cause, may grant a reasonable extension of the time allowed for response to an Order to Show Cause.

[36 FR 7820, Apr. 24, 1971, as amended at 36 FR 13387, July 21, 1971. Redesignated at 38 FR 26609, Sept. 24, 1973]

EDITORIAL NOTE: For FEDERAL REGISTER citations affecting § 1316.47, see the List of CFR Sections Affected, which appears in the Finding Aids section of the printed volume and at *www.govinfo.gov*.

§ 1316.48 Notice of appearance.

Any person entitled to a hearing and desiring to appear in any hearing, shall, if he or she has not filed a request for hearing, file within the time specified in the notice of proposed rulemaking, a written notice of appearance in the following format (see the Table of DEA Mailing Addresses in § 1321.01 of this chapter for the current mailing address):

(Date) __________
Drug Enforcement Administration, Attn: Hearing Clerk/OALJ

(Mailing Address) __________
Subject: Notice of Appearance

Dear Sir:

Please take notice that __________ (Name of person) will appear in the matter of: __________ (Identification of the proceeding).

(A) (State with particularity the interest of the person in the proceeding.).

(B) (State with particularity the objections or issues, if any, concerning which the person desires to be heard.).

(C) (State briefly the position of the person with regard to the particular objections or issues.).

All notices to be sent pursuant to this appearance should be addressed to:

(Name) __________
(Street Address) __________
(City and State) __________

Respectfully yours,
(Signature of Person) ____________________

[81 FR 97041, Dec. 30, 2016]

§ 1316.49 Waiver of hearing.

Any person entitled to a hearing may, within the period permitted for filing a request for hearing or notice of appearance, waiver of an opportunity for a hearing, together with a written statement regarding his position on the matters of fact and law involved in such hearing. Such statement, if admissible, shall be made a part of the record and shall be considered in light of the lack of opportunity for cross-examination in determining the weight to be attached to matters of fact asserted therein.

§ 1316.50 Appearance; representation; authorization.

Any person entitled to appear in a hearing may appear in person or by a representative in any proceeding or hearing and may be heard with respect to matters relevant to the issues under consideration. A representative must either be an employee of the person or an attorney at law who is a member of the bar, in good standing, of any State, territory, or the District of Columbia, and admitted to practice before the highest court of that jurisdiction. Any representative may be required by the Administrator or the presiding officer to present a notarized power of attorney showing his authority to act in such representative capacity and/or an affidavit or certificate of admission to practice.

[36 FR 7820, Apr. 24, 1971, as amended at 36 FR 13387, July 21, 1971. Redesignated at 38 FR 26609, Sept. 24, 1973]

§ 1316.51 Conduct of hearing and parties; ex parte communications.

(a) Hearings shall be conducted in an informal but orderly manner in accordance with law and the directions of the presiding officer.

(b) Participants in any hearing and their representatives, whether or not members of the bar, shall conduct themselves in accordance with judicial standards of practice and ethics and the directions of the presiding officer. Refusal to comply with this section shall constitute grounds for immediate exclusion from any hearing.

(c) If any official of the Administration is contacted by any individual in private or public life concerning any substantive matter which is the subject of any hearing, at any time after the date on which the proceedings commence, the official who is contacted shall prepare a memorandum setting forth the substance of the conversation and shall file this memorandum in the appropriate public docket file. The presiding officer and employees of the Administration shall comply with the requirements of 5 U.S.C. 554(d) regarding ex parte communications and participation in any hearing.

§ 1316.52 Presiding officer.

A presiding officer, designated by the Administrator, shall preside over all hearings. The functions of the presiding officer shall commence upon his designation and terminate upon the certification of the record to the Administrator. The presiding officer shall have the duty to conduct a fair hearing, to take all necessary action to avoid delay, and to maintain order. He shall have all powers necessary to these ends, including (but not limited to) the power to:

(a) Arrange and change the date, time, and place of hearings (other than the time and place prescribed in § 1301.56) and prehearing conferences and issue notice thereof.

(b) Hold conferences to settle, simplify, or determine the issues in a hearing, or to consider other matters that may aid in the expeditious disposition of the hearing.

(c) Require parties to state their position in writing with respect to the various issues in the hearing and to exchange such statements with all other parties.

(d) Sign and issue subpoenas to compel the attendance of witnesses and the production of documents and materials to the extent necessary to conduct administrative hearings pending before him.

(e) Examine witnesses and direct witnesses to testify.

(f) Receive, rule on, exclude, or limit evidence.

(g) Rule on procedural items pending before him.

(h) Take any action permitted to the presiding officer as authorized by this part or by the provisions of the Administrative Procedure Act (5 U.S.C. 551–559).

[36 FR 7820, Apr. 24, 1971. Redesignated at 38 FR 26609, Sept. 24, 1973, and amended at 42 FR 57457, Nov. 3, 1977; 62 FR 13970, Mar. 24, 1997]

§ 1316.53 Time and place of hearing.

The hearing will commence at the place and time designated in the notice of hearing published in the FEDERAL REGISTER but thereafter it may be moved to a different place and may be continued from day to day or recessed to a later day without notice other than announcement thereof by the presiding officer at the hearing.

§ 1316.54 Prehearing conference.

The presiding officer on his own motion, or on the motion of any party for good cause shown, may direct all parties to appear at a specified time and place for a conference for:

(a) The simplification of the issues.

(b) The possibility of obtaining stipulations, admission of facts, and documents.

(c) The possibility of limiting the number of expert witnesses.

(d) The identification and, if practicable, the scheduling of all witnesses to be called.

(e) The advance submission at the prehearing conference of all documentary evidence and affidavits to be marked for identification.

(f) Such other matters as may aid in the expeditious disposition of the hearing.

§ 1316.55 Prehearing ruling.

The presiding officer may have the prehearing conference reported verbatim and shall make a ruling reciting the action taken at the conference, the agreements made by the parties, the schedule of witnesses, and a statement of the issues for hearing. Such ruling shall control the subsequent course of the hearing unless modified by a subsequent ruling.

§ 1316.56 Burden of proof.

At any hearing, the proponent for the issuance, amendment, or repeal of any rule shall have the burden of proof.

§ 1316.57 Submission of documentary evidence and affidavits and identification of witnesses subsequent to prehearing conference.

All documentary evidence and affidavits not submitted and all witnesses not identified at the prehearing conference shall be submitted or identified to the presiding officer as soon as possible, with a showing that the offering party had good cause for failing to so submit or identify at the prehearing conference. If the presiding officer determines that good cause does exist, the documents or affidavits shall be submitted or witnesses identified to all parties sufficiently in advance of the offer of such documents or affidavits or witnesses at the hearing to avoid prejudice or surprise to the other parties. If the presiding officer determines that good cause does not exist, he may refuse to admit as evidence such documents or affidavits or the testimony of such witnesses.

§ 1316.58 Summary of testimony; affidavits.

(a) The presiding officer may direct that summaries of the direct testimony of witnesses be prepared in writing and served on all parties in advance of the hearing. Witnesses will not be permitted to read summaries of their testimony into the record and all witnesses shall be available for cross-examination. Each witness shall, before proceeding to testify, be sworn or make affirmation.

(b) Affidavits submitted at the prehearing conference or pursuant to § 1316.57 with good cause may be examined by all parties and opposing affidavits may be submitted to the presiding officer within a period of time fixed by him. Affidavits admitted into evidence shall be considered in light of the lack of opportunity for cross-examination in determining the weight to be attached to statements made therein.

[36 FR 7820, Apr. 24, 1971, as amended at 36 FR 13387, July 21, 1971. Redesignated at 38 FR 26609, Sept. 24, 1973]

§ 1316.59 Submission and receipt of evidence.

(a) The presiding officer shall admit only evidence that is competent, relevant, material and not unduly repetitious.

(b) Opinion testimony shall be admitted when the presiding officer is satisfied that the witness is properly qualified.

(c) The authenticity of all documents submitted in advance shall be deemed admitted unless written objection thereto is filed with the presiding officer, except that a party will be permitted to challenge such authenticity at a later time upon a showing of good cause for failure to have filed such written objection.

(d) Samples, if otherwise admissible into evidence, may be displayed at the hearing and may be described for purposes of the record, or may be admitted in evidence as exhibits.

(e) Where official notice is taken or is to be taken of a material fact not appearing in the evidence of record, any party, on timely request, shall be afforded opportunity to controvert such fact.

(f) The presiding officer shall file as exhibits copies of the following documents:

(1) The order to show cause or notice of hearing;

(2) Any notice of waiver or modification of rules made pursuant to § 1316.44 or otherwise;

(3) Any waiver of hearing (together with any statement filed therewith) filed pursuant to § 1316.49 or otherwise;

(4) The prehearing ruling, if any, made pursuant to § 1316.55;

(5) Any other document necessary to show the basis for the hearing.

§ 1316.60 Objections; offer of proof.

If any party in the hearing objects to the admission or rejection of any evidence or to other limitation of the scope of any examination or cross-examination, he shall state briefly the grounds for such objection without extended argument or debate thereon except as permitted by the presiding officer. A ruling of the presiding officer on any such objection shall be a part of the transcript together with such offer of proof as has been made if a proper foundation has been laid for its admission. An offer of proof made in connection with an objection taken to any ruling of the presiding officer rejecting or excluding proffered oral testimony shall consist of a statement of the substance of the evidence which the party contends would be adduced by such testimony; and, if the excluded evidence consists of evidence in documentary or written form a copy of such evidence shall be marked for identification and shall accompany the records as the offer of proof.

§ 1316.61 Exceptions to rulings.

Exceptions to rulings of the presiding officer are unnecessary. It is sufficient that a party, at the time the ruling of the presiding officer is sought, makes known the action that he desires the presiding officer to take, or his objection to an action taken, and his grounds therefor.

§ 1316.62 Interlocutory appeals from rulings of the presiding officer.

Rulings of the presiding officer may not be appealed to the Administrator prior to his consideration of the entire hearing without first requesting the consent of the presiding officer. Within ten (10) business days of receipt of a party's request for such consent, the presiding officer shall certify on the record or in writing his determination of whether the allowance of an interlocutory appeal is clearly necessary to prevent exceptional delay, expense or prejudice to any party, or substantial detriment to the public interest. If the presiding officer denies an interlocutory appeal, he shall, within three (3) business days, transmit his determination and the parties' filings related to the interlocutory appeal to the Administrator for the Administrator's discretionary review. If an interlocutory appeal is allowed by the presiding officer or if the Administrator determines that an appeal is warranted under this section, any party to the hearing may file a brief in quintuplicate with the Administrator within such period that the Administrator directs. No oral argument will be heard unless the Administrator directs otherwise.

[84 FR 18140, Apr. 30, 2019]

§ 1316.63 Official transcript; index; corrections.

(a) Testimony given at a hearing shall be reported verbatim. The Administration will make provision for a stenographic record of the testimony and for such copies of the transcript thereof as it requires for its own purpose.

(b) At the close of the hearing, the presiding officer shall afford the parties and witnesses time (not longer than 30 days, except in unusual cases) in which to submit written proposed corrections of the transcript, pointing out errors that may have been made in transcribing the testimony. The presiding officer shall promptly thereafter order such corrections made as in his judgment are required to make the transcript conform to the testimony.

[36 FR 7820, Apr. 24, 1971, as amended at 36 FR 13387, July 21, 1971. Redesignated at 38 FR 26609, Sept. 24, 1973, and amended at 50 FR 2046, Jan. 15, 1985]

§ 1316.64 Proposed findings of fact and conclusions of law.

Any party in the hearing may file in quintuplicate proposed findings of fact and conclusions of law within the time fixed by the presiding officer. Any party so filing shall also serve one copy of his proposed findings and conclusion upon each other party in the hearing. The party shall include a statement of supporting reasons for the proposed findings and conclusions, together with evidence of record (including specific and complete citations of the pages of the transcript and exhibits) and citations of authorities relied upon.

§ 1316.65 Report and record.

(a) As soon as practicable after the time for the parties to file proposed findings of fact and conclusions of law has expired, the presiding officer shall prepare a report containing the following:

(1) His recommended rulings on the proposed findings of fact and conclusions of law;

(2) His recommended findings of fact and conclusions of law, with the reasons therefore; and

(3) His recommended decision.

(b) The presiding officer shall serve a copy of his report upon each party in the hearing. The report shall be considered to have been served when it is mailed to such party or its attorney of record.

(c) Not less than twenty-five days after the date on which he caused copies of his report to be served upon the parties, the presiding officer shall certify to the Administrator the record, which shall contain the transcript of testimony, exhibits, the findings of fact and conclusions of law proposed by the parties, the presiding officer's report, and any exceptions thereto which may have been filed by the parties.

[36 FR 7778, Apr. 24, 1971. Redesignated at 38 FR 26609, Sept. 24, 1973 and amended at 44 FR 55332, Sept. 26, 1979]

§ 1316.66 Exceptions.

(a) Within twenty days after the date upon which a party is served a copy of the report of the presiding officer, such party may file with the Hearing Clerk, Office of the Administrative Law Judge, exceptions to the recommended decision, findings of fact and conclusions of law contained in the report. The party shall include a statement of supporting reasons for such exceptions, together with evidence of record (including specific and complete citations of the pages of the transcript and exhibits) and citations of the authorities relied upon.

(b) The Hearing Clerk shall cause such filings to become part of the record of the proceeding.

(c) The Administrative Law Judge may, upon the request of any party to a proceeding, grant time beyond the twenty days provided in paragraph (a) of this section for the filing of a response to the exceptions filed by another party if he determines that no party in the hearing will be unduly prejudiced and that the ends of justice will be served thereby. Provided however, that each party shall be entitled to only one filing under this section; that is, either a set of exceptions or a response thereto.

[44 FR 55332, Sept. 26, 1979]

§ 1316.67 Final order.

As soon as practicable after the presiding officer has certified the record to the Administrator, the Administrator shall cause to be published in the FEDERAL REGISTER his final order in the proceeding, which shall set forth the final rule and the findings of fact and conclusions of law upon which the rule is based. This order shall specify the date on which it shall take effect, which date shall not be less than 30 days from the date of publication in the FEDERAL REGISTER unless the Administrator finds that the public interest in the matter necessitates an earlier effective date, in which event the Administrator shall specify in the order his findings as to the conditions which led him to conclude that an earlier effective date was required.

[44 FR 42179, July 19, 1979, as amended at 44 FR 55332, Sept. 26, 1979]

§ 1316.68 Copies of petitions for judicial review.

Copies of petitions for judicial review, filed pursuant to section 507 of the Act (21 U.S.C. 877) shall be delivered to and served upon the Administrator in quintuplicate. The Administrator shall certify the record of the hearing and shall file the certified record in the appropriate U.S. Court of Appeals.

[36 FR 7820, Apr. 24, 1971. Redesignated at 44 FR 42179, July 19, 1979]

PART 1317—DISPOSAL

AUTHORITY: 21 U.S.C. 821, 822, 823, 827, 828, 871(b), and 958.

SOURCE: 79 FR 33565, Sept. 9, 2014, unless otherwise noted.

§ 1317.01 Scope.

This part sets forth the rules for the delivery, collection, and destruction of damaged, expired, returned, recalled, unused, or otherwise unwanted controlled substances that are lawfully possessed by registrants (subpart A) and non-registrants (subpart B). The purpose of such rules is to provide prompt, safe, and effective disposal methods while providing effective controls against the diversion of controlled substances.

Subpart A—Disposal of Controlled Substances by Registrants

§ 1317.05 Registrant disposal.

(a) *Practitioner inventory*. Any registered practitioner in lawful possession of a controlled substance in its inventory that desires to dispose of that substance shall do so in one of the following ways:

(1) Promptly destroy that controlled substance in accordance with subpart C of this part using an on-site method of destruction;

(2) Promptly deliver that controlled substance to a reverse distributor's registered location by common or contract carrier pick-up or by reverse distributor pick-up at the registrant's registered location;

(3) For the purpose of return or recall, promptly deliver that controlled substance by common or contract carrier pick-up or pick-up by other registrants at the registrant's registered location to: The registered person from whom it was obtained, the registered

manufacturer of the substance, or another registrant authorized by the manufacturer to accept returns or recalls on the manufacturer's behalf; or

(4) Request assistance from the Special Agent in Charge of the Administration in the area in which the practitioner is located.

(i) The request shall be made by submitting one copy of the DEA Form 41 to the Special Agent in Charge in the practitioner's area. The DEA Form 41 shall list the controlled substance or substances which the registrant desires to dispose.

(ii) The Special Agent in Charge shall instruct the registrant to dispose of the controlled substance in one of the following manners:

(A) By transfer to a registrant authorized to transport or destroy the substance;

(B) By delivery to an agent of the Administration or to the nearest office of the Administration; or

(C) By destruction in the presence of an agent of the Administration or other authorized person.

(5) In the event that a practitioner is required regularly to dispose of controlled substances, the Special Agent in Charge may authorize the practitioner to dispose of such substances, in accordance with subparagraph (a)(4) of this section, without prior application in each instance, on the condition that the practitioner keep records of such disposals and file periodic reports with the Special Agent in Charge summarizing the disposals. The Special Agent in Charge may place such conditions as he/she deems proper on practitioner procedures regarding the disposal of controlled substances.

(b) *Non-practitioner inventory.* Any registrant that is a non-practitioner in lawful possession of a controlled substance in its inventory that desires to dispose of that substance shall do so in one of the following ways:

(1) Promptly destroy that controlled substance in accordance with subpart C of this part using an on-site method of destruction;

(2) Promptly deliver that controlled substance to a reverse distributor's registered location by common or contract carrier or by reverse distributor pick-up at the registrant's registered location;

(3) For the purpose of return or recall, promptly deliver that controlled substance by common or contract carrier or pick-up at the registrant's registered location to: The registered person from whom it was obtained, the registered manufacturer of the substance, or another registrant authorized by the manufacturer to accept returns or recalls on the manufacturer's behalf; or

(4) Promptly transport that controlled substance by its own means to the registered location of a reverse distributor, the location of destruction, or the registered location of any person authorized to receive that controlled substance for the purpose of return or recall as described in paragraph (b)(3) of this section.

(i) If a non-practitioner transports controlled substances by its own means to an unregistered location for destruction, the non-practitioner shall do so in accordance with the procedures set forth at § 1317.95(c).

(ii) If a non-practitioner transports controlled substances by its own means to a registered location for any authorized purpose, transportation shall be directly to the authorized registered location and two employees of the transporting non-practitioner shall accompany the controlled substances to the registered destination location. Directly transported means the substances shall be constantly moving towards their final location and unnecessary or unrelated stops and stops of an extended duration shall not occur.

(c) *Collected controlled substances.* Any collector in lawful possession of a controlled substance acquired by collection from an ultimate user or other authorized non-registrant person shall dispose of that substance in the following ways:

(1) *Mail-back program.* Upon receipt of a sealed mail-back package, the collector shall promptly:

(i) Destroy the package in accordance with subpart C of this part using an on-site method of destruction; or

(ii) Securely store the package and its contents at the collector's registered location in a manner consistent with § 1301.75(c) of this chapter (for practitioners), or in a manner consistent with the security requirements for Schedule II controlled substances (for non-practitioners) until prompt on-site destruction can occur.

(2) *Collection receptacles.* Upon removal from the permanent outer container, the collector shall seal it and promptly:

(i) Destroy the sealed inner liner and its contents;

(ii) Securely store the sealed inner liner and its contents at the collector's registered location in a manner consistent with §1301.75(c) of this chapter (for practitioners), or in a manner consistent with §1301.72(a) of this chapter (for non-practitioners) until prompt destruction can occur; or

(iii) Securely store the sealed inner liner and its contents at a long-term care facility in accordance with §1317.80(d).

(iv) *Practitioner methods of destruction.* Collectors that are practitioners (*i.e.*, retail pharmacies and hospitals/clinics) shall dispose of sealed inner liners and their contents by utilizing any method in paragraph (a)(1), (a)(2), or (a)(4) of this section, or by delivering sealed inner liners and their contents to a distributor's registered location by common or contract carrier pick-up or by distributor pick-up at the collector's authorized collection location.

(v) *Non-practitioner methods of destruction.* Collectors that are non-practitioners (*i.e.*, manufacturers, distributors, narcotic treatment programs, and reverse distributors) shall dispose of sealed inner liners and their contents by utilizing any method in paragraph (b)(1), (b)(2), or (b)(4) of this section, or by delivering sealed inner liners and their contents to a distributor's registered location by common or contract carrier or by distributor pick-up at the collector's authorized collection location for destruction. Freight forwarding facilities may not be utilized to transfer sealed inner liners and their contents.

§1317.10 Registrant return or recall.

(a) Each registrant shall maintain a record of each return or recall transaction in accordance with the information required of manufacturers in §1304.22(a)(2)(iv) of this chapter.

(b) Each registrant that delivers a controlled substance in Schedule I or II for the purpose of return or recall shall use an order form in the manner described in part 1305 of this chapter.

(c) Deliveries for the purpose of return or recall may be made through a freight forwarding facility operated by the person to whom the controlled substance is being returned provided that advance notice of the return is provided and delivery is directly to an agent or employee of the person to whom the controlled substance is being returned.

§1317.15 Reverse distributor registration requirements and authorized activities.

(a) Any person that reverse distributes a controlled substance shall be registered with the Administration as a reverse distributor, unless exempted by law or otherwise authorized pursuant to this chapter.

(b) A reverse distributor shall acquire controlled substances from a registrant pursuant to §§1317.05 and 1317.55(a) and (c) in the following manner:

(1) Pick-up controlled substances from a registrant at the registrant's registered location or authorized collection site; or

(2) Receive controlled substances delivered by common or contract carrier or delivered directly by a non-practitioner registrant.

(i) Delivery to the reverse distributor by an authorized registrant directly or by common or contract carrier may only be made to the reverse distributor at the reverse distributor's registered location. Once en route, such deliveries may not be re-routed to any other location or person, regardless of registration status.

(ii) All controlled substance deliveries to a reverse distributor shall be personally received by an employee of the reverse distributor at the registered location.

(c) Upon acquisition of a controlled substance by delivery or pick-up, a reverse distributor shall:

(1) Immediately store the controlled substance, in accordance with the security controls in parts 1301 and 1317 of

this chapter, at the reverse distributor's registered location or immediately transfer the controlled substance to the reverse distributor's registered location for secure storage, in accordance with the security controls in parts 1301 and 1317 of this chapter, until timely destruction or prompt return of the controlled substance to the registered manufacturer or other registrant authorized by the manufacturer to accept returns or recalls on the manufacturer's behalf;

(2) Promptly deliver the controlled substance to the manufacturer or another registrant authorized by the manufacturer to accept returns or recalls on the manufacturer's behalf; or

(3) Timely destroy the controlled substance in a manner authorized in subpart C of this part.

(d) A reverse distributor shall destroy or cause the destruction of any controlled substance received for the purpose of destruction no later than 30 calendar days after receipt.

Subpart B—Disposal of Controlled Substances Collected From Ultimate Users and Other Non-Registrants

§ 1317.30 Authorization to collect from non-registrants.

(a) The following persons are authorized to collect controlled substances from ultimate users and other non-registrants for destruction in compliance with this chapter:

(1) Any registrant authorized by the Administration to be a collector pursuant to § 1317.40; and

(2) Federal, State, tribal, or local law enforcement when in the course of official duties and pursuant to § 1317.35.

(b) The following non-registrant persons in lawful possession of a controlled substance in Schedules II, III, IV, or V may transfer that substance to the authorized persons listed in paragraph (a) of this section, and in a manner authorized by this part, for the purpose of disposal:

(1) An ultimate user in lawful possession of a controlled substance;

(2) Any person lawfully entitled to dispose of a decedent's property if that decedent was an ultimate user who died while in lawful possession of a controlled substance; and

(3) A long-term care facility on behalf of an ultimate user who resides or resided at such long-term care facility and is/was in lawful possession of a controlled substance, in accordance with § 1317.80 only.

§ 1317.35 Collection by law enforcement.

(a) Federal, State, tribal, or local law enforcement may collect controlled substances from ultimate users and persons lawfully entitled to dispose of an ultimate user decedent's property using the following collection methods:

(1) Take-back events in accordance with § 1317.65;

(2) Mail-back programs in accordance with § 1317.70; or

(3) Collection receptacles located inside law enforcement's physical address.

(b) Law enforcement that conducts a take-back event or a mail-back program or maintains a collection receptacle should maintain any records of removal, storage, or destruction of the controlled substances collected in a manner that is consistent with that agency's recordkeeping requirements for illicit controlled substances evidence.

(c) Any controlled substances collected by law enforcement through a take-back event, mail-back program, or collection receptacle should be stored in a manner that prevents the diversion of controlled substances and is consistent with that agency's standard procedures for storing illicit controlled substances.

(d) Any controlled substances collected by law enforcement through a take-back event, mail-back program, or collection receptacle should be transferred to a destruction location in a manner that prevents the diversion of controlled substances and is consistent with that agency's standard procedures for transferring illicit controlled substances.

(e) Law enforcement that transfers controlled substances collected from ultimate users pursuant to this part to a reverse distributor for destruction should maintain a record that contains the following information: If a sealed inner liner as described in §1317.60 is used, the unique identification number of the sealed inner liner transferred, and the size of the sealed inner liner transferred (e.g., 5-gallon, 10-gallon, etc.); if a mail-back package as described in §1317.70 is used, the unique identification number of each package; the date of the transfer; and the name, address, and registration number of the reverse distributor to whom the controlled substances were transferred.

§1317.40 Registrants authorized to collect and authorized collection activities.

(a) Manufacturers, distributors, reverse distributors, narcotic treatment programs, hospitals/clinics with an on-site pharmacy, and retail pharmacies that desire to be collectors shall modify their registration to obtain authorization to be a collector in accordance with §1301.51 of this chapter. Authorization to be a collector is subject to renewal. If a registrant that is authorized to collect ceases activities as a collector, such registrant shall notify the Administration in accordance with §1301.52(f) of this chapter.

(b) Collection by registrants shall occur only at the following locations:

(1) Those registered locations of manufacturers, distributors, reverse distributors, narcotic treatment programs, hospitals/clinics with an on-site pharmacy, and retail pharmacies that are authorized for collection; and

(2) Long-term care facilities at which registered hospitals/clinics or retail pharmacies are authorized to maintain collection receptacles.

(c) Collectors may conduct the following activities:

(1) Receive and destroy mail-back packages pursuant to §1317.70 at an authorized registered location that has an on-site method of destruction;

(2) Install, manage, and maintain collection receptacles located at their authorized collection location(s) pursuant to §§1317.75 and 1317.80; and

(3) Promptly dispose of sealed inner liners and their contents as provided for in §1317.05(c)(2).

§1317.55 Reverse distributor and distributor acquisition of controlled substances from collectors or law enforcement.

(a) A reverse distributor is authorized to acquire controlled substances from law enforcement that collected the substances from ultimate users. A reverse distributor is authorized to acquire controlled substances collected through a collection receptacle in accordance with §§1317.75 and 1317.80.

(b) A distributor is authorized to acquire controlled substances collected through a collection receptacle in accordance with §§1317.75 and 1317.80.

(c) A reverse distributor or a distributor that acquires controlled substances in accordance with paragraph (a) or (b) of this section shall:

(1) Acquire the controlled substances in the manner authorized for reverse distributors in §1317.15(b)(1) and (2);

(2) Dispose of the controlled substances in the manner authorized for reverse distributors §1317.15(c) and (d); and

(3) Securely store the controlled substances in a manner consistent with the security requirements for Schedule II controlled substances until timely destruction can occur.

§1317.60 Inner liner requirements.

(a) An inner liner shall meet the following requirements:

(1) The inner liner shall be waterproof, tamper-evident, and tear-resistant;

(2) The inner liner shall be removable and sealable immediately upon removal without emptying or touching the contents;

(3) The contents of the inner liner shall not be viewable from the outside when sealed;

(4) The size of the inner liner shall be clearly marked on the outside of the liner (e.g., 5-gallon, 10-gallon, etc.); and

(5) The inner liner shall bear a permanent, unique identification number that enables the inner liner to be tracked.

(b) Access to the inner liner shall be restricted to employees of the collector.

(c) The inner liner shall be sealed by two employees immediately upon removal from the permanent outer container and the sealed inner liner shall not be opened, x-rayed, analyzed, or otherwise penetrated.

§ 1317.65 Take-back events.

(a) Federal, State, tribal, or local law enforcement may conduct a take-back event and collect controlled substances from ultimate users and persons lawfully entitled to dispose of an ultimate user decedent's property in accordance with this section. Any person may partner with law enforcement to hold a collection take-back event in accordance with this section.

(b) Law enforcement shall appoint a law enforcement officer employed by the agency to oversee the collection. Law enforcement officers employed and authorized by the law enforcement agency or law enforcement component of a Federal agency conducting a take-back event shall maintain control and custody of the collected substances from the time the substances are collected from the ultimate user or person authorized to dispose of the ultimate user decedent's property until secure transfer, storage, or destruction of the controlled substances has occurred.

(c) Each take-back event should have at least one receptacle for the collection of controlled substances. The collection receptacle should be a securely locked, substantially constructed container with an outer container and a removable inner liner as specified in § 1317.60 of this chapter. The outer container should include a small opening that allows contents to be added to the inner liner, but that does not allow removal of the inner liner's contents.

(d) Only those controlled substances listed in Schedule II, III, IV, or V that are lawfully possessed by an ultimate user or person entitled to dispose of an ultimate user decedent's property may be collected. Controlled and non-controlled substances may be collected together and be comingled, although comingling is not required.

(e) Only ultimate users and persons entitled to dispose of an ultimate user decedent's property in lawful possession of a controlled substance in Schedule II, III, IV, or V may transfer such substances to law enforcement during the take-back event. No other person may handle the controlled substances at any time.

§ 1317.70 Mail-back programs.

(a) A mail-back program may be conducted by Federal, State, tribal, or local law enforcement or any collector. A collector conducting a mail-back program shall have and utilize at their registered location a method of destruction consistent with § 1317.90 of this chapter.

(b) Only those controlled substances listed in Schedule II, III, IV, or V that are lawfully possessed by an ultimate user or person lawfully entitled to dispose of an ultimate user decedent's property may be collected. Controlled and non-controlled substances may be collected together and be comingled, although comingling is not required.

(c) Collectors or law enforcement that conduct a mail-back program shall make packages available (for sale or for free) as specified in this paragraph to ultimate users and persons lawfully entitled to dispose of an ultimate user decedent's property, for the collection of controlled substances by common or contract carrier. Any person may partner with a collector or law enforcement to make such packages available in accordance with this section. The packages made available shall meet the following specifications:

(1) The package shall be nondescript and shall not include any markings or other information that might indicate that the package contains controlled substances;

(2) The package shall be water- and spill-proof; tamper-evident; tear-resistant; and sealable;

(3) The package shall be preaddressed with and delivered to the collector's registered address or the participating law enforcement's physical address;

(4) The cost of shipping the package shall be postage paid;

(5) The package shall have a unique identification number that enables the package to be tracked; and

(6) The package shall include instructions for the user that indicate the process for mailing back the package, the substances that can be sent, notice that packages may only be mailed

from within the customs territory of the United States (the 50 States, the District of Columbia, and Puerto Rico), and notice that only packages provided by the collector will be accepted for destruction.

(d) Ultimate users and persons lawfully entitled to dispose of an ultimate user decedent's property shall not be required to provide any personally identifiable information when mailing back controlled substances to a collector. The collector or law enforcement may implement a system that allows ultimate users or persons lawfully entitled to dispose of an ultimate user decedent's property to notify the collector or law enforcement that they are sending one of the designated packages by giving the unique identification number on the package.

(e) A collector that conducts a mail-back program pursuant to paragraph (a) shall:

(1) Accept only those controlled substances contained within packages that the collector made available for the collection of controlled substances by mail and packages that are lawfully forwarded to the collector pursuant to paragraph (e)(3) of this section.

(2) Within three business days of receipt, notify the Field Division Office of the Administration in their area of the receipt of a package that likely contains controlled substances that the collector did not make available or did not agree to receive pursuant to subparagraph (e)(3) of this section.

(3) When discontinuing activities as a collector or ceasing an authorized mail-back program:

(i) Make a reasonable effort to notify the public prior to discontinuing such activities or ceasing the authorized mail-back program; and

(ii) Obtain the written agreement of another collector that has and utilizes at its registered location a method of destruction consistent with § 1317.90 of this chapter to receive all remaining mail-back packages that were disseminated but not returned and arrange for the forwarding of only such packages to that location.

(f) Only law enforcement officers employed by the law enforcement agency or law enforcement component of a Federal agency and employees of the collector shall handle packages received through an authorized mail-back program. Upon receipt of a mail-back package by a collector conducting a mail-back program, the package shall not be opened, x-rayed, analyzed, or otherwise penetrated.

§ 1317.75 Collection receptacles.

(a) Collectors or Federal, State, tribal, or local law enforcement may manage and maintain collection receptacles for disposal.

(b) Only those controlled substances listed in Schedule II, III, IV, or V that are lawfully possessed by an ultimate user or other authorized non-registrant person may be collected. Controlled and non-controlled substances may be collected together and be comingled, although comingling is not required.

(c) Collectors shall only allow ultimate users and other authorized non-registrant persons in lawful possession of a controlled substance in Schedule II, III, IV, or V to deposit such substances in a collection receptacle at a registered location. Collectors shall not permit an ultimate user to transfer such substance to any person for any reason. Once a substance has been deposited into a collection receptacle, the substance shall not be counted, sorted, inventoried, or otherwise individually handled.

(d) Collection receptacles shall be securely placed and maintained:

(1) Inside a collector's registered location, inside law enforcement's physical location, or at an authorized long-term care facility;

(2) At a registered location, be located in the immediate proximity of a designated area where controlled substances are stored and at which an employee is present (e.g., can be seen from the pharmacy counter). Except as follows:

(i) At a hospital/clinic: A collection receptacle shall be located in an area regularly monitored by employees, and shall not be located in the proximity of any area where emergency or urgent care is provided;

(ii) At a narcotic treatment program: A collection receptacle shall be located in a room: That does not contain any other controlled substances and is securely locked with controlled access;

(iii) At a long-term care facility: A collection receptacle shall be located in a secured area regularly monitored by long-term care facility employees.

(e) A controlled substance collection receptacle shall meet the following design specifications:

(1) Be securely fastened to a permanent structure so that it cannot be removed;

(2) Be a securely locked, substantially constructed container with a permanent outer container and a removable inner liner as specified in §1317.60 of this chapter;

(3) The outer container shall include a small opening that allows contents to be added to the inner liner, but does not allow removal of the inner liner's contents;

(4) The outer container shall prominently display a sign indicating that only Schedule II–V controlled and non-controlled substances, if a collector chooses to comingle substances, are acceptable substances (Schedule I controlled substances, controlled substances that are not lawfully possessed by the ultimate user, and other illicit or dangerous substances are not permitted); and

(f) Except at a narcotic treatment program, the small opening in the outer container of the collection receptacle shall be locked or made otherwise inaccessible to the public when an employee is not present (e.g., when the pharmacy is closed), or when the collection receptacle is not being regularly monitored by long-term care facility employees.

(g) The installation and removal of the inner liner of the collection receptacle shall be performed by or under the supervision of at least two employees of the authorized collector.

§1317.80 Collection receptacles at long-term care facilities.

(a) A long-term care facility may dispose of controlled substances in Schedules II, III, IV, and V on behalf of an ultimate user who resides, or has resided, at such long-term care facility by transferring those controlled substances into an authorized collection receptacle located at that long-term care facility. When disposing of such controlled substances by transferring those substances into a collection receptacle, such disposal shall occur immediately, but no longer than three business days after the discontinuation of use by the ultimate user. Discontinuation of use includes a permanent discontinuation of use as directed by the prescriber, as a result of the resident's transfer from the long-term care facility, or as a result of death.

(b) Only authorized retail pharmacies and hospitals/clinics with an on-site pharmacy may install, manage, and maintain collection receptacles at long-term care facilities and remove, seal, transfer, and store, or supervise the removal, sealing, transfer, and storage of sealed inner liners at long-term care facilities. Collectors authorized to install, manage, and maintain collection receptacles at long-term care facilities shall comply with all requirements of this chapter, including §§1317.60, 1317.75, and 1317.80.

(c) The installation, removal, transfer, and storage of inner liners shall be performed either: By or under the supervision of one employee of the authorized collector and one supervisor-level employee of the long-term care facility (e.g., a charge nurse or supervisor) designated by the authorized collector; or, by or under the supervision of two employees of the authorized collector.

(d) Upon removal, sealed inner liners may only be stored at the long-term care facility for up to three business days in a securely locked, substantially constructed cabinet or a securely locked room with controlled access until transfer in accordance with §1317.05(c)(2)(iv).

(e) Neither a hospital/clinic with an on-site pharmacy nor a retail pharmacy shall operate a collection receptacle at a long-term care facility until its registration has been modified in accordance with §1301.51 of this chapter.

§1317.85 Ultimate user delivery for the purpose of recall or investigational use of drugs.

(a) In the event of a product recall, an ultimate user in lawful possession of a controlled substance listed in Schedule II, III, IV, or V may deliver the recalled substance to the manufacturer of the substance or another registrant authorized by the manufacturer to accept recalled controlled substances on the manufacturer's behalf.

(b) An ultimate user who is participating in an investigational use of drugs pursuant to 21 U.S.C. 355(i) and 360b(j) and wishes to deliver any unused controlled substances received as part of that research to the registered dispenser from which the ultimate user obtained those substances may do so in accordance with regulations promulgated by the Secretary of Health and Human Services pursuant to 21 U.S.C. 355(i) and 360b(j).

Subpart C—Destruction of Controlled Substances

§ 1317.90 Methods of destruction.

(a) All controlled substances to be destroyed by a registrant, or caused to be destroyed by a registrant pursuant to § 1317.95(c), shall be destroyed in compliance with applicable Federal, State, tribal, and local laws and regulations and shall be rendered non-retrievable.

(b) Where multiple controlled substances are comingled, the method of destruction shall be sufficient to render all such controlled substances non-retrievable. When the actual substances collected for destruction are unknown but may reasonably include controlled substances, the method of destruction shall be sufficient to render non-retrievable any controlled substance likely to be present.

(c) The method of destruction shall be consistent with the purpose of rendering all controlled substances to a non-retrievable state in order to prevent diversion of any such substance to illicit purposes and to protect the public health and safety.

§ 1317.95 Destruction procedures.

The destruction of any controlled substance shall be in accordance with the following requirements:

(a) *Transfer to a person registered or authorized to accept controlled substances for the purpose of destruction.* If the controlled substances are transferred to a person registered or authorized to accept the controlled substances for the purpose of destruction, two employees of the transferring registrant shall load and unload or observe the loading and unloading of any controlled substances until transfer is complete.

(b) *Transport to a registered location.* If the controlled substances are transported by a registrant to a registered location for subsequent destruction, the following procedures shall be followed:

(1) Transportation shall be directly to the registered location (the substances shall be constantly moving towards their final location and unnecessary or unrelated stops and stops of an extended duration shall not occur);

(2) Two employees of the transporting registrant shall accompany the controlled substances to the registered location;

(3) Two employees of the transporting registrant shall load and unload or observe the loading and unloading of the controlled substances until transfer is complete;

(c) *Transport to a non-registered location.* If the controlled substances are transported by a registrant to a destruction location that is not a registered location, the following procedures shall be followed:

(1) Transportation shall be directly to the destruction location (the substances shall be constantly moving towards their final destruction location and unnecessary or unrelated stops and stops of an extended duration shall not occur);

(2) Two employees of the transporting registrant shall accompany the controlled substances to the destruction location;

(3) Two employees of the transporting registrant shall load and unload or observe the loading and unloading of the controlled substances;

(4) Two employees of the transporting registrant shall handle or observe the handling of any controlled substance until the substance is rendered non-retrievable; and

(5) Two employees of the transporting registrant shall personally witness the destruction of the controlled substance until it is rendered non-retrievable.

(d) *On-site destruction.* If the controlled substances are destroyed at a registrant's registered location utilizing an on-site method of destruction, the following procedures shall be followed:

(1) Two employees of the registrant shall handle or observe the handling of any controlled substance until the substance is rendered non-retrievable; and

(2) Two employees of the registrant shall personally witness the destruction of the controlled substance until it is rendered non-retrievable.

PART 1321—DEA MAILING ADDRESSES

AUTHORITY: 21 U.S.C. 871(b).

SOURCE: 75 FR 10685, Mar. 9, 2010, unless otherwise noted.

§ 1321.01 DEA mailing addresses.

The following table provides information regarding mailing addresses to be used when sending specified correspondence to the Drug Enforcement Administration.

TABLE OF DEA MAILING ADDRESSES

Code of Federal Regulations Section—Topic	DEA mailing address
DEA Administrator	
1308.43(b)—Petition to initiate proceedings for rulemaking. 1316.23(b)—Petition for grant of confidentiality for research subjects. 1316.24(b)—Petition for exemption from prosecution for researchers.	Drug Enforcement Administration, Attn: Administrator, 8701 Morrissette Drive, Springfield, VA 22152.
DEA Diversion Control Division	
1307.03—Exception request filing. 1307.22—Delivery of surrendered and forfeited controlled substances. 1310.21(b)—Sale by Federal departments or agencies of chemicals which could be used to manufacture controlled substances certification request.[2]	Drug Enforcement Administration, Attn: Diversion Control Division/DC, 8701 Morrissette Drive, Springfield, VA 22152.

TABLE OF DEA MAILING ADDRESSES—Continued

Code of Federal Regulations Section—Topic	DEA mailing address
DEA Regulatory Section	
1301.71(d)—Security system compliance review for controlled substances. 1309.71(c)—Security system compliance review for List I chemicals. 1310.03(c)—Mail-Order reports involving transactions with non-regulated persons or exports.[1] 1310.05(b)(1)—Unusual or excessive loss or disappearance of listed chemicals. 1310.05(b)(2)—Reports of domestic regulated transactions in a tableting machine or an encapsulating machine.[1] 1310.05(c)(1)—Reports of imports and exports of a tableting machine or an encapsulating machine.[1] 1310.05(c)(2)—Report of declared exports of machines refused, rejected, or returned. 1312.12(a)—Application for import permit (DEA Form 357).[1] 1312.18(b)—Import declaration (DEA Form 236) submission.[1] 1312.22(g)(8)—Request for return of unacceptable or undeliverable exported controlled substances.[1] 1312.27(a)—Controlled substances export declaration (DEA Form 236) filing.[1] 1312.31(b)—Controlled substances transshipment permit application. 1312.32(a)—Advanced notice of importation for transshipment or transfer of controlled substances. 1313.12(b)—Authorization to import listed chemicals (DEA Form 486/486A).[1] 1313.12(e)—Quarterly reports of listed chemicals importation. 1313.21(b)—Authorization to export listed chemicals (DEA Form 486).[1] 1313.21(e)—Quarterly reports of listed chemicals exportation. 1313.22(c)—Notice of declared exports of listed chemicals refused, rejected or undeliverable.[1] 1313.31(b)—Advanced notice of importation for transshipment or transfer of listed chemicals. 1313.32(b)(1)—International transaction authorization (DEA Form 486).[1] 1314.110(a)(1)—Reports for mail-order sales. 1314.110(a)(2)—Request to submit mail-order sales reports.	Drug Enforcement Administration, Attn: Regulatory Section/DRG, 8701 Morrissette Drive, Springfield, VA 22152.
DEA Drug & Chemical Evaluation Section	
1308.21(a)—Exclusion of nonnarcotic substance. 1308.23(b)—Exemption for chemical preparations. 1308.24(d)—Exempt narcotic chemical preparations importer/exporter reporting. 1308.24(i)—Exempted chemical preparations listing. 1308.25(a)—Exclusion of veterinary anabolic steroid implant product application. 1308.26(a)—Excluded veterinary anabolic steroid implant products listing. 1308.31(a)—Exemption of a nonnarcotic prescription product application. 1308.32—Exempted prescription products listing. 1308.33(b)—Exemption of certain anabolic steroid products application. 1308.34—Exempted anabolic steroid products listing. 1310.13(b)—Exemption for chemical preparations. 1310.05(d)—Bulk manufacturer of listed chemicals reporting.	Drug Enforcement Administration, Attn: Drug & Chemical Evaluation Section/DRE, 8701 Morrissette Drive, Springfield, VA 22152.
UN Reporting & Quota Section	
1303.12(b)—Application for controlled substances procurement quota (DEA Form 250) filing and request.	Drug Enforcement Administration, Attn: UN Reporting & Quota Section/DRQ, 8701 Morrissette Drive, Springfield, VA 22152.

TABLE OF DEA MAILING ADDRESSES—Continued

Code of Federal Regulations Section—Topic	DEA mailing address
1303.12(d)—Controlled substances quota adjustment request. 1303.22—Application for individual manufacturing quota (DEA Form 189) filing and request for schedule I or II controlled substances. 1304.31(a)—Manufacturers importing narcotic raw material report submission. 1304.32(a)—Manufacturers importing coca leaves report submission. 1315.22—Application for individual manufacturing quota for ephedrine, pseudoephedrine, phenylpropanolamine (DEA Form 189) filing and request. 1315.32(e)—Application for procurement quota for ephedrine, pseudoephedrine, phenylpropanolamine (DEA Form 250) filing and request. 1315.32(g)—Procurement quota adjustment request for ephedrine, pseudoephedrine, and phenylpropanolamine. 1315.34(d)—Application for import quota for ephedrine, pseudoephedrine, phenylpropanolamine (DEA Form 488) request and filing. 1315.36(b)—Request import quota increase for ephedrine, pseudoephedrine, or phenylpropanolamine.	
Pharmaceutical Investigations Section	
1304.04(d)—ARCOS separate central reporting identifier request. 1304.33(a)—Reports to ARCOS.	Drug Enforcement Administration, Attn: ARCOS Unit/DOPT, P.O. Box 2520, Springfield, VA 22152–2520 OR Drug Enforcement Administration, Attn: ARCOS Unit, 8701 Morrissette Drive, Springfield, VA 22152.
DEA Registration Section	
1301.03—Procedures information request (controlled substances registration). 1301.13(e)(2)—Request DEA Forms 224, 225, and 363. 1301.14(a)—Controlled substances registration application submission. 1301.18(c)—Research project controlled substance increase request. 1301.51—Controlled substances registration modification request. 1301.52(b)—Controlled substances registration transfer request. 1301.52(c)—Controlled substances registration discontinuance of business activities notification. 1309.03—List I chemicals registration procedures information request. 1309.32(c)—Request DEA Form 510. 1309.33(a)—List I chemicals registration application submission. 1309.61—List I chemicals registration modification request.	Drug Enforcement Administration, Attn: Registration Section/DRR P.O. Box 2639, Springfield, VA 22152–2639.
DEA Hearing Clerk	
1301.43—Request for hearing or appearance; waiver. 1303.34—Request for hearing or appearance; waiver. 1308.44—Request for hearing or appearance; waiver. 1316.45—Hearings documentation filing. 1316.46(a)—Inspection of record. 1316.47(a)—Request for hearing. 1316.48—Notice of appearance.	Drug Enforcement Administration, Attn: Hearing Clerk/OALJ, 8701 Morrissette Drive, Springfield, VA 22152.

TABLE OF DEA MAILING ADDRESSES—Continued

Code of Federal Regulations Section—Topic	DEA mailing address
DEA Federal Register Representative	
1301.33(a)—Filing of written comments regarding application for bulk manufacture of Schedule I and II substances.[2] 1301.34(a)—Filing of written comments regarding application for importation of Schedule I and II substances.[2] 1303.11(c)—Filing of written comments regarding notice of an aggregate production quota.[2] 1303.13(c)—Filing of written comments regarding adjustments of aggregate production quotas.[2] 1303.13(c)—Filing of written comments regarding adjustments of aggregate production quotas.[2] 1308.43(g)—Filing of written comments regarding initiation of proceedings for rulemaking.[2]	Drug Enforcement Administration, Attn: Federal Register Representative/DRW, 8701 Morrissette Drive, Springfield, VA 22152. *http://www.regulations.gov/.*

[1] Applications/filings/reports are required to be filed electronically in accordance with this chapter.
[2] Applications/filings/reports may be filed electronically in accordance with this chapter.

[81 97041, Dec. 30, 2016]

PARTS 1322–1399 [RESERVED]

CHAPTER III—OFFICE OF NATIONAL DRUG CONTROL POLICY

PART 1400 [RESERVED]

PART 1401—PUBLIC AVAILABILITY OF INFORMATION

AUTHORITY: 5 U.S.C. 552, as amended.

SOURCE: 64 FR 69901, Dec. 15, 1999, unless otherwise noted.

§ 1401.1 Purpose.

The purpose of this part is to prescribe rules, guidelines and procedures to implement the Freedom of Information Act (FOIA), as amended, 5 U.S.C. 552.

§ 1401.2 The Office of National Drug Control Policy—organization and functions.

(a) The Office of National Drug Control Policy (ONDCP) was created by the Anti-Drug Abuse Act of 1988, 21 U.S.C. 1501 *et seq.*, and reestablished under 21 U.S.C. 1701 *et seq.* The mission of ONDCP is to coordinate the anti-drug efforts of the various agencies and departments of the Federal government, to consult with States and localities and assist their anti-drug efforts, to conduct a national media campaign, and to annually promulgate the National Drug Control Strategy.

(b) ONDCP is headed by the Director of National Drug Control Policy. The Director is assisted by a Deputy Director of National Drug Control Policy, a Deputy Director for Supply Reduction, a Deputy Director for Demand Reduction, and a Deputy Director for State and Local Affairs.

(c) Offices within ONDCP include Chief of Staff, and the Offices of Legal Counsel, Strategic Planning, Legislative Affairs, Programs Budget and Evaluation, Supply Reduction, Demand Reduction, Public Affairs, State and Local Affairs, and the Financial Management Office.

(d) The Office of Public Affairs is responsible for providing information to the press and to the general public. If members of the public have general questions about ONDCP that can be answered by telephone, they may call the Office of Public Affairs at (202) 395–6618. This number should not be used to make FOIA requests. All oral requests for information under FOIA will be rejected.

§ 1401.3 Definitions.

For the purpose of this part:

(a) All the terms defined in the Freedom of Information Act apply.

(b) *Commercial-use request* means a request from or on behalf of one who seeks information for a cause or purpose that furthers the commercial, trade or profit interests of the requester or the person or institution on whose behalf the request is made. In determining whether a requester properly belongs in this category, ONDCP will consider the intended use of the information.

(c) *Direct costs* means the expense actually expended to search, review, or duplicate in response to a FOIA request. For example, direct costs include 116% of the salary of the employee performing work and the actual costs incurred while operating equipment.

(d) *Duplicate* means the process of making a copy of a document. Such copies may take the form of paper, microform, audio-visual materials, or machine-readable documentation. ONDCP will provide a copy of the material in a form that is usable by the requester.

(e) *Educational institution* means preschool, a public or private elementary or secondary school, an institution of undergraduate higher education, an institution of graduate higher education, an institution of professional education, or an institution of vocational education that operates a program or programs of scholarly research.

(f) *Noncommercial scientific institution* means an institution that is not operated on a commercial basis as that term is defined in this section, and that is operated solely for the purpose of conducting scientific research not intended to promote any particular product or industry.

(g) *Records* and any other terms used in this part in reference to information includes any information that would be an agency record subject to the requirements of this part when maintained in any format, including electronic format.

(h) *Representative of the news media* means any person actively gathering news for an entity that is organized and operated to publish or broadcast news to the public. News is information about current events or information that would be of interest to the public. Examples of the news media include television or radio stations that broadcast to the public at large and publishers of news periodicals that make their products available to the general public for purchase or subscription. Freelance journalists may be regarded as working for the news media where they demonstrate a reasonable basis for expecting publication through that organization, even though not actually employed by it.

(i) *Request* means a letter or other written communication seeking records or information under FOIA.

(j) *Review* means the process of examining documents that are located during a search to determine if any portion should lawfully be withheld. It is the processing of determining disclosability.

(k) *Search* means to review, manually or by automated means, agency records for the purpose of locating those records responsive to a request.

§ 1401.4 Access to information.

The Office of National Drug Control Policy makes available information pertaining to matters issued, adopted, or promulgated by ONDCP, that are within the scope of 5 U.S.C. 552(a)(2). A public reading area and the ONDCP FOIA Handbook are located at *http://www.whitehousedrugpolicy.gov/about/about.html*.

§ 1401.5 How to request records.

(a) Each request must reasonably describe the record(s) sought including the type of document, specific event or action, originator of the record, date or time period, subject matter, location, and all other pertinent data.

(b) Requests must be received by ONDCP through the mail or by electronic facsimile transmission. Mailed requests must be addressed to Executive Office of the President, Office of National Drug Control Policy, Office of Legal Counsel, Washington, DC 20503. The applicable fax number is (202) 395–5543.

(c) The words "FOIA REQUEST" or "REQUEST FOR RECORDS" must be clearly marked on the cover-letter, letter and envelope. The time limitations imposed by § 1401.7 will not begin until the Office of the General Counsel identifies a letter or fax as a FOIA request.

§ 1401.6 Expedited process.

(a) Requests and appeals will be given expedited treatment whenever ONDCP determines either:

(1) The lack of expedited treatment could reasonably be expected to pose an imminent threat to the life or physical safety of an individual; or

(2) An urgency to inform the public about an actual or alleged federal government activity occurs and the request is made by a person primarily engaged in disseminating information.

(b) A request for expedited processing may be made at the time of the initial request for records or at a later time.

(c) A requester who seeks expedited processing must submit a statement, certified to be true and correct to the best of that person's knowledge and belief, explaining in detail the basis for requesting expedited processing. A requester within the category in paragraph (a)(2) of this section also must establish a particular urgency to inform the public about the government activity involved in the request, beyond the public's right to know about government activity generally. The formality of certification may be waived as a matter of administrative discretion.

(d) Within ten days of receipt of a request for expedited processing, ONDCP will decide whether to grant it and will notify the requester of the decision. If a request for expedited treatment is granted, the request will be given priority and will be processed as soon as practicable. If a request for expedited processing is denied, any appeal of that decision will be acted on expeditiously.

§ 1401.7 Prompt response.

The General Counsel, or designee, will determine within 20 days (excepting Saturdays, Sundays and legal public holidays) after the receipt of a FOIA request whether it is appropriate to grant the request and will provide written notification to the person making the request. If the request is denied, the written notification will include the names of the individuals who participated in the determination, the reasons for the denial, and that an appeal may be lodged within the Office of National Drug Control Policy.

§ 1401.8 Extension of time.

(a) In unusual circumstances, the Office of General Counsel may extend the time limit prescribed in § 1401.7 or § 1401.9 by written notice to the FOIA requester. The notice will state the reasons for the extension and the date a determination is expected. The extension period may be divided among the initial request and an appeal but will not exceed a total of 10 working days (excepting Saturdays, Sundays, or legal public holidays).

(b) The phrase "unusual circumstances" means:

(1) The requested records are located in establishments that are separated from the office processing the request;

(2) A voluminous amount of separate and distinct records are demanded in a single request; or

(3) Another agency or two or more components in the same agency have substantial interest in the determination of the request.

(c) Where unusual circumstance exist, ONDCP may provide an opportunity for amendment of the initial request so that the request may be timely processed. Refusal by the person to reasonably modify the request or arrange an alternative time frame shall be considered as a factor for purposes of 5 U.S.C. 552 (a)(6)(C).

(d) ONDCP may aggregate requests by a requester or a group of requestors where multiple requests reasonably appear to be a single request.

§ 1401.9 Appeals.

An appeal to the ONDCP must explain in writing the legal and factual basis for the appeal. It must be received by mail at the address specified in § 1401.5 within 30 days of receipt of a denial. The Director or designee will decide the appeal within 20 days (excepting Saturdays, Sundays, and legal public holidays). If the Director or designee deny an appeal in whole or in part, the written determination will contain the reason for the denial, the names of the individuals who participated in the determination, and the provisions for judicial review.

§ 1401.10 Fees to be charged—general.

ONDCP will recoup the full allowable costs it incurs in response to a FOIA request.

(a) *Manual search for records.* ONDCP will charge 116% of the salary of the individual(s) making a search.

(b) *Computerized search for records.* ONDCP will charge 116% of the salary of the programmer/operator and the apportionable time of the central processing unit directly attributed to the search.

(c) *Review of records.* ONDCP will charge 116% of the salary of the individual(s) conducting a review. Records or portions of records withheld under an exemption subsequently determined not to apply may be reviewed to determine the applicability of exemptions not considered. The cost for a subsequent review is assessable.

(d) *Duplication of records.* Request for copies prepared by computer will cost 116% of the apportionable operator time and the cost of the tape or disk. Other methods of duplication will cost 116% of the salary of the individual copying the data plus 15 cents per copy of 8½ × 11 inch original.

(e) *Other charges.* ONDCP will recover the costs of providing other services such as certifying records or sending records by special methods.

§ 1401.11 Fees to be charged—miscellaneous provisions.

(a) Remittance shall be mailed to the Office of Legal Counsel, ONDCP, Washington DC 20503, and made payable to the order of the Treasury of the United States on a postal money order or personal check or bank draft drawn on a bank in the United States.

(b) ONDCP may require advance payment where the estimated fee exceeds $250, or a requester previously failed to pay within 30 days of the billing date.

(c) ONDCP may assess interest charges beginning the 31st day of billing. Interest will be at the rate prescribed in section 3717 of title 31 of the United States Code and will accrue from the date of the billing.

(d) ONDCP may assess search charges where records are not located or where records are exempt from disclosure.

(e) ONDCP may aggregate individual requests and charge accordingly for requests seeking portions of a document or documents.

§ 1401.12 Fees to be charged—categories of requesters.

(a) There are four categories of FOIA requesters: commercial use requesters; educational and non-commercial scientific institutions; representatives of the news media; and all other requesters.

(b) The specific levels of fees for each of these categories are:

(1) *Commercial use requesters.* ONDCP will recover the full direct cost of providing search, review and duplication services. Commercial use requesters will not receive free search-time or free reproduction of documents.

(2) *Educational and non-commercial scientific institution requesters.* ONDCP will charge the cost of reproduction, excluding charges for the first 100 pages. Requesters must demonstrate the request is authorized by and under the auspices of a qualifying institution and that the records are sought for scholarly or scientific research not a commercial use.

(3) *Requesters who are representatives of the news media.* ONDCP will charge the cost of reproduction, excluding charges for the first 100 pages. Requesters must meet the criteria in § 1401.3(h), and the request must not be made for a commercial use. A request that supports the news dissemination function of the requester shall not be considered a commercial use.

(4) *All other requesters.* ONDCP will recover the full direct cost of the search and the reproduction of records, excluding the first 100 pages of reproduction and the first two hours of search time. Requests for records concerning the requester will be treated under the fee provisions of the Privacy Act of 1974, 5 U.S.C. 552a, which permits fees only for reproduction.

§ 1401.13 Waiver or reduction of fees.

Fees chargeable in connection with a request may be waived or reduced where ONDCP determines that disclosure is in the public interest because it is likely to contribute significantly to public understanding of the operations or activities of the Government and is not primarily in the commercial interest of the requester.

PART 1402—MANDATORY DECLASSIFICATION REVIEW

Sec.

AUTHORITY: Section 3.4, E.O. 12356 (3 CFR, 1982 Comp., p. 166), and Information Security Oversight Office Directive No. 1 (32 CFR 2001.32).

SOURCE: 57 FR 55089, Nov. 24, 1992, unless otherwise noted.

§ 1402.1 Purpose.

Other government agencies, U.S. citizens or permanent resident aliens may request that classified information in files of the Office of National Drug Control Policy (ONDCP) be reviewed for possible declassification and release. This part prescribes the procedures for such review and subsequent release or denial.

§ 1402.2 Responsibility.

All requests for the mandatory declassification review of classified information in ONDCP files should be addressed to the Security Officer, Office of National Drug Control Policy, Executive Office of the President, Washington, DC 20500, who will acknowledge receipt of the request. When a request does not reasonably describe the information sought, the requester shall be notified that unless additional information is provided, or the scope of the request is narrowed, no further action will be taken.

§ 1402.3 Information in the custody of ONDCP.

Information contained in ONDCP files and under the exclusive declassification jurisdiction of ONDCP will be reviewed by the Director of the Office of Planning, Budget, and Administration of ONDCP and/or the office of primary interest to determine whether, under the declassification provisions of section 3.1 of Executive Order 12356 (3 CFR, 1982 Comp., p. 166), the requested information may be declassified. If the information may not be released, in whole or in part, the requester shall be given a brief statement as to the reasons for denial, a notice of the right to appeal the determination to the Director of ONDCP, and a notice that such an appeal must be filed within 60 days in order to be considered.

§ 1402.4 Information classified by another agency.

When a request is received for information that was classified by another agency, the Director of the Office of Planning, Budget, and Administration of ONDCP will forward the request and a copy of the document(s) along with any other related materials, to the appropriate agency for review and determination as to release. Recommendations as to release or denial may be made if appropriate. The requester will be notified of the referral, unless the receiving agency objects on the grounds that its association with the information requires protection.

§ 1402.5 Appeal procedure.

Appeals reviewed as a result of a denial will be routed to the Director of ONDCP, who will take action as necessary to determine whether any part of the information may be declassified. If so, the Director shall notify the requester of this determination and shall make any information available that is declassified and is otherwise releasable. If continued classification is required, the requester shall be notified by the Director of ONDCP of the reasons therefore.

§ 1402.6 Fees.

There will normally be no fees charged for the mandatory review of classified material for declassification under this part.

§ 1402.7 Suggestions and complaints.

Suggestions and complaints regarding the information security program of ONDCP should be submitted, in writing, to the Security Officer, Office of National Drug Control Policy, Washington, DC 20500.

PARTS 1403–1499 [RESERVED]

FINDING AIDS

A list of CFR titles, subtitles, chapters, subchapters and parts and an alphabetical list of agencies publishing in the CFR are included in the CFR Index and Finding Aids volume to the Code of Federal Regulations which is published separately and revised annually.

Table of CFR Titles and Chapters

(Revised as of April 1, 2020)

Title 1—General Provisions

Title 2—Grants and Agreements

Title 2—Grants and Agreements—Continued

Chap.	
XXVII	Small Business Administration (Parts 2700—2799)
XXVIII	Department of Justice (Parts 2800—2899)
XXIX	Department of Labor (Parts 2900—2999)
XXX	Department of Homeland Security (Parts 3000—3099)
XXXI	Institute of Museum and Library Services (Parts 3100—3199)
XXXII	National Endowment for the Arts (Parts 3200—3299)
XXXIII	National Endowment for the Humanities (Parts 3300—3399)
XXXIV	Department of Education (Parts 3400—3499)
XXXV	Export-Import Bank of the United States (Parts 3500—3599)
XXXVI	Office of National Drug Control Policy, Executive Office of the President (Parts 3600—3699)
XXXVII	Peace Corps (Parts 3700—3799)
LVIII	Election Assistance Commission (Parts 5800—5899)
LIX	Gulf Coast Ecosystem Restoration Council (Parts 5900—5999)

Title 3—The President

I	Executive Office of the President (Parts 100—199)

Title 4—Accounts

I	Government Accountability Office (Parts 1—199)

Title 5—Administrative Personnel

I	Office of Personnel Management (Parts 1—1199)
II	Merit Systems Protection Board (Parts 1200—1299)
III	Office of Management and Budget (Parts 1300—1399)
IV	Office of Personnel Management and Office of the Director of National Intelligence (Parts 1400—1499)
V	The International Organizations Employees Loyalty Board (Parts 1500—1599)
VI	Federal Retirement Thrift Investment Board (Parts 1600—1699)
VIII	Office of Special Counsel (Parts 1800—1899)
IX	Appalachian Regional Commission (Parts 1900—1999)
XI	Armed Forces Retirement Home (Parts 2100—2199)
XIV	Federal Labor Relations Authority, General Counsel of the Federal Labor Relations Authority and Federal Service Impasses Panel (Parts 2400—2499)
XVI	Office of Government Ethics (Parts 2600—2699)
XXI	Department of the Treasury (Parts 3100—3199)
XXII	Federal Deposit Insurance Corporation (Parts 3200—3299)
XXIII	Department of Energy (Parts 3300—3399)
XXIV	Federal Energy Regulatory Commission (Parts 3400—3499)
XXV	Department of the Interior (Parts 3500—3599)
XXVI	Department of Defense (Parts 3600—3699)

Title 5—Administrative Personnel—Continued

Chap.	
LXXIV	Federal Mine Safety and Health Review Commission (Parts 8400—8499)
LXXVI	Federal Retirement Thrift Investment Board (Parts 8600—8699)
LXXVII	Office of Management and Budget (Parts 8700—8799)
LXXX	Federal Housing Finance Agency (Parts 9000—9099)
LXXXIII	Special Inspector General for Afghanistan Reconstruction (Parts 9300—9399)
LXXXIV	Bureau of Consumer Financial Protection (Parts 9400—9499)
LXXXVI	National Credit Union Administration (Parts 9600—9699)
XCVII	Department of Homeland Security Human Resources Management System (Department of Homeland Security—Office of Personnel Management) (Parts 9700—9799)
XCVIII	Council of the Inspectors General on Integrity and Efficiency (Parts 9800—9899)
XCIX	Military Compensation and Retirement Modernization Commission (Parts 9900—9999)
C	National Council on Disability (Parts 10000—10049)
CI	National Mediation Board (Part 10101)

Title 6—Domestic Security

I	Department of Homeland Security, Office of the Secretary (Parts 1—199)
X	Privacy and Civil Liberties Oversight Board (Parts 1000—1099)

Title 7—Agriculture

	SUBTITLE A—OFFICE OF THE SECRETARY OF AGRICULTURE (PARTS 0—26)
	SUBTITLE B—REGULATIONS OF THE DEPARTMENT OF AGRICULTURE
I	Agricultural Marketing Service (Standards, Inspections, Marketing Practices), Department of Agriculture (Parts 27—209)
II	Food and Nutrition Service, Department of Agriculture (Parts 210—299)
III	Animal and Plant Health Inspection Service, Department of Agriculture (Parts 300—399)
IV	Federal Crop Insurance Corporation, Department of Agriculture (Parts 400—499)
V	Agricultural Research Service, Department of Agriculture (Parts 500—599)
VI	Natural Resources Conservation Service, Department of Agriculture (Parts 600—699)
VII	Farm Service Agency, Department of Agriculture (Parts 700—799)
VIII	Agricultural Marketing Service (Federal Grain Inspection Service, Fair Trade Practices Program), Department of Agriculture (Parts 800—899)

Title 8—Aliens and Nationality

Chap.

I Department of Homeland Security (Parts 1—499)

V Executive Office for Immigration Review, Department of Justice (Parts 1000—1399)

Title 9—Animals and Animal Products

I Animal and Plant Health Inspection Service, Department of Agriculture (Parts 1—199)

II Agricultural Marketing Service (Federal Grain Inspection Service, Fair Trade Practices Program), Department of Agriculture (Parts 200—299)

III Food Safety and Inspection Service, Department of Agriculture (Parts 300—599)

Title 10—Energy

I Nuclear Regulatory Commission (Parts 0—199)

II Department of Energy (Parts 200—699)

III Department of Energy (Parts 700—999)

X Department of Energy (General Provisions) (Parts 1000—1099)

XIII Nuclear Waste Technical Review Board (Parts 1300—1399)

XVII Defense Nuclear Facilities Safety Board (Parts 1700—1799)

XVIII Northeast Interstate Low-Level Radioactive Waste Commission (Parts 1800—1899)

Title 11—Federal Elections

I Federal Election Commission (Parts 1—9099)

II Election Assistance Commission (Parts 9400—9499)

Title 12—Banks and Banking

I Comptroller of the Currency, Department of the Treasury (Parts 1—199)

II Federal Reserve System (Parts 200—299)

III Federal Deposit Insurance Corporation (Parts 300—399)

IV Export-Import Bank of the United States (Parts 400—499)

V (Parts 500—599) [Reserved]

VI Farm Credit Administration (Parts 600—699)

VII National Credit Union Administration (Parts 700—799)

VIII Federal Financing Bank (Parts 800—899)

IX Federal Housing Finance Board (Parts 900—999)

X Bureau of Consumer Financial Protection (Parts 1000—1099)

XI Federal Financial Institutions Examination Council (Parts 1100—1199)

XII Federal Housing Finance Agency (Parts 1200—1299)

XIII Financial Stability Oversight Council (Parts 1300—1399)

Title 12—Banks and Banking—Continued

Chap.	
XIV	Farm Credit System Insurance Corporation (Parts 1400—1499)
XV	Department of the Treasury (Parts 1500—1599)
XVI	Office of Financial Research (Parts 1600—1699)
XVII	Office of Federal Housing Enterprise Oversight, Department of Housing and Urban Development (Parts 1700—1799)
XVIII	Community Development Financial Institutions Fund, Department of the Treasury (Parts 1800—1899)

Title 13—Business Credit and Assistance

I	Small Business Administration (Parts 1—199)
III	Economic Development Administration, Department of Commerce (Parts 300—399)
IV	Emergency Steel Guarantee Loan Board (Parts 400—499)
V	Emergency Oil and Gas Guaranteed Loan Board (Parts 500—599)

Title 14—Aeronautics and Space

I	Federal Aviation Administration, Department of Transportation (Parts 1—199)
II	Office of the Secretary, Department of Transportation (Aviation Proceedings) (Parts 200—399)
III	Commercial Space Transportation, Federal Aviation Administration, Department of Transportation (Parts 400—1199)
V	National Aeronautics and Space Administration (Parts 1200—1299)
VI	Air Transportation System Stabilization (Parts 1300—1399)

Title 15—Commerce and Foreign Trade

	SUBTITLE A—OFFICE OF THE SECRETARY OF COMMERCE (PARTS 0—29)
	SUBTITLE B—REGULATIONS RELATING TO COMMERCE AND FOREIGN TRADE
I	Bureau of the Census, Department of Commerce (Parts 30—199)
II	National Institute of Standards and Technology, Department of Commerce (Parts 200—299)
III	International Trade Administration, Department of Commerce (Parts 300—399)
IV	Foreign-Trade Zones Board, Department of Commerce (Parts 400—499)
VII	Bureau of Industry and Security, Department of Commerce (Parts 700—799)
VIII	Bureau of Economic Analysis, Department of Commerce (Parts 800—899)
IX	National Oceanic and Atmospheric Administration, Department of Commerce (Parts 900—999)
XI	National Technical Information Service, Department of Commerce (Parts 1100—1199)

Chap.

XIII East-West Foreign Trade Board (Parts 1300—1399)

XIV Minority Business Development Agency (Parts 1400—1499)

SUBTITLE C—REGULATIONS RELATING TO FOREIGN TRADE AGREEMENTS

XX Office of the United States Trade Representative (Parts 2000—2099)

SUBTITLE D—REGULATIONS RELATING TO TELECOMMUNICATIONS AND INFORMATION

XXIII National Telecommunications and Information Administration, Department of Commerce (Parts 2300—2399) [Reserved]

Title 16—Commercial Practices

I Federal Trade Commission (Parts 0—999)

II Consumer Product Safety Commission (Parts 1000—1799)

Title 17—Commodity and Securities Exchanges

I Commodity Futures Trading Commission (Parts 1—199)

II Securities and Exchange Commission (Parts 200—399)

IV Department of the Treasury (Parts 400—499)

Title 18—Conservation of Power and Water Resources

I Federal Energy Regulatory Commission, Department of Energy (Parts 1—399)

III Delaware River Basin Commission (Parts 400—499)

VI Water Resources Council (Parts 700—799)

VIII Susquehanna River Basin Commission (Parts 800—899)

XIII Tennessee Valley Authority (Parts 1300—1399)

Title 19—Customs Duties

I U.S. Customs and Border Protection, Department of Homeland Security; Department of the Treasury (Parts 0—199)

II United States International Trade Commission (Parts 200—299)

III International Trade Administration, Department of Commerce (Parts 300—399)

IV U.S. Immigration and Customs Enforcement, Department of Homeland Security (Parts 400—599) [Reserved]

Title 20—Employees' Benefits

I Office of Workers' Compensation Programs, Department of Labor (Parts 1—199)

II Railroad Retirement Board (Parts 200—399)

III Social Security Administration (Parts 400—499)

Title 20—Employees' Benefits—Continued

Chap.

IV Employees' Compensation Appeals Board, Department of Labor (Parts 500—599)

V Employment and Training Administration, Department of Labor (Parts 600—699)

VI Office of Workers' Compensation Programs, Department of Labor (Parts 700—799)

VII Benefits Review Board, Department of Labor (Parts 800—899)

VIII Joint Board for the Enrollment of Actuaries (Parts 900—999)

IX Office of the Assistant Secretary for Veterans' Employment and Training Service, Department of Labor (Parts 1000—1099)

Title 21—Food and Drugs

I Food and Drug Administration, Department of Health and Human Services (Parts 1—1299)

II Drug Enforcement Administration, Department of Justice (Parts 1300—1399)

III Office of National Drug Control Policy (Parts 1400—1499)

Title 22—Foreign Relations

I Department of State (Parts 1—199)

II Agency for International Development (Parts 200—299)

III Peace Corps (Parts 300—399)

IV International Joint Commission, United States and Canada (Parts 400—499)

V Broadcasting Board of Governors (Parts 500—599)

VII Overseas Private Investment Corporation (Parts 700—799)

IX Foreign Service Grievance Board (Parts 900—999)

X Inter-American Foundation (Parts 1000—1099)

XI International Boundary and Water Commission, United States and Mexico, United States Section (Parts 1100—1199)

XII United States International Development Cooperation Agency (Parts 1200—1299)

XIII Millennium Challenge Corporation (Parts 1300—1399)

XIV Foreign Service Labor Relations Board; Federal Labor Relations Authority; General Counsel of the Federal Labor Relations Authority; and the Foreign Service Impasse Disputes Panel (Parts 1400—1499)

XV African Development Foundation (Parts 1500—1599)

XVI Japan-United States Friendship Commission (Parts 1600—1699)

XVII United States Institute of Peace (Parts 1700—1799)

Title 23—Highways

I Federal Highway Administration, Department of Transportation (Parts 1—999)

Title 24—Housing and Urban Development

Title 25—Indians

Chap.

I Bureau of Indian Affairs, Department of the Interior (Parts 1—299)

II Indian Arts and Crafts Board, Department of the Interior (Parts 300—399)

III National Indian Gaming Commission, Department of the Interior (Parts 500—599)

IV Office of Navajo and Hopi Indian Relocation (Parts 700—899)

V Bureau of Indian Affairs, Department of the Interior, and Indian Health Service, Department of Health and Human Services (Part 900—999)

VI Office of the Assistant Secretary, Indian Affairs, Department of the Interior (Parts 1000—1199)

VII Office of the Special Trustee for American Indians, Department of the Interior (Parts 1200—1299)

Title 26—Internal Revenue

I Internal Revenue Service, Department of the Treasury (Parts 1—End)

Title 27—Alcohol, Tobacco Products and Firearms

I Alcohol and Tobacco Tax and Trade Bureau, Department of the Treasury (Parts 1—399)

II Bureau of Alcohol, Tobacco, Firearms, and Explosives, Department of Justice (Parts 400—699)

Title 28—Judicial Administration

I Department of Justice (Parts 0—299)

III Federal Prison Industries, Inc., Department of Justice (Parts 300—399)

V Bureau of Prisons, Department of Justice (Parts 500—599)

VI Offices of Independent Counsel, Department of Justice (Parts 600—699)

VII Office of Independent Counsel (Parts 700—799)

VIII Court Services and Offender Supervision Agency for the District of Columbia (Parts 800—899)

IX National Crime Prevention and Privacy Compact Council (Parts 900—999)

XI Department of Justice and Department of State (Parts 1100—1199)

Title 29—Labor

SUBTITLE A—OFFICE OF THE SECRETARY OF LABOR (PARTS 0—99)

SUBTITLE B—REGULATIONS RELATING TO LABOR

I National Labor Relations Board (Parts 100—199)

Title 29—Labor—Continued

Chap.

II Office of Labor-Management Standards, Department of Labor (Parts 200—299)

III National Railroad Adjustment Board (Parts 300—399)

IV Office of Labor-Management Standards, Department of Labor (Parts 400—499)

V Wage and Hour Division, Department of Labor (Parts 500—899)

IX Construction Industry Collective Bargaining Commission (Parts 900—999)

X National Mediation Board (Parts 1200—1299)

XII Federal Mediation and Conciliation Service (Parts 1400—1499)

XIV Equal Employment Opportunity Commission (Parts 1600—1699)

XVII Occupational Safety and Health Administration, Department of Labor (Parts 1900—1999)

XX Occupational Safety and Health Review Commission (Parts 2200—2499)

XXV Employee Benefits Security Administration, Department of Labor (Parts 2500—2599)

XXVII Federal Mine Safety and Health Review Commission (Parts 2700—2799)

XL Pension Benefit Guaranty Corporation (Parts 4000—4999)

Title 30—Mineral Resources

I Mine Safety and Health Administration, Department of Labor (Parts 1—199)

II Bureau of Safety and Environmental Enforcement, Department of the Interior (Parts 200—299)

IV Geological Survey, Department of the Interior (Parts 400—499)

V Bureau of Ocean Energy Management, Department of the Interior (Parts 500—599)

VII Office of Surface Mining Reclamation and Enforcement, Department of the Interior (Parts 700—999)

XII Office of Natural Resources Revenue, Department of the Interior (Parts 1200—1299)

Title 31—Money and Finance: Treasury

SUBTITLE A—OFFICE OF THE SECRETARY OF THE TREASURY (PARTS 0—50)

SUBTITLE B—REGULATIONS RELATING TO MONEY AND FINANCE

I Monetary Offices, Department of the Treasury (Parts 51—199)

II Fiscal Service, Department of the Treasury (Parts 200—399)

IV Secret Service, Department of the Treasury (Parts 400—499)

V Office of Foreign Assets Control, Department of the Treasury (Parts 500—599)

VI Bureau of Engraving and Printing, Department of the Treasury (Parts 600—699)

VII Federal Law Enforcement Training Center, Department of the Treasury (Parts 700—799)

Title 31—Money and Finance: Treasury—Continued

Title 32—National Defense

Title 33—Navigation and Navigable Waters

Title 34—Education

Title 34—Education—Continued

Title 35 [Reserved]

Title 36—Parks, Forests, and Public Property

Title 37—Patents, Trademarks, and Copyrights

Title 38—Pensions, Bonuses, and Veterans' Relief

Chap.

I Department of Veterans Affairs (Parts 0—199)

II Armed Forces Retirement Home (Parts 200—299)

Title 39—Postal Service

I United States Postal Service (Parts 1—999)

III Postal Regulatory Commission (Parts 3000—3099)

Title 40—Protection of Environment

I Environmental Protection Agency (Parts 1—1099)

IV Environmental Protection Agency and Department of Justice (Parts 1400—1499)

V Council on Environmental Quality (Parts 1500—1599)

VI Chemical Safety and Hazard Investigation Board (Parts 1600—1699)

VII Environmental Protection Agency and Department of Defense; Uniform National Discharge Standards for Vessels of the Armed Forces (Parts 1700—1799)

VIII Gulf Coast Ecosystem Restoration Council (Parts 1800—1899)

Title 41—Public Contracts and Property Management

SUBTITLE A—FEDERAL PROCUREMENT REGULATIONS SYSTEM [NOTE]

SUBTITLE B—OTHER PROVISIONS RELATING TO PUBLIC CONTRACTS

50 Public Contracts, Department of Labor (Parts 50–1—50–999)

51 Committee for Purchase From People Who Are Blind or Severely Disabled (Parts 51–1—51–99)

60 Office of Federal Contract Compliance Programs, Equal Employment Opportunity, Department of Labor (Parts 60–1—60–999)

61 Office of the Assistant Secretary for Veterans' Employment and Training Service, Department of Labor (Parts 61–1—61–999)

62—100 [Reserved]

SUBTITLE C—FEDERAL PROPERTY MANAGEMENT REGULATIONS SYSTEM

101 Federal Property Management Regulations (Parts 101–1—101–99)

102 Federal Management Regulation (Parts 102–1—102–299)

103—104 [Reserved]

105 General Services Administration (Parts 105–1—105–999)

109 Department of Energy Property Management Regulations (Parts 109–1—109–99)

114 Department of the Interior (Parts 114–1—114–99)

115 Environmental Protection Agency (Parts 115–1—115–99)

128 Department of Justice (Parts 128–1—128–99)

129—200 [Reserved]

SUBTITLE D—OTHER PROVISIONS RELATING TO PROPERTY MANAGEMENT [RESERVED]

Chap.

SUBTITLE E—FEDERAL INFORMATION RESOURCES MANAGEMENT REGULATIONS SYSTEM [RESERVED]

SUBTITLE F—FEDERAL TRAVEL REGULATION SYSTEM

300 General (Parts 300-1—300-99)

301 Temporary Duty (TDY) Travel Allowances (Parts 301-1—301-99)

302 Relocation Allowances (Parts 302-1—302-99)

303 Payment of Expenses Connected with the Death of Certain Employees (Part 303-1—303-99)

304 Payment of Travel Expenses from a Non-Federal Source (Parts 304-1—304-99)

Title 42—Public Health

I Public Health Service, Department of Health and Human Services (Parts 1—199)

IV Centers for Medicare & Medicaid Services, Department of Health and Human Services (Parts 400—699)

V Office of Inspector General-Health Care, Department of Health and Human Services (Parts 1000—1099)

Title 43—Public Lands: Interior

SUBTITLE A—OFFICE OF THE SECRETARY OF THE INTERIOR (PARTS 1—199)

SUBTITLE B—REGULATIONS RELATING TO PUBLIC LANDS

I Bureau of Reclamation, Department of the Interior (Parts 400—999)

II Bureau of Land Management, Department of the Interior (Parts 1000—9999)

III Utah Reclamation Mitigation and Conservation Commission (Parts 10000—10099)

Title 44—Emergency Management and Assistance

I Federal Emergency Management Agency, Department of Homeland Security (Parts 0—399)

IV Department of Commerce and Department of Transportation (Parts 400—499)

Title 45—Public Welfare

SUBTITLE A—DEPARTMENT OF HEALTH AND HUMAN SERVICES (PARTS 1—199)

SUBTITLE B—REGULATIONS RELATING TO PUBLIC WELFARE

II Office of Family Assistance (Assistance Programs), Administration for Children and Families, Department of Health and Human Services (Parts 200—299)

Title 45—Public Welfare—Continued

Chap.

III Office of Child Support Enforcement (Child Support Enforcement Program), Administration for Children and Families, Department of Health and Human Services (Parts 300—399)

IV Office of Refugee Resettlement, Administration for Children and Families, Department of Health and Human Services (Parts 400—499)

V Foreign Claims Settlement Commission of the United States, Department of Justice (Parts 500—599)

VI National Science Foundation (Parts 600—699)

VII Commission on Civil Rights (Parts 700—799)

VIII Office of Personnel Management (Parts 800—899)

IX Denali Commission (Parts 900—999)

X Office of Community Services, Administration for Children and Families, Department of Health and Human Services (Parts 1000—1099)

XI National Foundation on the Arts and the Humanities (Parts 1100—1199)

XII Corporation for National and Community Service (Parts 1200—1299)

XIII Administration for Children and Families, Department of Health and Human Services (Parts 1300—1399)

XVI Legal Services Corporation (Parts 1600—1699)

XVII National Commission on Libraries and Information Science (Parts 1700—1799)

XVIII Harry S. Truman Scholarship Foundation (Parts 1800—1899)

XXI Commission of Fine Arts (Parts 2100—2199)

XXIII Arctic Research Commission (Parts 2300—2399)

XXIV James Madison Memorial Fellowship Foundation (Parts 2400—2499)

XXV Corporation for National and Community Service (Parts 2500—2599)

Title 46—Shipping

I Coast Guard, Department of Homeland Security (Parts 1—199)

II Maritime Administration, Department of Transportation (Parts 200—399)

III Coast Guard (Great Lakes Pilotage), Department of Homeland Security (Parts 400—499)

IV Federal Maritime Commission (Parts 500—599)

Title 47—Telecommunication

I Federal Communications Commission (Parts 0—199)

II Office of Science and Technology Policy and National Security Council (Parts 200—299)

III National Telecommunications and Information Administration, Department of Commerce (Parts 300—399)

Title 47—Telecommunication—Continued

Chap.

IV National Telecommunications and Information Administration, Department of Commerce, and National Highway Traffic Safety Administration, Department of Transportation (Parts 400—499)

V The First Responder Network Authority (Parts 500—599)

Title 48—Federal Acquisition Regulations System

1 Federal Acquisition Regulation (Parts 1—99)

2 Defense Acquisition Regulations System, Department of Defense (Parts 200—299)

3 Department of Health and Human Services (Parts 300—399)

4 Department of Agriculture (Parts 400—499)

5 General Services Administration (Parts 500—599)

6 Department of State (Parts 600—699)

7 Agency for International Development (Parts 700—799)

8 Department of Veterans Affairs (Parts 800—899)

9 Department of Energy (Parts 900—999)

10 Department of the Treasury (Parts 1000—1099)

12 Department of Transportation (Parts 1200—1299)

13 Department of Commerce (Parts 1300—1399)

14 Department of the Interior (Parts 1400—1499)

15 Environmental Protection Agency (Parts 1500—1599)

16 Office of Personnel Management, Federal Employees Health Benefits Acquisition Regulation (Parts 1600—1699)

17 Office of Personnel Management (Parts 1700—1799)

18 National Aeronautics and Space Administration (Parts 1800—1899)

19 Broadcasting Board of Governors (Parts 1900—1999)

20 Nuclear Regulatory Commission (Parts 2000—2099)

21 Office of Personnel Management, Federal Employees Group Life Insurance Federal Acquisition Regulation (Parts 2100—2199)

23 Social Security Administration (Parts 2300—2399)

24 Department of Housing and Urban Development (Parts 2400—2499)

25 National Science Foundation (Parts 2500—2599)

28 Department of Justice (Parts 2800—2899)

29 Department of Labor (Parts 2900—2999)

30 Department of Homeland Security, Homeland Security Acquisition Regulation (HSAR) (Parts 3000—3099)

34 Department of Education Acquisition Regulation (Parts 3400—3499)

51 Department of the Army Acquisition Regulations (Parts 5100—5199) [Reserved]

52 Department of the Navy Acquisition Regulations (Parts 5200—5299)

53 Department of the Air Force Federal Acquisition Regulation Supplement (Parts 5300—5399) [Reserved]

Chap.

54 Defense Logistics Agency, Department of Defense (Parts 5400—5499)

57 African Development Foundation (Parts 5700—5799)

61 Civilian Board of Contract Appeals, General Services Administration (Parts 6100—6199)

99 Cost Accounting Standards Board, Office of Federal Procurement Policy, Office of Management and Budget (Parts 9900—9999)

Title 49—Transportation

SUBTITLE A—OFFICE OF THE SECRETARY OF TRANSPORTATION (PARTS 1—99)

SUBTITLE B—OTHER REGULATIONS RELATING TO TRANSPORTATION

I Pipeline and Hazardous Materials Safety Administration, Department of Transportation (Parts 100—199)

II Federal Railroad Administration, Department of Transportation (Parts 200—299)

III Federal Motor Carrier Safety Administration, Department of Transportation (Parts 300—399)

IV Coast Guard, Department of Homeland Security (Parts 400—499)

V National Highway Traffic Safety Administration, Department of Transportation (Parts 500—599)

VI Federal Transit Administration, Department of Transportation (Parts 600—699)

VII National Railroad Passenger Corporation (AMTRAK) (Parts 700—799)

VIII National Transportation Safety Board (Parts 800—999)

X Surface Transportation Board (Parts 1000—1399)

XI Research and Innovative Technology Administration, Department of Transportation (Parts 1400—1499) [Reserved]

XII Transportation Security Administration, Department of Homeland Security (Parts 1500—1699)

Title 50—Wildlife and Fisheries

I United States Fish and Wildlife Service, Department of the Interior (Parts 1—199)

II National Marine Fisheries Service, National Oceanic and Atmospheric Administration, Department of Commerce (Parts 200—299)

III International Fishing and Related Activities (Parts 300—399)

IV Joint Regulations (United States Fish and Wildlife Service, Department of the Interior and National Marine Fisheries Service, National Oceanic and Atmospheric Administration, Department of Commerce); Endangered Species Committee Regulations (Parts 400—499)

V Marine Mammal Commission (Parts 500—599)

Alphabetical List of Agencies Appearing in the CFR

(Revised as of April 1, 2020)

Agency	CFR Title, Subtitle or Chapter
Administrative Conference of the United States	1, III
Advisory Council on Historic Preservation	36, VIII
Advocacy and Outreach, Office of	7, XXV
Afghanistan Reconstruction, Special Inspector General for	5, LXXXIII
African Development Foundation	22, XV
Federal Acquisition Regulation	48, 57
Agency for International Development	2, VII; 22, II
Federal Acquisition Regulation	48, 7
Agricultural Marketing Service	7, I, VIII, IX, X, XI; 9, II
Agricultural Research Service	7, V
Agriculture, Department of	2, IV; 5, LXXIII
Advocacy and Outreach, Office of	7, XXV
Agricultural Marketing Service	7, I, VIII, IX, X, XI; 9, II
Agricultural Research Service	7, V
Animal and Plant Health Inspection Service	7, III; 9, I
Chief Financial Officer, Office of	7, XXX
Commodity Credit Corporation	7, XIV
Economic Research Service	7, XXXVII
Energy Policy and New Uses, Office of	2, IX; 7, XXIX
Environmental Quality, Office of	7, XXXI
Farm Service Agency	7, VII, XVIII
Federal Acquisition Regulation	48, 4
Federal Crop Insurance Corporation	7, IV
Food and Nutrition Service	7, II
Food Safety and Inspection Service	9, III
Foreign Agricultural Service	7, XV
Forest Service	36, II
Information Resources Management, Office of	7, XXVII
Inspector General, Office of	7, XXVI
National Agricultural Library	7, XLI
National Agricultural Statistics Service	7, XXXVI
National Institute of Food and Agriculture	7, XXXIV
Natural Resources Conservation Service	7, VI
Operations, Office of	7, XXVIII
Procurement and Property Management, Office of	7, XXXII
Rural Business-Cooperative Service	7, XVIII, XLII
Rural Development Administration	7, XLII
Rural Housing Service	7, XVIII, XXXV
Rural Utilities Service	7, XVII, XVIII, XLII
Secretary of Agriculture, Office of	7, Subtitle A
Transportation, Office of	7, XXXIII
World Agricultural Outlook Board	7, XXXVIII
Air Force, Department of	32, VII
Federal Acquisition Regulation Supplement	48, 53
Air Transportation Stabilization Board	14, VI
Alcohol and Tobacco Tax and Trade Bureau	27, I
Alcohol, Tobacco, Firearms, and Explosives, Bureau of	27, II
AMTRAK	49, VII
American Battle Monuments Commission	36, IV
American Indians, Office of the Special Trustee	25, VII
Animal and Plant Health Inspection Service	7, III; 9, I
Appalachian Regional Commission	5, IX
Architectural and Transportation Barriers Compliance Board	36, XI

Agency	CFR Title, Subtitle or Chapter
Arctic Research Commission	45, XXIII
Armed Forces Retirement Home	5, XI; 38, II
Army, Department of	32, V
Engineers, Corps of	33, II; 36, III
Federal Acquisition Regulation	48, 51
Bilingual Education and Minority Languages Affairs, Office of	34, V
Blind or Severely Disabled, Committee for Purchase from People Who Are	41, 51
Broadcasting Board of Governors	22, V
Federal Acquisition Regulation	48, 19
Career, Technical, and Adult Education, Office of	34, IV
Census Bureau	15, I
Centers for Medicare & Medicaid Services	42, IV
Central Intelligence Agency	32, XIX
Chemical Safety and Hazard Investigation Board	40, VI
Chief Financial Officer, Office of	7, XXX
Child Support Enforcement, Office of	45, III
Children and Families, Administration for	45, II, III, IV, X, XIII
Civil Rights, Commission on	5, LXVIII; 45, VII
Civil Rights, Office for	34, I
Council of the Inspectors General on Integrity and Efficiency	5, XCVIII
Court Services and Offender Supervision Agency for the District of Columbia	5, LXX
Coast Guard	33, I; 46, I; 49, IV
Coast Guard (Great Lakes Pilotage)	46, III
Commerce, Department of	2, XIII; 44, IV; 50, VI
Census Bureau	15, I
Economic Analysis, Bureau of	15, VIII
Economic Development Administration	13, III
Emergency Management and Assistance	44, IV
Federal Acquisition Regulation	48, 13
Foreign-Trade Zones Board	15, IV
Industry and Security, Bureau of	15, VII
International Trade Administration	15, III; 19, III
National Institute of Standards and Technology	15, II; 37, IV
National Marine Fisheries Service	50, II, IV
National Oceanic and Atmospheric Administration	15, IX; 50, II, III, IV, VI
National Technical Information Service	15, XI
National Telecommunications and Information Administration	15, XXIII; 47, III, IV
National Weather Service	15, IX
Patent and Trademark Office, United States	37, I
Secretary of Commerce, Office of	15, Subtitle A
Commercial Space Transportation	14, III
Commodity Credit Corporation	7, XIV
Commodity Futures Trading Commission	5, XLI; 17, I
Community Planning and Development, Office of Assistant Secretary for	24, V, VI
Community Services, Office of	45, X
Comptroller of the Currency	12, I
Construction Industry Collective Bargaining Commission	29, IX
Consumer Financial Protection Bureau	5, LXXXIV; 12, X
Consumer Product Safety Commission	5, LXXI; 16, II
Copyright Royalty Board	37, III
Corporation for National and Community Service	2, XXII; 45, XII, XXV
Cost Accounting Standards Board	48, 99
Council on Environmental Quality	40, V
Court Services and Offender Supervision Agency for the District of Columbia	5, LXX; 28, VIII
Customs and Border Protection	19, I
Defense Contract Audit Agency	32, I
Defense, Department of	2, XI; 5, XXVI; 32, Subtitle A; 40, VII
Advanced Research Projects Agency	32, I
Air Force Department	32, VII
Army Department	32, V; 33, II; 36, III; 48, 51

Agency	CFR Title, Subtitle or Chapter
Defense Acquisition Regulations System	48, 2
Defense Intelligence Agency	32, I
Defense Logistics Agency	32, I, XII; 48, 54
Engineers, Corps of	33, II; 36, III
National Imagery and Mapping Agency	32, I
Navy, Department of	32, VI; 48, 52
Secretary of Defense, Office of	2, XI; 32, I
Defense Contract Audit Agency	32, I
Defense Intelligence Agency	32, I
Defense Logistics Agency	32, XII; 48, 54
Defense Nuclear Facilities Safety Board	10, XVII
Delaware River Basin Commission	18, III
Denali Commission	45, IX
Disability, National Council on	5, C; 34, XII
District of Columbia, Court Services and Offender Supervision Agency for the	5, LXX; 28, VIII
Drug Enforcement Administration	21, II
East-West Foreign Trade Board	15, XIII
Economic Analysis, Bureau of	15, VIII
Economic Development Administration	13, III
Economic Research Service	7, XXXVII
Education, Department of	2, XXXIV; 5, LIII
Bilingual Education and Minority Languages Affairs, Office of	34, V
Career, Technical, and Adult Education, Office of	34, IV
Civil Rights, Office for	34, I
Educational Research and Improvement, Office of	34, VII
Elementary and Secondary Education, Office of	34, II
Federal Acquisition Regulation	48, 34
Postsecondary Education, Office of	34, VI
Secretary of Education, Office of	34, Subtitle A
Special Education and Rehabilitative Services, Office of	34, III
Educational Research and Improvement, Office of	34, VII
Election Assistance Commission	2, LVIII; 11, II
Elementary and Secondary Education, Office of	34, II
Emergency Oil and Gas Guaranteed Loan Board	13, V
Emergency Steel Guarantee Loan Board	13, IV
Employee Benefits Security Administration	29, XXV
Employees' Compensation Appeals Board	20, IV
Employees Loyalty Board	5, V
Employment and Training Administration	20, V
Employment Policy, National Commission for	1, IV
Employment Standards Administration	20, VI
Endangered Species Committee	50, IV
Energy, Department of	2, IX; 5, XXIII; 10, II, III, X
Federal Acquisition Regulation	48, 9
Federal Energy Regulatory Commission	5, XXIV; 18, I
Property Management Regulations	41, 109
Energy, Office of	7, XXIX
Engineers, Corps of	33, II; 36, III
Engraving and Printing, Bureau of	31, VI
Environmental Protection Agency	2, XV; 5, LIV; 40, I, IV, VII
Federal Acquisition Regulation	48, 15
Property Management Regulations	41, 115
Environmental Quality, Office of	7, XXXI
Equal Employment Opportunity Commission	5, LXII; 29, XIV
Equal Opportunity, Office of Assistant Secretary for	24, I
Executive Office of the President	3, I
Environmental Quality, Council on	40, V
Management and Budget, Office of	2, Subtitle A; 5, III, LXXVII; 14, VI; 48, 99
National Drug Control Policy, Office of	2, XXXVI; 21, III
National Security Council	32, XXI; 47, II
Presidential Documents	3
Science and Technology Policy, Office of	32, XXIV; 47, II

Agency	CFR Title, Subtitle or Chapter
Trade Representative, Office of the United States	15, XX
Export-Import Bank of the United States	2, XXXV; 5, LII; 12, IV
Family Assistance, Office of	45, II
Farm Credit Administration	5, XXXI; 12, VI
Farm Credit System Insurance Corporation	5, XXX; 12, XIV
Farm Service Agency	7, VII, XVIII
Federal Acquisition Regulation	48, 1
Federal Aviation Administration	14, I
Commercial Space Transportation	14, III
Federal Claims Collection Standards	31, IX
Federal Communications Commission	5, XXIX; 47, I
Federal Contract Compliance Programs, Office of	41, 60
Federal Crop Insurance Corporation	7, IV
Federal Deposit Insurance Corporation	5, XXII; 12, III
Federal Election Commission	5, XXXVII; 11, I
Federal Emergency Management Agency	44, I
Federal Employees Group Life Insurance Federal Acquisition Regulation	48, 21
Federal Employees Health Benefits Acquisition Regulation	48, 16
Federal Energy Regulatory Commission	5, XXIV; 18, I
Federal Financial Institutions Examination Council	12, XI
Federal Financing Bank	12, VIII
Federal Highway Administration	23, I, II
Federal Home Loan Mortgage Corporation	1, IV
Federal Housing Enterprise Oversight Office	12, XVII
Federal Housing Finance Agency	5, LXXX; 12, XII
Federal Housing Finance Board	12, IX
Federal Labor Relations Authority	5, XIV, XLIX; 22, XIV
Federal Law Enforcement Training Center	31, VII
Federal Management Regulation	41, 102
Federal Maritime Commission	46, IV
Federal Mediation and Conciliation Service	29, XII
Federal Mine Safety and Health Review Commission	5, LXXIV; 29, XXVII
Federal Motor Carrier Safety Administration	49, III
Federal Prison Industries, Inc.	28, III
Federal Procurement Policy Office	48, 99
Federal Property Management Regulations	41, 101
Federal Railroad Administration	49, II
Federal Register, Administrative Committee of	1, I
Federal Register, Office of	1, II
Federal Reserve System	12, II
Board of Governors	5, LVIII
Federal Retirement Thrift Investment Board	5, VI, LXXVI
Federal Service Impasses Panel	5, XIV
Federal Trade Commission	5, XLVII; 16, I
Federal Transit Administration	49, VI
Federal Travel Regulation System	41, Subtitle F
Financial Crimes Enforcement Network	31, X
Financial Research Office	12, XVI
Financial Stability Oversight Council	12, XIII
Fine Arts, Commission of	45, XXI
Fiscal Service	31, II
Fish and Wildlife Service, United States	50, I, IV
Food and Drug Administration	21, I
Food and Nutrition Service	7, II
Food Safety and Inspection Service	9, III
Foreign Agricultural Service	7, XV
Foreign Assets Control, Office of	31, V
Foreign Claims Settlement Commission of the United States	45, V
Foreign Service Grievance Board	22, IX
Foreign Service Impasse Disputes Panel	22, XIV
Foreign Service Labor Relations Board	22, XIV
Foreign-Trade Zones Board	15, IV
Forest Service	36, II
General Services Administration	5, LVII; 41, 105
Contract Appeals, Board of	48, 61
Federal Acquisition Regulation	48, 5

Agency	CFR Title, Subtitle or Chapter
Federal Management Regulation	41, 102
Federal Property Management Regulations	41, 101
Federal Travel Regulation System	41, Subtitle F
General	41, 300
Payment From a Non-Federal Source for Travel Expenses	41, 304
Payment of Expenses Connected With the Death of Certain Employees	41, 303
Relocation Allowances	41, 302
Temporary Duty (TDY) Travel Allowances	41, 301
Geological Survey	30, IV
Government Accountability Office	4, I
Government Ethics, Office of	5, XVI
Government National Mortgage Association	24, III
Grain Inspection, Packers and Stockyards Administration	7, VIII; 9, II
Gulf Coast Ecosystem Restoration Council	2, LIX; 40, VIII
Harry S. Truman Scholarship Foundation	45, XVIII
Health and Human Services, Department of	2, III; 5, XLV; 45, Subtitle A
Centers for Medicare & Medicaid Services	42, IV
Child Support Enforcement, Office of	45, III
Children and Families, Administration for	45, II, III, IV, X, XIII
Community Services, Office of	45, X
Family Assistance, Office of	45, II
Federal Acquisition Regulation	48, 3
Food and Drug Administration	21, I
Indian Health Service	25, V
Inspector General (Health Care), Office of	42, V
Public Health Service	42, I
Refugee Resettlement, Office of	45, IV
Homeland Security, Department of	2, XXX; 5, XXXVI; 6, I; 8, I
Coast Guard	33, I; 46, I; 49, IV
Coast Guard (Great Lakes Pilotage)	46, III
Customs and Border Protection	19, I
Federal Emergency Management Agency	44, I
Human Resources Management and Labor Relations Systems	5, XCVII
Immigration and Customs Enforcement Bureau	19, IV
Transportation Security Administration	49, XII
HOPE for Homeowners Program, Board of Directors of	24, XXIV
Housing and Urban Development, Department of	2, XXIV; 5, LXV; 24, Subtitle B
Community Planning and Development, Office of Assistant Secretary for	24, V, VI
Equal Opportunity, Office of Assistant Secretary for	24, I
Federal Acquisition Regulation	48, 24
Federal Housing Enterprise Oversight, Office of	12, XVII
Government National Mortgage Association	24, III
Housing—Federal Housing Commissioner, Office of Assistant Secretary for	24, II, VIII, X, XX
Housing, Office of, and Multifamily Housing Assistance Restructuring, Office of	24, IV
Inspector General, Office of	24, XII
Public and Indian Housing, Office of Assistant Secretary for	24, IX
Secretary, Office of	24, Subtitle A, VII
Housing—Federal Housing Commissioner, Office of Assistant Secretary for	24, II, VIII, X, XX
Housing, Office of, and Multifamily Housing Assistance Restructuring, Office of	24, IV
Immigration and Customs Enforcement Bureau	19, IV
Immigration Review, Executive Office for	8, V
Independent Counsel, Office of	28, VII
Independent Counsel, Offices of	28, VI
Indian Affairs, Bureau of	25, I, V
Indian Affairs, Office of the Assistant Secretary	25, VI
Indian Arts and Crafts Board	25, II
Indian Health Service	25, V

Agency	CFR Title, Subtitle or Chapter
Industry and Security, Bureau of	15, VII
Information Resources Management, Office of	7, XXVII
Information Security Oversight Office, National Archives and Records Administration	32, XX
Inspector General	
Agriculture Department	7, XXVI
Health and Human Services Department	42, V
Housing and Urban Development Department	24, XII, XV
Institute of Peace, United States	22, XVII
Inter-American Foundation	5, LXIII; 22, X
Interior, Department of	2, XIV
American Indians, Office of the Special Trustee	25, VII
Endangered Species Committee	50, IV
Federal Acquisition Regulation	48, 14
Federal Property Management Regulations System	41, 114
Fish and Wildlife Service, United States	50, I, IV
Geological Survey	30, IV
Indian Affairs, Bureau of	25, I, V
Indian Affairs, Office of the Assistant Secretary	25, VI
Indian Arts and Crafts Board	25, II
Land Management, Bureau of	43, II
National Indian Gaming Commission	25, III
National Park Service	36, I
Natural Resource Revenue, Office of	30, XII
Ocean Energy Management, Bureau of	30, V
Reclamation, Bureau of	43, I
Safety and Enforcement Bureau, Bureau of	30, II
Secretary of the Interior, Office of	2, XIV; 43, Subtitle A
Surface Mining Reclamation and Enforcement, Office of	30, VII
Internal Revenue Service	26, I
International Boundary and Water Commission, United States and Mexico, United States Section	22, XI
International Development, United States Agency for	22, II
Federal Acquisition Regulation	48, 7
International Development Cooperation Agency, United States	22, XII
International Development Finance Corporation, U.S.	5, XXXIII; 22, VII
International Joint Commission, United States and Canada	22, IV
International Organizations Employees Loyalty Board	5, V
International Trade Administration	15, III; 19, III
International Trade Commission, United States	19, II
Interstate Commerce Commission	5, XL
Investment Security, Office of	31, VIII
James Madison Memorial Fellowship Foundation	45, XXIV
Japan–United States Friendship Commission	22, XVI
Joint Board for the Enrollment of Actuaries	20, VIII
Justice, Department of	2, XXVIII; 5, XXVIII; 28, I, XI; 40, IV
Alcohol, Tobacco, Firearms, and Explosives, Bureau of	27, II
Drug Enforcement Administration	21, II
Federal Acquisition Regulation	48, 28
Federal Claims Collection Standards	31, IX
Federal Prison Industries, Inc.	28, III
Foreign Claims Settlement Commission of the United States	45, V
Immigration Review, Executive Office for	8, V
Independent Counsel, Offices of	28, VI
Prisons, Bureau of	28, V
Property Management Regulations	41, 128
Labor, Department of	2, XXIX; 5, XLII
Employee Benefits Security Administration	29, XXV
Employees' Compensation Appeals Board	20, IV
Employment and Training Administration	20, V
Employment Standards Administration	20, VI
Federal Acquisition Regulation	48, 29
Federal Contract Compliance Programs, Office of	41, 60
Federal Procurement Regulations System	41, 50

Agency	CFR Title, Subtitle or Chapter
Labor-Management Standards, Office of	29, II, IV
Mine Safety and Health Administration	30, I
Occupational Safety and Health Administration	29, XVII
Public Contracts	41, 50
Secretary of Labor, Office of	29, Subtitle A
Veterans' Employment and Training Service, Office of the Assistant Secretary for	41, 61; 20, IX
Wage and Hour Division	29, V
Workers' Compensation Programs, Office of	20, I, VII
Labor-Management Standards, Office of	29, II, IV
Land Management, Bureau of	43, II
Legal Services Corporation	45, XVI
Libraries and Information Science, National Commission on	45, XVII
Library of Congress	36, VII
Copyright Royalty Board	37, III
U.S. Copyright Office	37, II
Management and Budget, Office of	5, III, LXXVII; 14, VI; 48, 99
Marine Mammal Commission	50, V
Maritime Administration	46, II
Merit Systems Protection Board	5, II, LXIV
Micronesian Status Negotiations, Office for	32, XXVII
Military Compensation and Retirement Modernization Commission	5, XCIX
Millennium Challenge Corporation	22, XIII
Mine Safety and Health Administration	30, I
Minority Business Development Agency	15, XIV
Miscellaneous Agencies	1, IV
Monetary Offices	31, I
Morris K. Udall Scholarship and Excellence in National Environmental Policy Foundation	36, XVI
Museum and Library Services, Institute of	2, XXXI
National Aeronautics and Space Administration	2, XVIII; 5, LIX; 14, V
Federal Acquisition Regulation	48, 18
National Agricultural Library	7, XLI
National Agricultural Statistics Service	7, XXXVI
National and Community Service, Corporation for	2, XXII; 45, XII, XXV
National Archives and Records Administration	2, XXVI; 5, LXVI; 36, XII
Information Security Oversight Office	32, XX
National Capital Planning Commission	1, IV, VI
National Counterintelligence Center	32, XVIII
National Credit Union Administration	5, LXXXVI; 12, VII
National Crime Prevention and Privacy Compact Council	28, IX
National Drug Control Policy, Office of	2, XXXVI; 21, III
National Endowment for the Arts	2, XXXII
National Endowment for the Humanities	2, XXXIII
National Foundation on the Arts and the Humanities	45, XI
National Geospatial-Intelligence Agency	32, I
National Highway Traffic Safety Administration	23, II, III; 47, VI; 49, V
National Imagery and Mapping Agency	32, I
National Indian Gaming Commission	25, III
National Institute of Food and Agriculture	7, XXXIV
National Institute of Standards and Technology	15, II; 37, IV
National Intelligence, Office of Director of	5, IV; 32, XVII
National Labor Relations Board	5, LXI; 29, I
National Marine Fisheries Service	50, II, IV
National Mediation Board	5, CI; 29, X
National Oceanic and Atmospheric Administration	15, IX; 50, II, III, IV, VI
National Park Service	36, I
National Railroad Adjustment Board	29, III
National Railroad Passenger Corporation (AMTRAK)	49, VII
National Science Foundation	2, XXV; 5, XLIII; 45, VI
Federal Acquisition Regulation	48, 25
National Security Council	32, XXI
National Security Council and Office of Science and Technology Policy	47, II

Agency	CFR Title, Subtitle or Chapter
National Technical Information Service	15, XI
National Telecommunications and Information Administration	15, XXIII; 47, III, IV, V
National Transportation Safety Board	49, VIII
Natural Resources Conservation Service	7, VI
Natural Resource Revenue, Office of	30, XII
Navajo and Hopi Indian Relocation, Office of	25, IV
Navy, Department of	32, VI
Federal Acquisition Regulation	48, 52
Neighborhood Reinvestment Corporation	24, XXV
Northeast Interstate Low-Level Radioactive Waste Commission	10, XVIII
Nuclear Regulatory Commission	2, XX; 5, XLVIII; 10, I
Federal Acquisition Regulation	48, 20
Occupational Safety and Health Administration	29, XVII
Occupational Safety and Health Review Commission	29, XX
Ocean Energy Management, Bureau of	30, V
Oklahoma City National Memorial Trust	36, XV
Operations Office	7, XXVIII
Patent and Trademark Office, United States	37, I
Payment From a Non-Federal Source for Travel Expenses	41, 304
Payment of Expenses Connected With the Death of Certain Employees	41, 303
Peace Corps	2, XXXVII; 22, III
Pennsylvania Avenue Development Corporation	36, IX
Pension Benefit Guaranty Corporation	29, XL
Personnel Management, Office of	5, I, IV, XXXV; 45, VIII
Human Resources Management and Labor Relations Systems, Department of Homeland Security	5, XCVII
Federal Acquisition Regulation	48, 17
Federal Employees Group Life Insurance Federal Acquisition Regulation	48, 21
Federal Employees Health Benefits Acquisition Regulation	48, 16
Pipeline and Hazardous Materials Safety Administration	49, I
Postal Regulatory Commission	5, XLVI; 39, III
Postal Service, United States	5, LX; 39, I
Postsecondary Education, Office of	34, VI
President's Commission on White House Fellowships	1, IV
Presidential Documents	3
Presidio Trust	36, X
Prisons, Bureau of	28, V
Privacy and Civil Liberties Oversight Board	6, X
Procurement and Property Management, Office of	7, XXXII
Public Contracts, Department of Labor	41, 50
Public and Indian Housing, Office of Assistant Secretary for	24, IX
Public Health Service	42, I
Railroad Retirement Board	20, II
Reclamation, Bureau of	43, I
Refugee Resettlement, Office of	45, IV
Relocation Allowances	41, 302
Research and Innovative Technology Administration	49, XI
Rural Business-Cooperative Service	7, XVIII, XLII
Rural Development Administration	7, XLII
Rural Housing Service	7, XVIII, XXXV
Rural Utilities Service	7, XVII, XVIII, XLII
Safety and Environmental Enforcement, Bureau of	30, II
Saint Lawrence Seaway Development Corporation	33, IV
Science and Technology Policy, Office of	32, XXIV
Science and Technology Policy, Office of, and National Security Council	47, II
Secret Service	31, IV
Securities and Exchange Commission	5, XXXIV; 17, II
Selective Service System	32, XVI
Small Business Administration	2, XXVII; 13, I
Smithsonian Institution	36, V
Social Security Administration	2, XXIII; 20, III; 48, 23
Soldiers' and Airmen's Home, United States	5, XI

List of CFR Sections Affected

All changes in this volume of the Code of Federal Regulations (CFR) that were made by documents published in the FEDERAL REGISTER since January 1, 2015 are enumerated in the following list. Entries indicate the nature of the changes effected. Page numbers refer to FEDERAL REGISTER pages. The user should consult the entries for chapters, parts and subparts as well as sections for revisions.

For changes to this volume of the CFR prior to this listing, consult the annual edition of the monthly List of CFR Sections Affected (LSA). The LSA is available at *www.govinfo.gov*. For changes to this volume of the CFR prior to 2001, see the "List of CFR Sections Affected, 1949–1963, 1964–1972, 1973–1985, and 1986–2000" published in 11 separate volumes. The "List of CFR Sections Affected 1986–2000" is available at *www.govinfo.gov*.

2015

21 CFR

80 FR Page

Chapter II

1308 Policy statement..........27854, 70658
Technical correction 70680, 78657
1308.11 (h)(29), (30) and (31) added..........5047
(h)(1) through (8) removed; (h)(9) through (31) redesignated as new (h)(1) through (23)..........14844
(h)(24) added..........42385
1308.12 (b)(1) introductory text revised..........3470
(b)(4) revised..........54718
1308.14 (g)(3) added..........69864
1308.22 Table amended; interim..........65634, 65637

Chapter III

1403 Regulation at 79 FR 76106 confirmed..........57383
1404 Regulation at 79 FR 76106 confirmed..........57383
1405 Regulation at 79 FR 76106 confirmed..........57383

2016

21 CFR

81 FR Page

1300.01 (b) amended..........97018
1300.02 (b) amended..........97019
1301 Policy statement..........53846
1301.12 (b)(3) revised..........97019
1301.24 (a)(1) revised..........97019

21 CFR—Continued

81 FR Page

1301.26 (b) introductory text revised..........97019
1301.29 Removed..........9766
1301.34 (c)(2) revised..........97019
1301.74 (g) revised; interim..........58839
(c) introductory text revised..........97020
1301.75 (e) revised; interim..........58839
1302.07 Revised..........97020
1303.12 (b) and (d) amended..........97020
1303.22 Introductory text amended..........97020
1304.02 Revised..........97020
1304.21 (d) revised..........97020
1304.31 (a) amended..........97020
1304.32 (a) amended..........97020
1304.33 (a) and (f)(1) revised..........97020
1305.07 Introductory text and (a) revised; interim..........58839
1305.17 (d) revised; interim..........58839
1308 Authority citation revised..........97021\
1308 Policy statement..........6175, 11429
1308.01 Revised..........97021
1308.11 (b)(3) through (55) redesignated as (b)(4) through (56); new (b)(3) added..........22025
(d)(48), (49) and (50) added; (h)(1), (2) and (3) removed; (h)(4) through (25) redesignated as new (h)(1) through (22)..........29145
(h)(26) and (27) added..........29496

21 CFR—Continued

21 CFR—Continued

2017

21 CFR

21 CFR—Continued

82 FR Page

Chapter II—Continued

1301.34 Regulation at 81 FR 97019 eff. date delayed to 3-21-17 8688
1301.74 Regulation at 81 FR 97020 eff. date delayed to 3-21-17 8688
1302.07 Regulation at 81 FR 97020 eff. date delayed to 3-21-17 8688
1303.12 Regulation at 81 FR 97020 eff. date delayed to 3-21-17 8688
1303.22 Regulation at 81 FR 97020 eff. date delayed to 3-21-17 8688
1304.02 Regulation at 81 FR 97020 eff. date delayed to 3-21-17 8688
1304.21 Regulation at 81 FR 97020 eff. date delayed to 3-21-17 8688
1304.31 Regulation at 81 FR 97020 eff. date delayed to 3-21-17 8688
1304.32 Regulation at 81 FR 97020 eff. date delayed to 3-21-17 8688
1304.33 Regulation at 81 FR 97020 eff. date delayed to 3-21-17 8688
1308 Policy statement 8590
Regulation at 81 FR 97021 eff. date delayed to 3-21-17 8688
1308.01 Regulation at 81 FR 97021 eff. date delayed to 3-21-17 8688
1308.11 (h)(23) through (28) correctly removed 2218
(d)(59) through (68) added; (h)(1) through (10), (20), (21) and (22) removed; (h)(11) through (19) redesignated as new (h)(1) through (9) 12177
(h)(10) through (15) added (temporary) 17123
(h)(16) added (temporary) 20547
(h)(4) removed; (b)(3) through (56) and (h)(5) through (15) redesignated as (b)(4) through (57) and (h)(4) through (14); new (b)(3) and new (15) added 26351
(h)(17) added (temporary) 32457
(d)(69), (70) and (71) added; (h)(1), (2) and (3) removed; (h)(4) through (17) redesignated as (h)(1) through (14) 47974
(h)(15) through (21) added (temporary) 49508
(h)(18) added (temporary) 51158
(b)(40) through (57) redesignated as (b)(41) through (58); new (b)(40) added 58559
1308.12 (f)(2) added; interim 14820
(b)(1) introductory text revised 45438
Regulation at 82 FR 14820 confirmed 55506

21 CFR—Continued

82 FR Page

Chapter II—Continued

1308.15 Regulation at 81 FR 29491 confirmed 13069
1308.21 Regulation at 81 FR 97021 eff. date delayed to 3-21-17 8688
1308.23 Regulation at 81 FR 97021 eff. date delayed to 3-21-17 8688
1308.25 Regulation at 81 FR 97021 eff. date delayed to 3-21-17 8688
1308.31 Regulation at 81 FR 97021 eff. date delayed to 3-21-17 8688
1308.33 Regulation at 81 FR 97021 eff. date delayed to 3-21-17 8688
1308.49 Regulation at 81 FR 97021 eff. date delayed to 3-21-17 8688
1309.26 Regulation at 81 FR 97021 eff. date delayed to 3-21-17 8688
1309.32 Regulation at 81 FR 97021 eff. date delayed to 3-21-17 8688
1309.46 Regulation at 81 FR 97021 eff. date delayed to 3-21-17 8688
1309.51 Regulation at 81 FR 97021 eff. date delayed to 3-21-17 8688
1309.71 Regulation at 81 FR 97021 eff. date delayed to 3-21-17 8688
1310 Regulation at 81 FR 97022 eff. date delayed to 3-21-17 8688
1310.02 (a)(1) through (30) redesignated as (a)(2) through (31); new (a)(1) added 32460
1310.03 Regulation at 81 FR 97022 eff. date delayed to 3-21-17 8688
1310.04 (g)(1)(i) through (x) redesignated as (g)(1)(ii) through (xi); new (g)(1)(i) added 32460
1310.05 Regulation at 81 FR 97022 eff. date delayed to 3-21-17 8688
1310.06 Regulation at 81 FR 97023 eff. date delayed to 3-21-17 8688
1310.09 (n) added 32460
1310.12 (c) table amended 32460
1310.13 Regulation at 81 FR 97025 eff. date delayed to 3-21-17 8688
1312.03 Regulation at 81 FR 97025 eff. date delayed to 3-21-17 8688
1312.11 Regulation at 81 FR 97026 eff. date delayed to 3-21-17 8688
1312.12 Regulation at 81 FR 97026 eff. date delayed to 3-21-17 8688
1312.13 Regulation at 81 FR 97027 eff. date delayed to 3-21-17 8688
1312.14 Regulation at 81 FR 97027 eff. date delayed to 3-21-17 8688
1312.15 Regulation at 81 FR 97027 eff. date delayed to 3-21-17 8688
1312.16 Regulation at 81 FR 97027 eff. date delayed to 3-21-17 8688

21 CFR—Continued

82 FR Page

Chapter II—Continued

1312.18 Regulation at 81 FR 97028 eff. date delayed to 3-21-17 8688
1312.19 Regulation at 81 FR 97029 eff. date delayed to 3-21-17 8688
1312.21 Regulation at 81 FR 97029 eff. date delayed to 3-21-17 8688
1312.22 Regulation at 81 FR 97029 eff. date delayed to 3-21-17 8688
1312.23 Regulation at 81 FR 97032 eff. date delayed to 3-21-17 8688
1312.24 Regulation at 81 FR 97032 eff. date delayed to 3-21-17 8688
1312.25 Regulation at 81 FR 97032 eff. date delayed to 3-21-17 8688
1312.26 Regulation at 81 FR 97033 eff. date delayed to 3-21-17 8688
1312.27 Regulation at 81 FR 97033 eff. date delayed to 3-21-17 8688
1312.28 Regulation at 81 FR 97035 eff. date delayed to 3-21-17 8688
1312.31 Regulation at 81 FR 97035 eff. date delayed to 3-21-17 8688
1312.32 Regulation at 81 FR 97036 eff. date delayed to 3-21-17 8688
1313.03 Regulation at 81 FR 97036 eff. date delayed to 3-21-17 8688
1313.12 Regulation at 81 FR 97036 eff. date delayed to 3-21-17 8688
1313.13 Regulation at 81 FR 97036 eff. date delayed to 3-21-17 8688
1313.14 Regulation at 81 FR 97037 eff. date delayed to 3-21-17 8688
1313.15 Regulation at 81 FR 97037 eff. date delayed to 3-21-17 8688
1313.16 Regulation at 81 FR 97037 eff. date delayed to 3-21-17 8688
1313.17 Regulation at 81 FR 97037 eff. date delayed to 3-21-17 8688
1313.21 Regulation at 81 FR 97038 eff. date delayed to 3-21-17 8688
1313.22 Regulation at 81 FR 97038 eff. date delayed to 3-21-17 8688
1313.23 Regulation at 81 FR 97038 eff. date delayed to 3-21-17 8688
1313.26 Regulation at 81 FR 97039 eff. date delayed to 3-21-17 8688
1313.27 Regulation at 81 FR 97039 eff. date delayed to 3-21-17 8688
1313.31 Regulation at 81 FR 97039 eff. date delayed to 3-21-17 8688
1313.32 Regulation at 81 FR 97039 eff. date delayed to 3-21-17 8688
1313.33 Regulation at 81 FR 97040 eff. date delayed to 3-21-17 8688

21 CFR—Continued

82 FR Page

Chapter II—Continued

1313.34 Regulation at 81 FR 97040 eff. date delayed to 3-21-17 8688
1313.35 Regulation at 81 FR 97040 eff. date delayed to 3-21-17 8688
1314.110 Regulation at 81 FR 97040 eff. date delayed to 3-21-17 8688
1315 Regulation at 81 FR 97041 eff. date delayed to 3-21-17 8688
1316.47 Regulation at 81 FR 97041 eff. date delayed to 3-21-17 8688
1316.48 Regulation at 81 FR 97041 eff. date delayed to 3-21-17 8688
1321.01 Regulation at 81 FR 97041 eff. date delayed to 3-21-17 8688

2018

21 CFR

83 FR Page

Chapter II

1301 Authority citation revised 3074
1301.28 (b)(1)(i), (ii) and (iii) revised 3074
1303.11 (b)(4) amended; (b)(5) redesignated as (b)(7); new (b)(5) and (6) added; (c) revised 32789
1303.12 (b) amended 32790
1303.13 (b)(1) and (c) revised 32790
1303.21 (a) amended 32790
1303.22 (c)(2) amended; (d) added 32790
1303.23 (a)(2) and (b)(2) amended 32790
1303.32 (a) amended 32790
1308 Policy statement 4411, 21834
1308.11 (h)(22) added (temporary) 472
(h)(23) through (29) added (temporary) 4584
(h)(30) added (temporary) 5191
(h)(23) and (29) revised; eff. through 2-1-20 10368
(b)(18) through (58) redesignated as (b)(19) through (59); new (b)(18) and (60) added; (h)(2) and (4) removed 17488
(h)(31) through (35) added (temporary) 31882

21 CFR—Continued

83 FR Page

Chapter II—Continued

(b) introductory text amended; (b)(57) through (60) redesignated as (b)(62) through (65); (b)(46) through (56) redesignated as (b)(50) through new (60); (b)(32) through (45) redesignated as (b)(35) through (48); (b)(4) through (31) redesignated as (b)(5) through (32); new (b)(4), new (33), new (34), new (49), and new (61) added; (h)(5), (13), (14), (20), and (29) removed 61323

(h)(36) added (temporary) 44478

1308.15 (f) added....48953

1312 Authority citation revised....48953

1312.30 Introductory text revised; (b) added....48953

2019

21 CFR

84 FR Page

Chapter II

1301.25 (f)(3) amended....68342

1301.74 Regulation at 81 FR 58839 confirmed....28214

1301.75 Regulation at 81 FR 58839 confirmed....28214

1305.05 (d) revised; (f) added....51374

1305.07 Regulation at 81 FR 58839 confirmed....28214

1305.11 Revised 51374

1305.12 (a) revised....51374

1305.13 (a), (b), (d), and (e) revised....51374

1305.14 (a) and (b) amended....51375

1305.15 (b) and (d) revised....51375

1305.16 (a) and (d) revised....51375

1305.17 Regulation at 81 FR 58839 confirmed....28214

1305.17 (a), (b), and (c) revised; (e) added....51375

1305.18 Revised 51375

1305.19 (a) revised....51375

1305.20 Added....51375

1308 Policy statement....16397

1308 Temporary regulations 58045

1308.11 Regulation at 67 FR 17123 eff. date extended to 4-10-20 13796

21 CFR—Continued

84 FR Page

Chapter II—Continued

(b)(51) through (66), (41) through (50), and (22) through (40) redesignated as (b)(55) through (70), (43) through (52), and (23) through (41); new (b)(22), new (42), new (53), and new (54) added; (h)(19), (21), (22), and (24) removed....57326

(d)(72) added; (h)(1) removed 448

(b) introductory text revised 20023

(b)(16) through (65) redesignated as (b)(17) through (66); new (b)(16) added; (h)(3) removed 20027

(h)(37) through (41) added (temporary) 15511

(h)(42) through (47) added (temporary) 34297

1308.12 Regulation at 81 FR 58839 confirmed....28214

(g)(3) revised....2449

(b)(1)(x) through (xviii) redesignated as (b)(1)(xi) through (xix); new (b)(1)(x) added....41914

1308.14 (c)(4) through (55) redesignated as (c)(5) through (56); new (c)(4) added 27943

(f)(12) redesignated as (f)(13); new (f)(12) added....27947

Correction: (f)(12) amended 60333

1316.62 Revised 18140

2020

(Regulations published from January 1, 2020, through April 1, 2020)

21 CFR

85 FR Page

Chapter II

1308 Regulation at 84 FR 27943 confirmed 4219

1308 Policy statement 5321

1308.11 (d)(73) through (78) added; (h)(6) through (11) removed....4215

(d)(79) added; (h)(18) removed....17497

1308.12 (b)(1) introductory text revised 4217

1308.14 Regulation at 84 FR 27947 confirmed....645

21 CFR—Continued

21 CFR—Continued

○

CPSIA information can be obtained
at www.ICGtesting.com
Printed in the USA
LVHW011512070822
725377LV00022B/170

9 781641 435819